Photoshop Elements 11

the missing manual®

The book that should have been in the box®

Barbara Brundage

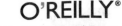
O'REILLY®

Beijing | Cambridge | Farnham | Köln | Sebastopol | Tokyo

Photoshop Elements 11: The Missing Manual

by Barbara Brundage

Published by O'Reilly Media, Inc.,
1005 Gravenstein Highway North, Sebastopol, CA 95472.

O'Reilly books may be purchased for educational, business, or sales promotional use. Online editions are also available for most titles (*http://my.safaribooksonline.com*). For more information, contact our corporate/institutional sales department: (800) 998-9938 or *corporate@oreilly.com*.

September 2012:   First Edition.

Revision History for the First Edition:
   2012-09-04   First release

See *http://oreilly.com/catalog/errata.csp?isbn=9781449316136* for release details.

ISBN-13: 978-1-449-31613-6

Contents

Part One: Introduction to Elements

Part Four: **Artistic Elements**

Part Seven: **Appendixes**

NOTE   Head to this book's Missing CD page at *www.missingmanuals.com/cds* to download two more appendixes: "The Organizer, Menu by Menu" and "The Editor, Menu by Menu."

The Missing Credits

ABOUT THE AUTHOR

 Barbara Brundage is the author of *Photoshop Elements 10: The Missing Manual*, an Adobe Community Expert, and a member of Adobe's prerelease groups for Elements 3–11. She's been teaching people how to use Photoshop Elements since it came out in 2001. Barbara first started using Elements to create graphics for use in her day job as a harpist, music publisher, and arranger. Along the way, she joined the large group of people finding a renewed interest in photography thanks to digital cameras. If she can learn to use Elements, you can, too! You can reach her at *barb@barbarabrundage.com* and read her blog at *www.barbarabrundage.com* (sometimes it's even about Photoshop Elements).

ABOUT THE CREATIVE TEAM

Dawn Mann (editor) is associate editor for the Missing Manual series. When not working, she beads, hikes, and causes trouble (though not all at the same time). Email: *dawn@oreilly.com*.

Melanie Yarbrough (production editor) lives, works, and does pretty much everything else in Cambridge, MA. When not ushering books through production, she's writing or baking up whatever she can imagine. Email: *myarbrough@oreilly.com*.

Sara Froehlich (tech reviewer) has been in love with computer graphics and digital photography since she discovered them in 1995 and has been teaching online classes in Photoshop Elements since its first release. (You can see her classes at *www.lvsonline.com*.) She's also the author of *Microsoft Expression Design Step by Step*. Sara enjoys traveling with her husband, Tom, and their papillon, Jasmine, and is especially fond of Florida, where she can get away from Minnesota winters! Website: *www.northlite.net*. Email: *northie@hickorytech.net*.

Francine Schwieder (tech reviewer) has used Macs and Photoshop since 1994 and has run many Mac Workshops focused on using Macs in general and graphics programs in particular. She has traveled, works on her home and yard, and brings all her varied interests together on her website at *http://pinkmutant.com*.

Julie Van Keuren (proofreader) quit her newspaper job in 2006 to move to Montana and live the freelancing dream. She and her husband, M.H. (who is living the novel-writing dream), have two sons, Dexter and Michael. Email: *little_media@yahoo.com*.

Ron Strauss (indexer) lives and works in Northern California. He moonlights as a classically trained violist. Email: *rstrauss@mchsi.com*.

ACKNOWLEDGMENTS

Many thanks to Sara Froelich and Francine Schwieder for reading this book and giving me the benefit of their advice and corrections. I'm also grateful for the help I received from everyone at Adobe, especially Bob Gager, Gaurav Jain, Deepak Sawant, Akshaya Saxena, Sanchit Loma, and Neeraj Chaudry.

Special thanks also to graphic artist Jodi Frye (*lfrye012000@yahoo.com*) for allowing me to reproduce one of her Elements drawings to show what can be done by those with more artistic ability than I have. My gratitude also to Florida's botanical gardens, especially McKee Botanical Garden (*www.mckeegarden.org*), Historic Bok Sanctuary (*www.boktower.org*), Heathcote Botanical Gardens (*www.heathcotebotanicalgardens.org*), and Harry P. Leu Gardens (*www.leugardens.org*) for creating oases of peace and beauty in our hectic world. Finally, I'd like to thank everyone in the gang over at the Adobe Photoshop Elements support forum for all their help and friendship.

THE MISSING MANUAL SERIES

Missing Manuals are witty, superbly written guides to computer products that don't come with printed manuals (which is just about all of them). Each book features a handcrafted index and cross-references to specific pages (not just chapters). Recent and upcoming titles include:

- *Access 2010: The Missing Manual* by Matthew MacDonald
- *Adobe Edge Preview 7: The Missing Manual* by Chris Grover
- *Buying a Home: The Missing Manual* by Nancy Conner
- *Creating a Website: The Missing Manual, Third Edition*, by Matthew MacDonald
- *CSS: The Missing Manual, Second Edition*, by David Sawyer McFarland
- *David Pogue's Digital Photography: The Missing Manual* by David Pogue
- *Dreamweaver CS6: The Missing Manual* by David Sawyer McFarland
- *Droid 2: The Missing Manual* by Preston Gralla
- *Droid X2: The Missing Manual* by Preston Gralla
- *Excel 2010: The Missing Manual* by Matthew MacDonald
- *FileMaker Pro 12: The Missing Manual* by Susan Prosser and Stuart Gripman
- *Flash CS6: The Missing Manual* by Chris Grover
- *Galaxy S II: The Missing Manual* by Preston Gralla
- *Galaxy Tab: The Missing Manual* by Preston Gralla
- *Google+: The Missing Manual* by Kevin Purdy
- *HTML5: The Missing Manual* by Matthew MacDonald

- *iMovie '11 & iDVD: The Missing Manual* by David Pogue and Aaron Miller
- *iPad: The Missing Manual, Fourth Edition* by J.D. Biersdorfer
- *iPhone: The Missing Manual, Fifth Edition* by David Pogue
- *iPhone App Development: The Missing Manual* by Craig Hockenberry
- *iPhoto '11: The Missing Manual* by David Pogue and Lesa Snider
- *iPod: The Missing Manual, Tenth Edition* by J.D. Biersdorfer and David Pogue
- *JavaScript & jQuery: The Missing Manual, Second Edition* by David Sawyer McFarland
- *Kindle Fire: The Missing Manual* by Peter Meyers
- *Living Green: The Missing Manual* by Nancy Conner
- *Mac OS X Mountain Lion: The Missing Manual* by David Pogue
- *Microsoft Project 2010: The Missing Manual* by Bonnie Biafore
- *Motorola Xoom: The Missing Manual* by Preston Gralla
- *Netbooks: The Missing Manual* by J.D. Biersdorfer
- *NOOK Tablet: The Missing Manual* by Preston Gralla
- *Office 2010: The Missing Manual* by Nancy Connor, Chris Grover, and Matthew MacDonald
- *Office 2011 for Macintosh: The Missing Manual* by Chris Grover
- *Personal Investing: The Missing Manual* by Bonnie Biafore
- *Photoshop CS6: The Missing Manual* by Lesa Snider
- *Photoshop Elements 10: The Missing Manual* by Barbara Brundage
- *PHP & MySQL: The Missing Manual* by Brett McLaughlin
- *QuickBooks 2012: The Missing Manual* by Bonnie Biafore
- *Switching to the Mac: The Missing Manual, Lion Edition* by David Pogue
- *Windows 7: The Missing Manual* by David Pogue
- *Windows 8: The Missing Manual* by David Pogue
- *Your Body: The Missing Manual* by Matthew MacDonald
- *Your Brain: The Missing Manual* by Matthew MacDonald
- *Your Money: The Missing Manual* by J.D. Roth

For a full list of all Missing Manuals in print, go to *www.missingmanuals.com/library.html*.

Introduction

When Photoshop Elements was first released back in 2001, it became a runaway success. It's easy to see why: Elements gives people all the tools they need to get the very best from their photographs. It lets you take a ho-hum shot and give it some wow. If you run a graphics studio or a large professional photography business, then you definitely need the full version of Photoshop. But for most people who aren't creating images for commercial printing, Elements offers a very useful toolkit at an appealing price.

Since 2001, there's been a new version of the program released almost every year, and each time Adobe has tried to add new features to make the program more valuable. The problem was that just cramming all that extra stuff into the original program eventually started to make things pretty unwieldy, and Elements was already a tad intimidating to real beginners with no background in working with digital images.

So with Elements 11, Adobe introduces a significant re-imagining of the program, designed to make it easier to use. If you've used Elements before, you may be taken aback the first time you see the stripped-down design of the new version. Not to worry—all your favorite Editor features are still there, although it may take a little looking around to find them. There are plenty of interesting new features, too. Elements also includes a photo-organizing program (called the Organizer, logically enough), which is where Adobe has made the biggest changes. In fact, the changes to Elements 11 are probably the biggest since the Organizer was first included back in Elements 3. But regardless of whether you're a complete newbie or have been using Elements for the past decade, this book will quickly get you up to speed on Elements 11.

Why Photoshop Elements?

Adobe Photoshop is the granddaddy of all image-editing programs. It's the Big Cheese, the industry standard against which everything else is measured. Every photo you've seen in a book or magazine in the past 15 years or so has almost certainly passed through Photoshop on its way to being printed. You just can't buy anything that gives you more control over pictures than Photoshop does.

But Photoshop has some big drawbacks: It's darned hard to learn, it's horribly expensive, and many of the features in it are just plain overkill if you don't work on pictures for a living.

For several years, Adobe tried to find a way to cram many of Photoshop's marvelous powers into a package that normal people could use. Finding the right formula was a slow process. First came PhotoDeluxe, a program that was lots of fun but came up short when you wanted to fine-tune *how* the program worked. Adobe tried again with Photoshop LE, which many people felt included all the difficulty of full Photoshop, but still gave too little of what you needed to do top-notch work.

Finally—sort of like "Goldilocks"—Adobe got it just right with Photoshop Elements, which took off like crazy because it offers so much of Photoshop's power in a program that almost anyone can learn. With Elements, you, too, can work with the same wonderful tools that the pros use. Elements has been around for quite a while now and, in each new version, Adobe has added lots of push-button-easy ways to correct and improve your photos.

What You Can Do with Elements 11

Elements not only lets you make photos look great, but it also helps you organize your photos and gives you some pretty neat projects in which to use them. The program even comes loaded with lots of easy ways to share photos. The list of what Elements can do is pretty impressive. You can use it to:

- Enhance photos by editing, cropping, and color-correcting them, including fixing exposure and color problems.

- Add all kinds of special effects to images, like turning a garden-variety photo into a drawing, painting, or even a tile mosaic.

- Combine photos into a panorama or montage.

- Move someone from one photo to another, and even remove people (your ex?) from last year's holiday photos.

- Repair and restore old and damaged photos.

- Organize your photos and assign keywords to them so you can search by subject or name.

- Add text to images and turn them into things like greeting cards and flyers.

- Create slideshows to share with friends, regardless of whether they use Windows, a Mac, or even just a cellphone.

- Automatically resize photos so they're ready to send either as regular email attachments or in specially designed emails.

- Create digital artwork from scratch, even without a photo to work from.

- Create and share incredible online albums and email-ready slideshows that will make your friends actually *ask* to see your vacation photos.

- Create and edit graphics for websites.

- Create wonderful projects like collages and calendars that you can print or digitally share with friends. Scrapbookers—get ready to be wowed.

It's worth noting, though, that there are still a few things Elements *can't* do. While the program handles text quite competently, at least as photo-editing programs go, it's still no substitute for QuarkXPress, InDesign, or any other desktop-publishing program. And Elements can do an amazing job of fixing problems in photos, but only if you give it something to work with. If your photo is totally overexposed, blurry, and the top of everyone's head is cut off, there's a limit to what even Elements can do to salvage it. (C'mon, be fair.) The fact is, though, you're more likely to be surprised by what Elements *can* fix than by what it can't.

What's New in Elements 11

There are plenty of new features in Elements 11. It would take pages to list all the changes, but here are some of the highlights:

- **Lighter color scheme.** If you've been hanging onto your old copy of Elements 5 or earlier because you couldn't stand the dark color scheme in Elements versions 6 through 10, you'll be thrilled to know that in Elements 11, Adobe has opted for light gray instead.

- **Major changes to the Organizer.** If you've been using the Organizer's system of tags and categories to manage your photos, you're in for a pretty wild ride with the new Organizer's system of People, Places, and Events. Adobe is taking the first steps toward a more automated system of categorizing photos in Elements 11.

- **No more Photoshop.com.** Adobe has eliminated the tie-in to Photoshop.com for backing up and syncing your photos. If you already have images stored there, you can still use your Photoshop.com account via a web browser, but in Elements 11, the only free uploading is to Adobe's Photoshop Showcase (page 9), where you can post your projects to share them but not back up your photos. Instead, Adobe is emphasizing its new program Revel (page 9).

- **Actions panel.** For the first time, Elements lets you install and run actions as easily as you can in Photoshop. Actions (page 433) are little scripts, like macros, that automate complicated processes. You still can't *create* actions in Elements, but there are thousands of actions available on the Internet, and now it's much, much simpler to use them.

- **Updated Refine Edge.** This is another popular feature brought over from Photoshop. If you've used Elements before, you know how vexing it is to try to extract fuzzy animals or people with flyaway hair from photos without having horrible, cut-out looking edges. Elements 11 includes a more deluxe version of the Refine Edge dialog box (page 145), which makes it easy to get the most complicated fine detail in your selections.

- **Easier to add extra content.** People love to add stuff to Elements, like brushes, layer styles (page 461), actions, and effects (page 456), but for several years it's been a huge headache to do this. In Elements 11, it's a snap to add these extras.

- **New Guided Edits.** Elements 11's Guided Edit mode—where the program walks you through various photo projects and editing tasks—includes a bunch of popular new choices: High Key, Low Key, Vignette, and Tilt-Shift (a.k.a. miniature effect).

- **New Filters.** Elements 11 brings three wonderful new Sketch filters for making photos look like illustrations: Comic, Graphic Novel, and "Pen and Ink" (see page 441). And the new Lens Blur filter lets you create a shallower depth of field in your images (page 448).

- **Raw Converter 7.** If you shoot your photos in Raw format (page 264), you'll be delighted to know that Adobe has finally made the wonderful advances in version 7 of the Raw Converter available in Elements. (Elements still doesn't have as many features in its Raw Converter as Lightroom 4 and Photoshop do, but now you can use the processes from the new version in the Elements Converter.)

- **Online Content.** In Elements 11, very few of the graphics, album templates, and so on are installed on your computer when you install Elements. Instead, they're stored online, and you need an Internet connection the first time you use them (once Elements downloads them, you can use them anytime, whether you're connected to the Internet or not).

Elements vs. Photoshop

You could easily get confused about the differences between Elements and the full version of Adobe Photoshop. Because Elements is so much less expensive, and because many of its more advanced controls are tucked away, a lot of Photoshop aficionados tend to view Elements as some kind of toy version of their program (and probably even more will now, given the stripped-down appearance of Elements 11 the first time you open it). They couldn't be more wrong: Elements *is* Photoshop, but it's Photoshop adapted for use with a home printer and the Web.

The most important difference between Elements and Photoshop is that Elements doesn't let you work or save in CMYK mode, which is the format used for commercial color printing. (CMYK stands for Cyan, Magenta, Yellow, and blacK. Your inkjet printer also uses those ink colors to print, but it expects you to give it an RGB file, which is what Elements creates. Don't worry—this is all explained in Chapter 7.)

Elements also lacks several tools that are basic staples in any commercial art department, like Actions are included with this version. the extra color control you can get from Selective Color Adjustment layers and the Pen tool's special talent for creating vector paths. Also, for some special effects, like creating drop shadows and bevels, the tool you'd use—layer styles—doesn't have as many settings in Elements as it does in Photoshop. The same holds true for a handful of other Elements tools.

And although Elements is all most people need to create graphics for the Web, it doesn't come with the advanced tools in Photoshop, which let you do things like automatically slice images into smaller pieces for faster web display. If you use Elements, then you have to look for another program to help with that.

The Key to Learning Elements

Elements may not be quite as powerful as Photoshop, but it's still a complex program, filled with more features than most people ever use. The good news is that the Quick Fix window (Chapter 4) lets you get started right away, even if you don't understand every last option Quick Fix presents you with. And you also get Guided Edit mode (page 22), which provides step-by-step walkthroughs of some popular editing tasks, like sharpening a photo or cropping it to fit on standard photo paper.

As for the program's more complex features, the key to learning how to use Elements—or any other program, for that matter—is to focus only on what you need to know for the task you're currently trying to accomplish.

For example, if you're trying to use Quick Fix to adjust the color of your photo and crop it, don't worry that you don't get the concept of layers yet. You won't learn to do everything in Elements in a day or even a week. The rest will wait until you need it, so take your time and don't worry about what's not important to you right now. You'll find it much easier to master Elements if you go slowly and concentrate on one thing at a time.

If you're totally new to the program, then you'll find only three or four big concepts in this book that you really need to understand if you want to get the most out of Elements. It may take a little time for some concepts to sink in—resolution and layers, for instance, aren't the most intuitive concepts in the world—but once they click, they'll seem so obvious that you'll wonder why they were confusing at first. That's perfectly normal, so persevere. You *can* do this, and there's nothing in this book that you can't understand with a little bit of careful reading.

The very best way to learn Elements is just to dive right in and play with it. Try all the different filters to see what they do. Add a filter on top of another filter. Click around on all the different tools and try them. You don't even need to have a photo to do this. See page 40 to learn how to make an image from scratch in Elements, and keep an eye out for the many downloadable practice images you'll find at this book's companion website, *www.missingmanuals.com/cds*. Get crazy—you can stack up as many filters, effects, and layer styles as you want without crashing the program.

About This Book

Elements is a cool program and lots of fun to use, but figuring out how to make it do what you want is another matter. Elements' Help files are very good, but of course you need to know what you're looking for to use them to your best advantage. (Elements' Help files are online; you can download a PDF of them from Adobe's Elements support pages at *www.adobe.com/support/photoshopelements*.)

You'll find a slew of Elements titles at your local bookstore, but most of them assume that you know quite a bit about the basics of photography and/or digital imaging. It's much easier to find good intermediate books about Elements than books designed to get you going with the program.

That's where this book comes in. It's intended to make learning Elements easier by avoiding technical jargon as much as possible, and explaining *why* and *when* you'll want to use (or avoid) certain features of the program. That approach is as useful to people who are advanced photographers as it is to those who are just getting started with their first digital cameras.

> **NOTE** This book periodically recommends *other* books, covering topics too specialized or tangential for a manual about Elements. Careful readers may notice that not all of these titles are published by Missing Manual parent O'Reilly Media. While we're happy to mention other Missing Manuals and books in the O'Reilly family, if there's a great book out there that doesn't happen to be published by O'Reilly, we'll still let you know about it.

You'll also find instructions throughout this book that refer to files you can download from the Missing Manual website (*www.missingmanuals.com/cds*) so you can practice the techniques you're reading about. And in various spots, you'll find several different kinds of short articles (a.k.a. boxes). The ones labeled "Up to Speed" help newcomers to Elements do things, or they explain concepts with which veterans are probably already familiar. Those labeled "Power Users' Clinic" cover more advanced topics that won't be of much interest to casual photographers.

A Note About Operating Systems

This book covers using Elements with both Windows computers and Macs, and you'll see both platforms represented in the illustrations. (Frankly, you'll see more Mac screenshots here, simply because some things are easier to read in the Mac version of the program. For example, pop-out menus are more likely to have a white background on a Mac instead of a dark one.) The Editor (the part of Elements where you tweak photos) works exactly the same way regardless of what kind of computer you're using, but there are some differences in the Organizer and the projects available to you, and those are noted as necessary. Also, most of the keyboard shortcuts you use to run commands are different in Windows and on Macs; page xxii explains how those shortcuts are listed in this book.

> **NOTE** Alas, the version of Elements sold in the Mac App Store wasn't available when this book was written, and certain things are unique about that version, like many of the file paths to the various pieces of the program. If you have the App Store version, head to this book's Missing CD page at *www.missingmanuals.com/cds* for info about any differences between your version of the program and the standard version.

So remember: It doesn't matter which version of the program is shown in the illustrations; unless the book says otherwise, the differences are just slight cosmetic ones, like the fact that you close Mac program windows by clicking a button on their left, whereas in Windows the button is on the right.

> **NOTE** Adobe's video-editing program, *Premiere* Elements, also uses the Elements Organizer, and if you install both programs, your Photoshop Elements menus will show a lot of Premiere Elements choices, too. These are normally turned off when you install only Photoshop Elements, but if they get turned on by mistake, you can turn most of them off if you don't care to see them by going to Organizer→Edit→Preferences→Editing/Adobe Elements 11 Organizer→Preferences→Editing. (Appendix B, available at *www.missingmanuals.com/cds*, explains all the Organizer's menus. Appendix C, also online, covers the Editor's menus.)

About the Outline

This book is divided into seven parts, each focusing on a certain kind of task:

- **Part One.** The first part of this book helps you get started with the program. Chapter 1 shows how to navigate Elements' slightly confusing layout and mishmash of programs within programs. You'll learn how to decide where to start from and how to customize Elements so it best suits your working style. You'll also read about some important keyboard shortcuts, and where to look for help when you get stuck. Chapter 2 covers how to get photos into Elements, the basics of organizing them, and how to open files and create new images from scratch. You'll also find out how to save and back up images. Chapter 3 explains how to rotate and crop photos, and includes a primer on that most important digital imaging concept—resolution.

- **Part Two.** Chapter 4 shows how to use the Quick Fix window to dramatically improve your photos. Chapter 5 and Chapter 6 cover two key concepts that you'll use throughout this book: making selections and working with layers.

- **Part Three.** Having Elements is like having a darkroom on your computer. In Chapter 7, you'll learn how to make basic corrections, such as fixing exposure, adjusting color, sharpening images, and removing dust and scratches. Chapter 8 covers topics unique to people who use digital cameras, like Raw conversion and batch-processing photos. In Chapter 9, you'll move on to more sophisticated fixes, like using the Clone Stamp to make repairs, making photos livelier by adjusting their color intensity, and adjusting light and shadows in images. Chapter 10 shows you how to convert color photos to black and white, and how to tint and colorize black-and-white photos. Chapter 11 explains how to use Elements' Photomerge feature to create a panorama from several photos, and to correct perspective problems in images.

- **Part Four.** This part covers the fun stuff: painting on photos and drawing shapes (Chapter 12), using filters and effects to create more artistic looks (Chapter 13), and adding text to images (Chapter 14).

- **Part Five.** Once you've created a great image in Elements, you'll want to share it, so this part is about how to create fun projects like photo books (Chapter 15), how to get the most out of your printer (Chapter 16), how to create files to use on the Web and in email (Chapter 17), and how to make slideshows and share them online (Chapter 18).

- **Part Six.** You can get hundreds of plug-ins and additional styles, brushes, and other nifty tools to customize your copy of Elements and increase its abilities; the Internet and your local bookstore are chock-full of additional info. Chapter 19 offers a look at some of these resources, as well as information about using a graphics tablet with Elements, and suggests some places to turn after you finish this book.

- **Part Seven.** Appendix A helps you get your copy of Elements up and running, and suggests what to do if it starts misbehaving. Appendixes B and C—which you can download from this book's Missing CD page (see page xxiv)—cover all the menu items in the Organizer and Editor, respectively.

For Newcomers to Elements

This book contains a lot of information, and if you're new to Elements, it can be a little overwhelming. But you don't need to digest it all at once, especially if you've never used any kind of photo-editing software before. So what do you need to read first? Here's a simple five-step way to use this book if you're brand new to photo editing:

1. **Read all of Chapter 1.**

   That's important for understanding how to get around in Elements.

2. **If your photos aren't on your computer already, then read about the Photo Downloader in Chapter 2.**

   The Downloader gets photos from your camera's memory card into Elements.

3. **If you want to organize your photos, then read about the Organizer (also in Chapter 2).**

   It doesn't matter where your photos are right now. If you want to use the Organizer to label and keep track of them, then read Chapter 2.

4. **When you're ready to edit your photos, read Chapters 3 and 4.**

   Chapter 3 explains how to adjust your view of photos in the Editor. Chapter 4 shows you how to use the Quick Fix window to easily edit and correct photos. Guided Edit (page 22) can also be very helpful when you're just getting started. If you skipped Chapter 2 because you're not using the Organizer, then go back there and read the part about saving photos (page 65) so you don't lose your work.

5. **When you're ready to print or share your photos, flip to the chapters on sharing images.**

   Chapter 16 covers printing, both at home and from online services. Chapter 17 explains how to email photos, and Chapter 18 teaches you how to create slide-shows and post them to the Photoshop Showcase website.

That's all you need to get started. You can come back and pick up the rest of the info in the book as you get more comfortable with Elements and want to explore more of the wonderful things you can do with it.

The Very Basics

This book assumes that you know how to perform basic activities on your computer like clicking and double-clicking your mouse buttons and dragging objects onscreen. Here's a quick refresher: To *click* means to move the point of your mouse or trackpad cursor over an object on your screen, and then to press the left mouse or trackpad button once. To *right-click* means to press the right mouse button once, which calls up a menu of special features. To *double-click* means to press the left button twice, quickly, without moving the mouse between clicks. To *drag* means to click an object and then to hold down the left button while you use the mouse to move the object.

Most onscreen selection buttons are pretty obvious, but you may not be familiar with *radio buttons:* To choose an option, click the little empty circle next to it.

In Elements, you'll often want to use keyboard shortcuts to save time, and this book tells you about keyboard shortcuts when they exist (and Elements has a lot). In this book, unless otherwise specified, keyboard shortcuts are always presented as Windows keystroke/Mac keystroke. So if you see a sentence like, "Press Ctrl+S/⌘-S to save your file," that means that if you use Windows, you should hold down the Control key while pressing the S key, and if you have a Mac, you should hold down the ⌘ key while pressing the S key. There's one slight exception to this: When you see "right-click/Control-click," if you have a Mac and a two-button mouse, you can right-click. But if you have a one-button mouse, you can *Control-click* instead—that means to press the Control key on your keyboard and then press your mouse button once.

If you're comfortable with basic concepts like these, then you're ready to get started with this book.

About→These→Arrows

Throughout this book (and the Missing Manual series, for that matter) you see sentences like this: "In the Editor, select Filter→Artistic→Paint Daubs." This is a shorthand way of helping you find files, folders, and menu items without having to read through excruciatingly long, bureaucratic-style instructions. So the sample sentence above is a short way of saying this: "In the Editor component of Elements, in the menu bar at the top of the screen, click the word 'Filter.' In the menu that appears, choose the Artistic section, and then go to Paint Daubs in the pop-out menu." Figure I-1 shows you an example in action.

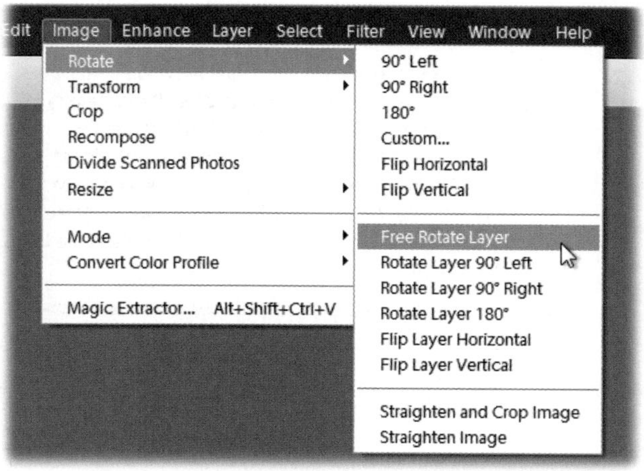

FIGURE I-1.

In a Missing Manual, when you see a phrase like "Image→Rotate→Free Rotate Layer," that's a quicker way of saying, "Go to the menu bar, click Image, slide down to Rotate, and then, from the pop-up menu, choose Free Rotate Layer."

Mac file paths are shown using the same arrows. Windows file paths, on the other hand, are shown in the conventional Windows style, so if you see, "Go to *C:\Documents and Settings\<your user name>\My Documents\My Pictures*," that means you should go to your C drive, open the Documents and Settings folder, look for your user account folder, and then find the My Documents folder. In that folder, open the My Pictures folder that's inside it.

When there are different file paths for Windows 7, Vista, and Windows XP, you'll find them all listed in this book. Like keyboard shortcuts, file paths are shown as Windows file path/Mac file path when all versions of Windows use the same file path. Otherwise, all the different versions are specified.

If you're using a Mac that's running OS X 10.7 (Lion) or 10.8 (Mountain Lion), there's one special challenge finding some of the files mentioned in this book; specifically, the ones located in the Library folders. (Figure I-2 explains.) Also, if you buy Elements from the Mac App Store, all the files are actually inside the application itself, which means your file paths will be different. (This book covers the version of Elements that was released in September 2012, so you won't see so much information about App Store–version file paths, since that information wasn't available when this book was written. Check this book's Missing CD page at *www.missingmanuals.com/cds* for updated information after the App Store version is released.)

NOTE The keyboard shortcuts given in this book are the official Adobe shortcuts. However, if you have a Mac with an abbreviated keyboard (without a 10-key section on the right), like a laptop keyboard or the smaller Bluetooth keyboards, you need to add the fn key to shortcuts that use the F-keys on the top row of your keyboard. So, for instance, while the shortcut for Full Screen View in the Organizer is ⌘-F11, on a MacBook Pro, you would use fn-⌘-F11.

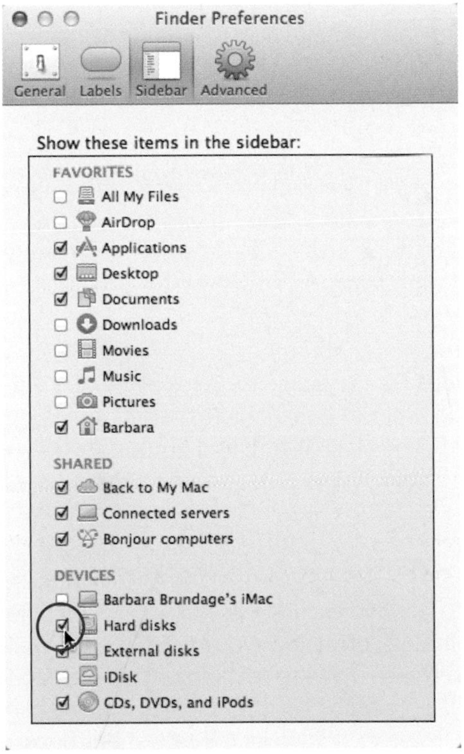

FIGURE I-2.

In OS X Lion and Mountain Lion, Apple has made it a little harder to find your Library folders. The one you'll need most often is the Library folder that resides at the very top level of your hard drive. This isn't exactly hidden in Lion and Mountain Lion,, but it never appears unless you change your settings to make it accessible. To do that, in the Finder, go to Finder→Preferences→Sidebar and, in the Devices section, turn on the "Hard disks" checkbox (circled). After that, you can always find the Library folder by just clicking the name of your hard drive in the list on the left side of a Finder window.

The other Library folder you may need is the one for your user account, which is a hidden file in Lion and Mountain Lion. To make it visible, in the Finder, open the Go menu and then press the Option key. Your account's Library folder will appear in the menu just below your Home folder.

NOTE If you're using a 64-bit version of Windows, you have two folders labeled Program Files. Windows puts 64-bit programs into the folder simply named Program Files, but Elements, like many programs you may install, is a 32-bit program, and Windows puts 32-bit programs into a folder named Program Files (x86). If you have a folder named Program Files (x86), then that's where you should always look for Elements' files. This book includes a reminder note every time this applies, such as, "Go to *C:\Program Files [Program Files (x86) if you have a 64-bit system]\Adobe\Elements 11 Organizer.*"

About the Online Resources

As the owner of a Missing Manual, you've got more than just a book to read. Online, you'll find example files so you can get some hands-on experience. You can also communicate with the Missing Manual team and tell us what you love (or hate) about the book. Head over to *www.missingmanuals.com/cds,* or go directly to one of the following sections.

Missing CD

This book doesn't have a CD pasted inside the back cover, but you're not missing out on anything. Go to *www.missingmanuals.com/cds* to download sample files mentioned in this book, as well as a few tutorials and two additional appendixes. And so you don't wear down your fingers typing long web addresses, this book's Missing CD page also offers a list of clickable links to the websites mentioned in these pages.

Registration

If you register this book at oreilly.com, you'll be eligible for special offers—like discounts on future editions of *Photoshop Elements 11: The Missing Manual.* Registering takes only a few clicks. To get started, type *http://oreilly.com/register* into your browser to hop directly to the Registration page.

Feedback

Got questions? Need more information? Fancy yourself a book reviewer? On our Feedback page, you can get expert answers to questions that come to you while reading, share your thoughts on this Missing Manual, and find groups for folks who share your interest in Elements. To have your say, go to *www.missingmanuals.com/feedback.*

Errata

In an effort to keep this book as up to date and accurate as possible, each time we print more copies, we'll make any confirmed corrections you've suggested. We also note such changes on the book's website, so you can mark important corrections into your own copy of the book, if you like. To report an error or view existing corrections, go to *http://missingmanuals.com/library.html,* click the title of this book, and then click the "View/Submit Errata" link on the right side of the page that appears.

■ Safari® Books Online

Safari Books Online is an on-demand digital library that lets you easily search over 7,500 technology and creative reference books and videos to find the answers you need quickly.

With a subscription, you can read any page and watch any video from our library online. Read books on your cellphone and mobile devices. Access new titles before they're available for print, and get exclusive access to manuscripts in development and post feedback for the authors. Copy and paste code samples, organize your favorites, download chapters, bookmark key sections, create notes, print out pages, and benefit from tons of other time-saving features.

Introduction to Elements

Finding Your Way Around Elements

P hotoshop Elements lets you do practically anything you want to digital images. You can colorize black-and-white photos, remove demonic red-eye stares, or distort the facial features of people who've been mean to you. The downside is that all those options can make it tough to find your way around Elements, especially if you're new to the program.

This chapter helps get you oriented. You'll learn what to expect when you launch the program and how to use Elements to fix photos with just a couple of keystrokes. You'll also learn how to use Guided Edit mode to get started editing photos. Along the way, you'll find out about some of Elements' basic controls and how to get to the program's Help files.

> **NOTE** Elements 11 is quite different from the previous versions of the program, so even if you're an Elements veteran, you'll want to read this chapter to get oriented. Much of the rest of the book may confuse you if you don't understand what's covered in this chapter.

■ Getting Started

Unlike some past versions of Elements, you launch Elements 11 pretty much the same way on both Mac and Windows computers.

When you install Elements in Windows, the installer creates a desktop shortcut for you. Just double-click that to launch Elements.

In the Mac version, you can launch Elements as the last step in the installation process (page 608 explains how to install Elements), or you can go to Applications→Adobe Photoshop Elements 11 and double-click its icon there. (Incidentally, the only other thing in there besides the uninstaller is a folder called Support Files. That's where you'll find the actual Editor application.) If you want to make a Dock icon for future convenience, start Elements and then go to the Dock and click the program's icon. Keep holding the mouse button down till you see a menu, and then choose Options→Keep in Dock.

Where the Heck Did Elements Go?

If you've installed Elements but can't figure out how to launch it, no problem.

Windows automatically creates a shortcut to Elements on your desktop when you install the program. (If you need help installing Elements, turn to Appendix A.) You can also go to the Start menu and then click the Adobe Photoshop Elements 11 icon. If you don't see Elements in the Start menu, then click the arrow next to All Programs, and you should see it in the pop-up menu.

On a Mac, go to Applications→Adobe Photoshop Elements 11.0, and then double-click the Adobe Photoshop Elements 11 icon.

NOTE People complained for years about the dark color scheme in Elements. Adobe has finally switched back to a lighter, easier-to-read version. Unfortunately, if you preferred the darker look, there's no way to change back to it.

Which Version of Elements Do You Have?

This book covers Photoshop Elements 11. If you're not sure which version you've got, the easiest way to find out is to look at the program's icon (the one you click to launch Elements). The icon for Elements 11 is a turquoise square with a stylized outline of two overlapping photographs on it in dark blue.

If you're still not sure, in Windows, click once on the Elements icon on your desktop, and Windows displays the full name of the program—including the version number—below the icon, if it wasn't already visible. You can also check the Windows Start menu, where Elements is listed along with its version number. On a Mac, check in your Applications folder to see the version number. Or, if Elements is already running, go to Help→About Photoshop Elements in Windows or Adobe Photoshop Elements Editor→About Photoshop Elements on a Mac.

You can still use this book if you have an earlier version of Elements because a lot of the basic editing procedures are the same. But Elements 11 has been updated in many ways, so you'd almost certainly feel more comfortable with a reference book for the version you have. There are Missing Manuals for Elements 3 through 10, too, and you may prefer to track down the book that matches your version of Elements. (For Elements 6 and 8, there are separate editions for the Mac and Windows versions.)

The Welcome Screen

When you launch Elements for the first time, you're greeted by the Welcome screen (Figure 1-1).

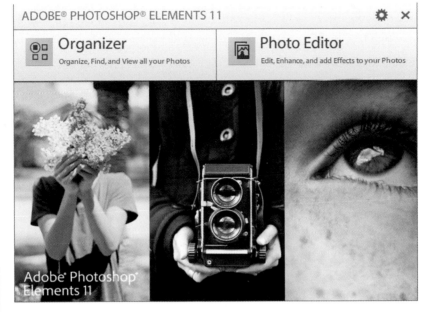

FIGURE 1-1.

Elements' Welcome screen. The images at the bottom are dynamic, meaning they change every three seconds or so, but the buttons at the top and the gear icon for the settings are always the same.

The Welcome screen is a launchpad that lets you choose which part of Elements you want to use:

- **Organizer button.** This starts the Organizer, which lets you store and organize your image files.

- **Photo Editor button.** Click this to start the Editor, which lets you modify images.

You can easily hop back and forth between the Editor and the Organizer—which you can think of as the two halves of Elements. But in some ways, they function as two separate programs. For example, if you start in the Organizer, then once you pick a photo to edit, you have to wait a few seconds while the Editor loads. And when you have both the Editor and the Organizer running, quitting the Editor doesn't close the Organizer—you have to close both parts of Elements independently.

At the bottom center of the Editor's main window is a button that you can click to launch the Organizer or switch over to it if it's already running. If you want to do the opposite—get photos from the Organizer over to the Editor—select the photo(s) and then click the Editor button at the bottom of the screen, or right-click/Control-click one of the selected thumbnails and choose "Edit with Photoshop Elements Editor." Either way, your photo(s) appear in the Editor so you can work on them. Once both programs are running, you can also just click the Editor's or the Organizer's icon in the Windows taskbar or the Mac Dock to switch from one to the other.

One helpful thing to keep in mind is that Adobe built Elements around the assumption that most people work on their photos in the following way: First, you bring photos into the Organizer to sort and keep track of them. Next, you open photos in the Editor to work on them, and then save them back to the Organizer when you've finished making changes. You can work differently, of course—by opening photos directly in the Editor and bypassing the Organizer altogether, for example—but you may feel like you're always swimming against the current if you choose a different workflow. (The next chapter has a few hints for disabling some of Elements' features if you find that they're getting in your way.)

Say Goodbye to the Welcome Screen

How do I get rid of the Welcome screen?

If you get to feeling welcomed enough, you may want to turn off the Welcome screen so you don't have to click through it every time you start Elements. To tell the Welcome screen you don't want to see it anymore, click Settings (the gear icon) in the screen's upper-right corner. This slides open a section of the window where you can choose to have the Editor or the Organizer launch from now on instead of the Welcome screen. Just choose the program you want from the list that appears.

If you change your mind later on about how you want Elements to open, go to Help→Welcome Screen in either the Editor or the Organizer, and then head back to the Settings menu described above and make your change.

You can also save a little of your system resources by making direct shortcuts to the Editor and Organizer programs and skipping the Welcome screen entirely. To do that, in Windows go to *C:\Program Files [Program Files (x86) for 64-bit systems]\ Adobe*, and then right-click the icon for the program you want and choose Create Desktop Shortcut. On a Mac, the easiest way is to create a Dock icon or icons from the running program as explained on page 610.

Organizing Your Photos

The Organizer is where your photos come into Elements *and* go out again when it's time to print, edit, or email them. The Organizer catalogs and keeps track of your photos, and you automatically come back to it for many activities that involve sharing photos, like emailing them (page 564) or creating an online gallery of them (page 571). The Organizer's main window (Figure 1-2) lets you view your photos, sort them into albums, and assign keyword labels to them.

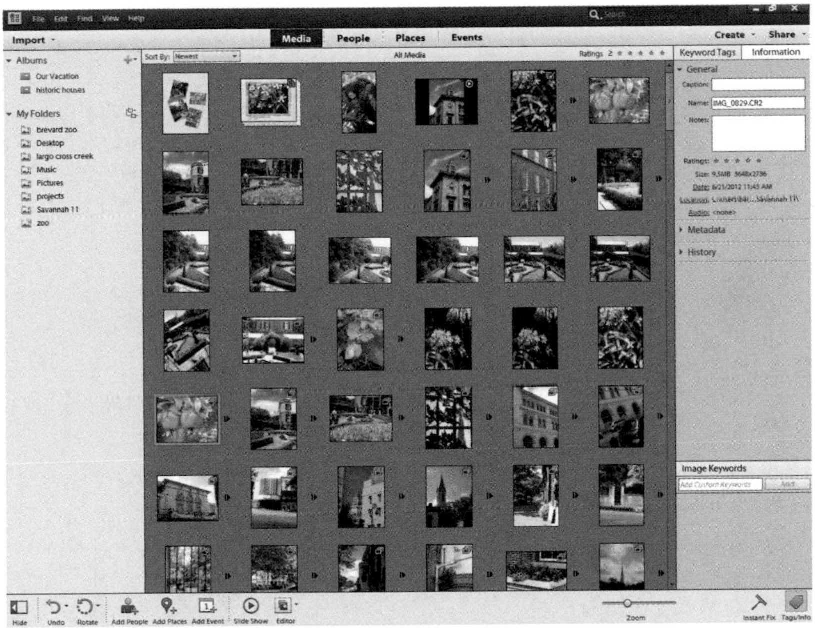

FIGURE 1-2.

The all-new Organizer, which lets you arrange and sort photos by the people, places, and events they represent, in addition to using keyword tags and categories. This is the Media room, which is where your photos go when you first import them to the Organizer. (Adobe calls the different areas of the Organizer "rooms" now.)

The Organizer got a complete makeover in Elements 11, so even if you've used the Organizer before, it's pretty much a whole new ballgame this time. The next chapter shows you how to use the Organizer to import and organize photos, and online Appendix B covers all the Organizer's different menu options (head to *www. missingmanuals.com/cds*). However, it's important to understand that you don't *have* to use the Organizer if you don't want to. Lots of people don't, for a variety of reasons. Page 43 explains some of the arguments for and against it.

Photo Downloader

Elements has yet another component that you may have seen already if you've plugged a camera into your computer after installing Elements: the Photo Downloader (Figure 1-3), which helps get photos into the Organizer directly from your camera's memory card.

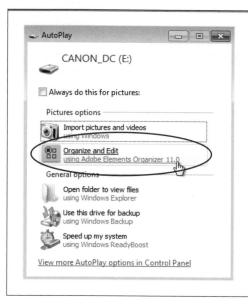

FIGURE 1-3.

Adobe's Photo Downloader is yet another program you get when you install Elements. Its job is to pull photos from your camera (or other storage device) into the Organizer. To use the Downloader in Windows 7 or Vista, just click "Organize and Edit using Adobe Elements Organizer 11.0" (circled) when this AutoPlay dialog box appears. (If you use Windows XP, you'll see a dialog box with similar options.) After the Downloader does its thing, you end up in the Organizer.

In Windows, the Downloader is one of your options in the Windows dialog box that you see when you connect a device. If you want to use the Downloader, then just choose it from the list.

On a Mac, you launch the Downloader from the Organizer by going to File→"Get Photos and Videos"→"From Camera or Card Reader." There's no way to make the Downloader run automatically on a Mac—you have to go through the Organizer to start it.

You can read more about the Downloader in Chapter 2. If you plan to use the Organizer to catalog photos and assign keywords to them, then reading the section on the Downloader (page 30) can help you avoid hair-pulling moments.

Adios, Photoshop.com

For the past few versions of Elements, Adobe strongly urged everyone to use the Photoshop.com service, which let you post your photos online, back them up, and sync photos between computers. That's all gone in Elements 11. If you have photos at Photoshop.com, you can still get to them via a web browser, but there's no link to the site in Elements itself anymore.

Instead, you can upload photos and albums to Adobe's Photoshop Showcase website (*www.photoshopshowcase.com*). For syncing between devices, you can sign up for Adobe Revel (formerly Adobe Carrousel), a paid service ($6.95 a month) that lets you coordinate your images among all your computers;

iPhones and other gadgets that run iOS (the operating system used by Apple devices); and Android phones and devices. Go to *www.adobe.com/products/revel.html* to learn more.

Photoshop.com isn't going anywhere right away, but if you've been relying on it, it might be prudent to start making other plans.

Elements' Inspiration Browser (which let you view tutorials) is gone, too, but most of what was there is available through the links in the program's Help menu. On the plus side, those annoying little ads that used to skid in and out at the bottom of the Elements window are also history.

Editing Your Photos

The Editor is the other main component of Elements. This is the fun part of the program, where you get to adjust, transform, and generally glamorize photos, and where you can create original artwork from scratch with drawing tools and shapes.

You can operate the Editor in three different modes:

- **Quick Fix.** For many Elements beginners, Quick Fix (Figure 1-4) ends up being their main workspace. It's where Adobe has gathered together the basic tools you need to improve most photos. It's also one of the two places in Elements where you can choose to have a before-and-after view while you work (the other is Guided Edit, described next). Chapter 4 gives you all the details on using Quick Fix. The first time you launch the Editor, you start out in Quick Fix mode.

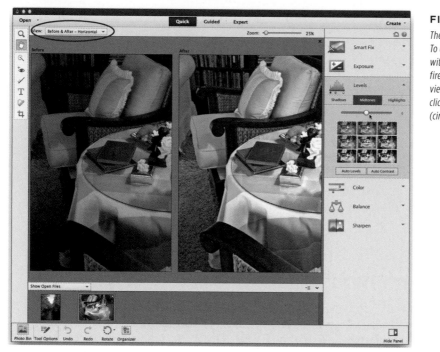

FIGURE 1-4.

The Quick Fix window. To compare your fixes with the original photo, fire up Before & After view, which you get to by clicking the View menu (circled).

- **Guided Edit.** This window can be a big help if you're a newcomer to Elements. It provides step-by-step walkthroughs of popular projects such as cropping photos and removing blemishes from them. It also hosts some fun special effects and workflows for more advanced users (see page 458).

- **Expert Mode.** This mode gives you access to Elements' most sophisticated tools. You have far more ways to work on your photo in Expert Mode than in Quick Fix, and if you're fussy, it's where you'll do most of your retouching work. Most of the Quick Fix commands are also available via menus in the Expert Mode window (shown in Figure 1-5).

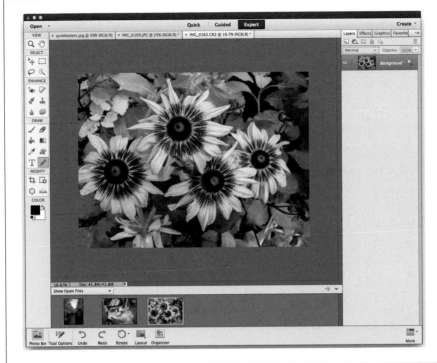

FIGURE 1-5.

The main Elements editing window, which Adobe calls Expert Mode. This is where you have access to all of Elements' editing features. This shows what you see on first entering the Custom Workspace, explained in the next section. You can customize your workspace quite a bit from this starting point.

Use the Quick, Guided, and Expert tabs at the top of the Elements window to switch modes. The rest of this chapter covers some of the Editor's basic concepts and key tools.

> **TIP** If you leave a photo open in the Editor, then when you switch back to the Organizer, you'll see a red band with a padlock across the photo's Organizer thumbnail as a reminder. To get rid of the lock and free up your image for Organizer projects, go back to the Editor and close the photo there.

Understanding Expert Mode

In Elements 11, once you click over to Expert Mode (click the tab at the top of the Editor to get there), you may be pretty puzzled as to how to proceed. There's a toolbox on the left, a row of icons across the bottom of the screen—and that's pretty much it. If you've ever used Elements before, you may be asking, "Where did everything go?" Not to worry. It's all still there, but you need to know how to make things work.

■ BASIC WORKSPACE

Expert Mode starts out in what Adobe calls the *Basic Workspace*, a new design that it hoped would be less confusing to beginners (Figure 1-6). On the left side of the screen is a double-columned toolbox. When you open a photo, a small *thumbnail* version of it appears in the area near the bottom of the window. This area is called the Photo Bin. However, what you see in this area changes depending on what you're doing. When you activate one of Elements' tools, this area is taken over by the Tool Options, where you see the settings for the tool you're currently using (more about that on page 14).

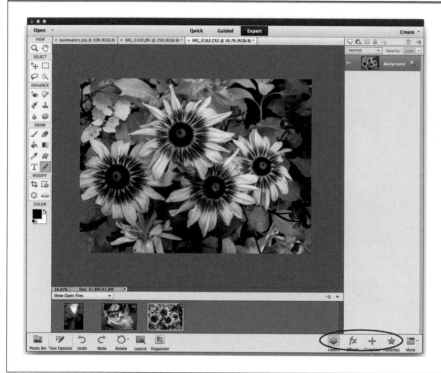

FIGURE 1-6.

When you first use the Editor in Expert Mode, the window looks like this, which Adobe calls the Basic Workspace. The buttons at the bottom right (circled) let you switch from one panel to another. You can see only one panel at a time, which is one reason why most folks prefer to use the Custom Workspace shown in Figure 1-5. It's explained in the next section.

At the bottom right of the screen are a series of buttons labeled Layers, Effects, Graphics, Favorites, and More. The first four are the names of Elements' most-used *panels*. Panels let you do things like keep track of what you've done to a photo (with the History panel) and apply special effects to your images (with the Effects and Graphics panels). You'll learn about the program's various panels in detail throughout this book.

Here's the thing about the Basic Workspace: When you click one of those panel buttons, that panel appears and fills the entire right of your screen (called the *Panel Bin*) from top to bottom, as the Layers panel does in Figure 1-6. When you're in the Basic Workspace, only the panels that have buttons at the bottom right of the screen can appear in the Panel Bin, and you can't see more than one of them at a time or resize them. To switch to another panel, you click its button and the previous panel disappears.

But the Editor has many more panels than just those four. If you need one of the others, like say the History panel (see page 25), you bring it up by clicking the More button in the window's lower-right corner. This brings up *all* the other panels in one floating group, and you click the tab of the panel you want to bring it to the front. You can move the group around on your screen, but you can't put it in the Panel Bin or take anything out of the Panel Bin to put in the group. You also can't remove any panels from the group, and you have no control over how big it is—it automatically resizes to fit the current panel. You can close the group by clicking the little X at its top right (in Windows) or top left (on a Mac).

> **TIP** If you click the tiny arrow on the right side of the More button you can choose a panel by name, but in the Basic Workspace you still get the whole clump. All choosing the name does is make sure that the panel you want is the front one when the grouped panels appear.

You can try running Expert Mode with the Basic Workspace, but odds are that in about 10 minutes this setup will have you raving and beating your head on your desk. Fortunately, Elements offers a *much* better way to use the Editor: the *Custom Workspace*.

■ CUSTOM WORKSPACE

If you've ever used Elements (or any graphics program) before, you'll be enormously relieved to know that you can make the Editor work much more efficiently than the Basic Workspace does. The secret is a well-hidden menu command that restores Elements to its full usefulness. To achieve this transformation, just click the tiny arrow on the right side of the More button and choose Custom Workspace.

Voilà! You just regained an enormous amount of freedom to set up things in the Editor the way you want them. In the Custom Workspace you can tear individual panels out of the panel group, put panels into the Panel Bin (and take them out), make your own panel groups, and so on.

Switch to the Custom Workspace right now. The rest of this book assumes that you'd like to see what you're doing and are using the Editor's Custom Workspace.

Bins, Panels, and Tabs

You're not stuck with the way things are initially laid out in the Custom Workspace (explained in the previous section). You can rearrange things quite a bit from where Adobe starts you out. This section explains the various ways you can customize the Editor workspace (assuming you're using the Custom Workspace, that is).

TIP You can hide *everything* in the workspace except for your images and the menu bar: no tools, panels, or anything else cluttering up your screen. This is handy when you want a good, undistracted look at what you've done to a photo. To do that, just press the Tab key; to bring everything back into view, press Tab again. (This also works in the Basic Workspace.)

■ THE PHOTO BIN/TOOL OPTIONS AREA

There's a long, narrow strip at the bottom of the Editor window that changes to display different things depending on what you're doing at the moment. When you first open a photo, you see the *Photo Bin* (Figure 1-7) in this area, which displays all your open files. But if you click a tool in the toolbox on the left side of the Editor window, the Photo Bin gets replaced with settings for that particular tool, called (logically enough) the *Tool Options*. There are buttons at the bottom left of the main Editor window that let you switch back and forth between the Photo Bin and Tool Options, so you can always change over to the one you want right now.

The Photo Bin/Tool Options area is fixed in place: You can't move it anywhere else or resize it. However, you can hide it by clicking the down-pointing arrow at the right end of the light-gray bar just above it. This gives you more space, but it also hides the settings for your tools, so it's hard to do much work with it hidden. To bring it back, click either the Photo Bin or Tool Options button at the bottom of the window. (This behavior is the same in both the Basic and Custom workspaces.)

There's more about how to use the Tool Options on page 21. The rest of this section is about the Photo Bin's useful features (Figure 1-7). The Photo Bin does a lot more than just show which photos you have open. You can drag photos' thumbnails in the bin to rearrange them if you want to use the images in a project. The bin also has two drop-down menus:

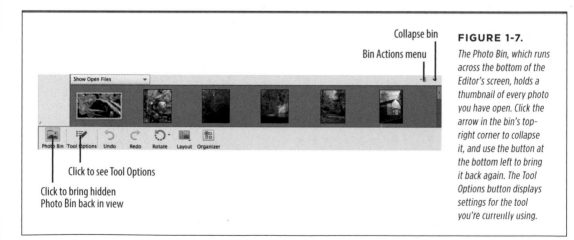

Collapse bin

Bin Actions menu

Click to see Tool Options

Click to bring hidden
Photo Bin back in view

FIGURE 1-7.

The Photo Bin, which runs across the bottom of the Editor's screen, holds a thumbnail of every photo you have open. Click the arrow in the bin's top-right corner to collapse it, and use the button at the bottom left to bring it back again. The Tool Options button displays settings for the tool you're currently using.

- **Show Open Files.** This menu at the bin's upper left lets you determine what the Photo Bin displays: the photos currently open in the Editor, selected photos from the Organizer, or any albums (page 55) you've made. This menu even lets you send files from the Organizer to the bin without actually opening them. Simply click photos to select them in the Organizer, and then come back over to the Editor, and switch this menu to "Show Files selected in Organizer"; you'll see the photos you selected in the Organizer waiting for you in the bin. Double-click one to open it for editing.

TIP If you regularly keep lots of photos open and you have an iPad, check out the Adobe Nav app (*www. photoshop.com/products/mobile/nav*), which lets you sort through open photos in Elements, see info about your photos, and switch tools without using your mouse. You can also use Adobe Revel to sync photos from all your i-devices to your computer (see page 9).

- **Bin Actions.** This is where the Photo Bin gets really useful, but it's not easy to spot this menu: It's the little four-line square in the bin's upper right. This menu lets you print the photos in the bin or make an album right there in the Photo Bin without ever going to the Organizer. If you don't use the Organizer, then the Photo Bin is a particularly great feature, because it lets you create groups of photos you can call up together: Just put them in an album (page 55), and then, from the bin's Show Open Files menu, select the album's name to see those photos. (You can also use this menu to reset the style source images you use in the Style Match feature, explained on page 376.) If you like things to be compartmentalized, the Show Grid menu item puts a thin black line around each thumbnail.

NOTE In the Photo Bin, you may notice strange little paintbrush icons appearing on the top-right corner of your photos' thumbnails. They indicate that you've edited a photo but haven't saved your changes.

■ THE PANEL BIN

When you're in Expert Mode, the right side of the Elements window displays the *Panel bin.* (In the Basic Workspace you won't see it till you click one of the panel buttons in the bottom-right corner of the Editor window.) When you first switch to the Custom Workspace (page 13), the Panel bin appears with four panels open: Layers, Effects, Graphics, and Favorites (Figure 1-8). These are the same four panels that have their own buttons in the Basic Workspace, but here you can close any of them that you don't need at the moment.

NOTE In older versions of Elements and Photoshop, panels were called "palettes." If you run across a tutorial that talks about the "Effects palette," for example, that's the same thing as the Effects panel.

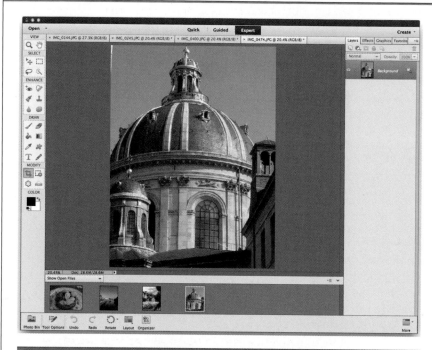

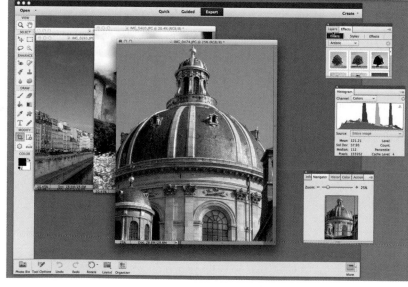

FIGURE 1-8.

Two different ways of working with the same images, panels, and tools. You can use any arrangement that suits you. (These images show the Mac version, in which the main menu bar is up at the top of the screen, out of the picture here. In Windows, it sticks to the top of the workspace.)

Top: The panels in the standard Custom Workspace arrangement, with the images in tabs.

Bottom: This image shows how you can customize your panels. The images here are in floating windows, and the Tool Options/Photo Bin is hidden. There's no Panel Bin, either, since all the panels are floating.

To pull a panel out of the bin, drag the panel's top tab (the one with its name on it); you've now got yourself a floating panel. (You can float panels even if you haven't turned on floating image windows as explained on page 95.) Figure 1-9 shows how to make panels even smaller once they're out of the bin by collapsing them in one of two ways. You can also combine panels, as shown in Figure 1-10; this works with both panels in the bin and freestanding panels you've dragged out of the bin.

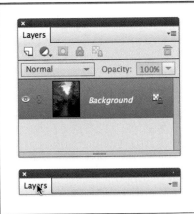

FIGURE 1-9.

You can free up lots of space by collapsing panels accordion-style once they're out of the bin.

Top: A full-sized panel.

Bottom: A panel collapsed by double-clicking the panel's tab (where the cursor is here). Be sure to click in the name of the panel, not in the blank area to the right of the tab.

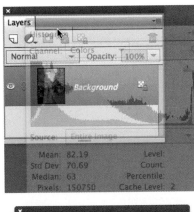

FIGURE 1-10.

You can combine two or more panels once you've dragged them out of the Panel Bin.

Top: Here, the Histogram panel is being combined with the Layers panel. To combine panels, drag one of them (by clicking the tab at the top of the panel) onto the other. When the moving panel becomes ghosted and you see the blue outline shown here, they'll combine as soon as you let go of your mouse button.

Bottom: To switch from one panel to another after they're grouped, just click the tab of the one you want to use. Here you see the mouse ready to click the Layers panel's tab to switch over to it from the Histogram panel. To remove a panel from a group, simply drag its tab out of the group. To return everything to how it looked when you first entered the Custom Workspace, go to Window→Reset Panels.

The first time you call up one of the panels that's not initially displayed in the Custom Workspace (by selecting its name in either the Window menu or the menu that appears when you click the down arrow on the right side of the More button), you get the same floating panel clump that you get in the Basic Workspace (page 12). Luckily, you can fix this in a jiffy. Just pull the panels you want loose from the clump. From now on, Elements will remember what you did, and those panels will appear right where you left them last time. So the first time you call up the History panel, for instance, you get the six-panel group. But if you separate the History panel from the group, from then on if you go to Window→History or click the arrow next to the More button and choose History, all you get is the panel you want, not the whole clump. You can put the panel in the bin, leave it floating, or combine it with another panel, and that's exactly how it will appear next time.

> **NOTE** If you've floated any panels, clicking the More button closes them. You can click the arrow on the right side of the button to bring up the pop-out menu and make choices there, but click the main part of the button and everything is gone. Click the button again to bring everything back again.

To close a floating panel, click its Close button (in Windows, the X at its upper right; on a Mac, at its upper left) or click the little white square made of four horizontal lines in the panel's upper right, and then choose Close from the menu that appears.

> **NOTE** Confusingly, Adobe sometimes refers to floating panels as "tabs" in Elements' menus. So, for example, when you click the four-lined square on a floating panel you see a Close Tab Group option instead of a Close Panel Group option.

In addition, when you're using the Custom Workspace, you can put floating panels into the Panel Bin. Where you drag the panel determines where it appears in the bin. If you want to see a panel's tab with the other tabs at the top of the bin, then drag the panel's top tab onto the other tabs at the top of the bin and let go when you see a blue outline. Since the Panel Bin in Elements 11 always fills the entire right side of the screen from top to bottom, you may also prefer to stack panels vertically so that you can see more than one at a time. To do that, drag the floating panel to the bottom of the bin. Once it's in, you can drag it farther up, and then add another panel at the bottom, if you wish. You can also drag it onto the tab of a panel that's already in the bin to create a combined panel.

One thing that's a bit tricky about the Custom Workspace is that you may wind up losing the Panel Bin completely. If you pull all the panels out of it, the bin feels unwanted and just disappears. This can be very handy because it gives you more space to spread out when working on photos, but if you want the bin back, you may find yourself dragging a panel all over the right side of the screen trying to make it dock back into the main window. The trick is to move the panel over the far right edge of the main Editor window. When you do this, the blue line appears along that edge. Let go of the panel, and the Panel Bin returns, with your panel in it.

All this panel organizing isn't as complicated as it sounds, and it's easier to learn by doing than by reading about it. So try dragging some panels around in the Custom Workspace. If you don't like the results of your handiwork or you move the panels around so much that you can't remember where you put things, just go to Window→Reset Panels, which puts all the panels back in their original spots.

■ IMAGE WINDOWS

You also get to choose how you want to view the images you're working on. Older versions of Elements used floating windows, where each image appears in a separate window that you could drag around. Elements now starts you out with a tabbed view—which uses something like the tabs in a web browser, or the tabs you'd find on paper file folders—but you can still put images into floating windows, if you prefer (page 95 explains how). The advantage of tabbed view is that it gives you plenty of workspace around your image, which is handy when you're working near the edges of a photo or using a tool that requires you to be able to get outside the image's boundaries. Many people switch back and forth between floating and tabbed windows as they work, depending on which is most convenient. All the things you can do with image windows—including how to switch between tabbed view and floating windows—are explained on page 93. (Incidentally, clicking Window→Reset Panels doesn't do anything to your image windows or tabs; it only resets your panels.)

> **NOTE** Because your view may vary, most of the illustrations in this book show only the image itself and the tool in use, without a window frame or a tab boundary around it.

Elements' Tools

Elements gives you an amazing array of tools to use when working on photos. You get almost two dozen primary tools to help select, paint on, and otherwise manipulate images, and some of the tools have as many as seven subtools. Bob Vila's workshop probably isn't any better stocked than Elements' virtual toolbox.

> **TIP** To explore every nook and cranny of Elements, you need to open a photo (in the Editor, choose File→Open). Lots of the menus are grayed out (unavailable) if you don't have a file open.

The long, skinny strip on the left side of the Editor window when you're in Expert Mode is the Tools panel (Figure 1-11). It stays perfectly organized so you can always find what you want without ever having to tidy it up. In Elements 11, the Tools panel is fixed in place—it's always in the same spot and you can't move it, resize it, or make it into a single column like you could in previous versions of the program.

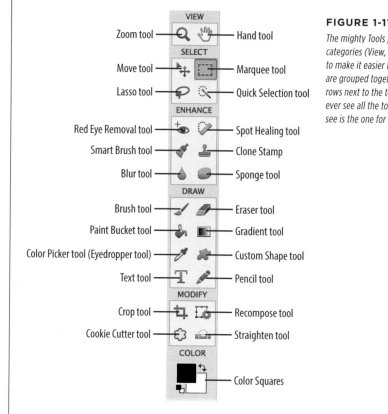

FIGURE 1-11.

The mighty Tools panel. In Elements 11, it's divided into six categories (View, Select, Enhance, Draw, Modify, and Color) to make it easier to find what you want. Because some tools are grouped together in the same slot (indicated by little arrows next to the tools' icons, shown in Figure 1-12), you can't ever see all the tools at once. For grouped tools, the icon you see is the one for the last tool in the group you used.

Many of the icons in the Tools panel actually represent tool *groups,* but in Elements 11, Adobe has chosen to play hide and seek with the subtools. Move your cursor over a section of the Tools panel, and you'll see teeny, tiny arrows above the icons of the tools in that section that have other tools nested with them (see Figure 1-12).

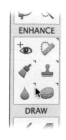

FIGURE 1-12.

When you move your mouse over a section of the toolbox that has subtools nested in with the visible tools, you see these minute arrows next to the tool icons. Here you can see that all the tools in the Enhance section *except* the Red Eye tool have more tools grouped with them. Unlike in earlier versions of Elements, you can't right-click a tool's icon or hold the mouse down to see the subtools; but you can cycle through all the tools that share a slot by Alt-clicking/Option-clicking the icon repeatedly, or just look in the Tool Options area at the bottom of the Elements window.

Incidentally, whether or not you see the category names (like the Enhance and Draw labels shown here) depends on your screen resolution. If your screen is so short that the Tools panel would be cut off if the names were displayed, Elements just doesn't show them.

When you click an icon in the Tools panel, the Tool Options area (page 14) displays settings for that tool, as well as icons for any subtools nested with that tool. If you forget what a particular icon is for, just put your cursor over it and a label (called a *tooltip*) will appear telling you the tool's name. To activate a tool, click its icon in either the Tools panel (if the icon is displayed there) or in the Tools Options area (if the tool is grouped with the currently active tool). Each tool comes with its own collection of options, as shown in Figure 1-13. The Tools panel remembers the last tool you used, so if you choose to use one of the nested tools, the next time you'll see the icon for *that* tool in the panel rather than the one for the tool that was there when you first started Elements. This seems complicated, but after a while you get pretty good at remembering where each tool lives.

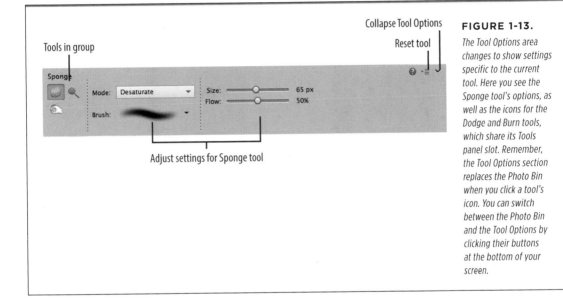

FIGURE 1-13.

The Tool Options area changes to show settings specific to the current tool. Here you see the Sponge tool's options, as well as the icons for the Dodge and Burn tools, which share its Tools panel slot. Remember, the Tool Options section replaces the Photo Bin when you click a tool's icon. You can switch between the Photo Bin and the Tool Options by clicking their buttons at the bottom of your screen.

Other windows in Elements, like Quick Fix and the Raw Converter, also have toolboxes, but none is as complete as Expert Mode's Tools panel. Don't worry about learning the names of every tool right now. It's easier to remember what a tool is once you've used it. And don't be overwhelmed by all of Elements' tools. You probably have a bunch of Allen wrenches in your garage that you use only every year or so. Likewise, you'll find that you tend to use certain Elements tools more than others.

TIP You can save a *ton* of time by activating tools with their keyboard shortcuts rather than by clicking their icons, since that way you don't have to interrupt what you're doing to trek over to the Tools panel. To see a tool's shortcut key, put your cursor over its icon; a label pops up indicating the shortcut key (it's the letter to the right of the tool's name). To activate the tool, just press the appropriate key. If the tool you want is part of a group then, all the tools in that group have the same keyboard shortcut, so just keep pressing that key to cycle through the group until you get to the tool you want.

The Always-On Toolbox

Do I always need to have a tool selected?

When you look at the Tools panel, you'll probably notice that one tool's icon is highlighted, indicating that the tool is active. You can deactivate it by clicking a different tool. But what happens when you don't want *any* tool to be active? How do you fix things so that you don't have a tool selected?

You don't. One tool always has to be selected, so you probably want to get in the habit of choosing a tool that won't do any damage to your image if you click accidentally. For instance, the Pencil tool, which leaves a spot or a line where you click, probably isn't a good choice. But the Marquee selection tool (page 139), the Zoom tool (page 98), and the Hand tool (page 99) are all safe bets. (When you open the Editor, Elements activates the tool you were using the last time you closed the program.)

Getting Help

Wherever Adobe found a stray corner in Elements, it stuck some help into it. You can't move anywhere in this program without being offered some kind of guidance. Here are a few of the ways you can summon assistance if you need it:

- **Help menu.** Choose Help→Photoshop Elements Help or press F1/⌘-?. When you do, Elements launches your web browser, which displays Elements' Help files, where you can search or browse a topic list and glossary. The Help menu also contains links to online video tutorials and Adobe's support forum for Elements.

- **Dialog box links.** Many dialog boxes have a few words of bright blue text somewhere in them. (Sometimes you'll see a question mark in a circle instead.) That text is actually a link to Elements Help. If you get confused about what the Remove Color Cast feature does, for instance, then, in the Remove Color Cast dialog box, click the blue words "color cast" for a reminder.

NOTE When Elements 11 is busy doing something that takes a while, it lets you know by displaying a notice in a dark gray oval that says something like "Undo Paint Bucket" or whatever the particular task is.

■ GUIDED EDIT

If you're a beginner, Guided Edit (Figure 1-14) can be a big help. It walks you through a variety of popular editing tasks, like cropping, sharpening, correcting colors, and removing blemishes. It also includes some features that are useful even if you're an old hand at Elements, like the High Key and Low Key edits (page 458). Guided Edit is really easy to use:

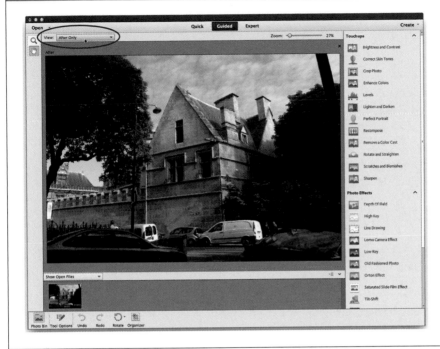

FIGURE 1-14.

Guided Edit gives you step-by-step help with basic photo editing. Just use the tools that appear in the right-hand panel once you choose an activity there. As with Quick Fix, you can change the view to Before & After; simply use the View menu (circled) to select the view you want.

1. **Go to Guided Edit.**

   At the top of the Editor window, click the Guided tab.

2. **Open a photo.**

   If you already have an image open when you click over to Guided Edit, then it appears in the main window automatically. If you need to open an image, press Ctrl+O/⌘-O and then, in the dialog box that appears, choose your photo. If you have several photos in the Photo Bin, then you can switch images by double-clicking the thumbnail of the one you want to work on. (If the Photo Bin disappears while you're working, just click its button at the bottom of the screen to bring it back again.)

3. **Choose what you want to do.**

   In the panel on the right side of the Guided Edit window, your options are grouped into major categories like Touchups and Photo Effects, with a variety of specific projects under each heading. Just click the task you want in the list, and the panel displays the relevant buttons and/or sliders for that task.

4. **Make your adjustments.**

Simply move the panel's sliders and click its buttons till you like what you see. If you need to adjust your view of the photo while you work on it, use the Hand (page 99) and Zoom (page 98) tools that appear in a little toolbox on the left side of the Guided Edit window.

If you want to start over, click the Reset Panel button, shown in Figure 1-15. If you change your mind about the whole project, click Cancel at the bottom of the panel.

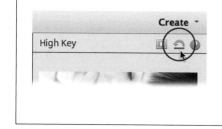

FIGURE 1-15.

Although Adobe tried to make Elements easier for beginners to use, it's a pretty good bet that you won't easily guess the purpose of this strange little icon, which appears in many places in Elements 11. This is the Reset button. In Guided Edit and Quick Fix, it's officially called Reset Panels, which is another way of saying, "Undo everything I've done since I entered this window." (Incidentally, the little button to its left lets you play a video tutorial on the particular edit you're performing.)

5. **Click Done to finish.**

Don't forget to save your changes (page 65). If you decide you don't like what you did, click Cancel. To close your photo, press Ctrl+W/⌘-W; or leave it open and switch to another tab to share it or use it in a project.

TIP Guided Edit shows you quick and easy ways to change an image, but it doesn't always get you the best possible results. It's a great tool for starting out; just remember that what you see there isn't necessarily the best you can make your images look. Once you're more comfortable in Elements, Quick Fix (Chapter 4) is a good next step. You'll find that most of the tools there will be familiar if you've been using Guided Edit.

Escape Routes

Elements has a couple of really wonderful features to help you avoid making permanent mistakes: the Undo command and the History panel. After you've gotten used to them, you'll probably wish it were possible to use these tools in all aspects of your life, not just Elements.

■ UNDO

No matter where you are in Elements, you can almost always change your mind about what you just did. Press Ctrl+Z/⌘-Z, and the last change you made goes away. This keystroke works even if you've just saved your photo, but only while the image is still open—if you close the file, your changes are permanent. Keep pressing Ctrl+Z/⌘-Z to keep undoing your work, step by step.

If you want to *redo* what you just undid, press Ctrl+Y/⌘-Y. These keyboard shortcuts are great for toggling changes on and off while you decide whether you want to keep them. The Undo/Redo keystrokes work in both the Organizer and the Editor.

> **NOTE** If you don't like Ctrl+Z/⌘-Z and Ctrl+Y/⌘-Y, you have a bit of control over the key combinations you use for Undo and Redo. Go to Edit→Preferences→General/Adobe Photoshop Elements Editor→Preferences→General, where the Step Back/Fwd menu gives you two other choices, both of which involve pressing the Z key in combination with the Control, Alt, and Shift keys in Windows, and with the ⌘, Option, and Shift keys on a Mac.

If you prefer buttons to keystrokes, you can use the Undo and Redo buttons in the bottom left of the Elements window instead. And if you want to use the keystrokes but forget what they are, they're listed at the top of the Edit menu.

■ THE HISTORY PANEL

In Expert Mode, you get even more control over the actions you can undo, thanks to the History panel (Figure 1-16), which you open by choosing Window→History. (In previous versions of Elements, this was called the *Undo* History panel.)

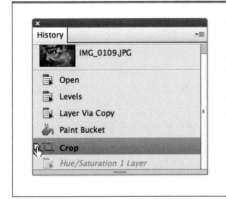

FIGURE 1-16.

For a little time travel, just drag the pointer on the left side of the panel (it's under the cursor in this image) up and watch your changes disappear. You can only go back sequentially. Here, for instance, you can't go back to the Paint Bucket without first undoing the Hue/Saturation Layer and the Crop. You can also hop to a given spot in the list by clicking the place where you want to go instead of using the pointer. Drag the pointer down to redo your work.

This panel holds a list of the changes you've made since you opened your image. Just drag the slider up and watch your changes disappear one by one. Like the Undo command, this panel works even if you've saved your file: As long as you haven't *closed* the file, the panel tracks every action you take. You can also drag the pointer down to redo changes that you've undone.

Be careful, though: You can back up only as many steps as Elements is set to remember. The program is initially set up to record 50 steps, but you can change that number by going to Edit→Preferences→Performance/Adobe Photoshop Elements Editor→Preferences→Performance and adjusting the History States setting. You can set it as high as 1,000, but remembering even 100 steps may slow your computer to a crawl if it doesn't have a super-powered processor, plenty of memory, and loads of disk space. If Elements runs slowly on your machine, then reducing the History States setting to, say, 20 may speed things up a bit.

■ THE ONE RULE OF ELEMENTS

As you're beginning to see, Elements lets you work in lots of different ways. What's more, most people who use the program approach projects in different ways; what works for your neighbor with her pictures may be quite different from how you'd work on the very same shots. But you'll hear one suggestion from almost every Elements veteran, and it's an important one: *Never, ever work on your original. Always, always, always make a copy of your image and work on that instead.*

The good news is that, if you store your photos in the Organizer, you don't need to worry about accidentally messing up your original. If you save your files as *version sets* (page 66), Elements automatically creates a copy when you edit a photo that's cataloged in the Organizer, so you can always revert to your original. Other image-management programs, like Apple's iPhoto and Adobe's Lightroom, also make versions for you if you set up Elements as your external editor (page 36).

But, as explained on page 43, you don't have to use the Organizer. If you've decided not to use it or version sets, then follow these steps to make a copy of your image in the Editor:

1. **Open the image you want to copy and then go to File→Duplicate.**

   The Duplicate Image dialog box appears.

2. **In the dialog box, name the duplicate and then click OK.**

   Elements opens the new, duplicate image in the main image window.

3. **Find the original image and click its Close button (the X or the red dot).**

   If you're using tabs (you are unless you've changed the settings described on page 93), the close X is on the right side of the image's tab in Windows, and on the left side on a Mac. If you have floating windows (page 16), the Close button is the standard Windows or Mac Close button you'd see in any window. Now the original is safely tucked out of harm's way.

4. **Save the duplicate by pressing Ctrl+S/⌘-S.**

   Choose Photoshop (.psd) as the file format when you save it. (You may want to choose another format after you've read Chapter 3 and understand more about your different format options.)

Now you don't have to worry about making a mistake or changing your mind, because you can always start over.

NOTE Elements doesn't have an autosave feature, so you should get into the habit of saving frequently as you work. This is true even if you're using a Mac running OS X 10.7 (Lion) or 10.8 (Mountain Lion)—Elements isn't currently able to use OS X's Auto Save feature. Page 65 has more about saving.

Getting Started in a Hurry

If you're the impatient type and you're starting to squirm because you want to be up and doing something to your photos, here's the quickest way to get started in Elements: Adjust an image's brightness and color balance all in one step.

1. **In Expert Mode or the Quick Fix window, open a photo.**

   Press Ctrl+O/⌘-O and navigate to the image you want, and then click Open.

2. **Press Alt+Ctrl+M/Option-⌘-M.**

   You've just applied Elements' Auto Smart Fix tool (Figure 1-17).

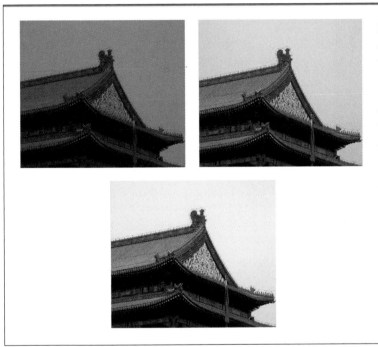

FIGURE 1-17.

Auto Smart Fix is the quickest, easiest way to improve the quality of a photo.

Top left: The original, unedited picture.

Top right: Auto Smart Fix makes quite a difference, but the colors are still slightly off.

Bottom: By using some of the other tools you'll learn about in this book (like Auto Contrast and Adjust Sharpness), you can make things look even better.

Voilà! You should see quite a difference in your photo, unless the exposure, lighting, and contrast were almost perfect before. (If you don't like what just happened to your photo, no problem—simply press Ctrl+Z/⌘-Z to undo the changes.) The Auto Smart Fix tool is one of Elements' many easy-to-use features.

If you're really raring to go, jump ahead to Chapter 4 to learn about using the Quick Fix commands. But it's worth taking the time to read the next two chapters so you understand which file formats to choose and how to make some basic adjustments to your images, like rotating and cropping them.

Don't forget to give Guided Edit a try if you see what you want to do in its list of topics. Guided Edit (page 22) can be a big help while you're learning your way around.

Importing, Managing, and Saving Photos

N ow that you've had a look around Elements, it's time to start learning how to get photos into the program and how to keep track of where they're stored. As a digital photographer, you don't have to deal with shoeboxes stuffed with prints, but you've still got to face the menace of photos piling up on your hard drive. Fortunately, Elements gives you some great tools for organizing your collection and quickly finding individual pictures.

In this chapter, you'll learn how to import photos from cameras, memory card readers, and scanners. You'll also find out how to import individual frames from videos, create new files from scratch, and open files already on your computer. Then you'll be ready for a quick tour of the redesigned Organizer, where you can sort and find pictures once they're in Elements. Finally, you'll learn about saving and backing up your precious files.

■ Importing from Cameras

Elements gives you lots of different ways to get photos from camera to computer, but if you use the Organizer, the simplest way is using Adobe's Photo Downloader. Later in this section, you'll learn about other ways to import photos.

> **NOTE** Take a moment to carefully read the instructions from your camera's manufacturer. If those directions conflict with anything you read here, follow the manufacturer's instructions.

The Photo Downloader

What happens when you plug a camera or memory card reader into your computer depends on your operating system. If you have Windows 7 or Vista, you get a standard Windows dialog box (shown on page 8) asking what you want to do. To use the Photo Downloader to get your photos into Elements, just click "Organize and Edit using Adobe Photoshop Elements Organizer 11.0." (If you're using Windows XP, choose Elements Organizer 11.0 from the dialog box that appears.)

> **NOTE** If you're using Windows and don't automatically see the dialog box described above when you plug your camera into your computer, then call up the Photo Downloader by heading to the Organizer and choosing File→"Get Photos and Videos"→"From Camera or Card Reader", or pressing Ctrl+G.

On a Mac, you won't see the Downloader at all unless you specifically tell your Mac to use it, which you do in the Organizer: "Go to File"→"Get Photos and Videos"→"From Camera or Card Reader", or press ⌘-G. You can't set the Mac Downloader to run automatically whenever you plug in a camera or card reader—you have to launch it from the Organizer.

> **NOTE** Although much of this chapter talks about importing pictures from a *camera*, most memory card readers work the same way. Use a card reader if you have one, since that will spare the camera's batteries and subject your camera to less wear and tear.

The Downloader's job is pretty straightforward: to shepherd your photos as they make the trip from camera to computer, and to make sure Elements knows where your images are stored. Your job is to help it along by adjusting the following settings (on display in Figure 2-1):

- **Get Photos from.** Your first step in downloading is to choose your camera or card reader from the list of available devices. (You may see a more generic "Camera or Card Reader" choice rather than the name of your camera; if that's all you see, then pick that option.) Just below this menu, the Downloader lists how many photos it found and how many duplicates (of images already in the Organizer) it plans to skip, if any.

- **Location.** Your photos usually get stored in a folder named for the date you shot them. In Windows 7 or Vista, this folder lives in *C:\Users\<your username>\Pictures*; in XP, it's *C:\<your user name>\My Documents\My Pictures\Adobe\Digital Camera Photos*. On a Mac, it's *[your hard drive]→Users→<your username>→Pictures*. If you want to change where your photos are headed, click the Browse button and choose another location. You can permanently change the standard save location by opening the Organizer and going to Edit→Preferences→"Camera or Card Reader"/Adobe Elements 11 Organizer→Preferences→"Camera or Card Reader" and changing the Save Files In setting; from then on, the Downloader will put your photos in the folder you chose.

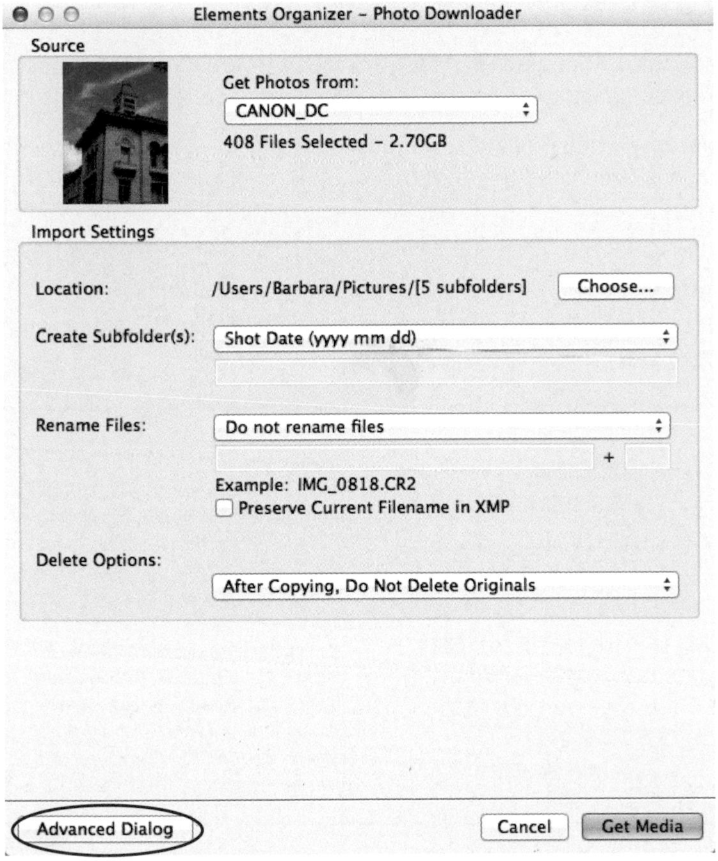

FIGURE 2-1.

When the Photo Downloader first launches, you see this dialog box, which lets you choose where Elements puts the photos and what it names them (say goodbye to names like IMG_0327. JPG). To start, choose your camera or card reader from the "Get Photos from" list at the top of the dialog box. If you want to import only specific images, click the Advanced Dialog button (circled) so you can choose which photos to grab and fine-tune other settings.

- **Create Subfolder(s).** If you want to have more levels of organization, you can put your image files into a subfolder *inside* the folder you chose for the Location. Use this drop-down menu to choose what Elements uses as the subfolder's name: today's date, the shot date (in your choice of several different formats), or a custom name. If you don't want to create a subfolder, choose None.

- **Rename Files.** Here you can choose to give all the files you're importing a custom name. If you select Custom Name from the drop-down menu and then type *obedience_school_graduation* in the box below it, for example, then you get photos named obedience_school_graduation_0001, obedience_school_graduation_0002, and so on. Or you can use just the shot date or today's date, or the name of the subfolder, or a combination of a custom name and the date you shot the photo. No matter which naming scheme you choose, Elements adds a four-digit number to the end of each file's name (as in the obedience-school example) to help you distinguish among them. You can also choose Advanced Rename to bring up a window where you can set a very complex group of parameters for naming your photos. If you leave the Rename Files field set to "Do not rename files," then Elements keeps the filenames and numbers your camera assigned.

- **Preserve Current Filename in XMP.** Turn this checkbox on if you want the photos' current filenames to be stored in the photos' *metadata* (page 48).

- **Open Organizer when Finished (Windows only).** If you're going to put your files in the Organizer, leave this checkbox turned on. Turn it off if you don't use the Organizer, or if you'd rather wait till later to get organized. (You won't see this checkbox if the Organizer is already running when you import your photos.)

- **Delete Options.** You can have the Downloader delete your files off your camera's memory card when it's done importing them. Figure 2-2 explains more about this option.

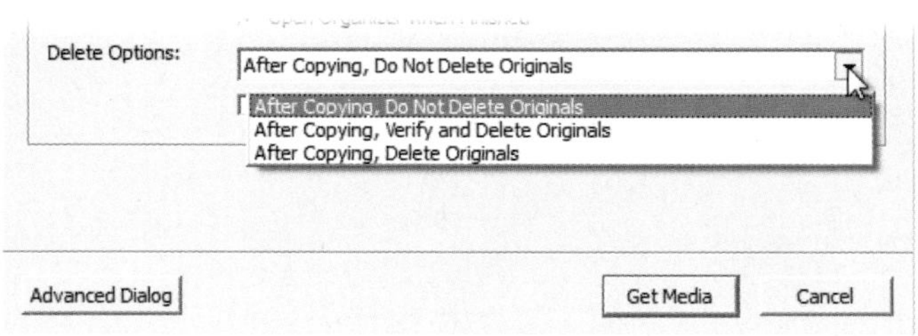

FIGURE 2-2.

The Photo Downloader can delete the files from your camera or memory card reader once it's done importing them. This feature seems handy, but think twice about using it. The Downloader is pretty reliable, but it's always good to wait until you've reviewed all your photos in Elements before deleting the originals. If you really want the Downloader to delete your files, at least choose "After Copying, Verify and Delete Originals" to make Elements check that it has copied your files correctly before vaporizing the originals.

- **Automatic Download (Windows only).** If you like to live dangerously, you can turn on this checkbox and Elements will download any new photos it detects without showing you the Photo Downloader dialog box. It's almost always best to leave Automatic Download off so that you have some control over what's going on. (This checkbox appears only after you've selected a device in the "Get Photos from" menu.) If you decide to take this risky route, you can tell Elements where to put your photos and whether it should delete the originals by going to the Organizer and choosing Edit→Preferences→"Camera or Card Reader."

The Downloader is smart enough to recognize any photos that it's already imported, and it doesn't reimport those. If you want to see these duplicates and for some reason download them again, or if you want to pick and choose which photos to import, then click the Advanced Dialog button at the bottom of the Downloader window to bring up the dialog box shown in Figure 2-3. (If you change your mind and want to switch back to the standard dialog box, then click the Standard Dialog button.)

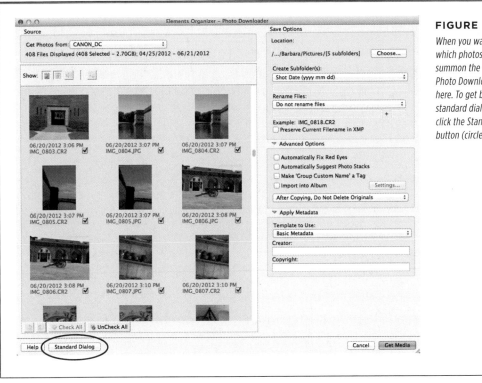

FIGURE 2-3.

When you want to select which photos to import, summon the advanced Photo Downloader, shown here. To get back to the standard dialog box, click the Standard Dialog button (circled).

The advanced dialog box gives you all the options found in the standard Photo Downloader, plus a few more. The advanced dialog box is divided into two main parts. On the left side are the thumbnails of your photos. The little checkmarks next to each image indicate which photos Elements plans to import; just turn off the checkboxes for the ones you don't want to bring into the Organizer. If you plan to import only a few images, save yourself some time by clicking Uncheck All below the preview area and then just turning on the checkboxes for the ones you want. (If you've already imported some of the images, the Organizer tells you so and doesn't import them again.) You can also import video and sound files.

The four buttons above the preview area (next to the word "Show") let you choose which files you see. From left to right, these are the buttons:

- **Show/Hide Images.** If you want to temporarily hide your photos (so you can look at just your video files, for instance), click this button or press Ctrl+M/⌘-M.

- **Video files.** This button is grayed out unless Elements finds any movie or video files on your memory card. If it does, you can hide them by clicking this button. You might do that if, say, you're only interested in importing still photos right now. To see the video files again, just click this button.

- **Audio files.** This button works just like the video button, but it becomes active when Elements finds audio files you may want to import.

- **Show Duplicates.** If Elements has already imported some of the photos on your memory card and you want to see those files again, then click this button and you can reimport them (or just see them for comparison's sake). In the preview area, the thumbnails of the files you've already imported display an icon that looks just like this button in their upper-right corners to indicate that they're duplicates.

> **NOTE** If you want to search for duplicates among the images already on your computer, you may think you've lucked out. Going to Find→By Visual Searches→"Search for Duplicate photos" in the Organizer sounds like just the ticket, doesn't it? Unfortunately, this is just a visually based search and, while Elements *may* find some duplicates this way (as well as a lot of photos you probably don't consider duplicates), there's no easy way to cull through the photos it finds, since you can't see any file information here to help you decide which of two visually identical images is the one you want to keep. All you can really do in the search results window is stack them.

The right side of the advanced dialog box is where you can adjust the settings for where your pictures are stored on your computer and how their folders are named. Most of these choices are the same ones you get in the Photo Downloader's standard dialog box, but you also get a few extras:

- **Automatically Fix Red Eyes.** If you turn this checkbox on, Elements searches through all your newly imported photos looking for people with red eyes (caused by camera flash) and fixes them automatically. It sounds great, but it's not 100 percent reliable and tends to "fix" things like bright white teeth as well. Fortunately, these changes aren't permanent because Elements makes a version set (page 66) with your original, so you can ditch the new version if you don't like what Elements did. But the extra time it takes for Elements to analyze all your photos *and* the time you'll waste looking for mistakes mean you're better off leaving this option turned off and using another method to fix red eyes later. See page 121 for more about Elements' Red Eye Removal tool. (You may find that you also need to turn off Automatically Fix Red Eyes in the Organizer by going to Edit→Preferences→"Camera or Card Reader" /Edit→Adobe Elements 11 Organizer→"Camera or Card Reader" to keep this setting from turning itself back on again.)

- **Automatically Suggest Photo Stacks.** The Organizer lets you group related photos together into *stacks*. Turn this checkbox on to use the auto-stack feature, where Elements automatically finds photos that should be grouped together.

This feature works best for photos taken in your camera's burst (rapid advance) mode—in other words, photos of the same subject taken in quick succession.

- **Make 'Group Custom Name' a Tag.** If you chose a custom name for your images, you can assign that name as a tag here. (Tags are explained on page 43.)

- **Import into Album.** Turn this checkbox on and Elements automatically adds the files you're currently downloading to the album you choose. Click the Settings button to select an existing album or to create a new one.

- **Apply Metadata.** If you want to write your name or copyright info right into the files' *metadata* (page 48) so that anyone who views your files will know they're yours, you can do that here.

Once you're done adjusting the Downloader's settings, click Get Media. The Downloader slurps down the photos and, in Windows, launches the Organizer (if it's not already running) so you can review your pictures.

> **TIP** In Windows, you can tell the Organizer to "watch" folders that you often bring graphics—or even sound files or videos—into. (Sorry, this feature isn't available on Macs.) For instance, you could tell Elements to watch your Pictures folder, which means the program will find all the new photos that you put there. But you can have it watch other folders, too. When you set a watched folder, Elements keeps an eye on it and, when new photos appear there, either imports the new files or tells you that they're waiting for you, depending on which option you choose. In the Organizer, go to File→Watch Folders, turn on the "Watch Folder and their Sub-Folder for new Files" checkbox. Then click the Add button, and *then* browse to the folder you want Elements to watch. And if you don't want Elements to watch a folder anymore, this is where you remove it from the list of watched folders. Also, if you want Elements to watch a folder that already contains photos in the Organizer, you can right-click its name in the Albums/Folders panel (page 49) and use the pop-out menu to tell Elements to watch it.

■ Opening Stored Images

If you've got photos already stored on your computer, you have several options for opening them with Elements. If you don't have Elements running but the file's format is set to open in Elements, then simply double-click the file's icon to launch Elements and open the image. (To change which files open automatically in Elements, see the box on page 38.) You've also got a few ways to open files from within Elements:

- **From the Organizer, for files not yet in the Organizer:** Go to File→"Get Photos and Videos"→"From Files and Folders" or press Ctrl+Shift+G/Shift-⌘-G, navigate to your photos, and then select them and click Get Media. (The other options in the "Get Photos and Videos from Files and Folders" dialog box—like fixing red eye and automatically suggesting photo stacks—are covered on page 34.) Then follow the steps in the next bullet point for opening your photos in the Editor.

- **From the Organizer, for files already in the Organizer:** You can select an image that's in the Organizer and open it in the Editor. To do so, in the Organizer, either click the file's thumbnail and then press Ctrl+I/⌘-I; right-click the thumbnail and choose "Edit with Photoshop Elements Editor"; or click the thumbnail and then click the Editor button at the bottom of the Organizer window. You can also Shift-click or Ctrl-click/⌘-click to select multiple photos before using any of these commands, and *all* those photos go to the Editor.

> **TIP** When your photos get to the Editor, they should appear in the main editing space. If you don't see anything there, go down to the Project Bin and, from the drop-down menu, choose "Show Files selected in Organizer."

- **From the Editor, for files anywhere on your computer:** Go to File→Open or press Ctrl+O/⌘-O and select your file(s). You can also drop a file right onto the Editor's main window and it'll open.

- **From other programs:** If you use another program to manage and organize your photos, like Lightroom, Aperture, or iPhoto, it's best to set Elements up as your external editor for that program and send your files to the Editor that way, rather than trying to use Elements' File→Open command. There are two reasons for this: First of all, the other program may be able to create and save *version sets* (page 66) like the Organizer does, but it won't be able to do that unless you send your files out for editing from within your other program. Also, the *library file* (the data the program stores about your photos) may be corrupted if you don't handle it exactly the way it's meant to be used. iPhoto's library is particularly resentful of being poked and prodded from outside the program itself.

The exact method for setting up an external editor depends on which program you're using, but there's typically a place to do that in the program's preferences. In Windows, you probably get to them by going to Edit→Preferences, and on a Mac, it's likely <Application name>→Preferences.

People who are new to Elements often get confused by the message shown in Figure 2-4, which appears in the Organizer when you leave a photo open in the Editor.

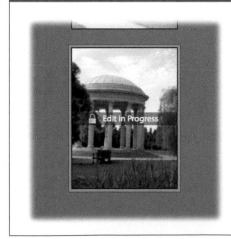

FIGURE 2-4.

This red "locked" band just means that you left your photo open in the Editor when you came back to the Organizer. To unlock it so that you have access to it in the Organizer, switch back to the Editor and close the photo by going to File→Close or pressing Ctrl+W/⌘-W.

Working with PDF Files

If you open a PDF file in Elements, you'll see the Import PDF dialog box (Figure 2-5), which lets you control how Elements treats the file. You can choose to import whole pages or just the images on the pages, import multiple pages (if the PDF is more than one page long), and choose the color mode (page 42) and the resolution of the imported files, as well as whether you want Elements to use anti-aliasing (page 156).

FREQUENTLY ASKED QUESTION

Picking the File Types That Elements Opens

How do I stop Elements from opening all my files?

Sometimes people are dismayed to discover that once they install Elements, it opens every time they double-click any kind of graphics file—whether they want the file to open in Elements or not. You can fix that easily enough:

In Windows: First, find a file of the type you want to change (like a JPEG, for example). Then, right-click the closed file's icon and, if you're using Windows 7 or Vista, select "Open with"→Choose Default Program from the pop-up menu. (If you're in Windows XP, select Open With→Choose Program instead.) In the list that

appears, select the program you want to use to open the file. Turn on the "Always use the selected program to open this kind of file" checkbox to set that program for all files of this type.

On a Mac: In the Finder, find a file of the type you want to change (like a JPEG, say). Click once to select it, and then press ⌘-I to bring up the Get Info window, which has lots of data about the file. Expand the "Open with" section by clicking the flippy triangle next to it, choose the program you want from the pull-down menu, and then click the Change All button. Voilà—from now on, those kinds of files will open in the program you chose.

Scanning Photos

Elements comes bundled with many scanners because it's the perfect program for making scans look their best. You have two main ways of getting scanned images into Elements. Some scanners come with a *driver plug-in,* a little program that lets you scan directly into Elements. Look on your scanner's installation software for info about Elements compatibility, or check the manufacturer's website for a Photoshop plug-in to download. (If the scanner lets you scan into Photoshop, you should be able to scan into Elements, too.) You may also be able to scan into Elements if your scanner uses the *TWAIN interface,* an industry standard used by many scanner manufacturers.

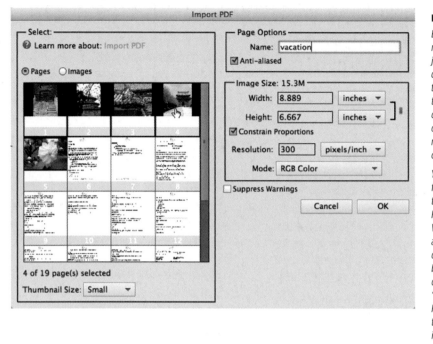

FIGURE 2-5.

*Elements can open
multipage PDFs. To open
just one page of the file,
double-click the page's
thumbnail. To open mul-
tiple pages, Ctrl-click/⌘-
click the ones you want,
or Shift-click to select a
range and then double-
click to open them.*

*You can catalog PDF
files in the Organizer,
too. To do that, go to
File→"Get Photos and
Videos"→"From Files
and Folders," and, in the
drop-down menu in the
bottom part of the win-
dow (on a Mac it's labeled
"Enable"), choose PDF
Files, and then navigate
to the PDF you want to
import.*

NOTE In Elements 11, you'll need to move the Adobe TWAIN driver (Twain_32.8ba), if your scanner requires it, before you can scan into Elements. In Windows, go to *C:\Program Files [Program Files(x 86) for 64-bit systems]\ Adobe\Photoshop Elements 11\Optional Plug-Ins\Import-Export*, find the Adobe TWAIN file, and move it to *C:\ Program Files [Program Files(x 86) for 64-bit systems]\Adobe\Photoshop Elements 11\Locales\en_US\Plug-Ins\ Import-Export* (the "en_US" part will be different if you aren't in the United States). If you don't want to hassle with this, you may be able to use WIA (the Windows system scanning) instead, from both the Editor and the Organizer.

On a Mac, go to Applications→Adobe Photoshop Elements 10→Support Files→Optional Plug-Ins→Import Modules, and move TWAIN.plugin from there into Applications→Adobe Photoshop Elements 10→Support Files→Plug-Ins→Import Modules.

If you have a Mac and you use OS X 10.6 (Snow Leopard), you need to be aware that not all Photoshop-compatible plug-ins will work with Elements 11. If you install your scanner, launch Elements, and then see a window that says, "One or more plug-ins are currently not available…" that usually means that your scanner plug-in isn't compatible with Elements 11, probably because you're trying to run a PowerPC plug-in on your Intel Mac. Here's why that's important: Beginning with Elements 8, Adobe decided not to let Elements run in Rosetta, the part of OS X that allows programs written for the older PowerPC Macs (G5 and earlier) to run on Intel Macs (newer Macs that use Intel processors). So your old scanner plug-in isn't going to work in Elements 11.

There are a couple of workarounds: If you're using Mac OS X 10.6 (Snow Leopard), you can keep an older version of Elements around for scanning, if you have one, or you can use the stand-alone scanner software that your scanner manufacturer may provide. (In OS X 10.7 [Lion] and 10.8 [Mountain Lion], Rosetta isn't available for *any* program.) In OS X 10.6, 10.7, and 10.8, you can also scan from Preview and send the scan straight to Elements. To do that, launch Preview with your scanner connected and then go to File→"Import from Scanner." You can even tell Preview to send the scan to Elements when you're done scanning. However, if you have a really old scanner, the scanning features in OS X 10.6, 10.7, and 10.8 may not acknowledge its existence, in which case you have to use the software provided by the manufacturer.

To control your scanner from within Elements, you can scan from the Editor and (in Windows) the Organizer. In the Editor, go to File→Import, and you'll see your scanner's name in the list that appears. In the Windows version of the Organizer, go to File→"Get Photos and Videos"→From Scanner, or press Ctrl+U. You should check out your available options for both locations because they're probably different. For instance, you may find that you have different file formats available to you in the Editor than in the Organizer.

If you have a Mac and you don't have an Elements plug-in for your scanner and the Adobe TWAIN driver doesn't work for you, then you'll need to use the software that came with your scanner. Then, once you've saved your scanned image in a format that Elements understands, like TIFF (.tiff, .tif) or Photoshop (.psd), open the file in Elements like you would any other photo. (Page 67 explains which formats Elements can use.)

TIP If you do a lot of scanning, check out the Divide Scanned Photos command (page 75), which lets you quickly scan in lots of photos at the same time. Also, you can save yourself a lot of drudgery in Elements if you make sure that both your scanner's glass and the prints you're scanning are as dust-free as possible before you start.

■ Capturing Video Frames

Elements lets you snag a single frame from a video and use it the way you would any still photo. This feature works only with movie files that are already on your computer (meaning you can't snag a frame from a video that's streaming to your computer from the Web). You're also limited to the formats that your operating system understands. So, for example, if you have a Mac, you may be able to watch videos in Windows Media (.wmv) format if you have Flip4Mac's free Windows Media Components for QuickTime (*http://tinyurl.com/crm9xx2*) installed, but you won't be able to import frames from those files, because OS X can't read them without a special program to help it out. Likewise, in Windows you can install QuickTime (it comes with iTunes, so you probably have it if you have an iPod, iPad, or iPhone), but you can't open QuickTime (.mov) files in Elements. And no matter what kind of computer you have, this Elements feature doesn't work with HD (high-definition) videos.

> **NOTE** Elements' video-capture tool isn't really designed for use with long movies. You'll get the best results with clips that are less than a minute or two long.

To import a video frame, in the Editor, go to File→Import→Frame From Video, and then in the Frame From Video dialog box do the following:

1. **Find the video that contains the frame you want to copy.**

    Click the Browse button and navigate to the movie file you want. After you choose the movie, its first frame appears in the dialog box's preview window.

2. **Navigate to the frame you want.**

    Either click the Play button (the single triangle), or use the slider below the preview to move through the movie until you see what you want.

3. **Copy the frame by clicking the Grab Frame button.**

    You can capture as many frames as you want by repeating this process. Each frame shows up in the Editor as a separate file.

4. **When you have everything you need, click Done.**

While grabbing video frames is fun, it does have certain limitations. Most important, any video frames you import will have a fairly low resolution, so don't expect to get a great print from a video frame.

Creating a New File

You may want to create a new, blank document when you're using Elements as a drawing program or when you're combining parts of images, for example.

To create a new file, go to the Editor, and choose File→New→Blank File, press Ctrl+N/⌘-N, or click the Open button at the upper left of your screen and choose New Blank File. No matter which method you use, you see the New dialog box. You have lots of choices to make each time you start a new file, including what to name it. All your other options are covered in the following sections.

> **TIP** You can't create a new, blank file in the Organizer, but Elements gives you a quick shortcut from the Organizer to the Editor so you can open up a new file there. In the Organizer, choose File→New→Photoshop Elements Image File, and Elements sends you over to the Editor and creates a virgin file for you. If you want to create a new file based on a photo that's in the Organizer, select the image's thumbnail, press Ctrl+C/⌘-C to copy the image, and then choose File→New→"Image from Clipboard." Elements switches you to the Editor, where you'll see your copied photo awaiting you, all ready to work on.

Picking a File Size

After you type a name for your file in the New dialog box, the next thing you need to decide is how big you want the image to be. There are two ways to do this:

- **Start with a Preset.** The Preset menu, the second item in the New dialog box, lets you choose the general kind of document you want. If you want to create a file for printing, pick from the menu's second group. The third group contains choices for onscreen viewing. Once you make a selection here, the next menu—Size—changes to show you suitable options for your choice. Figure 2-6 shows how this works.

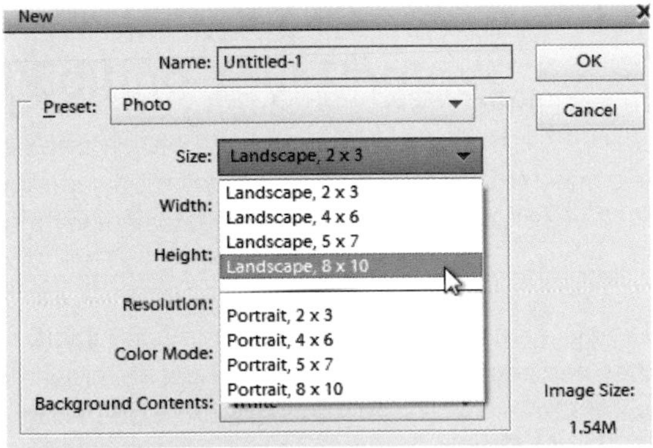

FIGURE 2-6.

Elements helps you pick an appropriate size when you use the Preset menu. Here, Photo is selected, so the Size menu includes standard sizes for photo paper, each available in either landscape or portrait orientation. (What Elements calls the "Default Photoshop Elements Size" is 6" x 4" at 300 pixels per inch, which works well if you're just playing around and trying things out.)

> **TIP** If you're into scrapbooking, you'll be pleased to see that Elements offers some standard scrapbook page sizes as presets.

- **Enter the numbers yourself.** If you prefer, just ignore the Preset and Size menus, and type what you want in the Width and Height boxes. The drop-down menus next to the boxes let you choose inches, pixels, centimeters, millimeters, points, picas, or columns as your unit of measurement.

Choosing a Resolution

If you decide not to use one of the size presets, you'll need to choose a resolution for your file. You'll learn a lot more about resolution in the next chapter (page 101), but a good rule of thumb is to go with 72 pixels per inch (ppi) for files that you'll look at only on a monitor, and 300 ppi for files you plan to print.

Selecting a Color Mode

Elements gives you lots of color choices throughout the program, but *color mode* is probably the most important one because it determines which tools and filters you can use on the document. These are your options:

- **RGB Color.** Choosing this mode (whose name stands for red, green, and blue) means that you're creating a color document, as opposed to a black-and-white one. (Page 230 has more about color in Elements.) You'll probably use this mode most of the time, even if you don't plan on having color in your image, because RGB gives you access to all of Elements' tools. That's right: You can use RGB Color mode for black-and-white images—and many people do, since it gives you the most options for editing your photo.

- **Bitmap.** Every pixel in a bitmap mode image is either black or white. Use Bitmap mode for *true* black-and-white images—shades of gray need not apply here.

- **Grayscale.** Black-and-white photos are technically called *grayscale* images because they're actually made up of many shades of gray. In Elements, you can't do as much editing on a grayscale photo as you can on an RGB one (for example, you can't use some of the program's filters on a grayscale image).

TIP Sometimes you may need to change the color mode of an existing file to use all of Elements' tools and filters. For example, there are quite a few things you can do only if your file is in RGB color mode. So if you need to use a filter (page 435) on a black-and-white photo and the menu item you want is grayed out, go to Image→Mode→RGB Color. Don't worry, changing the color mode won't suddenly colorize your photo; it just changes the way Elements handles the file. (You can always change back to the original color mode when you're done.) If you use Elements' "Convert to Black and White" feature (page 343), you'll still have an RGB-mode photo afterward, not a grayscale-mode image.

If your image is in RGB and you *still* don't have access to the filters, check to see if the file is 16 bit (page 282). If so, you need to convert it to 8-bit color to get everything working. Make that change by choosing Image→Mode→8 Bits/Channel. You're most likely to have 16-bit files if you import your images in Raw format (page 264), and some scanners also let you create 16-bit files. JPEG files are always 8-bit.

Choosing a Background

The last choice you have to make when creating a new file is the file's *background contents,* which tells Elements what color to use for the empty areas of the file, like, well, the background. You can be a traditionalist and leave the New dialog box's Background Contents menu set to white (almost always a good choice), or choose a particular color or *transparency* (more about transparency in a minute). To pick a color other than white, *before* you call up the New dialog box, use the background color square to pick the color you want, as shown in Figure 2-7; then select Background Color from the New dialog box's Background Contents menu.

FIGURE 2-7.
To choose a new background color, just click the background color square in the Tools panel (here, that's the blue one) to bring up the Color Picker. Then select the color you want. The new color appears in the square, and the next time you do something that involves using a background color, that's the shade you get. The color-picking process is explained in much more detail on page 247.

"Transparent" is the most interesting option. To understand transparency and why it's such a wonderful invention, you need to know that *every* digital image is either rectangular or square. Digital images *can't* be any other shape, but they can *appear* to be a different shape—sunflowers, sailboats, or German shepherds, for example. How? By placing an object on a transparent background so that it looks like it was cut out and only its shape appears, as shown in Figure 2-8. The actual photo is still a rectangle, but if you placed it into another image, you'd see only the shell and not the surrounding area, because the rest of the photo is transparent.

To keep the clear areas transparent when you close the image, you need to save it in a format that allows transparency. JPEGs, for instance, automatically fill transparent areas with solid white, so they're not a good choice. TIFFs, PDFs, and Photoshop (.psd) files, on the other hand, let the transparent areas stay clear. Page 553 has more about which formats allow transparency.

Using the Organizer

The Organizer is where you keep track of your photos and start most of the projects that involve sharing images with others (like posting them online, for example). You can see thumbnails of all your photos in the Organizer, assign them keywords (called *tags*) to make them easier to find, and search for them in lots of different ways.

In Elements 11, Adobe gave the Organizer a substantial makeover. It's based on two main ideas: Most people find organizing and tagging photos something of a chore; and most people want to organize photos by the people, places, or events they contain.

To try to deal with the drudgery of organizing, Elements 11 includes a lot more options to use various *smart* features, which let Elements do a lot of the heavy lifting for you. (If you've used a recent version of the Organizer, the face recognition system is one example of this, but there's a lot more of it in Elements 11.) You'll read about these new features in the sections of the Organizer where you find them.

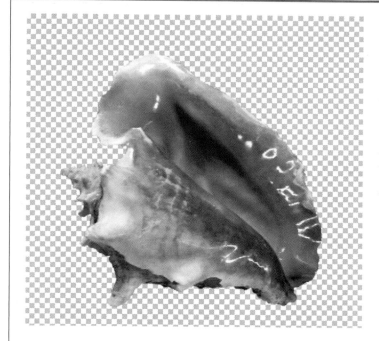

FIGURE 2-8.

This checkered background is Elements' way of indicating that an area is transparent. (It doesn't mean you've somehow selected a patterned background.) If you place this photo into another image, all you'll see is the seashell, without the checkerboard or the rectangular outline of the photo. If you don't like the size and color of the checkerboard pattern, you can adjust them in the Editor by going to Edit→Preferences→ Transparency/Adobe Photoshop Elements Editor→Preferences→Transparency.

To help deal with the second idea mentioned above, the new Organizer is divided into sections, which Adobe calls *rooms*. When you first import your photos, they come into the Media room (Figure 2-9), which is the part of Organizer where you can see all your photos all the time. From there, you can go into one of the other three rooms (People, Places, or Events) to do more organizing. You move from one room to another by clicking the tabs at the top of the window. To get the most out of Organizer, you need to understand how all the rooms work together.

However, there's one aspect of the new room system that you should understand before you start using the new Organizer. Each room has a more or less separate existence, so you can't always see the information you enter in one room in any of the others. So, for example, you can't see your list of keyword tags in the People room or in the Events room. This is different from previous versions of the Organizer where you could always see a master list of all your keywords (which Organizer calls *tags*). This may be enough to make you hesitate about spending a lot of effort on using the Organizer to categorize your photos. (Fortunately, you can do searches based on information from all the rooms, though. See page 63 for details.)

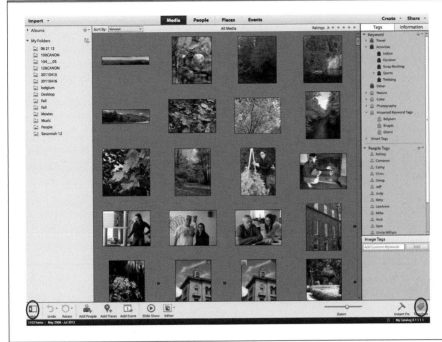

FIGURE 2-9.

The Media room is where you usually start off in the Organizer. If you don't see the useful panels on the sides, then click the buttons circled here to display them. The panel on the left shows your albums and folders, and the one on the right displays information about your photos.

The Instant Fix button (in the bottom-right corner of this window) calls up a panel where you can perform quick image fixes in the Organizer.

This section covers only the very basics of Elements' new organization system—there's lots more to it than there's room for here. Give the Organizer a good test drive to see if it works for you before you commit all your photos to it. You may hear from longtime Organizer users that they find the new Organizer more complicated than older versions, especially if they were used to the old setup. If you decide to bypass the new Organizer, at least until Adobe has refined it a little, there are many other programs you can use to organize your photos (Lightroom, Aperture, iPhoto, or iView MediaPro, for example), or you can just create your own filing system. If you decide to opt out for now, see the box on page 46 if you use Windows, or on page 47 for Macs, for how to work around it.

The Organizer stores information about your photos in a special database called a *catalog*. You don't have to do anything special to create your catalog—Elements creates it automatically the first time you import photos (and creatively names it *My Catalog*). It's possible to have more than one catalog, but most people don't because you can't search more than one catalog at a time. If for some reason you want to have more than one catalog, or if you ever want to start over with a new catalog, in the Organizer go to File→Manage Catalogs, and then click the New button. Enter a name for it and then click OK.

Avoiding the Organizer

People either love the Organizer or they hate it. If you're in the latter group and you have a Windows computer, try to see if you can come to terms with the Organizer, because it does have some useful features. You'll lose a lot if you give up the Organizer, as it's the only place in Elements where you get a visual preview of your images before opening them. Mac Organizer loathers, head over to the box on page 47; if you have a Windows computer, read on.

If you just can't abide the Organizer, or if you prefer to use a different program like Lightroom or Windows Live Photo Gallery to organize your photos—or you just like to be disorganized—then you can sidestep the Organizer. Simply adjust your settings on the Welcome screen as described on page 6 so that you always start up in the Editor. Also, remember to keep "Include in the Elements Organizer" and version sets turned *off* in the Save dialog box whenever you're saving a picture. Once you turn off the "Include in the Elements Organizer" setting, it stays off until you turn it back on, or until you open a photo from the Organizer (after which it turns itself back on). You may find you need to turn it off once every editing session (maybe

not, if you're lucky) but you don't have to keep turning it off every time you save.

If you want to be extra sure that Elements doesn't interpret any of your photo-related activities as a call for the Organizer, go to your computer's Control Panel→"System and Security"→Administrative Tools→Services and find Adobe Active File Monitor V11. (In Windows XP or Vista, you may need to choose Classic View first; and in Vista, you'll also see a dialog box or two asking for permission to continue.) This is a *service*, a small program that always runs in the background when your computer is on, even when Elements is closed. Click Adobe Active File Monitor, and then go to Action→Properties and set the "Startup type" option to Disabled.

If you've been using the Organizer in past versions of Elements, but you just can't come to grips with what Adobe has done to the Organizer in Elements 11, you can turn your tags into metadata keywords that other programs can read by selecting your photos in any version of the Organizer and going to File→"Save Metadata to File(s)." It might be a good idea to make tags for your categories before doing this to be sure they also come along.

Your catalog can include photos stored anywhere on your computer, and even photos that you've moved to external hard drives and CDs or DVDs. There aren't any limits on where you can keep your originals. That's how it's supposed to work, anyway. But in practice, Elements sometimes has a tough time finding files stored on network drives and other externals, so you may run into trouble if you want Elements to find photos you've saved on such devices. (The Mac Organizer, in particular, can't deal with network drives at all, although it should see removable drives, like FireWire or USB drives.)

Once your photos appear in the Organizer, if you want to move them, you have to use the Organizer to do that—as opposed to using another method like Windows Explorer—if you want the Organizer to know where they are. You aren't limited to photos, either—you can store videos and audio files in the Organizer as well.

Should You Use the Mac Organizer?

Starting with Elements 9, Adobe began including the Organizer in the Mac version of Elements instead of Adobe Bridge, which came with older versions of the program. So if you have a Mac, you need to decide whether to use the Organizer to keep track of your photos, and this is an even thornier question than it is in Windows.

If you've been using the Organizer in Windows and you just got a Mac, you probably want to use the Mac Organizer, since that's the easiest way to move everything over. However, you can only move catalogs made with Elements 9 or later from one operating system to the other, so if you have an older version of Elements for Windows, install Elements 11 in Windows and use it to upgrade your existing catalog. Next, make a full backup of your catalog to a removable hard drive. Then install Elements 11 on your Mac—you get both versions of the program in the same box—and restore the backup on the Mac (page 74 explains how). Once you're sure everything's working OK, you can deactivate Elements on the Windows computer (page 610) if you no longer need it. Also, if you have Premiere Elements, Adobe's video-editing program, the Organizer is much more important to that program than it is to Photoshop Elements.

If you use iPhoto, it's easy to siphon your images into the Organizer by choosing File→"Get Photos and Videos"→From iPhoto. You can import your *entire* iPhoto library or specific events (click More Options in the "Import from iPhoto" window to choose events) into Elements in a way that won't harm your photos. Elements reads your iPhoto library to get info about them, but if you create new files or edit existing ones, Elements saves that information in another folder outside the iPhoto library (page 65 has more about saving files). This is good, because the iPhoto library gets very cranky if you poke at it from outside iPhoto (don't try to make Elements save back into the iPhoto library or you could lose your photos entirely). Also, the Organizer has been known to make unexpected changes to the metadata (page 48) of files in the Organizer; if this happened to an image that's already in iPhoto, it's hard to tell what the effect might be. So if you're feeling brave, go ahead and give the Organizer a try. Just know that there's a slight risk involved.

If you want to move only some of your photos to the Organizer or just try it out, export your photos from the photo-management program you currently use, or create duplicate files to use as your test catalog. Put them where you want to keep them, and then import them by going to File→Get Photos→"From Files and Folders" in the Organizer.

The two big advantages to using the Organizer are that you can use all of Elements' features and Elements lets you save unlimited versions of your photos (see page 66). iPhoto, on the other hand, keeps only a single version plus the original. That means that if you edit a photo and then save it again, iPhoto overwrites the previous version (unless you import your saved files into iPhoto as new documents, which is a pain). The big disadvantages of using the Organizer are that it's not as smoothly integrated with other OS X programs as iPhoto is, and the Mac Organizer is still missing some major features that are in the Windows version. So while it's worth giving the Organizer a try, you may want to hold off until a later version of Elements before you commit to it for all your photos. Whatever you do, *don't* use both the Organizer and iPhoto to keep track of all your photos, because the two programs don't understand each other very well and you'll just get confused.

If you decide to avoid the Organizer, Adobe makes it easy to ignore it on a Mac. Just turn off the "Include in the Elements Organizer" checkbox in the Save As window (it should stay off, at least for that editing session). If photos accidentally get Organized, it's not a big deal, since the Organizer is just a database, which means it's not making copies of the photos and wasting gobs of space with duplicate images. If you're a fan of Adobe Bridge, you can keep using it. You just can't update it anymore, which is likely to be a problem if you shoot in Raw format (page 264) and buy a new model camera whose Raw format Bridge doesn't understand. (You can learn more about using Elements with iPhoto and using Bridge with later versions of Elements at *www.barbarabrundage.com*.)

TIP If you want to edit photos in programs other than Elements, the Organizer lets you do that. Just go to Edit→Preferences→Editing→Supplementary Editing Application/Adobe Elements 11 Organizer→Preferences→ Editing→Supplementary Editing Application and select your preferred program. (If you have Photoshop installed on your computer, it's automatically listed as an editing option.) This is handy if you want to supplement Elements with a program like PaintShop Pro or Pixelmator. Once you've chosen a supplemental editor, sending photos there is easy: Just select their thumbnails and then click the tiny arrow next to the Editor button at the bottom of the Organizer and choose External Editor. If you do decide to use a supplemental editor with the Organizer, be aware that Elements 11 doesn't automatically update your image thumbnails when you're through editing them. You need to do it manually. (Select the photos and go to View→Refresh, or just press F5.)

The Media Room

The Media room (Figure 2-9) is where your photos make their first appearance in the Organizer. There's a lot happening in this window, but once you learn your way around, it's all laid out pretty logically.

The center of the window shows thumbnails of all your photos. On the left side of the window is a panel which includes the names of any albums (page 55) you've made, and also a list of all the folders where your Organizer photos live. (This useful panel is visible in all the Organizer's rooms, not just the Media room.) You can hide this panel by clicking the Hide button at the bottom of the screen. When the panel is hidden, the button changes to say "Show"; click it again to bring back the panel.

TIP If you want to move photos that are in the Organizer from one place on your hard drive to another, you use Folder View, which is described starting on page 49.

You can use the Sort menu above the thumbnail area to see your photos by newest first, oldest first, or by the batches in which you imported them. To adjust the size of the thumbnails, use the Zoom slider below the thumbnail area. You can also quickly see any image in a larger view by double-clicking its thumbnail. This enlarges the image so it's the only one on your screen at a time. If you want to look through multiple photos in this single-image view, navigate through them by clicking the arrows above the image area. To get back to the regular grid view of all the thumbnails, click the Grid button at the upper left of the image area. (You can also view, organize, and edit your photos in Full Screen view, which is described on page 51.)

On the right side of the Organizer window is a panel with two tabs at its top: Keyword Tags and Information. (If you don't see this panel, click the Tags/Info button at the bottom right of the Organizer window.) If you click a photo's thumbnail, the Information panel shows you a *lot* of info about that photo—so much, in fact, that the panel is divided into three sections. Click the name of a section to expand it and see the information it contains. Here's what's in each one

- **General.** This section includes the photo's name, caption, any notes you've made, any rating (page 56), its size, date, location, and any audio associated with it.

- **Metadata.** This section includes all the information that your camera stores in the file. There are two little buttons at the upper right of this section. Normally

Elements starts you off showing the *brief* metadata, a short list of the most commonly used information, but if you click the right-hand button, you get the *full* metadata—all the info stored there. There's more about metadata on page 65.

- **History.** Here you can see when the file was last modified, when you imported it and from where, and the name of the volume (meaning "drive") where it's stored now.

At the bottom of the panel is a section labeled Image Keywords, where you can see any tags currently attached to the image and add your own tags. If you switch over to the Keyword Tags panel by clicking its tab, you also see the hierarchy of your tags and categories (page 52).

At the bottom right of the Organizer window is the Instant Fix button. Click it and the Keyword Tags and Information panels disappear and are replaced by the Photo Fix Options panel, which lets you apply a bunch of popular one-button fixes to your photos right in the Organizer, without sending the images over to the Editor. You can apply Auto Contrast, Auto Red Eye, Auto Color, Auto Sharpening, Auto Levels, and the Auto Smart Fix here. (Chapter 4 has more about how they all work.) You can also crop a photo here. When you use any of these fixes, the Organizer automatically creates version sets with your original photo, so it's not altered at all. To bring the other panels back when you're done using these instant fixes, just click the Tags/Info button at the bottom right of the Organizer window.

If some of your images came into the Organizer on their sides or upside down, you can get them upright by selecting their thumbnails and then clicking the Rotate button at the bottom of the window. This turns the photos counterclockwise; if you want to turn them the other way, click the tiny arrow on the right side of the Rotate button and then click the button that appears.

If you want to undo anything you've done in the Organizer, click the Undo button that's always at the bottom left of your screen, or just use the regular Ctrl+Z/⌘-Z keystroke. If you change your mind about undoing something, click the tiny arrow on the right of the Undo button and click the Redo button that appears, or just press Ctrl+Y/⌘-Y.

In addition, no matter which room you're in, you always have the option to import new files into the Organizer, start a Create project (page 509), or share your photos in a variety of ways (page 591). You can do all these things from the bar at the top of the Organizer window.

■ WORKING WITH FOLDERS

When you decide to use Organizer, you're putting it in charge of keeping track of your photos. But it can't do that if you move or delete photos from outside the Organizer; if you do, your photos become unconnected, and you have to help the Organizer reconnect them. So it's much better to do all moving and deleting from within the Organizer, which offers the handy Albums/Folders panel that makes it easy to move photos around while letting the Organizer keep track of them.

Folder view is part of the Albums/Folders panel on the left side of the Media room. (If you don't see it, click the Show button at the bottom left of the Organizer window.) At the top of the panel, you see the list of your albums, with a section labeled My Folders below. If you don't see any folders listed, click the flippy triangle to the left of the words "My Folders" to display them.

Adobe gives you two ways to see folders in the Organizer: Folder List view and Folder Hierarchy view. When you first start out in Folder view, you just see a list of the folders containing the photos currently in the Organizer. In this simple view (which Adobe calls *Folder List*,) you can move a photo by simply dragging its thumbnail from the preview area in the middle of the Organizer window onto the name of the folder you want to put it in. You can also right-click/Control-click any folder to display a pop-out menu that lets you see where it's located in Windows Explorer or the Mac Finder, watch the folder (if you use Windows—see page 35), rename it, delete it, or create an *Instant Album* based on it (an album of all the photos contained in that folder; Elements names the album the same thing as the folder).

That's all well and good, but what if you want to move a photo into a folder that doesn't yet contain any Organizer photos? Click the little yellow icon to the right of the words "My Folders" (it looks like two tiny folders) to see an expanded view of the folders on your hard drive. This hierarchical view, aptly called *Folder Hierarchy* view, lets you see all the folders on your hard drive, if you want, as Figure 2-10 explains. This is a great improvement over the Folder view in some past versions of Elements.

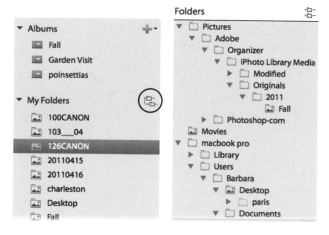

FIGURE 2-10.

Left: Here's the basic Folder List view the Organizer starts you out with. Click the tiny two-folder icon (circled) to see a more complete view of the folders on your hard drive.

Right: Folder Hierarchy view, where you can right-click/Control-click any folder to see a menu that has all the same options you get by doing this in Folder List view and lets you import photos from the folder you right-clicked/Control-clicked, as well as see all the subfolders within that folder. These options let you move a photo from anywhere on your hard drive to anywhere else you like, as long as the photo is already in the Organizer. If not, you'll need to import it before you can do anything with it here. (To get back to Folder List view, just click the two-folder icon.)

FULL SCREEN VIEW

One of the handiest features in the Organizer is Full Screen view. Once you get your photos into the Organizer, click the Slide Show button at the bottom of the screen, (keyboard shortcut: F11/⌘-F11) or use the secret "Compare Photos Side by Side" keystroke (F12/⌘-F12) to see a larger, slideshow-like view of your photos (either singly or in pairs, respectively) so you can pick the ones you want to print or edit. You can even choose music to accompany them. Figure 2-11 shows the difference between the two views. (If you don't want anything that elaborate, just double-click a thumbnail in the Media room to see that photo enlarged to fit the available space. Double-click it again to go back to thumbnail view.)

NOTE If you have a Mac with a keyboard without the 10-key pad on the right, like a laptop or the current Bluetooth keyboard, you always need to add the fn key to most keystroke combinations that use the top row of the keyboard. So if you have a MacBook Pro, for example, you'd use fn-⌘-F11 for Full Screen view.

Elements also lets you apply many editing commands right in Full Screen or "Side by Side" view. Just put your cursor over the Quick Edit panel's tab on the left side of the screen, and it pops out to give you access to all the one-button fixes available in the Editor's Quick Fix mode (page 113). You can also rate your photos here (page 56) using the stars at the top of the Quick Edit panel. The Quick Organize panel (also on the left side of the screen) lets you apply keyword tags in Tag Cloud view, or put photos into albums (page 55).

TIP The Organizer's Quick Edit and Quick Organize panels close back up each time a new image appears onscreen. To make a panel stay open, click the tiny pushpin icon on its right edge. To get rid of a panel entirely, click its Close button (the X in Windows, the dot on a Mac). To bring it back, use the controls at the bottom of the screen, which are described in detail on page 577.

You can even use Full Screen view as a quick slideshow to show off your latest images—see page 576 to learn how. To exit Full Screen view and get back to the Media room, press Esc.

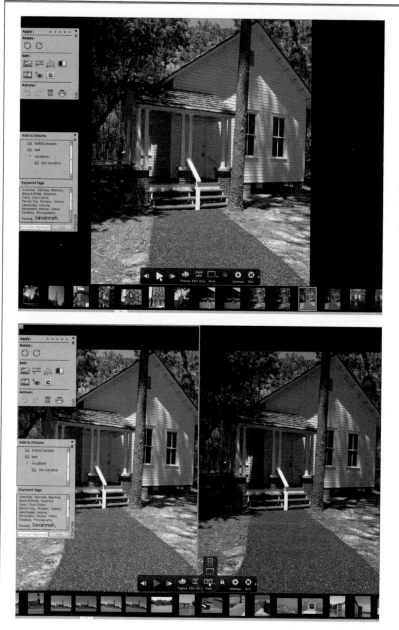

FIGURE 2-11.

Top: If you click the Slideshow button at the bottom of the Organizer window, you get this handy full-screen view of your images, where you can tag them or make quick edits using the panels on the left. (Usually you see only the panel's edges; click an edge to pop the panel open.)

Bottom: In "Side by Side" view, you can choose between comparing two images next to each other, as shown here, or click the View button (circled) to see one image above the other.

Creating Categories and Tags

The Organizer has a great system for quickly finding photos, but it works only if you use special keywords, called *tags,* that the Organizer uses to track down your pictures. A tag can be a word, a date, or even a rating (see the box on page 56). When you import photos to the Organizer, they're automatically tagged with the import date and any other tags you've specified in the Photo Downloader (see page 35). But you may want to add more tags to make it easier to search for the subject of the photo later on. You can give a photo as many tags as you like.

Elements lets you group tags into *categories.* You get a few preset categories—like Nature, Color, and Travel—and you can create your own, as well as make subcategories. For example, you can make a Vacations category with China Trip and Cozumel as subcategories. Your photos in those categories could have tags like "Jim and Helen," "silk factory," or "snorkeling."

You create some tags in the Media room. These basic tags are explained here, but tagging people, places, and events works a little differently in Elements 11. Those tags are explained in the following sections, beginning on page 57.

■ WORKING WITH BASIC TAGS AND CATEGORIES

Elements gives you a few generic tags to help get you started, but you'll want to learn how to create your own tags, too. After all, by the time you've got 5,000 or so photos in the Organizer, searching for "Family" probably isn't going to narrow things down much. Creating a new tag is as easy as can be:

- **Just type it.** In the Keyword Tags panel (page 48), head down to the box that contains the placeholder text "Add Custom Keywords" and start typing. At first you see a pop-up menu of all the existing tags, but if you keep typing, once Elements recognizes it as a new tag, the pop-up changes to say "Create new tag '<whatever you've typed>.'" Select the photo(s) you want to apply this new tag to and then click Add. Elements puts tags created this way in the Other category in the upper part of the Keyword Tags panel. To put it somewhere else, drag the tag's icon to the category where it belongs.

- **Keyboard shortcut.** When you're in the Organizer, press Ctrl+N/⌘-N.

- **Menu.** At the top of the Keyword Tags panel, click the green + sign and choose New Keyword Tag. (You can also create a new category or subcategory via this same menu.) When you create tags using this method, the Create Keyword Tag dialog box appears. Name the new tag by typing it in, and then assign it to a category using the drop-down menu. (You can change the category later if you want.)

When you create tags using either of the last two methods, the Create Keyword Tag dialog box appears. Name the new tag by typing it in, and then assign it to a category using the drop-down menu. (You can change the category later if you want.)

No matter which method you use, you can also edit the tag's icon, as explained in Figure 2-12. (Elements automatically assigns the first photo to which you apply the tag as the tag's icon image.) To assign the tag to a photo, simply drag the tag's icon from the Keyword Tags panel onto the photo's thumbnail. You can rearrange tags by dragging them to different categories in the Keyword Tags panel, and change tags to categories and categories to tags by right-clicking/Control-clicking them and choosing from the pop-up menu.

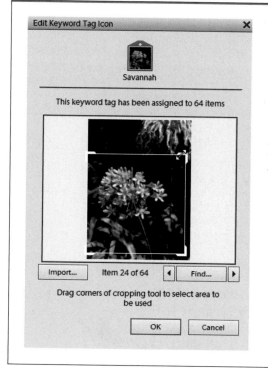

FIGURE 2-12.

Some people like to edit the icons that Elements uses to represent different tags to make it easy to search for a tag visually as well as by name. To change the picture associated with a tag, right-click/Control-click the tag in the Keyword Tags panel→Edit. In the Edit Keyword Tag dialog box that appears, click Edit Icon, and Elements opens the dialog box shown here. The arrows on either side of the Find button let you advance through all the photos that use that tag. (If you click the Find button, you see all those photos at once.) Or click the Import button to use a different image stored on your computer. Once you select the picture you want, drag the dotted square to choose which part of your photo appears on the tag.

When you move your cursor over a tag or keyword in the panel, you see an arrow to the right of its name. Clicking it opens the Advanced Search screen, which is explained on page 63.

To remove a tag you've assigned:

- **From a single photo.** Right-click/Control-click the photo's thumbnail and select Remove Keyword Tag→<name of tag>.

- **From a group of photos.** Select the photos, right-click/Control-click one of them, select "Remove Keyword Tag from Selected Items," and then choose the tag you want to remove.

TIP At the bottom of the list in the Keyword Tags panel is a category called Smart Tags. The Organizer includes a feature called the Auto Analyzer that can evaluate your photos and videos, pass judgment on them, and then assign corresponding Smart Tags, like High Quality or Blurred. If you only install Photoshop Elements, the Auto Analyzer is turned off unless you deliberately start it, but if you also have *Premiere* Elements on your computer, it's turned on automatically. In that case, disabling it should be one of the first things you do in Elements. Why? Because the Auto Analyzer is a real resource hog and it's very hard to remove a Smart Tag once the Auto Analyzer has applied it. Besides, for still photos, all it can do is evaluate blur, brightness, and contrast, and really, can't you tell that yourself? To shut it off, in the Organizer, go to Edit→Preferences→Media-Analysis→Auto Analyzer Options/Edit→Preferences→Media-Analysis→Auto Analyzer Options and turn off "Analyze Media for Smart Tags Automatically." You'll probably want to leave the People Recognition and Visual Search options turned on. Otherwise you can't use face recognition or perform visual-similarity or object searches (page 64).

Albums

Elements lets you group photos into *albums*, which are great for gathering together pictures taken at a particular event. They're also handy for preparing groups of photos that you want to use in a Create project like a slideshow or a photo collage (page 509).

When you create an album, you don't actually make a copy of all the photos included in it; you just create a group of virtual "pointers" to each image so Elements knows where to find them. That means albums can hold lots of pictures without taking up much space and, even better, you can easily include the same pictures in different albums. Photos in an album can appear in any order you choose, which is important if, for instance, you're preparing a slideshow.

Elements gives you several ways to create albums:

- **From the Organizer.** First Ctrl-click/⌘-click to select the photos you want to include. Then go to the Albums/Folders panel and click the green + sign. In the Add New Album panel that appears on the right side of the Organizer window, name your album and assign it to a *category* (explained in a moment) if you wish, and then click OK. Your new album joins the list of albums.

   You can also make an album from files anywhere on your computer, even if they're not in the Organizer, by heading to the Albums/Folders panel and clicking the tiny arrow to the right of the green + sign and then selecting "Import Albums from File."

   To create an online album (one that you might upload to Photoshopshowcase. com, for example), just head to the Share menu and choose Online Album.

- **From the Editor.** In the Editor, you can create an album from the Photo Bin's Bin Actions menu (page 15).

NOTE No matter which method you use to make an album, it will appear in the lists of albums in both the Organizer and in Editor (in the Photo Bin's Show menu).

Special Tags

Elements starts you off with two special kinds of tags:

- **Ratings.** These tags let you assign a one- to five-star rating to photos (a good way to mark the ones you want to print or edit). Ratings are a great search tool, because you can tell Elements to find, say, all your pictures rated four or more stars. To assign ratings, in the Organizer, go to View→Details and then just click the star under the photo's thumbnail that corresponds to your rating (the third star from the left for a three-star rating, say); or you can rate any photo in the Information panel's General section. To search by ratings, click the appropriate star at the top right of the Organizer and then choose a qualifier (like "and higher") by clicking the symbol to the left of the stars. You can search for all photos rated four stars or higher, for instance, or those rated two stars or lower, and so on. To change or remove a photo's rating, right-click/Control-click its thumbnail, choose Ratings from the menu that appears, and then pick the number of stars you want. You can also change a rating by clicking a different star

under the thumbnail (if you're in Details view).

- **Hidden.** When you apply this tag to a photo, the photo disappears from the Organizer window. The Hidden tag is useful for archiving photos that didn't come out quite right but that you're not ready to trash; that way, you can save these pictures (just in case) without having them cluttering up your screen while you're working with your good photos. To assign the Hidden tag, right-click/Control-click a photo and choose Visibility→"Mark as Hidden." To bring it back, go up to the View menu and choose Hidden Files→Show All Files, or right-click a visible photo and then choose Visibility→Show All Files, either of which makes even your hidden files visible. Then right-click/Control-click the photo again, and select Visibility→"Mark as Visible" to keep it in view. To put the rest of your hidden files back out of sight, choose View→Hidden Files→Hide Hidden Files. You can also see *only* your hidden files by going to View→Hidden Files→Show Only Hidden Files.

You can share any album online as you create it (see page 571 for more info). You can also share an existing album by right-clicking/Control-clicking its name in the list of albums and then choosing the export method you want to use. Elements gives you lots of options for displaying photos in a gallery and sharing them with friends. Chapter 18 has more about working with and sharing online albums.

> **NOTE** You can also burn albums to CD or DVD, or upload your slideshows and galleries to your own website. Page 574 explains how.

To see the photos in an album, just click its name in the Albums/Folders panel. To return to viewing all your photos, click the All Media button above the left side of the thumbnail area.

You can also create *album categories,* which are just what they sound like. If you have a lot of albums, you can group them into categories to make them easier to keep track of. To make an album category, go to the Albums/Folders panel and click the tiny arrow on the right of the green + sign and choose New Album Category. Name your category, and it appears in the Albums list. To add albums to it, just drag their icons onto the category's name. To remove an album from it, click the flippy triangle to the left of the category's name so you can see all the albums it contains, and then right-click the album you want to remove and choose Edit. In the Edit Album panel that appears on the right side of the Organizer window, click the Category drop-down menu and choose "None (Top Level)". Then click OK at the bottom of the Edit Album panel.

You can also create subcategories within categories. To do that, in the Albums/ Folders panel, click the tiny arrow on the right of the green + sign and choose New Album Category. Then name your subcategory and choose the main category under which you want it to appear from the Parent Album Category drop-down menu. The new category appears as a subcategory of the original one.

NOTE   If you're looking for the Smart Albums feature from previous editions of Elements, it's gone, but you can achieve pretty much the same thing with saved searches, which are described on page 64.

Tagging People

Elements has included *face recognition* technology for a while now. With face recognition, the Organizer analyzes your photos for faces and then shows you the ones it found, so that you can create tags for them. (Adobe calls this feature "people recognition," but it's designed to find only faces; it doesn't work so well on a photo of someone's back, for example.)

To use this feature, you first need to be sure that the Organizer is analyzing your photos. Go to Edit→Preferences→Media-Analysis/Adobe Elements 11 Organizer→ Preferences→Media-Analysis and make sure that "Analyze Photos for People Automatically" is turned on.

You start using face recognition in the Media room, but when you're done you go to the People room to see your results. Here's the process:

1. **At the bottom of the Media room window, click the Add People button.**

   A window asks if you're sure you want to find people. (Why else would you have clicked the button?) Click Yes. If you have any files where Elements didn't recognize anything in the photo as a person, you see a warning that Elements will skip those files.

2. **Tell Elements who the people it found are.**

   The People Recognition window opens with thumbnail images of different people that Elements found, with "Who is this?" beneath each one. Click that text and type a name for each person. Figure 2-13 shows what to do if Elements offers you an image that isn't a person.

   If you need to see a larger view to be sure who the person is, right-click/ Control-click the thumbnail and choose "Show in Full Size View." When you're done looking at the bigger view, click Back. Once you've filled in everyone's names, click Save.

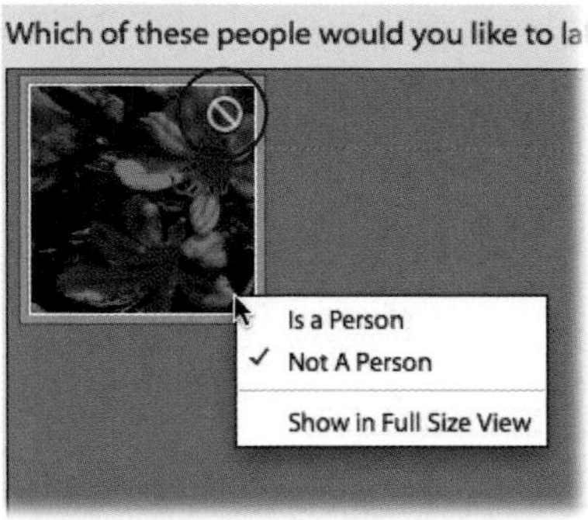

FIGURE 2-13.

If Elements makes a hopeful guess about something that isn't actually a person, either click the No symbol (circled) or click the tiny arrow at the thumbnail's bottom right and choose "Not a Person." If it is a person, choose "Is a Person" instead. If you need a better look to decide, choose "Show in Full Size View."

TIP   If you use Facebook, you have the option of downloading your Facebook friends list to help name people. Just click the button at the bottom left of the People Recognition window to start the process.

---

3. Tell Elements if it made mistakes in identifying anyone.

After you click Save in step 2, Elements shows you all the photos it found of each person and asks you to exclude anyone who doesn't belong in the group. If Elements misidentified someone—say. it thought one photo of your Uncle Fred was his brother Bill—click the arrow on the lower-right corner of the misidentified photo and choose "Not <name>." When you're done, click Save.

4. Identify more people.

Elements shows you another group of people. Repeat steps 2 and 3. It's easier this time because, when you click "Who is this?" Elements offers you a little pop-out with some of the people tags you've already created; just click a name to apply it to that photo. And if you start typing a name, you see a list of the names you've already entered that begin with that letter. When you're done, click Save.

5. Identify (or exclude) even *more* people.

When Elements is through with the people it's most sure about, it offers you a larger group of prospects that may well include lots of things that aren't people and asks, "Which of these people would you like to label?"

If Elements shows a photo that isn't a person you want to tag (or isn't a person at all), click the No symbol (the circle with a slash across it) in its upper-right corner. For photos that are people you want to tag, click the little arrow in their lower-right corners and choose "Is a Person." When you're done, click Save. Elements puts you through the identification process for your selections

When you're through, Elements displays a dialog box that says, "You have labeled everyone in your selection." Click OK and, if you like, you can switch over to the People room, shown in Figure 2-14, for a look at all the people you've tagged.

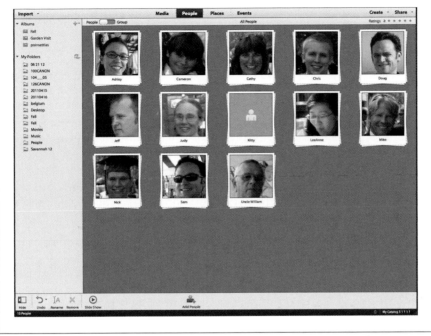

FIGURE 2-14.

When you're finished tagging the people in your photos, the Organizer's People room displays all your photos of people in neat stacks for each person.

The People room includes only images tagged with people tags. You can quickly scroll through all the images in a person's stack by moving your cursor over the stack. If you want the Organizer to use a different photo as the top image in the stack, right-click/Control-click the image when it appears and choose "Assign as Profile Picture."

To see all the photos in a stack at once, double-click the stack to expand it. If you want the Organizer to find additional photos of this person, click Find More at the bottom of the screen. (If you've already let the Organizer analyze all your photos for people, most likely it will just tell you there aren't any more.) Click the Back button at the top left of the preview area to go back to the main People room.

TIP   If you made a mistake naming someone—say you mistyped her name—you can fix that by clicking her photo stack and then clicking the Rename button at the bottom left of the Organizer window. A window pops up where you can type the name correctly or change it completely.

Once you've tagged everyone, the switch above the photo area reads People/Group. Click it to set it to Groups, and a Groups panel appears on the right side of the People room, where you can put people into groups if you want. (If you don't see the panel, click the Groups button at the bottom right of the Organizer window to display it.) You get some preset groups (Colleagues, Family, Friends), and you can create your own groups by clicking the green + button and choosing Add Group. However, there's a severe handicap to using groups: Nobody can be in more than one group. So if you put a friend from work into the Colleagues group and then add her to the Friends group, she disappears from Colleagues. You add people to groups by dragging their tags onto the name of the group. To remove a photo from a group, right-click/Control-click its thumbnail and choose "Move to Ungrouped."

You can manually add people tags to a particular photo, but there are some limitations. Just go back to the Media room and right-click/Control-click a photo and choose "Add a Person." A little window pops up where you can type in the name; type it and then click Add. When you're through adding people, click the window's Close button (the X in Windows, the red dot on Macs) to dismiss it. If you add a new person this way, she gets a stack, but no profile photo—you just see a gray box at the top of her stack. Photos of people with existing Elements-generated People tags that you tag this way should go right into their existing stacks. In either case, to see all the photos associated with the person, expand his stack by double-clicking it and, at the top let of the preview area, click the Faces/Photos switch to make sure it's set to Photos.

> **NOTE** Normally your Elements-generated people tags don't appear in the Media room, but if you prefer to tag the old-fashioned way by dragging and dropping, you can still do that. When you're in the Media room, go to View→"Show People in Tag Panel," and they'll appear so that you can use them just like any other tag.

Tagging Places

If your camera has a GPS system that automatically records the coordinates where you take each shot, then using the Places room is super easy. When you click the Places tab at the top of the Organizer window, you see all your GPS-enabled photos already tagged with the Google Maps information about where they were taken.

If your camera *doesn't* use GPS and you haven't added that data to any of your photos, then you see a blank window the first time you enter the Places room. Not to worry, though: You can manually tag your photos here by dragging them to locations on a Google Map. It's pretty easy to do:

1. **Call up the map.**

   Click the Add Places button at the bottom of either the Media room or the Places room. The Add Places window appears, where you see your photos in a strip along the top of the Google map. You can preselect photos or limit your search by clicking an album or a folder in the Albums/Folders panel (click the Show button at the bottom left of your screen if it's not visible) either before or after entering the Places room, or by clicking their thumbnails in the Media room before clicking Add Places. If you don't, then all your photos appear.

2. **Place your photos on the map.**

Figure 2-15 explains how to do this. You can adjust your view of the map using the drop-down menu at its upper right if you want a hybrid map/satellite view instead, for example. You can also search the map by typing the location you want to find into the search box above the map's left side.

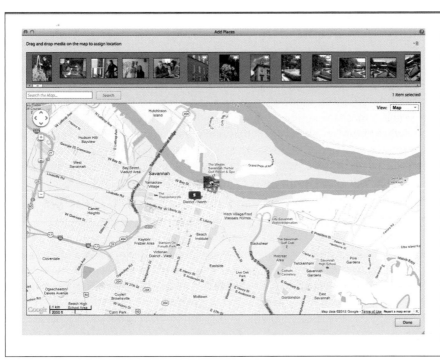

FIGURE 2-15.

Zoom and drag the map to the location where you want your photos, and then click a photo (or photos) and drag it from the top of the window onto the map. Once you've placed a photo, a red pin appears in that spot, showing the number of photos you placed there. Here you can see that this location already has five photos, and more are being dragged onto it. If you look at the thumbnails across the top of the window, you can see the little white tag symbol on some of them to indicate that they've already been placed.

3. **When you're finished placing photos, click Done.**

Elements takes you back to the Places room, where you see the message "Places have been assigned to media" and all the images you placed. (If you don't see your placed images, try clicking a different room's tab and then clicking the Places tab again.)

If you look at the Keyword Tags/Information panel (page 48), below the box where you can type in new keywords, you see the place tags assigned to your photos. As of this writing, that's at most four levels of tagging, because that's all the Organizer's map can do. So you might see something like United States, Georgia, Savannah, and Historic District-North. These tags are always visible in that spot when the Keyword Tags/Information panel is onscreen, so you can see them in the Media room as well as in the Places room.

Once your photos have been tagged with locations (by you or your camera), you can see them on the map again by clicking the Map button at the bottom right of the Places room window. This opens as a regular map view, which you can drag around and search to locate your photos. Click a pin to display a pop-up that says Show Media; click that to make the photos for that location appear in the image area. Click List up at the very top of the map window to see a list of all the place tags on your images instead of the map, and then click a tag to see the images associated with it.

The Places room also includes the Instant Fix button (page 49) so you can make quick corrections to your photos right there.

Working with Events

After learning about all the effort involved in tagging people and places (if your camera doesn't have GPS), you'll be pleased to know that Elements can deal with events automatically. The first time you enter the Events room by clicking its tab at the top of the Organizer window, you see a whole lot of empty gray space with no photos, and a message suggesting you try Smart Events. Click the Events/Smart Events switch at the top left of the window and presto! Elements fills the window with piles of photos, all neatly divided based on when they were taken. As with the other rooms, you can move your mouse across an event's pile to see preview thumbnails of all the photos, or double-click one to see an expanded view.

You can name an event to make it easier to search for later on. To do that, either right-click/Control-click the event's thumbnail and choose Name Event(s), or click the event to select it and then click the Name Event(s) button at the bottom of the screen. Either way, in the Name Event window that opens, type a name for the event and use the calendars to adjust the date(s) if Elements got them wrong. If you wish, you can add a description, too. (You can select multiple events before opening the Name Event window, but if you do, they all get assigned the same name. This is handy when Elements makes multiple events for one real event in your life.)

You can also create events manually. To do that, click the switch above the image area to set it to Events rather than Smart Events. Your smart events disappear, and you're back to the empty view. Next:

1. **Create a new event.**

   Click the Add Event button at the bottom of the window. (You can do this from the Media room, too.) The Organizer switches you to a view where you see all your photos, with the Add New Event panel on the right of your screen.

2. **Enter the info for your event.**

   In the top section of the panel, give the event a name, set the date(s) for the event, and enter a description, if you like.

3. **Add your photos.**

   You can control which photos are displayed in the middle of the Organizer by using the Albums/Folders panel on the left side of the screen. (If you don't see this panel, click the Show button in the lower left of your screen.) Click the name of a folder or an album and you only see the photos it contains. To get back to all photos, click the All Media button above the photo area's top-left corner.

To add photos to the event, drag their thumbnails to the lower part of the Add New Event panel (called the *Media Bin*) or select their thumbnails and click "Add to Media Bin" at the bottom of your screen. There are also buttons in the lower left of the screen to select or deselect all your photos. If you want to remove a photo after you've added it to the Media Bin, click it in the bin and then click the little trash can at the bin's lower left.

4. **When you're finished, click Done.**

If you decide not to create an event, click Cancel.

The Events room also lets you use a calendar to search for events by date. Click the Calendar button at the bottom right of the room, and the Calendar panel opens. Figure 2-16 explains how to use it. To close the panel, click the Calendar button again.

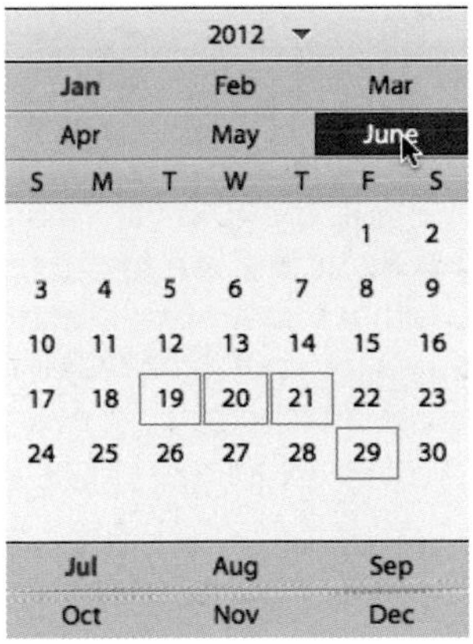

FIGURE 2-16.

When you click the Calendar button, this panel appears at the upper right of your screen. Initially the part that says "2012" here says All Years. Click it and choose the year you want. Here, you can tell that there are events for January and July because those months' names are displayed in blue rather than black. Click a month to see this daily calendar, where the days with events are outlined. Click a date to see its events. (If you've used Organizer in earlier versions of Elements, this is as close as you can get to the old Date View in Elements 11.)

Searching for Photos

After all that effort jumping from room to room tagging your photos, you'll be happy to know that Elements makes it easy to search for photos, offering you several different kinds of searches. The most basic method is to go to the search box at the upper right of the Organizer window and type a keyword or keywords into it. However, if you click the magnifying glass on the left of the box, you'll get a menu that gives you some more sophisticated ways to search for photos:

- **Advanced Search.** Figure 2-17 explains how this works. You can click the Options button above your search results (not shown in Figure 2-17) to save your search for future use. When you're through searching, click Clear to go back to where you were before you started searching.

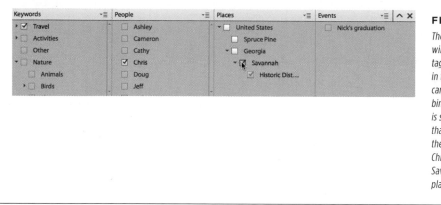

FIGURE 2-17.

The new Advanced Search window shows all the tags assigned in any room in the Organizer, so you can search for any combination. Here the search is set up to find images that have been assigned the Travel keyword, the Chris people tag, and the Savannah Historic District place tag.

- **Visual Similarity Search.** Select a photo (or photos) before choosing this menu item and the Organizer seeks out photos that it thinks look similar. You can fine-tune the results by dragging the slider at the top of the window. Drag it toward Color if you want Elements to give more weight to images with similar colors, and toward Shapes if you want it to emphasize similar shapes more than colors. Click All Media/Back when you're done searching.

- **Object Search.** You can show Elements a picture of your dog, your house, or just about anything and tell it to find more photos with the same subject. Select a photo of your desired object and then choose Object Search. In the "Mark an object for search" window that appears, drag the white frame around your subject and drag the corners so that it fits as precisely as possible. Then click Search Object. You can then drag the Color/Shape slider above the search results to tell Elements what to favor in its search.

- **Duplicate Search.** Choose this and the Organizer finds all the photos it thinks might be duplicates. Unfortunately, you can't delete duplicates here. You can stack them, though, by clicking the appropriate Stack button, and then expand the stack in the Media room by choosing Edit→Stack→"Expand Photos in Stack." This lets you look through the photos to see which one(s) you want to get rid of.

- **Saved Searches.** You can save any of the searches you make from this menu by using the Options button above the images in the search results window. Then choose this option from the search box's menu to call up your saved searches and use them again. These saved searches replace the old Smart Albums feature in earlier versions of Elements.

If you want to try a different search, click the Clear button above the right side of your search results and try again.

In addition to searching from the search box's menu, you can quickly search in the Keyword Tags panel (page 48). Just click the name of a tag or category, and Elements finds all the photos associated with that tag or category.

■ SEARCHING BY METADATA

As explained on page 48, your camera stores lots of information about your images in the form of *metadata*. In the Organizer, you can search by metadata to find, say, all the photos you took with a particular camera model at a certain aperture and exposure. Figure 2-18 explains how.

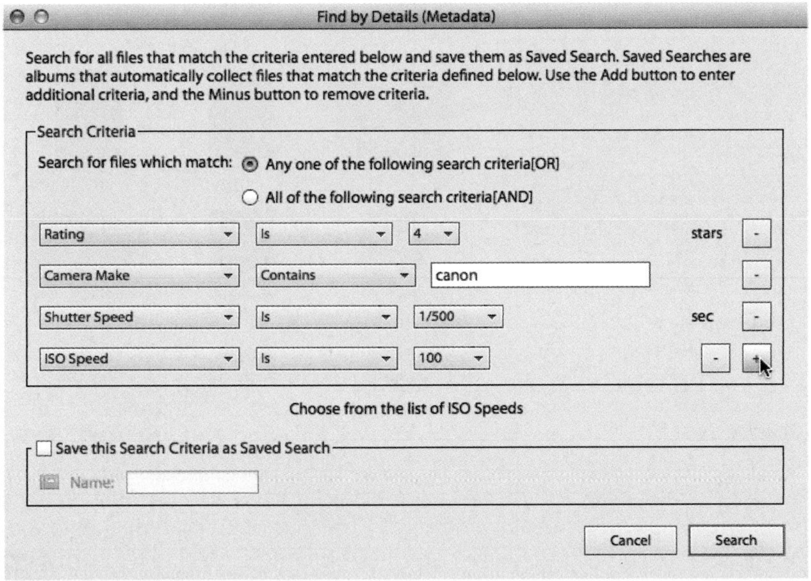

FIGURE 2-18.

To perform a search using your photos' metadata, go to Find→"By Details (Metadata)" to bring up this dialog box. Choose the category of metadata from the drop-down menu on the left, and then enter your term or choose the exact setting in the box on the right. Click the + button to add additional search terms (up to 10). To remove a criterion, click the search term's – button.

> **TIP** If you want to share your tag information with other people, it's easy to do. Just select the photos you want, and then go to File→"Write Keyword Tag and Properties Info to Photos." This transforms your tags into metadata keywords, which lots of programs can read. Or you can use the Organizer's Export command (File→"Export As New File(s)"), which also writes your tags into the metadata.

■ Saving Your Work

You've heard the advice before: Save files early and often. Happily, saving your work is easy in Elements. You don't need to do anything special to save information like tags or collections in the Organizer; that happens automatically. You just need to save images you've created or changed in the Editor. When you're ready to save a file, go to File→Save As or press Shift+Ctrl+S/Shift-⌘-S to bring up the Save As dialog box, shown in Figure 2-19.

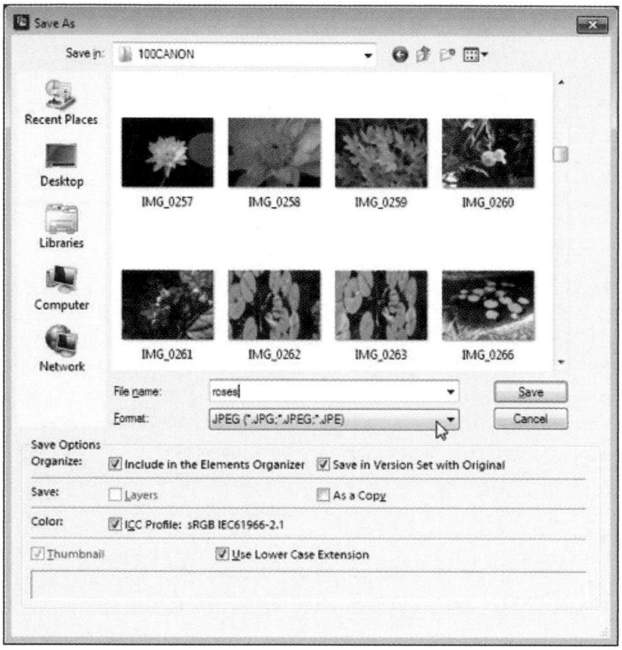

FIGURE 2-19.

Elements' Save As dialog box changes a little depending on what you're saving, but this example is pretty typical. When you click the Format drop-down menu (where the cursor is here), you'll see a long list of file formats to choose from.

The top part of the Save As dialog box is pretty much the same as it is for any program: You choose where you want to save the file, what to name it, and the file format you want. (More about file formats in a moment.) You also get some important choices that are unique to Elements:

- **Include in the Elements Organizer.** This checkbox is turned on the first time you use Elements. Leave it on and your photo gets saved in the Organizer. Turn it off if you don't want the new file to go to the Organizer. If you turn it off, Elements should remember to *leave* it off, at least for this editing session or until you save a photo that came from the Organizer.

- **Save in Version Set with Original.** This option tells the Organizer to save your image (including any edits you've made) as a new *version*, separate from the original. The image gets the same name as the original plus a suffix to indicate it's an edited version.

Elements lets you create as many versions as you want. That way, you can go directly to any state of the image that you've saved as a version, which is really handy. When you turn on this checkbox to start a version set, from then on, you'll be presented with the Save As dialog box every time you save. Elements does that to give you the chance to create a new version each time.

- **Layers.** If your image has *layers* (see Chapter 6), turn on this checkbox to keep them. If you turn this setting off, Elements usually forces you to save as a copy. To avoid having to do that, *flatten* the image (page 201) before saving it. But bear in mind that, once you close a flattened image, you can't get your layers back again—flattening is a *permanent* change.

- **As a Copy.** When you save an image as a copy, Elements makes the copy, names it "<Original filename> copy," and puts the copy away, but the original version remains open. If you want to work on the copy, you have to specifically open it. Sometimes Elements *forces* you to save an image as a copy—for instance, when you want to save a layered image and you turn off the Layers checkbox described in the previous bullet point.

- **ICC Profile.** Turn on this checkbox to make Elements embed a color profile (page 235) in your file.

- **Use Lower Case Extension (Windows only).** This setting makes Elements save the file as *yourfile.jpg* rather than *yourfile.JPG*. Leave this setting on unless you have a reason to turn it off. (You don't see this checkbox on a Mac because OS X always uses lowercase extensions.)

File Formats Elements Understands

Elements gives you loads of file format options in the Save As dialog box. Your best choice depends on how you plan to use the image:

- **Photoshop (.psd, .pdd).** It's a good idea to save your photos as .psd files—the native file format for Elements and Photoshop—before you work on them. A .psd file can hold lots of information, and you don't lose any data by saving in this format. It also lets you keep layers, which is important even if you haven't used them for much yet.

- **BMP (.bmp).** This format is an old Windows standby. It's the file format that the Windows operating system uses for many graphics tasks.

- **CompuServe GIF (.gif).** Everywhere except this menu, this format is known simply as GIF; Adobe adds "CompuServe" here because CompuServe invented and owns the code for this format. This format is used primarily for web graphics, especially files without a lot of subtle shadings of color. For more on when to choose GIFs, see Chapter 17. Page 561 explains how to animate GIFs.

Saving Options

Elements gives you several ways to save files. Before choosing one, you need to consider whether you want to create version sets (page 66) of your photos.

To tell Elements how to react to the Save command, in the Editor, go to Edit→Preferences→Saving Files/Adobe Photoshop Elements Editor→Preferences→Saving Files. The Preferences dialog box that appears includes the On First Save drop-down menu. By making a selection here, you can control (to some extent) when you'll see a dialog box offering you options for saving a file, and when Elements will behave like any other program and just save your changes without asking you for any input.

For most people, it's fine to leave this menu set to "Ask if Original" (explained below). But if you want more control over how Elements saves your photos (if you always want the option to create a new version set without having to remember to choose Save As, for instance), you can configure Elements to suit you. Here's what the three On First Save options do:

- **Always Ask.** Choose this setting and from then on, the first time you save a file by pressing Ctrl+S/⌘-S, or go to File→Save, Elements brings up the Save As dialog box—*if* this is the first time you've opened the file in this session of Elements. Close the file and reopen it while Elements is still running, and you won't see the Save As dialog box; Elements just saves the file. But once you exit Elements and launch it again, you get the Save As dialog box again the first time you press Ctrl+S/⌘-S. You can think of this option as short for "Always ask the first time I save a file in an editing session and then don't bug me anymore."

- **Ask If Original.** If you're editing your original file (as opposed to a version) and don't have any version sets, Elements opens the Save As dialog box the first time you save the file. On subsequent saves, or if you already have a version set, Elements just saves right over the existing version (unless you specifically do a Save As to create a new version). This option is meant to help you

avoid inadvertently creating dozens of versions of each file as you edit.

- **Save Over Current File.** When you select this option, Elements overwrites the existing file when you press Ctrl+S/⌘-S, without offering you the Save As dialog box at all. This is the way most other programs behave when saving—if you save a Word document, for instance, you don't get a dialog box; Word just saves your changes, writing over the previous saved version of the file. If you use Elements as the external editor for another photo-management program like iPhoto or Lightroom, this is the option you should use in order to create proper versions in the other program. If you choose this menu option and then, while you're working, decide you want to Save As instead of Save, press Shift+Ctrl+S/Shift-⌘-S (or just choose Save As from the Editor's File menu).

There are certain situations where Elements presents you with the Save As dialog box no matter *what* you choose in the On First Save menu. For instance, say you add layers (explained in Chapter 6) to a JPEG file. You can't save a JPEG with layers, so Elements brings up the Save As dialog box to let you choose a different file format for saving your work.

The File Saving Options section of the Saving Files Preferences dialog box has two other menus—Image Previews and File Extensions—but you probably won't ever need to change those settings.

You can also use the Saving Files Preferences dialog box to control how well your image file works with other programs. If you leave the Maximize PSD File Compatibility drop-down menu set to Always, Elements embeds a flattened image file for the benefit of programs that don't understand layers. That makes for a substantially larger file, but with disk space so cheap these days, it's usually best to let Elements maximize compatibility. If you choose Ask from this menu instead, then each time you save a layered PSD file, you'll see a dialog box that asks whether you want to maximize compatibility.

File Formats

After you've spent hours creating a perfect image, you'll want to share it with others. If everyone who wanted to view your images needed a copy of Elements, you probably wouldn't have a very large audience for your creations. So Elements lets you save in lots of different *file formats*.

What does that mean? It's pretty simple, really. A file format is a way in which your computer saves information so that another program or another computer can read and use the file.

Because there are many different kinds of programs and several different computing platforms (Windows, Linux, and Mac, for example), the kind of file that's best for one use may be a poor choice for doing something else. That's why many programs, like Elements, can save files in a variety of different formats. There are many formats, like TIFF and JPEG, that lots of different programs can read. Other formats—like the PUB files that Microsoft Publisher creates or the .pages files from Apple's Pages program—are easily read only by the program that created them.

• **Photo Project Format (.pse).** This special format is only for multipage Elements files (In Elements 11, you can create a multipage file in only a few of the Create projects, like a photo book. You can't create and work with multipage files in the Editor anymore.

• **JPEG (.jpg, .jpeg, .jpe).** Almost everyone who uses a computer has run into JPEGs, and most digital cameras offer this format as an option. Generally, when you bring a JPEG into Elements, you want to use another format when you save it to avoid losing data. Keep reading for more about why.

NOTE   If you're wondering why JPEG 2000 isn't on this list, see the box on page 71.

• **Photoshop PDF (.pdf, .pdp).** Adobe invented PDF (Portable Document Format), which lets you send files to people with Adobe Reader (a free program formerly called Acrobat Reader) so they can easily open and view the files. Elements uses PDF files to create presentations like slideshows. (People with Macs can also use OS X's Preview to view PDFs.)

• **PIXAR.** Yup, *that* Pixar. This is the special format for the movie studio's high-end workstations, although if you're working on one of those, it's extremely unlikely that you're reading this book.

• **PNG.** Here's another web-graphic format, created to overcome some of the disadvantages of JPEGs and GIFs. It has its own disadvantages, though; see page 560 for details.

• **TIFF (.tif, .tiff).** This is another format that, like PSD, preserves virtually all your photo's info and lets you save layers. Also like PSD files, TIFFs can be really big. This format is used extensively in print production, and some cameras let you choose it as a shooting option.

- **Digital Negative (.dng).** This format isn't an option listed in the Save As dialog box's Format menu; it's available only in the Raw Converter. This format was developed by Adobe in an attempt to create a more universal way to store all the different Raw file formats (page 264). You can download a special DNG Converter from Adobe's website (*www.adobe.com/downloads*) that lets you convert your camera's Raw formatted photos into DNG files. DNG files aren't ready to use the way JPEG or TIFF files are—you have to run them through the Raw Converter before you can use them in projects. Page 284 has more about DNG files.

■ ABOUT JPEGS

In the next chapter, you'll read about how throwing away pixels can lead to shoddy-looking pictures. It's also important to know that certain file formats are designed to make files as small as possible—and they do that by throwing out information by the bucketful. These formats are known as *lossy* because they discard, or lose, some of the file's data every time you save it, to help shrink the file. Sometimes you want that to happen, like when you need a small (and hence, fast-loading) file for a website. Because of that, many of the file formats that were developed for the Web, most notably JPEG, favor smallness above all.

> **NOTE** Formats that preserve all your data are called *lossless*. (You may also run across the term *non-lossy*, which means the same thing.) The most popular file formats for people who are looking to preserve all their photos' data are PSD and TIFF.

If you save a file in JPEG format, then every time you click the Save button and close the file, your computer squishes some of the data out of the photo. What kind of data? The info your computer needs to display and print the fine details. So you don't want to keep saving your file as a JPEG over and over again, because every time you do, the image loses a little more detail. You can usually get away with saving as a JPEG once or twice, but if you keep it up, sooner or later you'll start to wonder what happened to your beautiful picture.

It's OK that your camera takes photos and saves them as JPEGs—those are typically pretty enormous JPEGs. Just importing a photo as a JPEG won't hurt the picture, and neither will opening it to look at it, as long as you don't make any changes. But once you get your files into Elements, save your pictures as PSD or TIFF files while you work on them. If you want the final product to be a JPEG, then change the format back to JPEG *after* you're done editing it.

> **TIP** Your camera may give you several different JPEG compression options to help fit more pictures on your memory card. Always choose the *least* compression possible. This makes the files slightly larger, but the quality is much, much better, so it's worth sacrificing the space.

Bye-Bye, Old Formats

Elements used to be able to open a wide variety of obscure file formats, but in Elements 11 Adobe decided to remove the ability to open a lot of these. Mostly, they're formats hardly anyone uses anymore, and in some cases, like Photoshop Raw (which has nothing at all to do with the Raw files produced by cameras), they just caused confusion.

Here are the formats you can't open in Elements anymore: Filmstrip (FLM), Wireless BMP (WBM, WBMP), PCX, Targa (TGA, VDA, ICB, VST), Photoshop RAW (RAW), PICT (PCT, PICT), Scitex CT (SCT), Photoshop EPS (EPS), EPS TIFF Preview (EPS), Generic EPS (AI3, AI4, AI5, AI6, AI7, AI8, PS, EPS.AI, EPSF, EPSP), IFF Format, Photoshop 2.0, Alias PIX, and PICT Resource. Also, JPEG 2000 has been gone since Elements 9.

Fortunately, there are ways around this if you do need to open some of those formats. For example, here's how you can work with JPEG 2000 files (which are still used by many books that include practice images on discs and for a lot of downloadable artwork):

- **Windows:** Download the free ImageMagick program (*www.imagemagick.org*) and use it to convert your JPEG 2000 images to another lossless format.

- **Mac:** Use Preview (it's part of OS X) to open your JPEG 2000 files and save them in the format of your choice.

For the other old and obscure formats, in Windows, try IrfanView (*www.irfanview.com*), a wonderful free program that can open almost any Windows-compatible format. You can sometimes even use IrfanView to salvage damaged files, especially if you get an "invalid JPEG marker" error. If Elements balks at one of your files, first try opening and resaving the photo in IrfanView. If you're lucky, that may be all you need to do to make Elements recognize the file.

On a Mac, try GraphicConverter (*www.lemkesoft.com*), a great little program that can open darn near anything. It does great batch conversions, too, and even offers some basic image-editing features. GraphicConverter is shareware (it currently costs $40) with a generous demo period, and it's worth every penny.

Changing the File Format

It's super easy to change a file's format in Elements: Just press Shift+Ctrl+S/Shift-⌘-S or go to File→Save As and, from the Format drop-down menu, select the format you want. Elements makes a copy of your file in the new format and asks you to name it.

■ Backing Up Files

With computers, you just never know what's going to happen, so "Be prepared" is a good motto. If your computer crashes, it won't be nearly as painful if all your photos are safely backed up someplace else.

You'll be glad to know that Elements also makes it easy to save files to any add-on storage device—like an external hard drive—or to a CD or DVD (Windows only). The following section explains your options.

Organizer Backups

The Organizer offers a really helpful way to back up photos. It's one of Elements' best features, and it's certainly thorough, even going so far as to remind you to label the disc you create. You can back up your whole catalog or just specific photos. Simply follow these steps:

1. **Make sure your catalog is in tip-top shape.**

   In the Organizer, go to File→Manage Catalogs. In the Catalog Manager window, select your catalog in the list, and then click Repair. Next, click the window's Optimize button, which makes sure your catalog's database is in tip-top shape. Then close the Catalog Manager window.

   It's also not a bad idea to go to File→Reconnect→All Missing Files, although the Organizer warns you if you have unconnected files when you start your backup. (An *unconnected file* is a cataloged item that the Organizer can't find.)

   NOTE If you have multiple catalogs, you can back up only one at a time.

2. **Call up the Backup dialog box, and let Elements make sure your catalog is in backup-ready shape.**

   Go to File→Backup Catalog, or press Ctrl+B/⌘-B.

3. **Tell Elements what kind of backup to make.**

   In the dialog box that opens, you have to decide whether to back up your whole catalog or to make an incremental backup. The Full Backup option backs up *everything* in your catalog. Pick that option the first time you make a backup, or if you're backing up everything to move to a new computer.

   The Incremental Backup option finds only the stuff that's new since the last time you made a backup, and that's all it copies—a major time- and space-saver.

   NOTE You have to make a full backup at least once before Elements will let you do an incremental backup, and there seem to be more problems with incremental backups, so many people think it's prudent to do a full backup every time.

   Make your choice and then click Next to continue.

4. **Choose a destination for your files.**

   Your choices in the Select Destination Drive section include all your available hard drives. In the list, click the drive you want to use. If you're using Windows and you want to back up to CDs or DVDs, choose your disc drive in the list. Elements even pops the drive open for you.

   If you're backing up to a hard drive, click the Backup Path field's Browse button to select where you want Elements to put the backup. Navigate through the folders in the window that appears, and create a new folder if you'd like to keep your backups tidy (a good idea). Once you're done, the folder's *path* (a roadmap to where it lives) appears in the Backup window.

   If you're making an incremental backup, then you have to show Elements where to find your previous backup. Click the name of the drive where you made your previous backup, and then click the "Previous Backup file" field's Browse button to point Elements to the existing backup file.

5. **If you're backing up to a CD or DVD, insert a disc into the drive when Elements asks you to.** (If you're backing up to any other kind of media, including internal or external hard drives, then skip ahead to step 6.)

   Elements has to calculate how many discs it need to create your backup. As Elements burns each disc, it asks if you want it to verify the disc to be sure it's OK. You do. Elements prompts you to feed it more discs if the backup doesn't all fit on one disc.

   If you like, you can change the write speed for your disc. (A slower speed takes longer but may be more reliable.) Just choose one of the other speed options from the drop-down menu.

TIP Always check your backup discs once you've burned them, even if you verified them during backup. Do that by putting the disc in your computer and making sure all your files are there. If there's an error, you want to know about it *now*, not 6 months from now.

---

6. **Create the backup.**

   Click Done, and Elements generates the backup. If you decide you don't want to make a backup, click Cancel instead.

TIP These directions cover how to back up your images and your catalog. It's also a really good idea to back up your *catalog database* (the data file that the Organizer creates to keep track of where your photos are) every once in a while. To back up just the catalog information, in the Organizer, go to Help→System Info to see the file path to your current catalog (it's listed next to Catalog Location). Then burn those folders (including the files within them) to a CD or DVD or copy them to an external hard drive.

Be aware that a backup made using these steps is for *Elements'* use, not yours: If you look at the backup in Windows Explorer or a Mac's Finder, you'll see files with weird numerical names, and you can't just rummage around to find a particular photo you accidentally deleted. Instead, you have to let Elements handle restoring the files. Because you can't easily get individual files out of an official Elements backup, many people prefer to create their own backups, copying the catalog file (the preceding Tip explains where to find it) and their images. That way, you don't have to rely on Elements to retrieve lost photos for you.

If you want to switch your catalog to a new machine, you can install Elements and restore your existing backup. (This even works when moving from Windows to a Mac. If you want to move a catalog from one platform to another, use a removable hard drive for your backup.) To restore your catalog, in the Organizer, go to File→Restore Catalog, and then follow the onscreen directions.

NOTE   In Windows, you can also copy a few photos to CDs or DVDs rather than making a full backup of your catalog. To do that, go to File→"Copy/Move to Removable Drive." Leave the Move Files checkbox turned off, click Next, and then select your disc-burning drive in the list in the next window.

Macs don't let you do any kind of disc burning directly from Elements, but you can select photos in the Organizer and go to File→"Export as New File(s)" (page 528) to send them to the Finder for burning, if your Mac has an optical drive (one that can read and burn discs).

Rotating and Resizing Photos

I n the last chapter, you learned how to get photos *into* Elements. Now it's time to look at how to trim off unwanted areas and straighten crooked photos. You'll also learn how to change the overall size of images and how to zoom in and out to get a better look at things while you're editing.

NOTE From here through Chapter 14, you need to be in the Elements Editor. If you're still in the Organizer, press Ctrl+I/⌘-I to go to the Expert Mode window.

Straightening Scanned Photos

Anyone who's scanned printed photos can testify about the hair-pulling frustration you feel when your carefully placed pictures come out crooked onscreen. Whether you're feeding in precious memories one at a time or scanning batches of photos to save time, Elements can help straighten things out.

Straightening Two or More Photos at Once

If you've got a pile of photos to scan, save yourself some time and lay as many of them as you can fit on your scanner. Thanks to Elements' handy Divide Scanned Photos command, you can save them as individual image files in no time.

Start by scanning in the photos (Figure 3-1). It doesn't matter whether you scan directly into Elements or use the scanner's own software. (See page 37 for more about scanning images into Elements.) The only limit is how many can fit on your scanner at once.

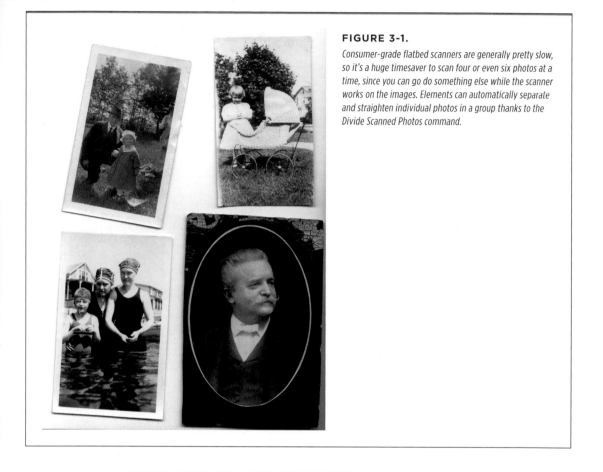

FIGURE 3-1.

Consumer-grade flatbed scanners are generally pretty slow, so it's a huge timesaver to scan four or even six photos at a time, since you can go do something else while the scanner works on the images. Elements can automatically separate and straighten individual photos in a group thanks to the Divide Scanned Photos command.

TIP   Sometimes it pays to be crooked. Divide Scanned Photos works best when your photos are fairly askew, so don't waste time trying to be precise when placing them on the scanner.

When you're done scanning, follow these steps:

1. **Open the scanned image file in the Editor.**

   It doesn't matter what file format you used when saving the scanned group of photos: TIFF, JPEG, whatever. Elements can read 'em all (unless you used JPEG 2000, in which case see page 71).

2. **Divide, straighten, and crop the individual photos.**

   Go to Image→Divide Scanned Photos, and then sit back and enjoy the view as Elements carefully calculates, splits, straightens out, and trims each image. You'll see the photos appear and disappear as Elements works through them.

3. **Name and save each separated image.**

When Elements is done, you'll have the original group scan as one image and a separate image file for each photo Elements carved out. All you need to do now is import the cut-apart photos into the Organizer (if you use the Organizer, that is). To do that, just make sure that "Include in the Elements Organizer" is turned on in the Save As dialog box (see page 66). If you don't use the Organizer, just save the images.

Elements usually does a crackerjack job splitting photos, but once in a while it chokes, leaving you with an image file that contains more than one photo. Figure 3-2 shows you what to do when Elements doesn't succeed in dividing things up.

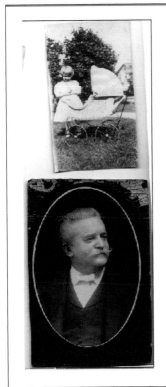

FIGURE 3-2.

Sometimes Elements just can't figure out how to split photos, and you wind up with something like these two not-quite-separated images. If that happens, rescan the photos that confused Elements, but this time make sure they're more crooked on the scanner and leave more space between them. Elements should then be able to split them correctly. Also, check for That doesn't seem to be a problem in this image. It was more evident in the previous figure, so I wonder if this one was straightened up when it shouldn't have been. Put a little more space between the photos so Elements can split them.

TIP Occasionally you may find that Elements can't accurately separate a group scan, no matter what you do. In that case, use the Rectangular Marquee tool (page 139) to select an individual image, copy it (Ctrl+C/⌘-C), paste it into its own document (File→New→"Image from Clipboard"), and then save it. You might also want to check your scanner driver—it may have a way to divide a group scan as part of the scanning process itself.

Straightening Individual Photos

Elements can also straighten and crop (trim) a single scanned image. After scanning the image and opening it in the Editor, simply choose Image→Rotate→"Straighten and Crop Image," and Elements tidies things up for you (choose Straighten Image instead if you'd rather crop the edges yourself). Better still, you can actually use the Divide Scanned Photos command (explained in the previous section) on a single image. (Cropping is explained on page 85.)

◼ Rotating Images

People scanning printed photographs aren't the only ones who sometimes need a little help straightening their pictures. Digital photos sometimes have to be rotated because some cameras don't include data in their image files that tells Elements (or any other image-editing program) the correct orientation. Certain cameras, for example, send portrait-oriented photos out on their sides, and it's up to you to straighten things out.

Fortunately, Elements has rotation commands all over the place. If all you need to get Dad off his back and stand him upright, here's a list of where you can perform a quick 90-degree rotation on any open photo:

- **Editor.** Click the Rotate button at the bottom of the screen to turn your image counterclockwise. (If you want to turn your photo clockwise instead, click the arrow next this button and then click the pop-out button that appears.) You can also right-click/Control-click a thumbnail in the Photo Bin and choose Rotate 90° Left (or Rotate 90° Right). Finally, in Expert Mode, you can also go to Image→Rotate→90° Left (or 90° Right)

- **Raw Converter.** Click the left or right arrow above the Preview window. (Flip to page 264 to learn about the Raw Converter.)

- **Organizer.** You can rotate a photo almost anytime in the Organizer by pressing Ctrl/⌘ plus the left or right arrow key. Another option is to choose Edit→Rotate 90° Left (or 90° Right). There are also Rotate buttons at the top of the Quick Edit panel in Full Screen view (page 51). Finally, there's a Rotate button at the bottom of the Media room window. (Just as in the Editor, if you want to rotate the other way, click the arrow to the right of this button and then click the button that appears.)

Those commands all get you one-click, 90-degree changes. But Elements has all sorts of other rotational tricks up its sleeve, as the next section explains.

Rotating and Flipping Options

Elements gives you several ways to change a photo's orientation. To see what's available, in the Editor, go to Image→Rotate. You'll notice two groups of rotate commands in this menu; for now, it's the top group you want to focus on. (The second group does the same things, only those commands work on layers, which are explained in Chapter 6.) The first group of commands includes:

- **90° Left/Right.** These commands do the same thing as the Rotate button explained earlier; use them to fix digital photos that arrive in Elements on their sides.

- **180°.** This turns your photo upside down and backward.

- **Custom.** Selecting this command brings up a dialog box where, if you're mathematically inclined, you can type in the precise number of degrees you want to rotate the photo.

- **Flip Horizontal.** Flipping a photo horizontally means that if your subject was gazing soulfully off to the left, now she's gazing soulfully off to the right.

- **Flip Vertical.** This command turns your photo upside down *without* changing the left/right orientation the way Rotate 180° does.

> **TIP** When you flip photos, remember you're making a mirror image of *everything* in the photo. So someone who's writing right-handed becomes a lefty, any text in the photo will be backward, and so on.

Figure 3-3 shows these commands in action.

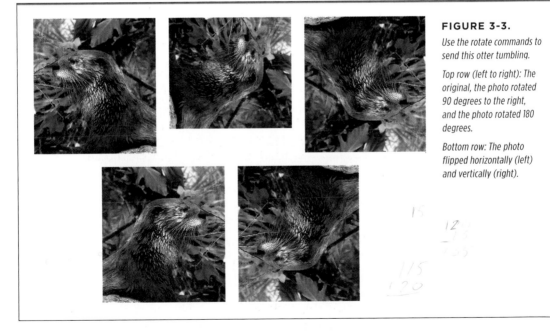

FIGURE 3-3.

Use the rotate commands to send this otter tumbling.

Top row (left to right): The original, the photo rotated 90 degrees to the right, and the photo rotated 180 degrees.

Bottom row: The photo flipped horizontally (left) and vertically (right).

If you want to position a photo at an angle (as you might in a scrapbook), use Free Rotate Layer, described on page 83.

Straightening the Contents of an Image

What about all those photos you've taken where the main subject (a person or a building, say) isn't quite straight? You can flip those pictures around forever, but if your camera was off-kilter when you snapped the shot, your subjects will still lean like a certain tower in Pisa. Elements can help with this problem, too. It includes a nifty Straighten tool that makes adjusting the horizon as easy as drawing a line.

> **TIP** Most of the time, the Straighten tool does the trick. But if you find the Straighten tool too fiddly or in the few cases where you can't get things looking perfect, you can use the old-school method: the Free Rotate Layer command, described on page 83.

Straighten Tool

If you can never seem to hold a camera perfectly level, you'll love Elements' Straighten tool. Here's how to straighten a crooked photo:

1. **Open a photo, and then activate the Straighten tool.**

   You'll find it at the lower right of the Modify section of the Tools panel; its icon is the carpenter's level. Or just press the P key.

2. **Make any necessary changes to the Tool Options settings.**

   Your choices are described after this list.

3. **Tell Elements where the image's horizon is.**

   Drag to draw a line in the photo to show Elements where horizontal *should* be. Figure 3-4 shows how—by drawing a line that traces the boundary between the ocean and the sky. The line appears at an angle when you draw it. That's fine, because Elements is going to level out the photo, making your line the true horizontal plane.

> **TIP** If you have a photo of trees, sailing ships, skyscrapers, or any other subject where you'd rather straighten vertically than horizontally, just hold down Ctrl/⌘ while you drag. That way, the line you draw determines the *vertical* axis of the photo. (It's important to press the mouse button *before* you press the Ctrl/⌘ key, or this trick won't work.)

4. **Elements automatically straightens your photo (and crops it, if you chose that setting in the Tool Options).**

   If you don't like what Elements did, press Ctrl+Z/⌘-Z to undo it and draw another line. If you're happy, you're all done, except for saving the file (Ctrl+S/⌘-S).

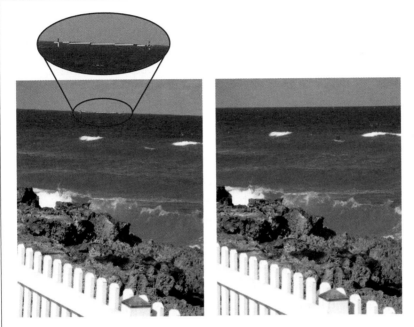

FIGURE 3-4.

Left: To correct the crooked horizon in this photo, simply draw a line along the part that should be level. It's easiest to do this by choosing a clearly marked boundary like the horizon here, but you can draw a line across anything you want to make level.

Right: Elements automatically rotates the photo to straighten its contents.

The Tool Options give you some control over how Elements handles the edges of your newly straightened photo. Once the picture is straightened, the edges are going to be a bit ragged, so you can choose what Elements should do about that:

- **Grow or Shrink** makes Elements add extra space (blank canvas) around the edges of the photo so that every bit of the original is still there. It's up to you to crop the image afterward (see page 85).

- **Remove Background** tells Elements to chop off the ragged edges to give you a nice, rectangular image. The downside to this option is that you lose some of the perimeter of your photo—though just a bit, so it's not usually a big deal.

- **Original Size** makes Elements keep the photo's dimensions exactly the same—even if that means including some blank space along the perimeter. You may also lose some of the edges of the image, particularly the corners.

If your photo has layers (see Chapter 6), you can use the Straighten tool to straighten just the active layer (page 181) by going to the Tool Options and turning off the Rotate All Layers checkbox. If you want Elements to straighten your whole photo, then leave this checkbox turned on.

The Straighten tool is best for photos where you were holding the camera crooked. If you try this tool and it makes things in your photo look very odd, then perhaps straightening isn't what it needs. Architectural photos, for instance, may look a bit crooked before you use this tool—but a lot worse afterward. If that house is *still* leaning even though you're sure the ground has been leveled correctly, then most likely your real problem is *perspective distortion* (a visual warping effect). To fix that, use Correct Camera Distortion (page 379) instead.

> **TIP** You can also straighten photos in the Raw Converter. There's a Straighten tool in its toolbox, right between the Crop tool and the Red Eye Removal tool. You use it just like the Editor's Straighten tool. Page 269 tells you more.

ON THE SQUARE

Grids, Guides, and Rulers

Elements gives you plenty of help when it comes to getting things straightened and aligned. In the Editor, you can turn on several features that make it really easy to create all kinds of projects:

- **Grid.** This option puts your entire image under a network of gridlines, as in Figure 3-5. This is really helpful when you're doing a free rotation (page 83) and you're not sure where straight is. Just go to View→Grid to toggle the grid on and off. You can adjust the grid's spacing in Edit→Preferences→Guides & Grid/Adobe Photoshop Elements Editor→Preferences→Guides & Grid. That's also where you can change the grid's color to make it show up better. To do that, click the color square in the grid preferences window, and then choose a color from the Color Picker (page 249).

- **Rulers.** If you want to measure something in an image, go to View→Rulers, and rulers appear along the sides of the image. You can change the unit of measurement by right-clicking/Control-clicking the ruler and choosing from the pop-out menu, or by going to Edit→Preferences→Units & Rulers/Adobe Photoshop Elements Editor→Preferences→Units & Rulers if you'd rather see, say, pixels or percents rather than inches.

- **Guides.** Guides are a great way to get things lined up. You can create as many guides as you want in an image. Just go to View→New Guide and choose a horizontal or vertical line; you can't change the orientation of a guideline once you create it. You can also specify a position in your image, or just create it anywhere by clicking OK, and then use the Move tool to drag it where you want it. (If the rulers are visible, you can just drag a guide from the ruler without going to the View menu.) Once you get your guidelines set up, you can keep yourself from accidentally moving them by going to View→Lock Guides. To remove your guides, go to View→Clear Guides.

If you save a photo with guides in it and send it to someone else using Photoshop or a version of Elements that can display guides (versions 6–11; Elements 6 and 7 can *see* guides, they just can't create them), that person will see your guides. If someone sends you a file with guides in it, you can see their guides if you turn them on in the View menu (View→Guides).

Guides are really handy, particularly for projects like scrapbooking, because you can make anything you add to a file *snap* (jump) right to the guide's location by choosing View→Snap To→Guides. If you decide you'd rather move objects freely, just select the same menu option again to toggle snapping off. (You can also have objects snap to the grid, but you can change this setting only when the grid is visible.)

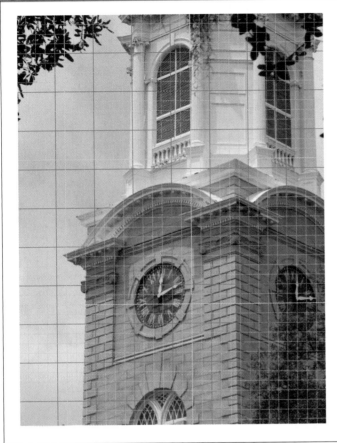

FIGURE 3-5.

If you need help figuring out where straight is, you can add a grid or guidelines in the Editor. The bright aqua lines are guides; the others are the grid. (Neither will show up when you print your photos.) Use the grid to help straighten an image. Guides are especially useful when you're adding items to a photo, since you can make things like text blocks (page 485) automatically line up by making them snap to the guidelines. The box on page 82 tells you how.

Free Rotate Layer

You can also use the rotate commands to straighten photos, or to turn them at angles for use in scrapbook pages or album layouts. The command that's best for this is Free Rotate Layer, which lets you grab a photo and spin it to your heart's desire. And if you aren't sure where straight is, Elements can help you figure it out, as the box on page 82 explains.

TIP You can use all the rotate commands on individual layers. Chapter 6 explains layers, but you don't have to understand them to use the Free Rotate Layer command.

To use Free Rotate Layer:

1. **Go to Image→Rotate→Free Rotate Layer.**

    If your image includes a Background layer, Elements automatically converts it to a regular layer for you. (You'll learn about layers in Chapter 6.)

2. **Drag to adjust your photo (see Figure 3-6).**

    Your picture may look kind of jagged while you're rotating. Don't worry about that—Elements will smooth things out once you're done.

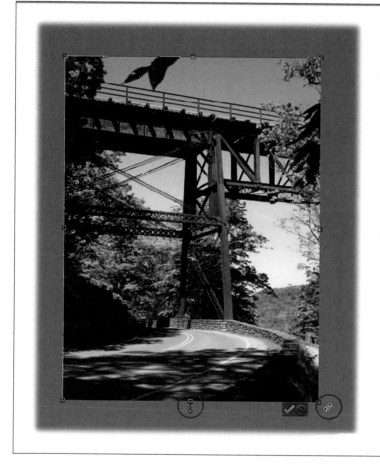

FIGURE 3-6.

Free Rotate Layer lets you straighten the contents of a photo—or even spin it around in a circle. Just grab either the handle at the bottom center of the photo or one of the square handles around its outside, both circled. (If you're on a Mac, you won't see the center handle, only the corner ones.) When you move your cursor near one of the handles, it turns into a curved, two-headed arrow.

When you've got ahold of a handle, drag to adjust your photo the way you'd straighten a crooked picture on the wall. Click the green checkmark below the image when you're happy with what you've done, or the red Cancel button to cancel.

3. **When you've got the image positioned where you want it, click the Commit button (the green checkmark) or press Enter.** (If you don't like what you did, click the Cancel button—the red No symbol—to cancel the rotation.)

    If you were straightening the photo (rather than angling it), you've got a nice straight picture, but the edges are probably pretty ragged, since the original had slanted, unrotated sides. You can take care of that by cropping the photo as explained next.

Cropping Pictures

Whether or not you straighten your digital photos, sooner or later you'll probably need to *crop* them—trim them to a certain size. Most people crop photos for one of two reasons: To print on standard-size photo paper, you usually need to cut away part of the image to make it fit the paper. Then there's the "I don't want *that* in my picture" reason. Fortunately, Elements makes it easy to crop away distracting background objects or people you'd rather not see.

A few cameras take photos that are proportioned exactly right for printing on standard-size paper like 4" x 6" or 8" x 10". (An image's width-to-height ratio is also known as its *aspect ratio*.) But most cameras create images that aren't the same proportions as any of the standard paper sizes. Figure 3-7 shows an example of cropping to fit on standard photo paper.

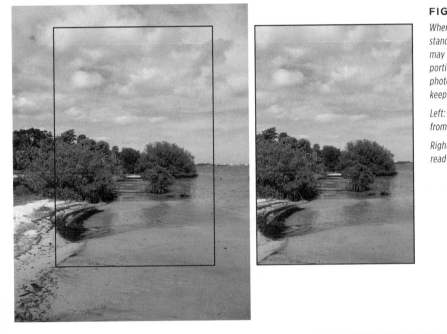

FIGURE 3-7.

When you print on standard-sized paper, you may have to choose the portion of your digital photo that you want to keep.

Left: The photo as it came from the camera.

Right: After cropping— ready for a 4" x 6" print.

The extra area most cameras provide gives you room to crop wherever you like. You can also crop out different areas for different size prints (assuming you save the original photo). If you'd like to experiment with cropping or changing resolution (explained on page 101), download the image in Figure 3-7 (*river.jpg*) from this book's Missing CD page at *www.missingmanuals.com/cds*.

If you're not sure how to crop an image, or if you need to meet some common requirements for photo contests, Elements offers some special crop overlays that can help crop photos to pleasing proportions. They're explained in the next section.

TIP   If your photo isn't in the Organizer or another image-management program that automatically protects the original, it's best to crop a *copy* of the image, since cropping throws away the pixels outside the area you choose to keep. And you never know—you may want those pixels back someday.

The Crop Tool

You can use the Crop tool in either Expert Mode or the Quick Fix window. This tool includes a helpful list of preset sizes to make your job easier (page 89 explains how to use them). In most cases, the presets work well, but if you want to crop to a custom size, here's what you do:

1. **Activate the Crop tool.**

   Click the Crop icon in the Tools panel (it's at the upper left of the Modify section) or press C.

2. **Drag in the image to select the area you want to keep.**

   When you let go of the mouse button, the area outside your selection gets covered with a dark shield to show what you'll discard. To move the area you've chosen, just click anywhere inside the *bounding box* (the marching-ants outline) and drag it wherever you want.

   If you change your mind, click the red Cancel button or press Esc. Elements undoes the selection so you can start over.

TIP   You may find the Crop tool a little crotchety sometimes. See the box on page 89 for help making it behave.

3. **If necessary, drag the handles on the sides and corners of the bounding box to resize it.**

   The handles look like little squares, as shown in Figure 3-8. You can drag in any direction, which lets you change the proportions of the crop, if you want to.

   You can also rotate the crop box to any angle (a handy way to straighten *and* crop in one go). To do so, put your cursor near a handle on the bounding box (the cursor turns into the curved, double-headed arrow circled in Figure 3-8), and then drag. For example, if your image is crooked, turn the crop box so that the outlines of the crop box are parallel to where straight should be in the photo and then crop; Elements straightens out your photo in the process.

   You can also choose a different crop overlay (explained below) to help you create a more appealing image, or turn the overlay off altogether if it bugs you. In the Tool Options area, just choose the one you want.

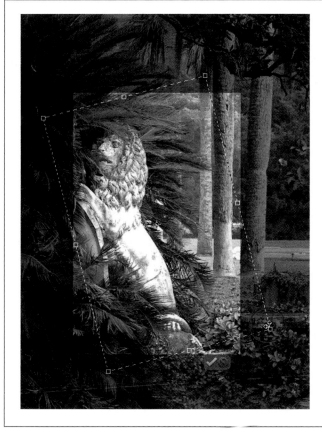

FIGURE 3-8.

To change your selection from horizontal to vertical or vice versa, just move your cursor outside the cropped area and it'll turn into the rotation arrows circled here. Then drag to rotate the crop box the same way you would a whole image.

Rotating your selection doesn't rotate the photo—just the boundaries of the crop. When you're done, press Enter/Return or click the green Commit checkmark to tell Elements you're satisfied. The red Cancel button cancels your crop. (The symbols appear when you let go of the mouse button.)

When you're sure you've got the crop you want, press Enter/Return, click the green Commit checkmark, or double-click inside the area you're going to keep, and you're done.

The Crop tool's various overlays can help you crop photos in the most visually pleasing way. Choose an option by clicking a thumbnail at the left end of the Tool Options area either before or after you've made a selection with the Crop tool (but before you *accept* the crop), and you'll see guidelines that help you decide where to crop. These are your options:

- **Rule of Thirds.** This is the option Elements chooses automatically the first time you use the Crop tool. The crop area is divided into thirds, both vertically and horizontally. Figure 3-9 explains how to use this overlay.

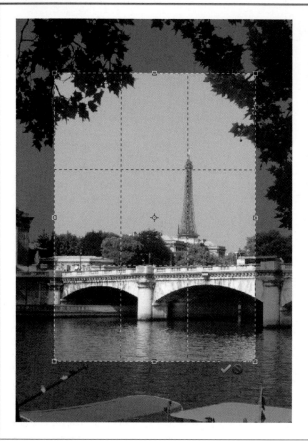

FIGURE 3-9.

The basic idea behind the Rule of Thirds is simple: Most people find images more pleasing to the eye if the main point of interest isn't placed squarely in the center. Instead, if you think of dividing a photo into thirds both horizontally and vertically (as this grid does), your subject will have more impact if it falls along one of those dividing lines or, even better, where two lines intersect. Here, the crop places the Eiffel tower on a vertical line, the bridge on a horizontal one, and the place where those two points of interest meet falls where the two lines intersect, making the cropped version better composed than the original photo.

- **Grid.** This puts the regular Elements grid (page 82) over your image.

- **Golden Ratio.** This is the most complex of the overlays, a complicated arrangement of rectangles, squares, and diagonal lines. The Golden Ratio has been used as the basis for pleasing proportions in art and architecture ever since the pyramids were built, and it's been used extensively by artists and photographers to create the most effective compositions. If you want to understand how it works, a good place to start is *http://tinyurl.com/6kuue7u,* which explains all about Fibonacci numbers (the basis for the Golden Ratio) in nature and art, as well as the math involved.

The most basic way to use this overlay is to make sure that the small busy area where the lines converge is on the focal point of your image, and to try to align the important features in the image with one of the dotted lines. So for instance, if you have a photo of a woman standing in a long line of people, put them along a dotted line and put the focal point over her face. If you want to flip this overlay so it aligns better with your image, just click the Flip button in the Tool Options area. To change the overlay's orientation, just click the arrows between the crop numbers, as shown in Figure 3-10.

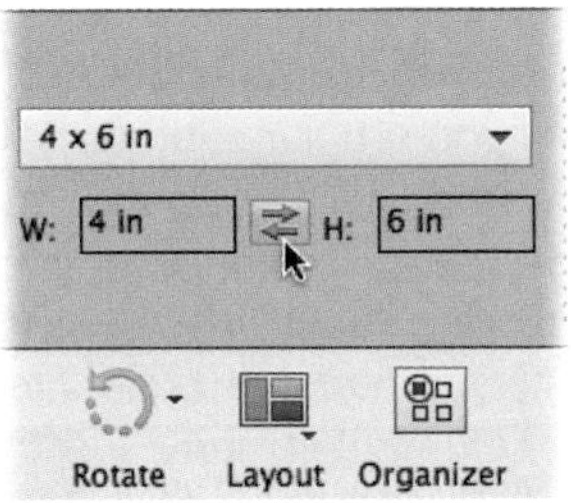

FIGURE 3-10.

To swap the crop box's width and height settings, just click these little arrows.

- **None.** This option gives you no visible overlay, just the empty crop box.

TROUBLESHOOTING MOMENT

Crop Tool Idiosyncrasies

The Crop tool is sometimes cantankerous. People have called it "bossy," and that's a good word for it. Here are some settings that may help you control it better:

- **Turn off Snap To Grid.** You may find that you just can't position a crop selection exactly where you want it. Does the edge keep jumping slightly away from where you put it? Like most graphics programs, Elements uses a grid of invisible lines—called the *autogrid*—to help place things exactly (see the box on page 82 for details). Sometimes this grid is a big help, but in situations like this, it's a nuisance.

  If you hold down Ctrl/⌘, you temporarily disable the autogrid. You can also turn off the grid or adjust its spacing. To turn it off, first make the grid visible by going to

View→Grid. Then choose View→Snap To→Grid. You can adjust the grid's settings—things like the spacing, color, and whether it uses solid or dotted lines—by going to Edit→Preferences→Guides & Grid/Adobe Photoshop Elements Editor→Preferences→Guides & Grid.

- **Clear the Crop tool.** Occasionally you may find that the Crop tool won't release a setting you entered, even after you clear the Tool Options settings. For example, if the tool won't let you drag where you want and keeps insisting on creating a particular-sized crop, you need to reset it. Simply click the little four-lined square at the far right of the Tool Options area, and then choose Reset Tool. If you want all your tools to go back to their original settings, choose Reset All Tools instead.

■ CROPPING AN IMAGE TO AN EXACT SIZE

You don't have to eyeball things when cropping a photo. You can enter any dimensions you want in the Tool Options area's W (width) and H (height) boxes or choose one of the presets from the Aspect Ratio menu (the unlabeled menu above the W and H boxes). The Aspect Ratio menu includes several standard photo sizes, like 4" x 6" and 8" x 10". It starts off set to No Restriction, which means you can drag freely. The menu's Use Photo Ratio option lets you crop your image by using the same width/height proportions (the *aspect ratio*) as the original. Figure 3-10 teaches you a timesaver: how to quickly swap the width and height numbers.

WARNING   If you enter a number in the Tool Options area's Resolution box that's different from your image's current resolution, the Crop tool *resamples* your image to match the new resolution. (Resolution is explained starting on page 101.) See page 107 to understand what resampling is and why it's not always a good thing.

Cropping with the Marquee Tool

The Crop tool is handy, but it decides several things you may want to control yourself. For instance, the Crop tool may decide to resample the image (see page 107) whether you want it to or not (and without any warning).

For better control, you may prefer the Rectangular Marquee tool. It's no harder to use than the Crop tool, but you get to make all the decisions yourself. But there's one other big difference between the two: With the Crop tool, all you can do to the selected area is crop it; the Rectangular Marquee tool, in contrast, lets you make lots of other changes to the selected area, like adjust its color, which you may want to do before you crop.

To make a basic crop with the Marquee tool:

1. **Open a photo and then activate the Marquee tool.**

    Click the little dotted rectangle near the top of the Tools panel or press M. Figure 3-11 shows you the shape choices you get in the Tool Options area for the marquee tools. For cropping, choose the Rectangular Marquee tool.

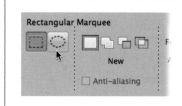

FIGURE 3-11.

Click the marquee tools, and then use these buttons to choose a shape—rectangle or ellipse. The Tools panel icon reflects the shape that's currently selected.

2. **Drag across the part of the photo you want to keep.**

    When you let go of the mouse button, Elements puts dotted lines like the ones shown in Figure 3-12 around the selected area. (Chapter 5 has more about making selections.) These dotted lines are sometimes called "marching ants." (Get it? The dashes look like ants marching around your picture.) The area inside the marching ants is the part that you're keeping. If you make a mistake, press Esc or Ctrl+D/⌘-D to get rid of the selection and start over.

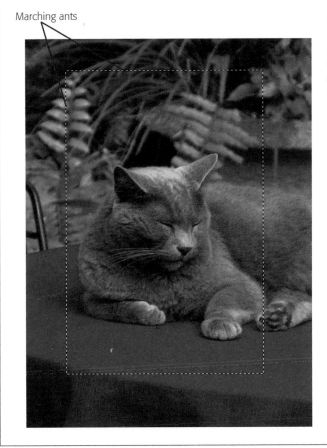

Marching ants

FIGURE 3-12.

When you let go after making your Marquee selection, you see the "marching ants" around the selection's edge. You can reposition the marquee by dragging it— just put your cursor anywhere inside the dotted outline and then drag it.

3. **Crop the photo.**

   Go to Image→Crop. The area outside your selection disappears, and Elements crops the photo to the area you selected in step 2.

If you want to crop a photo to a particular aspect ratio (proportion), you can do that easily. Once the Rectangular Marquee tool is active but before you drag to make a selection, go to the Tool Options area. Choose Fixed Ratio from the Aspect menu, and then enter the proportions you want in the W (width) and H (height) boxes. Finally, drag and crop as described in the previous list, and the photo will end up with the exact proportions you entered.

You can also crop to an exact size with the Rectangular Marquee tool:

1. **Check the resolution of your photo.**

   Go to Image→Resize→Image Size (or press Alt+Ctrl+I/Option-⌘-I) and make sure the Resolution number (ppi) is somewhere between 150 and 300 if you plan to print the cropped image (300 is best, for reasons explained on page 105.) If the number looks good, click OK and go to step 2. If the resolution is too low, change the number in the Resolution box to what you want. Make sure that the Resample Image checkbox is turned off, and then click OK. (If you don't plan to print the image, only the size matters, not the resolution in ppi.)

2. **Activate the Rectangular Marquee tool.**

   Click the Rectangular Marquee tool's icon (the dotted rectangle) in the Tools panel or press M. Check the Tools Options area to make sure you've got the Rectangular Marquee tool, not the Elliptical Marquee tool.

3. **Enter your Tool Options settings.**

   First, go to the Aspect menu and choose Fixed Size. Next, enter the dimensions you want in the W and H boxes. (You can also change the unit of measurement from pixels to inches or centimeters if you want; just change "px" to "in" or "cm.")

4. **Drag anywhere in your image.**

   You get a selection the exact size you chose in the Tool Options. You can reposition it by dragging or using the arrow keys.

5. **Crop the image.**

   Go to Image→Crop.

The Cookie Cutter tool also gives you a way to create really interesting crops, as shown in Figure 3-13.

TIP   If you're doing your own printing, there's no reason to restrict yourself to standard photo sizes like 4" x 6"—unless, of course, you need the image to fit a frame of that size. But most of the time, your images could just as well be square, or long and skinny, or whatever proportions you want. You can be especially inventive when sizing images for the Web. So don't feel that every photo you take has to be straitjacketed into a standard size.

■ Zooming and Repositioning Your View

Sometimes, rather than changing the size of a photo, all you want to do is change its appearance in Elements so you can get a better look at it. For example, you may want to zoom in on a particular area, or zoom out so you can see how edits you've made have affected the photo's overall look.

This section is about how to adjust your view of images. Nothing you do with the tools and commands covered in this section changes anything about the actual photo—just the way you see it. Elements gives you lots of tools and keystroke combinations to help with these views; soon you'll probably find yourself changing perspective without even thinking about it.

Image Views

Before you start changing your view of photos, it's good to get familiar with the different ways you can position images. Back in Chapter 1, you learned how to manage panels and bins. This section covers your options for image windows, which behave a little differently.

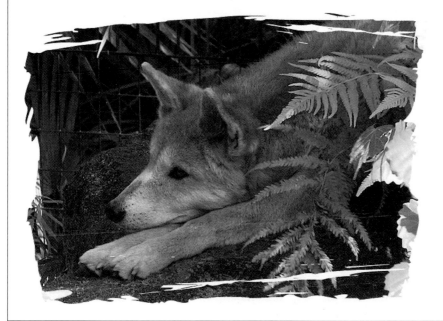

FIGURE 3-13.

With the Cookie Cutter tool, you don't have to be square. It lets you crop images to various shapes, from the kind of abstract border you see here, to heart- or star-shaped outlines. There's more on how to use this tool in Chapter 12.

You can choose between viewing images as tabs or in their own floating windows. Elements automatically starts out using tabs, but sometimes you may prefer to work with windows. For instance, if you want to use the Transform commands (page 385), putting the image into a tab gives you plenty of room to pull the handles that command places around the image, while you may find it easier to work with multiple images if each one is in its own window. There are a bunch of options for either view, and even if you're an Elements veteran but haven't quite gotten the hang of this relatively new system, you should read this section in case you accidentally wind up in a view you didn't want. Figure 3-14 shows the difference between tabs and windows.

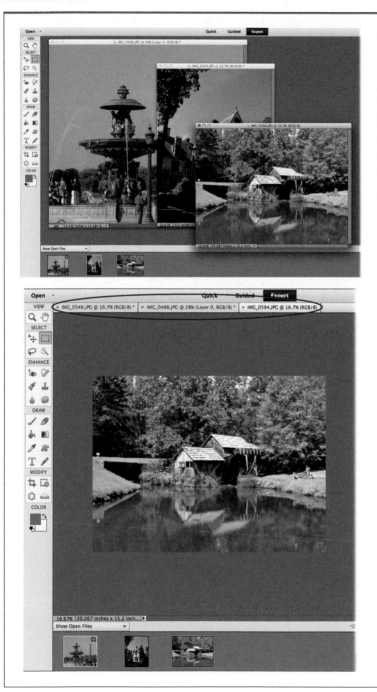

FIGURE 3-14.

Top: Three floating windows in Cascade view.

Bottom: The same three images as tabs. Notice that you see only one Image—the others are tucked away out of sight. To see one of the other images, click its tab near the top of the screen (circled). The tab's background will fill every part of the main Elements window that isn't occupied by bins, however large the area may be. The active image is easy to spot because its tab is lighter gray than the other images' tabs.

To give yourself maximum viewing flexibility, go to Edit→Preferences→General/
Adobe Photoshop Elements Editor→Preferences→General and turn on "Allow
Floating Documents in Expert Mode," and then click OK. When this setting is turned
off, you're stuck with tabs no matter what you choose in the Editor's menus. When
it's on, you can quickly switch back and forth between windows, tabs, or even a
combination of the two.

> **NOTE** You can also choose to let your images combine as tabs (just like image tabs in the main Editor
> window) within floating windows, so that you can have two or more photos in one floating window. This can help
> keep you organized when, for example, you're working on a project that involves a lot of photos; you can use
> this trick to group the ones you want to use together until it's time to work on them. To give yourself this option,
> go to Edit→Preferences→General/Adobe Photoshop Elements Editor→Preferences→General and make sure
> that "Enable Floating Document Window Docking" is turned on. On the other hand, if this feature has driven you
> crazy in the past couple of versions of Elements, you'll be pleased to know you can turn it *off* in Elements 11.

Since accurate image viewing is crucial in Elements, the Window, View, and Layout
menus all include options that let you control how the program displays images. The
Window and View menus are up at the top of your screen, and the Layout menu is
one of the buttons at the bottom left of the Editor's main window. When you go to
Window→Images, you get several choices of how to display images (a couple of
these options are available in only the Mac version of Elements, as noted below):

- **Tile.** Your image windows or tabs appear edge to edge so they fill the available desktop space. For example, with two photos open, each one gets half the
  workspace; with four photos, each one gets a quarter of it, and so on. With tabs,
  you have a lot of additional options when you use the Layout menu, described
  in Figure 3-15.

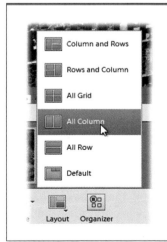

FIGURE 3-15.

*To arrange tabs to work with multiple images, click the Layout button at the bottom of the Expert
Mode window, and then choose the arrangement you want.*

*Default is the way tabs normally look, with only one visible and just the header tabs of the other
images in view. If you have only one image file open, all the other options in this menu are grayed
out. If you have only two images open, then the top three menu options (which are for three or more
photos) are grayed out. If you're using floating windows, clicking a layout's thumbnail consolidates
them all into tabs in the layout you choose here.*

- **Cascade.** Your image windows appear in overlapping stacks. Most people find cascading windows (Figure 3-14, top) the most practical view when they want to compare or work with two images. (This option is grayed out if you're working with tabs.)

- **Float in Window.** If you want to make a single image's tab into a window, click the image's tab to make it the active one, and then choose this option.

- **Float All in Windows.** If you have a bunch of tabs, choose this to turn them all into floating windows.

- **Consolidate All to Tabs.** Got a lot of windows that you want to turn back into tabs? Choosing this option does the trick.

- **New Window.** Choose this command and you get a separate, duplicate window for your active image. This view is a terrific help when you're working on fine details. You can zoom way in on one view while keeping the other window in a regular view so you don't lose track of where you are in the photo. (Don't worry about version control or remembering which window you're working in—both windows just show different views of the same image.) If you haven't turned on floating windows, this command creates a new tab instead, although that's not as useful.

- **Minimize (Mac only).** If you want to send the active image window to the Dock, choose this option or press ⌘-M. Click the image in the Dock to bring it back to Elements. (If you have image tabs, then the whole Elements window gets minimized when you choose this command.)

- **Bring All to Front (Mac only).** Use this command to bring all your open Elements image windows to the foreground (handy if you've got documents from several programs covering each other up).

- **Match Zoom.** Makes Elements display all your windows at the same magnification level as the active window (the one you're currently working in).

- **Match Location.** Elements makes the display in all your image windows match the active window so you see the same part of each image, like the upper-right corner or the bottom-left edge.

The View menu also gives you some handy commands for adjusting the view of your active image window or tab:

- **Zoom In/Out.** Zooming is explained on page 98. These menu commands are an alternative to using the Zoom tool.

TIP Keyboard shortcuts are the fastest way to zoom: Press Ctrl+=/⌘-= to zoom in and Ctrl-minus/⌘-minus to zoom out. The next section explains the Zoom tool in detail.

- **Fit on Screen.** This command makes your image as large as it can be while still keeping the whole photo visible. You can also press Ctrl+0/⌘-0 to get this view (that's the number zero, not the letter O), or double-click the Hand tool's icon in the Tools panel.

- **Actual Pixels.** For the most accurate look at the onscreen size of your photo, choose this option. If you're creating graphics for the Web, this view shows how big your image will be in a web browser. Keyboard shortcut: Ctrl+1/⌘-1. Or, double-click the Zoom tool's icon in the Tools panel.

- **Print Size.** This view is really just a guess by Elements, because it doesn't know exactly how big a pixel is on your monitor. But it's a rough approximation of the size the image would be if you printed it at its current resolution. (Resolution is explained on page 101.)

To adjust your view of a particular image, Elements gives you three useful tools: the Zoom tool, the Hand tool, and the Navigator panel, all of which are explained in the following sections. While you may find the whole tab vs. window business a little confusing at first, it gives you lots of ways to stay organized while working. The box below has some additional tips for keeping things under control.

ORGANIZATION STATION

Window Management Hints

In addition to the various menu commands discussed in this section, there's another way to control whether you have tabs or windows without trekking up to the menu bar: dragging. (You need to enable floating windows *and* floating window docking—page 95 tells you how—before these tricks will work.) Here are a few shortcuts:

- **Turn a tab into a window.** Just grab the tab's title bar and drag down. The tab pops off into a floating window.

- **Turn a window into a tab.** Drag the window up toward the top of the Elements workspace until you see a blue outline. This outline is Elements' way of telling you that, if you let go of the mouse button, it'll consolidate the window with the outlined area, just like it consolidates panels (see page 17).

- **Create tabs in a floating window.** If you want to put two images in one floating window (say you're working on combining elements from many different images, and it's getting hard to know which is where), just drag one

window's title bar onto another window's title bar and let go when you see the blue outline. You now have a floating window with two tabs. (Repeat this trick as many times as you want for a multitabbed window.)

- **Avoid making tabs.** When you're working with floating windows, if the tops of the windows move too close together, Elements wants to combine them. If you're dragging windows around and you see the telltale blue outline, just keep dragging till it disappears.

- **Undo accidental tabs.** If you create a tab you didn't mean to, grab the top of the image you want to turn back into a floating window, and then drag it loose from the tab group.

Just remember that in Elements, anytime you're dragging something and a blue outline appears, what you're dragging is going to get consolidated with something if you let go of the mouse. If you don't want that to happen, keep dragging till the outline disappears.

The Zoom Tool

Some of Elements' tools require you to get a really close look at your image to see what's going on. Sometimes you even need to see individual pixels as you work, as shown in Figure 3-16. The Zoom tool makes it easy to zoom your view in and out.

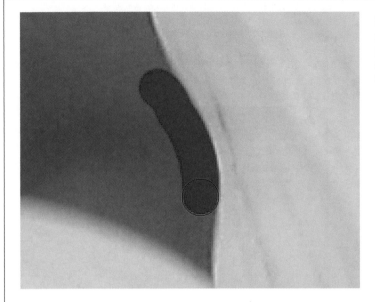

FIGURE 3-16.

There will be times when you want to zoom way, way in on an image. You may even need to go pixel by pixel in tricky spots, as shown here.

The Zoom tool lives at the very top of the Tools panel; its icon is a little magnifying glass. Click it or press Z to activate the tool. Once you do that, two magnifying glass buttons appear at the left end of the Tool Options area. To zoom in, click the one with the + sign on it, and then click the spot in your photo where you want the zoom to focus. The point you click becomes the center of your view, and the view size increases again each time you click. To zoom out, in the Tool Options, click the magnifying glass with the – sign on it instead.

> **TIP** Holding Alt/Option while you click makes the Zoom tool do the opposite of what it's currently set to do. For instance, if the tool is set to zoom in, then pressing this key makes it zoom out.

The Zoom tool has several other Tool Options settings:

- **Zoom.** You can either drag this slider or click the number to its right and then type what you want here and the view immediately jumps to that percentage. The maximum is 3200 percent, and the minimum is 1 percent.

- **Resize Windows To Fit.** Turn this checkbox on and the image windows get larger or smaller as you zoom, according to your current view. The image always fills the whole window with no gray space around it. (At least that's how it's *supposed* to work; sometimes it's a bit buggy.)

- **Zoom All Windows.** If you have more than one image window, turn this option on and the zoom level of all the windows changes simultaneously when you zoom in one window. (This option works with tabs, too, so be careful—you may zoom a hidden image when you don't want to.)

> **TIP** Holding down the Shift key while zooming in or out makes all your windows zoom together, just as if you'd turned on the Zoom All Windows checkbox.

- **Actual Pixels.** This button (which is labeled "1:1") has the same effect as choosing Actual Pixels from the View menu. It's explained on page 97.

- **Fit Screen.** This button does the same thing as the View menu's "Fit on Screen" command—see page 97.

- **Fill Screen.** This makes your photo fill Elements' whole viewing area, even if the image doesn't all fit onscreen at once.

- **Print Size.** This is a duplicate of the View menu command. See page 97 for the lowdown.

> **TIP** You don't need to bother with the Zoom tool at all—you can use your keyboard instead. Press Ctrl+=/⌘-= to zoom in and Ctrl+minus/⌘-minus to zoom out. Just hold down Ctrl/⌘ and keep tapping the equal or minus sign key until you see what you want. (You can zoom to 100 percent by double-clicking the Zoom tool's Tools panel icon.) It doesn't matter which tool you're using—you can always zoom in or out this way. Because you'll do a lot of zooming in Elements, these keyboard shortcuts are ones to remember.
>
> And if you have a mouse with a scroll wheel, you can use that to zoom, too. Go to Edit→Preferences→General/ Adobe Photoshop Elements Editor→Preferences→General and turn on "Zoom with Scroll Wheel."

The Hand Tool

With all that zooming, sometimes you can't see your whole image at once. The Hand tool lets you change which part of an image appears onscreen. It's super easy to use: Just click the little hand icon at the top of the Tools panel or press H to activate it. When you do, your cursor turns into the little icon shown in Figure 3-17. Simply drag your photo to move it around in the window. This tool is really helpful when you're zoomed way in or working on a large image.

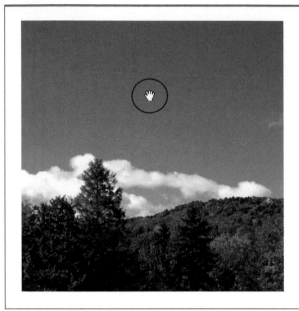

FIGURE 3-17.

The easiest way to activate the Hand tool is to press and hold the space bar on your keyboard. (You can tell when the Hand tool is active because you see this little white-gloved cursor.) No matter what you're doing in Elements, pressing the space bar calls up the Hand tool. When you let go of the space bar, Elements switches back to the tool you were previously using.

If you find that you can't back out of the Hand tool, just give your space bar a whack—it may be sticking.

The Hand tool gives you the same All Windows option you get with the Zoom tool (page 98), but you don't have to adjust the Tool Options settings to activate it. Just hold down Shift while using the Hand tool, and all your windows scroll in sync. The Hand tool also gives you the same four buttons as the Zoom tool (Actual Pixels [1:1], Fit Screen, Fill Screen, and Print Size); they're described on page 97.

Figure 3-18 shows the Hand tool's somewhat more sophisticated assistant, the Navigator panel, which is really useful for working on big photos or when you want to have a slider handy for micromanaging the zoom level. Go to Window→Navigator to call it up. (It appears as part of the grouped floating panel [page 11], but if you're in the Custom workspace [page 13] you can drag it out and close the rest of the group to get it out of your way.)

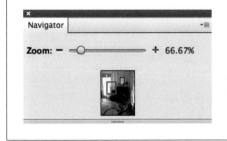

FIGURE 3-18.

Meet the Navigator, which is perfect for keeping track of where you are in a large image. You can travel around the image by dragging the little red rectangle shown here, which marks the area of the photo that's currently displayed onscreen. You can also adjust your zoom level by dragging the slider, clicking the percentage and typing a new number, or clicking the + and − buttons on either end of the slider.

Changing the Size of an Image

The previous section explained how to resize your *view* of an image—how it appears on your monitor. But sometimes you need to change the *actual* size of an image, and that's what this section is about.

Resizing photos brings you up against a pretty tough concept in digital imaging: *resolution,* which measures, in pixels, the amount of detail your image can show. What's confusing is that resolution for printing and for onscreen use (like email and the Web) are quite different.

You need many more pixels to create a good-looking print of an image than you do to view the image clearly onscreen. A photo that's going to print well almost always has too many pixels in it to display easily onscreen, and as a result, its file is usually pretty hefty for emailing. So you often need two copies of a photo for the two different uses. (If you want to know more about the nitty-gritty of resolution, a good place to start is *www.scantips.com*.)

This section gives you a brief introduction to both onscreen and print resolution, especially in terms of what decisions you'll need to make when using the Resize Image dialog box. You'll also learn how to add more canvas (more blank space) around photos, which you'd do to make room for a caption below an image, for instance, or when you want to combine two photos.

To get started, open a photo you want to resize and then go to Image→Resize→Image Size or press Alt+Ctrl+I/Option-⌘-I. Either way, you see the Image Size dialog box shown in Figure 3-19.

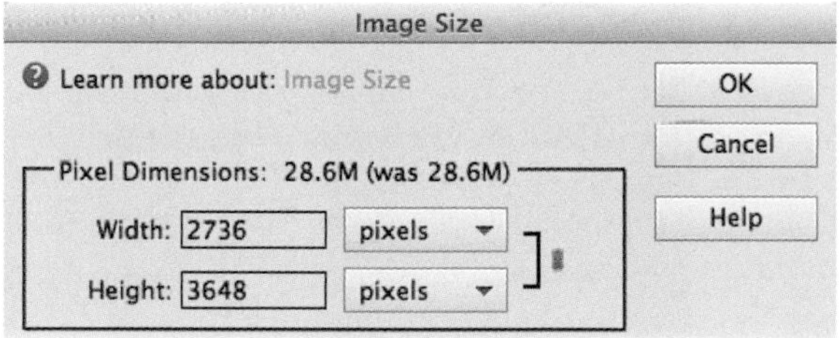

FIGURE 3-19.

This dialog box gives you two different ways to change the size of a photo. Use the Pixel Dimensions section (shown here) when preparing a photo for onscreen viewing. (The number next to Pixel Dimensions—here, 28.6M—tells you the current size of your file in megabytes or kilobytes.) Before you can make any changes here, you have to turn on the Resample Image checkbox at the bottom of the dialog box (not shown), since changing pixel dimensions always involves resampling (see page 107).

Resizing Images for Email and the Web

It's important to learn how to size photos so that they show up easily and clearly onscreen. Have you ever gotten an emailed photo that was so huge you could see only a tiny bit of it on your monitor at once? That happens when someone sends an image that isn't optimized for onscreen viewing. Happily, it's easy to avoid that problem once you know how to correctly size photos for onscreen use.

The Image Size dialog box has two main sections: Pixel Dimensions and Document Size. You'll use the Pixel Dimensions settings when you know the image is going to be viewed only onscreen. (The Document Size settings are for printing, which is covered in the next section.)

A monitor is concerned only with the size of a photo as measured in pixels, known as the *pixel dimensions*. On a monitor, a pixel is always the same size (unlike a printer, which can change the size of the pixels it prints). Your monitor doesn't know anything about pixels per inch (ppi), and it can't change the way it displays a photo even if you change the photo's ppi settings, as shown in Figure 3-20. (Graphics programs like Elements can change the size of your onscreen view by, say, zooming in, but most programs can't.) All you have to decide is how many pixels long and how many pixels wide you want the photo to be. You control those measurements in the Pixel Dimensions section of the Image Size dialog box.

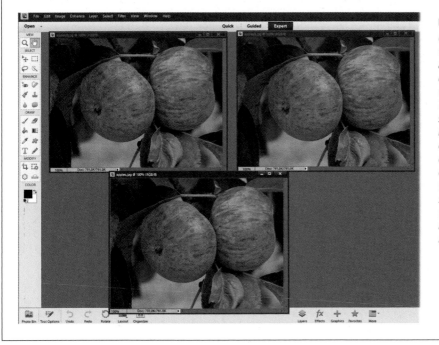

FIGURE 3-20.

One of these apple photos was saved at 3000 ppi, another at 300 ppi, and one at 3 ppi. Can you tell which is which? Nope. They all look exactly the same on your monitor because they all have exactly the same pixel dimensions, which is the only resolution setting your monitor understands. In other words, your monitor doesn't care about the ppi settings of an image.

What dimensions should you use? That depends on who's going to see your photos, but as a general rule, small monitors today are usually 1024 pixels wide by 768 pixels high, although netbook screens can be quite a bit smaller than that. And some monitors, like the largest Dell and Apple models, have many more pixels than that.

Still, if you want to be sure that people who view your photo won't have to scroll to see the whole thing, a good rule of thumb is to make the longest side of the photo no more than 650 pixels (it doesn't matter whether that's the width or the height). And if you want people to be able to see more than one image at a time, you may want to make your photos smaller than that. Also, some people still set their monitors to display only 800 pixels wide by 600 pixels high, so you may want to create even smaller images to send to them.

On the other hand, if you send really small pictures to people with deluxe, high-resolution monitors where the individual pixels are minuscule, they're likely to complain that the photos are too tiny to see in detail. So if you send to a varied group of folks, you may need to make different copies for different audiences. On the whole, it's better to err on the side of caution—nobody will have trouble receiving and opening an image that's too small, but an overly large attachment can cause problems for people with small mailboxes.

TIP   To get the most accurate look at how your photo displays on a monitor, go to View→Actual Pixels.

Also, although a photo always has the same pixel dimensions, you really can't control the exact physical dimensions at which those pixels display on other people's monitors. A pixel is always the same size on any given monitor (as long as you don't change the monitor's screen resolution), but different monitors have different-sized pixels. Figure 3-21 may help clarify this concept.

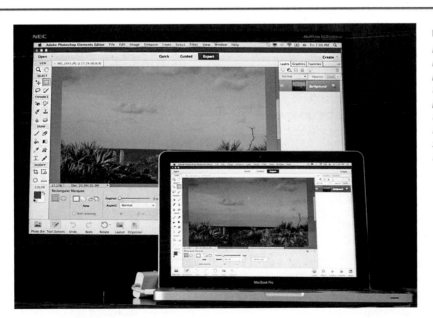

FIGURE 3-21.

Both these screens are running at 1280 x 800 pixels, but as you can see, the monitor in the back is physically much larger. At this resolution, each pixel is much bigger on that screen than on the laptop in front.

NOTE In the following sections, you'll learn what to do when you want to *reduce* the size of an image. It's much easier to get good results when making a photo smaller than larger. Elements can *increase* the size of an image using a technique called upsampling (page 107), but you often get mediocre results; page 107 explains why.

To resize a photo, start by making extra sure you're not resizing the original. You're going to be shedding pixels that you can't get back, so if your photo isn't already in the Organizer, resize a copy of it (File→Duplicate) rather than the original. Here's what you do:

1. **Call up the Image Size dialog box.**

   Go to Image→Resize→Image Size or press Alt+Ctrl+I/Option-⌘-I.

2. **Turn on the Resample Image checkbox at the bottom of the dialog box.**

   You won't be able to make any changes to the photo's pixel dimensions until you do this.

3. **In the Pixel Dimensions section, enter the dimension you want for the longer side of the photo.**

   As explained earlier, you usually want 650 pixels or fewer, unless you know for sure that your recipients have up-to-date equipment and broadband Internet connections. Be sure to choose pixels as the unit of measurement. You just need to enter a number for one dimension; Elements automatically figures the other dimension as long as the Constrain Proportions checkbox is turned on down near the bottom of the dialog box.

4. **Check the settings at the bottom of the dialog box.**

   Scale Styles doesn't matter, so leave it off. Constrain Proportions and Resample Image should be turned on. (*Resampling* means changing the number of pixels in an image.) The Resample Image menu lists the different resampling methods you can choose from. Adobe recommends Bicubic Sharper when you're making an image smaller, but you may want to experiment with the other options if you don't like the results Bicubic Sharper gives you. (The menu includes the suggested use for each method in parentheses after its name.) Just try one option, and then undo it and go back and try again with a different setting to see which you prefer.

5. **Click OK.**

   Elements resizes the photo, although you may not immediately see a difference onscreen. (Go to View→Actual Pixels before and after you resize and you'll see the difference.) Save the resized photo to make your changes permanent.

Sometimes Elements resizes an image automatically—for example, when you use the Organizer's E-Mail command (see page 564). But the method described here gives you more control than letting Elements make all the decisions for you.

TIP If you're also concerned about the file's size in megabytes or kilobytes, use Save For Web (see page 554) instead, which helps you create smaller files.

Resizing for Printing

If you want great prints, you need to think about a photo's resolution quite differently than you do for onscreen images. For printing, as a general rule, the more pixels the photo has, the better. That's the reason camera manufacturers keep packing more megapixels into their new models—the more pixels you have, the larger you can print a photo and still have it look terrific.

TIP Even before you take photos, you can do a lot toward making them print well if you always choose the largest size and the highest quality setting on your camera (typically Extra Fine, Superfine, or Fine).

When you print, you need to consider two things: the photo's size in inches (or whatever your preferred unit of measurement is) and its resolution in pixels per inch (ppi). These settings work together to determine the quality of your print.

Your printer is a virtuoso that plays pixels like an accordion: It can squeeze the pixels together and make them smaller, or spread them out and make them larger. Generally speaking, the denser the pixels (the higher the ppi), the higher the photo's resolution and the better it looks. If your photo doesn't have enough pixels, the print will look *pixelated*—jagged and blurry. The goal is to have enough pixels so that they'll be packed fairly densely—ideally about 300 ppi.

You usually don't get a visibly better result if you go over 300 ppi—you just have a larger file. And depending on your tastes, you may be content with your results at a lower ppi. For instance, some photos taken with Canon cameras come into Elements at 180 ppi, and you may be happy with how they print. But 200 ppi is usually considered about the lowest density for an acceptable print. Figure 3-22 shows why it's so important to have a high ppi setting.

To set the size of an image for printing:

1. **Call up the Image Size dialog box.**

   Go to Image→Resize→Image Size, or press Alt+Ctrl+I/Option-⌘-I.

2. **Check the image's resolution.**

   Take a look at the Document Size section of the dialog box (see Figure 3-23). Start by checking the Resolution (pixels/inch, a.k.a. ppi) setting. If it's too low, like 72 ppi, go to the bottom of the dialog box and turn off the Resample Image checkbox. Then enter the ppi you want in the Resolution field. When you increase the ppi setting, Elements should automatically lower the values in the Width and Height fields, making the document smaller because of the greater density of the pixels. If it doesn't, click OK, and then open the dialog box again.

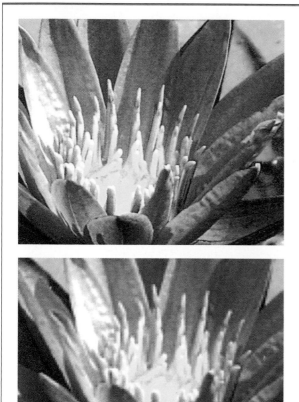

FIGURE 3-22.

Different resolution settings can dramatically alter print quality. These photos have been printed and then scanned so you can see the results of printing them.

Top: A photo with a resolution of 300 ppi.

Bottom: The same photo with a resolution of 72 ppi. Too few pixels stretched too far causes this kind of blocky, blurry print. When you can see individual pixels (like you can here), a photo is said to be "pixelated."

3. **Check the physical size of the photo.**

   Look at the Width and Height numbers in the Document Size area. Are they what you want? If so, you're all done. Click OK.

4. **If the size numbers aren't right, resize the photo.**

   If the proportions aren't what you want, crop the photo (page 85) and then come back to the Image Size dialog box. (Don't try to reshape an image using this dialog box.)

Once you've cropped the image and opened the dialog box again, turn on the Resample Image checkbox and, if you're making the photo larger, choose Bicubic Smoother from the drop-down menu at the bottom of the dialog box; if you're making the photo smaller, choose Bicubic Sharper instead. (These settings are Adobe's recommendation, but you may find that you prefer one of the other resampling choices.) Be sure to read the next section, "Resampling," to understand how you're affecting the photo when you do this.

Make sure that Constrain Proportions is turned on, and then enter the size you want for the width or height. (Elements calculates the other dimension for you.) Scale Styles doesn't matter, so leave it off.

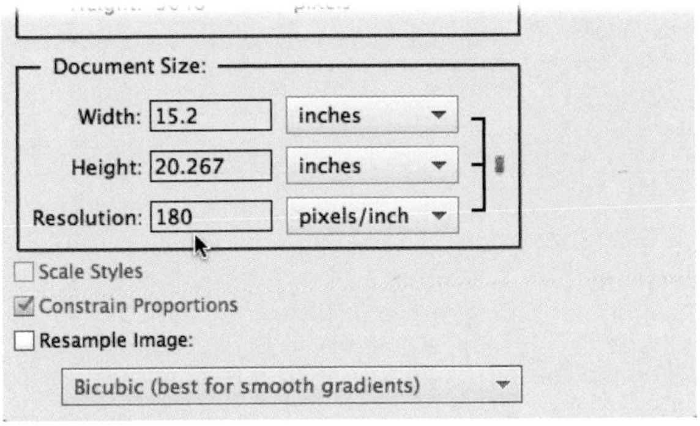

FIGURE 3-23.

Crop your image to the shape you want (see page 85), and then use this section of the Image Size dialog box to set its size for printing.

5. **Click OK.**

   Elements resizes the photo so it's ready for printing.

■ RESAMPLING

Resampling is an image-editing term for changing the number of pixels in an image. The results of resampling are permanent, so you want to avoid resampling an original photo if you can help it. As a rule, it's easier to get good results when you *downsample* (make a photo smaller) than when you *upsample* (make a photo larger).

When you upsample, you're *adding* pixels to the image. Elements has to get them from somewhere, so it makes them up. It's pretty good at doing this, but these pixels are never as good as the ones that were in the photo to begin with, as you can see in Figure 3-24. (Download the figure *russian_box.jpg* from this book's Missing CD page at *www.missingmanuals.com/cds* if you'd like to try this yourself. Zoom in really close so you can see the pixels.)

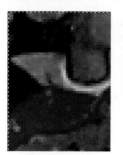 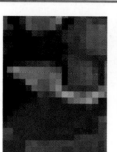 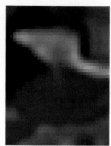

FIGURE 3-24.

Here's a close-up look at what happens to a photo when you resample it.

The photo as it came from the camera.

Downsampled to 72 ppi.

Upsampled back to the original resolution. See how soft the pixels look compared to the original?

When you enlarge an image to bigger than its original size, you'll definitely lose some quality. So, for example, if you try to stretch a photo that's 3" inches wide at 180 ppi to an 8" x 10" inch print, don't be surprised if the results look pretty bad.

Elements offers several resampling methods, and they do a really good job when you find the right one for your situation. You select them from the Resample Image menu at the bottom of the Image Size dialog box. Adobe recommends choosing Bicubic Smoother when you're upsampling (enlarging) images and Bicubic Sharper when you're downsampling (reducing) photos, but you may prefer one of the others. It's worth experimenting with them all to see which you like.

Adding Canvas

Just like the works of Monet and Matisse, your photos appear in Elements on digital "canvases." Sometimes you'll want to add more canvas to make room for text or to combine photos into a collage.

You can add canvas in either tabbed or window views by going to Image→ Resize→Canvas Size. You can change the canvas size using a variety of measurements. If you don't know exactly how much more canvas you want, then choose "percent" from the Width or Height drop-down menu (the other one changes automatically). Then you can guesstimate that you want, say, 2 percent more canvas or 50 percent more. Figure 3-25 shows how to get your photo into the right place on the new canvas.

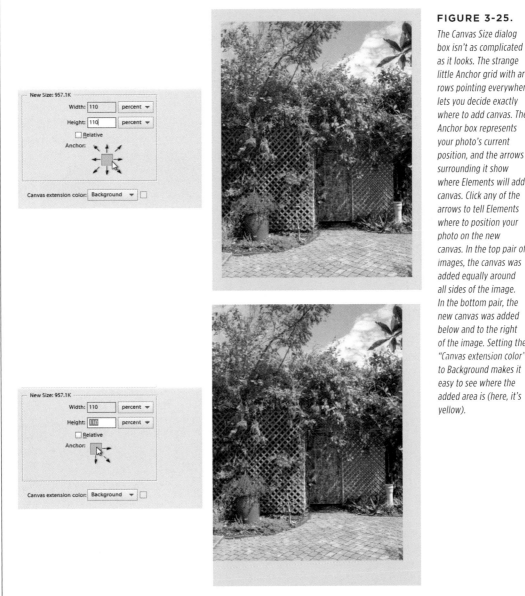

FIGURE 3-25.

The Canvas Size dialog box isn't as complicated as it looks. The strange little Anchor grid with arrows pointing everywhere lets you decide exactly where to add canvas. The Anchor box represents your photo's current position, and the arrows surrounding it show where Elements will add canvas. Click any of the arrows to tell Elements where to position your photo on the new canvas. In the top pair of images, the canvas was added equally around all sides of the image. In the bottom pair, the new canvas was added below and to the right of the image. Setting the "Canvas extension color" to Background makes it easy to see where the added area is (here, it's yellow).

Changing the size of the canvas doesn't change the size of your picture any more than pasting a postcard onto a full-size sheet of paper changes the size of the postcard. In both cases, all you get is more empty space around the picture. The "Canvas extension color" menu lets you make the new canvas your current foreground or background color, or white, black, gray, or "Other" (which brings up the Color Picker), so you can make the new canvas whatever color you like. You can see these options only if your image has a Background layer (see page 182); if not, the "Canvas extension color" menu doesn't expand when you click it, and Elements automatically makes the added canvas transparent.

The Relative checkbox is useful when you know, for instance, that you want your canvas to be 10 percent larger than it is now (so you'd enter 10 percent in the Width and Height boxes); if it's turned off you have to work with absolute numbers (so you'd enter 110 percent in those fields to do the same thing).

TIP If you just want to add canvas to the bottom of your image for a caption, check out the Captions action in the Actions panel (page 454).

Elemental Elements

The Quick Fix

With Elements' Quick Fix tools, you can dramatically improve a photo's appearance with just a click or two. The Quick Fix window gathers easy-to-use tools that help you adjust the brightness and color of your photos and make them look sharper. You don't even need to understand much about what you're doing—just click a button or move a slider, and then decide whether you like how it looks.

Even if you *do* know what you're doing, you may still find yourself using the Quick Fix window to tweak things like shadows and highlights because it gives you a handy before-and-after view as you work. Also, the new Vibrance slider and the Temperature and Tint sliders can come in very handy for advanced color tweaking, like finessing the overall color of an otherwise finished photo. You also get two tools—the Selection Brush and the Quick Selection tool—that let you easily change specific areas of photos.

Besides letting you make general fixes, the Quick Fix window also makes it a snap to whiten teeth and fix blemishes in your photo. You can even add text or crop your photo here. And Adobe has made it super easy to decide just what to do to an image by adding a number of *presets* to the adjustments; you'll learn about them on page 119. These presets are great if you need extra help—just pick one of them as a starting point and work from there.

In this chapter, you'll learn how (and in which order) to use the Quick Fix tools. If you have a newish digital camera, you may find that Quick Fix gives you everything you need to take your photos from pretty darn good to dazzling.

TIP If a whole chapter on Quick Fix is frustratingly slow, you can start off by trying out the ultrafast Auto Smart Fix—a quick-fix tool for the truly impatient. Page 27 tells you everything you need to know. Also, Guided Edit may give you enough help to accomplish what you want to do; page 22 has the full story.

The Quick Fix Window

When you first start Elements 11, you see the Quick Fix window. If you click away from it, it's easy to get back to, as long as you're in the Editor: Just click the word Quick at the top of your screen.

The Editor remembers which component you were last using (Quick, Guided, or Expert). So if you're working in the Organizer and want to send photos over to the Editor, if you right-click/Control-click a photo in the Organizer and choose "Edit with Photoshop Elements Editor," your photo will go right to the Quick Fix window if that's where you were the last time you used the Editor. If not, just click the Quick tab at the top of the screen.

You can also get to Quick Fix from some of the projects in Create mode: Just right-click/Control-click the photo you want to fix and choose Edit Quick; you get sent to Quick Fix with the photo ready for your adjustments. When you come into Quick Fix this way, you see a button at the left of the screen that says "Return to Creations." When you finish editing the image, click this button to go right back to where you left off in your project.

TIP You can also apply many quick fixes right from the Organizer, even in Full Screen view. See the box on page 116 for details.

The Quick Fix window looks like a stripped-down version of the Expert Mode window (see Figure 4-1). Your tools are neatly arranged on both sides of the image: On the left, there's an eight-item toolbox; on the right, the Quick Fix panel, which includes six sections for different adjustments you can make (Figure 4-2).

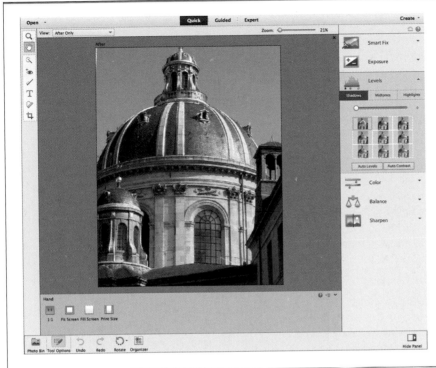

FIGURE 4-1.

The Quick Fix window. If you have several photos open when you launch this window, you can use the Photo Bin at the bottom to choose the image you want to edit. Just click the Photo Bin button at the bottom of your screen to make the bin's contents visible, and then double-click an image thumbnail and that photo becomes the active image—the one that's displayed front and center in the Quick Fix preview area. See Figure 4-2 for a close-up view of the quick-edit panels on the right side of this window.

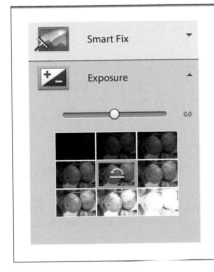

FIGURE 4-2.

Each section name here is actually a big button. When you click one, that section expands so that you can use the commands it contains. Click another section and the previously open one closes. Besides these handy fixes, you can also use most of the Expert Mode menu commands if you need something that's not included in the Panel Bin.

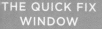
Below the left side of the image preview area is the same group of buttons you have in Expert Mode: Photo Bin, Tool Options, Undo, Redo, Rotate, Layout, and Organizer. They work the same way in Quick Fix as they do elsewhere in the Editor (page 14).

The following sections give you a quick overview of the tools Quick Fix offers, and then explain how to actually use them.

Quick Fixes in the Organizer

The Organizer gives you several ways to apply Quick Fix's auto corrections without launching the Editor. The Organizer's Photo Fix Options panel has buttons that let you apply Auto Smart Fix, Auto Color, Auto Levels, Auto Contrast, Auto Sharpen; fix red eye; or crop your photo. For more selective editing, you'll still want the Editor, but if Auto is your thing, you'll be very happy staying in the Organizer. And if you use the Organizer, you get the added benefit of having your fixes automatically made on a copy of your image, which Elements saves in a *version set* (page 66) with the original.

There are two ways to get to the Organizer's auto fixes:

- **Just click it.** In the main Organizer window, click the Media button at the top of the screen (if it's not already selected) and then click the Instant Fix button at the bottom right of the screen. When you're done editing, just click the Instant Fix button again to close the panel.

- **Use a different view.** In the Organizer, you can press F11/⌘-F11 for Full Screen view or F12/⌘-F12 for a side-by-side comparison (on a Mac, depending on your keyboard and version of OS X, you may need to add the fn key to these keyboard shortcuts), or click the Slideshow button at the bottom of the Organizer window. Once you do that, if you then click the arrow at the right of the control strip to show the hidden controls and then click Fix, a Quick Edit panel appears on the left side of your screen. (The panel tends to be shy and collapse against the left edge of the screen, so you may need to click it to pop it open). Each of the panel's icons is a button for one of the auto fixes. Just click one to apply that fix while you've got a large view of your photo—very handy for tweaking images as you preview a newly imported batch of photos, for example.

Read on for more about what these tools do. They work the same way in the Organizer as they do in the Editor.

TIP If you need extra help, check out Guided Edit (page 22), which walks you through each step of basic editing projects.

The Quick Fix Toolbox

The Quick Fix window's toolbox holds an easy-to-navigate subset of the tools available in Expert Mode. All the tools work the same in both modes, and you can use the same keystrokes to switch tools. And just as in Expert Mode, when you click a tool, its Tool Options replace the Photo Bin. (To bring the Photo Bin back into view, just click the Photo Bin button at the bottom of the screen.) From top to bottom, here's what you get:

- **The Zoom tool** lets you telescope in and out on your image—perfect for getting a good, close look at details or pulling back to see the whole photo. (See page 98 for more on this tool.) You can also zoom by using the Zoom slider in the upper-right corner of the image preview area.

- **The Hand tool** helps move your photo around in the image window—just like grabbing it and moving it with your own five fingers. There's more about this tool on page 99.

- **The Quick Selection tool** lets you apply Quick Fix commands to specific portions of the image. Once you make a selection with this tool, the commands you use will change only the selected area, not the entire photo. You can also use the regular Selection Brush in Quick Fix; just activate the Quick Selection tool and then click the Selection Brush icon in the Tool Options area (the brush that's pointed down, like it's painting).

  What's the difference between the two tools? The Selection Brush lets you paint a selection exactly where you want it (or mask out part of your photo to keep it from changing), while the Quick Selection tool makes Elements figure out the boundaries of your selection based on marks you make on the image (which don't have to be precise). Also, the Quick Selection tool is far more automatic than the regular Selection Brush. You can read more about these tools beginning on page 151. (To get the most out of them, you need to understand the concept of selections; Chapter 5 tells you everything you need to know.)

- **The Red Eye Removal tool** lets you darken those demonic-looking red flash reflections in people's eyes. See page 121 to learn how.

- **The Whiten Teeth Tool.** This handy tool makes it super simple to brighten your subject's pearly whites. Page 131 explains how to use it.

- **The Type Tool.** Just click in your photo with this tool and start typing to add text. The Tool Options at the bottom of the window make it easy to choose a different font and change the size and color of the text. In the Quick Fix window, you can do anything that doesn't require access to the Layers panel, including bending and warping text (see page 488). Chapter 14 is all about the many things you can do with text in Elements.

- **The Healing Brushes.** The Spot Healing Brush lets you make truly invisible corrections to fix blemishes in a snap. Page 307 explains all about using this helpful tool. For now, if you're a beginner, first zoom in so you can see what you're doing, and then use the slider in the Tool Options to choose a brush size that just barely covers the spot you want to fix. Click that spot and Elements fixes it right up so it blends with the surrounding area.

  You can also use the regular Healing Brush in Quick Fix—just click its icon in the Tools Options area, which looks like a Band-Aid *without* a dotted semicircle next to it. Page 311 explains how to use this tool.

- **The Crop tool** lets you change the size and shape of a photo by cutting off the areas you don't want (see page 86).

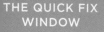

TIP If the contents of your photo need straightening (see page 80), usually it's easier to do that in Expert Mode before switching to Quick Fix, since the Quick Fix toolbox doesn't include the Straighten tool. However, there's a sneaky way to straighten with the Crop tool that you can use in Quick Fix, too—see page 86.

The Quick Fix Panel

When you switch to Quick Fix, the Quick Fix panel appears on the right side of your screen. This is where you make the majority of your adjustments. Elements helpfully arranges everything into five panels—Smart Fix, Levels, Color, Balance, and Sharpness. In most cases, it makes sense to start with the top section and work your way down until you get the results you want. (See page 133 for more suggestions on what order to work in.)

NOTE There's one exception to this top-to-bottom order of operations: You may want to use the Red Eye Removal tool (which is in the toolbox on the left of the window) *before* you do other editing. Page 121 has details on using it.

The panel fills the right side of the Quick Fix screen. If it's in your way, you can make it disappear by clicking the Hide Panel button at the bottom right of the window. That changes the button to say Show Panel; click it again to bring back the panel. You can also expand and collapse sections within the panel as you work, as explained in Figure 4-3.

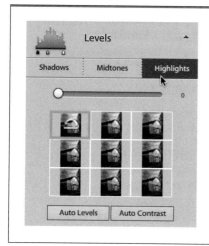

FIGURE 4-3.

Clicking the name of a section in the panel collapses or expands that section. In Elements 11, you can see the tools and commands for only one section at a time, so when you click another section, the previous one closes. In sections like this one that offer multiple editing options, just click the tabs at the top of the section to see what's available. Here, for example, if you click Highlights, you'll see the previews and thumbnails for adjusting the brightest areas of the photo.

■ USING PRESETS

Elements has a handy feature to help the undecided: *presets*. When you click a section in the panel, a grid of nine tiny thumbnails appears below the slider (see Figure 4-4). Each thumbnail represents a different preset for that slider.

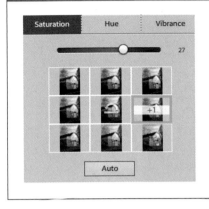

FIGURE 4-4.

Put your cursor over any of the thumbnails to see its effect displayed on your photo. To adjust the strength of the effect, click the thumbnail that's closest to what you want and keep pressing your mouse button; then drag left or right (this is called scrubbing*) and watch as your image changes (let go of your mouse when the image looks good). When you start scrubbing, your cursor disappears and you see a white band with numbers that change as you scrub, as you can see in the middle-right thumbnail here. If you decide not to make any changes, just click the thumbnail with the curved arrow over a line on it (the center image here) to return your photo to how it looked when you opened that section.*

If you don't have super-micro vision, these thumbnails are probably too darn small for you to be able to tell the difference—but not to worry: Place your cursor over a thumbnail and Elements previews that setting on your image itself so you can get a good view. You can even use scrubbing to adjust the effect, as explained in Figure 4-4. Once you like what you see, click the thumbnail to apply that change to your photo, although if you've been scrubbing you may find, you've already made the change. To reset your image back to what it looked like when you began using the current group of presets, click the thumbnail with the curved arrow on it. (If you've already moved on to another preset group, you can use the Undo button at the bottom of the window, or just use the standard Undo command [Ctrl+Z/⌘-Z] instead.)

TIP As you make changes with the sliders or the presets, Elements displays a numeric value to the right of the slider. If you have several similar photos to fix, note what this number is for the first photo when you get it how you like it. Then, when you open the next photo, just click the number for that setting (it turns into a text box) and type in the value you want.

Different Views: After vs. Before and After

When you open an image in Quick Fix, your picture appears by itself in the main window with the word "After" above it to let you know that you're in After Only view. Elements keeps the Before view—your original photo—tucked out of sight. But you have three other layout options, which you can choose anytime: Before Only, "Before & After - Horizontal," and "Before & After - Vertical." Both of the before-and-after views are especially helpful when you're trying to figure out whether you're improving your picture, as shown in Figure 4-5. You switch between views by picking the one you want from the View pop-up menu just above your image.

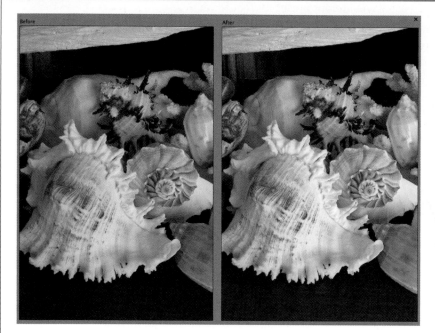

FIGURE 4-5.

The Quick Fix window's before-and-after views make it easy to see how you're changing a photo. Here you see "Before & After - Horizontal," which displays the views side by side. To see them one above the other, choose "Before & After - Vertical" instead. If you want a more detailed view, use the Zoom tool or the Zoom slider at the top of the screen to focus on just a portion of the image.

Editing Your Photos

As this section explains, the Quick Fix window's tools are pretty easy to use. You can try one or all of them—it's up to you. And whenever you're happy with how your photo looks, you can leave Quick Fix and go back to the Expert Mode window or the Organizer.

TIP To rotate a photo, click the Rotate button below the image preview area. If you want to rotate in the opposite direction, click the tiny arrow to the right of the Rotate button and then click the button that appears. (See page 78 for more about rotating photos.)

In Quick Fix, any changes you make are automatically applied—you don't have to do anything to accept them. If you're tweaking an image and decide you don't like how it's turning out, click the Reset button at the top of the Panel to return your photo to the way it looked *before* you started working in Quick Fix. The Reset button looks like an arrow arching over a straight line, and it's just below the word "Create" (which, incidentally, lets you start a Create project [Chapter 15] right from the Quick Fix window). Keep in mind that this button undoes *all* Quick Fix edits, so don't use it if you want to undo only a single action. For that, just click the Undo button at the bottom of the window, or use the regular Undo command: Choose Edit→Undo, or press Ctrl+Z/⌘-Z. When you make a change and then close a section, your image remains changed, so remember to undo that edit or reset the photo if you're just experimenting and don't want to keep that change when you go to the next section.

Fixing Red Eye

Anyone who's ever taken a flash photo has run into the dreaded problem of *red eye*—those glowing, demonic pupils that make your little cherub look like a character from an Anne Rice novel. Red eye is even more of a problem with digital cameras than with film, but luckily Elements has a simple and terrific tool for fixing it. All you need to do is click the red spots with the Red Eye Removal tool, and your problems are solved.

This tool works the same in both Quick Fix and Expert Mode. Here's what you do:

1. **Open a photo and zoom in so you can see where you're clicking.**

   Use the Zoom tool to magnify the eyes. (Switch to the Hand tool if you need to drag the photo around so the eyes are front and center.)

2. **Activate the Red Eye Removal tool by clicking the red-eye icon in the toolbox or by pressing Y.**

3. **Click the red part of the pupil (see Figure 4-6).**

   That's it! Just one click should fix the problem. If it doesn't, press Ctrl+Z/⌘-Z to undo it, and then try *dragging* over the pupil instead. Sometimes one method works better than the other. And, as explained in a moment, you can also try adjusting this tool's two settings: Darken Amount and Pupil Size.

4. **Repeat the process on the other eye, and you're done.**

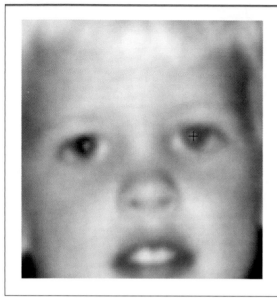

FIGURE 4-6.

Zoom in when using the Red Eye Removal tool so you get a good look at the pupils. Don't worry if your photo is so magnified that it loses definition—just make the red area large enough so you can hit it right in the center.

The left eye here has already been fixed. Notice what a good job this tool does of keeping the highlights (called catch lights) in the eye that's been treated.

> **TIP** You can also apply the Organizer's Auto Red Eye Fix in Quick Fix and Expert Mode. In either window, just press Ctrl+R/⌘-R or go to Enhance→Auto Red Eye Fix. (In Expert Mode, you can also activate the Red Eye Removal tool, and then click the Auto button in the Tool Options area.) The only tradeoff to using Auto Red Eye Fix in the Editor is that you don't *automatically* get a version set like you do when using the tool in the Organizer, but you can create a version set when you save your changes, as explained on page 66.

If you need to adjust how the Red Eye Removal tool works, the Tool Options gives you two controls, although 99 percent of the time you can ignore them:

- **Pupil Radius.** Drag this slider to tell Elements how large an area to consider part of the pupil.

- **Darken.** If the result is too light, drag this slider to the right.

> **TIP** You can also fix red eye right in the Raw converter (page 264) if you're dealing with Raw files.

Another Red-Eye Fix

The Red Eye Removal tool does a great job most of the time, but it doesn't always work, and it doesn't work on animals' eyes. Expert Mode gives you a couple of other ways to fix red eye that work in almost any situation. Here's one:

1. **Zoom way, way in on the eye.** You want to be able to see the individual pixels.

2. **Use the Eyedropper tool (page 251) to sample the color from a good area of the eye, or from another photo.** Check the foreground color square (page 247) to make sure you've got the color you want.

3. **Activate the Pencil tool (page 404) and set its size to 1 pixel.**

4. **Click the bad or empty pixels of the eye to replace their color with the correct shade.** Remember to leave a couple of white pixels for a catch light (the pupil's glinting highlight).

This process works even if the eye is *blown out* (that is, all white with no color info left).

If you're a layers fan, you can also fix red eye by selecting the bad area, creating a Hue/Saturation Adjustment layer (page 209), and then desaturating the red area. However, this method doesn't work so well if the eye is blown out.

Smart Fix

The Quick Fix window's secret weapon is the Smart Fix command, which automatically adjusts a picture's lighting, color, and contrast, all with one click. You don't have to figure anything out—Elements does it all for you. This command generally works better on photos that are underexposed (too dark) than overexposed (too bright), but it doesn't hurt to give it a try even on overexposed shots.

You'll find the Smart Fix command in the aptly named Smart Fix section of the Panel Bin, and it's about as easy to use as hitting the speed-dial button on your phone: Click the Auto button and, if the stars are aligned, your picture will immediately look better. (Figure 4-7 gives you a glimpse of its capabilities. If you want to try this fix for yourself, download *iris.jpg* from this book's Missing CD page at *www.missingmanuals.com/cds*.)

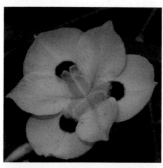
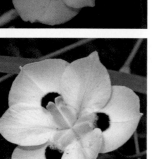

FIGURE 4-7.

Top: This photo, taken in the shade, is pretty dark.

Bottom: The Auto Smart Fix button improved it significantly with just one click. You might want to use the tools in the Balance section (page 129) to really fine-tune the color.

TIP You'll find Auto buttons scattered throughout Elements. When you click one, the program makes a best-guess attempt to apply whatever change the Auto button is next to (Smart Fix, Levels, Contrast, and so on). It never hurts to at least try clicking these buttons; if you don't like what you see, you can always perform the magical undo: Edit→Undo or Ctrl+Z/⌘-Z.

If you're happy with Auto Smart Fix's changes, you can move on to another photo, or try sharpening the same photo a little if the focus appears a bit soft (see page 130). You don't need to do anything to accept the Smart Fix changes, but if you're not thrilled with the results, take a good look at your picture. If you like what Auto Smart Fix did but the effect is too strong or too weak, press Ctrl+Z/⌘-Z to undo it, and then try one of the tool's presets or play with the Smart Fix slider instead. This slider does the same thing as the Auto Smart Fix button, only *you* control the degree of change. Watch the image as you drag the slider to the right. (If your computer is slow, there will be a certain amount of lag, so go slowly to give it a chance to catch up.) If you overdo it, click the Undo button at the bottom of the window and start again.

TIP You'll usually get better results by moving the Smart Fix slider in several small increments rather than in one big sweeping movement.

Incidentally, these are the same Smart Fix commands you see in the Editor's Enhance menu: Enhance→Auto Smart Fix (Alt+Ctrl+M/Option-⌘-M) has the same effect as clicking the Auto button in the Smart Fix section of the Quick Fix panel, and Enhance→Adjust Smart Fix (Shift+Ctrl+M/Shift-⌘-M) displays a Smart Fix slider you can tweak.

Sometimes Smart Fix just isn't smart enough to do everything you want, and sometimes it does things you *don't* want. Fortunately, you still have several other editing options that are covered in the following sections. (If you don't like what Smart Fix has done to your photo, remember to undo its effect before making other changes.)

TIP Auto Smart Fix is one of the commands you can apply from within the Organizer, so there's no need to launch the Editor if all you want to do is run this command. See the box on page 116 for more about making fixes from the Organizer.

Adjusting Exposure

The Exposure section is new to the Quick Fix window in Elements 11. You can use the presets or the slider to make adjustments to your photo's overall exposure. You may want to use this section first, if you think your image needs it. But if the image's exposure looks fine, you can skip this section and move on to the Levels section.

Adjusting Lighting and Contrast

The Levels section lets you make sophisticated adjustments to photos' brightness and contrast. You might be surprised: Sometimes problems you thought stemmed from exposure or even focus can be fixed with these commands.

■ LEVELS

If you want to understand how Levels works, you're in for a long, technical ride. But if you just want to know what it can do for your photos, the short answer is that it adjusts their brightness by redistributing their color information. Levels changes (and hopefully fixes!) both brightness and color at the same time.

If you've never used a photo-editing program before, this may sound rather mysterious, but photo pros will tell you that Levels is one of the most powerful commands for fixing and polishing pictures. To find out if its magic works for you, click the Auto Levels button at the bottom of the Levels section. Figure 4-8 shows what a big difference it can make. If you'd like to give it a try, download *ocean.jpg* from this book's Missing CD page at *www.missingmanuals.com/cds*.

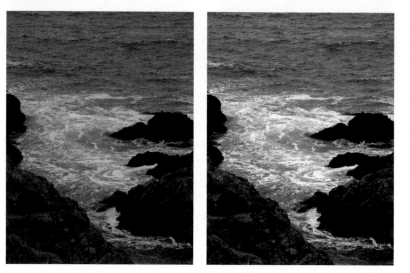

FIGURE 4-8.

A quick click of the Auto Levels button can make a dramatic difference.

Left: The original photo isn't bad, and you may not realize that the colors could be better.

Right: Here you can see how much more effective the photo is once Auto Levels has balanced the colors.

What Levels does is complex. Chapter 7 has loads more details about what's going on behind the scenes and how you can apply this command more precisely.

NOTE Although the Auto Levels and Auto Contrast buttons appear at the bottom of each tab in the Levels section (Shadows, Midtones, and Highlights), they always work on your *entire* image, so you get the same result no matter which tab is displayed when you click these buttons.

■ CONTRAST

In Quick Fix, the main alternative to Auto Levels is Auto Contrast. Most people find that their images tend to benefit from one or the other of these options. Contrast adjusts the relative darkness and lightness of an image without changing its color, so if Levels made the colors go all goofy, try adjusting the contrast instead. You apply Contrast the same way you apply Levels: Just click the Auto Contrast button.

Calibrating Your Monitor

Why do my photos look awful in Elements?

You may find that your images look really terrible when you open them in Elements even though they look decent in other programs. Maybe they look all washed out, or reddish or greenish, or even black and white. If that's the case, you need to calibrate your monitor, as explained on page 230. It's easy to do, and it makes a big difference.

The reason for this is that Elements is what's known as a *color-managed* program. You can read all about color management on page 230. For now, you just need to know that color-managed programs pay much more attention to the settings for your monitor than other programs (like word processors) do. Color-managed programs are a little more trouble to set up initially, but the advantage is that you can get truly wonderful results if you invest a little time and effort when you're getting started.

TIP After you apply Auto Contrast, look closely at the edges of the objects in your photo. If your camera's contrast was already high, you may see a halo or a sharp line around the photo's subject. In that case, the contrast is too high; undo Auto Contrast (Ctrl+Z/⌘-Z) and try another fix instead.

■ SHADOWS, MIDTONES, AND HIGHLIGHTS

The other Levels fixes do an amazing job of bringing out details that are lost in the shadows or bright areas of your photo. Figure 4-9 shows what a difference they can make.

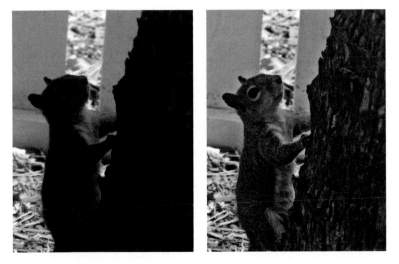

FIGURE 4-9.

Left: This image has overly bright highlights and shadows that are much too dark.

Right: After adjusting the shadows and highlights, you can see there's plenty of detail here. (Use the color sliders—described in the next section—to get rid of the orange tone.)

Although there are presets for each of these, you'll probably find you have more control by using the sliders. Here's what each fix controls:

- **Shadows.** Nudge this slider to the right, and you'll see details emerge from murky black shadows as Elements lightens the dark areas of your photo.

- **Midtones.** Use this fix *after* you've adjusted the photo's shadows and highlights, which can make an image look flat—like it doesn't have enough contrast between dark and light areas. This slider can help bring back a more realistic look.

- **Highlights.** Use this slider to dim the brightness of overexposed areas.

> **TIP** You may think you need only lighten shadows in a photo, but sometimes just a smidgen of Highlights may help, too. Don't be afraid to experiment by using this slider even if you've got a relatively dark photo.

Go easy: Getting overenthusiastic with these sliders can give your photos a flat, washed-out look.

Adjusting Color

The Color panel lets you—surprise, surprise—play around with the colors in your images. In many cases, if you've been successful with Auto Levels or Auto Contrast, you won't need to use this panel.

■ AUTO COLOR

Here's another one-click fix. Actually, in some ways Auto Color should be up in the Levels section. Like Levels, it simultaneously adjusts color and brightness, but it looks at different information in photos to decide what to do.

When you're first learning to use Quick Fix, you may want to try Auto Levels, Auto Contrast, and Auto Color to see which generally works best for your photos. Undo the changes after you use each one and compare your results. Most people find they prefer one of the three most of the time.

Auto Color may be just the ticket for your photos, but you may also find that it shifts colors in strange ways. Click it and see what you think. If it makes your photo look worse, just click Reset or press Ctrl+Z/⌘-Z to undo it, and go back to Auto Levels or Auto Contrast. If they *all* make your colors look a little wrong, or if you want to tweak the colors in your photo, move on to the Color sliders and presets instead.

■ THE COLOR SLIDERS

If you want to adjust the colors in your photo without changing its brightness, try the Color sliders. For instance, your digital camera may produce colors that don't quite match what you saw when you took the picture; you may have scanned an old print that's faded or discolored; or you may just want to change the colors in a photo for the heck of it. Whatever the case, the sliders in the Color panel are for you (you can click preset thumbnails, too). Just click the appropriate tab near the top of the panel to see each one:

- **Saturation** controls the intensity of the image's color. For example, you can turn a color photo to black and white by moving this slider all the way to the left. Move it too far to the right and everything glows with so much color that it looks radioactive.

- **Hue** changes the color from, say, red to blue or green. If you aren't aiming for realism, you can have fun using this slider to create funky color changes.

- **Vibrance** used to be available only in the Raw Converter (see Chapter 8), but it's such a useful tool that Adobe decided to add it to Quick Fix, too. While Saturation adjusts all colors equally, the Vibrance slider is much smarter: It increases the intensity of the duller colors while holding back on colors that are already so vivid they may oversaturate. If you want to make colors pop, try this slider first.

You probably won't use all these sliders on a single photo, but you can if you like. To fine-tune the color, you may want to move on to the next panel: Balance. In fact, in many cases you'll need only the Balance fixes.

Balancing Color

Photos often have the right amount of saturation, but suppose there's something about the color balance that just isn't right, and moving the Hue slider makes everything look funky. The Balance section contains two very useful controls for adjusting the overall colors in an image:

- **Temperature** lets you adjust colors from cool (bluish) on the left to warm (orangeish) on the right. Use this slider for things like toning down the warm glow you see in photos taken in tungsten lighting, or just for fine-tuning color balance.

- **Tint** adjusts the green/magenta balance of your photo, as shown in Figure 4-10.

There are presets for these adjustments, too, but you may find that they're all much too exaggerated if you're after realistic color, so you're probably better off using the sliders.

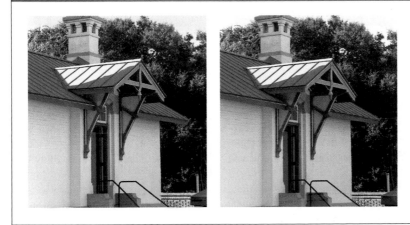

FIGURE 4-10.

Left: This kind of greenish tint is a common problem with many digital cameras, especially cellphone cameras.

Right: A little adjustment of the Tint slider clears it up in a jiffy. It's not always as obvious as it is here that you need a tint adjustment. If you aren't sure, the sky can be a dead giveaway: Is it robin's egg blue like the left photo here? If so, tint is what you need.

TIP In early versions of Elements, these sliders were grouped with the Color sliders, since you'll often use a combination of adjustments from both groups. Chapter 7 has lots more about how to use the full-blown Editor to really fine-tune your image's colors.

Sharpening

Now that you've finished your other corrections, it's time to sharpen your photo, so move down to the Sharpen panel. Sharpening gives the effect of better focus by improving the edge contrast of objects in photos. Once again, an Auto button is at your service: Click the Sharpen panel's Auto button to get things started. Figure 4-11 shows what you can expect.

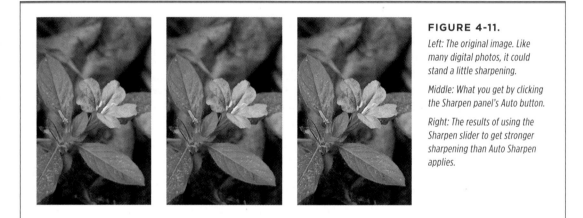

FIGURE 4-11.

Left: The original image. Like many digital photos, it could stand a little sharpening.

Middle: What you get by clicking the Sharpen panel's Auto button.

Right: The results of using the Sharpen slider to get stronger sharpening than Auto Sharpen applies.

The sad truth is that there really isn't any way to improve the focus of a photo once you click the shutter. Photo-editing programs like Elements sharpen by increasing the contrast where they perceive edges of objects, which is why it's best to make sharpening your last editing step (sharpening first can have strange effects on other editing tools you apply later).

TIP If you see funny halos around objects in your photos or strange flaky spots (making your photo look like it has eczema), those are a sure sign of oversharpening; reduce the Sharpen settings till they go away. In fact, many modern cameras apply a pretty hefty dose of sharpening right in the camera, so you may decide you like your photo best with no extra sharpening at all.

Always look at the actual pixels (View→Actual Pixels) when you sharpen, because that gives you the clearest sense of what you're doing to your picture. If you don't like what Auto Sharpen does (a distinct possibility), you can undo it (use the Undo button or press Ctrl+Z/⌘-Z) and try the Sharpen slider instead. Zero sharpening is all the way to the left; moving to the right increases the amount of sharpening Elements applies. You can also click the preset thumbnails, but it's probably easier to use the slider here. As a general rule, you want to sharpen photos you plan to print more than images destined for use online. Page 254 has lots more info about sharpening.

NOTE If you've used photo-editing programs before, you may be interested to know that the Auto Sharpen button applies Adjust Sharpness (page 257) to photos. The difference is that, unlike applying Adjust Sharpness from the Enhance menu, you don't have any control over the settings. But the good news is that if you want to use Adjust Sharpness, or even if you prefer to use Unsharp Mask (page 254), you can get that control from within Quick Fix. Just go to the Enhance menu and choose the sharpener of your choice.

At this point, all that's left to do is crop your photo; page 85 tells you everything you need to know. However, you can also give your photo a bit more punch by using the Touch Up tools explained in the next section.

TIP If you have a Mac, OS X has some pretty sophisticated sharpening tools built right in. Preview lets you apply Luminance Channel sharpening, a complex technique you might like better than Elements' sharpening options. Open a photo in Preview and give it a try (Tools→Adjust Color→Sharpness) to see whether you prefer it to what Quick Fix can do.

Whitening Teeth

The Quick Fix toolbox contains a special tool to help whiten dull or discolored teeth. It's very easy to use—just drag over the area you want to change, and Elements makes a detailed selection of the area and applies the change for you. Here are the details:

1. **Open a photo and make your other corrections first.**

If you're an old hand at using Elements, use Whiten Teeth *before* sharpening. But if you're a beginner and not comfortable with layers (see Chapter 6), sharpen first. (See page 131 for more about why.)

2. **Click the Whiten Teeth icon.**

   It's the one that looks like a toothbrush. You can also activate this tool by pressing the F key. Either way, your cursor turns into a circle with crosshairs in it.

3. **Drag across the area you want to whiten.**

   Just drag over the teeth in your photo. Elements automatically creates a selection that includes the entire object it thinks you want. (It works just like the Quick Selection tool [page 143], only it also whitens the selected area.) You'll see the marching ants appear (page 138) around the area Elements is changing (see Figure 4-12).

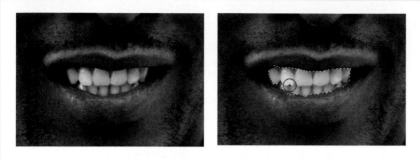

FIGURE 4-12.

Just a quick swipe across these teeth selected and whitened them while keeping them looking realistic.

4. **If Elements included too much or too little, tweak the selection's size.**

   In the Tool Options area, you'll see three little brush icons. Click the top icon to start another new selection, click the middle one and drag to add to the existing selection, or click the bottom one and then drag over an area you want to remove from the existing selection. (You don't have to use the Tool Options: You can also just drag to extend your selection, or Alt-drag/Option-drag if Elements whitened too much area and you need to remove some of it.)

5. **Once you're happy with the change, you're done.**

   You can back up by clicking the Undo button or pressing Ctrl+Z/⌘-Z to undo your changes step by step. Just keep going to eliminate the whitening completely if you don't like it.

> **NOTE** The Whiten Teeth and Text tools create a layered file. If you understand layers (Chapter 6), you can go back to Expert Mode and make changes after you use these tools to do things like adjust the opacity or blend mode of the new layer. You can always discard your changes by discarding the layer they're on. And for the Whiten Teeth tool, you can even edit the area affected by the changes by editing the layer mask it creates, as explained on page 205, or using the Smart Brush tool (page 225) in Expert Mode.

As mentioned above, after you work with this tool, Elements leaves you with a layered file. Normally that isn't a problem, even if you don't know anything about layers, but once in a while you may find that nothing happens when you try to make further changes to your photo. In that case, click the Expert button at the top of the screen to go back to Expert Mode. In the Layers panel (if you can't find it, go to Window→Layers to bring it back), look for the word "Background" and click it. Once you do, that part of the panel should turn blue (if it doesn't, click it again). Now you can go back to the Quick Fix window (by clicking the Quick button at the top of the window) and do whatever you want to your photo. However, the whitened teeth may behave differently from the rest of the photo. If that happens and you haven't closed the photo since using Whiten Teeth, use the History panel (page 25) to back up to before you used it.

Quick Fix Suggested Workflow

There are no hard-and-fast rules for what order you need to work in when using the Quick Fix tools. As mentioned earlier, Elements lays out the tools in the Panel Bin in the order that usually makes sense. But you can pick and choose whichever tools you want, depending on what you think your photo needs. If you're the type of person who likes a set plan for fixing photos, here's one order in which to apply the commands:

1. **Rotate your photo (if needed) using the buttons below the image preview.**

2. **Fix red eye (if needed) as explained on page 121.**

3. **Fix any blemishes with the Spot Healing Brush (page 307).**

4. **Crop the image.**

   If you know you want to crop your photo, now's the time. Doing so gets rid of any problem areas before they affect other adjustments. For example, say your photo has a lot of overexposed sky that you want to crop out. If you leave it in, that area may skew the effects that the Levels and Color fixes have on your image. So if you already know where you want to crop, do it before making other adjustments for more accurate results. (It's also okay to wait till later to crop if you aren't yet sure what you want to trim.)

5. **Try Auto Smart Fix and/or the Smart Fix slider; use the Undo command if you don't like the results.**

   Pretty soon you'll get a good idea of how likely it is that this fix will do a good job on your photos. Some people love it; others think it makes their pictures too grainy.

6. **If Smart Fix didn't do the trick, work your way down through the other levels and color fixes until you like the way your photo looks.**

   Read the sections earlier in this chapter to understand what each command does to your photo.

7. **Sharpen your image.**

   Try to make sharpening your last adjustment, because other commands can give you funky results on photos you've already sharpened. But if you're a beginner and not comfortable with layers, you can sharpen *before* using the Whiten Teeth tool. (See page 131 for more about why you'd wait to use it.)

TIP When you're in Quick Fix mode, you can switch back to Expert Mode at any point if you want tools that aren't available in Quick Fix. If you want to close your photo from the Quick Fix window, click the X at the top right of the preview area or press Ctrl+W/⌘-W.

Adjusting Skin Tones

If you're like most amateur photographers, your most important photos are pictures of people: your family, your friends, or even just fascinating strangers. Elements gives you yet another tool for making fast fixes—one that's designed especially for correcting photos with people in them: the "Adjust Color for Skin Tone" command, available from the menu in both the Quick Fix and Expert Mode windows.

This command's name is a bit confusing. What it actually does is adjust your *whole* image based on the skin tone of someone in the photo. The idea is that you're likely much more interested in the way the people in your photos look than in how the background looks, so "Adjust Color for Skin Tone" makes good skin color its top priority. This is another automatic fix, but there's a dialog box where you can tweak the results once you've previewed Elements' suggested adjustments. Here's how to use this command:

1. **Call up the "Adjust Color for Skin Tone" dialog box (Figure 4-13).**

   In either Quick Fix or Expert Mode, go to Enhance→Adjust Color→"Adjust Color for Skin Tone." (You may need to move the dialog box that appears out of the way so you can see what's happening in your photo.) Generally, you want to use this command *after* making any overall changes to your photo, but *before* you sharpen it.

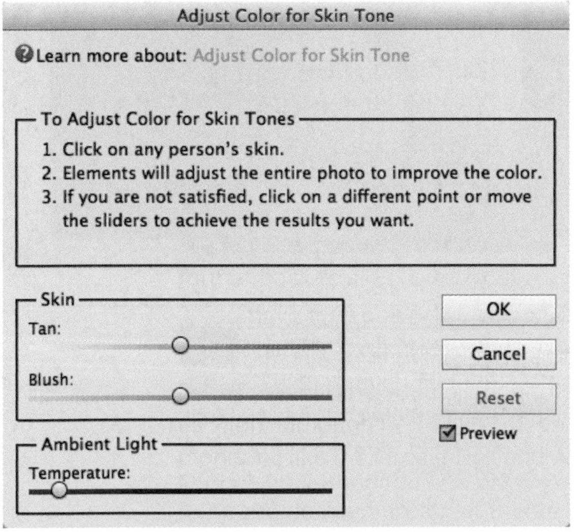

Adjust Color for Skin Tone

❷ **Learn more about:** Adjust Color for Skin Tone

To Adjust Color for Skin Tones
1. Click on any person's skin.
2. Elements will adjust the entire photo to improve the color.
3. If you are not satisfied, click on a different point or move the sliders to achieve the results you want.

Skin
Tan:
Blush:

Ambient Light
Temperature:

OK
Cancel
Reset
☑ Preview

FIGURE 4-13.

When this dialog box appears, your cursor turns into a little eyedropper when you move it over your photo. Just click the best-looking area of skin you can find. Clicking different spots gives different results, so you may want to experiment by clicking various places.

You can't drag the dialog box's sliders until you click. After Elements adjusts the photo based on your click, use the sliders to fine-tune the results.

2. **Tell Elements which patch of skin to use for calculating color adjustments.**

Find a portion of your photo where your subject's skin has relatively good color, and click it.

3. **Tweak the results.**

Elements is often a bit overenthusiastic in its adjustments. Use the sliders in the dialog box to get a more pleasing, realistic color. You can get an idea of which way to move them by looking at the colors in their tracks. The Tan slider increases or decreases the browns and oranges in the skin tones. Blush increases the rosiness of the skin as you move the slider right and decreases it as you move it left. The Ambient Light slider works just like the Temperature slider in the Quick Fix Panel Bin. You may get swell results with your first click or have to use all the sliders to get a truly realistic result. It simply depends on the photo.

You can preview the changes right in your photo as you work. If you mess up and want to start again, click the dialog box's Reset button. If you decide you'd rather use another tool instead, click Cancel.

4. **When you like what you see, click OK.**

Elements applies your changes. If you want to undo them, press Ctrl+Z/⌘-Z.

"Adjust Color for Skin Tone" seems to work better on fair skin than on darker skin tones. It's also better at making fairly subtle adjustments.

TIP If you understand layers (Chapter 6), you may want to make a duplicate layer and apply this command to the duplicate. That way you can adjust the intensity of the result by adjusting the layer's opacity (see page 188). You can also apply a layer mask (page 202) to protect areas you don't want changed.

Also, notice that not just the skin tones change—Elements adjusts *all* the colors in the photo (Figure 4-14). You may find your image has acquired quite a color cast by the time you've got the skin just right (see page 244). If this bothers you, try a different tool. On the other hand, you can create some very nice late-afternoon light effects with this command.

While "Adjust Color for Skin Tone" is really meant as a kind of alternative fast fix, you may find it's most useful for making small, final adjustments to photos you've already edited using other tools.

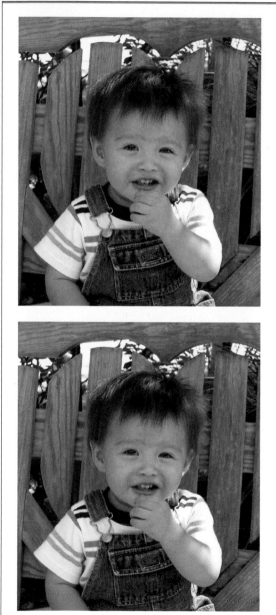

FIGURE 4-14.

Top: This photo has a slight greenish cast, giving the little boy a somewhat unappealing skin tone.

Bottom: "Adjust Color for Skin Tone" warms up his skin tones and even removes the greenish tinge from the bench he's sitting on.

Making Selections

One of Elements' most impressive talents is its ability to let you select part of an image and make changes only to that area. Selecting something tells Elements, "Hey, *this* is what I want to work on—don't touch the rest of it."

You can select a whole image or any part of it. Using selections, you can fine-tune images in very sophisticated ways: Change the color of just one rose in a bouquet, for instance, or change your nephew's festive purple hair back to something his grandparents would appreciate. Graphics pros will tell you that good selections make the difference between shoddy, amateurish work and a slick, professional job.

Elements includes a whole bunch of different selection tools. You can draw a rectangular or circular selection with the marquee tools; paint to create a selection with the Selection Brush; or just drag in your photo with the Quick Selection tool and let Elements figure out the exact boundaries of your selection. When you're looking to pluck a particular object (a beautiful flower, say) from a photo, the Magic Extractor works wonders. The Transform Selection command lets you resize selections in a snap. And Elements 11 brings a wonderful new tool to help with difficult selections like hair or fur—the upgraded Refine Edge dialog box that debuted in Photoshop CS5 (see page 145).

For most jobs, there's no right or wrong tool. With experience, you may find that you prefer working with certain tools more than others, and you'll often use more than one tool to create a perfect selection. Once you've read this chapter, you'll understand all the different selection tools and how to use each one.

TIP It's much easier to select an object that's been photographed against a plain, contrasting background. So if you know you're going to want to select a bicycle, for example, shoot it in front of a blank wall rather than, say, a hedge.

Selecting Everything

Sometimes you just want to select a whole photo, like when you want to copy and paste it. Elements gives you some useful commands that help you easily make basic selections:

- **Select All** (Select→All or Ctrl+A/⌘-A) tells Elements to select your whole image. You'll see "marching ants" (Figure 5-1) around the outer edge of the picture.

Marching ants

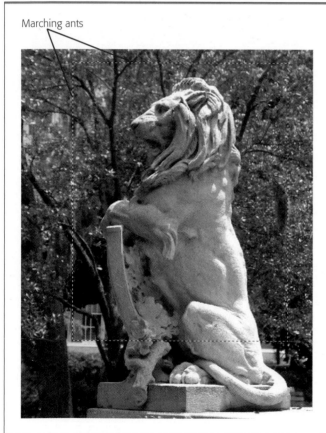

FIGURE 5-1.

The popular name for these dotted lines is "marching ants" because they march around your selections to show you where the edges lie. When you see the ants, your selection is active, meaning that whatever you do next will apply only to the selected area.

If you want to copy your image into another picture or program, Select All is the fastest way to go. If the photo contains layers—which you'll learn about in Chapter 6—you may not be able to get everything you want with the Select All command. In that case, use Edit→Copy Merged, or press Shift+Ctrl+C/Shift-⌘-C instead.

- **Deselect Everything** (Select→Deselect, Esc, or Ctrl+D/⌘-D) removes any current selection. Remember this keystroke combination, because it's one you'll probably use a lot.

- **Reselect** (Select→Reselect or Shift+Ctrl+D/Shift-⌘-D) tells Elements to reactivate the selection you just canceled. Use Reselect if you realize you still need a selection you just got rid of (Ctrl+Z/⌘-Z works, too).

- **Hide/View a Selection** (Ctrl+H/⌘-H) keeps your selection active while hiding its outline. This is handy because sometimes the marching ants are distracting or make it hard to see what you're doing. To bring the ants back, press Ctrl+H/⌘-H a second time.

> **TIP** If a tool acts goofy or won't do anything, start your troubleshooting by pressing Ctrl+H/⌘-H to make sure you don't have a hidden selection you forgot about.

■ Selecting Rectangular and Elliptical Areas

Selecting a whole photo is all well and good, but many times your reason for making a selection is precisely because you don't want to make changes to the whole image. How do you select just part of a picture?

The easiest way is to use the marquee tools. You already met the Rectangular Marquee tool back in Chapter 3 in the section on cropping (page 85). If you want to select a block, circle, or oval in your image, the marquee tools are the way to go. As the winners of the Most Frequently Used Selection Tools Award, they get top spot in the Select area of the Editor's Tools panel. You can modify how they work, like telling them to create a square instead of a rectangle, as explained in Figure 5-2. Here's how to use them:

1. **Press M or click the marquee tools' icon in the Tools panel to activate it.**

   The Rectangular Marquee tool is the little dotted rectangle at the upper right of Select section of the Tools panel. (You may see a little dotted oval instead if you used the Elliptical Marquee tool last.)

2. **Choose the shape you want to draw: a rectangle or an ellipse.**

   In the Tool Options area, click the rectangle or the ellipse to set the shape, or just tap the M key again to switch between the two shapes.

3. **Adjust the Feather slider in the Tool Options area if you want the object's outline softened.**

Feathering makes the edges of a selection softer or fuzzier for better blending (when you're trying, say, to replace Brad Pitt's face with yours). The box on page 156 explains how feathering works.

4. **Drag within your image to make a selection.**

Wherever you initially click becomes one of the corners of your rectangular selection or a point just beyond the outer edge of your ellipse (you can also draw perfectly circular or square selections, as Figure 5-2 explains). The selection's outline expands as you drag.

If you make a mistake, just press Esc. You can also press either Ctrl+D/⌘-D to get rid of *all* current selections, or Ctrl+Z/⌘-Z to remove the most recent one.

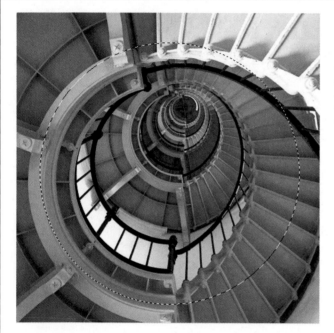

FIGURE 5-2.

To make a perfectly circular or square selection—rather than an elliptical or rectangular one, respectively—hold down the Shift key while you drag. You can reposition your selection after it's drawn by dragging it or tapping the arrow keys on your keyboard. You can also adjust it with Transform Selection, explained on page 169.

The items in the Tool Options area's Aspect drop-down menu give you three ways to control the size of your selection: Normal lets you manually control it; Fixed Ratio lets you enter proportions in the Width and Height boxes; and Fixed Size lets you enter specific dimensions in these boxes. The Anti-aliasing checkbox is explained in the box on page 156.

Once you've made a selection, you can move it around in the photo by dragging it or using the arrow keys to nudge it in the direction you want to move it. And the Transform Selection command lets you drag a selection larger or smaller, or change its shape; page 169 tells you how.

UP TO SPEED

Paste vs. Paste Into Selection

Newcomers to Elements are often confused by the fact that the program has two Paste commands: Paste and Paste Into Selection. Knowing what each one does will help you avoid problems.

- Ninety-nine percent of the time, **Paste** is the one you want. This command simply places your copied object wherever you paste it. Once you've pasted the object, you can move it by moving the selected area.

- **Paste Into Selection** is a special command for pasting a selection into *another* selection. Your pasted object appears only *within* the bounds of the selection you paste it into. When you use this command, you can still move what you paste, but it won't be visible anywhere outside

the edges of the selection you pasted it into.

For example, say you want to put a beautiful mountain view outside a window: First, select and copy the mountain (Ctrl+C/⌘-C). Next, select the window, and then choose Edit→Paste Into Selection to add the view. After that you can maneuver the mountain photo around till it's properly centered. But if you move it outside the boundary of your window selection, it just disappears. And, once you deselect, your material is permanently in place; you can't move it again.

If you understand layers (see Chapter 6), here's another way to think about the difference: Paste creates a new layer, while Paste Into Selection puts what you paste on the existing layer.

Selecting Irregularly Sized Areas

It would be nice if you could get away with making only simple rectangular and elliptical selections, but life is never that neat. If you want to change the color of one fish in your aquarium picture, for example, selecting a rectangle or an oval just isn't going to cut it.

Thankfully, Elements gives you other tools that make it easy to create very precise selections—no matter their size or shape. In this section, you'll learn how to use the rest of the selection tools. But first you need to understand the basic controls that they (almost) all share.

Controlling the Selection Tools

If you never make mistakes or change your mind, you can skip this section. If, on the other hand, you're human, you need to know about the mysterious little squares you see in the Tool Options area when the selection tools are active (see Figure 5-3).

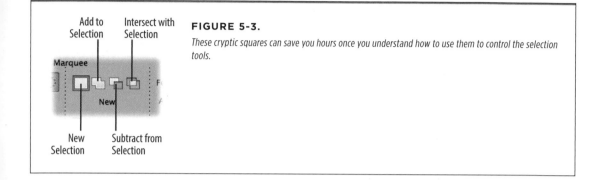

FIGURE 5-3.

These cryptic squares can save you hours once you understand how to use them to control the selection tools.

These squares don't look like much, but they tell the selection tools how to do their jobs: whether to start a new selection with each click, to add to what you've already got, or to remove things from the current selection. They're available for all the selection tools except the Selection Brush and the Quick Selection tool, which have their own sets of options. From left to right, here's what they do:

- **New** is the standard selection mode that you'll probably use most of the time. When you click this button and start a new selection, your previous selection disappears.

- **Add** tells Elements to add what you select to whatever you've *already* selected. Unless you have an incredibly steady mouse hand, this option is a godsend because it's not easy to get a perfect selection on the first try. (Holding down the Shift key while you use any selection tool temporarily switches you to this mode.)

- **Subtract** removes what you select next from any existing selection. (Holding down Alt/Option while selecting the area you want to remove does the same thing.)

- **Intersect** is a bit confusing. It lets you take a selected area, make a new selection, and wind up with only the area where the selections overlap, as shown in Figure 5-4. (The keyboard equivalent is Shift+Alt/Shift-Option) Most people don't need this one much, but it can be useful for things like creating special shapes. If you need a selection shaped like a quarter of a pie, for instance, create a circular selection, and then switch to "Intersect with Selection" and drag a rectangular selection from the circle's center point. You'll wind up with just the arc-shaped area where they intersect.

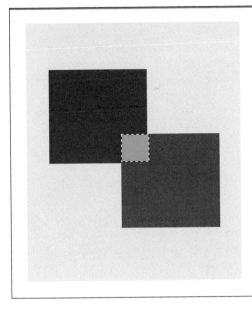

FIGURE 5-4.

Intersect mode lets you take two separate selections and select only the area where they intersect. If you have an existing selection, then when you select again, your new selection includes only the overlapping area. Here, the top blue square was the first selection, and the bottom fuchsia square was the second. The bright green area is the final selection.

Selecting with a Brush

Elements gives you two very special brushes for making selections. The Selection Brush has been around since Elements 2, so if you've used the program before, you probably know how handy it is. These days it often takes a backseat to the amazing Quick Selection tool, which makes even the trickiest selections as easy as doodling. The Quick Selection tool automatically finds the bounds of the objects you drag it over, while the Selection Brush selects only the area directly under the brush cursor. Using the Quick Selection tool in combination with the new version of the Refine Edge dialog box makes it incredibly simple to create the kinds of selections that would have driven you half-crazy trying to get them right in previous versions of Elements.

These two brushes are grouped together in the Tools panel, and they're available in both Expert Mode and Quick Fix because they're so useful. You may well find that with these two brushes, you rarely need the other selection tools.

It couldn't be easier to use the Quick Selection tool:

1. **Activate the Quick Selection tool.**

   It shares a Tools panel slot with the Selection Brush and the Magic Wand, just below the marquee tools. Click this slot in the Tools panel, and then—if the Selection Brush or Magic Wand is active instead—click the Quick Selection tool's icon in the Tool Options area or tap the A key until you see its icon. Look carefully at the Tool Options—the Quick Selection tool looks like a wand with a dotted line around the tip and it points up; the regular Selection Brush points down; and the Magic Wand icon has a yellow starburst tip.

2. **Drag within your photo.**

As you move the cursor, Elements calculates where it thinks the selection's edges should be, and the selection outline jumps out to surround that area. It's an amazingly good guesser. You don't even need to cover the entire area or go around the edges of the object—Elements does that for you.

This tool has a few Tool Options settings, which are explained below, but you mostly won't need to think about them, at least not till you've finished making your selection. Then you'll probably want to try using the Refine Edge dialog box (explained in the next section).

3. **Adjust the selection.**

Odds are that you won't get a totally perfect selection that includes everything you wanted on the first try. To increase the selection area, drag in the direction where you want to add to the selection. A small move usually does it, and the selection jumps outward to include the area that Elements thinks you want, as shown in Figure 5-5.

To remove an area from the selection, hold Alt/Option while dragging or clicking the area you don't want.

Once you're happy with your selection, that's it—unless you want to tweak the edges using Refine Edge (see the next section), and you probably do.

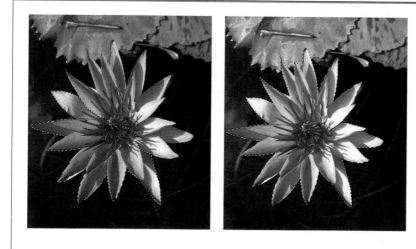

FIGURE 5-5

Left: It would be tough to select this water lily by hand because of the many pointy-edged petals. The first drag with the Quick Selection tool produced this partial selection. Notice how well the tool found the petals' edges.

Right: Another drag across the lily told Elements to select the whole blossom. Creating this selection took less than 5 seconds. (Notice that the tool missed a little bit on the edges in a couple of spots. Reduce the brush size when dragging to add those, or switch to the regular Selection Brush to finish up.)

The Quick Selection tool has a few Tool Options settings, but you really don't need most of them:

- **New, Add, Subtract.** These three icons let you choose a selection mode, as described in the previous section (page 141), but you don't need to use them. The Quick Selection tool automatically adds to your selection if you drag over an unselected area. Shift-drag to select multiple areas that aren't contiguous, or Alt-drag/Option-drag to remove areas from your selection.

- **Brush Settings.** You can make all kinds of adjustments to your brush by clicking this drop-down menu, although you'll rarely need to tweak any of these except maybe the brush size once in a while. The additional brush settings you find here are explained on page 395.

- **Refine Edge.** This option lets you tweak the selection's edges so you get more realistic results when changing the selected area or copying and pasting it. (This button is grayed out until you actually make a selection.) It's also wonderful for improving selections of things like hair or animal fur. It's explained in detail in the next section.

- **Sample All Layers.** Turn this checkbox on, and the Quick Selection tool selects from all visible layers in your image, rather than just the active layer. (Chapter 6 explains all about layers.)

- **Auto-Enhance.** This setting tells Elements to automatically smooth out the selection's edges. It's a more automated way to make some of the same sorts of edge adjustments you can make manually with Refine Edge.

TIP Depending on what you plan to do with your selection, you may want to check out the Smart Brush tool. It works just like the Quick Selection tool, but it goes further than simply completing your selection for you: It also automatically applies the color correction or special effect you choose from its pop-out menu. See page 225 for more about the Smart Brushes.

The Quick Selection tool doesn't work for every selection, but it's a wonderful tool that's worth trying first for any irregular selection. You can use the Selection Brush or one of the other selection tools to clean up afterward, if needed, but be sure to give Refine Edge a chance to see what it can do for your selection's edges.

Refining Selection Edges

The Refine Edge dialog box is another tremendously helpful Elements feature, and it's gotten a huge power boost in Elements 11. In the days before Refine Edge, people used to spend a lot of money on fancy plug-ins to help them create difficult selections and extractions, but now it's amazingly simple to do even the toughest selection job right in the Refine Edge dialog box. And before Elements 11, this dialog box was useful for helping you create smooth, feathered, plausible edges on any selection—a must when you want to realistically blend edited sections into the rest of an image.

But if you've ever tried selecting a girl with flyaway hair or a Golden Retriever, you know how hard it can be to get a selection that includes the edges of the hair or fur so that it doesn't look impossibly cut out. Enter the upgraded Refine Edge dialog box, which makes the most difficult selections as easy as pie, as Figure 5-6 shows.

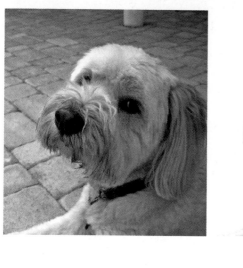
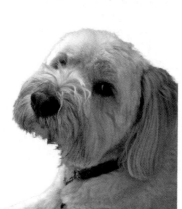

FIGURE 5-6.

Left: If you want to remove this puppy from its distracting background, Refine Edge is just the ticket. Extracting the dog to use in another image would have been impossibly tough in earlier versions of Elements, but the new Refine Edge dialog box makes it a snap to select soft, furry edges.

Right: Here's the extracted dog shown against a plain background so you can see what a good job Refine Edge did.

You can call up the Refine Edge dialog box by clicking the Refine Edge button that appears in the Tool Options for most of the selection tools. Or you can summon it by going to Select→Refine Edge whenever you have an active selection. Either way, here's how to use it:

1. **Choose how you want to view your selection.**

   You may need to drag the Refine Edge dialog box out of the way if Elements plops it right on top of your image. Once you can see your image, you can use the dialog box's controls to pick a way to view the selection. Your many view options are explained at the end of this list. Most of the time you can leave the options in the View Mode section the way Adobe set them. The View Mode section also has a little two-item toolbox at the upper left, including your old friends the Hand and Zoom tools, so you can get a very precise look at how you're changing your selection.

TIP If you inadvertently selected some areas that you don't want, you've got a couple of options. If the unwanted area is touching the stuff you do want selected (for instance, you've included a big chunk of the floor as well as your subject), it's best to click Cancel in the Refine Edge dialog box, edit your selection, and then come back again. But if the unwanted areas *aren't* touching the stuff you want to keep, you can usually go back once you're through in the Refine Edge dialog box and use the Eraser tool (if you choose to output a selection—see step 3) or edit the layer mask (if you choose to output a masked layer) to get rid of the unwanted areas. Bottom line: Your selection doesn't need to be absolutely perfect before you use the Refine Edge dialog box, but it's going to be harder to edit the selection's edges once you're done in Refine Edge.

2. **Use the options in the dialog box's Edge Detection and Adjust Edge sections to refine the edges of your selection.**

   These tools and sliders, explained in the list that follows, let you tweak and polish the selection's edges. Sometimes it may take Refine Edge a few seconds to catch up to you, so go slowly and watch to see just how you're changing the edges. It usually doesn't take much to get all the soft edges. If you go too far, you may see more of the background color bleeding through, or Elements may even decide to omit some flyaway hairs or other fine details.

TIP If you just want to adjust the edges of an easy-to-select object like a kayak or a toaster, you can skip right down to the dialog box's Adjust Edge section, tweak those sliders, and then click OK. But for tricky selections, you'll need the help of the Edge Detection settings, too.

3. **In the Output section, use the Output To drop-down menu to choose what kind of selection you want and where you want it to appear (in the current document or a new one) once you're done in Refine Edge.**

   You get six different choices that are all explained below. You can even save your extracted selection to a brand-new file, if you want.

4. **When you like what you've done, click OK.**

   If you decide not to refine the edges after all, click Cancel. To undo all the changes you've made in this dialog box and start over, Alt-click/Option-click the Cancel button to turn it into a Reset button.

The Refine Edge dialog box is packed with options. It may look a bit confusing at first, but like most things in Elements, everything is actually very logically arranged. The dialog box is divided into four main sections: View Mode, Edge Detection, Adjust Edge, and Output. As in the Quick Fix window, you don't need to use all the adjustments, only the ones you want, and generally your best bet is to start at the top and work down.

The first section, View Mode, is full of useful ways to get the best possible look at your selection. As mentioned above, you have the Hand and Zoom tools on the left, and then the View menu, which gives you seven different ways to see your selection. Each view has a keyboard shortcut that makes it easy to switch among them without using your mouse:

- **Marching Ants (keyboard shortcut: M)** shows the regular selection outline that you normally see.

- **Overlay (V)** displays the red mask overlay you get when using the Selection Brush in Mask mode (see page 152). The red area is the *unselected* part of your image. This view is a good way to check for holes and jagged edges.

- **On Black (B)** shows just the selected area against a black background.

- **On White (W)** displays your selection against a white background. In most cases, this view works well. Refine Edge usually starts you off in this view the first time you use this feature. (After you've used the Refine Edge dialog box, Elements remembers the view you were using the last time you used Refine Edge.)

- **Black and White (K)** shows only the outline of the selection in white against a black background so you aren't distracted by the details in your image.

- **On Layers (L)** shows your selection against the transparency checkerboard (see page 44).

- **Reveal Layer (R)** shows the current layer (or the whole image if you aren't working with layers yet) with the selection outline hidden. In other words, this view shows what you would see with no selection at all.

This section also includes two special checkboxes to give you even more help:

- **Show Radius (keyboard shortcut: J).** Turn this on and you see only the edge outline of your selection, the part you're adjusting with the Refine Edge tools. It's helpful to turn this option on after you've used the Radius slider in the Edge Detection section; doing so lets you see exactly the area that Elements is analyzing for Smart Radius (explained below).

- **Show Original (P).** When you turn this on, Elements displays your original image without a visible selection. If your image isn't layered, you'll see the same thing you'd see in Reveal Layer view described above. This is a great way to go back and see where you started to make sure you like what you're doing.

The next section is Edge Detection. If your selection is fine except for needing a little feathering or smoothing, you can skip this section, but for tricky selections, this is where the magic starts:

- **Smart Radius.** Turn on this checkbox and Elements goes to work analyzing the edges of your selection to see whether they're hard or soft, and figure out what it needs to do to improve them. You can control the results (to some extent) by using the other options in this section. Figure 5-7 shows Smart Radius at work.

(This setting may be turned on when you open the Refine Edge dialog box, but it doesn't affect anything until you move the Radius slider, described next.)

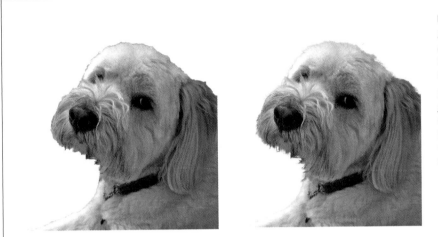

FIGURE 5-7.

Left: Here's what the edge of this rough selection looks like when you first launch Refine Edge.

Right: As you can see, adjusting the Smart Radius slider makes Elements think a lot harder about where the real edges of the selection should be.

- **Radius.** This setting tells Elements how far from your original marching ants to search for potential edges. You can adjust this setting either by dragging the slider or clicking where it says 0.0 and typing a number of pixels. Increasing the Radius setting will soften the edges of your selection to some extent. So if you selected the edge of a roof or other hard object, for instance, you'd want to leave this set to 0.0 (unless the roof is thatched, maybe). The fuzzier the object you selected, the further to the right you'll probably want to move this slider.

There's also a little two-item toolbox with two special tools to help you fine-tune your selection even more; press the E key to toggle between them:

- **Refine Radius.** If Elements isn't quite finding everything you want to select, then run this tool over the spots on the edge of your selection where you want the program to pay more attention. This will force Elements to refine its calculations for that region, making the selection more precise. Brushing over soft edges like hair or fur increases the amount of detail in the edges of the selection.

- **Erase Refinements.** On the other hand, if Elements starts taking in too much of the surrounding area when you use the Refine Radius tool, this tool acts like an eraser to tell Elements to ignore the area where you drag.

As if all those weren't enough, the Adjust Edge section gives you even more ways to tweak your selection's outline. The first two, Smooth and Feather, are most helpful for hard-edged selections where you don't need the other Refine Edge tools so much. To adjust the following settings, you can either drag the slider or type a number in pixels (Smooth, Feather) or a percentage (Contrast, Shift Edge).

- **Smooth.** This setting gets rid of jagged edges in your selection. Be careful: A little smoothing goes a long way. If you've increased the Smart Radius setting, you probably won't want to use this option, too.

- **Feather.** Feathering (which also softens edges) is explained in the box on page 156.

- **Contrast.** Use this slider if you find that everything you've done to your selection has melted away all the edge differentiation between your subject and the background, and you want to increase the contrast between your selection and the surrounding area again. Usually, though, you're better off going back to the Edge Detection section and adjusting your selections there.

- **Shift Edge.** This slider adjusts the size of your selection. Move the slider left to contract the selection or right to expand it. The main use for this slider is to help when you've included too much of the contrasting background in your selection, although Decontaminate Colors (explained next) may be able to fix that better than this slider. Sometimes it also helps Smart Radius to do its job better if you shift the edges a bit.

Finally, the Output section gives you another immensely helpful tool for tweaking the coloration of your selection's edges: the Decontaminate Colors checkbox. After all that edge adjusting, your final selection may still include some of the background color you don't want, like the blue shirt of the person who was holding the fuzzy duckling in your original photo. Turn on this checkbox and then use the Amount slider to tell Elements how much to try to replace any color fringes with nearby colors (not necessarily the colors of your selection). Move the slider right and Elements changes more pixels; move it left and Elements changes fewer. Using the View menu to switch back and forth between your current view and Reveal Layer view is a good way to monitor how the Amount slider is affecting the colors in your photo.

The Output section also lets you send your perfected selection out for use in a great many different ways. After all that work refining it, you'll want to get the most use out of your exquisite selection, so the Output To menu lets you choose what you want Elements to do when you click OK in the Refine Edge dialog box:

- **Selection** If you simply want a plain ol' selection, only a much-improved one, choose this.

- **Layer Mask.** If you understand layers and masks (see Chapter 6, especially page 202), then select this option and Elements will turn your selection into a mask for your original layer.

- **New Layer.** Select this option if you want to save your selected object on its own layer in your original image. Elements cuts it out and puts it on a transparent background in your image.

- **New Layer with Layer Mask.** Choose this and you get a duplicate layer in your image that includes a layer mask based on the selection.

- **New Document.** If you want to cut out your selected object to use on its own, this option creates a brand-new file containing nothing but your selection on a transparent background.

- **New Document with Layer Mask.** Choose this option and Elements copies the entire original layer (the one that was the basis for your selection) into a new document that includes a layer mask based on the selection.

NOTE   If you used Decontaminate Colors, you can't choose Selection or Layer Mask from the Output To menu—you have to choose one of the New Layer or New Document options instead. That's because Decontaminate Colors changes the color of pixels in your image, so it does more than just change the edges of a selection. Adobe created this restriction to help you preserve your original image.

There aren't any particular Refine Edge settings that apply to every selection. Most of the time you'll need to play around with several of its sliders to get the best result. But if you want the Refine Edge dialog box to always open with the same settings (you always want Smart Radius turned on, say), turn on the Remember Settings checkbox at the bottom of the dialog box, and the next time you launch Refine Edge, all the settings should be just the way you left them.

The Selection Brush

The Selection Brush is great for creating complex selections when you want to be totally in charge (without the help you get from the Quick Selection tool), and for cleaning up selections made with other tools, especially if you're trying to fix holes within such a selection. You can use it on its own or as a complement to the Quick Selection tool, described in the previous section.

The Quick Selection tool is awesome, but sometimes it doesn't put the edges of your selection exactly where you want them. The Selection Brush gives you total control because it selects only the area you drag your cursor over. You can even let go of the mouse button, and each time you drag again, Elements automatically adds to your selection; you don't need to change modes in the Tool Options or to hold down the Shift key, as with other selection tools.

The Selection Brush also has a Mask mode, in which Elements highlights what *isn't* part of your selection. Mask mode is great for finding tiny spots you've missed and for checking the accuracy of your selection's outline. In Mask mode, anything you paint over gets *masked* out; in other words, it's protected from being selected. Masking is a little confusing at first, but you'll soon see how useful it is. Figure 5-8 shows the same selection made with and without Mask mode.

The Selection Brush is pretty simple to use:

1. **Click the Selection Brush's icon in the Tools panel or press A.**

   You may not see the Selection Brush at first because it shares a Tools panel slot with the Quick Selection tool and the Magic Wand. If you see one of those tools' icons instead, just click it, then click the Selection Brush's icon in the Tool Options area; it's the brush that looks like it's painting—its tip points down.

2. **In the Tool Options area, choose either Selection mode or Mask mode and the brush size and hardness you want.**

   Your Tool Options choices are explained in the list below.

3. **Drag over the area you want to select.**

   If you're in Selection mode, the area you drag over becomes part of your selection, and Elements puts marching ants around it. If you're in Mask mode, the area you drag over is *excluded* from becoming part of your selection, and Elements puts a red film over it.

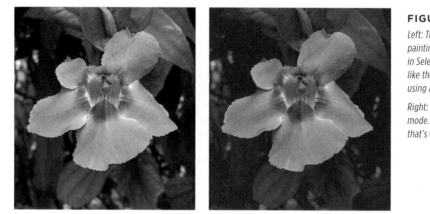

FIGURE 5-8.

Left: This flower was selected by painting with the Selection Brush in Selection mode. It looks just like the selections you can make using any of the selection tools.

Right: The same selection in Mask mode. The red covers everything that's not part of the selection.

The Selection Brush gives you several choices in the Tool Options:

- **Mode.** This unlabeled drop-down menu is where you tell Elements whether you want to create a selection (Selection) or exclude an area from being part of a selection (Mask).

- **Brush thumbnail.** Click the triangle to the right of this squiggly line and you can choose from lots of different brushes. (For more about brushes, see page 395.)

- **Size.** To change the brush cursor's size, drag this slider or click the pixel value and then type in a new one. Or press the close bracket key (]) to enlarge the cursor (keep tapping it until you get the size you want) or the open bracket key ([) to shrink it. You can also put your cursor over the word "Size" and scrub to the left or right to make the brush smaller or larger, respectively. (Don't know how to scrub? For more on this nifty feature, see page 189.)

> **TIP** The bracket key shortcuts work with any brush, not just the Selection Brush.

- **Hardness.** This setting controls the sharpness of the brush cursor's edge, which affects your selection (see Figure 5-9).

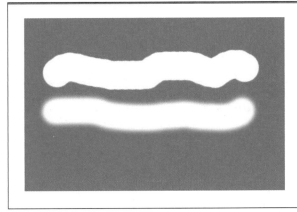

FIGURE 5-9.

These two brushstrokes show the way the Hardness setting affects the edges of a selection. Here, two different selections were made in the green rectangle. The top selection was made at 100 percent hardness, and the bottom one at 50 percent. (The selected area was then deleted to show the outline more clearly.)

Switching between Selection and Mask mode is a good way to see how well you've done when you finish making a selection. In Mask mode, the areas of your image that *aren't* part of the selection have a red film over them, so you can clearly see the selected area.

> **TIP** You don't have to live with a red mask. To change the mask's color, in the Tool Options area, click the color square below the Overlay slider (the Selection Brush has to be active and in Mask mode). In the window that pops up, either click a color swatch or click the multicolored circle in the window's bottom right, and then use the Color Picker to choose a different hue. You can also use the Overlay Opacity slider (labeled simply "Overlay" in the Tool Options area) to adjust how well your image shows through the mask.

You can temporarily make the Selection Brush do the opposite of what it's been doing by holding down Alt/Option while you drag. This can save a lot of time when you're making a tricky selection, since you don't have to keep hopping down to the Tool Options area to change modes, and you can keep the view (either your selection or the mask) the same. For example, if you're in Selection mode and you've selected too large an area, Alt-drag/Option-drag over the excess to remove it. If you're masking out an area, Alt-drag/Option-drag to add to the selection. This may sound confusing, but it'll make sense once you try it. Some things are easier to learn just by doing them.

TIP   The Selection Brush is useful for fine-tuning selections you've made with the other selection tools. Quickly switching to the Selection Brush in Mask mode is a great way to check for spots you've missed—the red makes it really easy to spot them.

The Magic Wand

The Magic Wand is a slightly temperamental—and occasionally highly effective—tool for selecting an irregularly shaped but uniformly colored (or nearly so) part of an image. If there's a big area of a particular color, the Magic Wand can find its edges in one click. This tool isn't actually all that magical: All it does is search for pixels with similar color values. But if it works for you, you may decide Adobe should keep "magic" in its name because it's a great timesaver when it cooperates, as Figure 5-10 shows.

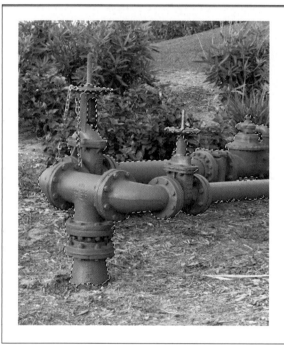

FIGURE 5-10.

Just one click with the Magic Wand created this nearly perfect selection. If there isn't a big difference between the color of the area you want to select and the colors of neighboring areas, this tool won't be as effective as it was here.

You'll find the Magic Wand in the same Tools panel slot as the Quick Selection tool and the Selection Brush, just below the marquee tools. Its icon is an upward-pointing wand with a yellow starburst tip. To activate it, either press the A key repeatedly or click whichever tool from the group is active and then click the Wand's icon in the Tool Options area. Using the Magic Wand is pretty straightforward: Just click anywhere in the area you want to select. Depending on the Wand's *tolerance* setting (explained in the following list), you may nail the selection right away, or it may take several clicks to get everything. If you need to click more than once, remember to hold down Shift so that each click adds to your selection.

As mentioned above, the Magic Wand does best when you offer it a good, solid block of color that's clearly defined and doesn't have a lot of different shades in it. But it's frustrating to use to select colored areas that have any shading or tonal gradations—you have to click and click and click.

Elements includes some special Tool Options settings that can help the Wand do a better job:

- **Tolerance** controls how many shades the tool selects. A higher setting includes more shades (resulting in a larger selected area), while a lower setting gets you fewer shades (and a more precise selection). If you set the tolerance too high, you'll probably select a lot more of your image than you want.

- **Sample All Layers.** If you have a layered file (you'll learn about layers in the next chapter), turn this checkbox on to make the Wand select the color in *all* the image's layers. If you want it to select the color only in the active layer, then leave this setting turned off.

- **Contiguous** makes the Magic Wand select only similarly colored areas touching one another. This checkbox is on by default, but sometimes you can save a lot of time by turning it off, as Figure 5-11 explains.

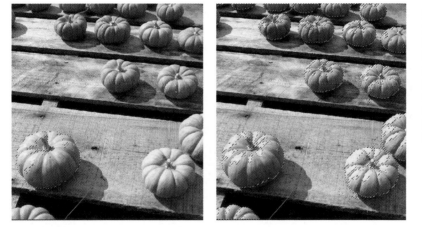

FIGURE 5-11.

In the left photo, the Contiguous checkbox is turned on. By turning it off, as in the photo at right, you can select all the pumpkins with just one click. Then you can use the Selection Brush (page 151) to quickly clean up the selection.

- **Anti-aliasing** is explained in the box on page 156.

The Tool Options for the Magic Want also give you access to the Refine Edge dialog box so you can fix up the edges of your selection, as explained on page 145.

The big disadvantage to the Magic Wand is that it tends to leave unselected contrasting areas around the edge of your selection that are a bit of a pain to clean up. So you may want to give the Quick Selection tool (page 143) a spin before trying the Magic Wand, especially if your goal is to select a range of colors. However, if you put a Magic Wand selection on its own layer (see Chapter 6), you can use Refine Edge or the Defringe command (page 167) to help clean up the edges.

The Lasso Tools

The Magic Wand is pretty handy, but it works well only when your image has clearly defined areas of color. If you want to select something from a cluttered background, the Magic Wand just won't cut it. In cases like that, the easiest option is to draw around the object you want to select.

Enter the Lasso tool. Elements actually has three lasso tools: the Lasso, the Polygonal Lasso, and the Magnetic Lasso. Each one lets you select an object by tracing around it.

You activate the lasso tools by clicking their icon in the Tools panel (it's just below the Move tool), and then selecting the particular variation you want in the Tool Options area, or by repeatedly pressing the L key till you see the right tool. Then just drag around the outline of an object to make your selection. The following sections cover each lasso tool in detail. All three let you apply feathering and anti-aliasing as you make a selection (see the box below), and the basic Lasso and Polygonal Lasso give you access to Refine Edge (page 145) right in their Tool Options settings.

Feathering and Anti-Aliasing

If you're old enough to remember what supermarket tabloid covers looked like before Photoshop, you probably had a good laugh at the obviously faked photos. Anyone could see where the art department had physically glued a piece cut from one photo onto another picture. Nowadays, the pictures of Brangelina's vampire baby from Mars look *much* more believable because Photoshop (and Elements) let you can add *anti-aliasing* and *feathering* when you make selections.

Anti-aliasing is a way of smoothing the edges of a digital image so they don't look jagged. When you make selections, the Lasso tools and the Magic Wand let you decide whether to use anti-aliasing. It's best to leave anti-aliasing on unless you want a really hard-looking edge on your selection.

Feathering, on the other hand, blurs the edges of a selection. When you make a selection that you plan to move to a different photo, a tiny bit of feathering can do a lot to make it look like it's always been part of the new photo. Some selection tools, like the marquee tools, let you set a feather value before using them. And you can feather existing selections by going to Select→Feather or pressing Alt+Ctrl+D/Option-⌘-F.

Generally, a 1- or 2-pixel feather gives your selection a natural-looking edge without visible blurring. A larger feather gives a soft edge to photos, as you can see in Figure 5-12. If you apply a feather value that's too high for the size of your selection, you see a warning that reads, "No pixels are more than 50% selected." Reduce the feather number to placate Elements.

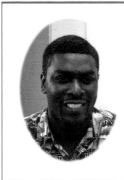

FIGURE 5-12.

Old-fashioned vignettes like this one are classic examples of when you'd want a fairly large feather. In this figure, the feather is 15 pixels wide. The higher the feather value, the softer the edge. (Incidentally, there's also a Vignette Effect in Guided Edit if you need more help.)

■ THE BASIC LASSO TOOL

The idea behind the basic Lasso tool is simple: Activate the tool (your cursor changes to the lasso shape shown in Figure 5-13) and then click your photo and drag around the outline of what you want to select. When the end of your outline gets back around and joins up with the beginning, you've got a selection. (If the start and end points don't meet up, then when you let go of your mouse, Elements connects them with a straight line, which may not be what you want.)

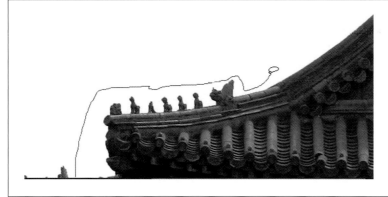

FIGURE 5-13.

The end of the cursor's "rope," not the lasso's loop, is the selection-drawing part of the basic Lasso tool. If the cursor's shape bothers you, press the Caps Lock key to change it to crosshairs instead.

It's not always easy to make an accurate selection with the Lasso, especially if you're using a mouse. A graphics tablet (page 595) is a big advantage when using this tool, since tablets let you draw with a pen-shaped pointer. But even if you don't have a graphics tablet lying around, you can make all of Elements' tools work just fine with your mouse once you get used to their quirks.

It helps to zoom way in and go very slowly when using the Lasso. (See page 92 for more info on changing your view.) Many people use the regular Lasso tool to quickly select an area that roughly surrounds an object (as in Figure 5-13), and then go back with the other selection tools—like the Selection Brush or the Magnetic Lasso—to clean things up.

> **TIP** If you need to draw a straight line for part of your selection border, hold down Alt/Option and click the points where you want the line to start and end. So if you're selecting an arched Palladian window, for instance, once you get around the curve at the top and reach the straight side, press Alt/Option and click at the bottom of the side to get the whole side all in one go. You need to have already clicked in your image with the tool at least once before you press this key, though, or this trick won't work.

Once you've created a selection, you can click the Refine Edge button in the Tool Options to adjust and feather the edges (see page 145). Press Esc or Ctrl+D/⌘-D to get rid of your selection if you decide you don't want it anymore.

■ THE MAGNETIC LASSO

The Magnetic Lasso is a very handy tool, especially if you were the kind of kid who never could color inside the lines or cut paper chains out neatly. This tool snaps to the outline of any clearly defined object you're trying to select, so you don't have to follow the edge exactly.

As you might guess, the Magnetic Lasso works best on objects with well-defined edges, so you won't get much out of it if your subject is a furry animal, for instance. This tool also likes a good, strong contrast between the object and the background.

Click to start a selection, and then move your cursor around the perimeter of what you want to select. (Just as with the basic Lasso tool, you can change the cursor's shape by pressing the Caps Lock key.) Then double-click again back where you began to finish your selection. You can also Ctrl-click/⌘-click at any point, and the Magnetic Lasso will immediately close up whatever area you've surrounded. The Tool Options settings let you adjust how many *anchor points* the Magnetic Lasso puts down and how sensitive it is to the edge you're tracing, as shown in Figure 5-14.

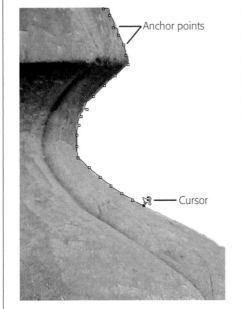

Anchor points

Cursor

FIGURE 5-14.

One nice thing about the Magnetic Lasso is that it's easy to back up as you're creating a selection. As you drag, it lays down tiny boxes called anchor points, as shown here. If you make a mistake, pressing Backspace/Delete takes you back one point each time you press the key. (If you want to completely get rid of a Magnetic Lasso selection you've begun but not completed, press Esc.) If the Magnetic Lasso skips a spot or won't grab onto a spot you want it to, you can force it to put down an anchor point by clicking once where you want the anchor to go.

In addition to Feather and Anti-aliasing (explained in the box on page 156), the Magnetic Lasso has four other Tool Options settings:

- **Width** tells the tool how far to look when it's trying to find an edge. This value is in pixels, and you can set it as high as 256.

- **Contrast** controls how sharp a difference the Magnetic Lasso should look for between the outline and the background. A higher number makes Elements look for sharper contrasts, and a lower number makes it look for softer ones.

- **Frequency** controls how often Elements puts down the anchor points shown in Figure 5-14.

- **Use tablet pressure to change pen width**—the little icon of a pen tip at the right of the other Tool Options settings—works only if you have a graphics tablet (page 595). When you turn this setting on, how hard you press with the stylus controls how Elements searches for the edge of objects you're trying to select: When you bear down harder, it's more precise; when you press more lightly, you can be a bit sloppier, and Elements will still find the edge.

Many people live full and satisfying lives paying no attention whatsoever to these settings, so don't feel that you have to fuss with them. You can usually ignore them unless the Magnetic Lasso misbehaves.

TIP You get better results with the Magnetic Lasso if you go more slowly than if you speed around an object. Like most people, the Magnetic Lasso does better work if you give it time to be sure where it's going.

■ THE POLYGONAL LASSO

At first, this may seem like a totally useless tool. It works something like the Magnetic Lasso in that it puts down anchor points (though you have to click each time you want it to add an anchor point), but it creates only perfectly straight line segments. So you may think, "That's great if I want to select a stop sign, but otherwise, what's the point?"

Actually, if you're one of those people who just plain *can't* draw, and you even have a hard time following the edge of an object onscreen, this is the tool for you. The trick is to move your cursor very short distances between clicks. Figure 5-15 shows the Polygonal Lasso in action.

The big advantage of this tool over the Magnetic Lasso is that it's much easier to keep it from getting into a snarl. Your only Tool Options settings for this tool are Feather and Anti-aliasing (which are explained in the box on page 156), as well as Refine Edge (page 145).

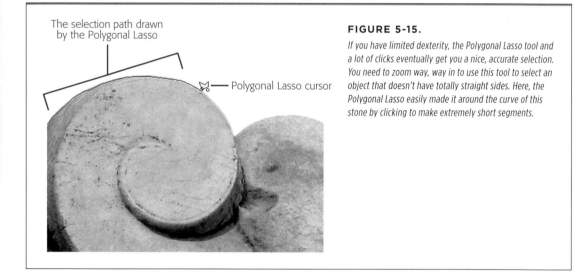

The selection path drawn by the Polygonal Lasso

Polygonal Lasso cursor

FIGURE 5-15.

If you have limited dexterity, the Polygonal Lasso tool and a lot of clicks eventually get you a nice, accurate selection. You need to zoom way, way in to use this tool to select an object that doesn't have totally straight sides. Here, the Polygonal Lasso easily made it around the curve of this stone by clicking to make extremely short segments.

◼ Extracting Objects from Images

Ever feel the urge to pluck an object out of a photo so you can use it on its own or somewhere else? For example, maybe you want to take an amazing shot you got of the moon and stick it in another photo. The traditional way of doing that is to make your selection, invert it (page 167), and then delete the rest of the image. But Elements streamlines this process with another "magic" tool—the Magic Extractor.

In Elements 11, you probably want to give the Refine Edge dialog box (page 145) first crack at extracting your object, especially if it's got tricky edges. But if you like more visual feedback about what you're doing, and if the object has well-defined edges, the Magic Extractor may be easier if you're a beginner. It works much like the Quick Selection tool in that you just give Elements a few hints and it does the rest. When the Magic Extractor is done, your selection is isolated in all its lonely glory, surrounded by transparency and ready for use on its own. Like the Quick Selection tool, this tool does a surprisingly good job—most of the time. To conduct your own experiments, download the practice photo *figurine.jpg* from this book's Missing CD page at *www.missingmanuals.com/cds*.

> **TIP** You may find it faster to use the Quick Selection tool (page 143) to select the object, invert your selection as explained on page 167, and then either delete the background area or use Refine Edge. The deluxe new Refine Edge dialog box can also do fancy extracting, including saving your extracted object to a masked layer or a new document, so you may want to give it a whirl before the Magic Extractor. If that doesn't work, then it's time to try the Magic Extractor.

The Magic Extractor has an elaborate dialog box with tools found nowhere else in Elements. The dialog box includes a toolbox on the left, instructions across the top, a preview of your image, and a set of controls on the right. It looks complicated, but it's really just a bunch of easy-to-use options for tweaking what you've got before Elements extracts your object. Here's how to use this timesaving tool:

1. **Go to Image→Magic Extractor, or press Shift+Alt+Ctrl+V/Shift-Option-⌘-V.**

   Your image appears in the preview area of the Magic Extractor dialog box (Figure 5-16). (If you want, you can make a selection *before* you launch the Magic Extractor. If you do that, the unselected area appears under a red mask.)

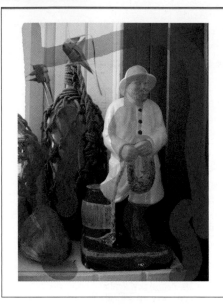

FIGURE 5-16.

Manually removing this figurine from its background would be a mighty long process. With the Magic Extractor, these few marks are all the help Elements needs to make the selection for you.

NOTE The Magic Extractor sometimes has problems with very large files. So if you need to extract an object from a hefty image, you may get better results if you crop away any unnecessary areas first. (See page 85 for more about cropping.)

2. **If necessary, change the marker colors.**

   On the right side of the dialog box, in the Tool Options section, are two colored boxes. Usually, you'll see red for the Foreground Brush (the one you use to mark what you want to keep) and blue for the Background Brush (the one that tells Elements what to discard). To make the brushstrokes easier to see (if your image happens to include a lot of red and blue, say), click the boxes to bring up the Color Picker (page 249) and choose new hues. This section also has a setting that lets you adjust the brush cursor's size, but that's hardly ever necessary unless the brush is bigger than the area you want to select.

3. **Click the Foreground Brush's icon (see Figure 5-18) or press B to activate it, and then to tell Elements what you want to extract.**

   Make some marks on the object you want to keep. You can draw lines, as shown in Figure 5-16, but making dots on your object may work just as well. With a little practice, you'll soon know what kind of marks you need for each object.

4. **Click the Background Brush's icon or press P (Figure 5-18) and then tell Elements what to exclude.**

   Use this tool to make some marks in the areas you *don't* want Elements to include in your selection.

5. **Click the Preview button.**

   In the preview area, Elements shows what it thinks you want selected. If what you see isn't even close, then click the Reset button at the bottom of the dialog box and hop back to step 3.

6. **If necessary, use the dialog box's various tools to adjust the boundaries of your selection.**

   For example, if Elements left off an area you want, usually just one click with the Foreground Brush is enough to add it. If there are spots missing within the selection, click the Fill Holes button. To get a better view of your work, use the Zoom and Hand tools (both of which are explained in more detail starting on page 89).

7. **Fine-tune the edges of your selection if you wish.**

   Feather (page 156), defringe (page 167), or smooth the edges of the selection with the Smoothing Brush (explained in a moment).

8. **When you like what you see, click OK.**

   If you want to give up and try another method, click the Cancel button instead. Figure 5-17 shows what the Magic Extractor can do.

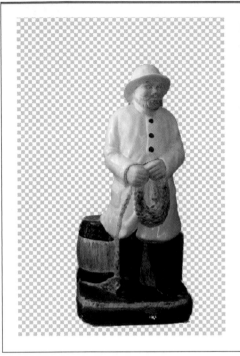

FIGURE 5-17.

Just the few marks you saw in Figure 5-16 produce this perfectly extracted selection, all ready to move to another image. (If you look really closely, there's a tiny bit of the purple background next to his beard, but a click with the Eraser tool [page 415] should fix that in a jiffy.)

> **NOTE** Once you understand layers (Chapter 6), you'll know that the Magic Extractor works only on the active layer. If you want to extract an object without wrecking the rest of your photo, then make a duplicate layer (page 185) and work on that new layer. And in some cases, you may prefer to use a layer mask instead (see page 202).

The Magic Extractor gives you lots of ways to make sure Elements creates a perfect selection. Its dialog box contains a whole set of special tools that are unique to the Extractor, as you can see in Figure 5-18. Each has its own keyboard shortcut (noted in parentheses after the tool's name in the list below) to make it easy to switch tools while you work. From top to bottom, here's what you get:

- **Foreground Brush (Keyboard shortcut: B).** Use this brush to mark what you want to include in your extraction. You can change the brush's color by choosing a different foreground color on the dialog box's right side.

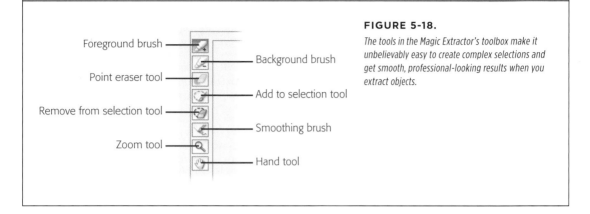

FIGURE 5-18.

The tools in the Magic Extractor's toolbox make it unbelievably easy to create complex selections and get smooth, professional-looking results when you extract objects.

- **Background Brush (P).** This brush tells Elements what you want to cut away from your selection. Like the Foreground Brush, you can pick a different color for this brush on the dialog box's right side.

- **Point Eraser tool (E).** If you mark something by mistake with the Foreground or Background Brush, use this tool to erase the marks.

- **"Add to Selection" tool (A).** For adding to your existing selection.

- **"Remove from Selection" tool (D).** Whatever you paint over with this tool gets omitted from your selection.

- **Smoothing Brush (J).** Once you've previewed your selection, you can use this tool to even out any ragged edges. But it's a good idea to try the Touch Up options on the right side of the dialog box (they're explained in a moment) first because, after you do, you may not need this brush.

- **Zoom tool (Z) and Hand tool (H).** These are the same trusty standbys you use to adjust your view elsewhere in Elements. See page 89 for more about these tools.

TIP Some of the fine-tuning tools, like the Smoothing Brush, work much better if you zoom in pretty close before using them.

To help you see exactly what you're doing, Elements gives you several ways to adjust the tools and your view of the image. The following settings, which are on the right side of the dialog box, become active only after you click the Preview button:

- **Preview.** These options let you choose whether to see just the selected area or your entire image. You can also pick what kind of background you want Elements to display your selection against. You can choose None (the standard transparency checkerboard), or a black, gray, or white matte to see a temporary solid-colored background that may make it easier to check the edges of your selection. Selecting Mask gives you the black-and-white view of a layer mask (see page 206); remember that what's masked *isn't* selected. Rubylith (the brand name of the original red masking film) is just a fancy name for the red mask view as opposed to the black-and-white view you get by choosing Mask.

- **Touch Up.** These settings are very helpful for making sure your selection is absolutely perfect:

  - **Feather.** Enter the amount, in pixels, you want Elements to feather the edge of your selection. (The box on page 156 explains feathering.) You can actually enter a value here before clicking Preview if you want, but you won't see the results until you do.

  - **Fill Holes.** If Elements left some gaps in your selection, you may be able to fill them by clicking this button. This works only for holes that are completely surrounded by selected material, though. So if the edges of your selection have bites out of them, use the Smoothing Brush instead, or give the area an extra click with the Foreground Brush.

  - **Defringe.** If your selection has a rim of contrasting pixels around it, this button can usually eliminate them. Figure 5-19 shows what a difference defringing can make. You can choose a different number of pixels for Elements to consider when applying this command by entering a value in the Defringe Width box, but the standard setting is usually fine. Elements is pretty good about making clean selections, so you probably won't click this button very often.

> **TIP** If the edges of your selection are ragged but the same color as the area you want to extract, or if defringing alone doesn't clean things up enough, try running the Smoothing Brush (page 165) along the edge of your selection to polish it until it's smooth.

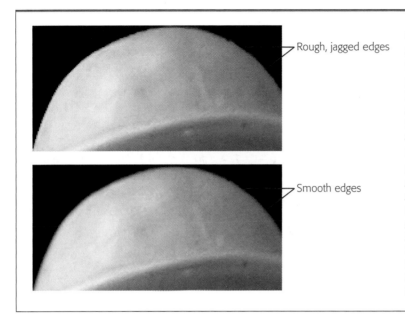

Rough, jagged edges

Smooth edges

FIGURE 5-19.

Defringing is a big help in cleaning up the edges of selections.

Top: Here's a close-up of the top of the little mariner's hat. The matte black background makes the ragged edges of the hat stand out. If you place this image into another graphic, it'll look like you cut it out with dull nail scissors.

Bottom: Here you can see how much softer the edges are after applying some defringing. Now you can place the figurine into another file without getting a cut-out effect; the hat will blend in believably. You don't need the Extractor to defringe, though; you can use this command on any layer by going to Enhance→Adjust Color→Defringe Layer.

Changing and Moving Selections

Now that you know all about making selections, it's time to learn some of the finer points of using and manipulating them. Elements gives you several options for changing the areas you've selected and for moving objects around after you select them. You can even save a tough selection so you don't have to do *that* again.

Inverting a Selection

One thing you often want to do with a selection is *invert* it. That means telling Elements, "You know the area I've selected? I want you to select everything *except* that area." Why would you want to do that? Because sometimes it's easier to select what you *don't* want. For example, suppose you have an object with a complicated outline, like the building in Figure 5-20. If you want to use just the building in a scrapbook of your trip to Europe, it's going to be difficult to select. But the sky is just one big block of color, so it's easy to select the sky with the Magic Wand.

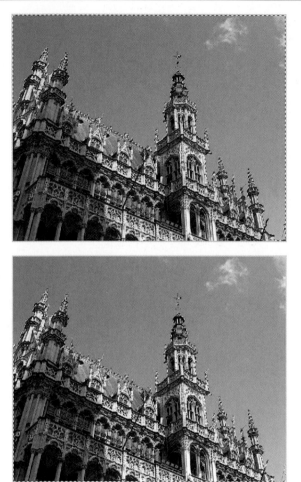

FIGURE 5-20.

Top: Say you want to make some adjustments to this building. You could spend half an hour meticulously selecting all that Gothic detail, or just select the sky with a couple of clicks of the Magic Wand and then invert your selection to get the building. Here, the marching ants around the sky show that it's the active selection—but that's not what you want.

Bottom: Inverting the selection (Select→Inverse) puts the ants around the building instead, without you going to the trouble of tracing over all the elaborate, lacy details of the roofline.

To invert a selection, simply make a selection with any tool that suits your fancy, and then go to Select→Inverse or press Shift+Ctrl+I/Shift-⌘-I. Now the part of your image that you *didn't* select is selected. Easy, huh?

Resizing a Selection

What if you want to tweak the size of your selection? For example, say you want to move the outline of your selection outward a few pixels to expand it. Elements gives you a really handy way to do that: the Transform Selection command.

With Transform Selection, you can easily drag any selection larger or smaller, rotate it, squish it narrower or shorter, or pull it out longer or wider (imagine smooshing a circular selection into an oval, for instance). As its name implies, Transform Selection does all these things to the *selection*, not to the object you've selected. (If you want to distort an object, you can use the Move tool [page 173] or the Transform commands [page 385] instead.) This is really handy, as you can see in Figure 5-21.

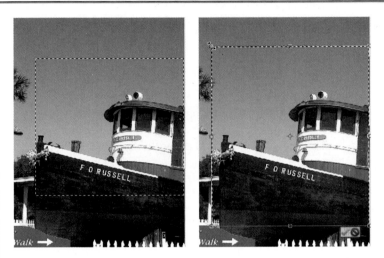

FIGURE 5-21.

Left: Sometimes it's tough to draw exactly the selection you want. Here, attempting to avoid the sign and the palm fronds led to cutting off part of the rope bumper on the boat's bow.

Right: After you've decided that it would be easier to clone out any unwanted fronds (page 314 explains how), Transform Selection makes it easy to resize the selection to include the whole rope.

To use Transform Selection:

1. **Make a selection.**

   Use the selection tool(s) of your choice. Transform Selection is especially handy when you've used one of the marquee tools and didn't hit the selection quite right, but you can use it on any selection.

2. **Go to Select→Transform Selection.**

   A bounding box with little square handles appears around your image, as shown in Figure 5-21. The Tool Options change to show the settings for this feature, which are the same as those for the Transform tools (page 385). Most of the time you won't need to worry about these settings.

3. **Grab a handle and adjust the area covered by your selection.**

   The different ways you can adjust a selection are explained in the list below.

4. **When you get everything just right, click the green checkmark or press Enter/Return to accept your changes.**

   If you mess up or change your mind about the whole thing, click Cancel (the red No symbol) or press Esc to revert to your original selection.

You can change your selection in most of the same ways you learned about back in the section on cropping (page 85):

- **To make the selection wider or narrower,** drag one of the side handles.

- **To make the selection taller or shorter,** drag a top or bottom handle.

- **To make the selection larger or smaller,** drag a corner handle. Before you start, take a quick look at the Tool Options to be sure the Constrain Proportions checkbox is turned on if you want the selection's shape to stay exactly the same. If you want the shape to change, then turn the checkbox off.

- **To rotate the selection,** move your mouse near a corner handle till you see the curved arrows, and then click and drag to spin the selection's outline to the angle you want.

Transform Selection is a great feature, but it only expands or contracts your selection in the same ways the Transform tools can change things. In other words, you can change the selection's width, height, and proportions, but you can't change a star-shaped selection into a dog-shaped one, for example. Elements gives you a number of other ways to adjust a selection's size, which may work better for you in certain situations, although in most cases Transform Selection is probably the easiest.

But what do you do if you just want to enlarge the selection to include surrounding areas of the same color? Elements has you covered. Figuring out which of the following commands to use can be confusing because the two ways to enlarge a selection sound really similar: Grow and Expand. You might think they do the same thing, but there's a slight but important difference between them:

- **Grow** (Select→Grow) moves your selection outward to include more similar, contiguous colors, no matter what shape your original selection was. This command doesn't care about shape; it just finds more matching contiguous pixels.

- **Expand** (Select→Modify→Expand) preserves the shape of your selection and just enlarges it by the number of pixels you specify.

- **Similar** (Select→Similar) does the same thing as Grow but looks at all the pixels in your image, not just ones adjacent to the current selection.

- **Contract** (Select→Modify→Contract) shrinks a selection by the number of pixels you specify.

So what's the big distinction between Grow and Expand? Figure 5-22 shows how differently they behave.

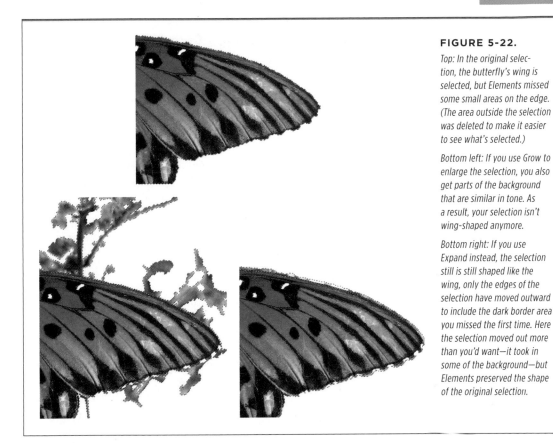

FIGURE 5-22.

Top: In the original selection, the butterfly's wing is selected, but Elements missed some small areas on the edge. (The area outside the selection was deleted to make it easier to see what's selected.)

Bottom left: If you use Grow to enlarge the selection, you also get parts of the background that are similar in tone. As a result, your selection isn't wing-shaped anymore.

Bottom right: If you use Expand instead, the selection still is still shaped like the wing, only the edges of the selection have moved outward to include the dark border area you missed the first time. Here the selection moved out more than you'd want—it took in some of the background—but Elements preserved the shape of the original selection.

Moving Selected Areas

So far you've learned how to move selections themselves (the marching ants), but often you make selections because you want to move *objects* around—like putting that dreamboat who wouldn't give you the time of day next to you in a class photo. You can move a selected object in several ways. Here's the simplest, tool-free way to move something from one image to another:

1. **Select the object you want to move.**

   Make sure you've selected everything you want—it's really annoying when you paste a selection from one image to another and then find that you missed a spot.

2. **Press Ctrl+C/⌘-C to copy it.**

   You can use Ctrl+X/⌘-X if you want to cut it out of your original; just remember that Elements leaves a hole if you do that.

3. Decide where to put the selected object.

If you want to dump the object into its very own document, choose File→New→"Image from Clipboard." Doing so creates a new document with just your selection in it.

If you want to place the object into an existing photo, then use Ctrl+V/⌘-V to paste it into another image in Elements.

> **TIP** You can also use Refine Edge to select, cut out, and paste your object into a new file, all in one go. Flip back to page 145 to learn how.

Once the object is where you want it, you can use the Move tool (explained next) to position it, rotate it, or scale it to fit the rest of the photo. You can even paste it into a document in another program.

> **TIP** If you copy and paste a selection and then notice that it's got partially transparent areas in it, back up and go over your selection with the Selection Brush using a hard brush cursor. Then copy and paste again.

POWER USERS' CLINIC

Smoothing and Bordering

Most of the time, you'll probably use Refine Edge to fine-tune your selections, but Elements gives you two other ways to tweak selection outlines:

- **Smoothing** (Select→Modify→Smooth) is a not-always-dependable way to clean up ragged spots in a color-based selection (the kind you'd make with the Magic Wand, for instance). You enter a pixel value in the Smooth Selection dialog box, and Elements evens out your selection based on that number by searching for similarly colored pixels.

  For example, if you enter *5,* Elements looks at a 5-pixel radius around each pixel in your selection. In areas where most of the pixels are already selected, it adds in the others. In areas where most pixels *aren't* selected, it deselects

the ones that were selected to get rid of jagged edges and holes in the selection. This is handy, but smoothing is sometimes hard to control. Usually it's easier to clean up your selection by hand with the Selection Brush.

- **Bordering** (Select→Modify→Border) adds an anti-aliased, transparent border to your selection. You can think of this command as selecting the selection's outline. You might use it when your selection's edges are too hard and you want to soften them, although you're probably better off using Refine Edge instead. But if you go this route, enter a border width in the Border Selection dialog box and then click OK. Elements then selects only the border, so you can also apply a slight Gaussian blur (see page 446) to soften that part of the photo.

▦ THE MOVE TOOL

You can also move things around within a photo using the Move tool, which lets you cut or copy selected areas. Figure 5-23 shows how to use the Move tool to conceal distracting details.

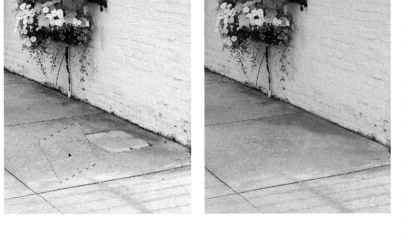

FIGURE 5-23.

Left: Say you want to get rid of the meter access hatch in this photo to keep it from drawing attention away from the lovely flowerboxes. To do that, select a piece of the sidewalk, and then activate the Move tool and hold down the Alt/Option key while dragging to copy the selected area. (If you use the Move tool without *holding down Alt/Option, Elements cuts out the selection instead, leaving a hole in your photo.)*

Right: After using the Clone Stamp (page 314) to blend in the new piece, you'd never know that slab of sidewalk wasn't solid.

The Move tool lives at the very top of the Expert Mode Tools panel. To use it to relocate an object, first select the object and then do the following:

1. **Activate the Move tool.**

   Click the Move tool's icon or press V. Your selection stays active but is now surrounded by a rectangle with square handles on it.

2. **Move the selection and then press Enter when you're satisfied with its position.**

   As long as the selection is active, you can work on your photo in other ways and then come back and reactivate the Move tool. (If you're worried about losing a complex selection, save it as described in the next section.) If you're not happy with what you've done, just press Ctrl+Z/⌘-Z as many times as needed to back up and start over again.

You can move a selection in several different ways:

- **Drag it.** If you simply move a selection by dragging it, you leave a hole in the background where the selection was, because the Move tool *truly* moves the selection. So unless you have something under it that you want to show through, that's probably not what you want to do.

- **Copy it and then move the copy.** If you press the Alt/Option key as you drag with the Move tool, you'll copy the selection so the original stays where it is. But now you have a duplicate to move around and play with, as shown in Figure 5-23, left.

- **Resize it.** You can drag the handles that the Move tool puts over your selection to resize or distort the selected material, which is great when you need to change the size of your selection. The Move tool lets you do the same things as Free Transform (see page 390).

- **Rotate it.** You can also rotate a selection the same way you can rotate a picture using Free Rotate (page 83): Just grab a corner handle and turn it.

> **TIP** You can save a trip to the Tools panel and move selections without activating the Move tool. To move a selection without copying it, just place your cursor in the selection, hold down Ctrl/⌘, and then drag the selection. To move a copy of a selection so you don't damage the original, do the same thing, but hold down the Alt/Option key as well. To move *multiple* copies, just let go, press Ctrl+Alt/⌘-Alt again, and drag once more.

The Move tool is also a great way to manage and move objects that you've put on their own layers (Chapter 6). Page 193 explains how to use the Move tool to arrange layered objects.

Saving Selections

You can tell Elements to remember the outline of a selection so that you can reuse it again later on. This is a wonderful, easy timesaver for particularly intricate selections. It's also very handy if the "Text on Selection" tool (page 501) misbehaves, forcing you to restart Elements to get it working again; just save the selection before you quit Elements and then reload it to pick up where you left off.

> **NOTE** Elements' saved selections are the equivalent of Photoshop's *alpha channels*. Keep that in mind if you decide to try tutorials written for the full-featured Photoshop. Incidentally, alpha channels saved in Photoshop show up in Elements as saved selections, and vice versa. You can save a selection, load it again, and save the file with the selection active to have it appear as an alpha channel in a program like Microsoft Word or Apple's Pages.

To save the current selection, choose Select→Save Selection, name your selection, and then click OK. When you want to use that selection again, go to Select→Load Selection, and there it is waiting for you.

> **TIP** When you save a feathered selection and then change your mind about how much feather you want, use the Refine Edge dialog box to adjust it. You can also save a hard-edged selection, load it, and then go to Select→Feather to add a feather if you need one. That way you can change the feather amount each time you use the selection, as long as you remember not to save the *change* to the selection.

■ EDITING A SAVED SELECTION

It's probably just as easy to start your selection over if you need to tweak a saved selection, but you can make changes if you want. This can save you time if the original selection was really tricky to create.

Say you've got a full-length photo of somebody, and you've created and saved a selection of the person's face (and named it, naturally enough, Face). Now, imagine that after applying a filter to that selection, you decide it would look silly to change only the face and not the person's hands, too. So you want to add the hands to your saved selection.

You have a couple of ways to do this. The simplest is just to load up Face, activate your selection tool of choice, put the tool in "Add to Selection" mode, select the hands, and then save the selection again with the same name.

But what if you have the hands selected and you want to add them to the existing, saved Face selection? Here's what you'd do:

1. **Go to Select→Save Selection.**

   In the Save Selection dialog box, choose Face from the Selection drop-down menu. When you do, all the radio buttons in the dialog box become active.

2. **In the Operation section of the dialog box, select "Add to Selection" and then click OK.**

   Elements adds what you just selected (the hands) to the saved Face selection and saves the whole shebang, so now the Face selection includes the hands, too.

> **TIP** If you find yourself frequently making changes to saved selections, you might want to consider using layer masks (page 202) instead, as they're much quicker to modify than selections.

Layers: The Heart of Elements

I f you've been working mostly in the Quick Fix window so far, you've probably noticed that once you close a file, the changes you've made are permanent. You can undo stuff while the file is still open, but once you close it, you're stuck with what you've done.

In Elements, you can keep your changes (most kinds, anyway) and still revert to the original image if you use *layers,* a nifty system of transparent sheets that keeps each component of the image on a separate sliver that you can edit. Layers are one of the greatest image-editing inventions ever: By putting each change you make on its own layer, you can rearrange an image's composition and add or subtract changes whenever you want.

If you use layers, then you can save a file and quit Elements, come back days or weeks later, and *still* undo what you did or change things around some more. There's no statute of limitations for the edits you make using layers.

Some people resist learning about layers because they fear layers are too complicated. But they're actually really easy to use once you understand how they work. And once you get started with layers, you'll realize that using Elements without them is like driving a Ferrari in first gear. This chapter gives you the info you need to get comfortable working with layers.

Understanding Layers

Imagine that you want to figure out the various ways you can redecorate a room in your house. The first thing you do is create a bare-bones drawing of the room. Now imagine you've also got a bunch of transparent plastic sheets that each contain an image that changes the room's look: a couch, a few different colors of carpeting, a standing lamp, and so on. Your decorating work is now pretty easy, since you can add, remove, and mix and match the transparencies with ease.

Layers in Elements work pretty much the same way: They let you add and remove objects, and make changes to the way the image looks. And you can modify or discard any of these changes later on.

Figure 6-1 shows an Elements file that includes layers. Each object in the flyer is on a different layer, so it's a breeze to remove or rearrange things. (If you want to follow along and work with a layers-heavy file, download *gardenparty.psd* from this book's Missing CD page at *www.missingmanuals.com/cds*.)

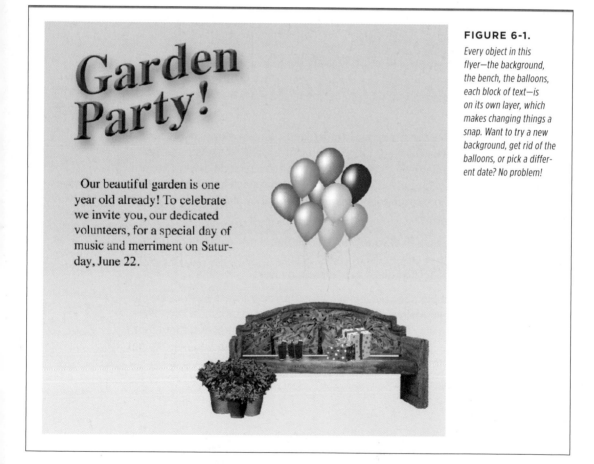

FIGURE 6-1.

Every object in this flyer—the background, the bench, the balloons, each block of text—is on its own layer, which makes changing things a snap. Want to try a new background, get rid of the balloons, or pick a different date? No problem!

NOTE It's important to understand that photos from your camera start out with just one layer. That means if you've got a photo like the one in Figure 6-2 left, all the objects—the two people, the ground they're standing on, and so on—are on the same layer. (Until you select an object and place it on its own layer, that is.)

That said, Elements often generates layers *for* you when you need them. For example, Elements automatically creates layers when you do things like move an object from one photo to another or use the Smart Brush tool (page 225), which thoughtfully puts its changes on their own layer.

You can also use layers for many adjustments to your photos, which lets you tweak or eliminate those changes later on. For instance, say you used Quick Fix's Hue slider to adjust the colors in your image, but the next day decide you don't like what you did—you're stuck (unless you can dig out a copy of your original image). But if you'd used a *Hue/Saturation Adjustment layer* (page 210) to make the change instead, you could just throw out that layer and keep all your other edits. Pretty neat, huh? You can also use layers to combine parts of different photos, as shown in Figure 6-2.

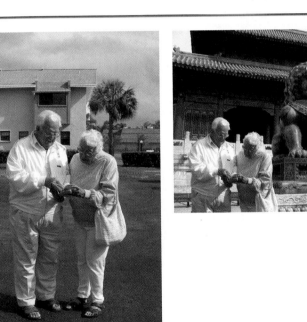

FIGURE 6-2.

Layers make it easy to combine elements from different images. Maybe you can't afford to send your grandparents on a real trip to China, but once you understand layers, you can give them a virtual vacation. When you copy part of one photo into another image, as was done here, Elements automatically places the pasted-in material on its own layer. You don't have to do anything to create the layer—it just appears when you paste. (Page 211 has more about combining elements from different photos.)

Once you understand how to use layers, you'll feel much more comfortable making radical changes to images, since any mistakes will be simple to fix. Not only that, but by using layers, you also can easily make lots of sophisticated edits that are otherwise very difficult and time-consuming. But the main reason to use layers is for creative freedom: They let you easily add lots of special effects that would be tough to create any other way.

The Layers Panel

The Layers panel is your control center for any layer-related action you want to perform, like adding, deleting, or duplicating layers. Figure 6-3 shows the Layers panel for an image with lots of layers. It includes each layer's name and a little thumbnail of the layer's contents. You can adjust the size of the thumbnails or even turn them off altogether, as explained in Figure 6-4.

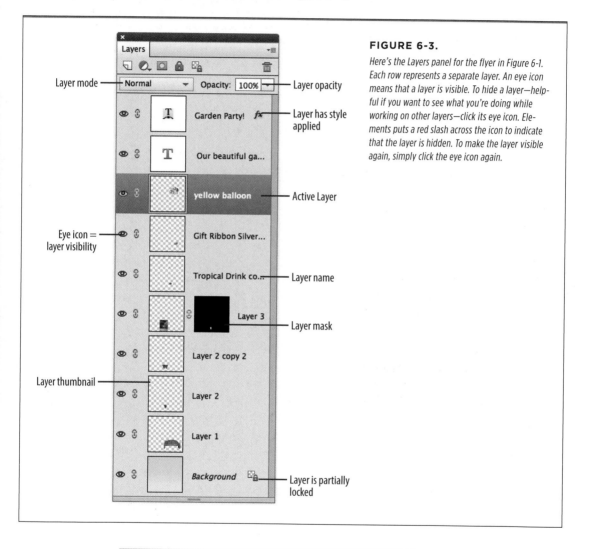

FIGURE 6-3.

Here's the Layers panel for the flyer in Figure 6-1. Each row represents a separate layer. An eye icon means that a layer is visible. To hide a layer—helpful if you want to see what you're doing while working on other layers—click its eye icon. Elements puts a red slash across the icon to indicate that the layer is hidden. To make the layer visible again, simply click the eye icon again.

Labels in figure:
- Layer mode
- Layer opacity
- Layer has style applied
- Active Layer
- Eye icon = layer visibility
- Layer name
- Layer mask
- Layer thumbnail
- Layer is partially locked

Panel contents: Normal / Opacity: 100% / Garden Party! / Our beautiful ga... / yellow balloon / Gift Ribbon Silver... / Tropical Drink co... / Layer 3 / Layer 2 copy 2 / Layer 2 / Layer 1 / Background

TIP It helps to keep the Layers panel handy whenever you work with layers, not only for the info it gives you, but also because you can usually manipulate layers more easily in the panel than directly in the image. And many changes, like renaming a layer, you can make *only* in the panel.

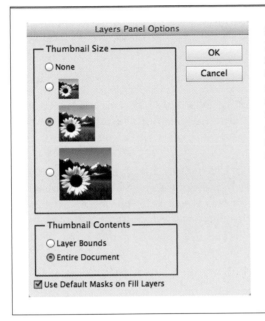

FIGURE 6-4.

To change the size of the thumbnails in the Layers panel, click the little square made up of horizontal lines (in the panel's upper-right corner, above the Opacity setting) to open the panel's pop-out menu. At the bottom of the menu, choose Panel Options, and this dialog box appears. (Here, medium-sized icons are selected.) If you change the Thumbnail Contents setting from Entire Document to Layer Bounds, you get a larger view of any objects surrounded by transparency (the object enlarges as much as it can within the thumbnail without showing all the empty space around it), which is helpful for keeping track of objects in a file with lots of layers.

The Layers panel usually contains one layer that's *active*, meaning that anything you do, like painting, will affect only that layer. You can tell which layer is active by looking at the Layers panel. The active layer is blue (as shown in Figure 6-3).

> **NOTE** If you use the layer-selection tricks described on page 198, then you can wind up with multiple active layers or none, but you generally want to have only one active layer.

When you look at a layered image, you're looking down on the stack of layers from the top, just as if you were looking at overlays on a drawing. The layers appear in the same order as in the Layers panel—the top layer of your image is at the top of the panel. Layer order is important because what's on top can obscure what's beneath it.

Elements lets you do lots of slick maneuvers right in the Layers panel: You can make a layer's contents invisible and then visible again, change the order in which layers are stacked, link layers together, change layers' opacity, add and delete layers—the list goes on and on. The rest of this chapter covers all these options and more.

> **TIP** The Layers panel is really important, so most people like to keep it around. In the Basic Workspace (page 12), this is easy: It's so important that it's the first of the panel buttons at the lower right of the Editor's main window. In the Custom Workspace (page 13), you can use any of the panel-management techniques described on page 17 to put it where it's easy to get to while you work.

The Background

The bottom layer of any image is a special kind of layer called the *Background*. When you first open an image or photo in Elements, its one existing layer is named Background (assuming nobody has already edited the file in Elements and changed things, that is). The name Background is logical because whatever else you do will happen on top of this layer.

> **NOTE** There are two exceptions to the first-layer-is-always-the-Background rule. First, if you create a new image by copying something from another picture, then you just have a layer named Layer 0. Second, Background layers can't be transparent, so if you choose the Transparency option when creating a file from scratch, then you have a Layer 0 instead of a Background layer.

As far as content, the Background can be totally plain or busy, busy, busy. A Background layer doesn't literally contain only the background of your photograph—your whole photo can be on a Background layer. It's entirely up to you what's on the Background layer, and what you place on other, new layers you add. With photographs, people often keep the original photo on the Background layer, and then perform adjustments and embellishments on other layers.

You can do a lot to Background layers, but there are a few things you *can't* do: change their blending modes (see page 190), opacity (page 188), or position in the layer stack. If you want to do any of those things, then you need to convert the background into a regular layer first.

To change a Background layer into a regular layer, double-click it in the Layers panel or go to Layer→New→Layer From Background. Or, if you try to make certain kinds of changes to the background (like applying a Layer Style [page 461]), then Elements prompts you to change the Background layer into a regular layer. But Elements often just creates a regular layer when you need it without bothering to ask you about it, like when you use the Transform commands (page 385).

> **TIP** The Background Eraser and Magic Eraser automatically turn a Background layer into a regular layer when you click a background with them. For example, say you have a picture of an object on a solid background and you want transparency around the object. One click with the Magic Eraser turns the Background layer into a regular layer, eliminates the solid-colored background, and replaces it with transparency. (There's more on the Eraser tools on page 415.)

You can also transform a regular layer into a Background layer if you want, but you need to start with an image that has no Background layer. In real life, it's unlikely that you'll ever need to do this in Elements, but, if you want to try it, here's how:

1. **In the Layers panel, click the layer you want to convert to a Background layer.**

2. **Select Layer→New→Background From Layer.**

   It may take a few seconds for Elements to finish calculating and to respond. When it's done thinking, the layer you've changed moves down to the bottom of the layer stack in the Layers panel and Elements renames it Background.

NOTE If you create a Background layer from a masked layer (page 202), the layer mask gets permanently applied to the image, since Background layers can't be masked.

COMPATIBILITY CORNER

Which File Types Can Use Layers?

You can add layers to any file you can open in Elements, but not every file format lets you *save* layers.

For instance, if your camera shoots JPEGs, you can open those JPEGs in Elements and add layers to them. But when you try to save these files, Elements presents you with the Save As dialog box instead of just saving. If you turn off the dialog box's Save Layers checkbox, a warning tells you that you have to save as a copy. That's Elements' way of telling you that you can't have layers in a JPEG file, so you need to save the image in another format to keep the layers.

You usually want to choose either Photoshop (.psd) or TIFF as your format when saving a layered image because they both let you keep your layers. (PDF files can also have layers.) But if you don't need the layers, then just save your JPEG as a copy, close the original file, and say No when Elements asks if you want to save your changes.

If someone using the full-featured Photoshop sends you a layered image, then you'll see the layers in the Layers panel when you open the file in Elements. Likewise, Photoshop folks can see layers you create in Elements.

If you open a Photoshop file with a layer that says "indicates a set" when you move your cursor over it in the Layers panel, that's what Photoshop calls a *layer group* or *layer set* (a way of grouping layers into what are essentially folders in the Layers panel), depending on which version of Photoshop created the file. Elements doesn't understand layer sets, so ask the sender to expand the sets and then send you the file again. Alternatively, you can use the Layer→Simplify command to convert the set to a single layer, which may or may not be editable. Or you can search the Internet for add-on toolsets (page 598) or look for scripts that will let you expand the set in Elements. Elements+ (page 598) is one option.

■ Creating Layers

As you learned earlier in the chapter, your image doesn't automatically have multiple layers. Lots of newcomers to Elements expect the program to be smart enough to put each object in a photo onto its own layer, which is a lovely dream, but Elements isn't that brainy. To experience the joy of layers, you first need to add at least one layer to your image; you'll learn how in the next few sections.

TIP It may help you to follow along through the next few sections, so get out a photo of your own or create a new file to use for practice. (See page 40 for details on how to create a new file; if you go that route, choose a white background.) Or you can download either *gardenparty.psd* or *daisies.jpg* from this book's Missing CD page at *www.missingmanuals.com/cds*.

Adding Layers

Elements gives you several ways to add a new layer:

- Choose Layer→New→Layer.

- Press Shift+Ctrl+N/Shift-⌘-N.

- In the Layers panel, click the "Create a new layer" icon (the little square shown in Figure 6-5).

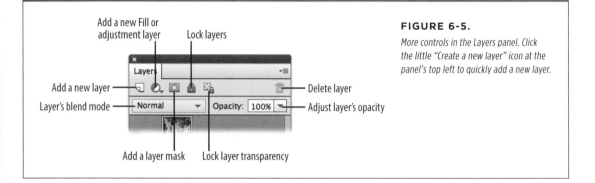

Add a new Fill or
adjustment layer   Lock layers

Add a new layer

Layer's blend mode   Normal   Opacity: 100%

Delete layer

Adjust layer's opacity

Add a layer mask   Lock layer transparency

FIGURE 6-5.

More controls in the Layers panel. Click the little "Create a new layer" icon at the panel's top left to quickly add a new layer.

When you create a new layer using any of these commands, the layer starts out empty. You won't see anything in your image change until you use the new layer for something (you paint on it, for example). In the Layers panel, the new layer is just above the layer that was active when you added the layer. Elements always puts new layers directly above the active layer, so if you want a new layer at the top of the stack, click the current top layer to make it active before creating the new layer.

> **TIP** The only practical limit to the number of layers your image can have in a document is your computer's processing power. But if you find yourself regularly creating projects with upwards of 100 layers, you may want to upgrade to Photoshop, which has tools that make it easier to manage lots of layers.

Some things you do create new layers automatically. For instance, if you copy and paste an object from another photo (see page 211 for instructions) or add artwork from the Content panel, then the object automatically arrives on its own layer. That's really handy because it lets you put the new item right where you want it without disturbing the rest of your composition.

Sometimes you want to manually create new layers. For example, you'd do that when you want to clone something (explained on page 314). If you don't make a separate layer to clone on, then your changes go right onto your existing layer and become part of it; once you save and close the file, you can't undo any of that cloning. But if you put your changes on a separate layer, you can always go back and discard that layer if you change your mind.

Deleting Layers

If you decide you don't want a particular layer anymore, you can easily delete it. Figure 6-6 shows the simplest method, though Elements also gives you a few other ways to delete a layer:

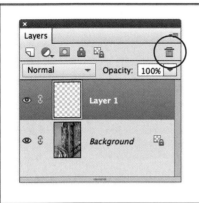

FIGURE 6-6.

To get rid of a layer, either drag it to the trash can icon on the Layers panel or select the layer and then click the trash can (circled). Elements asks if you want to delete the active layer; say yes, and it's history. After you delete a layer, as long as you haven't closed the file, you can get that layer back by using one of the Undo commands. But once you close the file, the layer is gone forever.

- Select Layer→Delete Layer.

- Right-click/Control-click the layer in the Layers panel, and then choose Delete Layer.

- Click the button at the upper right of the Layers panel (the square made of horizontal lines), and then choose Delete Layer.

Duplicating Layers

Creating a copy of a layer can be really useful. Many Elements features, like filters and color-modification tools, don't work on brand-new, *empty* layers. But if you apply such changes to your original photo layer, they alter it in ways you can't undo later. The workaround is to create a *duplicate* of the image layer and then make your changes on the copy. That way you can ditch the duplicate later if you change your mind, and your original layer is unchanged. If you use layer masks (page 202), you'll often duplicate existing layers while working with them.

If all this seems annoyingly theoretical, try going to Enhance→Adjust Color→Adjust Hue/Saturation, for example, when you're working on a new blank layer. You get the stern dialog box shown in Figure 6-7.

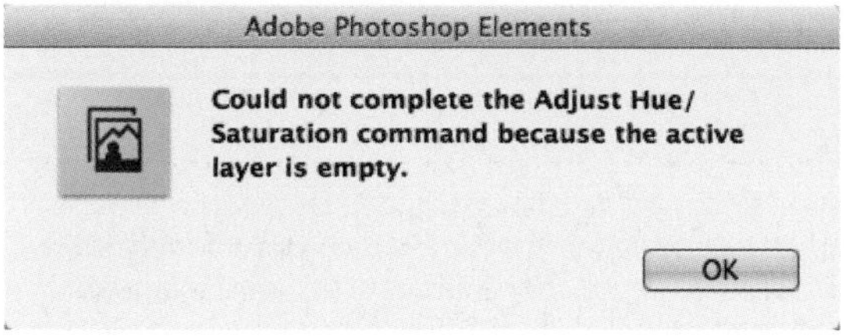

FIGURE 6-7.

Elements is usually pretty helpful when you try to do something that just won't work, like applying a Hue/Saturation adjustment to an empty layer. The solution here is just to switch the Layers panel's focus to a layer that has something in it.

TIP Very rarely, you may encounter the dreaded "no pixels are more than 50% selected" warning. Several things can cause this, but the most common are too large a feather value on a selection (see the box on page 156) or trying to work in the empty part of a layer that contains objects surrounded by transparency.

Elements gives you several ways to duplicate a layer and its content. In the Layers panel, click the layer you want to copy to make it active, and then do one of the following:

- Press Ctrl+J/⌘-J. (Be sure you don't have any active selections when you do this, or Elements copies only the *selection* to the new layer.)

- Choose Layer→Duplicate Layer.

- In the Layers panel, drag the layer you want to copy onto the "Create a new layer" icon.

- In the Layers panel, right-click the layer and, from the pop-up menu, choose Duplicate Layer.

- Click the little four-line square at the upper right of the Layers panel, and then choose Duplicate Layer.

All these methods copy everything in the active layer into the new layer. You can then mess with the duplicate as much as you want without damaging the original. Also, all of them except the keyboard shortcut and dragging onto the New Layer icon bring up a dialog box where you can name the new layer and even choose to use it in a new file or in another image (if you have more than one image open).

Copying and Cutting from Layers

You can also make a new layer that consists of only a *piece* of an existing layer. This is helpful when you want to do things like apply a layer style to one object on the layer. But first you need to decide whether you want to *copy* your selection or *cut* it out and place it on the new layer.

What's the difference? It's pretty much the same as copying versus cutting in your word-processing program. When you use the "New Layer via Copy" command, the area you select appears in the new layer and remains in the old layer, too. "New Layer via Cut," on the other hand, removes the selection from the old layer and places it on the new layer, leaving a corresponding hole in the old layer. Figure 6-8 shows the difference.

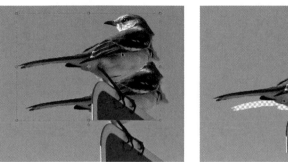 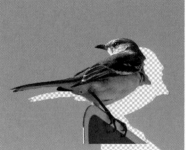

FIGURE 6-8.

The difference between "New Layer via Copy" and "New Layer via Cut" is obvious when you move the new layer to see what's beneath it.

Left: With "New Layer via Copy," the original bird is still in place in the underlying layer.

Right: When you use "New Layer via Cut," the excised bird leaves a hole behind.

GEM IN THE ROUGH

Naming Layers

You may have noticed that Elements isn't terribly creative when it comes to naming layers: You get Layer 1, Layer 2, and so on. Fortunately, you don't have to live with those titles.

Renaming layers may sound like a job for people with way too much time on their hands, but if you're working on a project that has lots of layers, you may find it easier to pick out the layers you want if you give them descriptive names. (Incidentally, you can't rename a Background layer; you have to change it into a regular layer first. Also, Elements helps you

out with Text layers by naming them using the first few words of text they contain.)

To rename a layer:

1. **Double-click its name in the Layers panel.** The name becomes an active text box.

2. **Type the new name.** You don't even need to highlight the text—Elements does that for you automatically.

As with any other change, you have to save your image afterward if you want to keep the new name.

Once you've selected what you want to copy or cut using one of the techniques described in Chapter 5, your new layer is only a couple of keystrokes away:

- **New Layer via Copy.** To copy your selection to a new layer, press Ctrl+J/⌘-J or go to Layer→New→"Layer via Copy." (If you don't select anything beforehand, then Elements copies your *whole* layer, making this a good shortcut for creating a duplicate layer.)

- **New Layer via Cut.** To cut your selection out of your old layer and put it on a new layer by itself, press Shift+Ctrl+J/Shift-⌘-J or go to Layer→New→"Layer via Cut." Just remember that this command leaves a hole in the original layer. (On a Background layer, the hole is filled with the current background color.) If you want to cut and move *everything* on a layer, press Ctrl+A/⌘-A before you cut, although usually it's easier just to move the layer instead. To do that, drag the layer up or down the stack in the Layers panel to put it where you want it.

> **TIP** Elements gives you a quick way to use a layer as the basis for a new document. Instead of copying and pasting, you can create a new document by going to Layer→Duplicate Layer or by clicking the four-lined square in the upper right of the Layers panel and choosing Duplicate Layer. Either way, you get a dialog box with a Document drop-down menu that lets you place the duplicate layer into the file you're currently working on, into any image currently open in the Editor, or into a new document of its own. You can also create a new document with only part of a layer by selecting the area you want, pressing Ctrl+C/⌘-C to copy it, and then going to File→New→"Image from Clipboard."

■ Managing Layers

The Layers panel lets you manipulate layers in all kinds of ways, but first you need to understand a few more of the panel's cryptic icons. Some of the things you can do with layers may seem obscure when you first read about them, but once you actually use layers, you'll quickly see why these options exist. The next few sections explain how to manipulate layers in several different ways: Hide them, group them together, change the way you see them, and combine them.

Hiding Layers

You can turn layers' visibility off and on at will, which is tremendously useful. If the image you're working on has a busy background, for example, it can be hard to see what you're doing when working on a particular layer. Making the Background layer invisible can help you focus on the layer you're interested in. To turn off a layer's visibility, head over to the Layers panel and click the eye icon to the layer's left. To make the layer visible again, just click the eye icon again.

> **TIP** If you have a bunch of hidden layers and decide you don't want them anymore, click the Layers panel's upper-right button (the little four-line square) and choose Delete Hidden Layers to get rid of all of them at once.

Adjusting Layer Opacity

Your choices for layer visibility aren't limited to on and off. You can create immensely cool effects by adjusting the *opacity* of your layers. In other words, you can make a layer partially transparent so that what's underneath it shows through.

To adjust a layer's opacity, click the layer in the Layers panel, and then do one of the following:

- Click the Opacity box, and then type in the percentage you want.

- Click the triangle to the right of the Opacity box and then drag the pop-out slider, or put your cursor on the word "Opacity" and *scrub* (drag) left for less opacity or right for more. (Figure 6-9 explains the advantage of scrubbing.) If you'd like to experiment with creating Fill and Adjustment layers (page 208) and changing their modes and opacity, download *daisies.jpg* from this book's Missing CD page at *www.missingmanuals.com/cds*.

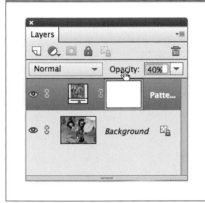

FIGURE 6-9.

You can watch the opacity of your layer change on the fly if you drag your cursor back and forth over the word "Opacity." Blend modes (page 190) often give the best effect if you adjust the opacity of their layers.

In addition to letting you change the opacity of existing layers, Elements also lets you set the opacity of a layer when you create it (though you can change it later using the methods described above). When you create a layer by pressing Shift+Ctrl+N/Shift+⌘+N or choosing Layer→New→Layer, you can set the new layer's opacity in the New Layer dialog box that appears. Alternatively, you can Alt-click/Option-click the Layers panel's New Layer icon to bring up the New Layer dialog box so you can set the opacity.

NOTE You can't change a Background layer's opacity. You first have to convert it to a regular layer; page 182 explains how.

Locking Layers

If you've gotten a layer just perfect and you don't want to accidentally change it, you can *lock* that layer to protect you from yourself. Locking keeps you from changing a layer's contents.

To lock *everything* on a layer so you can't make any changes to it, make sure the layer is active and then click the blue padlock at the top of the Layers panel. When you do, a matching blue padlock appears in the Layers panel to the right of the layer's name, and Elements puts a dark-gray outline around the padlock icon at the top of the panel. Now if you try to paint on that layer or use any other tools on it, your cursor turns into a No symbol (a circle with a diagonal line through it) to remind you that you can't edit that layer. To unlock the layer, just click the blue padlock icon at the top of the panel again.

> **NOTE** Locking a layer only keeps you from *editing* that layer. It doesn't stop you from flattening it or merging it into another layer, or from cropping your image.

You can also lock only the transparent parts of a layer—helpful when you want to modify an object that sits atop a transparent layer, like the seashell in Figure 6-10. When you do that, the transparent parts of your layer stay transparent no matter what you do to the rest of it.

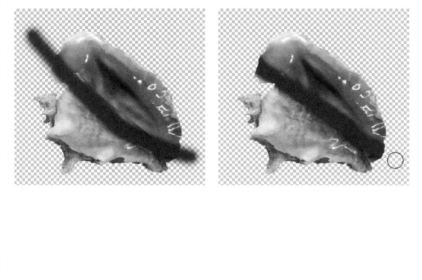

FIGURE 6-10.

After isolating an object on its own layer, you may want to paint only on that object—and not on the transparent part of the layer. Elements lets you lock the transparent portion of a layer, making it easy to paint just the object.

Left: On a regular layer, paint goes wherever your brush does.

Right: With the layer's transparency locked, the brushstroke stops at the edge of the seashell, even though the brush cursor (the circle) is now on the transparent part of the layer.

To lock the transparent parts of a layer, select the layer, and then, at the top of the Layers panel, click the "Lock transparent pixels" icon—the smaller blue padlock with a checkerboard next to it. (It's grayed out if the active layer doesn't have any transparent parts.) When you do, the same icon appears in the Layers panel to the right of the layer's name, and Elements puts a gray border around the icon at the top of the panel. To unlock the layer, select it in the Layers panel and then click the padlock-and-checkerboard icon at the top of the panel again.

Blend Modes

At the top of the Layers panel is a drop-down menu that usually says Normal (and, in the New Layer dialog box, there's a Mode menu that's usually set to Normal). This is your *blend mode* setting. When used with layers, blend modes control how the objects on a layer combine, or *blend,* with the objects on the layer beneath it. By using different blend modes, you can make your image lighter or darker, or even make it look like a poster with just a few bold colors in it. Blend modes can also control how some tools—those with Blend Mode settings—change your image. Tweaking a tool's blend mode can sometimes dramatically change your results.

Blend modes are an awful lot of fun once you understand how to use them. They can help you fix under- or overexposed photos and create all kinds of special visual effects. You can also use some tools, like the Brush tool, in different blend modes to achieve different effects. The most common blend mode is Normal, in which everything you do behaves just the way you'd expect: An object shows its regular colors, and paint acts just like, paint.

Page 409 has lots more about how to use blend modes. For now, take a look at Figure 6-11, which shows how you can totally change the way a layer looks just by changing its blend mode.

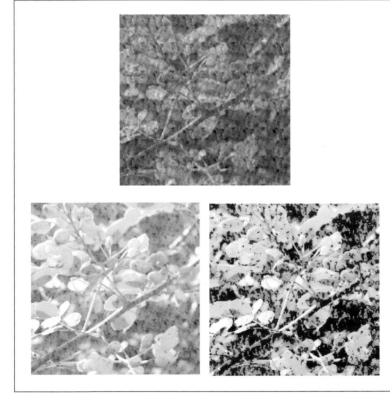

FIGURE 6-11.

This photo of cassia flowers has a Pattern Fill layer over it. (Page 207 has more about Fill layers.) Here you see the effect of changing the pattern layer's blend mode. In Normal blend mode at 100 percent opacity, the pattern would completely hide the leaves, but by changing the blend mode and opacity of the pattern layer, you can create very different looks. The modes shown here are Normal (top), Linear Dodge (bottom left), and Hard Mix (bottom right). Notice how Linear Dodge makes everything much lighter and Hard Mix produces a vivid, posterized effect.

Not every blend mode makes a visible change to every image; some of them may seem to do nothing. That's to be expected. It just means that you don't have a condition in your image that responds to that particular mode change. See page 259 for one example of a situation where a mode change makes an enormous difference.

Fading in Elements

One great thing you get in the full-featured Photoshop that Elements lacks is the ability to *fade* special effects and filters. Fading gives you fine control over how much these tools change an image. For example, filters often generate harsh-looking results, so Photoshop's Fade command lets you adjust a filter's effect until it's what you intended.

Happily, you can approximate the Fade command in Elements: First, apply filters, effects, or layer styles to a duplicate layer. Then, reduce that layer's opacity till it blends in with what's below (and change the blend mode if necessary) to get exactly the result you want.

Rearranging Layers

One of the truly amazing things you can do with Elements is move layers around. Changing the order in which layers are stacked lets you make different objects appear in front of or behind each other. For example, if you've got two objects and each is on its own layer, you can position one object behind the other. To do so, in the Layers panel, just grab a layer and drag it to where you want it.

> **TIP** Remember, you're always looking down onto the layer stack when you view your image, so moving something up in the Layers panel's list moves it toward the front of the picture.

Figure 6-12 shows the early stages of the garden party invitation from Figure 6-1. The potted plants are already in place, and the bench was brought in from another image. But the bench came in at the top of the layer stack, in front of the flowers. To put the bench behind the plants, simply drag the bench layer below the plants layer in the Layers panel.

> **NOTE** Background layers are the only kind of layer you can't move. If you want to put a Background layer in another spot in the layer stack, first convert it to a regular layer (page 182), and *then* move it.

You can also move layers by going to Layer→Arrange, and then choosing one of these commands:

- **Bring to Front** (Shift+Ctrl+]/Shift-⌘-]) sends the selected layer to the top of the stack so the layer's contents appear in your image's foreground.

- **Bring Forward** (Ctrl+]/⌘-]) moves the layer up one level in the Layers panel, so it appears one step closer to the front of your image.

- **Send Backward** (Ctrl+[/⌘-[) moves the layer down one level so it's one step farther back in the image.

- **Send to Back** (Shift+Ctrl+[/Shift-⌘-[) puts the layer directly above the Background layer so it appears as far back as possible.

- **Reverse** (no keyboard shortcut) switches two layers' locations in the stack. You have to select two layers in the panel (by Ctrl-clicking/⌘-clicking them, for example) before using this command.

> **TIP** These commands (except Reverse) are also available from the Move tool's Tool Options or by right-clicking/Control-clicking in your photo when the Move tool is active. As a matter of fact, using the Move tool is a great way to rearrange layers in your image, as the next section explains.

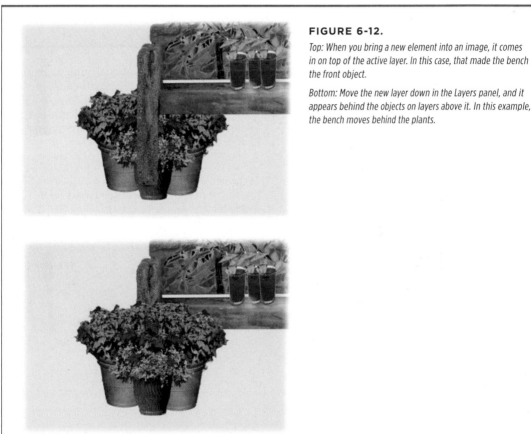

FIGURE 6-12.

Top: When you bring a new element into an image, it comes in on top of the active layer. In this case, that made the bench the front object.

Bottom: Move the new layer down in the Layers panel, and it appears behind the objects on layers above it. In this example, the bench moves behind the plants.

■ ARRANGING LAYERS WITH THE MOVE TOOL

You can use the Move tool to select and arrange layers right in the image window, without trekking all the way over to the Layers panel. (If you need a refresher on Move tool basics, flip to page 173.) Say you've got an image that has several different objects in it, and each object is on its own layer. To arrange layers with the Move tool:

1. **Activate the Move tool by clicking its icon in the Tools panel or pressing V.**

2. **Select the layer(s) you want to move.**

    As soon as you activate the Move tool, you see a bounding box (solid dark lines) around the contents of the active layer in your image. As you move your cursor over the image, you see a blue outline around the object the cursor is over—no matter how far down the layer stack the object's layer is (see Figure 6-13). When you click to select the layer you want to move, a bounding box with large square handles on it appears around that layer. Shift-click to select objects on multiple layers, and the bounding box expands to include everything you've selected. You can also drag a selection around multiple objects and choose them that way. (For instance, you could drag over both the balls and the mitt to move them as a group, so you don't have to rearrange them afterward.)

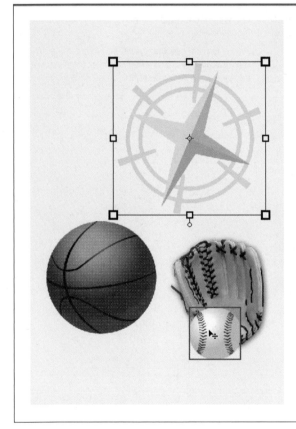

FIGURE 6-13.

The Move tool lets you select objects that are on any layer, not just the active one. When you move the cursor over an object, you see a blue outline around its layer. Here, the compass is the active layer (you can see the bounding box around it), but the Move tool is ready to select the baseball (you can see the blue box around it), even though it's not on the active layer. If all these outlines annoy you, you can get rid of them by heading to the Tool Options area and turning off the Show Bounding Box and "Show Highlight on Rollover" checkboxes. If you want to force the Move tool to concentrate only on the active layer, then turn off the Auto Select Layer checkbox, too.

3. **Move the layer(s).**

You can do this by clicking the Tool Options area's Arrange icon, choosing Layer→Arrange, or right-clicking inside the bounding box in the image. Whichever method you use, you see all the choices described in the previous section ("Bring to Front," Bring Forward, and so on) except for Reverse, which is available only from the Layer menu. You can also use keyboard shortcuts (again, except for Reverse).

> **NOTE** If you selected multiple layers, you may find that some of the commands are grayed out (that is, you can't choose them). If that's a problem, just click elsewhere in the image to deselect the layers, and then move the layers one at a time instead of as a group.

Aligning and Distributing Layers

You can also use the Move tool to arrange objects in an image. The tool's *aligning* feature can arrange the items on each layer so that they line up straight along their top, bottom, left, or right edges, or through their centers. So, for example, if you align the top edges, then Elements makes sure that the top of each object is exactly in line with the tops of all the others.

> **TIP** Don't forget that you can add guidelines (page 82) to help position objects just so in an image.

You'll also find it a breeze to evenly distribute the *spacing* between multiple objects. The Move tool's *distribute* feature spaces out objects based on their edges or centers. If you distribute the top edges, for example, Elements makes sure there's an even amount of space from the top edge of one object to another. Figure 6-14 shows examples of aligned and distributed guitars.

> **NOTE** Distributing objects is especially handy when you're creating projects like those described in Chapter 15.

Aligning and distributing layers with the Move tool works much like rearranging layers:

1. **Activate the Move tool by clicking its icon in the Tools panel or pressing V.**

2. **Select the objects you want to align.**

   This maneuver works only if each object is on its own layer. If you have multiple objects on one layer, then move them to their own layers one at a time by selecting each object, and then pressing Ctrl+Shift+J/⌘-Shift-J.

Once all the objects are on their own layers, Shift-click inside the blue outline that appears around each object when you put your cursor over it to select each layer you want to work with, or Shift-click or Ctrl-click/⌘-click in the Layers panel to select the layers you want.

3. **Choose how you want to align or distribute the objects by clicking the option you want in the Tool Options area.**

   The Align and Distribute sections both offer the same choices: Top, Center, Bottom, Left, Middle, and Right. The little thumbnails (each of which is actually a button) show you how your objects will line up. Just click the one that matches what you're going for.

> **NOTE** You can apply as many different align and distribute commands as you like, as long as the layers you're working with are still selected. Figure 6-14 shows how these commands work.

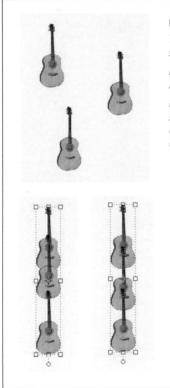

FIGURE 6-14.

Top: Each of these guitars is on its own layer, but they need to be tidied up if you want them in a neat stack.

Bottom left: Here's the result of selecting the guitars with the Move tool and then picking Align→Center. As you see, the guitars' centers are aligned, but they're not evenly distributed.

Bottom right: The same guitars after a trip to Distribute→Middle. Note that they're evenly spaced but still overlapping. That's because Distribute doesn't add any additional space between the outermost objects. If you want wider spacing between objects, then make sure they're farther apart before you distribute them.

Linking and Clipping Layers

What if you want to move several layers at once? For instance, in the garden party image back on page 178, two layers contain potted plants in terra-cotta pots. It's kind of a pain to drag each plant layer individually if you want to move them both in front of the bench. Fortunately, Elements gives you a way to keep your layers united.

■ LINKING LAYERS

Sometimes, you'll want to move a couple of layers as a group, while still keeping the layers separate. In that case, you can *link* two or more layers together so they travel as a unit, as shown in Figure 6-15.

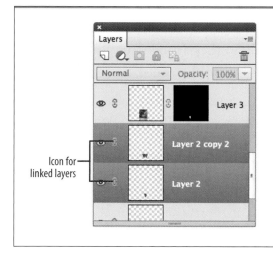

Icon for
linked layers

FIGURE 6-15.

In the Layers panel, Shift-click or Ctrl-click/⌘-click to select the layers you want to link, and then click the little chain icon next to one of the layers' thumbnails to link them together. The chain icon turns orange on each of the linked layers to let you know they're connected.

To unlink them, simply click one of the linked layers in the Layers panel, and then click the chain icon again.

You can also merge the layers (as explained in the next section) into one layer. Or you can use the layer selection choices described in the box on page 198 and skip linking altogether; as long as the layers all stay selected, they travel as a group. But the advantage of linking is that the linked layers stay associated until you unlink them—you don't need to worry about accidentally clicking somewhere else in the panel and losing your selection group.

Selecting Layers

You can quickly choose multiple layers when you want to do things like link, move, or delete layers. For your quick-selection pleasure, Elements gives you a whole group of layer-selection commands, which you'll find in the Select menu. Here's what they do:

- **All Layers.** Choose this command and Elements selects every layer except the Background layer. Even if you've turned off a layer's visibility (page 188), it still gets selected.

- **Deselect Layers.** When you're done working with layers as a group, pick this command and you won't have any layers selected until you click one.

- **Similar Layers.** This command is the most useful in the group. Choose it and every layer that's the same type as

the active one gets selected, no matter where it is in the stack. For example, if you have a Text layer active when you choose Similar Layers, then Elements selects *all* the Text layers in the file you're working on. Or if you have an Adjustment layer active, it selects all the Adjustment layers. You can use this command to quickly select a stack of Adjustment layers you want to drag to another image, for instance, using the technique described on page 211.

You can also Shift-click to select multiple layers that are next to one another in the Layers panel, or Ctrl-click/⌘-click to select layers that are separated. That way, you can avoid the Select menu altogether. Once you're done working with the layers you selected, you can either use the Deselect Layers command or just click another layer to make it the active layer.

■ CLIPPING LAYERS TOGETHER

An even more powerful way to combine layers is to group them together using a *clipping mask*. This technique sounds complex, but it's actually quite easy and very powerful. With this kind of grouping, one layer (the clipping mask layer) influences the other layers it's grouped with.

> **NOTE** This technique used to be called "grouping," but starting with Elements 8, Adobe changed it to "clipping," which is what it's called in Photoshop. The behavior is exactly the same as the old grouped layers—only the name is different.

Clipping layers isn't anything like linking them. You can probably understand the process most easily by looking at Figure 6-16, which shows how to crop the image on one layer using the shape of an object on another layer.

> **NOTE** If you clip two layers together, Elements applies the bottom layer's Opacity setting to both layers.

Once the layers are clipped together, you can still slide the top layer around with the Move tool to reposition it so that you see exactly the part of it that you want. So in Figure 6-16, for example, the ocean layer was positioned so the breaking wave appears at the bottom of the shell shape.

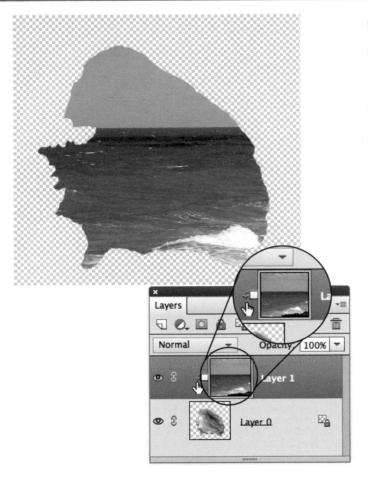

FIGURE 6-16.

This image began life as a picture of a seashell on one layer and an ocean scene on the layer above it. Because the ocean layer was above the shell layer in the Layers panel, the ocean image totally hid the shell. But interesting things happen when you clip these layers together: The ocean layer automatically gets cropped to the shape of the bottom layer, the seashell. The fancy way to say that is the shell now acts as the clipping mask for the ocean image.

The tiny downward-bent arrow with the white square next to it just above the cursor in the Layers panel shown here indicates that the ocean layer is clipped.

To clip two layers together, position the two layers next to each other in the Layers panel by dragging. (Put the one you want to act as the mask *below* the other image.) Then make the top layer (of the two you want to clip) the active layer. Then choose Layer→Create Clipping Mask or press Ctrl+G/⌘-G.

You can also clip right in the Layers panel: Hold down Alt/Option, and then, in the panel, move your cursor over the dividing line between the layers you want to clip. When two linked circles appear by your cursor, click once and Elements groups those layers together with a clipping mask.

If you get tired of the layer grouping or want to delete or change one of the layers, then select one of the clipped layers and go to Layer→Release Clipping Mask or press Ctrl+G/⌘-G again to undo the grouping.

> **TIP** Elements gives you an even easier way to group layers: The New Layer dialog box has a "Use Previous Layer to Create Clipping Mask" checkbox. Turn it on, and Elements pre-clips your new layer with the layer below it.

Merging and Flattening Layers

By now, you probably have some sense of how useful layers are. But there's a downside to having layers in an image: They take up a lot of storage space, especially if you have lots of duplicate layers. (In other words, layers make files bigger.) Fortunately, you don't have to keep layers in your files forever. You can reduce a file's size quite a bit—and sometimes also make things easier to manage—by merging layers or flattening the image.

■ MERGING LAYERS

Sometimes you may have two or more separate layers that really could be treated as one layer, like the plants in Figure 6-17. You aren't limited to just linking those layers together; once you've got everything arranged just right, you can *merge* them together into a single layer. Also, if you want to copy and paste your image, standard Copy and Paste commands typically copy only the top layer, so it helps to get everything into one layer, at least temporarily. You'll probably merge layers quite often when you're working with multilayer files (for example, when you've got multiple objects that you want to edit simultaneously).

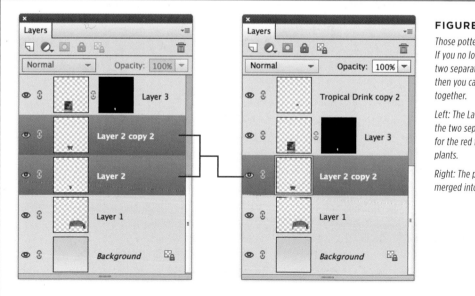

FIGURE 6-17.

Those potted plants again. If you no longer need two separate plant layers, then you can merge them together.

Left: The Layers panel with the two separate layers for the red flowering plants.

Right: The plant layers merged into one.

You have a couple of different ways to merge layers, depending on what's active in your image. You can run either of the following commands by heading up to the Layer menu, clicking the Layers panel's upper-right button (the four-lined square), or by using keyboard shortcuts:

- **Merge Down** (Ctrl+E/⌘-E) combines the active layer with the layer immediately beneath it. If the layer just below the active layer is hidden, then you can't run this command.

- **Merge Visible** (Shift+Ctrl+E/Shift-⌘-E) combines all the visible layers in the current document into one layer. If you want to combine layers that are far apart, then just temporarily turn off the visibility of the ones in between (and any other layers that you don't want to merge) by clicking their eye icons.

It's important to understand that once you merge layers and then save and close your file, you can't just unmerge them. While your file is still open, you can use any of the Undo commands, but once you exceed the history states limit you've set in Preferences (page 25), you're stuck with your merged layers.

TIP   The box on page 202 explains how to combine all your layers while still keeping separate copies of the individual layers.

Sometimes, when a layer contains text or shapes drawn with a shape tool, you can't merge that layer right away; Elements needs to *simplify* the layer first. Simplifying means converting its contents to a *raster object*—a bunch of pixels subject to the same resizing limitations as any photo. So, for example, after you rasterize a Text layer, then you can apply filters to the text or paint on it, but you can't edit the words anymore. (See page 422 for more about simplifying and working with shapes, and Chapter 14 to learn about working with text.) Unlike previous versions of Elements, if you try to merge a layer that needs to be simplified first, Elements 11 doesn't ask you if you want to do this—it just automatically simplifies the layer and merges it with the others you selected before applying the Merge command.

■ FLATTENING AN IMAGE

Layers are simply swell when you're working on an image, but they're a headache when you want to share the file, especially if you're sending it to a photo-printing service (their machines usually don't understand layered files). Even if you're printing at home, the large size of a multilayer file can make it take forever to print. And if you plan to use your image in other programs, very few non-Adobe programs are totally comfortable with layers, so you may get some odd results.

In these cases, you can squash everything in your picture into a single layer. You do this by *flattening* your image: Go to Layer→Flatten Image or, in the Layers panel, click the four-lined-square and choose Flatten Image. Or, to keep your original intact, go to File→Save As, and in the Save As dialog box, turn *off* the Layers checkbox (which will turn *on* the "As a Copy" checkbox) before clicking the Save button.

TIP Saving your image as a JPEG file automatically gets rid of layers, too.

There's no keyboard shortcut for flattening because it's something you don't want to do by accident. Like merging, flattening is a permanent change. Cautious Elements veterans always do a Save As (instead of a plain Save) before flattening. That way you have a flattened copy *and* a working copy with the layers intact, just in case. Organizer version sets (page 66) can help you here, too, because they let you save an image in different states, so you can have both a layered and a flattened version.

NOTE Flattening creates a Background layer out of the existing layers in an image, which means that you lose transparency, just as with a regular Background layer. If you want to create a single layer *with* transparency, then use the Merge Visible command (page 201) instead.

POWER USERS' CLINIC

Stamp Visible

Sometimes you want to perform an action on all your image's visible layers without permanently merging them together. You can do this quickly and easily—even if your file contains dozens of layers—with the Stamp Visible command, which combines the contents of all your visible layers into a new layer at the top of the stack. Stamp Visible is great because it lets you work on the new combined layer while leaving your existing layers untouched, in case you want them back later.

Make sure the top layer is selected, and then just press Shift+Alt+Ctrl+E/Shift-Option-⌘-E or hold down Alt/Option while selecting the Merge Visible command from the Layer menu or from the Layers panel's menu, which you open by clicking the square made of four horizontal lines. However you run the command, Elements creates a new layer at the top of the Layers panel and fills it with the combined contents of all your other layers. To keep a layer or two from being included in this new layer, just turn off the visibility of the layers you want to exclude before running Stamp Visible.

Layer Masks

Elements gives you an incredibly powerful tool for getting the most out of layers: *layer masks.* What are they and why are they such a big deal?

As their name implies, layer masks let you hide (or "mask") parts of layers. Back in Chapter 5, you learned about selecting parts of photos and using Refine Edge or the Magic Extractor to cut objects out of an image, and earlier in this chapter you learned how to cut or copy something to a new layer. Those are all fine techniques, but if next week you change your mind about exactly what you want to include, you have to start all over again. Wouldn't it be cool if you could just make the parts of your photo that you don't want vanish, and then make them reappear later on if you change your mind?

Layer masks let you do exactly that: They're like a cloak of invisibility for layers, and it's totally up to you how much shows. When you mask part of a layer, the visible part looks just like an object that's been cut out and surrounded by transparency, but the rest of the layer is all still there—it's just hidden away. What's more, showing or hiding more of what's on the layer is as easy as painting on it, and there's no statute of limitations—you can come back to the layer and adjust things whenever you want. Figure 6-18 helps explain why this is such a great way to work.

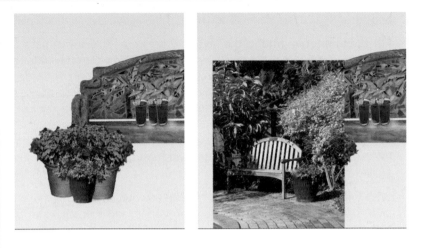

FIGURE 6-18.

Left: Here's part of that flyer from Figure 6-1. The blue pot in the front looks right at home, doesn't it?

Right: The blue pot actually came from this poolside photo. To isolate the pot, a layer mask was placed over the rest of the photo, hiding it. (The mask was turned off here to show you the original image.) If you wanted to, you could go back and edit the mask to reveal more of the photo or change what the mask covers if, for instance, you'd rather use one of the bushes behind the pot in your flyer instead.

In full Photoshop, layer masks have been *de rigueur* for all sorts of changes for years now because they're incredibly powerful and easy to use. The only downside to layer masks is that the extra content makes your file somewhat larger, but that's a small price to pay for so much flexibility.

NOTE Adjustment and Fill layers (which you'll learn about in the next section) come with layer masks already attached to them; you don't have to do anything to add them.

Layer masks are a tad confusing at first, but you'll quickly get the hang of them and learn how much they can do for you. The easy way to remember what they do is to think of them as Halloween masks for your layers: Whatever is behind the mask is hidden, while you can see everything that's not covered by the mask.

You can add a layer mask to any layer except a Background layer. Here's how:

1. **Make sure the layer you want to mask is active.**

    If it's not, click it in the Layers panel.

2. **Add a layer mask.**

    You have several choices for how the mask should start off:

- **Empty, showing all the layer's contents.** To create a "blank" layer mask (in other words, one that starts out not covering anything in the layer), just click the "Add layer mask" icon at the top of the Layers panel (it looks like a circle within a square; you can see it back in Figure 6-5) or choose Layer→Layer Mask→Reveal All. When you do, a pure white mask thumbnail appears in the Layers panel to the right of the active layer's thumbnail.

- **Filled, completely hiding the layer.** To create a "full" layer mask that covers everything in the active layer, Alt-click/Option-click the "Add layer mask" icon in the Layers panel or choose Layer→Layer Mask→Hide All. Elements adds a black mask thumbnail to the Layers panel. You'd use this option if you wanted to hide most of the layer. That way, you can just reveal ("unmask") the areas you want to keep visible, like the eyes and lips of a portrait, for example. That's faster than painting over everything else in the layer. (You'll learn how to edit layer masks in a moment so you can hide exactly what you want.)

- **With only a selection visible.** To hide all but certain areas of the active layer, select the parts you want to keep visible, and then click the "Add layer mask" icon or go to Layer→Layer Mask→Reveal Selection. Elements masks everything but your selection, leaving only the selected area(s) visible. The result looks exactly like you used the Magic Extractor on the layer; the difference is that everything else is *still there*—it's just hidden.

- **With only a selection hidden.** To hide only a few bits of the layer, select those parts and then Alt-click/Option-click the "Add layer mask" icon or go to Layer→Layer Mask→Hide Selection and Elements hides the selected area(s).

TIP Remember, you can create masks and masked layers from selections right in the Refine Edge dialog box, too (page 145).

You'll learn how to edit the area covered by a mask in a moment, but first here are a few other useful things you can do with a layer mask:

- **Disable it.** If you want to see your layer without the mask, in the Layers panel, just right-click/Control-click the mask's thumbnail and choose Disable Layer Mask, or go to Layer→Layer Mask→Disable. Everything that the mask was hiding reappears and Elements puts a big red X over the mask's thumbnail to remind you that it's disabled.

NOTE When you disable a layer mask, your menu choice changes to read "Enable" instead. Just choose it to toggle the mask back on.

- **Merge it into the layer.** If you decide that you really, really don't need to edit a layer mask anymore, right-click/Control-click its thumbnail in the Layers panel and then choose Apply Layer Mask (or go to Layer→Layer Mask→Apply instead), and the mask becomes a permanent, uneditable part of the layer it's attached to. Basically, doing this puts you in the same situation you'd be in if you used the "Layer via Copy" command or if you'd selected something and then deleted the rest of the layer (meaning you lose all the flexibility you get by using a layer mask), so this isn't something you'll do often.

- **Unlink it.** When you add a layer mask, a little chain appears in the Layers panel between the layer's thumbnail and the mask's thumbnail to indicate that they work as a unit. But if you unlink them, you can move the mask separately from the layer itself. This is handy when you've got a mask the size and shape of the area you want to see perfectly masked out, only it's not quite over the right part of the image. In that case, unlink the mask from the layer so you can drag the mask without moving the layer's contents. To do that, just click the chain icon or go to Layer→Layer Mask→Unlink. The chain disappears and you can now use the Move tool to rearrange things. To relink them, click the spot where the chain icon was or choose the menu item again (which now says "Link" instead).

- **Delete it.** To get rid of a layer mask and return the layer to its unmasked state, in the Layers panel, right-click/Control-click the mask's thumbnail and choose Delete Layer Mask, or go to Layer→Layer Mask→Delete.

▪ EDITING A LAYER MASK

Now that you have a mask, it's time to learn how to change the area it covers. You do this by simply painting on it with black or white. Painting with black increases the masked area; painting with white increases the visible area. "Black conceals and white reveals" is an old Photoshop saw that helps remind you what each color does.

You can work on the mask by painting directly in the main image window, or make the layer mask visible and work in either of two special mask views, which are sometimes helpful when the objects in your image have tricky edges, or if you need to check for missed spots. Here's the simplest way to make changes to the area covered by a layer mask:

1. **Make sure the masked layer is active.**

   If it isn't, click it in the Layers panel. This step is important: If the masked layer isn't active, you'll add paint to the actual image.

2. **In the Layers panel, click the layer mask's thumbnail.**

   You tell Elements whether you want to work directly on the layer or on the layer *mask* by clicking the thumbnail of the one you want. (You can tell which one is active because Elements puts an extra little outline around its thumbnail.) The foreground and background color squares change to black and white, respectively, as soon as you click the thumbnail. If for some reason they don't, just press D.

3. Paint directly on your image.

Use the Brush tool to paint on the image. Paint an area black to hide it or white to show it. Remember: Black conceals and white reveals. (An easy way to switch between your foreground and background colors is to press X.)

You can also use the selection tools the same way you would on any other selection to change the mask's area. (See Chapter 5 if you need help making selections.) If you watch the layer mask's thumbnail in the Layers panel, you'll see that it changes to show where you've painted.

To make a layer mask visible in the main image window (rather than just as a thumbnail in the Layers panel), you simply click it in the Layers panel while holding down certain key combinations. Elements gives you a choice of two different ways to see the masked area, as shown in Figure 6-19. If you Alt-click/Option-click the mask's thumbnail, you see the black-and-white layer mask (instead of your photo) in the image window. Add the Shift key when you click to see a red overlay on the photo instead of the black-and-white view. Press the same keys again while clicking the thumbnail (or just click the left thumbnail) to get back to a regular view of your image.

The black-and-white mask view shows only the mask itself, not your photo beneath it. This is a good choice when you want to check how clean the edges of your selection are. But if you're adding or subtracting areas of your photo, use the red-overlay view instead so you can see the objects in your photo as you paint over them. You can use the method described earlier to paint in either view.

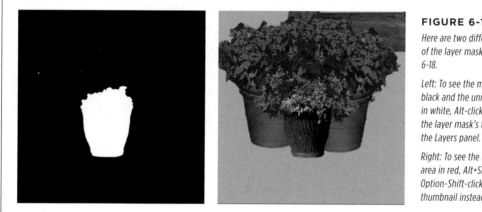

FIGURE 6-19.

Here are two different views of the layer mask from Figure 6-18.

Left: To see the masked area in black and the unmasked area in white, Alt-click/Option-click the layer mask's thumbnail in the Layers panel.

Right: To see the masked area in red, Alt+Shift-click/ Option-Shift-click the mask's thumbnail instead.

TIP You can use shades of gray to adjust a layer mask's transparency. Simply paint on your mask with gray to change the opacity of the area revealed on the layer. The darker the gray, the less shows through; the lighter the gray, the more of what you're painting shows through the mask. Paint with dark gray, for example, for a faint, ghosted effect, the sort of thing you might use to create a background for stationery.

Layer masks are incredibly powerful, and this section has just covered the very basics, but there are literally *thousands* of different uses for them. You can paint the edges of a photo with grunge brushes, for instance, to create interesting borders, or apply a black-to-white gradient to a layer mask to make the layer fade on one edge. There are entire books written about masking techniques, and once you get started you'll want to explore more ways you can use this powerful feature to help your creativity soar. If you want to learn how to mask a particular object (like hair, say), just Google "mask hair photoshop" and you'll get more tutorials than you could work through in a lifetime. Katrin Eismann's *Photoshop Masking & Compositing* (New Riders Press) is one of the most complete books on the subject, although a fair amount of the book (like the parts about using the Pen tool) pertains only to Photoshop.

TIP Full Photoshop also has another kind of mask, called the Quick Mask. If you try a tutorial written for Photoshop that calls for Quick Mask, just use the Selection Brush in Mask mode instead.

■ Adjustment and Fill Layers

Adjustment layers and *Fill layers* are special types of layers. Adjustment layers let you manipulate the lighting, color, or exposure of the layers beneath them. If you're mainly interested in using Elements to spruce up your photos, then you'll probably use Adjustment layers more than any other kind of layer. They're great because they let you undo or change your edits later on.

You can also use Adjustment layers to take the changes you've made to one photo and apply those same changes to another photo (see the box on page 208). And after you've created an Adjustment layer, you can limit future edits so they change only the area of the photo affected by the Adjustment layer. You'll find out about all the things you can do with Adjustment layers in the next few chapters. For now, you just need to learn how to create and manipulate them, which the next section explains.

Fill layers are exactly what they sound like: layers filled with a color, pattern, or *gradient* (a rainbow-like range of colors—see page 465). Fill layers are great when you've cut an object out of its original image and want to put some color behind it, for example.

One cool thing about both Adjustment and Fill layers is that they automatically come with layer masks, as shown in Figure 6-20.

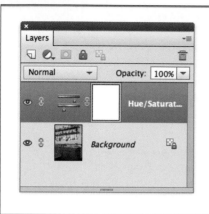

FIGURE 6-20.

Adjustment and Fill layers, like the Hue/Saturation Adjustment layer shown here, always display two things in the Layers panel: an icon on the left and a thumbnail on the right. The thumbnail represents the layer's layer mask, which you can use to control the area that's affected by the adjustment. As for the icons, each type of Adjustment layer and Fill layer has its own unique icon. With Adjustment layers, just click the layer you want to change to make it the active layer, and then go to the Adjustments panel to tweak things. With Fill Layers, double-click the icon to bring up a dialog box that lets you make changes to the layer's settings.

> **TIP**   Digital photographers should check out Photo Filter Adjustment layers, which let you make the sort of adjustments to photos that used to require you to put a colored piece of glass over your camera's lens. Page 294 has more about photo filters.

GEM IN THE ROUGH

Adjustment Layers for Batch Processing

Page 295 shows you how to perform *batch* commands—that is, simultaneously applying adjustments to groups of photos by using the Process Multiple Files command. The drawback of Process Multiple Files is that it gives you access to only some of the Auto commands, so your editing options are really limited.

So what if you're a fussy photographer who's got 17 shots that are all pretty much the same and you'd like to apply the same fixes to all of them—do you have to edit each one from scratch? Nope. Simply open the photos you want to fix, and then drag an Adjustment layer from the first photo onto each of the other photos. (Page 211 shows you how to drag layers between images.) That way, each photo gets the same adjustments at the same settings. It's not as fast as true batch processing, but it takes a lot less time than editing each photo from scratch.

Adding Fill and Adjustment Layers

Creating an Adjustment or Fill layer is easy: In the Layers panel, just click the half-black/half-white circle to display the menu shown in Figure 6-21. The menu includes all your Adjustment and Fill layer options (the first three items are Fill layers; the rest are Adjustment layers).

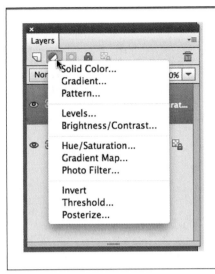

FIGURE 6-21.

To create a new Adjustment or Fill layer, click the half-black/half-white circle to see this menu, and then pick the type of layer you want. If you'd rather work from the menu bar, then go to Layer→New Adjustment Layer (or Layer→New Fill Layer) and choose a type.

■ FILL LAYERS

Elements can create three types of Fill layers: Solid Color, Gradient (a rainbow-like range of colors—see page 465), and Pattern (page 320 has more about patterns). When you create a Fill layer, Elements displays a dialog box that lets you tweak the layer's settings. After you make your choices, click OK, and the new layer appears.

You can change a Fill layer's settings by selecting it in the Layers panel and then going to Layer→Layer Content Options, or, in the Layers panel, double-clicking the layer's left-hand icon. Either way, the layer's dialog box reappears so you can tweak its settings.

■ ADJUSTMENT LAYERS

When you create an Adjustment layer, the layer automatically appears in your image, and the Adjustments panel appears so you can tweak the layer's settings (Figure 6-22). (The exception is the Invert Adjustment layer—if you create one of those, you see the Adjustments panel but it doesn't include any settings you can change.) Confusingly, you won't see the word "Adjustments" at the top of this panel; instead, the heading reflects the type of Adjustment layer you added: Levels, Hue/Saturation, or whatever. The exact settings in the panel also depend on the type of Adjustment layer you added. In Basic mode, the Adjustments panel is always floating—you can't put it into the Panel Bin.

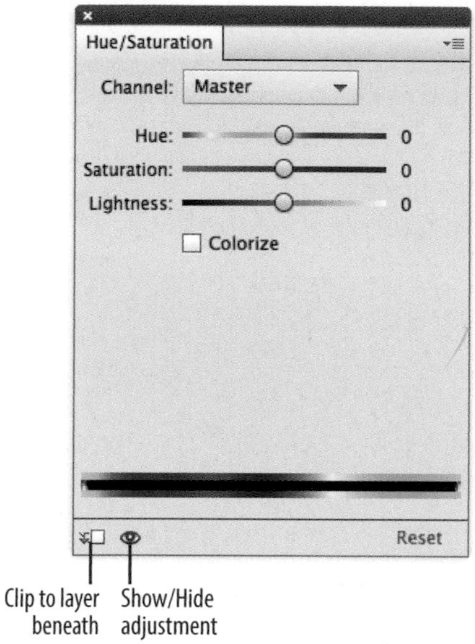

FIGURE 6-22.

The Adjustments panel appears when you create a new Adjustment layer. The icons at the bottom let you view your image with and without the Adjustment layer, so you can judge how you're changing things. You can also clip the Adjustment layer to the layer beneath it in the Layers panel, or unclip it (see page 198).

The Adjustments panel is really handy because it lets you see the settings for any Adjustment layer anytime. In the Layers panel, just double-click the left-hand icon on the Adjustment layer you want to change, and Elements displays the Adjustments panel showing the settings for that layer. Double-click a different Adjustment layer's icon to see its settings instead.

Elements lets you add the following kinds of Adjustment layers:

- **Levels.** This is a much more sophisticated way to apply Levels than using the Auto Levels button in Quick Fix or the Enhance menu's Auto Level command. For most people, Levels is *the* most important type of Adjustment layer. Page 236 has more about using Levels.

- **Brightness/Contrast.** This does pretty much the same things as the Quick Fix adjustment (covered on page 126).

- **Hue/Saturation.** Again, this is much like the Quick Fix command (page 129), only with slightly different controls.

- **Gradient Map.** This one is tricky to understand and is explained in detail on page 476. It maps each tone in your image to a new tone based on the gradient you select. That means you can apply a gradient so that the colors aren't just distributed in a straight line across your image.

- **Photo Filter.** Use this type of layer to adjust the color balance of photos by adding warming, cooling, or special-effects filters, just like you might attach to the lens of a film camera. See page 294 for more info.

- **Invert.** This Adjustment layer reverses the colors in your image to their opposite values, for an effect similar to a film negative; page 341 has details.

- **Threshold.** Use this kind of layer to make everything in a photo pure black or white (with no shades of gray). See page 342.

- **Posterize.** This one reduces the numbers of colors in an image to create a poster-like effect, as explained on page 341.

You can edit an Adjustment layer's layer mask the same way you edit any other layer mask (page 205). The only difference is what happens when you edit the mask: Instead of showing or hiding the objects in your photo, you show and hide the *effects* of the adjustment, since this kind of a layer contains an adjustment instead of an image.

In Elements 11 you delete Adjustment and Fill layers the way you delete any other layer—no more extra steps, as there were in earlier versions of Elements. Simply drag the layer to the Layer panel's trash can and it's gone. You can also go to the Layer menu, right-click the layer in the Layers panel, or click the Layers panel's upper-right menu button (the square made of four horizontal lines). All these routes give you a Delete Layer option.

■ Moving Objects Between Images

Layers let you easily combine parts of different photos. If you're using tabs (page 93), the simplest way to do this is by copying and pasting: Select what you want to move (press Ctrl+A/⌘-A if you want to move the whole photo), and then press Ctrl+C/⌘-C to copy it. Next, make the destination image the active image by double-clicking it in the Photo Bin, and then press Ctrl+V/⌘-V to paste. The pasted material comes in on its own layer, and you can then use the Move tool to rearrange it in its new home.

You can also move objects between images by dragging. To do this, you need to choose one of the tiled views if you're using tabs (page 95), or Tile or Cascade (Window→Images→Tile or Cascade) if you're using floating windows (page 93). Just put what you want from Photo A into its own layer, and then drag it onto Photo B. You can use the Move tool to move the object from one image to another, or you can just drag it. The trick is that you have to drag the layer from Photo A's *Layers panel.* If you try to drop one photo directly onto another photo's window, then you'll just wind up with a lot of windows stacked on top of one another. Figure 6-23 shows you how to execute this maneuver.

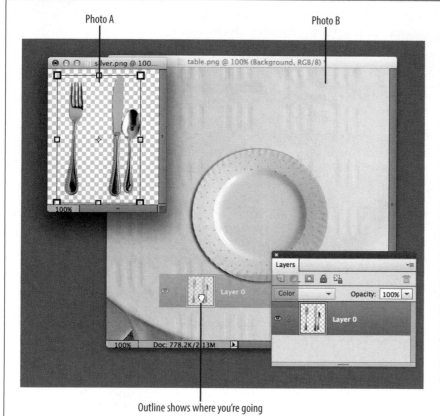

Photo A

Photo B

FIGURE 6-23.

The goal here is to get the silverware from Photo A (whose Layers panel is visible) onto the tablecloth in Photo B. You always drag from the Layers panel onto a photo window when combining parts of different images. (If you try to drag from a photo to a photo, it won't work unless you activate the Move tool first.) When you do this, you may see a shadowy version of what was in the Layers panel for Photo A (as shown here) or just the little clutching hand cursor and no outline at all, depending on the version of your operating system. Use the Move tool to reposition your object once you've dropped it into the image.

Outline shows where you're going

TIP You can also drag a photo directly from the Photo Bin onto another image. This is really useful for projects like scrapbooking where you have many objects, each in its own file, that you want to combine on a single page in Elements.

But what if, rather than moving a whole layer, you just want to move a particular object—say, a person—to another photo? Just follow these steps:

1. **Open both photos in Expert Mode.**

   You can pull off this maneuver in a tabbed view, but most people find it easier to use floating windows. To use floating windows, first go to Edit→Preferences→General/ Adobe Photoshop Elements Editor→Preferences→General and make sure that "Allow Floating Documents in Expert Mode" is turned on. Next, go to Window→Images→"Float All in Windows," and then go back to Window→Images and choose Tile or Cascade.

If you want to use tabs instead, go to the Layout menu below the Photo Bin and choose a layout that gives you a view of all your images.

2. **Prepare both photos for combining.**

   Go to Image→Resize→Image Size, and then make sure both photos have the same Resolution (ppi) setting (see page 101 for a refresher on resizing and resolution). Why? If one photo is way bigger than the other, then the moved object could easily blanket the entire target image.

   You don't absolutely *have* to do this size balancing, but it'll make your life a lot easier, since it helps avoid having an enormous or tiny pasted object. (Keep reading for more advice about resolution when moving objects and layers.)

3. **Select what you want to move.**

   Use the selection tool(s) of your choice (see Chapter 5 if you need help making selections). Add a 1- or 2-pixel feather to the selection to avoid a hard, cut-out-looking edge.

4. **Move the object.**

   There are several ways to move what you selected to the other image:

   - **Copy and paste.** Press Ctrl+C/⌘-C to copy the object from the first photo. Next, click the second photo to make it active, and then press Ctrl+V/⌘-V to paste what you copied.

   - **Use the Move tool.** Activate the Move tool, and then drag the selection to the other photo. As you're moving, you may see a hole in the original where the selection was, but as long as you keep your mouse button pressed till you get over the second photo, this fills back in after you let go of your mouse. (If seeing this hole bothers you, just Alt-drag/Option-drag to move a *copy* of the selection instead.)

   - **Drag the layer.** If the object you want to move is already on its own layer and surrounded by transparency, then you can just drag the layer from the first photo's Layers panel into the destination photo's main image window or tab.

   It doesn't matter which method you use—Elements puts whatever you moved on its own layer in the combined image.

5. **If necessary, use the Move tool to position or scale the transported object, as shown in Figure 6-24.**

   See page 173 for more about using the Move tool.

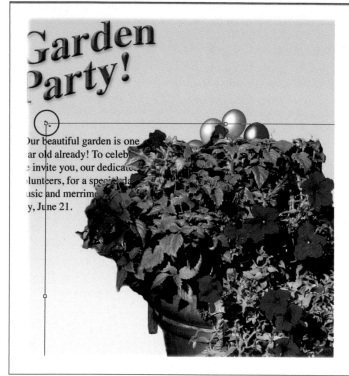

FIGURE 6-24.

If you forget to balance out the relative sizes and resolutions of the photos you're combining, then you can wind up with a giant object in your photo, like these flowers. The solution is simple: Just activate the Move tool and then Shift-drag a corner of the oversized item's resizing box (circled). (You may need to drag the new object around a bit in order to expose a corner.) Don't forget that you can use all the Move tool's features (page 193) on your new object.

6. **Save your work.**

   If you may want to make further adjustments to the object you moved, then save the combined image as a TIFF or Photoshop (.psd) file to keep the layers. (Remember that if you save it as a JPEG, then you lose the layers and you can't easily change or move the new object anymore.)

Here are a few things to keep in mind when copying from one image to another:

• **Watch out for conflicting resolution settings (see page 105).** The destination image (that is, the one receiving the moved layer or object) controls the resolution. So if you bring in a layer that's set to 300 pixels per inch (ppi) and place it on an image that's set to 72 ppi, then Elements sets the object you're moving to 72 ppi; its overall apparent size will increase proportionately as the pixels get spread out more.

TIP It's tricky to work with multiple images in tabs. Instead, try creating floating windows (go to Window→Images→"Float All in Windows"), and then go back to the same submenu and choose Tile or Cascade. Cascade gives you the most flexibility for positioning photos. (You'll need to turn on floating windows in the Editor's preferences *before* you can do this; see page 95.)

- **Lighting matters.** Objects that are lit differently stand out if you try to combine them. If possible, plan ahead and use similar lighting for photos you're thinking about combining.

- **Center the moved layer.** If you're dragging a layer and want Elements to center it in the new image, then Shift-drag the layer.

- **Feather with care.** A little feathering goes a long way toward creating a realistic combined image.

- **Watch your settings.** When you move an object from one image to another, it keeps the blend mode and opacity it had in the first image. For example, if you drag over an object that was at 40% opacity and in Dissolve mode, it will have those same settings in the new image, so you may need to make adjustments.

TIP If you'd like more practice using layers and moving objects between photos, visit this book's Missing CD page at *www.missingmanuals.com/cds* and download the table tutorial, which walks you through most of the basic layer functions.

Retouching

Basic Image Retouching

You may be perfectly happy using Elements only in Quick Fix mode. And that's fine, as long as you understand that you've hardly scratched the surface of what the program can do. Sooner or later, though, you'll probably run across a photo where your best Quick Fix efforts just aren't enough. Or maybe you're simply curious what else Elements has under its hood. That's when you finally get to put all your image-selecting and layering skills to good use.

Elements gives you loads of ways to fix photos beyond the limited options in Quick Fix. This chapter guides you through fixing basic exposure problems, shows you various ways of sharpening photos, and (most importantly) explains how to improve the colors in your images. You'll also learn how to use the amazing Smart Brush tool that lets you apply many common fixes by just brushing over the problem area.

To get the most out of Elements, you need to understand a little about how your camera, computer, and printer think about color. Along with resolution (page 101), color is one of the most important concepts in Elements. After all, almost all the adjustments that image-editing programs make involve changing the color of pixels. So quite a bit of this chapter is about understanding how Elements—and by extension, you—can manipulate images' color.

> **TIP** Most of Elements' advanced-fix dialog boxes have a Preview checkbox that lets you watch what's happening as you adjust the settings. It's a good idea to keep these checkboxes turned on so you can decide whether you're improving things. And for a handy "before" and "after" comparison, simply toggle the checkbox on and off.

Fixing Exposure Problems

Incorrectly exposed photos are *the* number one problem that photographers face. No matter how carefully you set up a shot and how many different settings you try on your camera, it always seems like the picture you really want to keep is the one that's over- or underexposed.

The Quick Fix commands (page 113) can really help photos, but if you've tried using them to bring back a picture that's badly over- or underexposed, you've probably run into the limitations of what Quick Fix can do. Similarly, the Shadows/Highlights command (page 127) can do a lot, but it's not intended to fix a photo whose exposure is totally botched—just ones where the contrast between light and dark areas needs a bit of help. And if you push Smart Fix (page 123) to its limits, the results may be a little strange. In those situations, you need to move on to some of Elements' more powerful tools to help improve the image's exposure.

> **TIP** In this section, you'll learn about the more traditional ways of correcting exposure in Elements, as well as how to use the Smart Brush tool for corrections. But be sure to also check out the Elements Camera Raw Converter (page 264), which can help with your JPEG and TIFF images, too. Your results with non-Raw photos may vary, but the Raw Converter just might turn out to be your best choice.

UP TO SPEED

Understanding Exposure

What exactly *is* exposure, anyway? You almost certainly know a poorly exposed photo when you see one: It's either too light or too dark. But precisely what has gone wrong?

Exposure refers to the amount of light your film (or the sensor in your digital camera) received when you released the shutter. A properly exposed photo shows details in *all* parts of the image—light and dark. Shadows aren't just pits of blackness, and bright areas show more than washed-out splotches of white.

Deciding Which Exposure Fix to Use

When you open a poorly exposed photo in Elements, the first thing to do is figure out what's wrong with it, just like a doctor diagnosing a patient. If the exposure isn't perfect, what exactly is the problem? Here's a list of common symptoms to help figure out what to do next:

- **Everything is too dark.** If your photo is really dark, try adding a Screen layer, as explained on page 221. If it's just a bit too dark, try using Levels (page 236).

- **Everything is too light.** If the whole photo looks washed out, try adding a Multiply layer (page 221). If it's just a bit too light, try Levels (page 236).

- **The photo is mostly OK, but the subject is too dark or the light parts of the photo are too light.** Try the Shadows/Highlights command (page 223) or the Smart Brush tool (page 225).

If you're lucky (or a really skilled photographer), you may not see any of these problems, in which case, skip to page 236 if you want to make the image's colors pop. And if you're lucky enough to have *bracketed* exposures (multiple exposures of exactly the same image), then check out the Exposure Merge feature (page 286), which makes it simple to blend those into one properly exposed image.

> **NOTE** You may have noticed that Brightness/Contrast wasn't mentioned in the preceding list. A lot of people jump for the Brightness/Contrast controls when facing a poorly exposed photo. That's logical—after all, these dials usually help improve the picture on your TV. But in Elements, about 99 percent of the time, you've got a whole slew of powerful tools—like Levels and the Shadows/Highlights command—that can do much more than Brightness/Contrast can, but feel free to give it a try when you need to make only very subtle changes.

Fixing Major Exposure Problems

If your photo is completely over- or underexposed, you need to add special layers to correct the problem. You follow the same steps to fix either issue; the only difference is the layer blend mode (page 190) you use: *Multiply* darkens an image's exposure while *Screen* lightens it. Figure 7-1 shows Multiply in action and gives you a sense of the limitations of this technique if your photo's exposure is *really* far gone. You can download the file *brickwindow.jpg* from this book's Missing CD page at *www.missingmanuals.com/cds* if you'd like to try the different exposure fixes yourself.

Be careful, though: If only part of your photo is out of whack, using Multiply or Screen can ruin the exposure of the parts that were OK to start with, because these layers increase or decrease the exposure of the *whole* photo. So if the exposure problem doesn't affect the entire image, try the Smart Brush (page 225) or Shadows/Highlights command (page 223) first. You can also use a layer mask to restrict your changes to only part of the image; see page 202 to learn how.

If the whole photo needs an exposure correction, here's how to use layers to fix it:

1. **Duplicate your image layer.**

   Open your photo and press Ctrl+J/⌘-J or go to Layer→Duplicate Layer. Check to be sure the duplicate layer is the active layer.

2. **In the Layers panel, change the new layer's blend mode.**

   In the drop-down menu in the panel's upper left, choose Multiply if the photo is overexposed or Screen if it's underexposed. (Make sure you change the *duplicate* layer's mode, not the original layer's.)

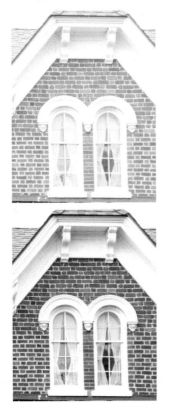

FIGURE 7-1.

In photography terms, each Multiply layer you add is roughly equivalent to stopping your camera down one f-stop, at least as far as the dark areas are concerned.

Top: This photo is totally overexposed, and it looks like there's no detail there at all.

Bottom: Multiply layers darken things enough to bring back a lot of the washed-out areas and bring out quite a bit of detail. But as you can see here, even Elements can't do much in areas where there's no detail at all, like the sky and the white framing around these windows.

3. **If needed, adjust the layer's opacity.**

   If the effect of the new layer is too strong, then in the Layers panel, lower the Opacity setting to reduce the new layer's opacity.

4. **If you decide that part of the image was actually better exposed** *before* **you added the new layer, mask out the areas where the exposure was OK.**

   Add a mask to the duplicate layer, and then paint out the areas where the original image was properly exposed, so that the background layer shows through (page 205 explains how). Remember that you can also paint with shades of gray to control how much of the original shows through. That can be very helpful in getting the most realistic results from this technique.

5. **Repeat as necessary.**

You may have to use as many as five or six layers if your photo is in really bad shape. If you need extra layers, you'll probably want them at 100 percent opacity, so you can just keep pressing Ctrl+J/⌘-J to duplicate the current top layer, including its layer mask (if you added one). You're more likely to need several layers to fix overexposure than underexposure. And, of course, there are limits to what Elements can do for a blindingly overexposed image. Overexposure is usually tougher to fix than underexposure, especially if the area is blown out, as explained in the box below.

Avoiding Blowouts

An area of a photo is *blown out* when it's so overexposed that it appears plain white—in other words, your camera didn't record any data at all for that area. (Elements isn't great with total underexposure—pure black—either, but that doesn't happen quite as often. Most underexposed photos have *some* tonal gradations in them, even if you can't see them very well.)

A blowout is as disastrous in photography as it is when you're driving. Even Elements can't fix blowouts, because there's no data for it to work with. So you're stuck with the fixes discussed in this chapter, which are never as good as a properly exposed original.

When you're taking pictures and choosing camera settings, remember that it's generally easier to correct underexposure than overexposure. So if you live where there's really bright sunlight most of the time, you may want to make a habit of backing your exposure compensation down a hair. Depending on your camera, subject, and the average ambient glare, try starting with the exposure compensation set at −.3 and adjusting from there.

You can also try *bracketing* shots—taking multiple photos of exactly the same subject with different exposure settings. Then you can combine several exposures for maximum effect using Elements' Exposure Merge feature (page 286).

The Shadows/Highlights Command

This command is one of Elements' best features. It's an incredibly powerful tool for adjusting only the dark or light areas of a photo without messing up the rest of it. Figure 7-2 shows what a great help it can be.

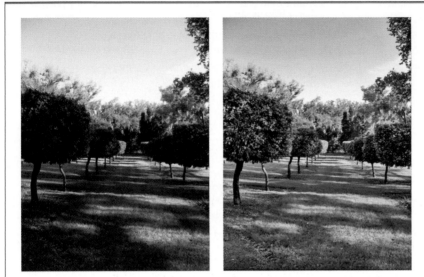

FIGURE 7-2.

The Shadows/Highlights command can bring back details in photos where you were sure there was no information at all—but sometimes at a cost.

Left: The sky and the grass aren't bad, but you'd never know there were oranges on these trees.

Right: A dose of Shadows/Highlights unearths plenty of details, although the overall effect is a bit flat when you push this command this far. This photo needs lots more work, but at least now you can see what kind of trees they are.

The Shadows/Highlights command in Expert Mode works pretty much the same way it does in Quick Fix (page 127). The single flaw in this great feature is that you can't apply it as an Adjustment layer (page 207), so you may want to apply Shadows/Highlights to a duplicate layer. That way, you can discard the changes later on if you want to take another whack at adjusting the photo. In any case, it's easy to make amazing changes to your photos with Shadows/Highlights. Here's how:

1. **Open a photo and duplicate the image layer (Ctrl+J/⌘-J) if you want to.**

   If you haven't edited the photo before, this is usually the Background layer, but you can use this command on any layer. Duplicating the image layer makes it easier to undo Shadows/Highlights later if you change your mind.

2. **Go to Enhance→Adjust Lighting→Shadows/Highlights.**

   Elements opens the Shadows/Highlights dialog box and makes your photo about 30 shades lighter. Don't panic—as soon as you select this command, the Lighten Shadows setting automatically jumps to 35 percent, which is way too much for most photos. Just shove the slider back to 0 to undo this change before you start making corrections.

3. **Adjust the sliders in the Shadows/Highlights dialog box until you like the result.**

   The sliders do exactly what they say: Lighten Shadows makes the dark areas of the photo lighter, and Darken Highlights makes the light areas darker. (Midtone

Contrast is discussed in a moment.) Dragging the sliders to the right increases their effect.

4. **When your photo looks good, click OK.**

> **TIP** If you're applying Shadows/Highlights on a duplicate layer, you can use a layer mask (page 202) to restrict your changes to only certain areas of the image.

The Shadows/Highlights dialog box is a cinch to use because you just make decisions based on what you're seeing. When you're using it, keep these tips in mind:

- **You may want to add a smidgen of the opposite tool to balance things out.** For example, if you're lightening shadows, you may get better results by giving the Darken Highlights slider a teeny nudge, too.

- **The Midtone Contrast slider can help keep your photo from looking flat after you're done with Shadows/Highlights, especially if you've made big adjustments.** Move the Midtone Contrast slider to the right to increase the photo's contrast. Doing so usually adds a bit of a darkening effect, so you may need to adjust one of the other sliders after you use it.

- **You can overdo the Shadows/Highlights feature.** If you see halos around the objects in your photo, you've pushed the settings too far.

> **TIP** If the Shadows/Highlights feature washes out your photo's colors—making everyone look like they've been through the laundry too many times—adjust the color intensity with one of the Saturation commands, either in Quick Fix or Expert Mode (as described on page 129). Watch people's skin tones when increasing the saturation—if the subjects in your photo start looking like sunless-tanning-lotion disaster victims, you've gone too far. Also, check out the Vibrance slider in Quick Fix (page 129), or try adjusting colors with Color Curves (page 325).

Correcting Part of an Image

The Shadows/Highlights command is great if you want to adjust *all* the light or dark areas of a photo, but what if you want to tweak the exposure only in certain areas? Or what if you like the photo's background just fine, but you want to tweak the subject a little? You can use a layer mask on a duplicate layer and make adjustments there, or select the area you want to tweak (see Chapter 5 for more about selecting), copy the selection to a new layer, and then make adjustments to that layer. But Elements gives you an even simpler way to apply a correction to just the area you want: the Smart Brush tools.

■ CORRECTING COLOR WITH A BRUSH

The Smart Brush is actually two different tools—the Smart Brush and the Detail Smart Brush—that work just like the Quick Selection tool and the regular Selection Brush, respectively. Only instead of merely selecting part of your photo, they also *edit* it as you brush. So you may be able to make targeted adjustments to different areas of your photo just by drawing a line over them. (The smart brushes don't always work, but they're truly amazing when they do.) The smart brushes always put the changes they make on new layers, so it's easy to edit the areas they affect, and they don't alter your original image.

This section explains how to correct exposure with the Smart Brush, but you have a whole menu of different things you can do with the Smart Brush: Change the color of someone's jacket, apply different special effects, put a little lipstick on someone, convert an area to black and white—the list goes on and on. As a matter of fact, if you've been using Quick Fix, you may well have met the Smart Brush already, although it doesn't go by that name there: The Whiten Teeth tool in the Quick Fix window uses the Smart Brush to apply its effects.

Here's how to put this nifty pair of tools to work:

1. **Open a photo in Expert Mode, and then activate the Smart Brush.**

   Click its icon in the Tools panel (it's in the Enhance section: the wide house-painter's brush just below the Red Eye tool) or press F. Check the Tool Options to be sure you have the regular Smart Brush. It shares its Tools panel slot with the Detail Smart Brush, which works like the Selection Brush in that it changes only the area directly under the brush cursor instead of automatically expanding your selection to include the whole object you brush over. For now, see if the regular Smart Brush is smart enough to select the area you want.

2. **Choose the correction you want to apply.**

   In the Tool Options area, click the thumbnail to the right of the brush icons and then choose from the drop-down menu. (Both smart brushes have the same Tool Options settings, discussed below. The important one is explained in Figure 7-3.) Adobe calls these choices Smart Paint.

3. **Drag over the area you want to change.**

   This step is just like using the Quick Selection tool (page 143). You don't need to make a careful selection, since Elements calculates the area it thinks you want to include and creates the selection for you. A simple line should do it.

4. **Tweak the selection, if necessary.**

   If Elements didn't quite select everything you want, then add to the selection by brushing again. Your adjustment disappears while you brush, unless you've got the Inverse checkbox turned on, in which case your selected area looks the same as the rest of the photo. (If you're doing an inverse black and white, for example, your colored area becomes black and white like the rest of the photo till you let go of the mouse button.)

   If you *still* need to modify the selection, then use the selection-editing tools explained in Figure 7-4. If you're really unhappy with the Smart Brush's selection talents, then head back to the Tool Options area and switch to the Detail Smart Brush instead.

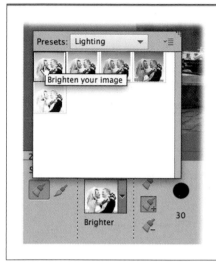

FIGURE 7-3.

Your Smart Paint options (the things you can do with the Smart Brush) are grouped into the categories listed in this drop-down menu. Each thumbnail image shows that option applied to a photo. For exposure issues, start by looking at the Lighting options (choose Lighting from the drop-down menu at the top of the palette). You can choose to make the area you're about to paint darker or brighter, increase or decrease the contrast, or even put a spotlight effect on it. Just put your cursor over each thumbnail to find the effect you want and then click it to select it.

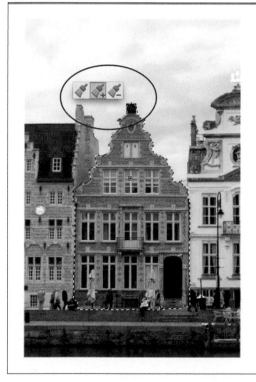

FIGURE 7-4.

Once you've used the Smart Brush, a little icon called a pin (the red icon in the circled area) appears in your photo to let you know that the selected region is now under the power of the Smart Brush. Click the pin and you see a trio of icons (circled) that let you edit the selected area. From left to right, the icons mean New Selection, "Add to Selection," and "Subtract from Selection."

If you're pressed for time, there's an even quicker way to modify your selection: Just drag again to expand the area affected by the Smart Brush (or to use the same adjustment on another part of your photo). The Smart Brush always adds new areas when you click again; it doesn't start a new selection each time you click the way the regular selection tools do. Alt-drag to remove changes from an area.

You'll see the pin anytime the Smart Brush is activated again, even after you've closed and saved your photo.

You can invert a selection by turning on the Inverse checkbox in the Tool Options. Then what you brush over is *excluded* from your selection, and everything else is included. You can turn on the checkbox before or after using the Smart Brush, as long as it's still the active tool. If you come back to the Smart Brush after using another tool, then you need to reactivate your Smart Brush selection by clicking the pin shown in Figure 7-4 before you can invert the selection, thus inverting the area covered by the effect.

5. **Once the right area is selected, adjust the effect (if necessary).**

The Smart Brush gives you several ways to change what it's done:

- **Choose a different adjustment.** Just head to the Tool Options and choose a different Smart Paint adjustment. Elements automatically updates your image.

- **Add another Smart Paint adjustment.** If you want to tweak your image in a second way, head to the right end of the Tool Options area, click the little four-lined square, and then choose Reset Tool. Then you can drag in your image again and the Smart Brush will put down an *additional* adjustment instead of just changing what you've already done. You can also use this to double up an effect—to add Lipstick twice, for instance, if you thought the first pass was too faint. Each Smart Brush adjustment gets its own pin, so if you have two Smart Brush adjustments in your photo, then you'll have two pins in it, too. (Each pin is a different color.) You can add as many different adjustments as you like.

- **Change the settings for Smart Paint you've already applied.** Rather than adding another Smart Paint layer to increase the effect, you can adjust the settings for the changes you've already made. Right-click/Control-click the pin in your image, and then choose Change Adjustment Settings. Depending on the kind of adjustment you've made, a window or panel pops up showing the current settings so you can adjust the effect you're brushing on. Since the Smart Brush uses Adjustment layers to make most of its changes, the available settings are the same as they would be if you had created a regular Adjustment layer. For example, if you're using the Brighter option, as shown in Figure 7-3, then you get the settings for a Brightness/ Contrast Adjustment layer.

NOTE If you're using certain of the black-and-white adjustments, you may not be able to edit them afterward. If you try, you'll just see a weird message telling you that the layer was created in the full version of Photoshop, even though you know it wasn't. You can delete the Adjustment layer or edit its layer mask, but that's all. Also, if you apply Effects (page 456) with the Smart Brush (the thumbnails for Effects look like a tree instead of the photo thumbnails you normally see—the Artistic Effects are all Effects, for example, although Reverse Effects and Special Effects aren't), you can't do anything to those with the brush once you're done, except change the area they cover.

6. **When you're happy with how things look, you're done.**

You can always go back to your Smart Paint edits again. Just activate the Smart Brush (click it in the Tools panel or press F) and the pin(s) appear so you can easily change what you've done. You can eliminate Smart Brush changes by right-clicking/Control-clicking the adjusted area and then choosing Delete Adjustment (the Smart Brush needs to be active), or by going to the Layers panel and discarding their layers (you can do this anytime, whether the Smart Brush is active or not). You can also edit a Smart Brush adjustment's layer mask the way you'd edit any other layer mask, as described on page 205. But usually it's easier just to click the pin and then adjust your selection.

The Smart Brush is especially handy for projects like creating images that are part color and part black-and-white, or even for silly special effects like making one object from a photo look like it's been isolated on a '60s-style psychedelic background.

> **TIP** Check out the textures available for the smart brushes—they're handy for creating backgrounds for isolated objects. To find them, head to the Tool Options area, click the Smart Paint thumbnail, and in the palette that appears, choose Textures from the Presets drop-down menu.

The Smart Brush has several Tool Options settings, but you usually don't need to use them:

- **Smart Paint.** Click this thumbnail image for a pop-out menu of all the possible Smart Brush adjustments, grouped into categories. (If you put your cursor over the thumbnail, the tooltip that appears says "Choose a Preset," but Adobe calls these settings Smart Paint in the Elements Help files and elsewhere.)

- **New selection.** Click the left brush icon to add the same effect elsewhere in your photo. (Just clicking someplace else with the brush does the same thing. Be careful, though: The brush may think that the new area is a continuation of your previous selection, so it may combine the two. If that happens, try using a smaller brush.)

- **Add to selection.** Click this next brush icon to put the Smart Brush in add-to-selection mode (the brush enters this mode automatically even if you don't click this icon).

- **Subtract from selection.** Did the Smart Brush take in more area than you wanted? Click the rightmost brush icon before brushing away what you don't want, or just Alt-drag/Option-drag.

- **Brush Size.** If you have trouble getting a good selection, then try adjusting the size of your brush.

- **Brush Settings.** Click this button to change the brush's size, hardness, spacing, angle, or roundness. If you have a graphics tablet, the Size setting in this panel gives you a couple of options to control brush size on the fly.

- **Inverse.** If you want to apply the adjustment to the area you *didn't* select with the Smart Brush, then turn on this checkbox.

- **Refine Edge.** Click this button if you want to make the edges of your effect sleeker, or to extract the area you've edited for use elsewhere. Page 145 has details.

TIP If you like the *idea* of the Smart Brush but never seem to find exactly the adjustments you want, or if you always want to change the settings you apply, then you can create your own Smart Paint options, as described in the box on page 231.

◼ Controlling the Colors You See

You want your photos to look as good as possible and to have beautiful, breathtaking color. That's probably why you bought Elements. But now that you've got the program, you're likely having a little trouble getting things to look the way you want. Does the following situation sound familiar?

- Your photos look great onscreen, but your prints are washed out, too dark, or the colors are all a little wrong.

- Your photos look fine in programs like Word or Windows Explorer, but they look awful in Elements.

What's going on? The answer has to do with the fact that Elements is a *color-managed* program. That means Elements uses information about your monitor when deciding how to display images. Color management is the science of making sure that the color in your images is always exactly the same, no matter who opens your file or what kind of hardware they're viewing it on or printing it with. If you think of all the different monitor and printer models out there, you get an idea of what a big job this is.

Graphics pros spend their whole lives grappling with color management, and you can find plenty of books about the finer points of it. At its most sophisticated, color management is complicated enough to make you curl up in the fetal position and swear never to create another picture. Luckily, Elements makes color management easy. Most of the time, you have only two things to deal with: your monitor calibration and your color space. The following pages cover both.

NOTE There are a couple of other color-related settings for printing, too, but you can deal with those when you're ready to print. Chapter 16 explains them.

Calibrating Your Monitor

Most programs pay no attention to your monitor's color settings, but color-managed ones like Elements rely on the *profile*—the information your computer stores about your monitor's settings—when it decides how to display a photo onscreen or how to print it. If that profile isn't accurate, the color in Elements won't be either.

So you may need to *calibrate* your monitor, which is a way of adjusting its settings. A properly calibrated monitor makes all the difference in the world in getting great-looking results. If your photos look bad only in Elements or if your printed pictures don't look anything like they do onscreen, then calibrating is a good way to begin fixing the problem.

Making Smart Paint

While the Smart Brush offers a lot of different Smart Paint presets, you may find it slightly frustrating that Elements doesn't have a setting for the particular corrections you use most frequently. No problem—as long as you can use Adjustment layers (page 207) to achieve the effect you want, you can create your own Smart Paint presets, and they'll appear in the menus right along with the ones from Adobe.

To get started in Windows 7 or Vista, go to *C:\ProgramData\Adobe\Photoshop Elements\11.0\Photo Creations\adjustment layers*. (In XP, it's *C:\Documents and Settings\All Users\Application Data\Adobe\Photoshop Elements\11.0\Photo Creations\adjustment layers*.) These files are hidden, so you need to turn on hidden files to see them (the tip on page 600 tells you how). On a Mac, go to *[your hard drive]\Library\Application Support\Adobe\Photoshop Elements\11.0\Photo Creations\adjustment layers*. (If you use OS X 10.7 [Lion] or 10.8 [Mountain Lion], see page xxiii.) No matter what your operating system, you see three files for each Smart Paint preset:

- **A PSD file** containing the preset's actual settings.
- **A thumbnail file,** which you need if you want to have a little preview in the menu.
- **An XML file** that tells Elements where in the menus to display the preset, like whether to show it in the "Black and White" or Lighting category, for instance. These files all have the word "metadata" in their names.

Basically, you need to edit *copies* of these files to make new ones for each preset you want to add. Here's how:

1. **Open one of the PSD files in the Editor.** Pick the one that's the closest to what you want. The PSD file is a 160-pixel square image with an Adjustment layer on it. Save the file with a new name so you don't mess up the original.

2. **Change the settings.** In the Layers panel, click the Adjustment layer to select it, and then—in the Adjustments panel—tweak its settings. Then save the file.

3. **Create a new thumbnail.** You can just save the original thumbnail with a new name. (Thumbnails are 74-pixel square JPEGs, in case you want to make a new one from scratch.)

4. **Create a new XML file.** Open the XML file and do a Save As, changing the name to that of the new Smart Paint choice you just created. (In Windows, open the file with Notepad, a text editor; in the Save As dialog box, choose All Files in the "Save as type" menu. On a Mac, use TextEdit, but be sure to save the file as plain text [.txt].) Then look through the contents of the file for a line like this:

```
<name value="$$$/content/adjustmentlayers/
ContrastHigh=Contrast High" />
```

In this example, you'd be adapting the Contrast High preset, so you just find the two instances of its name (note that there's no space in the first one), and then change them to the name of your new preset. You can also edit the preset's tooltip (the text that appears when you point to its thumbnail) and the category (you can use an existing category or create a new one).

When you're finished making changes, save the file. Name it *[my effect].metadata* (replace "my effect" with the preset's actual name). Make sure all three files are in the "adjustment layers" folder. Next, in Windows 7 or Vista, go to *C:\ProgramData\Adobe\Photoshop Elements\11.0\Locale\en_US* (this path is different if you aren't in the United States), and delete *MediaDatabase.db3* to refresh the list of presets. (Note that deleting this file will also delete all items in your Favorites panel [page 525].) In XP, it's in *C:\Documents and Settings\All Users\Application Data\Adobe\Photoshop Elements\11.0\Locale\en_us* (or your location). In Mac OS X, it's *[your hard drive]/Library/Application Support/Adobe/Photoshop Elements/11.0/Locale/en_US* (or your location). If you use OS X 10.7 (Lion) or 10.8 (Mountain Lion), see page xxiii. The next time you start Elements, you should see your new Smart Paint preset alongside the ones that came with Elements.

■ GETTING STARTED WITH CALIBRATING

Calibrating a monitor sounds intimidating, but it's actually not that difficult—some people think it's even kind of fun. And it's worth it, because afterward your monitor may look about a thousand times better than you thought it could. Calibrating may even make it easier to read text in Word, for instance, because the contrast is better. Your calibrating options, from best to only OK, are:

- **Use a colorimeter.** This method may sound disturbingly scientific, but it's actually the easiest. A *colorimeter* is just a device with special software that does the calibration for you. Using such a device is much more accurate than calibrating by eye. For a long time, only pros could afford colorimeters, but these days if you shop around, you can find the Pantone Huey or the Spyder2express for about $70. More professional calibrators like the i1Display Pro or the ColorMunki Display aren't much more expensive. If you're serious about controlling colors in Elements, this is by far your best option.

> **NOTE** The colorimeter software will probably ask you to set your monitor's brightness and contrast before you begin calibrating, even though most LCD monitors don't have adjustable dials for these settings. If you're happy with your monitor's current brightness and contrast, you can safely ignore this step. Unless you have a reason to use different settings, for an LCD monitor, you usually want to set the white point to 6500 (Kelvin) and your gamma to 2.2.

- **Software.** Whether you have a Windows computer or a Mac, you likely have some kind of software that can help you improve what you see:

    - **Windows:** There's a good chance that the drivers (software) for your computer's graphics card include some kind of calibration tool. Go to Control Panel→Appearance and Personalization→Display→Calibrate Color to use the Windows calibrator (in Windows XP: Display→Properties→Settings→ Advanced) to see what you have.

    - **Mac:** If you go to System Preferences→Displays→Color→Calibrate, you can use Apple's Display Calibrator Assistant to calibrate your monitor—sort of (see Figure 7-5). You can also find lots of calibration programs online, but most of them aren't much, if any, better than the Assistant.

- **Adobe Gamma.** If you have an older Windows version of Elements (Elements 5 or earlier), you may have this program, which used to come with Elements. It's pretty ancient, was never meant to work with anything but old CRT monitors (the big, fat ones like old-fashioned televisions), and doesn't work in Windows 7 or Vista. If you happen to have Adobe Gamma, it's better than nothing, but it's probably less useful than any other program you might have for adjusting your display.

If your photos still look a little odd even after you've calibrated your monitor, you may need to turn on the Ignore EXIF setting in the Editor's preferences; see Figure 7-6.

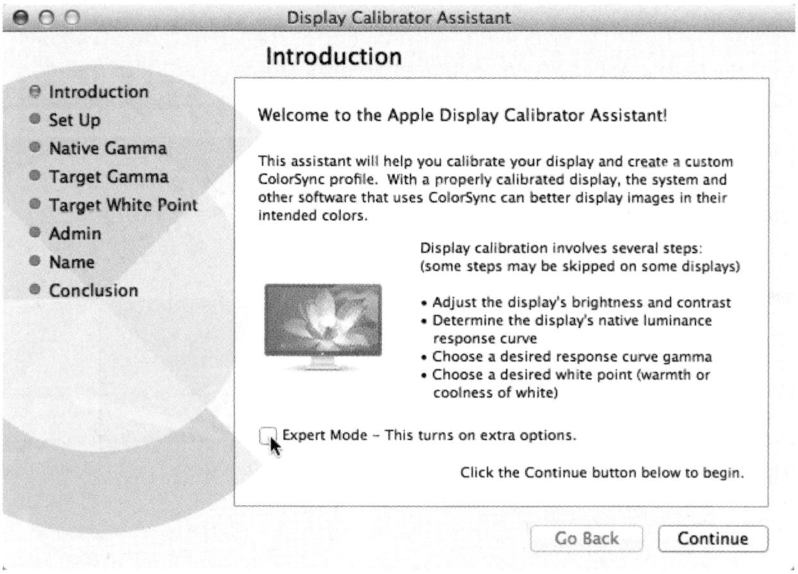

FIGURE 7-5.

Using the Display Calibrator Assistant is pretty simple. You can do a basic calibration that sets your gamma and white point, or turn on the Expert Mode checkbox for a more elaborate color-balancing process. In Expert Mode, you look at a series of apples (of course!) on a striped background and adjust things till the apples blend into the background. The problem is that it's almost impossible to get accurate results from a visual calibration. The Calibrator Assistant is better than nothing, but a colorimeter is a much better option.

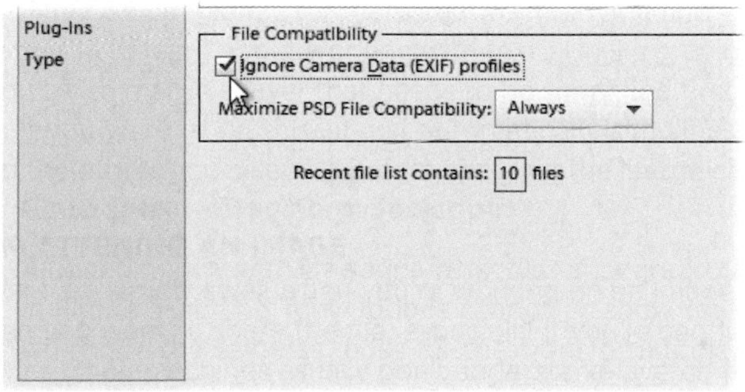

FIGURE 7-6.

If all the images from your digital camera have a color cast (usually red or yellow), go to Edit→Preferences→Saving Files/Adobe Photoshop Elements Editor→Preferences→Saving Files, and turn on "Ignore Camera Data (EXIF) profiles." Some cameras embed nonstandard color information in their files, so this setting tells Elements to pay no attention to it, which should make your photos display and print properly.

Choosing a Color Space

The other thing you may need to do to get good color from Elements is to check which *color space* the program is using. Color spaces are standards that Elements uses to define your colors. That may sound pretty abstruse, but they're simply ways of defining what colors mean. For example, when someone says "green," what do you envision: a lush emerald color, a deep forest green, a bright lime, or something else?

Choosing a color space helps make sure that everything that handles a digital file—Elements, your monitor, your printer, and so on—sees the file's colors the same way. Over the years, the graphics industry has agreed on standards so that everyone has the same understanding of what you mean when you say "red" or "green"—as long as you specify which color space (set of standards) you're using.

Elements gives you only two color spaces to pick from: *sRGB* (also called *sRGB IEC61966-2.1* if you want to impress your geek friends) and *Adobe RGB*. When you choose one, you're telling Elements which set of standards you want it to apply to your photos.

If you're happy with the colors you see on your monitor in Elements and you like the prints you're getting, you don't need to make any changes. If, on the other hand, you aren't satisfied with what Elements is showing you, you'll probably want to modify your color space, which you can do in the Color Settings dialog box (Figure 7-7). Go to Edit→Color Settings or press Shift+Ctrl+K/Shift-⌘-K. Here are your choices:

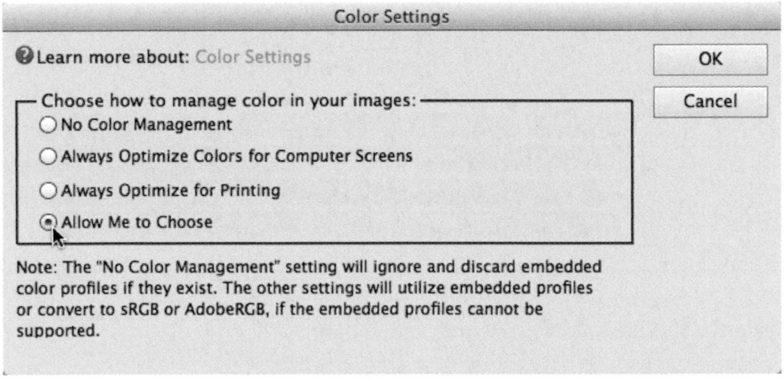

FIGURE 7-7.

If you select the "Allow Me to Choose" option here, you see the Missing Profile dialog box each time you open a previously untagged image. (You'll learn about color tags in a sec.)

- **No Color Management.** This setting makes Elements ignore any information that your file already contains, like color space data from your camera, and doesn't attempt to add any color info to the file. (When you do a Save As, there's a checkbox that offers you the option of embedding your monitor profile. Don't turn on this checkbox, since your monitor profile is best left for the monitor's own use, and putting the profile into the file can cause trouble if you ever send it someplace else for printing.)

- **Always Optimize Colors for Computer Screens.** This option selects the sRGB color space, which is what most web browsers use; this is a good choice when you're preparing graphics for the Web. Many online printing services also prefer sRGB files. (If you've used an early version of Elements, this is the same as the old Limited Color Management option.)

- **Always Optimize for Printing.** This option uses the Adobe RGB color space, which is wider than sRGB, meaning it allows more color gradations. This is sometimes your best choice for printing—but not always. Don't be afraid to try one of the other settings instead. Many home inkjet printers actually cope better with sRGB or no color management than with Adobe RGB. (For Elements veterans, this setting used to be called Full Color Management.)

- **Allow Me to Choose.** This option assumes that you're using the sRGB color space, but lets you assign either an Adobe RGB tag, an sRGB tag, or no tag at all (color tags are explained in a moment). After you select this option, each time you open a file that isn't sRGB, you see the dialog box shown in Figure 7-7 which you can use to assign a different profile to a photo. Just save the image once without a profile (turn off the ICC [International Color Consortium] Profile checkbox in the Save As dialog box), and then reopen it and choose the profile you want from this dialog box. Or, the box on page 236 explains an easier way to convert a color profile if you need to make a change.

So what's your best option? Once again, if everything looks good, leave it alone. Otherwise, for general use, you're probably best off starting with No Color Management, and then trying the others if that doesn't work.

When you save the file, Elements attempts to embed it with a *color tag*, info about the file's color space—either Adobe RGB or sRGB. (This kind of tag isn't related to the Organizer tags you read about in Chapter 2.) If you don't want a color tag—also known as an *ICC Profile*—in your file, just turn off the ICC Profile checkbox before saving the file. Figure 7-8 shows where to find the profile information in the Save As dialog box, and how to turn the whole process off.

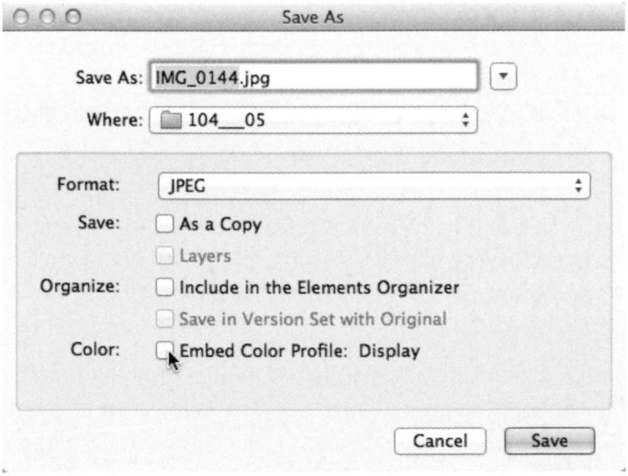

FIGURE 7-8.

When you save a file, Elements offers to embed a color tag in it. You can safely turn off the ICC Profile checkbox and leave the file untagged. (Assigning a profile is helpful because then any program that sees the file knows what color standards you're working with. But if you're new to Elements, you'll usually have an easier time if you don't start embedding profiles in files without a good reason.)

NOTE Elements automatically opens files tagged with a color space other than the one you're working in without letting you know what it's just done, so you won't know that there's a mismatch between the file's ICC profile and the color space you're using in Elements. (If, on the other hand, you try to open a file in a color *mode* that Elements can't handle, like CMYK, then Elements offers to convert it to a mode you can use.) For example, if you have an Adobe RGB file and you're working in "Always Optimize Colors for Computer Screens," Elements doesn't warn you about the profile mismatch the way early versions of the program did—it just opens the file. So if you consistently get strange color shifts when you open your Elements-edited files in other programs, check to be sure there isn't a profile mismatch between your images and Elements.

POWER USERS' CLINIC

Converting Profiles in Elements

If you're a color-management maven, Elements gives you a feature you'll really appreciate—the ability to convert an image's ICC profile from one color space to another. If you've been working in, say, sRGB and now you want your photo to have the Adobe RGB profile, you can convert it by going to Image→Convert Color Profile→"Convert to Adobe RGB Profile." If you're in Adobe RGB, you'll see "Convert to sRGB Profile" instead; your current color profile choice is grayed out. The same submenu also lets you remove the current image profile.

This is a true conversion: It correctly maps out your image's colors for the new profile, so they don't shift the way they might if you were just to tag a photo with a different profile. Why would you want to do such a conversion? If, for example, you use Adobe RGB when editing photos, but you're sending them to an online printing service that wants sRGB instead, then you may want to think about converting them.

Using Levels

People who've used Elements for a while will tell you that the Levels command is one of the program's most essential tools. You can fix an amazing array of problems simply by adjusting the level of each *color channel*. Each color displayed on your monitor is composed of three channels: red, green, and blue. In Elements, you can make very precise adjustments to images by adjusting these channels separately.

Just as its name suggests, Levels adjusts the amount, or level, of each color in an image. You can make several different adjustments with Levels, from generally brightening a photo's colors to fixing a color cast (page 244 has more about color casts). Many digital photo enthusiasts treat almost every picture they take to a dose of Levels because there's no better way to polish up the color in a photo.

The way Levels works is fairly complex. Start by thinking of the possible ranges of brightness in any photo on a scale from 0 (black) to 255 (white). Some photos may have pixels in them that fall at both those extremes, but most photos don't. Even the ones that do may not have the full range of brightness in each individual color channel. Most of the time, you'll find some empty space at one or both ends of the scale.

When you use Levels, you tell Elements to consider the range of colors available in your photo as the *total* tonal range it has to work with, and Elements redistributes the image's colors accordingly. Basically, you just get rid of the empty space at the ends of the scale of possibilities. This can dramatically change the color distribution in a photo, as you can see in Figure 7-9.

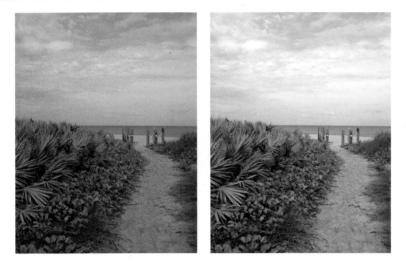

FIGURE 7-9.

A simple Levels adjustment can make a huge difference in the way your photos look.

Left: The gray-green cast to this photo makes everything rather dull.

Right: Levels not only gets rid of the color cast, but it also helps give the photo better contrast and sharpness.

Fortunately, it's much, much easier to *use* Levels than to understand it, as you know if you've tried Auto Levels in Quick Fix (page 125). That command is great for quick fixes. But if you really need to massage an image, Levels has a lot more under the hood than you can access in Quick Fix. The next section shows you how to get at these settings.

Understanding the Histogram

Before you get started adjusting Levels, you need to understand the heart, soul, and brain of the Levels dialog box: the histogram, shown in Figure 7-10. (You can call up this dialog box by pressing Ctrl+L/⌘-L.)

The histogram is the black bumpy mound in the middle of the dialog box. It's really nothing more than a bar graph indicating the distribution of the colors in your photo—there's just no space between the bars, which is why it looks like mountains.

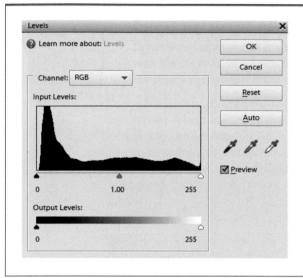

FIGURE 7-10.

One of the scariest sights in Elements, the Levels dialog box is actually your friend. If it frightens you, take comfort in knowing that you can always click the Auto button here, which is the same Auto Levels command as in Quick Fix. But it's worth persevering because the other options here give you much better control over the end results.

From left to right, the histogram shows the brightness range from dark to light (the 0 to 255 mentioned earlier in this section). The height of the "mountain" at any given point shows how many pixels in your photo have that particular brightness. You can tell a lot about a photo by where the mound is before you adjust it, as explained in Figure 7-11.

Above the histogram is the Channel menu. If you click it, you can choose to see a separate histogram for each individual color channel. You can adjust all three channels at once with the RGB setting, or change each channel separately for maximum control.

The histogram contains so much info about your photo that Adobe also makes it available in the Expert Mode in its own panel (Figure 7-12), so you can always see it and use it to monitor how you're changing the colors in an image. Once you get fluent in reading Histogramese, you'll probably want to keep this panel around.

The histogram is just a graph, and you don't do anything to it directly. When you use Levels, you use the histogram as a guide so that you can tell Elements what to consider the black and white points—that is, the darkest and lightest points—in your photo. (Remember, you're thinking in terms of brightness values, not shades of color, for these settings.)

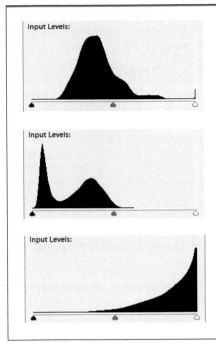

FIGURE 7-11.

Top: If the bars in the histogram are all smooshed together like this, your photo doesn't have a lot of tonal range. As long as you like how the photo looks, that's not important. But if you're unhappy with the photo's color, it's usually harder to get it exactly right in this kind of photo than in one that has a wider tonal range.

Middle: If the mound is bunched up on the left side, your photo is underexposed.

Bottom: If you just have a big lump on the right side, your photo is overexposed.

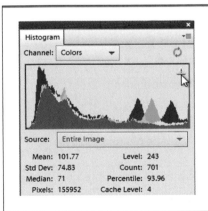

FIGURE 7-12.

If you keep the histogram available, you can always see what effect your changes are having on the photo's color distribution. To get this nifty Technicolor view, go to Window→Histogram and then choose Colors from the panel's Channel drop-down menu. To update the histogram to reflect any changes you've made to the image, click the triangle in its upper right as shown here, or the circling arrows above it. If you're really into statistics, there are a bunch of them at the bottom of this panel, but if you're not a pro, you can safely ignore these numbers.

Once you've set these end points (you'll learn how in a moment), you can adjust the *midtones*—the tones in between that would appear gray in a black-and-white photo. If that seems complicated, it's not—at least, not when you're actually doing it. Once you've made a Levels adjustment, the next time you open the Levels dialog box, you'll see that your histogram now runs the whole length of the scale because you've told Elements to redistribute your colors so that they cover the full dark-to-light range.

The next two sections show you—finally!—how to actually adjust an image with Levels.

> **TIP** Once you learn how to interpret the histograms in Elements, you can try your hand with your camera's histogram (if it has one). It's really hard to judge how well your picture turned out when all you have to go by is your camera's tiny LCD screen, so your camera's histogram can be a big help in figuring out how well exposed your shot was. Alas, you'll need to check your owner's manual to figure out how to display the histogram on your particular camera.

Adjusting Levels: The Eyedropper Method

One way to adjust Levels is to set the image's black, white, and/or gray points by using the eyedroppers in the Levels Adjustments panel. It's quite simple—just follow these steps:

1. **Bring up the Levels Adjustments panel by selecting Layer→New Adjustment Layer→Levels.**

   If you like, you can name the layer in the New Layer dialog box that appears, or just click OK to get on with it and create the layer. If you don't want a separate layer for your Levels adjustment, go to Enhance→Adjust Lighting→Levels or press Ctrl+L/⌘-L instead. (You'll get a dialog box instead of the panel, but it works exactly the same way.) But making the Levels changes on an Adjustment layer gives you more flexibility for making future changes.

2. **If necessary, move the Adjustments panel or the Levels dialog box out of the way so you have a good view of your photo.**

   The dialog box loves to plunk itself down smack in the middle of the most important part of your image. Just grab it by the top bar and drag it somewhere else.

3. **In the Adjustments panel or Levels dialog box, click the black eyedropper.**

   In the Adjustments panel, from top to bottom, the eyedroppers are black, gray, and white. In the dialog box they're arranged from left to right instead.

4. **Move your cursor over your photo and click an area that should be black.**

   Should be, not *is*. That's a mistake lots of people make the first time they use the Levels eyedroppers: They click a spot that's the same color as the eyedropper rather than one that ought to be that color. For instance, if your photo includes a wood carving that looks black but you know it should be dark brown, that's a bad place to click. Try clicking a black coffee mug or belt, instead. This is called "setting a black point."

5. **Repeat with the other eyedroppers for their respective colors.**

   Now find a spot that should be white (like maybe a cloud that's a little off-white now) and one that should be gray to set your white and gray points. That's the way it's supposed to work, anyway, but you can't always use all the eyedroppers in a given photo. Experiment to see what gives you the best-looking results.

TIP   You don't always need to set a gray point. If you try to set it and think your photo looked better without it, just skip that step.

---

6. **If you're using the dialog box, when you're happy with what you see, click OK.**

   If you're working with the Adjustments panel, you don't have to do anything: Elements has already applied your changes, so you're done.

See, it's not so hard. If you mess up, just click the dialog box's Reset button to start over again. In the Adjustments panel, click the word Reset at the bottom right (it doesn't look like a button until you move your mouse over it).

Adjusting Levels: The Slider Controls

The eyedropper method works fine if your photo has spots that should be black, white, or gray, but sometimes your pictures won't have any of these colors. Fortunately, the Levels sliders give you yet another way to apply Levels. It's by far the most popular method, and it gives you maximum control over your colors.

In the Levels dialog box (press Ctrl+L/⌘-L to open it), right below the histogram are three little triangles called *Input sliders.* The left slider sets the black point in your photo, the right slider sets the white point, and the middle slider adjusts the midtones (gray). You just drag them to make changes to the color levels in your photo, as shown in Figure 7-13.

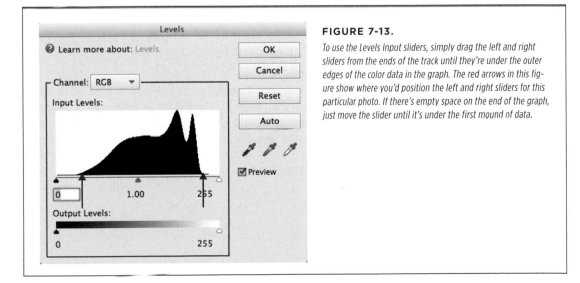

FIGURE 7-13.

To use the Levels Input sliders, simply drag the left and right sliders from the ends of the track until they're under the outer edges of the color data in the graph. The red arrows in this figure show where you'd position the left and right sliders for this particular photo. If there's empty space on the end of the graph, just move the slider until it's under the first mound of data.

When you move the left Input slider, you tell Levels, "Take all the pixels from this point down and consider them black." With the right slider, you're saying, "Make this pixel and all higher values white." The middle slider adjusts the brightness values that are considered medium gray. All three adjustments improve the contrast of your image.

> **TIP** If there are small amounts of color data (flat lines) at the ends of the histogram, or if all the data is clumped in the middle of the graph, watch your photo as you move the left and right Input sliders to decide how far in you should bring them. Moving them all the way in may be too drastic. Your own taste should always be the deciding factor when adjusting a photo.

Here's the easiest way to use the Levels sliders:

1. **Bring up the Levels dialog box or the Levels Adjustments panel.**

   Use one of the methods described in step 1 of the eyedropper method (page 240). If necessary, move the dialog box or Adjustments panel so you've got a clear view of your photo.

2. **Grab the black Input slider.**

   That's the one below the left end of the histogram.

3. **Drag it to the right, if necessary.**

   Move it over until it's under the farthest left part of the histogram that has a mound in it. For the histogram in Figure 7-13, for example, you'd move the left slider just a tiny bit, to where the left red arrow is. (Incidentally, although you're adjusting the image's colors, the Levels histogram is always black and white—you don't see any color in the dialog box itself.)

   You may not need to move the slider at all if there's already a good bit of data at the left end of the histogram. It's not mandatory to adjust all the sliders for every photo.

4. **Grab the white slider (the one on the right) and drag it left, if necessary.**

   Bring it under the farthest right area of the histogram that has a mound in it.

5. **Now adjust the gray slider.**

   This is the *midtones* slider, and it adjusts the midtones of your image. Move it back and forth while watching your photo until you like what you see. This slider has the most impact on the overall result, so take some time to play with it.

6. **If you're using the Levels dialog box, click OK.**

You can adjust the whole image at once or each color channel individually. The most accurate way is to open the Levels dialog box and to choose each color channel separately from the Channel drop-down menu. Adjust the end points for each channel, and then choose RGB from the menu and tweak just the midtones (gray) slider.

TIP If you know the numerical value of the pixels you want to designate for any of these settings, you can type that information into the unlabeled Input Levels boxes below the histogram. You can set the gray value from 0.10 to 9.99 (it's set at 1.00 automatically), and the other two boxes anywhere from 0 to 255.

The last control you may want to use in the Levels dialog box or Levels Adjustments panel is the Output Levels slider, which works roughly the same way as the brightness and contrast controls on your TV. Moving these sliders makes the darkest pixels darker and the lightest pixels lighter. Image pros call this "adjusting the tonal range of a photo."

Adjusting levels can improve almost every photo, but if your image has a bad *color cast*—if it's too orange or too blue, say—you may need something else. The next section explains how to get rid of color like that.

FREQUENTLY ASKED QUESTION

Levels Before Curves

I never know where to start adjusting the colors in my photos. Some photo mavens talk about using Levels, others about Curves. Which should I use?

Elements includes a much-requested feature from Photoshop—*Color Curves*. Despite the name, the Curves tool isn't some kind of arc-drawing tool; it's a sophisticated way of adjusting the colors in photos. Curves works something like Levels, but with many more points of correction.

In Elements, you get a simplified version of Photoshop's Curves dialog box, with a few preset settings. Because this version doesn't have quite as many adjustment points, you get some of the advanced color control of Curves without all the complexity.

Generally speaking, a quick Levels adjustment is usually all you need to achieve good, realistic color. But if you still aren't satisfied with the contrast in your image or you want to create funky artistic effects, check out page 325, which explains Color Curves in detail.

Removing Unwanted Color

It's not uncommon for an otherwise good photo to have a *color cast*—that is, to have all its tonal values shifted so it's too blue, like Figure 7-14, or too orange.

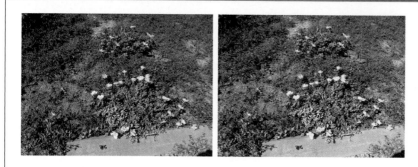

FIGURE 7-14.

Left: You may wind up with photos like this every once in a while if you forget to change your camera's white balance—a special setting for the type of lighting conditions you're shooting in (common settings are daylight, fluorescent, and so on). This is an outdoor photo taken with the camera set for tungsten indoor lighting.

Right: Elements fixes that wicked color cast in a jiffy. The photo still needs other adjustments, but the color is back in the right ballpark.

Elements gives you several ways to correct color-cast problems:

- **Auto Color Correction** doesn't give you any control over the changes, but it often does a good job. To use it, go to Enhance→Auto Color Correction or press Shift+Ctrl+B/Shift-⌘-B.

- The **Raw Converter** (page 264) may be the easiest way to fix problems, though it works only on Raw, JPEG, and TIFF files. Just run your photo through the Raw Converter and adjust its white balance there as described on page 271.

- **Levels** gives you the finest control of all. You can often eliminate a color cast by adjusting the individual color channels (as explained in the previous section) till the extra color is gone. The drawbacks are that Levels can be very fiddly for this sort of work; sometimes this method doesn't work if the problem is severe; and it can take much longer than the other methods.

- **Remove Color Cast** is a command designed specially for correcting a color cast with one click. The next section explains how to use it.

- The **Color Variations dialog box** can help you figure out which colors you need more or less of, but it has some limitations. It's covered on page 246.

- The **Photo Filter command** gives you much more control than the Remove Color Cast command, and you can apply Photo Filters as Adjustment layers, too. See page 294 for details.

- The **Average Blur filter,** used with a blend mode, lets you fix color casts. As you'll read on page 452, it's something like creating a custom photo filter.

- The **Adjust Color for Skin Tone** feature makes Elements adjust a photo based on the skin colors in the image. In practice, this adjustment is often more likely to *introduce* a color cast than to correct one, but if your photo has a slight bluish cast that's visible in the subject's skin (as explained on page 134), it may do the trick. This option works best for slight, annoying casts that are too subtle for the other techniques in this list.

You can use any of these methods, but a good bet is to start with Levels and then move on to the Remove Color Cast or Photo Filter command. To practice any of the fixes you're about to learn, download the photo *duneflowers.jpg* from this book's Missing CD page at *www.missingmanuals.com/cds*.

The Remove Color Cast Command

This command uses an eyedropper to adjust the colors in a photo based on the pixels you click. With this method, you show Elements where a neutral color should be. As you saw with the flowers in Figure 7-14, Remove Color Cast can make a big difference with just one click. To use it:

1. **Go to Enhance→Adjust Color→Remove Color Cast.**

   Your cursor should change to an eyedropper when you move it over your photo. If it doesn't, go to the dialog box and click the eyedropper icon.

2. **Click an area that should be gray, white, or black.**

   You only have to click once in your photo for this feature to work. As with the Levels eyedropper tool, click an area that *should be* gray, white, or black (as opposed to looking for an area that's *currently* one of these colors). If the image you're trying to fix has several of these areas, try clicking different spots in the photo. Just click Reset between each click on the photo until you find the spot that gives you the most natural-looking color.

3. **Click OK.**

Remove Color Cast works pretty well if your image has areas that should be black, white, or gray, even if they're tiny. The tricky thing is when you have an image that doesn't have any areas that should be one of those colors. If that's the case, consider using the Photo Filter command (page 294) instead.

> **TIP** If you generally like what Auto Levels does for your photos but feel like it leaves behind a slight color cast, a click with Remove Color Cast may be just the right finishing touch.

Using Color Variations

The Color Variations dialog box (Figure 7-15) appeals to many Elements beginners because it gives you visual clues about how to fix the color in a photo. You just click the little preview thumbnail that shows the color balance you like best and Elements applies the necessary change to make the photo look like that thumbnail.

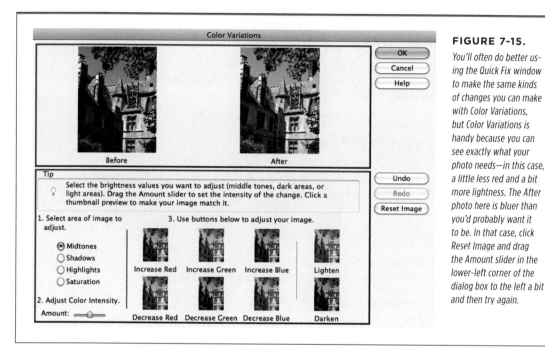

FIGURE 7-15.

You'll often do better using the Quick Fix window to make the same kinds of changes you can make with Color Variations, but Color Variations is handy because you can see exactly what your photo needs—in this case, a little less red and a bit more lightness. The After photo here is bluer than you'd probably want it to be. In that case, click Reset Image and drag the Amount slider in the lower-left corner of the dialog box to the left a bit and then try again.

But Color Variations has some pretty severe limitations, most notably the microscopic size of the thumbnails. Because of that, it's hard to see what you're doing, so even newcomers can usually get better results in Quick Fix (page 113).

Still, Color Variations is useful when you know something isn't right with a photo's color, but you can't quite figure out what to do about it. And because it's adjustable, Color Variations is good for when you *do* know what you want, but want to make only a tiny change to a photo's color. To use Color Variations:

1. **Open a photo and create a duplicate layer.**

   You probably want to make a duplicate layer for the adjustments by pressing Ctrl+J/⌘-J. That way, you'll have the option of discarding the changes if you're not happy with them. If you decide not to work on a duplicate, remember that you won't be able to undo these changes after you close the file.

2. **Go to Enhance→Adjust Color→Color Variations.**

   Elements displays the dialog box pictured in Figure 7-15.

3. **In the "Select area of image to adjust" area of the dialog box, click a radio button to let Elements know whether to adjust the midtones, shadows, highlights, or saturation.**

Color Variations automatically selects Midtones, which is usually what you want. But experiment with the other settings to see what they do. The Saturation button works just like Saturation in Quick Fix (page 129).

4. **Use the Amount slider at the bottom of the dialog box to control how drastic the change should be.**

The farther right you drag the slider, the more dramatic the change. Usually, just a smidgen is enough to make a noticeable change.

5. **Below where it says "Use buttons below to adjust your image," click one of the thumbnails to make your photo look like it.**

You can always click the Undo or Redo buttons on the right side of the dialog box, or click Reset Image to put your photo back the way it was when you started.

6. **When you're happy with the result, click OK.**

Choosing Colors

So far, the color corrections you've read about in this chapter have all done most of the color assigning for you. But a lot of the time, you want to *tell* Elements what colors to work with—like when you're selecting the color for a Background or Fill layer, or when you want to paint on an image.

Although you can use any of the millions of colors your screen can display, Elements loads only two colors at a time. You choose these colors using the foreground and background color squares at the bottom of the Tools panel (see Figure 7-16).

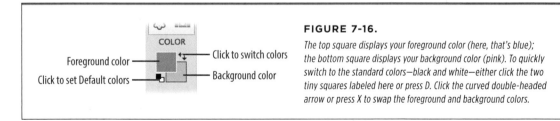

FIGURE 7-16.

The top square displays your foreground color (here, that's blue); the bottom square displays your background color (pink). To quickly switch to the standard colors—black and white—either click the two tiny squares labeled here or press D. Click the curved double-headed arrow or press X to swap the foreground and background colors.

Foreground and background mean just what they sound like—use the foreground color with tools like the Brush or the Paint Bucket, and the background color to fill in backgrounds. You can use as many colors in your images as you want, of course, but you can only use two at any given time.

The color-picking tools at the bottom of the Tools panel let you control the color you're using in a number of different ways:

- **Reset default colors.** Click the tiny black and white squares below the foreground square to return to the standard settings: black for the foreground color and white for the background color. Pressing the D key does the same thing.

- **Switch foreground and background colors.** Click the little curved two-headed arrow above the color squares and the background color becomes the foreground color, and vice versa. This is helpful when you've inadvertently made your color selection in the wrong box. Say you set the foreground color to yellow, but you actually meant to make the *background* color yellow; just click these arrows and you're all set. You can also press X instead.

- **Change either the foreground or background color to whatever color you want.** Click either square to call up the Color Picker (explained on page 249) to make your new choice. There's no limit on the number of colors you can select in Elements. (Well, technically there is, but it's in the millions, so you should find enough choices for anything you want to do.)

You have a few different ways to select foreground and background colors. The next few sections show you how to use the Color Picker, the Eyedropper tool, and the Color Swatches panel.

When working with some of Elements' tools, like the type tools, you can choose a color in the tool's Tool Options area. Adobe knows that, given a choice, most people prefer to work with either Color Swatches or the Color Picker, so it's come up with a way to accommodate both camps, as shown in Figure 7-17.

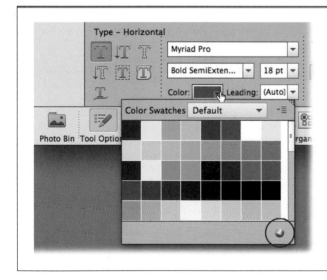

FIGURE 7-17.

Whether you prefer using Color Swatches or the Color Picker, you can choose your favorite (for most tools) in the Tool Options. Click the color sample in the box to bring up the Color Swatches. If you prefer the Color Picker, click the multicolored circle (circled). (This is different from how things worked in previous versions of Elements.)

TIP If you have an iPad, you've got another way to create colors for Elements. Adobe's Color Lava app lets you use your fingers to blend colors and then send them to Elements. Head to *www.photoshop.com/products/ mobile/colorlava* for more info about this app. (That web page says you need Photoshop to use Color Lava, but it works with Elements, too.)

The Color Picker

Figure 7-18 shows the Color Picker, which has an intimidating number of options, but most of the time you don't need them all. Choosing a color is as simple as clicking wherever you see the color you want. Here's how:

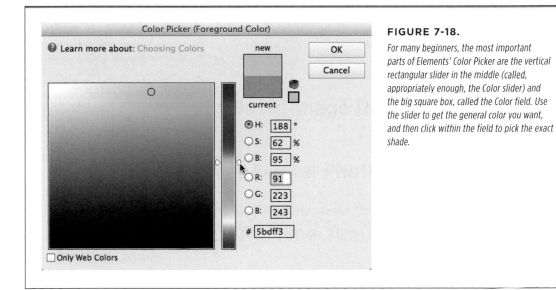

FIGURE 7-18.

For many beginners, the most important parts of Elements' Color Picker are the vertical rectangular slider in the middle (called, appropriately enough, the Color slider) and the big square box, called the Color field. Use the slider to get the general color you want, and then click within the field to pick the exact shade.

1. **Click the foreground or background color square in the Tools panel.**

   Elements launches the Color Picker. Some tools—like the Paint Bucket (page 405) and the Selection Brush's mask color option—also use the Color Picker. It works the same way no matter how you get to it.

2. **Choose the color range you want to select from.**

   Use the vertical Color slider in the middle of the dialog box to slide through the spectrum until you see the color you want in the big, square Color field.

3. **Click the spot in the Color field where you see the exact shade you want.**

   You can keep clicking around and watch the color in the window's "new" box change to reflect what you click. The "current" box shows your original color for comparison.

4. Click OK.

The color you selected now appears in the foreground or background square in the Tools panel (depending on which one you clicked in step 1).

That's the basic way to use the Color Picker. The box below explains how to enter a numeric value for a color if you know it and how to change the shades the Color Picker offers you.

> **NOTE** You're not limited to Elements' Color Picker. You can use your operating system's Color Picker instead, if you prefer (maybe you're used to working with the Windows Picker, for example).

- **Windows:** To change the Color Picker, in the Elements Editor, go to Edit→Preferences→General. At the top of the dialog box, choose Windows from the Color Picker menu. Now when you click a color square, the Windows Color Picker opens up looking pretty feeble, with just a few colored squares and some white ones. But if you click Define Custom Colors, it expands, giving you access to most of the same features as in the Adobe picker. (The plain white squares are like little pigeonholes where you can save your color choices.)

- **Mac:** Go to Adobe Photoshop Elements Editor→Preferences→General and select Apple from the Color Picker menu at the top of the dialog box. You might prefer Apple's color picker if you like to choose colors from a color wheel. There's even a fun view where you choose from a box of crayons. You can save colors in Apple's color picker by dragging them from the color field at the top of the window onto the squares at the bottom. Then click a square to choose that color the next time you want it.

Paint by Number

Elements' Color Picker includes some sophisticated controls that most folks can ignore. But in case you're curious, here's what the rest of the Color Picker does:

- **H, S, and B radio buttons.** These numbers determine the hue, saturation, and brightness of a color, respectively. They control pretty much the same values as the Hue/Saturation adjustment (page 129).

- **R, G, and B radio buttons.** These numbers let you specify the amount of red, green, and blue you want in the color you're picking. Each field can have a numerical value anywhere from 0 to 255; a lower number means less of the color, a higher number means more. For example, 128 R, 128 G, 128 B is neutral gray. By changing the numbers, you change the blend of the color.

- **# (hex number).** Below the radio buttons is a box where you can enter a special six-character *hexadecimal* code that you'd use when creating web graphics. This code tells web browsers which colors to display. You can also click a color in the window to see the hex number for that shade.

- **Only Web Colors checkbox.** Turning on this setting ensures that the colors you see in the main Color field are drawn only from the 216 colors that antique web browsers can display. For example, if you're creating a website and you're really worried about color compatibility with Netscape 4.0, this box is for you. If you see a tiny cube just to the right of the color sample box (as in Figure 7-18), the color you're using isn't deemed web safe. These days, it's hard to think of a time when you'd want to bother turning on this setting.

The Color Picker/Eyedropper Tool

If you've ever repainted your house, you've probably had the frustrating experience of spotting the *exact* color you want somewhere, but not having a way to capture that color. That's one problem you'll never run into in Elements thanks to the handy Eyedropper tool, which lets you sample any color on your monitor and make it your foreground color. If you can get a color onto your computer, Elements can grab it.

Sampling a color (that is, snagging it for your own use) couldn't be simpler with the Eyedropper: Just move your cursor over the color you want and then click. It even works on colors that aren't in Elements, as explained in Figure 7-19. Sampling is perfect for projects like scrapbook pages where you want to use, say, the color from an event program cover as a theme color for the project. Just scan the program and then sample the color with the Color Picker tool.

This tool used to go by the sensible name of Eyedropper, but for some incomprehensible reason Adobe now calls it the Color Picker tool, although it has nothing to do with the regular Color Picker (page 249), at least not directly. To avoid confusion, this book calls this tool by its old name. If you go looking for it in the Tools panel, just look for the eyedropper icon in the Draw section.

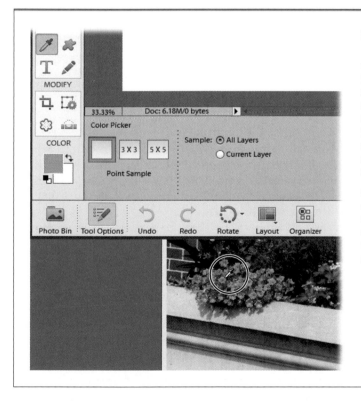

FIGURE 7-19.

To use the Eyedropper tool to sample colors outside of Elements, start by clicking anywhere in your Elements file. Then, while still holding your mouse button down, move your cursor over to the non-Elements object (a web page, for instance), until it's over the area you want to sample. When you let go of your mouse, the new color appears in Elements' foreground color square. (If you let go before you get to the non-Elements object, this trick won't work.)

Here, the Eyedropper (circled) is sampling the aqua color from a photo in Windows 7's Windows Photo Viewer. If you don't have a big monitor, it can take a bit of maneuvering to get the program windows positioned so you can perform this procedure.

Whatever you call it, it's one of the easiest tools to use:

1. **Click the Eyedropper in the Tools panel or press I.**

   Your cursor changes into a tiny eyedropper.

2. **Put your cursor over the color you want to sample.**

   If you want to watch the color in the foreground color square change as you move the Eyedropper tool around, hold the mouse button down as you go. If you have a layered file, you can use the radio buttons in the Tool Options area to tell Elements whether to sample from all the layers of the image or just the current layer.

3. **Click (or let go of your mouse button) when you see the color you want.**

   Elements loads your color choice as the foreground color so it's ready to use. (To set the background color instead, Alt-click/Option-click the color you want.)

If you want to keep the new color around so you can use it later without having to get the Eyedropper out again, save it in the Swatches panel. The next section teaches you how.

> **TIP** Unless you tell it otherwise, the Eyedropper tool selects the color of the exact pixel you click. But since there may be some slight pixel-to-pixel variation in a color, you can set the Eyedropper to sample a little block of pixels instead and then average them. In the Eyedropper's Tool Options you can choose between the exact pixel you click (Point Sample), a 3-pixel square average, or a 5-pixel square average. Just click the one you want. Oddly enough, this Eyedropper setting also applies to the Magic Wand (page 154). Change it here and you change it for the wand, too.

The Color Swatches Panel

The Color Swatches panel holds several preloaded groups of colors for you to choose from. Go to Window→Color Swatches to call it up. You can park it in the Panel Bin just like any other panel or leave it floating on your desktop. When you're ready to choose a color, just head to the panel and click the swatch you want, and it appears in the Tools panel's foreground color square or in the color box of the tool you're using.

The Color Swatches panel is really handy when you want to keep certain colors at your fingertips. For instance, you can put your logo colors into it, and then you always have them available for any graphics or ads you create in Elements.

Elements starts you off with several different *libraries* (groups) of color swatches; click the drop-down menu in the panel to see them all. Any swatch you create using the techniques in the next section appears at the bottom of the current library; you can save it there or create your own swatch libraries.

Using the Color Swatches panel to select your foreground or background color is as easy as using the Eyedropper tool. Figure 7-20 shows you how. And you can change the way the Color Swatches panel displays swatch information, as explained in Figure 7-21.

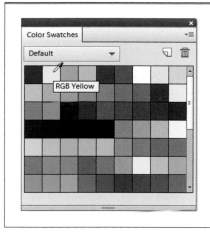

FIGURE 7-20.

When you move your cursor over the Color Swatches panel, it changes to an eyedropper. Simply click to select a foreground color, or Ctrl-click/⌘-click to pick a background color. If you're using a preloaded color library, you'll see labels appear as you move over each square.

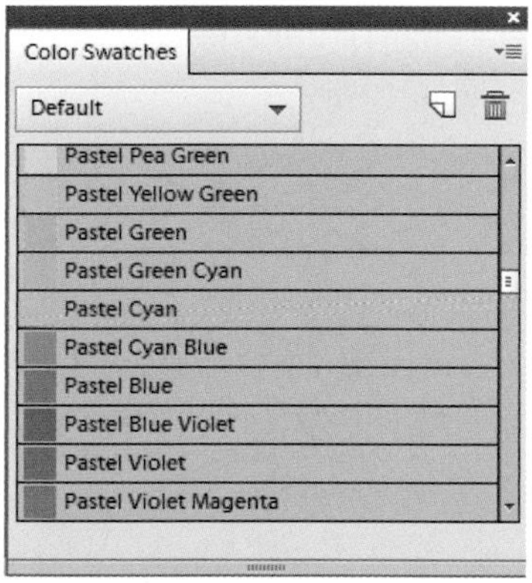

FIGURE 7-21.

To see swatch information displayed like this, click the four-line square at the top right of the panel and select Small List. Depending on the library you're using, you'll see the names or hex numbers of each color in addition to a small thumbnail of it.

■ SAVING COLORS IN THE SWATCHES PANEL

You can save any colors you've picked using the Color Picker or Eyedropper tool. (If you don't save them, you lose them as soon as you select a different swatch library or close the panel.) After sampling a color, you can save it as a swatch by doing one of two things:

- Click the New Swatch icon at the top of the Color Swatches panel. (It looks like a piece of paper with a folded corner.) After the swatch appears, if you want to give it a more descriptive name than "Color Swatch 1," right-click/Control-click it and then choose Rename Color Swatch.

- Click the little square made up of four lines at the panel's upper right and then choose New Swatch. A window appears where you can name and save your new swatch.

The name of the new swatch shows up as a pop-up label when you put your cursor over that swatch in the panel. Your swatch appears at the bottom of the current swatch library. To delete a swatch that you've saved, Alt-click/Option-click it or drag it to the trash can icon in the Color Swatches panel.

You can create your own swatch libraries if you want to keep your swatches separate from the ones that come with Elements. To do that, click the four-line square at the Color Swatches panel's upper right and pick Save Swatches. Then give the new library a name and save it. You can also find downloadable swatch libraries online (see page 598 for some suggestions about where to look). The best way to load these into Elements is to use the Preset Manager, explained on page 600.

NOTE When you create a new swatch library, it doesn't show up in the list of libraries until the next time you start Elements.

▉ Sharpening Images

Digital cameras are wonderful, but it's often hard to tell how well-focused your photos are until you download them to a computer. And because of the way cameras' digital sensors process information, most digital image data needs to be *sharpened*.

Sharpening is an image-editing trick that makes pictures look more clearly focused. Elements includes some almost miraculous tools for sharpening images. (It's pretty darned good at blurring them, too, if that's what you want; see page 446.)

Unsharp Mask

Although it sounds like the last thing you'd ever want to use on a photo, Unsharp Mask reigned as the Supreme Sharpener for generations of image correction, despite having the most counterintuitive name in all of Elements.

To be fair, it's not Adobe's fault. *Unsharp mask* is an old darkroom term, and it actually does make sense if you know how our film ancestors used to improve a picture's focus. It refers to a complicated darkroom technique that involved making a blurred copy of the photo at one point in the process.

For several versions of Elements, Unsharp Mask ranked right up there with Levels as a contender for most useful tool in Elements, and some people still think it's the best way to sharpen photos. Figure 7-22 shows how much a little Unsharp Mask can do for your pictures.

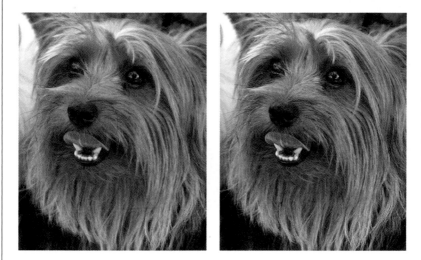

FIGURE 7-22.

Left: The photo as it came from the camera.

Right: The same photo treated with a dose of Unsharp Mask. Notice how much clearer the individual hairs in the dog's coat are and how much better defined the eyes and mouth are.

To use Unsharp Mask, first finish all your other corrections and changes. A good rule of thumb for sharpening is "last and once." Unsharp Mask (or any sharpening tool) can undermine other adjustments you make later on, so always make sharpening your last step. And repeatedly applying sharpening can degrade your image's quality.

TIP　An exception to the rule about sharpening only once is when you're converting Raw images (page 264): You can usually sharpen both in the Raw Converter and then again as a last step without causing problems.

If you're sharpening an image that has layers, be sure the active layer has something in it. (Applying sharpening to a Levels Adjustment layer, for example, won't do anything.) Also, perform any format conversions before sharpening. Finally, you may want to sharpen a duplicate layer just in case you decide to undo your changes later. Press Ctrl+J/⌘-J to create the duplicate layer.

NOTE　It's helpful to understand just exactly what Elements does when it "sharpens" a photo. It doesn't magically correct the focus. As a matter of fact, it doesn't really sharpen anything. What it does is increase the contrast where colors meet, giving the *impression* of crisper focus. So while Elements can dramatically improve a shot that's a little soft, it can't fix that old double exposure or a shot where the subject is just a blur of motion.

When you're ready to apply Unsharp Mask:

1. **Go to Enhance→Unsharp Mask.**

    You can use Unsharp Mask in either Expert Mode or Quick Fix.

2. **Adjust the settings in the Unsharp Mask dialog box until you like what you see.**

   Move the sliders until you're happy with your photo's sharpness (the following list explains what each slider does). In the preview part of the dialog box, you can zoom in and out and grab the photo to adjust which part you see. It's also a good idea to drag the dialog box off to the side so that you can watch your actual image for a more global view of the changes you're making. You get the most accurate look at how you're affecting the image if you set the view to 100 percent or Actual Pixels.

3. **When you're satisfied, click OK.**

The Unsharp Mask sliders work much like other tools' sliders:

- **Amount** tells Elements how much to sharpen, in percent terms. A higher number means more sharpening.

- **Radius** lets Elements know how far from an edge it should look when increasing the contrast.

- **Threshold** controls how different a pixel needs to be from the surrounding pixels before Elements considers it an edge and sharpens it. If you leave this setting at zero—which is the standard setting—Elements sharpens *all* the image's pixels.

There are many, many different schools of thought about where to move the sliders or which values to plug into each box. Whatever works for you is fine. The one thing you want to watch out for is *oversharpening*. Figure 7-23 explains how to know if you've gone too far.

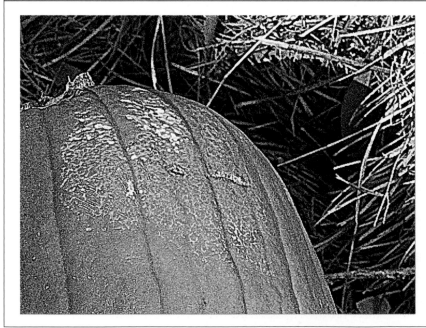

FIGURE 7-23.

The perils of oversharpening.

This is just a normal pumpkin, not a diseased one, but oversharpening gives it a flaky appearance and makes the straw in the background look sketched in rather than real. The presence of halos (like those along the edge of the pumpkin) is often your best clue that you've oversharpened an image.

You'll probably need to experiment a bit to find out which settings work best for you. Photos you plan to print usually need to be sharpened to an extent that makes them look oversharpened on your monitor, so you may want to create two separate versions of your photo: one for onscreen viewing and one for printing. Version sets in the Organizer are great for keeping track of multiple copies like this; see page 66.

Adjust Sharpness

The Unsharp Mask technique was around long before digital imaging. A lot of people (including the folks at Adobe) have been thinking that, in the computer age, there's got to be a better way to sharpen, and happily there is. The latest tool in the war on poor focus is Adjust Sharpness.

The Unsharp Mask tool helps boost a photo's sharpness by a process something like reducing Gaussian blur (page 246). Problem is, Gaussian blurring is rarely the cause of a picture's poor focus, so there's only so much Unsharp Mask can do. In real life, blurry photos are usually caused by one of two things:

- **Lens blur.** Your camera's prime focal point isn't directly over your subject, or your lens isn't quite as sharp as you'd like it to be.

- **Motion blur.** You moved the camera—or your subject moved—while you pressed the shutter.

Adjust Sharpness is as easy to use as Unsharp Mask, and it gives you settings to correct all three kinds of blur—Gaussian, lens, and motion. When you first open the Adjust Sharpness dialog box, its settings are almost identical to those of Unsharp Mask. It's the extra things Adjust Sharpness can do that make it a more versatile tool. Here's how to use it:

1. **Make sure the layer you want to sharpen is the active layer.**

   See Chapter 6 if you need a refresher on layers.

2. **Go to Enhance→Adjust Sharpness.**

   You can reach this menu item from either Expert Mode or Quick Fix.

3. **Make your changes in the Adjust Sharpness dialog box.**

   As shown in Figure 7-24, the dialog box gives you a nice big preview. It's usually best to stick with 50 or 100 percent zoom (use the plus and minus buttons below the preview to zoom) for the most accurate view. The other settings are explained in detail after this list.

4. **When you like the way your photo looks, click OK.**

The first two settings in the Adjust Sharpness dialog box, Amount and Radius, work exactly the same way they do in Unsharp Mask (page 254). Here's what the other settings do:

- **Remove.** This is where you choose what kind of fuzziness to fix: Gaussian, lens, or motion blur. If you aren't sure which you want, try all three and see which works best.

- **Angle.** If you're dealing with motion blur, you can improve your results by telling Elements the angle of the motion. For example, if your grip on the camera slipped, the direction of motion would be downward. Move the line in the little circle or type a number in degrees to approximate the angle. (It's awfully tricky to get the angle exactly right, so you may find it easier to sharpen without messing with this setting.)

- **More Refined.** Turn on this checkbox and Elements takes a tad longer to apply sharpening since it sharpens more details. Generally you'll want to leave this setting off for photos with lots of little details, like leaves or fur (and people's faces, unless you like to look at pores). But you might want it on for bold desert landscapes, for example, or other subjects without lots of fiddly small parts. Noise, artifacts, and dust become much more prominent when you turn on this setting, since they get sharpened along with the details of the photo. Experiment and watch the main image window as well as the preview to see how this setting affects your photo.

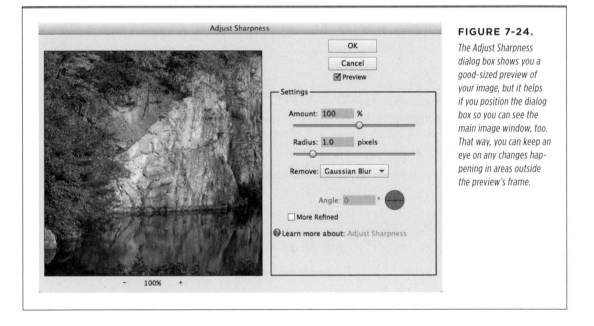

FIGURE 7-24.

The Adjust Sharpness dialog box shows you a good-sized preview of your image, but it helps if you position the dialog box so you can see the main image window, too. That way, you can keep an eye on any changes happening in areas outside the preview's frame.

TIP Although the Amount and Radius settings in the Adjust Sharpness dialog box control the same things as they do in Unsharp Mask, that doesn't necessarily mean that you can just plug your favorite Unsharp Mask settings into the Adjust Sharpness dialog box and get the same results. You may prefer very different numbers for these settings for the two tools.

Some people who've used Smart Sharpening in the full-featured Photoshop swear they'll never go back to Unsharp Mask. Try out Adjust Sharpness—Elements' version of Smart Sharpening—and see if you, too, like it better than Unsharp Mask. To give you an idea of the difference between the two methods, Figure 7-25 shows the dog from Figure 7-22 again, only this time with a dose of Adjust Sharpness instead of Unsharp Mask. Some people consider Adjust Sharpness too darned fiddly to use, so feel free to go back to Unsharp Mask if it works better for you. (And Mac folks, don't forget that you also have the option of sharpening in Preview [page 131]).

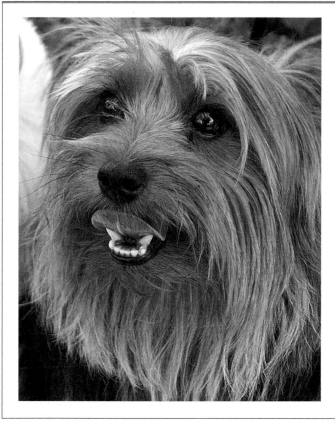

FIGURE 7-25.

Here's the terrier from page 255, only this time he's been sharpened using Adjust Sharpness. Notice how much each hair in his coat stands out, and how much more detail you can see in his nose and mouth.

The High-Pass Filter

Unsharp Mask is definitely the traditional favorite, and Adjust Sharpness is the latest thing in sharpening, but there's an alternative method that many people prefer because you apply it on a dedicated layer, which means you can lessen the effect later by adjusting the layer's opacity. Moreover, you can use this method to punch up the colors in a photo as you sharpen. It's called *high-pass sharpening*.

All sharpening methods have their virtues, and you may find that you choose a technique according to the content of your photo. Try the following procedure by downloading the photo *tiles.jpg* from this book's Missing CD page at *www.miss-ingmanuals.com/cds*:

1. **Open a photo and make sure the layer you want to sharpen is the active layer.**

2. **Duplicate the layer by pressing Ctrl+J/⌘-J.**

   If you have a multilayered image and you want to sharpen *all* the layers, first flatten the image or use the Stamp Visible command (see the box on page 202) so everything is on one layer.

3. **Go to Filter→Other→High Pass.**

   Your photo now looks like the victim of a mudslide, buried in featureless gray. Don't panic—that's what's supposed to happen.

4. **In the High Pass dialog box, move the slider until you can barely see the outline of your subject.**

   Usually that means picking a setting between roughly 1.5 and 3.5. If you can see colors, your setting is probably too high. (If you can't quite eliminate every trace of color without totally losing the outline, a tiny bit of color is OK.) Keep in mind that the edges you see through the gray are the ones that will get sharpened the most. Use that as your guide for how much detail to include.

5. **Click OK.**

6. **In the Layers panel, set the blend mode for the new layer to Overlay.**

   Ta-da! Your subject is back again in glowing, sharper color, as shown in Figure 7-26.

TIP   There's yet another way to create "pop" in photos: the Clarity setting in the Raw Converter (page 277), which sharpens and enhances contrast at the same time. (If you know what "local contrast enhancement" means, this setting does something similar.) You can use it on Raw, JPEG, and TIFF files. It's especially useful for clearing haze from shots.

The Sharpen Tool

Elements also gives you a dedicated Sharpen tool for working on specific areas of a photo rather than the entire image. It's a special brush that sharpens the areas you drag it over; Figure 7-27 shows it in action. To get to it, click the Blur tool's icon in the Tools panel or press R, and then choose the Sharpen tool (the triangle) in the Tool Options.

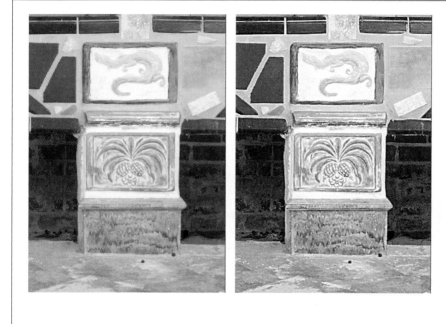

FIGURE 7-26.

Left: A close-up look at the original photo.

Right: High-pass sharpening using the Vivid Light blend mode makes the colors stand out more, but it also makes all the tiles a bit coarser and rougher looking than they were in the original. For high-pass sharpening, you can use any of the blend modes in the group with Overlay, except Hard Mix and Pin Light. Vivid Light can make your colors pop, but watch out for sharpening artifacts (page 256), since they'll be more vivid, too. Overlay gives you a softer effect.

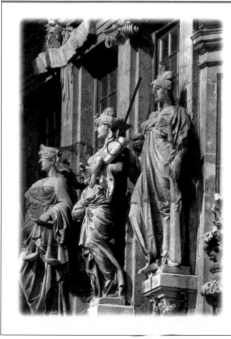

FIGURE 7-27.

The Sharpen tool isn't meant for sharpening whole photos, but it's great for sharpening details. Here it's being used to touch up the details in the middle statue. (The red arrow helps you find the circular cursor.)

Approach this tool with caution: It's super easy to overdo it. One pass too many or too high a setting and you'll start seeing artifacts.

The Sharpen tool has some of the same Tool Options settings as the Brush tool (see page 395 for more about brush settings), as well as a few all its own:

- **Mode** lets you increase the visibility of an object's edge by choosing from several different blend modes; Normal typically gives the most predictable results.

- **Brush.** You can choose a different brush if you want, but usually the one Elements selects is OK.

- **Strength** controls how much the brush sharpens what it passes over. A higher number means more sharpening.

- **Size.** You need to be fairly precise about the size of the brush you use so you can target the details you want to sharpen without affecting the surrounding areas.

- **Sample All Layers** makes the Sharpen tool work on all the image's visible layers. Leave this checkbox off if you want to sharpen only the active layer.

- **Protect Detail.** This setting helps you avoid *pixelation* (blockiness) while you enhance the details in your photo. At least that's how it's supposed to work, but in reality this setting doesn't always have much effect. Adobe suggests leaving it turned on unless you're after an exaggerated sharpening effect.

Elements for Digital Photographers

If you're a fairly serious digital photographer, you'll be delighted to know that Adobe hasn't just loaded Elements with easy-to-use features. The program also includes a collection of pretty advanced tools pulled straight from the full-featured Photoshop.

Number one on the list is the Adobe Camera Raw Converter, which lets you convert and edit *Raw files*—a format some cameras use to give you maximum editing control. In this chapter, you'll learn lots more about the Raw format and why you may (or may not) want to use it. But don't skip to the next chapter if your camera only shoots JPEGs: You can use the Raw Converter to edit JPEG and TIFF images, too, which can come in really handy, as you'll see shortly.

> **NOTE** Whereas JPEG and TIFF are acronyms for technical photographic terms, the word "Raw"—which you may occasionally see in all caps (RAW)—actually refers to the pristine, unprocessed quality of these files.

Adobe recently gave the Raw Converter a major update, and the version included with Elements 11 includes new, improved processes for converting files. It's a huge improvement over past versions of the Converter. If you've used Elements before and decided that you prefer your camera manufacturer's conversion software to what's available in Elements, it's time to give Elements' Raw Converter another try.

This chapter also explains Exposure Merge, which lets you combine different versions of a photo to create a single image with a higher dynamic range (a wider range of correctly exposed areas) than you can get from a single shot. You'll also get to know the Photo Filter command, which helps adjust colors by replicating the old-school effect of placing filters over camera lenses. And Elements has some truly useful batch-processing tools that let you do things like rename groups of files, convert them to different formats, and even apply basic retouching to multiple photos. Read on to learn about all these features.

The Raw Converter

Probably the most useful thing Adobe has done for photography buffs is to include the Adobe Camera Raw Converter in Elements. For many people, this feature alone is worth the price of the program, since you just can't beat the convenience of being able to perform conversions in the same program you use for editing.

If you don't know what Raw is, it's just a file format (a group of formats, really, since every camera maker has its own Raw format with its own file extension), but it's a very special one. Your digital camera actually contains a little computer that processes your photos right inside the camera. If you shoot in JPEG format, for instance, your camera makes some decisions about things like sharpness, color saturation, and contrast before it saves the JPEG files to its memory card.

But if your camera lets you shoot Raw files, then you get the *unprocessed* data straight from the camera. Shooting in Raw lets you make your own decisions about how your photos should look, to a much greater degree than with any other format. It's something like getting a negative from your digital camera—what you do to it in your digital darkroom is up to you.

That's Raw's big advantage—total control. The downside is that every camera manufacturer has its own proprietary Raw format, and the format varies even among models from the same manufacturer. No regular graphics program can edit these files, and very few programs can even open them. Instead, you need special software to convert Raw files to a format you can work with. In the past, that usually meant you needed software from the manufacturer before you could move your photo into an editing program like Elements.

Enter Adobe Camera Raw, which lets you convert your files right in Elements. Not only that, but the Adobe Camera Raw plug-in that comes with Elements lets you make sophisticated corrections to your photos before you even open them. Many times, you can do everything you need right in the Converter, so that you're done as soon as you open the converted file. (You can, of course, still use any of Elements' regular tools once you've opened a Raw file.) Using Adobe Camera Raw saves you a ton of time, and it's compatible with most cameras' Raw files.

> **NOTE** Adobe regularly updates the Raw Converter to work with new proprietary Raw formats produced by different cameras and to include updated profiles for existing cameras. So if your camera's Raw files don't open, check for a newer version of the Converter by going to Help→Updates in the Editor. (Normally, when you install Elements, it's set to periodically check for updates automatically, but you can also check manually.) If you aren't sure which version of the Raw Converter you have (you can't remember whether you've applied the latest update, for instance), go to Help→About Plug-In→Camera Raw/Adobe Photoshop Elements Editor→About Plug-In→Camera Raw to check.

Using the Raw Converter

For all the options it gives you, the Raw Converter is really easy to use. Adobe designed it to automatically calculate and apply what it thinks are the correct settings for exposure, shadows, brightness, and contrast. You can accept the Converter's decisions or override them and do everything yourself—it's your call.

While you may find all the Converter's various settings, tools, and tabs a little overwhelming at first, it's actually laid out quite logically. Here's a quick overview of how to use it (you'll get details in a moment):

1. **Open a file in the Raw Converter (Figure 8-3).**

   You can call up the Raw Converter from either the Organizer or the Editor's Expert Mode window just by opening a Raw file. (If you've previously edited the file in an older version of the Raw Converter, the first time you open it in Elements 11, you may see the warning shown in Figure 8-1.)

> **NOTE** If you run Elements on a screen that's less than 768 pixels high (like on a netbook, say, or if you've reduced your monitor's resolution to less than that), the Raw Converter window may not appear. Elements just automatically converts your file and opens it straight into the Editor without giving you a chance to tweak anything.

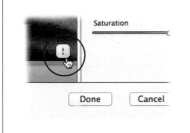

FIGURE 8-1.
If your Raw file has been edited before with an older version of Adobe Camera Raw, you'll see this warning at the lower right of the image preview area the first time you launch the converter in Elements 11. The exclamation point means that the file is set to use the older version's conversion process. Just click the exclamation point to update to the latest process and see the new sliders.

2. **Adjust your view and do any necessary rotating, straightening, and cropping.**

   The Raw Converter has its own tools for all these tasks, so you don't need to go into the Editor for any of them.

3. **Adjust the image's settings.**

   This is the best part of shooting Raw format images: You can tweak settings for things like lighting and color. The Converter also lets you apply final touchups like noise reduction, sharpening, and so on.

4. **Leave the Converter and go to the Editor.**

   The Raw Converter is a powerhouse for improving your photo's fundamental appearance, but to perform all the other adjustments Elements lets you make—applying filters, adding effects, and so on—you need to move your image to the

Editor, which is also where you save the file in the standard graphics format of your choice (like TIFF, PSD, or JPEG).

If you'd like some practice with the Converter, you can download a sample Raw image (*Raw_practice.mrw*) from this book's Missing CD page at *www.missingmanuals. com/cds*, but be warned: It's a big file (7.2 MB).

To start converting a Raw file, in the Organizer, right-click/Control-click the file, and then choose "Edit with Photoshop Elements Editor" (or press Ctrl+I/⌘-I) to bring up the Converter window. (If you select multiple Raw files and the Converter doesn't open automatically when you send them to the Editor, you can find your files in the Photo Bin by going to the menu above the bin and choosing "Show Files selected in Organizer." Select them all, and then double-click one thumbnail to display them in the Converter.) If you're starting from the Editor, just go to File→Open. Figure 8-2 explains how to work with multiple files in the Raw Converter.

> **NOTE** In Windows, you may not be able to open Raw files by double-clicking them outside Elements (on the Windows desktop, for instance). If you try that, you'll probably see a message to the effect that your computer has no idea what program to use to open that file. (Windows may also offer to take you to a website where you can download the files necessary to let Windows display your Raw photos.) To make your computer always use Elements to open Raw files, follow the steps on page 37.
>
> On a Mac, you can usually open Raw files in Preview using the built-in Raw support in OS X, unless you have a very new camera or one of the few models that Apple doesn't support.

One important point to remember about Raw files: Elements never overwrites the original file. As a matter of fact, Elements *can't* modify the original Raw file in any way. So your original is always there if you want to try converting it again later using different settings. It's something like having a negative from which you can always get more prints. This also applies to *any* image you edit in the Raw Converter, not just Raw files. You can crop a JPEG file here, for instance, and your original JPEG doesn't get cropped—only the copy you open from the Converter. (There's more about working with non-Raw files in the Converter on page 282.)

> **TIP** If you shoot Raw+JPEG (where your camera takes one photo and saves it as both a Raw file and a JPEG file), you may find that the Photo Downloader (page 30) gets very confused by this scenario. If you have problems importing these files into the Organizer, try using one of the other methods discussed on page 35 to get the photos onto your computer, then use File→Get Photos and Videos→"From Files and Folders" to bring them into the Organizer.

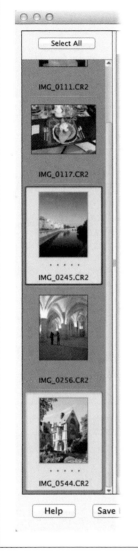

FIGURE 8-2.

When you have several files open in the Raw Converter, you get this handy filmstrip view down the left side of the window. You can select a single image from the group by clicking it, and then your changes apply only to that file. Shift-click or Ctrl-click to select multiple images (or use the Select All button at the top of the list), and all the selected files get changed along with the one in the main preview area.

When you finish your tweaks and click Open, all the selected files appear in the Editor's Photo Bin. If you want to save a group of them in another format, then use the Process Multiple Files command (page 295).

■ ADJUSTING THE VIEW

When the Raw Converter opens, you see something like Figure 8-3. Before you decide whether to accept the automatic settings that Elements offers or to do your own tweaking, you need to get a good close look at the image. The Converter makes it easy to do this by giving you a large preview of the image and a handful of tools to help adjust what you see:

- **Zoom and Hand tools.** These are in the toolbox in the top left of the Converter window. You use them here exactly the same way as elsewhere in Elements. (You'll find more about the Zoom tool on page 99; the Hand tool is described on page 98. The keyboard shortcuts for adjusting the view and scrolling also work in the Raw Converter.)

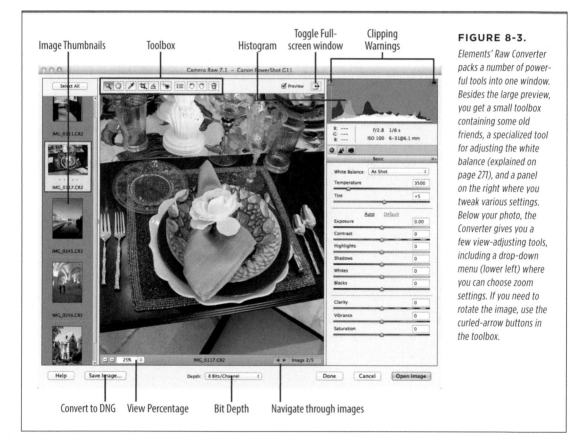

FIGURE 8-3.

Elements' Raw Converter packs a number of powerful tools into one window. Besides the large preview, you get a small toolbox containing some old friends, a specialized tool for adjusting the white balance (explained on page 271), and a panel on the right where you tweak various settings. Below your photo, the Converter gives you a few view-adjusting tools, including a drop-down menu (lower left) where you can choose zoom settings. If you need to rotate the image, use the curled-arrow buttons in the toolbox.

- **View percentage.** Below the lower-left corner of the preview window is a drop-down menu with preset sizes. Just choose the size you want, or click the + or – buttons to zoom in or out.

- **Full Screen.** Just above the upper-right corner of the preview area is an icon that looks like a page with a double-headed arrow on it. Click it to put the Raw Converter window into full-screen mode. Click it again to toggle back to the normal view.

- **Histogram.** In the upper-right corner of the Converter window is a histogram that helps you keep track of how your changes affect the colors in the photo. (Flip back to page 237 for more on the fine art of reading histograms.)

> **TIP** Another handy feature in the Raw Converter is the panel just below the histogram, where you can see important shooting information about your photo, like the aperture and ISO speed (*ISO* is a digital camera's version of film speed). Put your cursor over a pixel in the image and the pixel's RGB values (page 250) appear here as well.

Once you've gotten a good close look at the photo, you have a decision to make: Did Elements do a good enough job of choosing settings for you? (In other words, do you like how your photo looks?) If so, you're done. Just click the Open Image button in the Converter's lower-right corner and Elements opens the photo in the Editor, ready for any artistic changes or cropping. If you prefer to make adjustments to the photo in the Converter, read on. (If you're happy with Elements' conversion but you want to sharpen the picture, then skip ahead to page 279.)

> **NOTE** Everyone gets confused by the Save Image button in the Converter's lower left. That button is actually the DNG Converter (see page 284), and all you can do when you click it is create a DNG file. To save your edited Raw file, click Done if you want to save your changes without actually opening the file, or click Open Image and then save it in the format of your choice in the Editor.

▓ ROTATING, STRAIGHTENING, AND CROPPING

Before tweaking your settings, you can make the following basic adjustments to photos right in the Raw Converter:

- **Rotate it.** Click one of the rotation arrows above the image preview.

- **Straighten it.** The Raw Converter has its own Straighten tool (page 80), which you use just like the one in the Editor's Tools panel, although it has a different icon and cursor. (It's just to the right of the Crop tool in the Raw Converter's toolbox.) However, you don't see the photo actually straighten out in the Converter—Elements just shows you the outline of where the edges of the straightened photo will be. Open the photo in the Editor to make Elements apply the straightening.

- **Crop it.** The Raw Converter has the same Crop tool as the Editor (page 86). To crop to a particular aspect ratio, click the Crop tool's icon for a drop-down menu of presets to choose from, or right-click/Control-click the image itself when the Crop tool is active. To crop to a particular size, choose Custom from the menu, and then, in the dialog box that appears, enter the dimensions. (You also need to select inches, centimeters, or pixels, or enter a custom aspect ratio.) Your cropping info gets saved along with the Raw file, so the next time you open the file in the Converter, you see the cropped version.

To Shoot in the Raw or Not

Should I shoot all my pictures in Raw format?

It depends. Using Raw format has pros and cons. You may be surprised to learn that some professional photographers *don't* use Raw. For example, many journalists don't, and it's not common with sports photographers, either.

Here's a quick look at the advantages and disadvantages, to help you decide whether to get involved with Raw. On the plus side, you get:

- **More control.** With Raw, you have a lot of extra chances to tweak your photos, and you get to call the shots, instead of your camera making the processing decisions.
- **More fixes.** If you're not a perfect photographer, Raw is more forgiving than other formats, so you can fix a lot of mistakes (though even Raw can't make a bad photo great).
- **No need to constantly fuss with white balance while shooting.** That said, you'll have better quality data to work with if your camera's white-balance settings are correct.
- **Nondestructive editing.** The edits you make in the Raw Converter don't change your original image one jot. It's always there if you need to make a fresh start.

But Raw also has some significant drawbacks. For one thing, you can't just open a Raw file and start editing it the way you do with JPEGs. You always have to convert it first, whether you use the Elements Converter or one supplied by the company that made your camera. Other disadvantages include the following:

- **Larger file size.** Raw files are smaller than TIFFs, but they're usually much bigger than the highest-quality JPEGs. Consequently, you need bigger (or more) memory cards if you regularly shoot Raw.

- **Slower speed.** It generally takes cameras longer to save Raw files than JPEGs—something to keep in mind when you're taking action shots. Most cameras these days have a buffer that holds several shots and lets you keep shooting while the camera is working, but you may hit the limit pretty quickly if you're using burst (rapid-advance) mode, especially with a pocket-sized point-and-shoot camera that uses Raw. In that case, you just have to wait. (Most digital single-lens reflex cameras are pretty fast with Raw these days, but they're generally even faster with JPEG.)
- **Worse in-camera preview.** Older cameras have some pretty significant limitations in terms of digitally zooming the view in the viewfinder when using Raw. Windows computers may not be able to display previews of your Raw files, either, without a special browser. Macs usually can, unless your camera model is new since the last time Apple updated OS X's Raw support (there are also a couple of cameras that never seem to get included), or so old that Apple drops it from the list.

You may want to try a few shots of the same subject in both Raw and JPEG to see whether you notice a difference in the results. Generally speaking, Raw offers the most leeway if you want to make significant edits, but you need to understand what you're doing. JPEG is easier if you're a beginner.

The bottom line: It's your call. Some excellent photographers wouldn't think of shooting in anything but Raw, while others think it's too time-consuming.

As with straightening, Elements just draws a mask over the cropped area in the Converter; you can still see the outline of the whole photo. To adjust your crop, in the Raw Converter's toolbox, click the Crop tool again, and then drag one of the handles that appear around the cropped area. To revert to the uncropped original later, activate the Raw Converter's Crop tool, and then right-click/Control-click inside the crop box's boundaries and choose Clear Crop.

> **TIP** You can also fix red eye in the Raw Converter. The Red Eye Removal tool is in the toolbox just to the right of the Straighten tool, and it works the same way it does everywhere else in Elements (see page 121).

Adjusting White Balance

The long strip down the right side of the Raw Converter window gives you lots of ways to tweak and correct photos' color, exposure, sharpness, brightness, and noise level. The strip is divided into three tabs. Start with the one labeled Basic, which contains, well, the *basic* settings for the major adjustments. (The Raw Converter automatically opens to this tab.)

First, check the White Balance setting at the top of the Basic tab. Adjusting white balance is often the most important change when it comes to making photos look their best. This setting adjusts all the colors in a photo by creating a neutral white tone. If that sounds a little strange, stop and think about it for a minute: The color you think of as *white* actually changes depending on lighting conditions. At noon there's no warmth (no orange/yellow) to the light because the sun is high in the sky. Later in the day when the sun's rays are lower, whites are warmer. Indoors, tungsten lighting is much warmer than fluorescent lighting, which makes whites rather bluish or greenish. Your eyes and brain easily compensate for these changes, but sometimes your camera may not, or may overcompensate, giving your photos a color cast. The Raw Converter's White Balance setting lets you create more accurate color by neutralizing the white tones.

Most digital cameras have their own collections of white-balance settings. Typical choices include Auto, Daylight, Cloudy, Tungsten, Fluorescent, and Custom. When you shoot JPEGs, picking the correct setting really matters, because it's tough to readjust white balance, even in a program like Elements (unless you tweak the JPEG with the Raw Converter as explained in the box on page 282, and even then the results may not be what you want). With Raw photos, you can afford to be a little sloppier about setting your camera's white balance, because you can easily fix things in the Raw Converter. Getting the white balance right can make a huge difference in how your photo looks, as you can see in Figure 8-4.

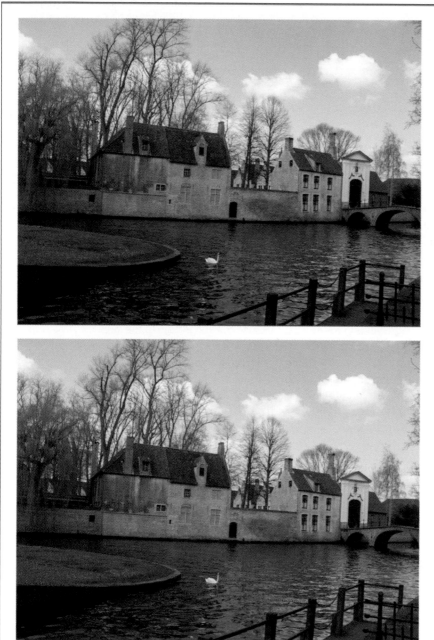

FIGURE 8-4.

Top: The lighting in this shot has a bluish cast that makes it look chilly.

Bottom: A single click on the swan with the White Balance tool makes the whole photo look warmer. (It could stand a little additional tweaking [including straightening], but the better white balance makes the photo more vivid and improves its contrast.)

The Raw Converter gives you several ways to adjust an image's white balance:

- **Drop-down menu.** The White Balance menu just below the histogram starts out set to As Shot, which means Elements is showing your camera's settings. You can use this menu to choose from Auto, Daylight, Cloudy, and so on. It's worth giving Auto a try because it picks the correct settings surprisingly often.

- **Temperature.** Use this slider to make the photo warmer (more orange) or cooler (more blue). Dragging the slider left cools the photo; dragging it right warms it. You can also type a temperature in the text box in degrees Kelvin (the official measurement for color temperature), if you're experienced in doing this by the numbers. Use the Temperature slider and the Tint slider (described next) together for a perfect white balance.

- **Tint.** This slider controls the green/magenta balance of the photo, pretty much the way it does in Quick Fix. Move it left to increase the amount of green in the photo, or right for more magenta.

- **White Balance tool.** The eyedropper icon up in the Converter window's toolbox is actually the White Balance tool. Activate it and then click any white or light-gray spot in your photo, and Elements calculates the white balance based on those pixels. This is the most accurate method in this list, but you may have a hard time finding neutral pixels to click with it. If you choose a blown-out area, Elements will warn you to pick another spot with more information in it.

If you're a good photographer, then much of the time a good white balance and a little sharpening may be all your photo needs before it's ready to go out into the world.

Adjusting Tone

The next group of six sliders—from Exposure down through Blacks—helps you improve an image's exposure and lighting (also known as *tone)*. If you like Elements to make decisions for you, click the word "Auto" above these sliders, and the program selects what it thinks are the best positions for each of the six sliders. If you don't click anything, then Elements starts you off with the Default settings. Here's the difference between Auto and Default:

- **Auto.** Elements automatically adjusts the photo using the same software-powered guesswork behind the other Auto buttons throughout the program. To make Elements always apply auto adjustments, see Figure 8-5.

- **Default.** The Raw Converter has a database of basic tone settings for each camera model. If you choose Default, then you see the baseline settings for your camera, and it's up to you to make further adjustments to the photo. If you want, you can set your own defaults (where the sliders are when your photo opens), too, as explained on page 277. If you don't like what you got with Auto, then just click Default to switch the photo back to how it was when you opened it.

After you've clicked Auto or Default, you can override any tone setting by moving its slider. If you go to the trouble of shooting Raw, then you may well prefer to do so, as Figure 8-6 demonstrates.

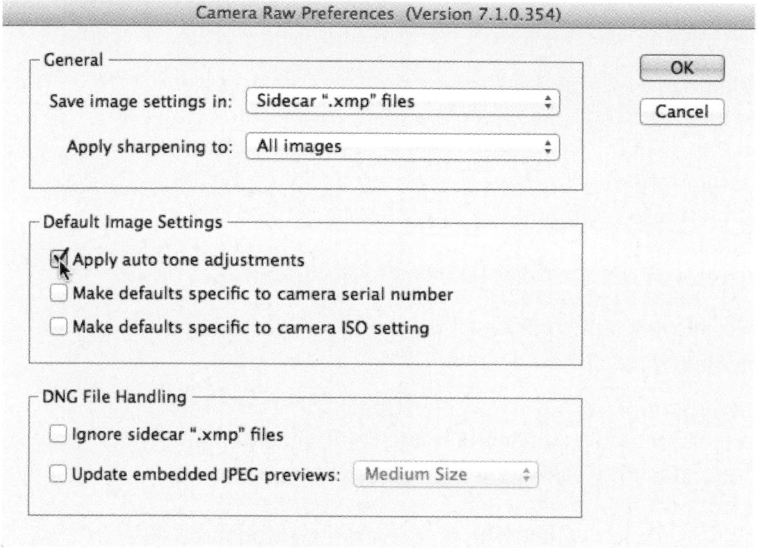

Camera Raw Preferences (Version 7.1.0.354)

General

Save image settings in: Sidecar ".xmp" files

Apply sharpening to: All images

OK
Cancel

Default Image Settings

☑ Apply auto tone adjustments
☐ Make defaults specific to camera serial number
☐ Make defaults specific to camera ISO setting

DNG File Handling

☐ Ignore sidecar ".xmp" files
☐ Update embedded JPEG previews: Medium Size

FIGURE 8-5.

To make the Raw Converter always open your photos with the Auto settings applied, open the Raw Converter Preferences dialog box by clicking the three-line icon in the Raw Converter's toolbox pressing Ctrl+K/⌘-K. In the dialog box, turn on the "Apply auto tone adjustments" checkbox, as shown here, and from now on, the Raw Converter is in Auto mode—at least for the tone settings.

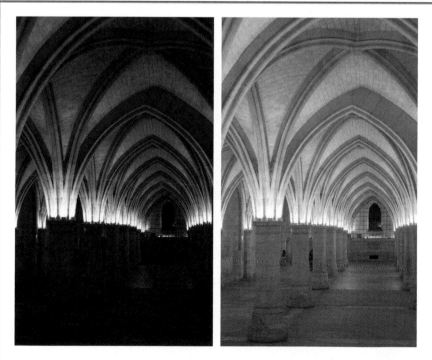

FIGURE 8-6.

Left: The Raw Converter's Auto settings make this photo look like a lost cause.

Right: With a little bit of manual adjustment, you can see that the camera actually captured plenty of details for the Raw Converter to bring out.

If you've converted Raw files in older versions of Elements, you'll notice that the sliders in the current version of the Raw Converter (version 7) are very different from what they were in older versions. Even the ones that have the same names work differently (and better) than they used to. For one thing, each slider starts out dead in the middle (at 0), giving you more ability to adjust it either up or down. Here's a rundown of what each one does :

- **Exposure.** A properly exposed photo shows the largest possible range of detail—shadows contain enough light to reveal details, and highlights aren't so bright that all you see is white. Move this slider left to decrease exposure or right to increase it. (This setting has the greatest effect on the midtones in your photo.)

- **Contrast.** This slider also adjusts the image's midtones; move it right for greater contrast in those tones, or left for less. People usually use this slider last, because things can shift pretty dramatically if you use other sliders after increasing contrast.

- **Highlights.** This clever slider can bring down overexposed highlights (recovering details that were lost in those areas) without underexposing the rest of the photo, or increase the brightness of highlights that are too dark. One of the changes in this version of the Raw Converter is that you can now move both this slider and the Shadows slider (explained next) way farther than you could before without causing problems in your image.

- **Shadows.** This slider increases the shadow values in the photo and determines which pixels become black. Increasing this setting may help improve the image's contrast. Drag the slider right to lighten shadows or left to darken them.

- **Whites.** Use this slider to set the photo's white point, more or less the way you do with Levels (page 236). ·

- **Blacks.** Use this slider to set your black point, again something like the way you do with Levels.

Most of the time, you'll use several of these sliders to get a perfectly exposed photo. However, in a change from the usual "work from the top down" way that most groups of controls in Elements work, you may want to start with Whites and Blacks and *then* go back up to Exposure and the others.

It's quite amazing how much more range you can pull out of a photo in the new Raw Converter than you could in older versions. For example, you can now process images like the one in Figure 8-6 as a single image file in the Raw Converter. In the past, you would have had to fix such photos with some kind of exposure blending or Elements' Exposure Merge feature (page 286).

One thing to watch for: Although you can make pretty large adjustments now, setting the tone sliders too high may still *clip* some of your highlights (meaning they'll be so bright that you won't see any detail in them). Figure 8-7 explains more about clipping.

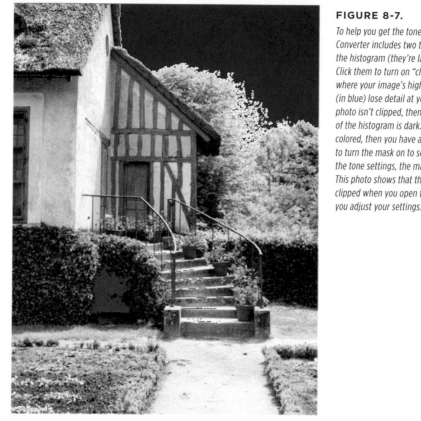

FIGURE 8-7.

To help you get the tone settings right, the Raw Converter includes two triangles above the ends of the histogram (they're labeled back in Figure 8-3). Click them to turn on "clipping warnings" that reveal where your image's highlights (in red) or shadows (in blue) lose detail at your current settings. If the photo isn't clipped, then the triangle for that end of the histogram is dark. If the triangle is white or colored, then you have a problem; click the triangle to turn the mask on to see the clipping. As you adjust the tone settings, the mask changes accordingly. This photo shows that the red and blue areas will be clipped when you open the photo in the Editor unless you adjust your settings.

Once you have things adjusted the way you want, you can move on to the Basic tab's other sliders and adjust the photo's clarity, vibrance, and saturation. You can also save your current settings for use with other photos, or undo all the changes you've made, as explained on page 277.

Adjusting Vibrance and Saturation

The final group of settings on the right side of the Raw Converter controls the vividness of your image's colors. Most Raw files have lower saturation to start with than you'd see in the same photo shot as a JPEG, so people often want to boost the saturation of their Raw images. Move the sliders right for more intense color, or left for more muted color. (If you know you'll *always* want to change the intensity of the color, then you can change the Raw Converter's standard setting by moving the slider until you have the intensity you want and then creating a new camera default setting as described on page 277.)

Here's what each of the three sliders does:

- **Clarity.** This slider is a bit different from the next two. Clarity isn't strictly a color tool, although it's an absolutely amazing feature. If you're an experienced Elements sharpener, you may have heard of the technique called *local contrast enhancement,* where you use the Unsharp Mask with a low Amount setting and a high Radius setting to eliminate haze and bring out details. That's sort of what this slider does: Through some incredibly sophisticated computing, it creates an edge mask for your photo that it uses to increase detail. It can do wonderful things for many—maybe even most—photos by improving contrast and adding punch. Give it a try, but be sure you're viewing your photo at 100 percent magnification (or more) so you can see how you're changing things. The calculations the Raw Converter does when you adjust this setting have changed quite a bit in Elements 11, so if you've used older versions and found you didn't like the effect it had on your photos, give the new version a try. You may be pleasantly surprised.

- **Vibrance.** The Raw Converter's Vibrance slider works the same way it does in the Quick Fix window: It increases the intensity of dull colors without oversaturating already-vivid ones. If you want to adjust an image's saturation, then try this slider first, before you move the Saturation slider.

- **Saturation.** This slider controls how vivid the image's colors are by changing the intensity of *all* its colors by the same amount.

■ SAVING YOUR SETTINGS

Most of the time, you'll only want to use the current Raw Converter settings on the specific photo(s) you're editing right now. But Elements gives you a bunch of ways to save time by saving settings for future use. Below the histogram, to the right of the word "Basic," are three tiny lines with a minute arrow at their bottom right. Click that icon to see a drop-down menu. Whatever you choose in this menu determines how Elements converts your photo. Here's what the choices mean:

- **Image Settings.** This is the "undo all my changes" option. If you've made some changes to your photo in the Converter but want to revert to the settings Elements originally presented you with, then choose this option.

- **Camera Raw Defaults.** The Raw Converter contains a profile of normal Raw settings for your camera model that it uses as its baseline for the adjustments it makes. That's what you get when you pick this option. You may have several profiles to choose from here (see the box on page 284).

- **Previous Conversion.** If you've already processed a photo and want to apply the same settings to the photo you're currently working on, then choosing this setting applies the settings from the last Raw image you opened (but only if it's from the same camera).

- **Custom Settings.** Once you start changing the Raw Converter's settings, this becomes the active option (the one with the checkmark next to it). You don't need to select it—Elements does that automatically as soon as you start making adjustments.

Since individual cameras—even if they're the same model—may vary a bit (as a result of the manufacturing process), the Camera Raw Defaults settings may not be the best ones for your camera. You can override the default settings and create your own set of defaults for any camera. Here's how:

- **To change your camera's settings:** If you know that you *always* want a different setting for one of the sliders—like maybe the Shadows setting should be at 5 instead of the basic Elements setting of 0—move any or all of the sliders to where you want them, and then choose Save New Camera Raw Defaults from the menu discussed above. From now on, Elements opens your photos with these settings as the starting point.

- **To revert to the original Elements settings for your camera:** If you want to go back to the way things were originally, then click the Settings button (the one with the three lines on it), and choose Reset Camera Raw Defaults.

> **TIP** You can apply the same changes to multiple photos at once. Page 266 explains how.

The Raw Converter's preferences include a couple of special settings that may interest you. To bring up the Camera Raw Preferences dialog box, in the Raw Converter's toolbox, click the icon with three lines. These preferences can be really useful, especially if you have more than one camera:

- **Make defaults specific to camera serial number.** Turn this on if you have more than one of a particular camera model; for instance, if you carry two bodies of the same model with different lenses when you shoot, or if both you and your spouse have the same camera model. This setting lets you have a different default for each camera body.

- **Make defaults specific to camera ISO setting.** Since you may shoot very differently at different ISO settings (ISO is the digital equivalent of film speed), you can use this setting to create a default that Elements applies only to photos shot at ISO 100, at ISO 1600, and so on.

> **TIP** If you regularly share photos with other people using Adobe programs, you'll be pleased to know that the Raw Converter's preferences let you choose whether your settings get saved in the Camera Raw database or in a sidecar XMP file that goes along with the image. If you choose the XMP option, then your settings become portable along with your photo—so if you send the image to someone else, the settings come along for the ride (as long as you send the XMP file, too).

You don't have to create default settings to save the changes you make to a particular photo. If you just want to save the settings for the photo or group of photos you're working on right now without having to open them all in the Editor and save them in another format, make your changes and then click the Raw Converter's Done button to update the settings for the image file(s).

TIP You can also choose a different camera profile for the Raw Converter to use as a basis for adjusting your photos. Page 284 explains how.

Adjusting Sharpness and Reducing Noise

Once you've got your image's exposure and white balance right, you may be almost done tweaking the photo. But in most cases, you'll want to click over to the Raw Converter's Detail tab to do a little sharpening: On the right side of the Raw Converter, above the word "Basic," click the icon that looks like two triangles.

None of the adjustments on this tab have Auto settings, although you can change the standard settings by moving their sliders where you want them and then creating a new camera default (page 278).

The first set of sliders on this tab is labeled Sharpening. Sharpening increases the edge contrast in a photo, which makes it appear more crisply focused. The sharpening tools in the Raw Converter are a bit different from those in the Editor, but some of the sliders should look familiar if you've sharpened before, since they're similar to the settings for Unsharp Mask and Adjust Sharpness:

- **Amount** controls how much Elements sharpens. The scale here goes from 0 (no sharpening) to 150 (usually way too much sharpening).

- **Radius** governs how wide an area Elements considers an edge. Its scale goes from 0.5 pixels to 3 pixels. Generally, the more fine detail in your photo, the lower the setting you want here.

- **Detail** controls how Elements applies sharpening. At 100—the right end of the scale—the effect is most similar to Unsharp Mask (in other words, you can overdo it if you aren't careful). At 0, you shouldn't see any sharpening halos at all.

- **Masking** is a very cool feature that reduces the area where sharpening takes place so that only edges get sharpened. With a setting of 0, everything in the photo gets sharpened equally. If you find that Elements is sharpening more details than you like, then use this slider to create an edge mask that keeps Elements from sharpening areas inside the edges. The farther you move this slider to the right, the more area you protect from sharpening. While you adjust this slider, Elements does some amazing behind-the-scenes calculations, so don't be surprised if there's a little lag in the preview when you move this slider.

The Masking and Detail settings work together to perform really accurate sharpening, which is why their sliders go so high—you won't like the effect from just one of them set all the way up, but by experimenting with both sliders, you can create excellent sharpening in your photo.

> **TIP** You can get an extremely helpful view of your image if you hold the Alt/Option key as you move the sliders, as explained in Figure 8-8. (Unlike in previous versions of the Converter, you no longer have to set your view to 100 percent or more to use this handy feature.)

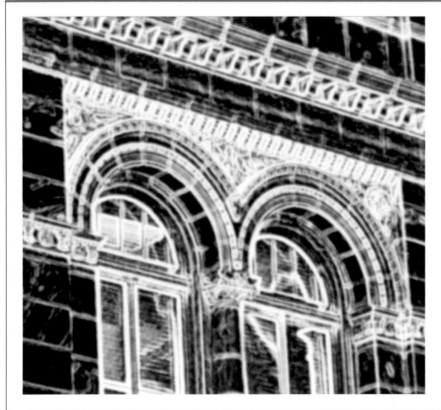

FIGURE 8-8.

If you've tried high-pass sharpening (page 259), then you won't have any trouble understanding this helpful view. Just Alt-drag/Option-drag the Detail tab's Masking slider to see this black-and-white view of your image. The lack of color in this view makes it easy to focus on what you're doing to the edge sharpness in the photo, so you get a highly accurate view of the effect each slider is having. (The other sliders also show a different view when you Alt-drag/Option-drag them, but it's more like what you see when applying the High Pass filter.)

If you're not planning on making any further edits to your photo when you leave the Raw Converter, then go ahead and sharpen your image here. On the other hand, some people prefer to wait and sharpen only after they finish all their other adjustments in the Editor, so they skip these sliders. But you can usually sharpen here and then sharpen again later (in the Editor) without any problems.

The second group of settings on this tab (under Noise Reduction) work together to reduce *noise* (graininess) in your photos. Noise is a big problem in digital photos, especially with 5-plus megapixel cameras that don't have the large sensors found in single-lens reflex cameras, and with cellphone cameras. Here's how these adjustments can help:

- **Luminance.** You can reduce grayscale noise, which gives photos an overall grainy appearance—something like what you see in old newspaper photos—by adjusting this slider. The slider always starts at 0, since you don't want to use more than you need—moving it to the right reduces noise but also softens the image's details.

- **Luminance Detail.** This helps set the threshold for luminance noise reduction. If you set it high, you preserve more details but may have a noisier photo. If you set it low, you have less noise, but maybe less detail, too.

- **Luminance Contrast.** Set this slider higher and you can preserve some of the contrast you might lose with the Luminance slider, but too high a setting here can produce blotches or mottling. Set this slider low and you get smoother results that preserve more of the image's texture, but you may lose some contrast.

- **Color.** If areas of your photo that should be evenly colored contain obvious clumps of different-colored pixels, this setting can help smooth things out. Drag this slider to the right to reduce the amount of color noise.

- **Color Detail.** This slider works on color noise the same way the Luminance Detail slider works on luminance noise. If you set this slider high, detailed color edges get preserved, but you might see some color speckling in your photo. Set it low and you'll have less color noise, but you may see some bleeding where colors meet.

In most cases, it may take a fair amount of fiddling with these sliders to come up with the best compromise between sharpness and smoothness. It helps if you zoom in to 100 percent or more when using these sliders.

Non-Raw Files in the Raw Converter

If your camera shoots JPEGs and you've always been curious about what this Raw business is all about, you can find out for yourself—sort of. You can open and process JPEG, PSD, and TIFF files with the Raw Converter. (If you want to try another kind of file, save it as a TIFF and *then* open it with the Raw Converter. That way you can take advantage of the Converter's special tools, like Vibrance or Clarity, for any photo.)

To open non-Raw files from the Editor, in Windows, go to File→Open As, select the image, and then choose Camera Raw as the format. (If you're on a Mac, go to File→Open, select the image, and then choose Camera Raw from the Format menu.) The image opens in the Converter, and you can work on it just like a real Raw file—well, almost. The thing about using other formats in the Converter is this: When your camera processed the JPEG file that it wrote to its memory card, it tossed out the info it didn't need for the JPEG, so Elements doesn't have the same amount of data to work with as it does for a true Raw

file. The Converter lets you create a DNG—digital negative—file (page 284) from a JPEG if you want, but it can't put back the info that wasn't included in the JPEG, so this feature isn't really very useful for most people.

Because non-Raw files don't have as much info as Raw files, working with them in the Raw Converter can lead to some iffy results. You may find that the Converter does a bang-up job on your photo, or you may decide you liked it better before you started messing with it. There are so many variables involved that it's really hard to predict the results you'll get, but it's definitely worth a try.

If you find you like using the Raw Converter for JPEGs, then you might want to experiment with reducing your camera's saturation, contrast, and sharpening settings, if possible. That's because you're more likely to get good results from the Raw Converter if your image is fairly neutral to start with.

Choosing Bit Depth

Once you've got your photo looking good, you have one more important choice to make: Do you want to open it as an 8-bit file or a 16-bit file? *Bit depth* refers to how many pieces of color data, or *bits,* each pixel in an image can hold. A single pixel of an 8-bit image can have 24 pieces of information in it—8 for each of the three color channels (red, green, and blue). A 16-bit image holds far more color info than an 8-bit photo. How much more? An 8-bit image can hold up to 16 million colors, which may sound like a lot, but a 16-bit image can hold up to 281 *trillion* colors.

> **TIP** You can adjust 16-bit images with microscopic precision, but your home printer only prints in 8-bit color. If you want to do all your editing (or at least 90 percent of it) in 16-bit color, then consider upgrading to Photoshop.

Most digital cameras produce Raw files with 10 or 12 bits per channel, although a few can shoot 16-bit files. Elements can save any of these original bit depths as either 8- or 16-bit files. You'd think it would be a good idea to save digital files at the largest possible bit depth, but you'll find quite a few restrictions on what you can do with 16-bit files in Elements. You can open them, make some corrections, and save them, but that's about it. You can't work with layers or apply the more artistic filters to 16-bit files, though you can use many of Elements' Auto commands. If you want to work with layers on 16-bit files, then you need to upgrade to Photoshop.

NOTE Your scanner may *say* it handles 24-bit color, but this is actually the same as what Elements calls 8-bit. Elements goes by the number of bits per color channel, whereas some scanner manufacturers try to impress you by giving you the total for all three channels (8 x 3 = 24). So when you see really high bit numbers on scanners—assuming they're not machines for commercial print shops—you can usually get the Elements equivalent by dividing by three.

Once you've decided between 8- and 16-bit color, make your selection in the Depth drop-down menu at the bottom of the Raw Converter window. This setting is "sticky," so all your images open in the color depth you choose until you change it. If you ever forget what bit depth you've chosen, your image's title bar or tab tells you, as shown in Figure 8-9.

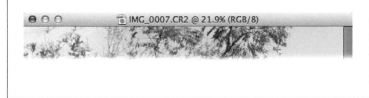

FIGURE 8-9.

You can always tell an image's bit depth by looking at the top bar or tab of its image window in the Editor. The 8 at the end of this title tells you that this is an 8-bit image.

TIP If you decide to create a 16-bit image and later become frustrated by your lack of editing options, then you can convert the image to 8-bit by choosing Image→Mode→8 Bits/Channel in the Editor. (You can't convert an 8-bit image to 16 bits, however.)

If you want to take advantage of any 16-bit files you have, you may want to convert a copy of the file to 8 bits, and then use either Save As or the Organizer's version set option when you save it. That way, you'll still have the 16-bit file for future reference. (Incidentally, your Save options are different for the two bit depths: JPEG, for instance, is available only for 8-bit files, because JPEGs are *always* 8-bit. Because of this, if you try to save a 16-bit file as a JPEG, Elements makes you save it as a copy.)

A popular choice when you're thinking about your order of operations (*workflow*, in photo industry–speak) is to first convert your Raw file as a 16-bit image to take advantage of the increased color information and make basic corrections, and then convert to 8-bit for the fancy stuff like adding artistic filters or layers in the Editor.

Finishing Up

Now that you've got your photo all tweaked, sleeked, and groomed to look exactly the way you want, it's time to get it out of the Raw Converter. To do that, click the Open Image button in the Converter's lower-right corner, which sends the image to the Editor, where you can save it in the format of your choice, like TIFF or JPEG. (Why not click the Raw Converter's Save Image button? Adobe should probably rename this button, which confuses everyone. The Save Image button is actually a link to the DNG Converter, discussed in the next section.)

If you just want to save your changes without opening the file, just click Done to close the Converter. The next time you open the Raw file, the Raw Converter will remember where you left off.

POWER USERS' CLINIC

Working with Profiles

The Raw Converter has yet another trick up its sleeve. (You can safely ignore this feature if you're a beginner, but it's pretty handy for Raw experts.) In addition to the Basic and Detail tabs, the Converter also has a Camera Calibration tab (its icon is a little camera). This tab includes a Process menu for choosing the process for your Raw conversion, and a Name drop-down menu.

Your choices in the Name menu depend on your particular camera model, but the list typically includes a group of profiles with names like Adobe Standard, Camera Portrait, Camera Neutral, and so on; some numbered profiles that seem to imply you're using an older version of Adobe Camera Raw; or a combination of both kinds of profiles. What's the point of this cryptic list? It lets you choose from the different *profiles* for your camera—basically, sets of parameters that the Raw

Converter uses to convert the Raw files from cameras into recognizable photos. (The Raw Converter can use any profile with any process you choose from this tab's Process menu.)

Just click through the profiles in the list to see their effects (watch how the preview of your image changes) and choose the one you like best. (You can edit these profiles in Photoshop, but not in Elements.) If you're wondering why the list shows older ACR (Adobe Camera Raw) versions like 4.2, that's because the list shows the version numbers for when the built-in Adobe Camera Raw profiles were last updated. (Not all camera models list these older profiles.) So if you've been thinking, "You know, I prefer the way my Raw files looked a couple of versions ago," no problem. Just pick the older profile version from the list to use that instead of the newest one.

Converting to DNG

A few years ago, there was a lot of buzz about Adobe's DNG (digital negative) format, and if you shoot Raw, you should know what it is. As you learned at the beginning of this chapter, every camera manufacturer uses a different format for Raw files. Even the formats for different cameras from the same manufacturer differ. It's a recipe for an industry-wide headache.

Adobe's solution is the DNG format, which the company envisions as a more standardized alternative to Raw files. Here's how it works: When you convert a Raw file to a DNG file, it still behaves like a Raw file—you can still tweak its settings in the Raw Converter, and you still have to save it in standard image formats like TIFF or JPEG to use it in a project. But the idea behind DNG is that if you save your Raw files in this format, then you don't have to worry about whether Elements 35 can open them. Adobe clearly hopes that all camera manufacturers will adopt this standard, putting an end to the mishmash of different formats that make Raw files such a nuisance to deal with. If all cameras used DNG, then when you bought a new camera you wouldn't have to worry about whether your programs could view the camera's images.

You can create DNG files from Raw files right in the Raw Converter. At the bottom left of the window, just click the Save Image button, and up pops the DNG Converter shown in Figure 8-10. Choose a destination (where you want to save the file), and then select how you want to name the DNG file. You get the same naming options as with Process Multiple Files (page 295), but since you can only use the DNG Converter to convert one file at a time here, you may as well keep the photo's current name and just add the .dng extension to the end of it.

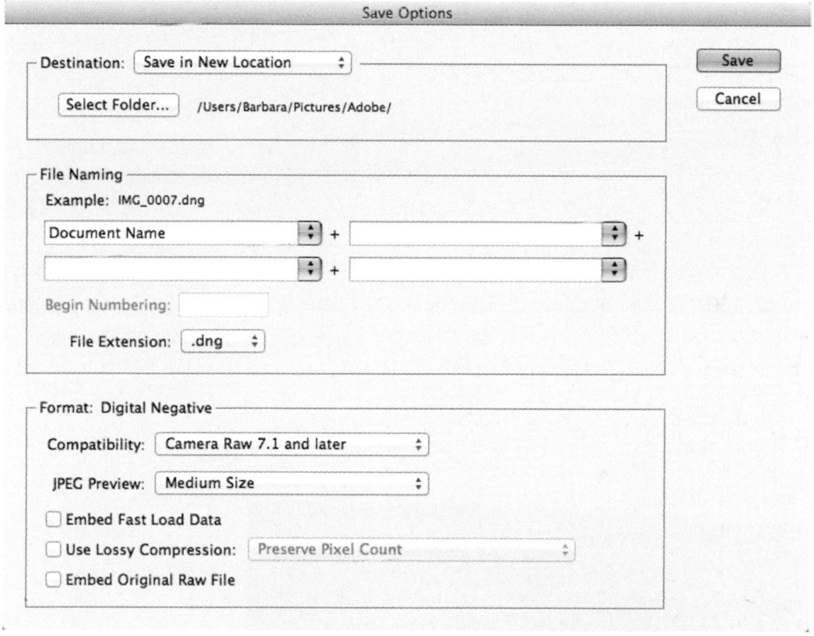

FIGURE 8-10.

Elements' DNG Converter. The bottom section of this window lets you tell Elements whether to compress the file, how to handle the image preview, and whether to embed your original Raw file in the new DNG file. Generally, you're best off leaving the settings in this section the way they are here.

The jury is still out on whether DNG is going to become the industry standard. But people have had other good ideas over the years like the JPEG 2000 format (see page 71) that never really took off. DNG hasn't proved to be quite as universal as Adobe had hoped, so a fair number of people are becoming a bit skeptical about the ultimate fate of DNG, and it's not nearly as popular now as it was a few years ago. Whether you create DNG files from your Raw files is up to you, but for now, it's probably prudent to hang onto the original Raw files as well, even if you decide in favor of DNG.

> **TIP** If you want to convert a group of Raw files to DNG in one batch, the easiest way is to go to Adobe's website (*www.adobe.com/downloads*), search for "DNG," and then download the stand-alone DNG Converter, and then make a shortcut to it on your desktop so it's always available. Then just drop a folder of Raw images onto its icon, and the DNG Converter processes the whole folder at once. You can also save all the images open in the Raw Converter at once by highlighting them in the list on the left side of the window and then clicking Save Images.

■ Blending Exposures

If you've been using a digital camera for any length of time, you know what a juggling act it can be to get a photo that's properly exposed everywhere, from its deepest shadows to its brightest highlights. With most digital cameras, you're likely to hit the clipping point (page 275) in an image much sooner than you want to: If you up the exposure so the shadows are nice and detailed, then about half the time you blow out the highlights. On the other hand, if you adjust the exposure settings down to favor the highlights, then your shadows are murkier than an old Enron annual report. Figure 8-11 shows the problem.

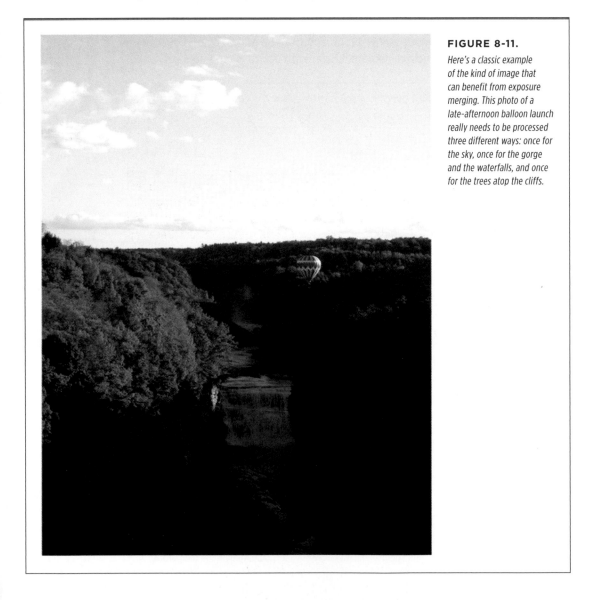

FIGURE 8-11.

Here's a classic example of the kind of image that can benefit from exposure merging. This photo of a late-afternoon balloon launch really needs to be processed three different ways: once for the sky, once for the gorge and the waterfalls, and once for the trees atop the cliffs.

Digital blending is a technique photographers use to get around these limitations. To use it, you *bracket* your shots, meaning you take two or more identical photos of your subject at different settings—one exposed for shadows and one for highlights—and then combine them, choosing the best bits of each one. People who are fanatical about getting their images truly perfect may combine several different exposures.

That technique is great for landscapes, but if you're shooting hummingbirds, roller-skating chimps, or toddlers, you know it's just about impossible to get two identical shots of a moving subject. And if you're like many people, you may not realize you didn't capture what you wanted until you see the shot on your computer at home. But even if you only have one photo of that perfect moment, you can sometimes cheat a bit and get a similar result from processing the photo twice in the Raw Converter (once to favor the shadowy areas, and once for the highlights) so you wind up with two exposures. The problem is figuring out how to combine them into one great image.

TIP The Raw Converter's new processing engine may be able to tease enough exposure range from your photo so that you don't need to blend two exposures, even if it's not a Raw file. Try that first. Page 282 explains how to work with non-Raw files in the Raw Converter.

If you can't make the Raw Converter's settings work, or if the Raw Converter just makes you nervous, Elements gives you another super simple way to blend images. It's called Photomerge Exposure, and it's as easy to use as any of the program's other Photomerge features (see Chapter 11). It can even be a one-click fix, if you want. Elements offers several ways to blend photos. Your main choice is between an automatic merge, where Elements makes most of the decisions, and a manual merge, which gives you more control but requires a little more effort.

NOTE Exposure merging isn't meant for blending two totally different photos together, like replacing the blown out sky in your photo of the Taj Mahal with a good sky from a photo of your dude-ranch trip. To use Photomerge Exposure, your photos should be pretty much identical except for their exposures. So use images you took with your camera's exposure bracketing feature, or even one shot you've processed twice or more to get one good version with properly exposed highlights, one with good shadows, and so on. Sadly, Elements actually does a better job with a single photo processed two ways than it does with multiple shots, so if you don't like what you get by blending two actual exposures, take the best one, process it two ways, and then use those files as the basis of your merge.

Automatic Merges

It's incredibly easy to combine photos using the Automatic Merge feature because Elements makes most of the decisions for you. (If that's not for you, you can opt for a manual merge, where you call the shots, as explained in the next section.) Here's what you do:

1. **Prepare, open, and select your images.**

   You can start with two or more photos where you used exposure bracketing on your camera, or with one image that you've processed in two (or more) different ways in the Raw Converter (page 264), for example, once favoring the shadows and once the highlights.

   Elements lets you combine up to 10 photos, so you can create as many different versions as you need to make sure every part of the image is properly exposed. Then select the photos you want to work with in the Photo Bin, and you're ready for the next step.

2. **Call up the Photomerge Exposure window.**

   You can get to it from the Editor in either Expert Mode or Guided Edit. In Expert Mode, go to Enhance→Photomerge→Photomerge Exposure, or Guided Edit→Photomerge→Exposure. Either way, the Photomerge Exposure window opens. It's a lot like the windows for Group Shot, Faces, and Scene Cleaner, if you've used any of those before, and it works much the same way.

3. **Tell Elements you want to perform an automatic merge.**

   Most of the time, the Exposure Merge window opens with the Automatic tab active, so you'll see the final, automatically merged image. If it doesn't, simply click that tab on the right side of the window. (It's easy to tell which tab is active without even looking at the right side of the window: In Automatic mode, you see only one image in the preview area on the left of the screen, while in Manual mode you see two.)

4. **Select a merge option and make any adjustments you want.**

   On the right side of the Exposure Merge window are two radio buttons that let you choose the type of automatic merge:

   - **Simple Blending.** Elements does everything—all you have to do is click Done.

   - **Smart Blending.** If you pick this option, you can use the three sliders on the right side of the window to adjust the merge. (The sliders are explained below.) Elements uses a different kind of analysis on your photo here than it does if you opt for the Simple Blending merge, so don't be surprised if the appearance of your image shifts a bit when you click this radio button.

   You can't use the sliders if you have Simple Blending selected; they become active only when you choose Smart Blending.

5. **When you're happy with what you see, click Done.**

   Elements blends the photos in a new file so that your originals are preserved. Don't forget to save the blended image.

That's all there is to it. Elements usually does a pretty good job (depending on your photos, of course), as shown in Figure 8-12. But you can help the program by nudging the Smart Blending sliders if you aren't quite satisfied with what Elements proposes for your image. Here's what each slider does:

- **Highlight Details** controls the way Elements blends the bright areas of the images.

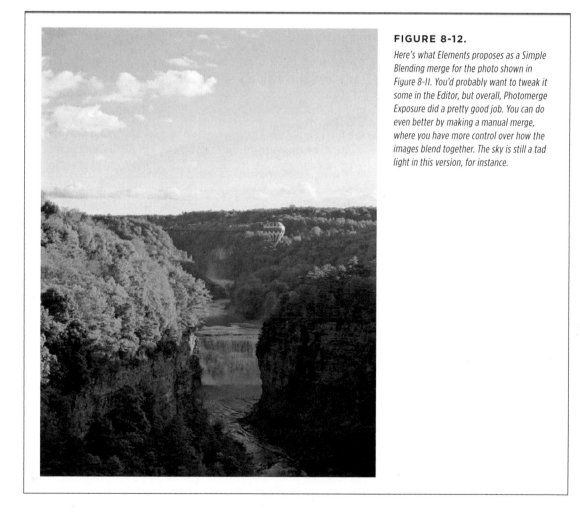

FIGURE 8-12.

Here's what Elements proposes as a Simple Blending merge for the photo shown in Figure 8-11. You'd probably want to tweak it some in the Editor, but overall, Photomerge Exposure did a pretty good job. You can do even better by making a manual merge, where you have more control over how the images blend together. The sky is still a tad light in this version, for instance.

• **Shadows** adjusts the blend of the darker areas.

TIP If you've used Shadows/Highlights (page 223), you already know everything you need to about these two sliders.

• **Saturation** adjusts the blended image's color intensity, which is handy if the blend made your photo look a little drab or oversaturated. It's similar to the Saturation slider in Quick Fix (page 129).

If you prefer to have more control over what Elements does, you can combine your photos manually instead, as explained next.

Manual Merges

Automatic merges are super easy to do, even for a beginner, but sometimes Elements doesn't get it right. Or maybe you just like telling Elements what to do rather than accepting its judgment about your images. Either way, manual merges are what you want.

You begin a manual merge the same way as an automatic one (follow steps 1 and 2 on page 288). Then, once you have the Photomerge Exposure window open, do the following:

1. **Choose to make a manual merge.**

   On the right side of the Photomerge Exposure window, click the Manual tab if it's not already active. When you do, Elements changes the preview area to display spaces for two photos.

2. **Choose a background photo.**

   This is the photo that's going to be the basis of your merge—the one you'll blend bits of other photos into. Usually, you'll want to pick the photo with the largest area of correct exposure, though the tip below describes an exception to this rule. (You can use up to 10 photos in a manual merge, but you only work with two at a time.) Drag your background photo of choice into the right-hand slot.

TIP If you're blending several exposures, you may get the best results if you choose the photo with the best midtones as your background photo, even if that's not the photo with the largest properly exposed area. That's because Elements likes to start from the middle and work out when blending several images (in other words, it does better if you let it figure out the midtones first before making it blend the shadows and highlights).

---

3. **Choose a foreground photo.**

This is the photo you'll copy bits from to put in the background photo. Double-click it to tell Elements it's the one you want to use. It appears in the left-hand slot. (Elements sometimes picks a foreground image for you, but it's not always a good guesser and you may want to override the choice it made.)

4. **Tell Elements what to copy.**

Click the Pencil Tool button on the right side of the window and drag over the areas in the foreground photo that you want to move to the background photo. This tool works like the Quick Selection tool in that it automatically expands the selection from the line or dot you make. (It's not like the regular Pencil tool in the Expert Mode Tools panel.) If it selects too much or if you drag over something by mistake, use the Eraser tool to remove some of your marks (see Figure 8-13).

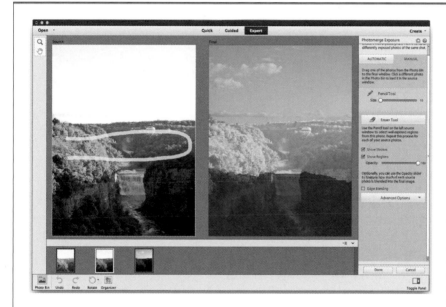

FIGURE 8-13.

Here's the midpoint of creating a manual merge of the image in Figure 8-11. (The Show Regions checkbox is turned on here to make it easier to see what Elements is doing.) Here, the trees on the cliffs are being brought over from the left image, as indicated by the yellow mask on the right-hand image. However, the balloon itself is a tad overexposed in spots in the left image, so you might want to go back with the Eraser tool and remove the marks over it so that it doesn't get copied over, or else zoom the view way in to erase only the blown-out white parts.

5. **If you need to, align the photos.**

   If your copied material is slightly out of alignment with the background photo (a common problem if you used exposure bracketing for live subjects), scroll down in the Manual tab and click the Advanced Option button, and then click the Alignment Tool button. When you do, three little target marks appear in each preview when you move your cursor over the photo. Drag the marks so they're in the same spot in each photo (like over a tiger's eyes and mouth in bracketed wildlife photos), and then click the Align Photos button. Elements figures out the difference in perspective between the two images and corrects for it.

6. **Tweak the blending.**

   You may be horrified by how crudely Elements blends the images at first, but that's OK. There are two settings in the Manual tab that you can use to fix things:

   - **Opacity.** Use this slider to adjust the foreground image's transparency for a more realistic effect.

   - **Edge Blending.** Turn on this checkbox and Elements automatically refines the edges of the blend to avoid a cut-and-pasted look. Try turning on this checkbox before adjusting the Opacity slider.

   TIP If you want a large view of your images while you're working, you can temporarily hide the Photomerge Exposure panel by clicking the button at the bottom right of the Elements window. To bring it back, click the button again.

7. **Repeat with other images, if you wish.**

   To add details from another image that you preselected, drag it to the foreground image slot and repeat the process. You can keep doing this to combine a total of 10 images. Each additional photo gets a different colored marker to help you keep track of what came from which photo.

8. **When you like what you see, click Done.**

   As with an automatic merge, Elements creates a new layered file for the blended image so your originals are untouched.

If you need to adjust the view while you're working on a merge, Elements gives you some help:

- **Zoom and Hand tools.** Your old friends the Zoom and Hand tools live in the little toolbox to the left of the images. They work the same way here as everywhere else in Elements.

- **Show Strokes.** This checkbox in the Manual tab lets you show or hide the marks you make with the Selection tool.

- **Show Regions.** Turn this on and Elements displays a blue-green mask over the background photo, with yellow over the areas where it's blending in material from the foreground photo, as you can see in Figure 8-13. The balloon and top of the cliffs are yellow because that's what's coming over from the foreground photo. (If you add more photos, each gets a mask colored to match its marker color.)

> **TIP** Photomerge Exposure is fun, but you may want something a bit more powerful. In that case, you should explore HDR (high dynamic range) programs and plug-ins. Regardless of whether you have a Windows computer or a Mac, a good place to start is *www.hdrlabs.com*. Mac folks should also check out Bracketeer from Pangeasoft (*www.pangeasoft.net*), an excellent exposure-blending program that produces wonderful results.

WORKAROUND WORKSHOP

Manually Blending Exposures

Elements' Photomerge Exposure tool makes it pretty easy to blend exposures, but you may not care for the final result, no matter how much effort you put into it. In that case, you can just blend the images yourself by stacking them up:

1. **Open both exposures.** You can only work with two images at once when you do it this way.

2. **Pick the photo with the largest amount of properly exposed area.** That's going to be the top layer of your combined image.

3. **Turn that photo into a regular layer.** Double-click it in the Layers panel to unlock it. You can give it a name, if you want, or just click OK to accept the one Elements gives it.

4. **Apply a layer mask to it.** Click the layer mask icon at the top of the Layers panel (it looks like a circle within a square).

5. **Combine the images.** From the Layers panel, drag the masked photo's layer thumbnail onto the main image window of the other image, or select it by pressing Ctrl+A/⌘-A, and then copy and paste it into the other image. (See page 211 for more about moving layers from one photo to another.)

6. **Edit the layer mask to combine the images.** On the layer mask, paint out the badly exposed areas of the masked photo to let the well-exposed parts of the other image show through. See page 205 for the details of how to do this.

To add additional exposures, merge the two existing layers first (page 200), and then repeat the process with another image.

■ Photo Filter

Elements' Photo Filter feature gives you a host of nifty filters to work with. They're the digital equivalent of the lens-mounted filters used in traditional film photography. They can help you correct problems with an image's white balance and perform a bunch of other fixes from the seriously photographic to the downright silly. For example, you can correct bad skin tone or dig out an old photo of your fifth-grade nemesis and make him green. Figure 8-14 shows the Photo Filter in action.

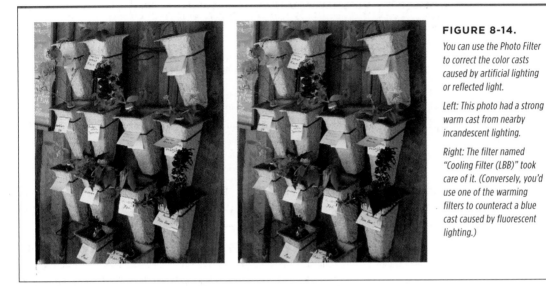

FIGURE 8-14.

You can use the Photo Filter to correct the color casts caused by artificial lighting or reflected light.

Left: This photo had a strong warm cast from nearby incandescent lighting.

Right: The filter named "Cooling Filter (LBB)" took care of it. (Conversely, you'd use one of the warming filters to counteract a blue cast caused by fluorescent lighting.)

Elements comes with 20 photo filters, but for most people, the first six in the list (see step 2 below) are the most important: three warming filters and three cooling filters, which you use to get rid of color casts caused by poor white balance (see page 271).

These filters sometimes work better than the Color Cast eyedropper (page 245) because you can control their strength using the Density slider (explained in a moment). You can also apply them as Adjustment layers, so you can tweak them later on.

To apply a photo filter:

1. **Open the Photo Filter dialog box, or create a new Adjustment layer.**

   Go to Filter→Adjustments→Photo Filter, or Layer→New Adjustment Layer→Photo Filter. Either way, you see the Photo Filter adjustment controls. If you're applying the Photo Filter directly to your image, you get a dialog box. If you go the Adjustment-layer route, the controls appear in the Adjustments panel instead (after you click OK to create the layer), but both offer exactly the same controls.

2. **Choose a filter from the drop-down list, or click the Color radio button and choose a color.**

   The drop-down list gives you a choice of filters in preset colors. (The numbers following the names of some filters correspond to the numbers of the equivalent glass filters you'd use on a film camera.)

   To pick your own custom color, click the Color button instead. Then click the color square next to it to bring up the "Select filter color" dialog box—which is really just the Color Picker (page 249)—and choose the shade you want. Pick a color for the filter, and Elements applies it to your image so you can decide whether you like it (you may have to drag the dialog box out of the way to see your image). When you've got the color you want, click OK to close the Color Picker.

3. **In the Adjustments panel or Photo Filter dialog box, move the Density slider to adjust the filter's intensity.**

   Moving the slider right increases the filter's effect; moving it left decreases it. If you leave the Preserve Luminosity checkbox turned on, then the filter doesn't darken the image. Turn off the checkbox and your photo gets darker when you apply the filter. Watch your image to see the effect.

4. **When your photo looks good, save it.**

Processing Multiple Files

If you're addicted to batch-processing photos, then you'll love Elements' Process Multiple Files feature. In addition to renaming files and changing their formats, you can do a lot of other very useful things with this tool, like adding copyright information or captions to multiple files, or even using some of Quick Fix's Auto commands.

To call up the batch-processing window, in Expert Mode, go to File→Process Multiple Files. You see yet another headache-inducing, giant Elements dialog box. Fear not—this one is actually pretty easy to understand. If you look closely, you see that it's divided into sections, each with a different specialty (see Figure 8-15).

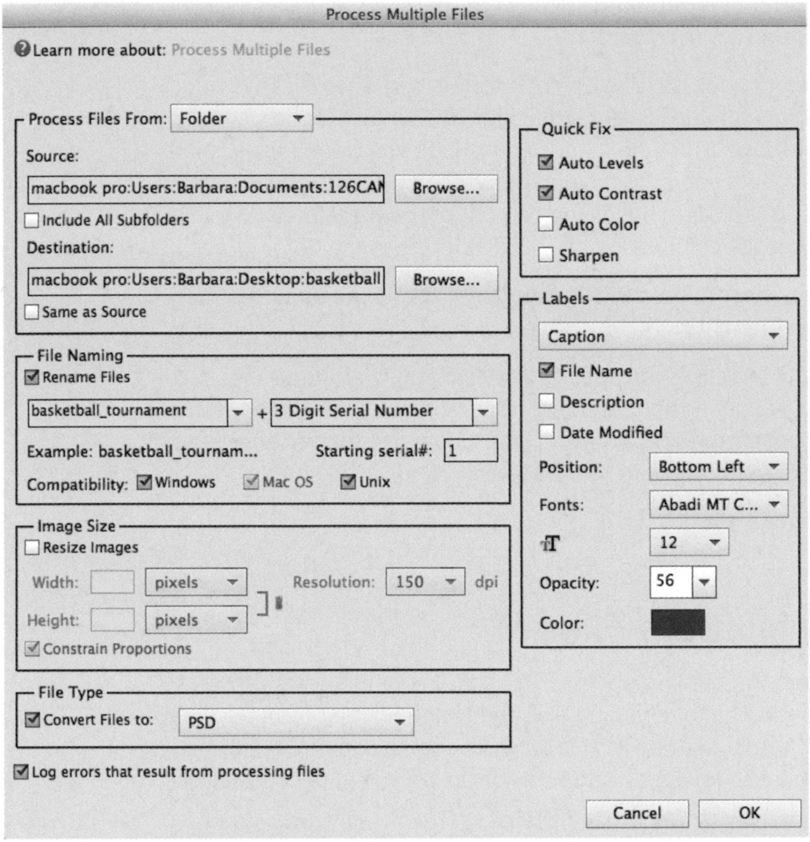

FIGURE 8-15.

You could call Process Multiple Files "Computer, Earn Your Keep," because it can make so many changes at once.

Here, the dialog box is set up to apply the following changes: Rename every file (from things like PICT8983 *to* basketball_tournament001, basketball_tournament002, *and so on), change the images to PSD format, apply Auto Levels and Auto Contrast, and add the filename as a caption. You make all that happen just by clicking OK.*

> **TIP**   Process *Multiple* Files is the name of this command, but you can run it on just one photo if you want (although you'll usually find it easier to use the Save As command instead; see Chapter 2 for more about saving files). Just open a photo, go to File→Process Multiple Files, and then, in the Process Files From drop-down menu, choose Opened Files. You can even opt to save the new version to the desktop so you don't overwrite the original.

The following sections cover each part of the Process Multiple Files dialog box. You *have* to use the first section (which tells Elements which files to process), but you'll probably want to use only one or two of the other sections at any given time (though you can use them all, as shown in Figure 8-15).

TIP If you're working in the Organizer, then you can do some batch-processing without opening the Editor. Select the files you want, and then go to File→Export As New File(s) (or press Ctrl+E). You get a dialog box that lets you change the files' format, pick a new size from a list of presets, set a destination for the new images, and choose a new "common base name" (if you want). If you choose this last option, then your files get the new name plus a sequential number. (By the way, this export feature is a great way to create a folder of JPEGs to send to an online photo service.)

Choosing Files

The upper-left section of the Process Multiple Files dialog box is where you tell Elements which files to convert and where to put them once it has processed them. You have several options here, which you select from the Process Files From drop-down menu: the contents of a folder, files you import directly from a camera or compatible scanner, or the currently open files. Choosing Import brings up the same options you get when you select File→Import; use this setting to convert files as you bring them into Elements—from a camera or scanner, for example.

TIP If you want to process files that are scattered around in different locations on your hard drive, then speed things up by opening the files first or gathering them into one folder. If you have a couple of folders' worth of photos to convert, put all those folders into one containing folder and then use the Include All Subfolders option explained in a moment; that way, all the files get converted at once.

Here's a step-by-step tour of the process:

1. **Choose the files you want to convert.**

   Use the Process Files From drop-down menu to select which kind of files you want: ones in a folder, ones imported from your camera or scanner, or ones that are currently open.

2. **If you chose Folder, then tell Elements which folder you want.**

   Click the Browse button next to the Source field and, in the dialog box that appears, choose a folder. (Files you want to process have to be in a folder if they aren't already open.) If you have folders *within* a folder and you want to operate on all those files, then turn on the Include All Subfolders checkbox. Otherwise, Elements changes only the files in the top-level folder.

3. **Pick a destination.**

   The Destination field tells Elements where to put the files after it processes them. Most of the time, you'll want a new folder for this, so click Browse to the right of this field, and then, in the window that opens, click New Folder. Or you can choose an existing folder in the Browse window, but a word of warning if you go this route: Be careful about choosing "Same as Source"; Figure 8-16 explains why.

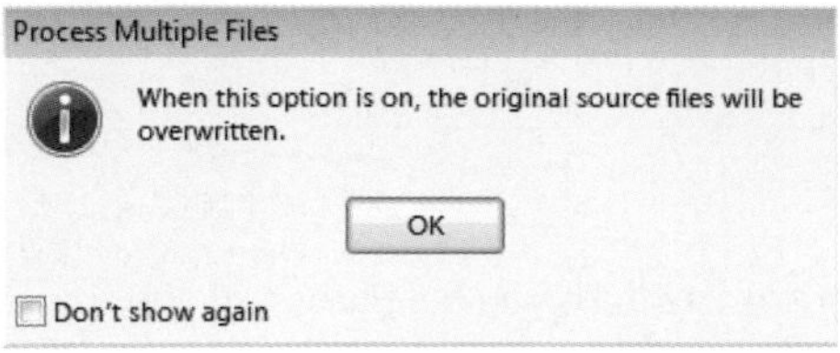

FIGURE 8-16.

If you turn on the "Same as Source" checkbox, then Elements warns you that it's going to replace your originals with the new versions. That can be a timesaver, but it's dangerous, too—if something goes wrong, then your originals are toast. Bottom line: Don't turn on "Same as Source" unless you have backup copies someplace else.

The following sections explain the various things Process Multiple Files can do to the files you've selected.

Renaming Files

Being able to rename a group of files in one fell swoop is a very cool feature, but it has a few limitations. If you think it means you can give each photo a unique name like "Keisha and Gram at the Park," followed by "Fred's New Newt," and so on, you're going to be disappointed. Instead, what Elements offers is a quick way of applying a similar name to a group of files. That means you can easily transform a folder filled with files named *DSCF001.jpg*, *DSCF0002.jpg*, and so on, into the slightly friendlier *Keisha and Gram001.jpg, and Keisha and Gram002.jpg*.

To rename files, turn on the Process Multiple Files dialog box's Rename Files checkbox. Below it are two text boxes with drop-down menus next to them (a + sign separates the menus). You can enter anything you like in these boxes, and it replaces every filename in the group. Or you can choose any of the options in the menus (both menus are the same).

> **TIP** If you turn on the "Same as Source" checkbox, then Elements grays out the Rename Files option. So if you want to put your renamed files in the same folder as the originals, leave "Same as Source" turned off, but select the same folder as the destination in the top part of the dialog box. That way Elements places your renamed files in the same folder as the originals without *replacing* the originals.

The menus offer you a choice of the document name (in three different capitalization styles), serial numbers, serial letters, dates, extensions, or nothing at all (which gives you just numbers without any kind of prefix). Figure 8-17 shows the many options.

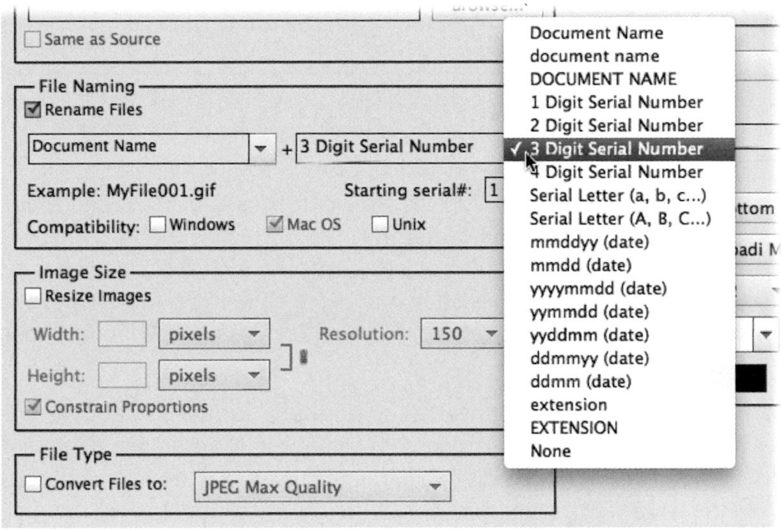

FIGURE 8-17.

Elements offers loads of naming options. If you select Document Name, for example, your photos retain their original names plus whatever you choose from the right-hand drop-down menu. DOCUMENT NAME gets you the same filenames in all capital letters, "1 Digit Serial Number" starts you off with the number 1, and so on.

TIP If you want to add serial numbers to your filenames, you can designate the starting number in the "Starting serial#" box. Elements always starts out by suggesting 1, but you can type over the 1 to change it to any number you please. Once you make a choice, just below the Document Name area, you see an example of how the filename will look. So if you type *tongue_piercing_day* into the first text box and choose 3 Digit Serial Number in the second, then Elements names your photos *tongue_piercing_day001.jpg, black tongue_piercing_day002. jpg*, and so on.

You also get to tell Elements which operating systems' naming conventions it should use when assigning the new names, as explained in Figure 8-18. If you send files to people or servers that run other operating systems, then you know how important this is. Your best bet is to play it safe and turn on all three checkboxes; you never know when you may need to send a photo to your nephew who uses Linux isn't a choice in the figure.

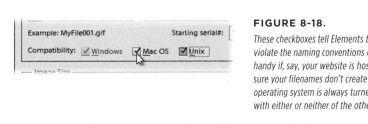

FIGURE 8-18.

These checkboxes tell Elements to watch out for any characters that would violate the naming conventions of the operating systems you select. This is handy if, say, your website is hosted on a Unix server and you want to be sure your filenames don't create problems for it. The checkbox for your own operating system is always turned on, and you can choose to be compatible with either or neither of the other operating systems.

Changing Image Size and File Type

The Image Size and File Type sections of the Process Multiple Files dialog box let you resize photos and change their file formats, respectively. The Image Size settings work best when you're trying to reduce file sizes (say you've got a folder of images that you've converted for Web use but found are still too large).

> **NOTE** Before you make any big changes to a group of files, it's important to understand how changes to an image's resolution and file size affect its appearance. See page 101 for a refresher.

To apply image-size changes, turn on the Resize Images checkbox, and then adjust the Width, Height, and Resolution settings, all of which work the same way as those described on page 105. You'll get better results with this command if you make sure all the images you run it on in one batch have the same orientation. In other words, use it on a group of landscape-oriented files and then on a group of portrait-oriented images.

The File Type section lets you convert files from one format to another. This is probably the most popular batch-processing activity. If, for example, your camera creates JPEGs and you want to edit TIFFs, then you can change a whole folder at once. From the drop-down menu, just select the type of files you want to create.

The final setting on the left side of the dialog box is a checkbox that makes Elements log any errors it runs into while processing your files. It's a good idea to turn this checkbox on, as explained in Figure 8-19.

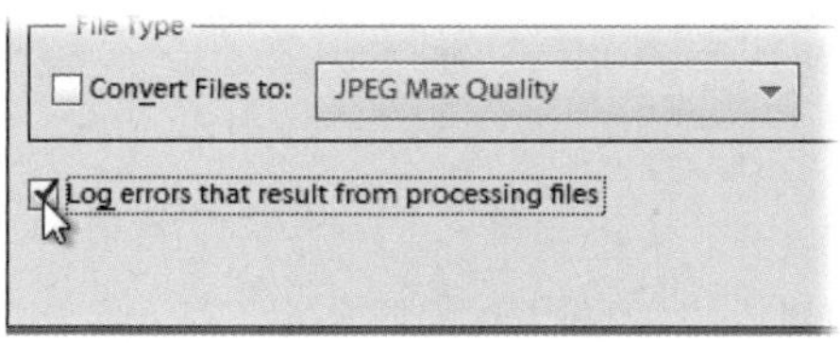

FIGURE 8-19.

If you turn on this checkbox, then Elements lets you know if it runs into any problems while converting the files. It creates a little text log file with the extension .txt and puts it in the folder with your completed images, whether there were problems or not. (If nothing went awry, the file is blank.)

Applying Quick Fix Commands

In the upper-right corner of the Process Multiple Files dialog box are some of the same Quick Fix commands you find in the regular Quick Fix window. If you consistently get good results with the Auto commands there, then you can use these checkboxes to run them on a whole folder at once.

You can run Auto Levels, Auto Contrast, Auto Color, Auto Sharpen, or any combination of those commands on all the files in the folder you're processing. If you need a refresher on what each one does, see Chapter 4, beginning on page 125.

Unfortunately, you can't batch-run the Auto Smart Fix command from this dialog box. If that's what you want to do, or if your only reason for bringing up the Process

Multiple Files dialog box is to use any of the editing options (without renaming, resizing, or using any of the dialog box's other features), then you can save time by selecting your photos in the Organizer and running those commands right from the Organizer's Instant Fix pane, as explained on page 116.

> **TIP** Don't forget that you can also batch-process corrections in the Raw Converter (see page 267). Then open the files in the Editor and use Process Multiple Files to save all the changed files at once.

Attaching Labels

The tools in the dialog box's Labels section let you add copyright notices, which Elements calls *watermarks*, and captions to images (see Figure 8-20). Watermarks and captions get imprinted right onto the photo itself. The process is the same for creating both; only the content differs. A watermark contains any text you choose, while a caption is limited to your choices from a group of checkboxes.

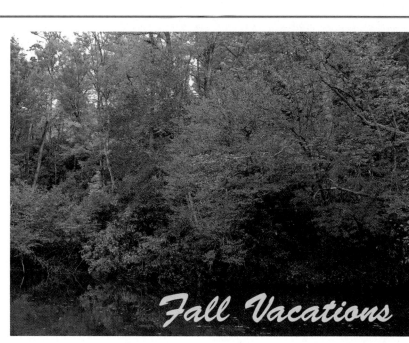

FIGURE 8-20.

The text "Fall Vacations" in this image is what Adobe calls a watermark. Elements is very flexible about the fonts and sizes you can choose for a watermark or a caption, but you don't get much say in where it goes on your photo if you use the Process Multiple Files feature. For maximum flexibility, use a type tool instead, as explained on page 479. The drawback: You can't batch-process using that method.

First, you need to choose between a watermark and a caption (select from the drop-down menu right below the Labels heading). You can't do both at once, so if you want both, add one, run Process Multiple Files, and then add the other and run Process Multiple Files again on the resulting images. You can download *fall.jpg* from this book's Missing CD page at *www.missingmanuals.com/cds* to practice adding your own watermarks and captions.

■ WATERMARKS

To create a watermark, enter some text in the Custom Text box and then choose where you want the text to go and what it should look like, as explained in a moment. Text you enter here gets applied to every photo in the batch, so this is a great way to add copyright or contact info that you want on every photo, as shown in Figure 8-21. (If you want different text on each photo, check out the I don't see this in either 8-20 or 8-21.

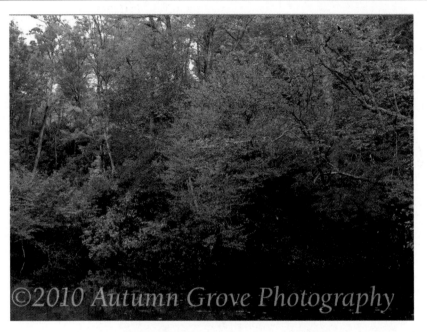

FIGURE 8-21.

You just can't beat Process Multiple Files for quickly adding copyright info to photos, although some other methods create a more sophisticated look, as described in the tip on page 303.

> **TIP** If you're on a Windows computer and want to include the copyright symbol (©), hold the Alt key while typing *0169* on the number pad (not the top row of the keyboard), or use the Character Map (choose Start→All Programs→Accessories→System Tools→Character Map). On a Windows laptop without a number pad, turn on Number Lock (you may need to press the Fn key to do this) and then hold down the Alt key while typing *0169* on the embedded number pad (those are the numbers on the letter keys, not at the top of the keyboard). On a Mac, just press Option-G.

Once you've decided what you want the custom text to say, you need to make some choices about its position and size. These options are the same whether you're adding a watermark or a caption, and if you switch from one to the other before actually running Process Multiple Files, then your previous choices appear:

- **Position.** This tells Elements where to put the text. Your options are Bottom Left, Bottom Right, or Centered. Careful: Centered doesn't mean "bottom center"—it puts the text smack in the middle of your image.

- **Font.** This menu lets you choose any font on your computer. (Chapter 14 has tons of info about fonts.)

- **Size.** This setting (whose icon is two Ts) determines the how big your text is. Click the menu next to the two Ts to choose from several preset sizes, up to 72 point.

- **Opacity.** Use this to adjust how solidly the text prints. Choose 100 percent for maximum readability, or click the down arrow and move the slider to the left for watermark text that lets the image underneath it show through.

- **Color.** Use this setting to select the text's color. Click the box to bring up the Color Picker (page 249) and make your choice.

> **TIP** If you want to use a logo as a watermark, the Process Multiple Files dialog box can't help you. But there *is* a way to apply a logo to a bunch of images in Elements: First, create the logo on a new layer in one of the images. Adjust the Layers panel's Opacity setting until you like the results, and then save the file. Now you can drag that layer from the Layers panel onto the image window for each photo where you need it. (If you Shift-drag the layer, then it goes to exactly the same spot on each image, assuming they're all the same size.) You can also do this with Adjustment layers, which give you a sort of batch-processing capability for applying the same adjustments to multiple files. Another option is to create a custom brush from your logo (page 403) and use that, and then adjust the opacity or apply a layer style (page 461) for a truly custom look.

■ ADDING CAPTIONS

For a caption, you can select any of the following, separately or in combination:

- **File Name.** You can choose to show the file's name as the caption. If you decide to use the Process Multiple Files dialog box's renaming feature at the same time, then Elements uses the new name you're assigning.

- **Description.** Turn this checkbox on to use any text you've entered in the Description section of the File Info dialog box (File→File Info) as your caption. This option is the most flexible one for entering text, and the only way to add different text to each photo you're batch-processing (see Figure 8-21). Just enter text in each photo's Description field before you use Process Multiple Files.

- **Date Modified.** This is the date the file was last changed. In practice, that means today's date, because you're modifying the file by running Process Multiple Files on it.

Your choices for how and where the caption will appear are the same as those listed above for watermarks.

Retouching: Fine-Tuning Images

Basic edits like exposure fixes and sharpening are fine if all you want to make are simple adjustments. But Elements also gives you tools for making sophisticated changes that are easy to apply, and that can make the difference between a ho-hum photo and a fabulous one. This chapter introduces you to some advanced editing maneuvers that can help you rescue damaged photos or give good ones a little extra zing.

The first part of the chapter shows how to get rid of blemishes—not only those that affect skin, but also dust, scratches, stains, and other photographic imperfections. You'll also learn some powerful color-improving techniques, including how to use the Color Curves tool, which is a great way to enhance an image's contrast and color.

Then you'll learn to use the exciting Recompose tool, which lets you change the size and shape of photos, eliminate empty areas between objects, and even remove unwanted elements from pictures, all without distorting the parts you want to keep. This amazing feature works so well that nobody seeing the results would ever suspect the photo wasn't originally shot that way.

■ Fixing Blemishes

It's an imperfect world, but in your photos, it doesn't have to look that way. Elements includes powerful tools for fixing your subject's flaws: You can erase crow's feet and blemishes, eliminate power lines in an otherwise perfect view, or even hide objects you wish weren't in the photo. Not only that, but these same tools are great for fixing problems like tears, folds, and stains—the great foes of photoscanning veterans. With a little effort, you can bring back photos that seem beyond help.

Two of the most important ways to do this are *cloning* and *healing*. Cloning lets you patch bad areas by hiding them with material from elsewhere in a photo. Healing is similar, but when you use this method Elements also evaluates the area around the spot you're fixing and then blends your repair into what's already there. You'll need to use both techniques to fix badly damaged photos. Figure 9-1 shows the kind of restoration you can accomplish with Elements (and a little persistence).

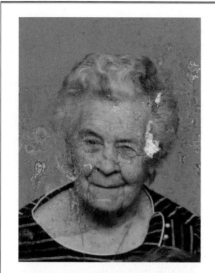

FIGURE 9-1.

Top: Here's a section of a water-damaged family portrait. The grandmother's face is almost obliterated.

Bottom: The same image after repairing it with Elements. It took a lot of cloning and healing to get this result, but if you keep at it, you can do the kind of work that would have required professional help before Elements. If you're interested in restoring old photos, check out Katrin Eismann's books on the subject (Photoshop Restoration and Retouching [New Riders, 2006] is a good one to start with). They cover full-featured Photoshop, but you can adapt most of the techniques for Elements. You might also want to read Matt Kloskowski's The Photoshop Elements 5 Restoration and Retouching Book (Peachpit Press, 2007). Although it's written for Elements 5 for Windows, you can still use the techniques in later versions of Elements for Mac or PC.

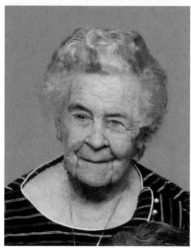

Elements gives you three main tools for this kind of work:

- **The Spot Healing Brush** is the easiest way to repair photos. Just drag over the spot you want to fix, and Elements searches the surrounding area and blends that info into the trouble spot, making it indistinguishable from the background. What's more, you get a Content-Aware option, bringing over one of the most popular features from Photoshop (although Elements' version is much more limited; see page 309). When you use the Content-Aware feature, Elements analyzes your photo so it can create new material that looks like part of the original image. This makes the Spot Healing Brush a truly versatile tool for making seamless fixes.

- **The Healing Brush** works much like the Spot Healing Brush, only you tell the Healing Brush which part of your photo to use as a source for the material you want to blend in. This tool is better suited to large areas, because you don't have to worry about inadvertently dragging in unwanted details (which can happen with the Spot Healing Brush).

- **The Clone Stamp** works like the Healing Brush in that you sample a good area and apply it to the spot you want to fix. But instead of blending the repair in, the Clone Stamp simply covers the bad area with the replacement. This tool is best for situations when you want to *completely* hide the underlying area, as opposed to letting any of what's already there blend into your repair (which is how things work with the Healing Brushes). The Clone Stamp is also your best option for creating a realistic copy of details that are elsewhere in a photo. You can clone some leaves to fill in a bare branch, for instance, or replace a knothole in a fence board with good wood.

All three tools work similarly: You drag each one over the area you want to change. It's as simple as using a paintbrush. In fact, each of these tools requires you to choose a brush like the ones you'll learn about in Chapter 12. Brush selection is pretty straightforward; you'll learn the basics in this chapter.

> **TIP** To smooth out blotchy or blemished skin, check out the Surface Blur filter, explained on page 453. It's a good one to try for minor touch-ups that affect large areas. In contrast, the tools described in this section are better for fixing individual imperfections, like pimples or scars.

The Spot Healing Brush: Fixing Small Areas

The Spot Healing Brush is great at fixing minor blemishes like pimples, lipstick smudges, stray lint, and so on. Simply paint over the area you want to repair, and Elements searches the surrounding regions and blends them into the spot you're brushing. Figure 9-2 shows what a great job this tool can do. (If you'd like to experiment with this tool, download the file *borage.jpg* from this book's Missing CD page at *www.missingmanuals.com/cds*.)

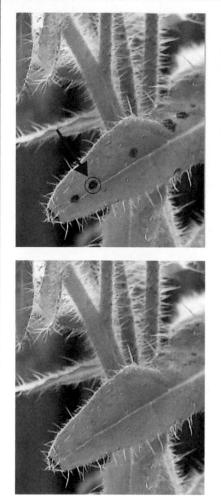

FIGURE 9-2.

The trick to using the Spot Healing Brush is to work on tiny areas. If you choose too large a brush or drag over too large an area, you're more likely to pick up undesired shades and details from the surrounding area.

Top: Say you want to show off your fine crop of borage, but something's been attacking the leaves. Simply grab a brush that's barely bigger than the blemish, like the one shown here.

Bottom: One click with the Spot Healing Brush and you have a truly invisible fix. It took only a few clicks to repair all the brown spots on this leaf.

The Spot Healing Brush's ability to borrow information from surrounding areas is great in some situations, but a drawback in others. The larger the area you drag the brush over, the wider Elements searches for replacement material. So if there's contrasting material close to the area you're trying to fix, it can get pulled into the repair. For instance, if you're trying to fix a spot on an eyelid, you may wind up with some of the color from the eye itself mixed in with your repair.

You get the best results from this brush when you choose a brush size that barely covers the spot you're trying to fix. If you need to drag to fix an oblong area, for instance, use the smallest brush width that covers the flaw. The Spot Healing Brush also works much better when there's a large surrounding area that looks the way you want your repaired spot to look.

TIP Sometimes you can help Elements out by making a selection first, to limit the area where the brush can search for replacement material.

You won't believe how easy it is to fix problem areas with this tool.

1. **Activate the Spot Healing Brush.**

   Click the Healing Brush icon (the Band-Aid) in the Tools panel or press J, and then choose the Spot Healing Brush—the one with the dotted selection lines extending from it—in the Tool Options area. (Both the Healing Brush and the Spot Healing Brush have a Band-Aid icon, but the one for the Spot Healing Brush has a little arc-shaped dotted line next to it.)

2. **Choose a brush just barely bigger than the flaw you're trying to fix.**

   You can adjust your brush size using the Size slider in the Tool Options, or by pressing] (the close bracket key) for a larger brush or [(the open bracket key) for a smaller brush.

   The Spot Healing Brush is set to Content-Aware (explained in a sec), and that's the best setting to try first.

3. **Click the bad spot.**

   If the brush doesn't quite cover the flaw, then drag over the blemished area instead.

4. **When you release the mouse button, Elements repairs the blemish.**

   You may see a weird dark-gray area as you drag. Don't worry—it's just there to show you where you're brushing, and it disappears when you let go.

The Spot Healing Brush has four Tool Options settings:

- **Type.** These radio buttons let you adjust how the brush works:

  - **Proximity Match** tells Elements to search the surrounding area for replacement pixels.

  - **Create Texture** tells it to blend only from the area you drag the cursor over.

  - **Content-Aware** tells the program to do some fancy figuring to invent new material to blend in with the existing photo (see Figure 9-3).

  Your best bet will usually be to try Content-Aware first. If that doesn't do a good job, undo what you did and try Proximity Match instead. Generally speaking, if Proximity Match doesn't work well, you'll get better results by switching to the regular Healing Brush than by choosing Create Texture, though Adobe suggests that you may like the results you get from Create Texture better if you drag over a spot more than once.

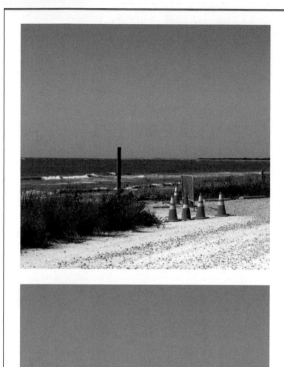

FIGURE 9-3.

The Content-Aware option for the Healing Brushes can give you amazing results with some photos, but it can also result in cases of "so close and yet so far," as you can see here.

Top: The only day you could get to the beach with your camera, there were traffic cones everywhere.

Bottom: The Content-Aware option did a great job of zapping the big wooden post, but large areas like all those cones make it confused about what to use as replacement material. You could keep trying the Spot Healing Brush over and over, but at this point it would be faster to use the Clone Stamp (page 314) for that area instead.

- **Brush.** You can use this drop-down menu to choose a different brush style (see Chapter 12 for more about brushes), but you're usually best off sticking to the standard brush that Elements starts with and just changing its size, if necessary.

- **Size.** Use this slider to adjust the brush's size. You want a brush just barely wide enough to cover the blemish you're healing.

- **Sample All Layers.** Turn this checkbox on if you want the brush to look for replacement material in all your photo's visible layers. If you leave it off, Elements uses material from only the active layer. (Another reason to turn this on: if you created a new, blank layer to heal on so you can blend your work in later by adjusting the healed area's opacity.)

Sometimes you get great results with the Spot Healing Brush on a larger area if it's surrounded by a field that's similar in tone to the spot you're trying to fix, especially if you use the Content-Aware option, but you may find that you need to do extra work for a perfect result (see Figure 9-3). Sometimes you can switch to Proximity Match and finish up, or you may need the regular Healing Brush (explained next) or the Clone Stamp (page 314) to get things just perfect.

The Healing Brush: Fixing Larger Areas

The Healing Brush lets you fix much bigger areas than you can usually manage with the Spot Healing Brush. The main difference between the two tools is that with the regular Healing Brush, *you* choose the area that gets blended into the repair. The blending makes the repair look natural, as Figure 9-4 shows.

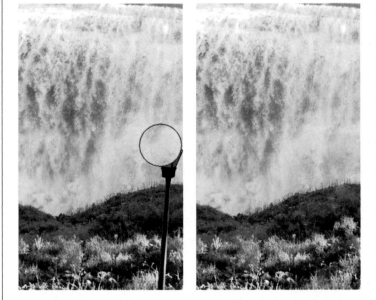

FIGURE 9-4.

Left: After you Alt-click/Option-click to choose your repair source, the source appears inside the brush's cursor. Here, for instance, the cursor contains the part of the waterfall you'll be blending in, rather than the lamppost you'll be covering up. (If this bothers you, see page 313 to learn how to get a regular, empty cursor.)

Right: It took three brushstrokes to eliminate this lamppost (one for the water, one for the grass, and one for where they intersect), but you can see how quickly this method gets you 99 percent of the way to a natural-looking fix. There's a little bit of haze in the grass right along the edge of the cliff that might benefit from a little touching up with the Clone Stamp (page 314), but fixing that only takes another click or two.

TIP You may want to give the Spot Healing Brush's Content-Aware option a try for larger areas, too. If it fails, then go with the regular Healing Brush instead. And sometimes you'll want to use both brushes. For example, in Figure 9-4, the regular Healing Brush does a good job hiding the lamppost where it was in front of the water and the ground, but you might want to try the Spot Healing Brush's Content-Aware option to get a good transition line between the two.

The basics of using the Healing Brush are similar to that of the Spot Healing Brush: Drag over the flaw you want to fix. The difference is that with the Healing Brush, you first need to Alt-click/Option-click where you want Elements to look for replacement pixels. The repair material (which Elements calls your "source") doesn't have to be nearby; in fact, you can sample from a totally different photo if you like (to do that, just arrange both photos in your workspace so you can easily move the cursor between them). Here are the details:

1. **Activate the Healing Brush.**

   Click the Healing Brush's icon (the Band-Aid) in the Enhance section of the Tools panel or press J and then choose it in the Tool Options area.

2. **Find a good spot to use in the repair and Alt-click/Option-click it.**

   When you Alt-click/Option-click the good spot, your cursor temporarily turns into a circle with crosshairs in it to indicate that this is the point from which Elements will retrieve your repair material. (If you want to use material from a different photo, both the source photo and the one you're repairing have to be in the same *color mode*—see page 42.)

3. **Drag over the area you want to repair.**

   You can see where Elements is sampling the repair material from because it puts a + in that spot. As with the Spot Healing Brush, the area you drag over shows the source material until you release the mouse button.

4. **When you let go of your mouse, Elements blends the sampled area into the problem area.**

   You often won't know how effective you were until Elements is through working its magic (it may take a few seconds for the program to finish its calculations and blend in the repair). If you don't like the result, press Ctrl+Z/⌘-Z to undo it and try again.

The Healing Brush offers quite a few Tool Options settings:

- **Brush** and **Size.** The standard brush generally works well, so you'll probably just need to adjust its size, but you can click the brush thumbnail to choose a different brush if you prefer.

- **Brush Settings.** Click this button for a pop-out palette that lets you customize the hardness and shape of your brush cursor (see page 395), as well as the spacing of the marks it makes (page 399). If you have a graphics tablet, you can use the Size menu to tell Elements whether you want to control the brush's size by how hard you press the stylus or by turning the stylus's scroll wheel.

- **Aligned.** If you leave this checkbox turned off, all the source material Elements uses comes from the spot that you Alt-clicked/Option-clicked, as long as you only click rather than dragging. Turn on this checkbox and Elements keeps sampling new source material as you use the tool; the sampling follows the direction of your brush. If you turn the Aligned setting off and *drag* in your photo, the brush behaves as though this setting were turned on.

  Generally, for both the Healing Brush and the Clone Stamp (explained next), it's easier to leave this setting turned off. You can still change the source point by Alt-clicking/Option-clicking another spot, but you often get better results if *you* make the decision about when to move on to another location rather than letting Elements decide.

- **Source.** If you leave this menu set to Sampled, Elements blends the source material into your image as explained above. If you change this menu to Pattern, Elements blends in a pattern instead. Using the Healing Brush with patterns is explained on page 319.

- **Mode.** You can choose from various blend modes (page 190) here, but most of the time, you want one of the top two options: Normal or Replace. Normal is usually your best choice, but if the replacement pixels give the area you're working on a visibly different texture than the surrounding area, choose Replace instead, which preserves the grain of the photo.

- **Clone Overlay.** Click this button for a pop-out palette where you can adjust what you see in the cursor when using this tool. When Show Overlay is turned on, you see a floating, ghostly overlay of the source area where you're sampling in relation to your original, so you can tell exactly how things line up for accurate healing. You can use the other settings here to adjust the overlay's opacity or invert it (make the light areas dark and the dark areas light so that you can see details more clearly) for a better view. The Clipped option pins the overlay to your brush so you see only a brush-sized piece of overlay rather than one that covers the entire image. Turning on the Auto Hide checkbox makes the overlay disappear when you click so it's not in your way as you work. When you first use the Healing Brush, it's set to use a clipped overlay. Just turn off all the settings in this palette if you want an empty circle for your cursor instead.

> **NOTE** The Clone Stamp (explained next) has the same Clone Overlay options as the Healing Brush, and the settings you choose for one tool also apply when you switch to the other tool.

- **Pattern thumbnail.** You won't see this setting unless you've set the Source menu to Pattern. If you did, click this box to select a pattern.

- **Sample All Layers.** This checkbox tells Elements to sample from all the visible layers in the area where you set your source point. Leave it turned off and Elements samples only from the active layer. You'd turn this setting on if you wanted to heal on a new, blank layer.

TIP If you like, you can heal on a separate layer. The advantage of doing so is that if you find the end result is a little too much—your granny suddenly looks like a Stepford wife, say—you can reduce the opacity of the healed layer to let the original show through. Just press Shift+Ctrl+N/Shift-⌘-N to create a new layer and then, in the Tool Options area, turn on the Sample All Layers checkbox. This is also a good plan when using the Clone Stamp (explained next).

The Clone Stamp

The Clone Stamp is like the Healing Brush in that it adds material from a source point that you select, but the Clone Stamp doesn't *blend in* the new material—it just covers up the underlying area. This makes the Clone Stamp great for when you don't want to leave any trace of what you're repairing. Figure 9-5 shows an example of when cloning is a better choice than healing.

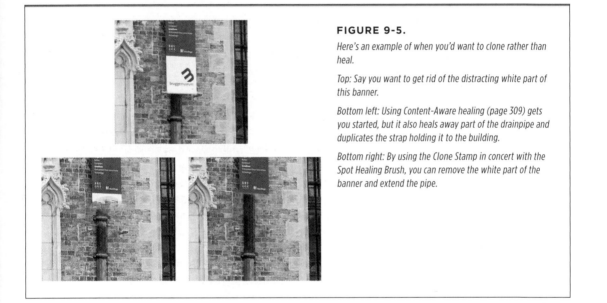

FIGURE 9-5.

Here's an example of when you'd want to clone rather than heal.

Top: Say you want to get rid of the distracting white part of this banner.

Bottom left: Using Content-Aware healing (page 309) gets you started, but it also heals away part of the drainpipe and duplicates the strap holding it to the building.

Bottom right: By using the Clone Stamp in concert with the Spot Healing Brush, you can remove the white part of the banner and extend the pipe.

Using the Clone Stamp is much like using the Healing Brush, but you get different results:

1. **Activate the Clone Stamp.**

   Click its icon (the rubber stamp) in the Tools panel's Enhance section or press S, and then choose it in the Tool Options. The Clone Stamp shares its spot in the Tools panel with the Pattern Stamp, which is explained on page 320. (You can easily tell which is which because the Pattern Stamp's icon has a little checkerboard to its left.)

TIP You can clone on a separate layer, just as you can use the Healing Brush on a dedicated layer. It's a good idea to clone on a separate layer, since cloning is so much more opaque than healing, plus doing so lets you adjust the opacity of your repair afterward. So before you start cloning, press Shift+Ctrl+N/Shift-⌘-N to create a new layer and then turn on Sample All Layers in the Tool Options area.

2. **Zoom in on the spot you want to repair.**

   You may need to zoom way, way in to get a good enough look at what you're doing. (Page 93 explains how to adjust your view.)

GEM IN THE ROUGH

Fixing Dust and Scratches

Scratched, dusty prints can create giant headaches when you scan them. Cleaning your scanner's glass helps, but lots of photos come with dust marks already in the print, or in the file itself if the lens or sensor of your digital camera was dusty.

A similar problem is caused by *artifacts*, blobbish areas of color caused by JPEG compression. If you take a close look at the sky in a JPEG photo, for instance, you may see that instead of a smooth swath of blue, there are lots of distinct little clumps of each shade of blue.

The Healing Brushes are usually your best first line of defense for fixing these problems, but if the specks are widespread, Elements offers a few other options.

The first is the Reduce Noise filter's JPEG artifacts option (page 444); if you're lucky, that will take care of things. If it doesn't, another possible solution is the Despeckle filter (Filter→Noise→Despeckle). And if *that* doesn't get everything, undo it and try the Dust & Scratches filter (Filter→Noise→Dust & Scratches) or the Median filter (Filter→Noise→Median) instead. The Radius setting for these last two filters tells Elements how far to search for pixels to use in its calculations; keep that number as low as possible. The downside to using these filters is that they smooth things out in a way that can make your image look blurred, so you'll probably want to make a selection first to confine their effects to the areas that need repair. Generally, Despeckle blurs images the least.

One final option: Try creating a duplicate layer (Layer→Duplicate), running the Surface Blur filter (page 453) on it and then, in the Layers panel, reducing the opacity of the filtered layer.

3. **Find a good spot to sample as a replacement for the bad area.**

   You want an area that has the same tone as the spot you're fixing. The Clone Stamp doesn't do any blending the way the Healing Brush does, so any tone difference will be pretty obvious.

4. **Alt-click/Option-click the spot you want to clone from.**

   When you click, the cursor turns into a circle with crosshairs in it, indicating the source point for the repair. (When you perform the next step, you'll see a + marking the source point.)

5. **Click the spot you want to cover.**

   Elements puts whatever you selected in the previous step on top of what you click, concealing the original. You can drag with the Clone Stamp, but that makes it act like it's in Aligned mode (described in the previous bulleted list), so it's often preferable to click several times for areas that are larger than your sample. (The only difference between real Aligned mode and what you get from dragging is that with dragging, when you let go of the mouse, your source point snaps back to where you started. If you turn on the Aligned checkbox, your source point stays where you stopped.)

6. **Continue until you've covered the area.**

   With the Clone Stamp, unlike the Healing Brush, what you see as you click is what you get—Elements doesn't do any further blending or smoothing.

The choices you make in the Clone Stamp's Tool Options are important in getting the best results:

- **Brush.** You can use this drop-down menu to select a different brush style (see Chapter 12 for more about brushes), but the standard style usually works pretty well. If the soft edges of the cloned areas bother you, you may be tempted to switch to a harder brush, but that will likely make your photo look like you threw confetti on it, because hard edges won't blend with what's already there.

- **Sample All Layers.** When you turn on this checkbox, Elements samples replacement material from all the visible layers in the area where you set your source point (step 4 above). When it's off, Elements samples only the active layer.

- **Size.** Choose a brush that's just big enough to select your sample without picking up other details that you don't want in your repair. It can be tempting to clone huge chunks to speed things up, but most of the time you'll do better using the smallest brush that gets the sample you want.

- **Opacity.** Elements automatically uses 100 percent opacity for cloning, but you can reduce this setting to let some details of the original show through.

> **TIP** You gain more control by placing your cloned material on another layer (see the tip in step 1 above) than by adjusting the Clone Stamp's Opacity setting.

- **Mode.** You can choose any blend mode (page 190) for cloning, but Normal is usually your best bet. Other modes can create interesting special effects.

- **Aligned.** This setting works exactly the way it does for the Healing Brush (page 313). Turn it on and Elements keeps sampling at a uniform distance from your cursor as you clone; turn it off and it keeps putting down the same source material. Figure 9-6 shows an example of when you'd turn on Aligned. (If you drag the Clone Stamp instead of clicking with it, Elements automatically turns on the Aligned checkbox.)

- **Clone Overlay.** The Clone Stamp starts out using a clipped overlay, the same way the Healing Brush does. Your options for adjusting the overlay are the same, too (page 313). If you want an empty cursor, just turn off all the options in this palette. The settings you choose here apply when you use the Healing Brush and vice versa.

The Clone Stamp is a powerful tool, but it's crotchety, too. The box below suggests some ways to make it behave.

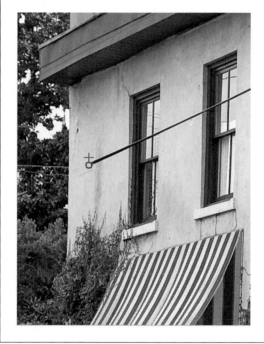

FIGURE 9-6.

One way to get rid of the power line in this photo is to use the Clone Stamp's Aligned option. (The thick power line originally entered this photo at the upper left, above the smaller lines you can still see in the background.) By choosing a brush barely larger than the thick power line and sampling just above the line, you can replace the entire thing in one long sweep, despite the many changes in the background behind it. Here, the round cursor is at the left end of what remains of the power line, and the sample point is the + right above the cursor.

TROUBLESHOOTING MOMENT

Keeping the Clone Stamp Under Control

The Clone Stamp is a great tool, but it sometimes has a mind of its own.

If you suddenly see spots of a different shade appearing as you clone, take a look at the Tool Options area's Aligned checkbox, which has a tendency to insist on staying turned on. Even if you turn it off, it can turn itself back on when you aren't looking.

Once in a great while, the Clone Stamp just won't reset itself when you try to select a new sample point. In that case, try clicking the little four-lined square at the right end of the Tool

Options and choosing Reset Tool, as shown in Figure 9-7. If that doesn't do it, quit the Editor and then relaunch it and delete Elements' preferences file. Here's how: Hold down Shift+Alt-Ctrl/Shift-Option-⌘ immediately after you launch the Editor. Keep these keys down till you see a dialog box asking if you want to delete the program's settings; click Yes. This returns all your Elements settings to where they were the first time you launched the program and usually cures about 80 percent of the problems you may run into in Elements.

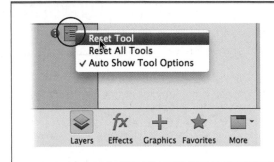

FIGURE 9-7.

Left: You can reset the Clone Stamp (or, for that matter, any Elements tool) by clicking the four-lined square at the right end of the Tool Options area (circled).

Right: From this menu, choose Reset Tool. (If you want to reset the whole Tools panel, choose Reset All Tools instead.) This clears up a lot of the little problems you may have when trying to make a tool behave.

Repairing Tears and Stains

With Elements, you can do a lot to bring damaged photos back to life. The Healing Brush and the Clone Stamp are major players when it comes to restoring pictures. It's fiddly work that takes some persistence, but you can achieve wonders if you have the patience.

If you're lucky and large parts of your photo are in good shape, you can use the Move tool to copy the good bits into the problem area. First, select the part you want to copy. Then press V to activate the Move tool and Alt-drag/Option-drag the good piece where you want it.

If you need a mirror image of something, you can use the Rotate commands to flip a selection. For example, if the left leg of a chair is fine but the right one is missing, try selecting and Alt-dragging/Option-dragging the left leg with the Move tool. When it's where you want it, go to Image→Rotate→Flip Selection Horizontal to turn the copied left leg into a new right leg.

If you don't need to rotate an object, sometimes you can just increase the Clone Stamp's brush size and then clone the object where you need a duplicate. However, this technique works well only when the background is the same in both areas.

■ Applying Patterns

In addition to solid colors, Elements also lets you add patterns to images. The program comes with quite a few built-in patterns, and you can download more (see page 598) or create your own. Patterns let you add interesting designs to images or give more realistic textures to certain repairs.

You can use the Healing Brush or the Pattern Stamp to apply patterns. As you learned earlier, the Healing Brush has a pattern setting in its Tool Options. The Pattern Stamp shares a Tools panel slot with the Clone Stamp, and it works much like the Clone Stamp but puts down a preselected pattern instead of a sampled area. The tool you use to apply the pattern makes a big difference, as you can see from Figure 9-8. The next two sections explain how to use both tools.

TIP   Elements gives you lots of ways to use patterns, including creating a Fill layer that's covered with the pattern you choose. (Fill layers are covered on page 207.) The Smart Brushes (page 225) also let you apply patterned effects to images, although Adobe officially calls these effects "textures" rather than "patterns." They're particularly nice for creating interest in a flat or empty background area. In the Smart brushes' Tool Options, just choose Textures from the thumbnails pop-out menu.

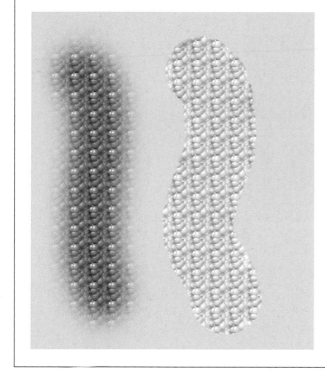

FIGURE 9-8.

The same pattern applied with the Pattern Stamp (left) and the Healing Brush (right). The Healing Brush blends the pattern in with the underlying color (and texture, when there is any), while the Pattern Stamp just plunks down the pattern exactly as it appears in the pop-out palette. To get a softer edge on the Healing Brush's pattern, choose a softer brush from the pop-out palette.

The Healing Brush

The Healing Brush's Pattern mode is great for things like improving the texture of someone's skin by applying texture from another photo.

Using patterns with the Healing Brush is just as easy and works the same way as using the tool in normal healing mode: Just drag across the area you want to fix. The only difference is that you don't have to choose a sampling point, since the *pattern* is your source: When you drag, Elements blends the pattern you selected into your photo.

After activating the Healing Brush (keyboard shortcut: J), in the Tool Options area's Source menu, choose Pattern, and then click the pattern thumbnail that appears to choose the one you want from the pop-out palette. You can see more patterns by selecting from the menu at the top of the palette, or you can create and save your own patterns. Figure 9-9 explains how to make custom patterns.

TIP Changing the blend mode (page 190) when using patterns can result in some interesting effects.

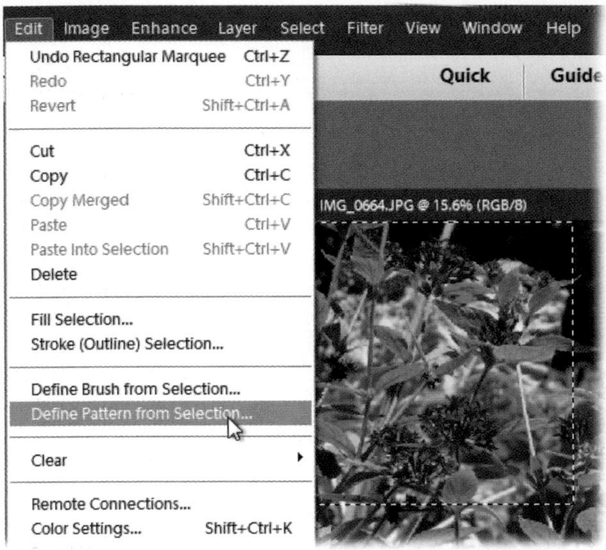

FIGURE 9-9.

It's easy to create your own patterns. In any image, simply make a rectangular, unfeathered selection, and then choose Edit→"Define Pattern from Selection." Your pattern appears at the bottom of the current pattern palette, and a dialog box pops up so you can name the new pattern. To use a whole image as a pattern, don't make a selection—just go to Edit→Define Pattern. To rename or delete a pattern later, right-click/Control-click it in the Pattern palette. You can also download hundreds of different patterns from various online sources (see page 598), and then use the Preset Manager (page 600) to make them available in Elements.

The Pattern Stamp

This tool is like the Clone Stamp, but instead of copying sampled areas, it puts down a predefined pattern that you select from the Pattern palette. The Pattern Stamp is useful when you want to apply a pattern to an image without mixing the pattern with what's already there. For instance, to see what your patio would look like if it were a garden, you could use the Pattern Stamp to paint a lawn and a flower border on a photo of your patio.

To get started, click the Clone Stamp in the Tools panel or press S, and then choose the Pattern Stamp in the Tool Options area. Then click the pattern thumbnail in the Tool Options to open the Pattern palette so you can pick one. Other options for this brush (like the size, hardness, and so on) are the same as for the Clone Stamp. The one extra option is the Impressionist checkbox demonstrated in Figure 9-10, which is mostly useful for creating special effects.

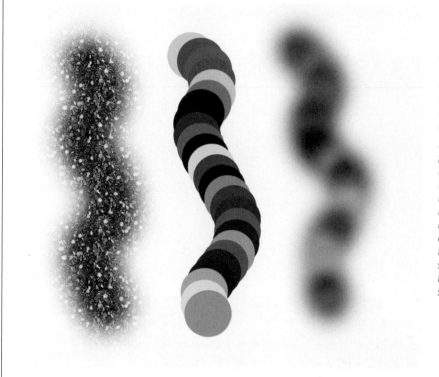

FIGURE 9-10.

If you turn on the Pattern Stamp's Impressionist checkbox, Elements blurs the pattern, creating an effect vaguely like an Impressionist painting—but only if you use a soft brush.

Here you see a pattern put down with the Pattern Stamp using different settings: I see the relationship between the middle and the right one, but the one on the left doesn't look anything like the others. Is it really the same Pattern Stamp as the other two? and a very soft brush (right).

Once you've selected a pattern, simply drag in your photo where you want Elements to put that pattern.

Recomposing Photos

The previous sections taught you how to remove flaws and objects you don't want in photos by manually covering them up bit by bit. But maybe you're thinking, "It seems so last-century to have to drudge away like that. There's got to be an easier way!" You're right—there is.

The Recompose tool is one of the coolest features in Elements. It lets you eliminate unwanted objects and people from a photo by just scribbling a line over them, and then moving the edges of the photo to reshape it. Amazingly, Elements can keep the rest of the photo undistorted as it makes the unwanted objects vanish. Take a look at Figure 9-11 to see what this tool can do. Want to get rid of your daughter's ex-boyfriend in that group shot? Just draw a line on him in the photo, push the image's edges closer together, and he's history. Couldn't get your feuding coworkers to stand close together in the holiday party photo? No problem—you can easily remove the empty space between them.

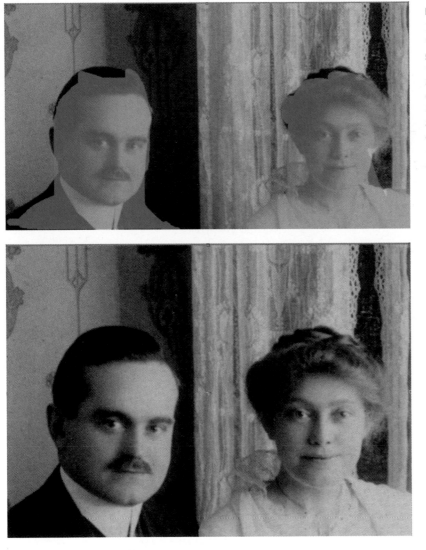

FIGURE 9-11.

Top: Say you only have a wide photo of your great grandparents, but you want to put it in a narrow frame. You could shrink it down till it fits, but then the image would be too small. Instead, just make a few marks on it with the Recompose tool (the green marks mean "Keep this").

To turn on the tool's Quick Highlight setting—which makes the tool automatically mark the whole area you drag over, the way the Quick Selection tool's selection expands to encompass a whole object—just right-click/Control-click your photo and choose Use Quick Highlight from the shortcut menu. The Normal Highlight setting (which this tool uses unless you change it) usually produces fairly similar results, but Quick Highlight makes it easier to see exactly what you're choosing. To recompose the image after adding these marks, just drag one of its edges toward the middle of the photo.

Bottom: The end result. Your ancestors will now fit nicely into their new frame.

You can also use the Recompose tool to alter the shape of a photo without cropping it. Have a landscape-oriented photo that you wish were portrait-oriented instead? Recompose can fix that. There are limits to what it can do, but with a suitable photo, you can just shove it into the proportions you want, and Elements will keep everything looking perfectly normal and not distorted.

Elements has to do an awesome amount of calculating to make this tool work, but it's actually one of the easier Elements tools to use:

1. **Open a photo and activate the Recompose tool.**

   The Recompose tool is at the upper right of the Tools panel's Modify section, next to the Crop tool. Its keyboard shortcut is W.

2. **Tell Elements which parts of the photo you *don't* want to change.**

   You use the Recompose tool's Protection Brush to indicate which areas you want preserved. To select this brush, head to the Tool Option area's Recompose section and make sure the blue brush with the + sign beside it is selected; then drag over the areas you want to keep. This is something like using the Quick Selection tool in that you don't have to select *everything;* just make enough marks so that Elements knows which objects you mean. However, this tool is more literal-minded than the Quick Selection tool, so you may need more marks when using it.

   If you make a mistake, click the eraser icon just below the brush icon (it also has a + sign beside it) to remove the marks you don't want.

> **TIP** The Recompose tool has a hidden menu to speed things up: Right-click/Control-click your photo when the tool is active and you can choose Use Quick Highlight (shown in Figure 9-11), which makes the whole process of telling Elements what to keep and what to eliminate go much faster. This setting also tends to produce better results.

   To automatically select the people in your photo, in the Tool Options area, click the "Highlight Skin tones" icon (the little green man to the right of the No Restriction button). Note, however, that this feature doesn't work on sepia images like the one in Figure 9-11.

3. **Tell Elements what you want to get rid of.**

   To delete specific objects or areas, drag over them with the Removal Brush (in the Tool Options, click the blue brush icon with the – sign next to it). Like the Protection Brush, the Removal Brush has its own eraser just below it (also with a – sign next to it) that you can use to correct any mistakes you make with the Removal tool.

> **TIP** You don't always need to use both of the Recompose tool's brushes. You can even try not marking anything at all, but you'll likely get better results if you give Elements a little guidance. If you make a mistake with either brush, use the corresponding eraser to remove the stray marks.

4. **Recompose the photo.**

Once you're through marking up your photo, use the bounding box around the image to resize it. It works just like the Move tool's bounding box: Grab a square handle or a corner and then drag to change the image's shape. There are also several Tool Options settings that you can use to make the photo a specific size; they're explained in a moment.

Watch the unwanted areas disappear as you drag the edges closer together.

> **TIP** If you want to make your image wider or taller than it is now (to make a portrait-oriented photo into a landscape one, for example), you first need to add canvas (page 108) to give the new width or height someplace to go. Just keep in mind that Elements isn't as good at removing objects when you're making the image larger as it is when you're shrinking it down.

5. **Finish up.**

When you're happy with how things look, click the Commit button (the green checkmark) or press Enter/Return. If you decide you don't want to recompose after all, or if you need to go back and adjust the marks you made on the picture, click the red Cancel button or press Esc. When you're done, crop off any extra blank space on the edges of the photo (see page 85).

> **TIP** You may find that some remnants of removed objects reappear after you press Enter/Return. Just use the Clone Stamp or Healing Brush to get rid of them.

The Recompose tool has several Tool Options settings to make your job easier:

- **Brushes and erasers.** There are four icons in the Recompose section of the Tool Options. In the top row are the "Mark for Removal" and "Mark for Protection" brushes, and in the bottom row are the two erasers: "Erase highlights marked for removal" (for erasing Removal Brush marks you made by mistake) and "Erase highlights marked for protection" (for erasing Protection Brush marks you don't want).

- **Size.** This is just like the size setting for any brush tool. To adjust this setting, drag the Size slider, click the numeric value and enter a size in pixels, put your cursor over the word "Size" and scrub (page 189), or use the bracket key shortcuts (page 396). Chapter 12 covers brushes in detail.

- **Threshold.** This setting tells Elements how much you want to protect the details from distortion. For best results, leave it at 100 percent.

- **Preset.** Normally this button is set to No Restriction (which lets you drag the bounding box any which way to resize the image), but if you click it, you can choose an option to recompose to the photo's current aspect ratio to one of several popular photo-paper sizes or the 16:9 aspect ratio popular for images used in high-definition videos. If you make a choice here or in the width and height boxes (explained next), Elements recomposes your photo to that size.

- **W (width) and H (height).** If you want your final image to be a custom size, enter it here. Click the arrows between the boxes to swap the numbers, just as you can with the Crop tool.

- **Highlight Skin tones.** Click this icon (the little green man) and, if you're lucky, Elements selects the people in your photo. It's kind of dicey, though—you may find Elements prefers other objects to the folks in your pictures, but it's worth a click, since you can always undo Elements' selection.

What's most amazing about this tool is the way your background still looks real when you're done. Someone seeing your Recomposed photo would never guess that it didn't start out looking just like it does now. Recomposing doesn't work for every photo, but when it does, the results are almost magical.

Color Curves: Enhancing Tone and Contrast

If you hang around photo-editing veterans, you'll hear how useful Photoshop's Curves tool is. Contrary to what you might think based on its name, Curves isn't a drawing tool. Instead, it works much like Levels (page 236), but with many more points of correction. Adobe includes a simplified version of this tool in Elements and calls it *Color Curves* to remind you what it's for.

Unlike Levels, which let you adjust an entire photo's white point, black point, and midtone settings, the Color Curves tool lets you target specific tonal regions. For instance, it lets you make only the shadows lighter or only the highlights darker. Maybe that's why some pros say that Color Curves is Levels on steroids. (The box on page 243 has advice on when to use Levels and when to use Color Curves.)

Since Curves, in its original-strength Photoshop version, is a pretty complicated tool, Adobe makes it easier to use in Elements. Elements starts you with a group of preset adjustments to choose from (see Figure 9-12). These presets are shortcuts to the types of basic enhancements you'll use most often; just click one to try it. If you like what it does, you're done. But if you aren't satisfied with any of the presets, you can easily make changes using the Adjust Color Curves dialog box's sliders.

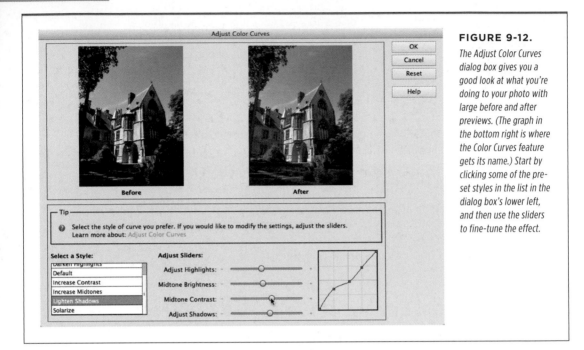

FIGURE 9-12.

The Adjust Color Curves dialog box gives you a good look at what you're doing to your photo with large before and after previews. (The graph in the bottom right is where the Color Curves feature gets its name.) Start by clicking some of the preset styles in the list in the dialog box's lower left, and then use the sliders to fine-tune the effect.

Here's how to improve a photo's appearance with Color Curves:

1. **Open a photo and make a duplicate layer.**

   Press Ctrl+J/⌘-J or go to Layer→Duplicate Layer. Elements doesn't let you use Color Curves as an Adjustment layer, so you're safer applying it to a duplicate layer in case you want to change something later.

   TIP   If you decide you'd like to restrict your adjustment to a particular area, you can apply a layer mask (page 202) to the duplicate layer and edit the mask so your adjustment changes only part of the photo. For instance, if you're happy with everything in your shot of Junior's Little League game *except* the catcher in the foreground, do a Color Curves adjustment on a duplicate layer and then mask out everything but him.

2. **Go to Enhance→Adjust Color→Adjust Color Curves.**

   Elements opens the Adjust Color Curves dialog box, where you see your original image on the left.

3. **Choose a Color Curves preset.**

Scroll through the "Select a Style" list and click the preset that seems closest to what you want. Feel free to experiment by clicking different presets. (As long as you're just clicking in the list, you don't need to click Reset between each one, since Elements starts from the original image each time you click.)

The dialog box gives you a decent-sized look at how you're changing things, but for important photos, you can also preview the effect right in the image. To do that, drag the dialog box out of the way and check the actual photo to see how you're changing things before you commit.

4. **Decide whether you like the changes.**

If you're satisfied, click OK. If not, continue on to the next step.

5. **Make any further adjustments.**

If you think your photo still doesn't look quite right, use the sliders shown in Figure 9-13 to tweak the photo. (The sliders are explained in a moment.) Click Reset if you want to undo the changes you've made with the sliders. Notice how subtle the preset curves are—a tiny nudge makes a big difference, so be gentle.

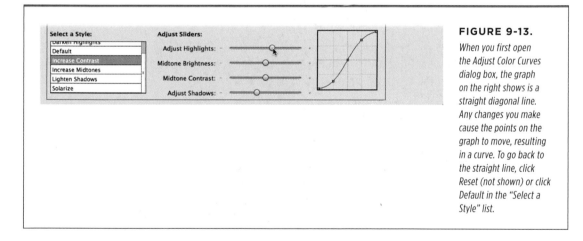

FIGURE 9-13.

When you first open the Adjust Color Curves dialog box, the graph on the right shows is a straight diagonal line. Any changes you make cause the points on the graph to move, resulting in a curve. To go back to the straight line, click Reset (not shown) or click Default in the "Select a Style" list.

6. **When you're happy with the photo's new look, click OK.**

Don't forget to save your changes. If you used a duplicate layer, you can always change your mind later on and start over on a fresh layer.

> **TIP** If you've used Curves add-ons in an old version of Elements—like those from Richard Lynch or Grant Dixon, for example—or if you've used Photoshop's Curves Adjustment layers (you power user, you!), the Color Curves tool may take a bit of getting used to, since you can't adjust the curve by dragging it. If not being able to drag drives you nuts, SmartCurve (*http://free.pages.at/easyfilter/curves.html*) is a popular, free, Windows-only add-on that lets you drag to your heart's content (unfortunately, there's no Mac equivalent). Also, some of the add-on toolsets for Elements let you make corrections on a graph rather than with the sliders. (See page 598 for more about add-ons.)

Once you have some Color Curves experience under your belt, you probably won't be satisfied with the presets, so don't hesitate to use the sliders to adjust different tonal regions in your photo:

- **Adjust Highlights.** Drag this slider left to darken the photo's highlights, or right to lighten them.

- **Midtone Brightness.** If you'd like the middle range of colors to be darker, move this slider left. Move it right to make the midtones brighter.

- **Midtone Contrast.** This slider works just like the one in Elements' Shadows/Highlights feature (page 223): Move it right to increase the photo's contrast, or left to decrease it.

- **Adjust Shadows.** If you want to lighten shadowy areas, move this slider right. To darken them, move it left.

As you drag the sliders, you can see the point you're adjusting move on the graph and watch the curve change shape. Although it's fun to watch the graph, pay more attention to what's happening in the photo.

Color Curves is such a potent tool that it can change a photo in ways you don't intend. So rather than using Color Curves to make huge adjustments, try another tool first, and then use Color Curves for the final, subtle tweaks. But if you *want* to create wild special effects, then Color Curves may be just the ticket; see Figure 9-14 for an example.

> **TIP** You can also apply the Solarize adjustment to part of a photo with the Smart Brush tool (page 225). But if you use the brush method, you can't edit the settings afterward, so you may prefer to apply Solarize using Color Curves on a duplicate layer.

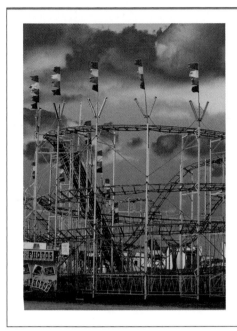

FIGURE 9-14.

Many people prefer to use Color Curves for artwork and special effects rather than adjusting photos. Jimi Hendrix fans may like the Solarize preset, which Adobe includes to give you a starting point for funky pictures like this one. (Others say this preset should serve as a warning about going overboard with this tool.)

Making Colors More Vibrant

Do you drool over the luscious photos in travel magazines, the ones of vivid desti-nations that make real life seem drab in comparison? What *is* it about those photos that makes them so dramatic? Often the answer is the *saturation,* or intensity, of the colors. Supersaturated color makes for darned appealing landscape and object photos, regardless of how the real thing may rate on the vividness scale.

There are various ways to adjust a photo's saturation. Some cameras have features that help control it, but Elements lets you do even more. For example, by increasing or decreasing a photo's saturation, you can shift the perceived focal point, change the image's mood, or just make the photo more eye-catching.

By increasing your subject's saturation and decreasing saturation in the rest of the photo, you can focus viewers' attention, even in a crowded photo. Figure 9-15 shows an example of this technique.

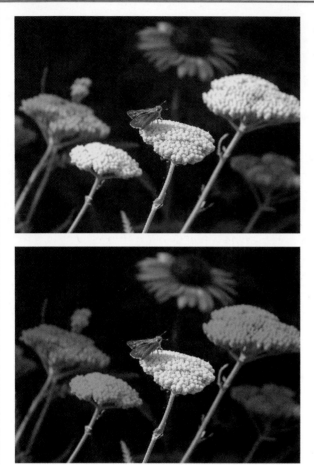

FIGURE 9-15.

Top: All the yellow flowers in this image are equally bright, including those in the background, so you might miss the insect on the front blossom.

Bottom: To make the insect and its flower stand out from the crowd, desaturate the rest of the image. Download the photo skipper.jpg *from this book's Missing CD page at* www.missingmanuals.com/cds *to try it yourself.*

It's easy to change saturation. You might want to start with the Quick Fix Vibrance slider (see page 129). If that doesn't work well, try using either of the more traditional methods, which are explained in the following sections: the Hue/Saturation dialog box or the Sponge tool. For big areas or when you want a lot of control, go with the Hue/Saturation dialog box. If you just want to quickly paint a different saturation level (either higher or lower) on a small spot in your photo, the Sponge tool is faster.

TIP Many consumer-grade digital cameras automatically crank the saturation of JPEG photos into the stratosphere. That's great if you love all the color, but if you prefer not to live in a Technicolor universe, you can desaturate photos in Elements to remove some of the excess color.

The Hue/Saturation Dialog Box

Hue/Saturation is one of the most popular commands in Elements. If you aren't satisfied with the results of a simple Levels adjustment, you may want to work on the hue or saturation as the next step toward getting eye-catching color.

Hue simply means the color of your image—whether it's blue or brown or purple or green. Most people use the saturation adjustments more than the hue controls, but both hue and saturation are controlled by the same dialog box. You can use the Hue slider to change the color of objects in photos, but you'll probably want to adjust saturation far more often than you'll want to shift an image's hue.

When you use Hue/Saturation, it's a good idea to make most of your other corrections first—like levels or exposure changes. Then follow these steps:

1. **If you want to adjust only part of the photo, select the area you want to change.**

   Use whatever selection tool(s) you prefer. (See Chapter 5 for a refresher on selections.)

2. **Call up the Hue/Saturation dialog box.**

   Go to Enhance→Adjust Color→Adjust Hue/Saturation, or to Layer→New Adjustment Layer→Hue/Saturation. As always, if you want to make changes that are easy to undo, use an Adjustment layer instead of working directly on the photo. (If you go the Adjustment layer route, you'll make your changes in the Adjustments panel rather than a dialog box, but your options are exactly the same.)

TIP Using an Adjustment layer gives you more flexibility because you can always come back and edit the layer's mask later on if you change your mind about what you want to modify. See page 209 for more info.

3. **In the dialog box or panel, move the sliders until you like what you see.**

   To adjust only saturation, ignore the Hue slider. Drag the Saturation slider right to increase the amount of color or left to decrease it. If necessary, move the Lightness slider left to make the color darker, or right to make it lighter.

   If you're using an Adjustment layer, that's all you have to do. (If you use the dialog box, click OK when you're satisfied.) Incidentally, you don't have to change all the colors in your photo equally; Figure 9-16 explains how to focus on individual color channels.

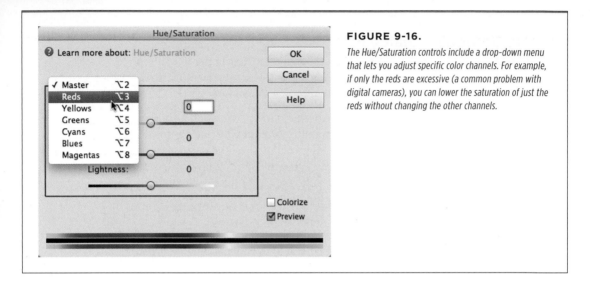

FIGURE 9-16.

The Hue/Saturation controls include a drop-down menu that lets you adjust specific color channels. For example, if only the reds are excessive (a common problem with digital cameras), you can lower the saturation of just the reds without changing the other channels.

> **TIP** Generally speaking, if you want to change a pastel to a more intense color, you'll need to increase the saturation *and* reduce the lightness (by moving the Lightness slider left) if you don't want the color to look radioactive.

Adjusting Saturation with the Sponge Tool

The Sponge tool gives you another way to adjust saturation. Even though it's called a sponge, this tool works like any other brush tool in Elements; the process of choosing the size and hardness is the same as choosing them for a brush (see page 395).

> **TIP** Although the Sponge tool is handy for working on small areas, all the dragging required gets old when you're working on a large chunk of an image. For those situations, use Hue/Saturation (page 331) instead.

To use the Sponge tool, just drag over the area you want to change. Figure 9-17 shows the kind of effect the Sponge has.

You may want to press Ctrl+J/⌘-J to create a duplicate layer before using the Sponge. That way you can throw out the duplicate layer later if you don't like the changes, or add a layer mask to restrict the area they affect (page 202). Here's how to use this tool:

1. **Activate the Sponge tool.**

   Press O (that's the letter, not the number) or click its icon in the Tools panel (it's in the Enhance section just below the Clone Stamp), and then choose the Sponge in the Tool Options. Then select the brush size and settings you want (they're explained in a sec).

2. **Drag over the area you want to change.**

If you aren't seeing enough of a difference, increase the Flow setting (explained in a moment) a little. If the effect is too strong, reduce the Flow number.

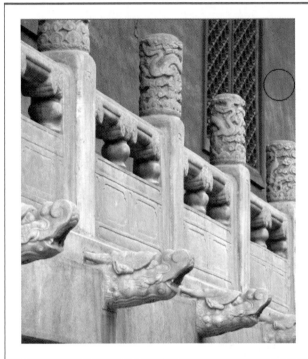

FIGURE 9-17.

The Sponge tool was applied to the upper-right part of this wall, increasing the color saturation and making the paint redder.

Approach the Sponge tool with caution: It can quickly start to degrade your image's quality, especially if you've made lots of other adjustments to it. So if you start to see noise (graininess), undo your sponging and try again at a reduced Flow setting.

> **TIP** If you have a hard time coloring (or decoloring) inside the lines, select the area you want before sponging. That way the tool won't have any effect outside the selection, so you can be as sloppy as you like.

The Sponge tool's Tool Options offer a couple of unique settings:

- **Mode.** Here's where you tell the Sponge whether to saturate (add color) or desaturate (remove color).

- **Flow.** This setting governs how intense the effect is; a higher number means more intensity.

Changing an Object's Color

In Chapter 4, you saw one way to change the color of an object: Select it and then use Quick Fix's Hue and Saturation sliders. Elements also gives you other ways to achieve the same result: You can use an Adjustment layer, the Replace Color command, or the Color Replacement tool. (The Smart Brush tools offer a whole menu of color changes, too; see the tip below for the lowdown.)

The method you should choose depends on your photo and personal preference. Using an Adjustment layer gives you the most flexibility if you want to make changes later. Replace Color is the fastest way to change a color that's widely scattered throughout your image. And the Color Replacement tool lets you quickly brush a replacement color over the one you want to change. Figure 9-18 shows the kind of complex color change you can make in a jiffy using any one of these methods.

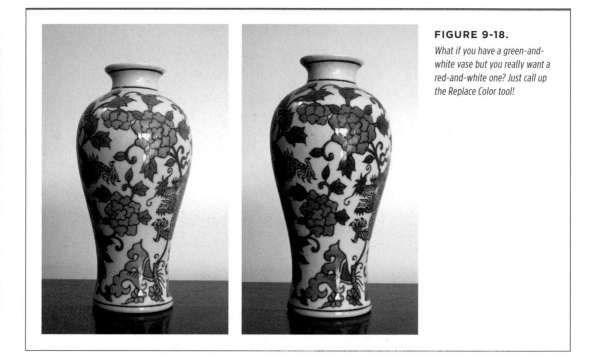

FIGURE 9-18.

What if you have a green-and-white vase but you really want a red-and-white one? Just call up the Replace Color tool!

> **TIP** The Smart Brush (page 225) lets you target an area and make a quick color adjustment, so you might think that sounds like a good tool for changing color. It can be, but its color presets are pretty limited (and pretty ugly). Also, the Smart Brush doesn't just apply a single color—it uses gradient maps (page 476) instead. If you can get the effect you like using the Smart Brush, go for it. But it's tough to adjust color with this tool, since you have to either pick a different gradient or edit the one the Smart Brush used (page 228 tells you how). On the whole, the methods described in the following pages are much easier to control.

Using an Adjustment Layer

You can use a Hue/Saturation Adjustment layer to make the kind of color changes you saw in Figure 9-18. The advantage of this method is that you can go back later and change your settings or the area affected by the layer (as opposed to changing the whole image). The process is the same as the one described on page 331, only this time you start by selecting what you want to change:

1. **Select the object whose color you want to change.**

   Use any of the selection tools (see Chapter 5). If you don't make a selection before creating the Adjustment layer, it'll change the whole photo.

2. **Create a new Hue/Saturation Adjustment layer.**

   Go to Layer→New Adjustment Layer→Hue/Saturation. The new layer affects only the area you selected.

3. **Use the Adjustments panel's sliders to tweak the color until it looks good, and then click OK.**

   Use the Hue slider first to pick the color you want. Then use the Saturation slider to adjust the color's vividness and the Lightness slider to adjust its darkness.

This method is fine if it's easy to select the area you want to change. But what if there are a bunch of widely scattered areas of color that need changing, or you want to change one shade everywhere it appears in a photo? For that, Elements offers the Replace Color command, explained next.

Replacing Specific Colors

Take a look at the green-and-white vase in Figure 9-18 again. Do you have to tediously select each green area if you want to make it a red-and-white vase? You *could* do it that way, but it's far easier to use the Replace Color command instead. When you run this command, you'll see one of those Elements dialog boxes that looks a bit intimidating, but it's a snap to use once you understand how it works. Replace Color changes every instance of the color you select, no matter where it appears in the image.

You don't need to start by making a selection when you use this command but, as usual, run it on a duplicate layer (Ctrl+J/⌘-J) if you want to keep your options open for future changes. And before you start, be sure the active layer isn't an Adjustment layer, or Replace Color won't work. Then:

1. **Open the Replace Color dialog box.**

   Go to Enhance→Adjust Color→Replace Color. The Replace Color dialog box in Figure 9-19 appears. You may need to drag it out of the way so you can see your whole photo.

TIP To protect a particular area of your chosen color from being changed, paint a mask on it by using the Selection Brush in Mask mode before you start.

---

2. **Move your cursor over your photo.**

The cursor changes to an eyedropper. Make sure that the leftmost eyedropper in the Replace Color dialog box (the one *without* a + or – sign next to it) is the active one, as in Figure 9-19.

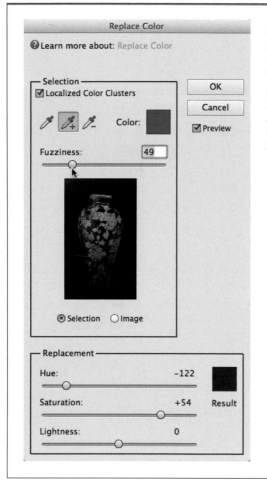

FIGURE 9-19.

The part of this dialog box that looks like a negative shows where the sliders will affect the image's color. The lighter areas are where Elements plans to substitute your new color.

Use the Hue and Saturation sliders to adjust the replacement color (shown in the Result box). The Fuzziness setting (explained in Figure 9-20) works a little like the Magic Wand's Tolerance setting, and the Localized Color Clusters checkbox is something like the Magic Wand's Contiguous setting—it restricts the selection to colors near where you click.

3. **Click an area of the color you want to replace.**

Elements selects all the areas that match the particular shade you selected, but you won't see marching ants in your image the way you do with the selection tools. If you click more than once, you *change* your selection instead of adding to it. To add to your selection (that is, to select additional shades), Shift-click in your photo.

Another way to add more shades is to select the middle eyedropper (the one with the + sign next to it) and click in your photo again. To remove a color, select the rightmost eyedropper (with the – sign) and click, or Alt-click/Option-click with the leftmost eyedropper. To undo your selecting and start over, Alt-click/Option-click the Cancel button to turn it into a Reset button.

4. **When you've selected everything you want to change, move the sliders to change the color.**

   The Hue, Saturation, and Lightness sliders work exactly the way they do in the Hue/Saturation dialog box (page 331). Move them and watch the Result box to their right to see what color you're concocting. You can also click the Result box to bring up the Color Picker and choose a shade there. If you need to tweak the area you're changing, use the Fuzziness slider to adjust the range of colors that Color Replacement affects, as shown in Figure 9-20.

   Look at the photo after you've chosen a replacement color. If the preview doesn't show that color in all the areas you want, click the missing spots with the dialog box's middle eyedropper to fix them.

5. **Click OK.**

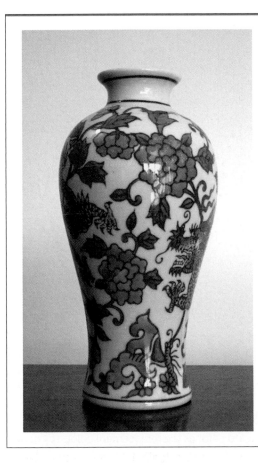

FIGURE 9-20.

Fuzziness is similar to the Magic Wand's Tolerance setting (page 155). Take a close look at the red parts of this vase—there's still a lot of green in the center of some of them. To change more pixels, set the Fuzziness higher by dragging it right (in this image, that change would make all the green spots turn red). If Elements is changing areas you don't want to, move the Fuzziness slider left instead.

The Color Replacement Tool

You can also brush on a color change. The Color Replacement tool lets you brush a different color onto the area you want to change without changing any colors besides the one you target.

For the past few versions of Elements, this tool had been pretty feeble because it was missing a very important setting that it had in earlier versions: options for sampling, which let you control how the tool seeks out colors to replace. In Elements 11, those options are back, so if you've thought this tool was a dud, give it another try. Figure 9-21 shows how it works in Elements 11.

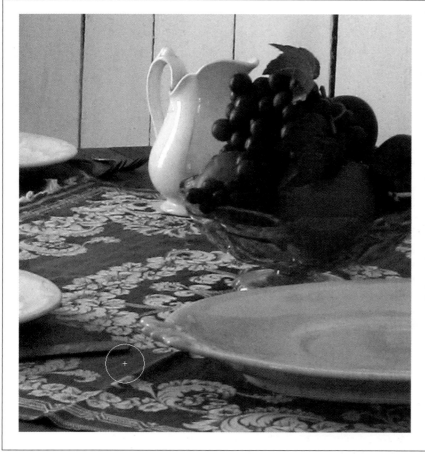

FIGURE 9-21.

Here's an example of when the Color Replacement tool comes in handy. Say you have a red tablecloth but you think this photo would look better if it were blue. In this particular photo, the Replace Color command (page 335) and the Magic Wand (page 154) would be hard to use, since the fruit is fairly similar in color to the tablecloth. But the Color Replacement tool lets you drag over the intricate pattern in the tablecloth without getting blue anywhere else. Here, the tool's mode is set to Hue, so that the blue matches the dullness of the original red.

Using the Color Replacement tool is straightforward:

1. **Pick the color to use as a replacement.**

    Elements uses the current foreground color as the replacement color. To change colors, click the foreground color square in the Tools panel and then choose a new hue from the Color Picker.

2. **Activate the Color Replacement tool and pick a brush size.**

Click the Brush tool in the Tools panel or press B and then, in the Tool Options area, choose the Color Replacement tool. Its icon is a brush with a color square next to it. For this tool, you usually want a fairly large brush, as shown in Figure 9-21. (See Chapter 12 to learn all about brushes.)

3. **Click or drag in your photo to change the color.**

Elements targets the color that's under the crosshairs in the center of the brush cursor. So in Figure 9-21, for example, keeping the crosshairs inside the tablecloth ensures that only the tablecloth changes.

> **TIP** You may want to use the Color Replacement tool on a duplicate layer (Ctrl+J/⌘-J) so you can adjust the layer's opacity to control the effect.

The Tool Options settings make a big difference in the way this tool works:

- **Brush Thumbnail.** You can't choose a different brush here; this thumbnail just gives you a preview of the size.

- **Size.** Use the slider to adjust the brush's size.

- **Tolerance.** This is like the Magic Wand's Tolerance setting: The higher the number, the more shades of color Elements changes. This setting is the key to getting good results with this tool.

- **Mode.** This controls the tool's blend mode (page 190). Generally you'll want to choose Color or Hue, although you can get some funky special effects with Saturation.

- **Limits.** This setting tells Elements which areas of the photo to look at when it searches for color. Discontiguous means the tool changes only instances of the color immediately beneath the brush's center. Contiguous means it also changes similar areas that are touching the area under the brush.

- **Brush Setting.** Most of the settings you see when you click this button (Hardness, Spacing, Roundness) are the same as for any brush (see Chapter 12 for more about brushes). In addition, you can choose to let your mouse's scrollwheel or the pressure of your stylus on a graphics tablet (page 595) control the size of the brush or the Tolerance setting (above).

- **Sampling.** These three eyedroppers are the secret to why this tool is back on form in Elements 11. They tell the Color Replacement *how* to look for colors to replace. Here's what they do, from left to right:

  - **Continuous** tells the brush to keep replacing every color you drag over.

  - **Once** tells it to replace the color where you first click with it and ignore other colors it passes over.

- **Background Swatch** tells it to look for the color that's currently in the background color square and replace that color—and *only* that color—whenever you brush over it. If you use this setting, be sure the background color is set to the one you want to change; use the Eyedropper (page 251) to sample the color before you switch to the Color Replacement brush.

- **Antialiasing.** This setting smooths the edges of the replacement color; it's best to leave it turned on.

Special Effects

Elements gives you some other useful ways of drastically changing the look of an image. You can apply these effects as Adjustment layers (Layer→New Adjustment Layer) or by going to Filter→Adjustments (there's much more about filters in Chapter 13). Either route gives you the same options (except for Equalize, which is available only as a filter); you can see them in action in Figure 9-22.

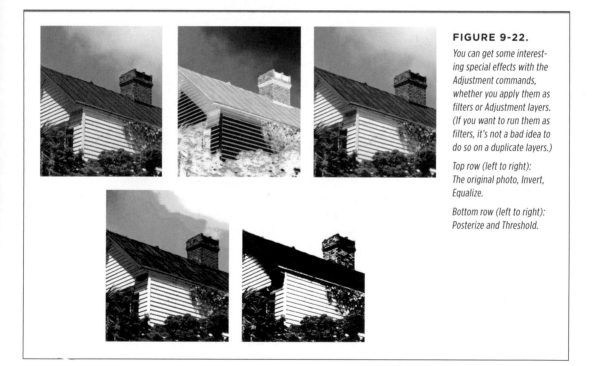

FIGURE 9-22.

You can get some interesting special effects with the Adjustment commands, whether you apply them as filters or Adjustment layers. (If you want to run them as filters, it's not a bad idea to do so on a duplicate layers.)

Top row (left to right): The original photo, Invert, Equalize.

Bottom row (left to right): Posterize and Threshold.

In most cases, you use these adjustments as steps along the way in a more complex treatment of a photo, but they're effective by themselves, too. Here's what each one does (listed in the order they appear in the Filter menu):

- **Equalize** makes the darkest pixel in the photo black and the lightest one white, and then redistributes the brightness values of all the colors in the photo to give them all equal weight. If you have an active selection when you run this filter, Elements brings up a dialog box that lets you choose whether you want it to equalize the whole photo or equalize it based on the selection. For example, say you have an image with dark woods and a bright sky and you've selected part of the sky. If you tell Elements to equalize based on the selection, the program brightens the whole image to the level of the pixels in the sky selection without including the dark, wooded areas in its calculations. So the resulting equalized photo is much brighter than it would have been if you'd told Elements to base its calculations on the *whole* photo. Equalize doesn't always work, but sometimes it does a great job of increasing the brightness of a dim photo.

- **Gradient Map** is pretty complicated. According to Adobe, it "maps the gray-scale range of an image to the colors of a specified gradient fill." (If you want to know what the heck *that* means, turn to page 476.) Basically, it lets you apply a gradient based on the light and dark areas of the photo; the gradient's colors replace the existing colors. Give it a shot and see whether you like the result.

- **Invert** makes the photo look like a negative. It's so useful in doing artistic things to photos that Elements lets you invert images anytime just by pressing Ctrl+I/⌘-I. To invert just part of an image, check out the Smart Brush tools (page 225), which have some interesting variations on inversion in their Special Effects menus, or use a duplicate layer with a layer mask (page 202) and edit the area that's covered by the mask.

> **NOTE** If you think choosing the Invert option sounds like a great way to turn negatives you scanned in with a basic flatbed scanner into positive images, that won't work unless your negatives are black and white. Color negatives have an orange mask on them that Elements can't easily undo, so you're best off with a dedicated film scanner that's designed to cope with negatives, or at least a scanner that has software for dealing with the mask.

- **Posterize** reduces the total number of colors in the photo, creating a less de-tailed, more poster-like image. The lower the number you enter in the dialog box, the fewer colors you get and the more extreme the result. If you want blocky, poster-like edges in a photo, try Filter→Artistic→Poster Edges instead of—or in addition to—this adjustment.

- **Threshold** turns every pixel in the photo pure white or pure black—you won't find any shades of gray here. Figure 9-23 explains how to tweak this adjustment's settings.

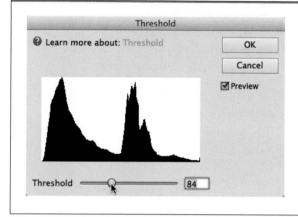

FIGURE 9-23.

This graph is a histogram (page 237) showing the light-to-dark distribution of the pixels in the image. The slider controls the dividing point between black and white pixels in a Threshold adjustment. Slide it left if you want more white pixels, or right for more black ones.

- **Photo Filter** makes color corrections, like removing color casts. Page 294 explains this filter in detail.

Removing and Adding Color

A stunning black-and-white image is so much more than just a color photo without color. If you love classic black-and-white photography or yearn to be the next Ansel Adams, you'll be over the moon with the high-quality black-and-white conversions Elements can do. If, on the other hand, you can't imagine why anyone would willingly abandon color, consider that in a world crammed with eye-popping colors, black and white really stands out. Or say you need to have something printed where you can't use color illustrations. And for artistic photography, there's nothing like black and white, where tone and contrast make or break the photo, without colors to distract you from its underlying structure.

In this chapter, you'll learn how to turn a color photo black and white, and how to create images that are partly in color and partly black and white. You'll also learn how to reverse the process and colorize black-and-white images.

■ Method One: Making Color Photos Black and White

Generally, just removing the color from a photo produces an image that's flat and uninteresting. A good black-and-white photo usually needs more contrast than you'll get if you simply zap the color. You can create different effects and moods in a photo, depending on what you decide to emphasize in the black-and-white version.

Black-and-white conversion has traditionally been a pretty complicated process. If you do a Google search, you'll find dozens of recipes for doing conversions. Fortunately for you, Elements makes it easy to perform this task, and even to do sophisticated tweaking of the different color channels. Just follow these steps:

1. **Open a photo and make sure it's ready to convert.**

   If the file has multiple layers, flatten it (Layer→Flatten Image) or make sure the layer you want to convert is the active layer (click it in the Layers panel). To convert only part of the photo, select the area you want to make black and white or create a duplicate layer (Ctrl+J/⌘-J) and then, after you do the conversion, use a layer mask to adjust the visible black and white area. (As always, it's best to do this on a copy, not on your original photo.)

2. **Go to Enhance→"Convert to Black and White," or press Alt+Ctrl+B/Option-⌘-B.**

   The "Convert to Black and White" dialog box appears. It includes helpful before and after previews of the image, and the controls shown in Figure 10-1.

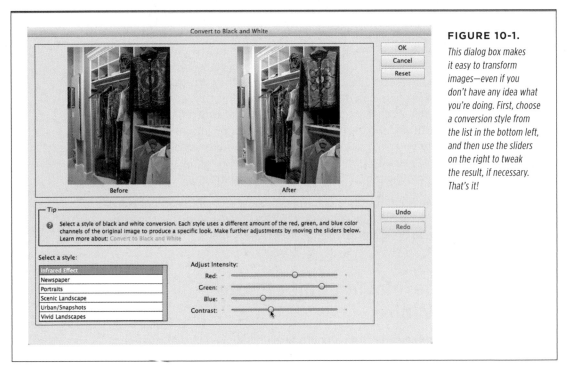

FIGURE 10-1.

This dialog box makes it easy to transform images—even if you don't have any idea what you're doing. First, choose a conversion style from the list in the bottom left, and then use the sliders on the right to tweak the result, if necessary. That's it!

3. **Choose a conversion style.**

   Elements gives you various preset styles for the conversion. Click a style in the list to apply it to your photo. Try each one to find your favorite.

4. Tweak the conversion, if necessary.

Use the dialog box's sliders (Red, Green, Blue, and Contrast) to increase or decrease the prominence of each color channel (page 236). You don't need to understand color channels to do this; just move the sliders around and see what they do (the After image shows how you're changing things). Go gently—it doesn't take much to make a big difference.

Once you move a slider, the Undo and Redo buttons on the right side of the dialog box become clickable. Use them to step backward and forward through your changes. To start from scratch, click Reset.

5. When you're satisfied with how the photo looks, click OK.

Be sure to carefully examine your actual image before clicking OK. Don't just rely on the smallish preview window—move the dialog box around your screen so you can see the whole photo before accepting the conversion. If you decide against creating a black-and-white image, click Cancel.

If you used a duplicate layer and you decide you want only a partially black-and-white image, then after you click OK, apply a layer mask (page 202) and paint away the areas you want to leave in color (page 205 explains how to edit the mask). Just remember: "Black conceals, white reveals."

TIP You may want to emphasize certain details in the photo without making additional changes to its overall tonality. To do that, use the Dodge and Burn tools (page 406) once you've completed the conversion.

The different conversion styles have descriptive names, like Portraits and Scenic Landscape, but don't put too much stock in those names. They're simply less intimidating ways of describing preset collections of color-channel settings. Be sure to test out the various styles to see which works best on your photo. For instance, you may prefer the way Uncle Julio looks when you choose Newspaper style instead of the Portraits style.

But wait a minute: Changes to the color channels? That's right. Back in Chapter 7, you read about how photos consist of three separate color channels: red, blue, and green. In your camera's original file, each of these channels is recorded as variations of light and dark tones—in other words, as a black-and-white image. This image file tells your computer or printer to render a particular channel as all red, blue, or green, and the blending of the three monotone channels makes all the colors you see.

When you convert a photo back to black and white, each of these channels contains varying amounts of details from your photo, depending on the color of your original subject. So, the green channel might have more detail from your subject's eyelashes, while the red channel may have more detail from the bark on the tree she's standing under. (Remember, the color channels themselves don't necessarily correspond to the color of the objects you see in the final photo. Or, put another way: Your camera uses a mixture of red, blue, and green to create what looks like bark to us humans.) And there's often more *noise* (graininess) in one channel than the others.

The "Convert to Black and White" dialog box's Red, Green, and Blue sliders let you increase or decrease the presence of each color channel so you can adjust how prominent various details are in the photo. These adjustments can greatly change the appearance of the final conversion. The Contrast slider, not surprisingly, adjusts the contrast (page 126) of the combined channels.

That's the theory behind those color channel sliders, but fortunately, you don't have to understand it to use them effectively. Just be sure you have a good view of your photo (zoom in and, if necessary, move the dialog box) and then move the sliders till you're happy with what you see. If you plan to print your converted photo, the note on page 348 has some tips on how to get a good black-and-white print from a color inkjet printer.

> **TIP** Elements gives you an even easier way to convert a photo to black and white (but it's an all-or-nothing scenario—you can't adjust the tones in the image): the Effects panel's black-and-white tint effect. Go to the Effects panel (if it's not already visible, click the Effects button at the bottom right of the Editor's main window), and then click the Effects tab at the top of the panel. From the panel's drop-down menu, choose Monotone Color, and then double-click the black-and-white tree to apply the effect. Also, some frames in the Frames section of the Graphics panel (page 524)—like a few of the Color Tint frames—automatically convert a photo to black and white when you place it in the frame. Page 514 explains how to use these frames.

◼ Method Two: Removing Color from a Photo

Because one size never fits all, Elements gives you a few other, totally different ways to remove color from images. The instructions in the preceding section are usually your best bet when you want to convert a whole photo to black and white. But if you're in a hurry or you're looking to do something artistic, like change a color photo into a drawing or a painting, try one of these three methods:

- **Switch color modes.** You may remember from page 42 that you need to choose a color mode for your photos: RGB, Bitmap, or Grayscale. You can remove the color from a photo simply by changing its mode to Grayscale: Go to Image→Mode→Grayscale. This method is quick, but it's also a bit destructive, since you can't apply it to a layer: The whole photo is either grayscale or not, and once you save and close the photo, the color info is gone for good.

- **Remove Color.** You can keep a photo in RGB mode and drain its color by going to Enhance→Adjust Color→Remove Color, or by pressing Shift+Ctrl+U/Shift-⌘-U. This command removes the color only from the active layer, so if the file has more than one layer, you need to flatten it first (Layer→Flatten Image) or the other layers will keep their colors.

The Remove Color command is really just another way to completely desaturate a photo—like you might do when using the Hue/Saturation command (described next). Remove Color is faster but doesn't give you as much control as the Hue/Saturation command. Figure 10-2 shows the difference between applying the Remove Color command and converting an entire image to grayscale as explained in the previous bullet.

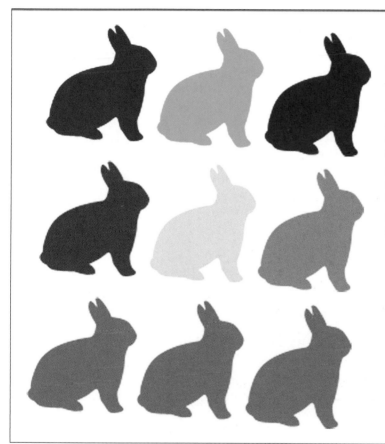

FIGURE 10-2.

Uncoloring your photo can generate very different results depending on the method you use.

Top: Each of these rabbits has a pure color value of 255. In other words, you're looking at rabbits that are 100 percent blue, green, and red, with zero as the value for the other two color channels.

Middle: The same images with the mode converted to grayscale (Image→Mode→ Grayscale).

Bottom: Using the Remove Color command gives you quite different results.

- **Hue/Saturation.** You can also call up the Hue/Saturation dialog box (page 331) by going to Enhance→Adjust Color→Adjust Hue/Saturation, and then moving the Saturation slider all the way to the left or typing *–100* into the Saturation box. The advantage of this method is that, if you don't care for the shade of gray you get, you can desaturate each color channel separately by using the dialog box's drop-down menu.

TIP   If you're planning to print the results of your black-and-white conversion, the paper you use can make a *big* difference in the results. If you don't like the gray tones you get with your usual paper, try a different weight or brand. You'll need to experiment, because the inks for various printer models interact differently with various brands of paper. And if you plan on printing lots of black-and-white photos, you may want to look into buying a photo printer that lets you substitute several shades of gray for your color cartridges.

Creating Spot Color

Removing almost all the color from a photo but leaving one or two objects in vivid tones, called *spot color,* is an effective artistic device that's long been popular in the print industry. (In the commercial printing business, "spot color" means something else—it refers to the use of special inks for a particular color in a multicolor image.) Figure 10-3 shows an example. (To practice the maneuvers you're about to learn, download the practice file *caboose.jpg* from this book's Missing CD page at *www. missingmanuals.com/cds.*)

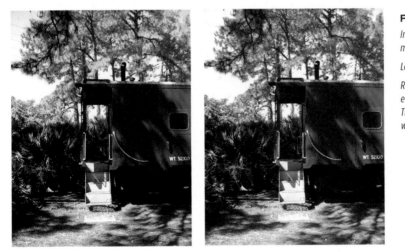

FIGURE 10-3.

In Elements, you can easily remove color from part of an image.

Left: The original photo.

Right: Now the color is gone from everything except the caboose. This section explains three easy ways to create this effect.

This section walks you through three of the easiest methods for creating spot color.

TIP   Check your camera's special effects settings for a spot or accent color option. Many cameras can now create black-and-white images with only one shade left in color.

Brushing Away Color

Creating black-and-white areas in a color photo is super easy in Elements. One way is to use the Smart Brush to convert an area to black and white while making a selection (see Figure 10-4). In other words, you paint the object you want to make black and white, and Elements selects and converts it—all while preserving the color in the rest of your photo. If you want to keep most of the image in color and convert only small portions of it to black and white, or vice versa, definitely try this method first.

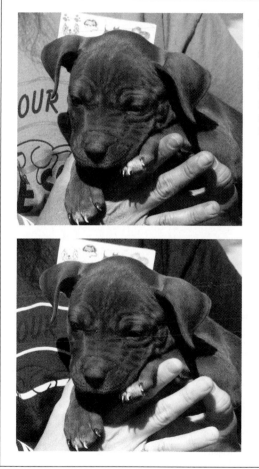

FIGURE 10-4.

With the Smart Brush, converting part of a photo to black and white is as simple as making a selection.

Top: The puppy is really cute, but the bright blue shirt draws your eye away from him.

Bottom: Drag over the puppy with the Smart Brush with the Inverse option turned on, and he stays in color while the rest of the photo turns black and white.

To paint away color with the Smart Brush:

1. **Open a photo in Expert Mode, and then activate the Smart Brush.**

   Press F or click its icon (the housepainter's brush) in the Tools panel. Check the Tool Options to be sure you have the regular Smart Brush activated and not the Detail Smart Brush. Happily, the Smart Brush puts its changes on their own layer, so you don't need to create a duplicate layer before using it.

2. **Choose the style of black-and-white conversion you want.**

   The thumbnail in the Tool Options area is actually the pop-out menu for the Smart Brush's presets. Click the thumbnail and then, in the palette that appears, click the drop-down menu and choose "Black and White." Then click the thumbnail that looks most like what you want (if you don't like it once it's applied, you can change it). Elements has a number of different conversion styles, and the names don't mean much, so it's best to go by the thumbnail preview when choosing one. To make the thumbnails a little easier to see, click the four-line square in the palette's upper right and choose Large Thumbnail.

3. **Drag over the object in your photo that you want to make black and white.**

   The Smart Brush should select the object and convert it, all in one go. If you have a hard time getting a good selection, go back to the Tool Options and switch to the Detail Smart Brush (page 225) instead. (It works like the regular Selection Brush, changing only the area directly under the cursor, so you'll have more work to do, but you'll get a more accurate selection.)

That's all there is to it. If you don't like the conversion style you chose or want to change the area the brush affects, click the pin icon that appears in your photo when you switch back to the Smart Brush and then make your changes. (See page 228 for more about how to fine-tune Smart Brush edits.) You can also adjust the affected area by editing the Smart Brush's layer mask, as explained on page 205.

The Smart Brush is great when you want a photo that's mostly in color with only a small area of black and white. If you want the opposite—a photo that's mostly black and white with only a small area of color—then turn on the Tool Options' Inverse checkbox (which reverses the area changed by the effect), and then brush over the area you want to keep in color. That way, the part you brush stays in color, while the rest of the photo turns black and white as soon as you start brushing. You can also use one of the methods listed in the following sections.

> **TIP** The Smart Brush's black-and-white conversion settings aren't always editable. Instead, you may see a confusing message that claims that the Adjustment layer was created in Photoshop, even though you just created it in Elements. That's because Adobe uses the Smart Brush to make some Photoshop-only conversion styles available in Elements so you can *apply* them but not tweak them once you're done.

Erasing Colors from a Duplicate Layer

If you don't want to use a layer mask (page 202), you can easily remove colors from parts of an image with the Eraser tool. (See page 415 for more about Elements' different erasers.) With this method, you place a color-free layer over the colored original, and then erase bits of the top layer to let the color below show through. Here's how:

1. **Open a photo and then create a duplicate layer.**

   Press Ctrl+J/⌘-J or go to Layer→Duplicate Layer. This layer will become the black-and-white version.

2. **Remove the color from the new layer.**

   Make sure the top layer (the new one you just created) is the active layer, and then go to Enhance→"Convert to Black and White," or to Enhance→Adjust Color→Remove Color. You should now see a black-and-white version of your image.

3. **Erase the areas of the top layer where you want to see color.**

   Use the Eraser tool (page 415) to remove parts of the top layer so the colored layer underneath it shows through. Usually you'll get the best results with a fairly soft brush.

If you want an image that's mostly colored with only a few black-and-white areas, reverse this technique: Remove the color from the bottom layer and leave the top layer in color; then erase as described above.

When you're finished, you can flatten the layers if you want. But by keeping them separate, you have the option of going back and erasing more of the top layer later on, or starting over by trashing the layer you erased.

Removing Color from Selections

If you don't want your image to have multiple layers, you can make a selection and then use the Enhance menu's "Convert to Black and White" option or Remove Color command. Just make sure you perform this technique on a copy, *not* the original—you don't want to risk wrecking the original photo.

While the Smart Brush is the handiest tool for uncoloring small areas, as explained above, the method described here is best if you don't like any of the Smart Brush's presets or if you're dead set against adding a new layer. Here's what you do:

1. **Mask out the area of the image where you want to keep the color.**

   Use the Selection Brush in Mask mode (see page 151) and paint over the area where you want to *keep* the color, to protect it from being changed in step 2. In other words, you'll make everything black and white *except* where you paint with the Selection Brush.

   If you want to keep the color in most of your photo and remove it from only one or two objects, then paint over them with the brush in Selection mode instead, or use the Quick Selection tool.

2. **Remove the color from the selected area.**

Go to Enhance→"Convert to Black and White," or to Enhance→Adjust Color→Remove Color. Either way, Elements removes the color from the areas not protected by the mask, but leaves the part under the mask untouched. (You can also do this by going to Enhance→Adjust Color→Adjust Hue/Saturation, and then moving the Saturation slider all the way to the left.) If you have trouble seeing what you've done, temporarily switch from Mask mode to Selection mode, or just click another tool and then click back to the Selection Brush to make any changes.

You should now see color only in the areas you didn't select. This method is the least flexible of all the ones described in this chapter because, once you close your image, the change is permanent. That's why you definitely don't want to use this method on the original photo.

Using an Adjustment Layer and the Saturation Slider

Finally, you can remove color using a Hue/Saturation Adjustment layer. This method doesn't offer you the tone adjustments you can make when using the Enhance menu's "Convert to Black and White" option, but using an Adjustment layer lets you both add and subtract areas of color later on. Here's what you do:

1. **Select the area where you want to remove the color.**

Use any selection tool you like (see Chapter 5 for a refresher). If it's easier to select the area where you want to *keep* the color, do that, and then press Shift+Ctrl+I/Shift-⌘-I to invert your selection so the area that will lose its color is selected instead.

2. **Create a Hue/Saturation Adjustment layer.**

Go to Layer→New Adjustment Layer→Hue/Saturation, or click the Layers panel's New Adjustment Layer icon (the half-black, half-white circle) and choose Hue/Saturation.

3. **In the Adjustments panel, move the Saturation slider all the way to the left to get rid of the color.**

With this method, you can go back and edit the Hue/Saturation Adjustment layer's layer mask to change the amount of colored area, including letting only partial color show, as you can see in Figure 10-5. But most of the time you'll get a better-looking black-and-white conversion with the duplicate layer technique described on page 351.

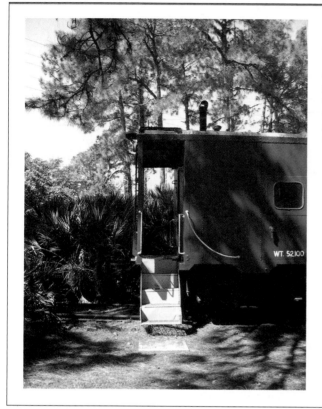

FIGURE 10-5.

By painting with different shades of gray on the layer mask, you can make the adjustment's effect partially transparent. Here, a fairly light gray was used to paint over the trees and ground on the left side of the image so that a little green and brown shows through, but it's not the bright, saturated color of the original photo. (Only part of the left side of the image was painted so you can see the contrast with what was there before.)

Colorizing Black-and-White Photos

So far, you've read about ways to make color photos black and white. But what about when you want to add color to a black-and-white image? Elements lets you do that, too. For instance, you can give an old photo the sort of hand-tinted effect you sometimes see in antique prints, as shown in Figure 10-6.

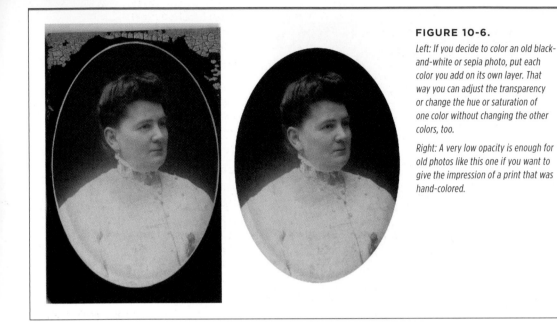

FIGURE 10-6.

Left: If you decide to color an old black-and-white or sepia photo, put each color you add on its own layer. That way you can adjust the transparency or change the hue or saturation of one color without changing the other colors, too.

Right: A very low opacity is enough for old photos like this one if you want to give the impression of a print that was hand-colored.

You can easily color things in Elements. But before you start tinting a photo, first make any needed repairs. (See page 306 for repair strategies, or page 220 for exposure fixes.) When the image is in good shape, here's how to color it:

1. **Make sure the photo is in RGB mode.**

   Go to Image→Mode→RGB Color. If your photo is in any other mode, you won't be able to color it.

2. **Create a new layer in Color blend mode.**

   Go to Layer→New→Layer and, in the New Layer dialog box that appears, select Color from the Mode menu. With the layer in this blend mode, you can paint on the layer and the image's details will still show through.

3. **Paint on the layer.**

   Activate the Brush tool (page 395) and choose a color for the Tools panel's foreground color square. Keep changing the foreground color as needed. If the color goes on too heavy, reduce the brush's opacity using the slider in the Tool Options area.

4. **Repeat steps 2 and 3 for each additional color you want to add.**

   This makes it easier to go back later and fix just one thing without risking the rest of your hard work.

You can also paint directly on the original layer (if you do, try switching the brush's blend mode to Color). But if you do that, you'll find it far more difficult to fix things if you make a mistake. Working on the original layer also doesn't give you much of an out if you decide later that, say, the lip color you painted on doesn't look so great with the skin color you just chose.

SPECIAL EFFECTS

Hints for Coloring Old Photographs

If you want to add some color to an antique black-and-white image, it's easier to create a separate layer for each part of a face you're going to color—lips, eyes, cheeks, skin—than to try to control different shades on one layer. That way, you can easily change just one color later on. (You can always merge the layers—by choosing Layer→Merge Visible or Layer→Merge Down—when you're done working on the photo.)

Here are some other tips for when you're aiming for that 19th-century look:

- To create a photo that looks like it was hand-colored a century ago, paint at less than 100 percent opacity—the tinting on old photos is very transparent.

- If you select an area before painting, you don't have to worry about getting color where you don't want it, because the paint is confined to your selection.

- Skin colors are really hard to create in the Color Picker. Instead, try sampling skin tones from another photo. If it's a family photo, the odds are good that the current generation's skin tones are reasonably close to Great-Granddad's. (If you're comfortable using Elements' more advanced features, a gradient map [page 476] can be an excellent way to create realistic skin shading, although it usually takes lots of gradient editing to get things just right. The face in Figure 10-6 was colored using a low-opacity gradient map based on the copper gradient that comes with Elements.)

The steps just described are handy when you want to use many different colors on a photo, but if you want to add only a single color to part of the photo, the easiest way is to use the Smart Brush:

1. **Be sure the photo is in RGB mode.**

   Go to Image→Mode→RGB Color. If the image isn't in RGB mode, the Smart Brush will paint only in shades of gray rather than in the color you select.

2. **Activate the Smart Brush and then choose a color to paint with.**

   Press F or click the Smart Brush's icon in the Tools panel. Then head to the Tool Options area and click the thumbnail to the right of the Smart Brush icon. On the palette that appears, choose Color from the drop-down menu. Then click one of the palette's thumbnails to select the color you want.

3. **Drag over what you want to color.**

   The Smart Brush automatically creates a selection and colors it.

TIP If you don't get a good selection with the regular Smart Brush, try the Detail Smart Brush instead.

---

4. Tweak the effect.

The brush tends to apply color pretty heavily, so you may prefer to go to the Layers panel and reduce the Smart Brush layer's opacity (see page 188 for more about layer opacity).

The Smart Brush works well if you happen to like one of its available color choices. But if you don't, use the new-layer method described earlier in this section, which is much more flexible, since you can choose any color you want.

Tinting a Whole Photo

You can give an entire photo an overall tint, even if the original is a grayscale photo. Tinting is a great way to create a variety of different moods.

Elements gives you two basic ways to tint photos. (There are actually a lot more than two, but these should get you started.) The first method described in this section (layer style) is faster, but the second (Colorize) lets you tweak the settings more. Figure 10-7 shows the results of using the layer-style method on a color photo.

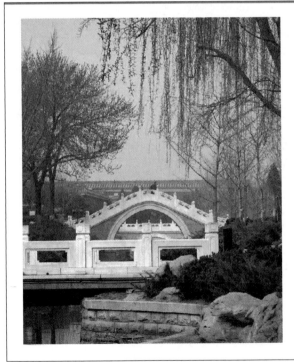

FIGURE 10-7.

The easiest way to create a monochrome color scheme is to use the Photographic Effects layer styles, which are explained in Chapter 13. This image had the Red Tone style applied to the original color photo. Elements removed the existing color and recolored the image in one click. The downside is that you can't edit the color once you're done if you later decide you'd rather have, say, blue.

TIP For a more subtle effect, you can use Photo Filters, described on page 294. Photo Effects (page 456) also has some terrific monotone tint effects.

For either method, if you want to keep the original color (or lack thereof) in part of the photo, use the Selection Brush in Mask mode to mask out the area you don't want to change.

> **TIP** Some of the Graphics panel's frame effects automatically add tints to photos when you apply them.

■ USING A LAYER STYLE

Although many people never dig down far enough to find them, Elements includes Photographic Effects layer styles that make tinting a photo as easy as double-clicking. You'll learn more about layer styles on page 461, but this section tells you all you need to know to use the Photographic styles. It's a simple process:

1. **Create a duplicate layer.**

   Go to Layer→Duplicate Layer or press Ctrl+J/⌘-J. (If you don't create a dupli-cate layer and your original has only a Background layer, Elements will ask if you want to convert it to a layer when you apply the style in step 3; click OK.)

2. **If necessary, change the image's mode to RGB.**

   Go to Image→Mode→RGB Color. It doesn't matter whether the original image is in color; the layer style gets rid of the original color and tints the photo all at the same time.

3. **Choose a layer style.**

   Go to the Effects panel and, at the top of the panel, click the word "Styles." Then, from the panel's drop-down menu, choose Photographic Effects. Double-click the color square you like or drag it onto the photo. You can click around and try different colors to see which you prefer. Undo (Ctrl+Z/⌘-Z) after each style you try, since sometimes an existing layer style can change the way a new one affects your photo.

4. **When you like what you see, you're done.**

The drawback to this method is that you can't easily go back and edit the layer style's color. Even if you call up the Style Settings dialog box (see page 462), you don't get any active checkboxes, because these styles don't use those settings. Instead, you need to use a Hue/Saturation adjustment (see page 331) or Color Variations (page 246) to go back later and change the layer style's tint color.

■ THE GRAPHICS PANEL'S TINT EFFECTS

The Graphics panel includes some frames that automatically apply tints to photos, as shown in Figure 10-8. (Go to Window→Graphics to display the panel if it's not already visible.) These range from simple all-over colors like Sepia to fading gradi-ents. (See page 465 for more about gradients.)

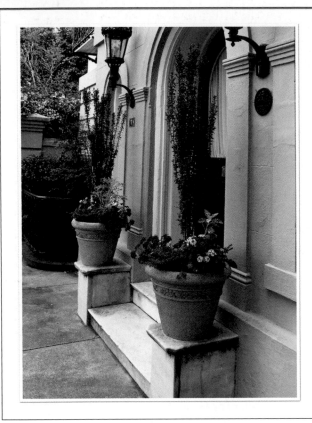

FIGURE 10-8.

Using the Graphics panel, you can apply elaborate effects—like this fading gradient, drop shadow, and frame—just by dropping your photo into a frame. The effect used here is the Color Tint Blue Fadeout 20px.

You can read more about using the Graphics panel's frames on page 514. To tint a photo, choose By Type in the panel's left drop-down menu and Frames in its right one, and then scroll down the list of thumbnails. If there's a color like blue, red, or sepia inside the frame instead of gray, it means your photo will be tinted that color when you apply the frame to it.

TIP The Photo Effects section of the Effects panel also has some very effective color tints. Page 456 explains how to apply effects.

■ USING COLORIZE

To add a color tint to a grayscale photo or to change the color of a photo that already has color in it, you can use the Colorize checkbox in either the Hue/Saturation dialog box or the Adjustments panel. With this method, you can choose any color you like, as opposed to the limited color choices of the layer styles explained in the previous section. And once you've selected the shade you want, you can adjust the color's intensity with the Saturation slider. Figure 10-9 explains how the Colorize setting changes the way the Hue/Saturation command works.

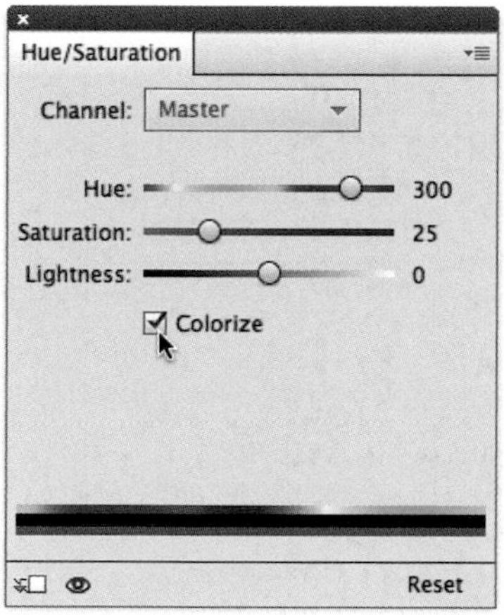

FIGURE 10-9.

To color something that doesn't have any color info in it, like a white shirt or a grayscale image, in the Adjustments panel, turn on the Colorize checkbox. (If you don't use an Adjustment layer, you get the same checkbox in the Hue/Saturation dialog box.)

If you don't turn on this checkbox, you can adjust the hue, saturation, and lightness of white all day long, but all it'll do is go from white to gray to black because there's no color info there for Elements to work with. Also, if something is pure white (that is, contains no color data at all), you may need to darken it by moving the Lightness slider to the left before any color shows up.

Here's how to work with the Colorize checkbox:

1. **Make sure your photo is in RGB mode.**

    Go to Image→Mode→RGB Color.

2. **Colorize the photo on a new layer.**

    Go to Layer→New Adjustment Layer→Hue/Saturation and then, in the Adjustments panel, turn on the Colorize checkbox. If you don't like the color Elements chose, that's OK—you're going to change it in the next step.

3. **Adjust the color until it looks the way you want it to.**

    Move the Hue, Saturation, and Lightness sliders until you get the look you want. Figure 10-10 shows the results. (If you selected and masked an area, that part should still show the original color.)

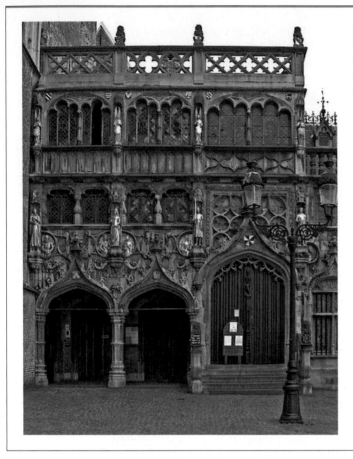

FIGURE 10-10.

This photo was tinted purple by turning on the Colorize checkbox in the Hue/Saturation dialog box. (The gold ornaments were masked out so they stayed in full color.)

TIP Want to turn a full-color photo to a monotone image in a hurry? Just turn on the Colorize checkbox—you don't need to remove the photo's color first—and Elements reduces the image to just one color. The advantage to using this method rather than a layer style is that you can use the sliders to select any color you want.

If you change your mind about the colorizing, head to the Layers panel and double-click the Hue/Saturation layer's left icon (the sliders). Doing so brings up the controls for the Hue/Saturation adjustment again so you can change the settings. You can also edit the layer mask, as described on page 205, if you want to change the area that's affected by the Adjustment layer.

When you're done, if you merge all the image's layers (or press Shift+Alt+Ctrl+E/ Shift-Option-⌘-E to produce a new merged layer above the existing layers), you can then use Levels, Color Variations, and Elements' other color-editing tools to tweak the tint effect.

Photomerge: Creating Panoramas, Group Shots, and More

Everyone's had the frustrating experience of trying to photograph an awesome view—like a city skyline or a mountain range—only to find that it's too wide to fit into one picture. Elements, once again, comes to the rescue. With the Photomerge command, you can stitch together a group of photos you shot while panning across the horizon to create a panorama that's much larger than any single photo your camera can take. Panoramas can become addictive once you've tried them, and they're a great way to get those wide, wide shots that are beyond the capability of your camera lens.

Elements includes the same great Photomerge feature that's part of Photoshop, which makes it incredibly easy to create super panoramas. Not only that, but Adobe also gives you a few fun twists on Photomerge that are unique to Elements: Faces, which lets you easily move features from one face to another; Group Shot, which lets you replace folks in group photos; and Scene Cleaner, for those times when your almost-perfect vacation shot is spoiled by strangers walking into the frame. You also get Style Match, which lets you copy the overall look of one photo into another. Like the Ansel Adams-ish look you came up with for one of your images? With Style Match, you can just tell Elements to copy that onto a different photo.

> **NOTE** Elements includes one more kind of merge: Photomerge Exposure, which lets you blend differently exposed versions of the same scene (like photos taken using your camera's exposure bracketing feature) to create one image that's perfectly exposed from the deepest shadows to the brightest highlights. You can learn all about it on page 286.

Finally, if you're into photographing buildings (especially tall ones), you know that you often need to do some perspective correcting because structures can appear to lean backward or sideways as a result of distortion caused by your camera's lens. This chapter shows you how to use the Correct Camera Distortion filter to straighten things back up. You'll also learn how to use the Transform commands to adjust or warp images.

Creating Panoramas

It's incredibly simple to make panoramas in Elements. You just tell the program which photos to use, and Elements automatically stitches them together. Figure 11-1 shows what a great job it does. (If you'd like to try it for yourself, you'll find *mountainA.jpg*, *mountainB.jpg*, *mountainC.jpg*, and *mountainD.jpg www* at *missingmanuals.com/cds*.)

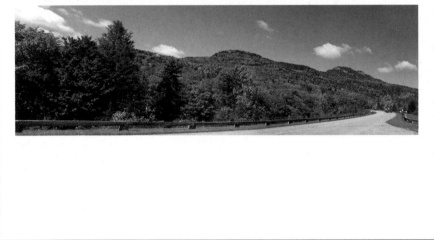

FIGURE 11-1.

With subjects like the Smoky Mountains, you can never capture the entire scene in one shot. Here's a four-photo panorama made with Photomerge. The individual photos had big variations in exposure and were taken without a tripod, but Elements still managed to take them straight from the camera with no adjusting and blend them seamlessly.

Elements can merge as many photos as you want to include in a panorama. The only real size limitation comes when you want to print your compositions. If you create a five-photo horizontal panorama but your paper is letter size, for example, your printout will only be a couple of inches high, even if you rotate the panorama to print lengthwise. However, if you're a panorama addict, you can buy a special printer with attachments that let you print on rolls of paper, so that there's no limit to the image's longest dimension. You can also use an online printing service, like Shutterfly, to get larger prints than you can make at home. (See page 538 for more about ordering prints online.)

You'll get the best panoramas if you plan ahead when shooting your photos. The pictures should be side by side, of course, and they should overlap one another by at least 30 percent. Also, you'll minimize the biggest panorama problem—matching the color between photos—if you make sure they all have identical exposures. While Elements can do a lot to blend exposures that don't match well, for the best results, adjust your photos *before* you start creating a panorama (see Chapter 7). It helps to keep them side by side so you can compare them as you work. (See page 93 to learn how to arrange photos on the Elements desktop.) The box on page 366 has more tips for taking merge-ready shots. However, Elements has gotten pretty good at blending photos together even if they have somewhat different exposures, as you can see in Figure 11-2.

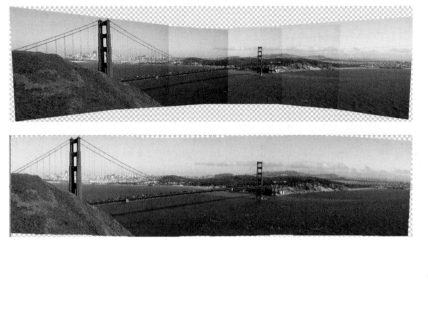

FIGURE 11-2.

Even if there's quite a difference in the color and exposures of your images, Elements can often do a fine job of combining them, as long as you turn on the Blend Images Together setting.

Top: Here's what you get with all the checkboxes in the Photomerge dialog box turned off. Not bad, but clearly stitched together.

Bottom: With Blend Images Together turned on, Elements does a fine job of smoothing the transitions between the photos. This image also shows what happens to your image's perspective if you turn on Geometric Distortion Correction (page 364).

When the photos you want to combine look good, you're ready to create a panorama. Just follow these steps:

1. **Go to Enhance→Photomerge→Photomerge Panorama.**

   The Photomerge dialog box appears.

2. **Tell Elements which photos to merge.**

   If the images you want to include are already open, click the Add Open Files button. Otherwise, in the Use drop-down menu, choose Files or Folder, and then click the Browse button to navigate to the photos you want. After you select them in the window that appears and click OK, Elements adds them to the list in the Photomerge dialog box. Add more files by clicking Browse again. To remove a file, click it in the dialog box's list, and then click Remove.

TIP You can merge directly from Raw files, although you don't get any controls for adjusting the file conversions (but you may get a pretty good merge anyway). Photomerge works only with 8-bit files (page 282), so you need to set the Raw converter to 8 bits before you start.

3. **From the Layout list on the left side of the Photomerge dialog box, choose a merge style.**

   Ninety-nine percent of the time you'll want to choose Auto, which works great in most cases; Elements takes care of everything and usually produces a nice panorama. You also get some other choices for special situations:

   • **Perspective.** When you select this option, Elements adjusts the rest of the images to match the middle one (Elements automatically figures out which image this is; you don't need to do anything to indicate it) by using skewing and other Transform commands to create a realistic view.

   • **Cylindrical.** Sometimes when you adjust perspective, you create a panorama shaped like a giant bow tie (as in Figure 11-2, top). Cylindrical *mapping* (the method Elements uses to plan out the panorama) corrects this distortion. (It's called "cylindrical" because it's like looking at the label on a bottle: the middle part seems the largest, and the image gets smaller as it fades into the distance, like a label wrapping around the sides of a bottle.) You may want to use this style for really wide panoramas.

NOTE If you choose Auto, Elements may use either Perspective or Cylindrical mapping when it creates your panorama, depending on what it thinks will work best for your photos.

   • **Spherical.** This option aligns and transforms your images as if you were standing inside a globe and pasting them on the wall. This is a good choice if your source images cover more than 180 degrees along the horizon. It's similar to Cylindrical but also corrects distortion on the vertical axis, not just side to side.

   • **Collage.** If you choose this option, Elements rotates your photos, if needed, to get them to align perfectly, but it doesn't make any perspective changes to them. If you want to combine your photos exactly as they are, this is your best bet. Elements usually crops the completed panorama, though.

   • **Reposition.** Elements overlaps your photos and blends the exposures, but it doesn't make any changes to the perspective.

   • **Interactive Layout.** This option lets you position your images manually in a window that's similar to the Photomerge window that was in early versions of Elements; the next section explains it in detail.

4. **Tell Elements how to combine the images.**

   At the bottom of the Photomerge dialog box are three checkboxes that can make a big difference in the final panorama:

- **Blend Images Together.** This option tells Elements to smooth the transitions between your photos and blend the colors in the images. Leave this setting on unless you have a good reason to turn it off.

- **Vignette Removal.** If you're merging photos that have some *vignetting* (shadowy corners caused by things like your camera's lens hood or the lens itself), turn this on and Elements will fix that while it merges the photos.

- **Geometric Distortion Correction.** The first photo in Figure 11-2 is shaped like a big bow tie, a common outcome when stitching lots of images together. Turn this setting on, and Elements squares things up a bit, as you can see in the bottom image of Figure 11-2. However, you may not like the result; it's totally up to you whether to turn this checkbox on.

NOTE You can't turn on Vignette Removal or Geometric Distortion Correction if you choose the Collage, Reposition, or Interactive Layout merge style.

5. **Click OK to create your panorama.**

   Elements whirls into action, combining, adjusting, and looking for the most invisible places to put the seams until it whips up a completed panorama for you. That's all there is to it.

NOTE Elements has a lot of complex calculations to make when creating a panorama, especially if you're combining lots of images or if there are big exposure differences between the photos, so this step may take awhile. Don't assume that Elements is stuck; it may just need a few minutes to finish working.

6. **Tell Elements whether or not to fill in any empty edges in the completed panorama.**

   When Elements finishes combining the images, you see a dialog box asking if you'd like the program to automatically fill in the edges of the panorama to make it rectangular. Elements uses Content-Aware filling (page 309) to do this, and sometimes you can get pretty amazing results.

   However, this requires Elements to do a lot of serious thinking, and if there's a lot of empty space in the panorama, you can expect your computer to slow to a crawl while Elements works. If the panorama is large, Elements may take many minutes to ponder it—and then announce that your computer doesn't have enough memory, anyway. If this happens, there are a couple of things to try. First, go to Edit→Preferences→Performance/Adobe Photoshop Elements Editor Preferences→Performance and increase the amount of RAM available for Elements to use. Second, click Cancel and try starting your Photomerge over, this time with Geometric Distortion Correction turned on or using the Collage merge style so there's less empty space to fill.

NOTE When Elements fills in edges, it creates a merged layer of all the photos in your panorama and works on that, so your file size will be much larger if you have Elements fill edges.

You'll probably want to crop the panorama, but otherwise, you're all done (except for saving the completed file). You can do anything to the panorama that you can do to any other photo. The Recompose tool (page 321) is especially useful for adjusting proportions in panoramas, if you need to do that.

TIP Elements creates layered panoramas, and if you look at the Layers panel you can see layer masks showing how much of each photo it used. Since you know how to edit layer masks (page 205), you can go back afterward and manually make changes, if you want.

IN THE FIELD

Shooting Tips for Good Merges

The most important part of creating an impressive and plausible panorama starts before you even launch Elements. You can save yourself a lot of grief by planning ahead when shooting photos.

Most of the time, you know *before* you shoot that you'll want to merge the photos. You don't often say, "Wow, I have seven photos of the Captain Jack Sparrow balloon at the Thanksgiving Day parade that just happen to be exactly in line and have a 30 percent overlap between each one. Guess I'll try a merge!"

So before you take pictures for a panorama, set your camera to be as much in manual mode as possible. The biggest headache in panorama making is trying to get the exposure, color, brightness, and so on to blend seamlessly (but Elements is darned good at blending the outlines of the physical objects in photos). So lock your camera's settings so that the exposure of each image is as identical as possible. Even small digital cameras that don't have much in the way of manual controls may have some kind of panorama setting—like Canon's Stitch Assist mode—that does the same thing.

(Your camera may actually be able to make merges that are at least as good as what Elements can do, because the camera does the image-blending internally. Check whether your model has a panorama feature.)

The more your photos overlap, the better. Elements does what it can with what you give it, but it's really happy if about a third of each image overlaps with the next.

Use a tripod if you have one, and *pan heads* (tripod heads that let you swivel the camera in an absolutely straight line). As long as your shots aren't wildly out of line, Elements can usually cope. But you may have to do quite a bit of cropping to get even edges on the finished result if you don't use a tripod.

Whether or not you use a tripod, keep the camera—rather than the horizon—level to avoid distortion. In other words, focus your attention more on leveling the body of the camera rather than what you see through the viewfinder. Use the same focal length for each image, and try not to use the zoom, unless it's manual, so you can keep it exactly the same for every image.

TIP Before you send your panorama out for printing, flatten it (Layer→Flatten Image), since most commercial printers don't accept layered files. Also, if you enlarge the view of your layered panorama and zoom in on the seams, you may see what look like hairline cracks. Merging or flattening the layers gets rid of these cracks.

Positioning Photos Manually

If you want to position your photos by hand, follow steps 1 and 2 above, and then in step 3 choose Interactive Layout from the Photomerge dialog box's Layout list.

When you click OK, Elements does its best to combine the photos and then presents them to you in the window shown in Figure 11-3.

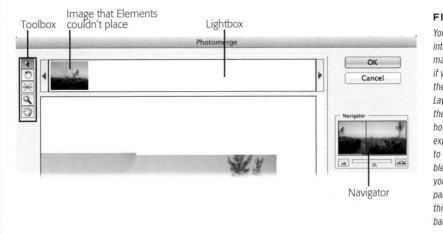

Toolbox Image that Elements couldn't place Lightbox

Navigator

FIGURE 11-3.

You don't often need to intervene when Elements makes a panorama, but if you want to control the process, Interactive Layout lets you position the photos by hand. Note how obvious the different exposures are here. Not to worry—Elements will blend the photos after you click OK, so the final panorama won't have this obvious exposure banding.

Your panorama in its current state appears in the large preview area, surrounded by special tools to help you get a better merge. On the window's left side is a toolbox, and on its right side are special controls. The lightbox across the top contains any photos that Elements couldn't figure out how to place. Use any combination of these features to improve your panorama. For example, you can manually drag files from the lightbox into the merged photos and reposition photos already in your panorama. Just grab them with the Select Image tool (explained below), and then drag them to the correct spot in the merge.

> **TIP** If you try to nudge a photo into position and it keeps jumping away from where you place it, turn off the "Snap to Image" checkbox on the right side of the window. Then you should be able to put the photo exactly where you want it. Just remember that Elements isn't doing the figuring for you anymore, so use the Zoom tool to get a good look at how you're aligning things. You may need to micro-adjust the photo's exact position.

Some of its tools at the top left of the window are familiar, and others are just for panoramas. From top to bottom, you get these:

- **Select Image (keyboard shortcut: A).** Use this tool to move individual photos into or out of your panorama or to reposition them. When this tool is active, you can drag photos into or out of the lightbox.

- **Rotate Image (R).** Elements usually rotates images automatically when it merges them, but if it doesn't or if it guesses wrong, activate this tool, and then click the photo you want to rotate. When you move your cursor close to a corner of the image, it turns into a curved double-headed arrow, just like the one you get with the regular Rotate commands. Simply click and drag to turn the photo until it fits in properly. Usually, you don't need to drastically change a photo's orientation, but this tool is handy for making small changes to line things up better.

- **Set Vanishing Point (V).** To understand what this tool does, think of standing on a long, straight, country road and looking off into the distance. The point at which the two parallel lines of the road seem to converge and meet the horizon is called the *vanishing point*. This tool tells Elements where you want that point to be in your finished panorama. Knowing the vanishing point helps Elements figure out the correct perspective; Figure 11-4 shows how it can change your results. (You need to turn on the Perspective option before you can use this tool. Page 364 explains how.)

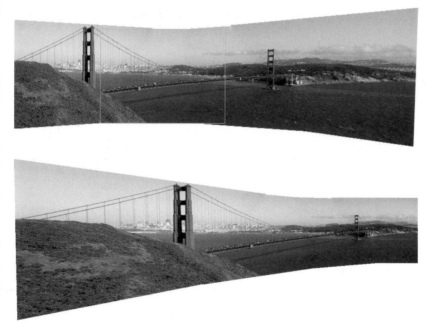

FIGURE 11-4.

Top: The result of clicking the center photo with the Set Vanishing Point tool.

Bottom: The result of clicking the right-hand image. Note that the tool selects a whole image, not a specific point within one of the photos. You can click any photo to put your vanishing point there, but if you then try to tweak things by clicking a higher or lower point in the same photo, nothing happens. To change the vanishing point, just click a different photo.

- **Zoom (Z).** This is the same Zoom tool you meet everywhere else in Elements.
- **Move View (H).** You use this tool the way you use the Hand tool when you need to scoot your *entire* merged image around to see a different part of it. (To move just one photo within your panorama, use the Select Image tool instead.)

To control your onscreen view of the panorama, use the Navigator on the right side of the Photomerge window. It works just like the regular Navigator described on page 100. Move the slider to resize your view; drag it right to zoom in on an area, or left to shrink the view so you can see the whole panorama at once. To target a particular spot, drag the red rectangle to control the area that's onscreen.

Also, on the bottom and right side of the preview window are arrow buttons. Click an arrow to move in the direction the arrow points (for example, click the right-facing arrow at the bottom of the window to slide your image to the right). At certain view sizes you'll also see scrollbars at the bottom and/or right side of the image. You can use them to manipulate the view, too.

Below the Navigator box are two radio buttons that adjust the viewing angle of your panorama:

- **Reposition Only.** This setting tells Elements to simply overlap the edges of the photos without changing the perspective. But if you don't like the way the angles in your panorama look, try clicking Perspective instead. (Elements always blends the exposures of your images to make the transitions smooth; there's no way to turn that off.)

- **Perspective.** If you click this button, Elements tries to apply perspective to the panorama to make it look more realistic. Sometimes the program does a bang-up job, but usually you get better results if you help it out by setting a vanishing point. If you still get a weird result, go ahead and create the merge anyway, and then correct the perspective afterward using one of the Transform commands covered in the next section.

Once you like how your photos are arranged, click OK and Elements creates the final panorama.

Merging Different Faces

Merging isn't just for making panoramas. One of the Elements-only tools that Adobe includes is Faces, a fun (OK, let's be honest—silly) feature that lets you merge parts of one person's face with another person's face. You can use it to create caricature-like photos, or to paste your new sweetie's face over your old sweetie's face in last year's holiday photo. Figure 11-5 shows an example of what Faces can do.

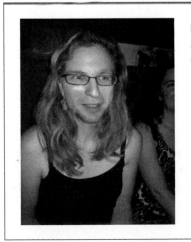

FIGURE 11-5.

Faces is really just for fun. You can create composite images like this one, and then use Elements' other tools to make the photo even sillier, if you like.

Although you'd be hard put to think of a serious use for Faces (it *may* work for something like copying a smile from one photo to another image of the same person with a more serious expression, but the result may not be top quality), it's fun to play with and simple to use:

1. **Choose the photos you want to combine.**

   You need to have at least two photos open in the Photo Bin before you start. You can Ctrl-click/⌘-click to preselect the photos you want to include.

2. **Call up the Faces window.**

   Go to Enhance→Photomerge→Photomerge Faces (you need to be in Expert Mode or this command is grayed out).

   If you didn't preselect images, a dialog box asks you to choose the photos you want to include. You can either click Cancel in the dialog box and then, in the Photo Bin, Ctrl-click/⌘-click the photos you want to use and choose the Photomerge Faces command again, or click Open All in the dialog box to include all the images in the Photo Bin. Elements then opens the Faces window, which has a preview area on the left and an instruction pane on the right.

3. **Pick a Final photo.**

   This is the photo into which you'll paste parts of a face from one or more other photos. Drag a photo from the bin into the Final area (the right-hand preview).

4. **Choose another Source photo if you don't like the one Elements selected.**

   This is the photo from which you'll copy part of a face to move to the Final image. Click an image in the Photo Bin, and it appears in the left-hand preview area. You can copy from many different photos, but you can work with only one Source photo at a time. (When you're done working with a Source photo, just click the next one you want. That way, you can use the ears from one photo, the nose from another, and so on.)

5. **Tell Elements how to align your photos.**

   This step is really important, because otherwise Elements can't adjust for any differences in size or angle between the two shots. Click the Alignment Tool button in the Photomerge Faces pane, and the three little targets shown in Figure 11-6 appear in each image. (You may need to move your cursor over a photo to see them.)

   Position the markers over the eyes and mouth in each photo. (If you need help seeing what you're doing, there's a little toolbox on the left with your old friends the Zoom and Hand tools, so you can reposition the photo for the best view.) Then click the Align Photos button, and Elements adjusts the images so they're the same size and sit at the same angle.

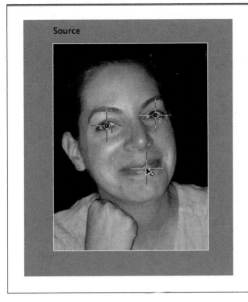

FIGURE 11-6.

To tell Elements how to align your photos, drag one of these three targets over each eye and the mouth in each photo. (You need to move your mouse over the photo to make the targets appear.) If you look very closely at the targets, you'll see that each one is numbered. Be sure to get the ones with the same numbers over the same features in both photos. For instance, don't put Target 1 over the left eye in one photo and the right eye in the other; put it over the left eye in both images.

6. **Tell Elements what features to move from the Source image to the Final image.**

   Click the Pencil tool in the Photomerge Faces pane and, in the Source photo, draw over the area you want to move. In a few seconds you should see the selected area appear in the Final photo. You only need to draw a quick line—don't try to color over all the material you want to move. In the Tool Options, you can adjust the size of the Pencil tool's cursor if it's hard to see what you're doing, or if the tool is grabbing too much of the surrounding area.

   If Elements moves too much stuff from the Source photo, use the Photomerge Faces pane's Eraser tool to remove part of your line. Watch the preview in the Final image to see how you're changing the selection. To start over, click the Reset button (the arching blue arrow over a line) at the top of the pane.

7. **When you're happy, click Done.**

   Elements creates your merge as a layered file. Now you can edit it using any tool to do things like clean up the edges or manually clone (page 314) a little more material than Elements moved. And you can make your image even sillier using the Transform commands (page 385), the Liquify filter (page 492), and so on.

You can adjust two settings in the Photomerge Faces pane:

- **Show Strokes.** If you want to see what you're selecting with the Pencil tool, leave this checkbox on.

- **Show Regions.** Turn this on to see a translucent overlay on the Final image, which makes it easier to tell which parts you're copying over from your Source photo. This is just like the regions options for Exposure Merge, which you can see on page 291.

It would be nice if you could use this feature to merge things besides faces, but it doesn't do a very good job of that. Even for faces, if you're doing something important, like repairing an old photo with parts from another picture of the same person, you may prefer to create your own selections and then manually move and adjust things (see page 173). But the Faces feature's alignment tools can simplify the process enough that it's worth giving it a try to see if it can do what you want.

Arranging a Group Shot

Have you ever tried taking photos of a bunch of people? Almost every time, you get a photo where everything is perfect—except for that one guy with his eyes shut. In another shot, that guy is fine, but other people are yawning or looking away from the camera. You probably thought, "Dang, I wish I could move Ed from that photo to this one. Then I'd have a perfect shot." Adobe heard you, and Group Shot is the result. It's designed for moving one person in a group from one photo to another, similar photo.

You launch Group Shot by going to Enhance→Photomerge→Photomerge Group Shot in either Quick Fix or Expert Mode. The steps for using Group Shot are the same as for Faces, except that you don't normally need to align the photos, since Group Shot is intended for situations where you were saying, "Just one more, everybody!" as opposed to moving people from photos taken at different times with different angles and lighting.

If you *do* need to align your photos, you can do that by clicking the Advanced Options button in the Photomerge Group Shot pane. Then just place the markers the same way you do in Faces (see Figure 11-6) and click Align Photos. Another advanced option is Pixel Blending, which adjusts the moved material to make it closer in tone to the rest of the Final image.

> **NOTE** It would be great if you could use Group Shot for things like creating a photo showing several generations of your family by combining parts of photos taken over many years. But Group Shot moves someone from the Source photo and pastes that person into the same spot in the Final photo, and then creates a composite layer in the completed merge. That means the relocated person is merged into the Background image, and isn't left as an extracted object, so you can't put that person in a different spot. So you need to tackle your generational-photo project the old-fashioned way: by moving each person onto a separate layer and then repositioning everybody where you want them.

Tidying Up with Scene Cleaner

You've probably had this experience when showing your vacation photos: "Here's a shot of Jodi and Taylor at the rim of the Grand Canyon. Those other people? No idea who they are; they just walked into the shot." Scene Cleaner was made to fix photos like that. It lets you eliminate unwanted people or elements in images to help you create photos like the ones you see in travel magazines that show famous sights in their lonely glory, without any tourists cluttering up the scene.

Scene Cleaner is quite easy to use, but you'll get better results if you can plan ahead when taking your photos. In order to get a people-less landscape (or one with only people you know), you need to shoot multiple photos from nearly the same angle, and all the areas you want to feature should be uninhabited in at least one photo. So, for instance, if you can get one shot of the Statue of Liberty where all the tourists are on the left side of her crown and one where they're on the right side, you're all set. Then you can use Scene Cleaner to create a more perfect world:

1. **Open the photos you want to combine.**

   In addition to being taken from nearly the same vantage point, the images should have similar exposures. For instance, if a cloud was passing overhead so that one photo is bright and one is shadowy, you'll have to do some fancy touch-ups afterward to blend the tones. In fact, it's usually easier to fix this beforehand. Chapter 7 has the full story on correcting exposures.

2. **Call up Scene Cleaner.**

   Go to Enhance→Photomerge→Photomerge Scene Cleaner. Elements automatically aligns the photos you chose, so there may be a slight delay before you see the Scene Cleaner window.

3. **Choose a Final image.**

   This is the base image into which you'll put parts of the other photo(s). Drag the photo you want from the Photo Bin into the Final preview area (the right-hand slot).

4. **Choose a Source image if you want to use a different photo than the one Elements picked.**

   Look through your photos to find one that's "clean" (meaning people- or object-free) in the area where the people or objects you want to remove from the Final photo are. For example, if your Final image is a photo of the Statue of Liberty with tourists on the left side of her crown, you'd want the Source photo to show the Statue of Liberty with *no* tourists on the left side of her crown. Click that photo in the Photo Bin, and it appears in the Source preview area (the left-hand slot). (As with Faces, you can use many Source images, but you work with only one at a time; just click the next Source photo when you're ready for it.)

5. **If necessary, align the photos manually.**

Usually you don't need to do this, but if Elements didn't do a good job of automatically aligning the photos, then in the Photomerge Scene Cleaner pane, click the Advanced Options button and you'll see the three markers described in the section on Faces (page 370). This time, instead of the eyes and mouth, place them over three similar locations in each photo. Each target has a tiny number next to it, so try to get the targets with the same numbers in the same place in each photo. (In other words, you don't want target 2 at the bottom of one photo and the top of the other.) Then click the Align Photos button.

6. **Tell Elements what you want to move.**

If the Pencil tool isn't active, click it in the Photomerge Scene Cleaner pane. Then, in the Source image, draw over the area you want to move to the Final photo. Just draw a quick line—Elements figures out exactly what to move. (You can also go to the Final preview and draw over the area you want to *cover*—Elements can figure it out either way.)

7. **If needed, adjust the areas.**

Use the Pencil tool again to add more areas, or the Eraser tool to remove bits if Elements moved too much. You can use the Eraser in either preview, Source or Final. If you have more than two photos to work with, in the Photo Bin, click another photo to display it in the Source slot, and then select the area(s) you want. If you need to see the edges of the areas that Elements is moving, turn on the Show Regions checkbox, explained in Figure 11-7. If the exposures don't blend well, click the Advanced Options button and turn on Pixel Blending for a smoother merge.

8. **When you're happy, click Done.**

Don't forget to save your work. If you want to start over, click Reset (the blue arrow-and-line icon at the top of the panel). If you decide to give up on the merge, click Cancel.

Most of the time, you need to use only Scene Cleaner's Pencil and Eraser tools, but Adobe gives you some additional options to help you out when necessary:

- **Show Strokes.** Leave this checkbox turned on or you can't see where you're drawing with the tools.

- **Show Regions.** If you turn this checkbox on, you can see a blue-and-yellow overlay showing the exact size of the material you're moving (see Figure 11-7).

- **Alignment Tool.** This advanced option lets you manually set the comparison points in case you don't like Elements' automatic choices. Step 5 above explains how to do so.

- **Pixel Blending.** Just as with Faces, you can turn on this setting when there's a discrepancy in the color or exposure of the photos so that they combine more seamlessly.

It's not always easy to get enough clear areas to blend, even with multiple photos. But when you have the right kind of Source photos, you can create the impression that you and your pals had a private tour of your favorite places.

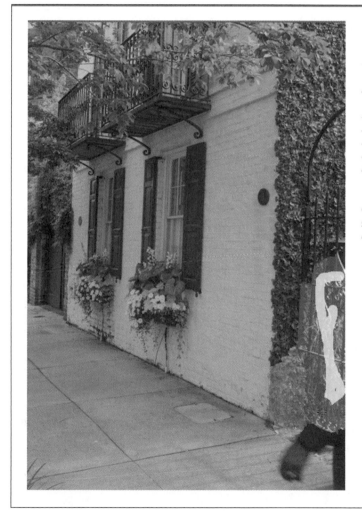

FIGURE 11-7.

When you turn on the Show Regions checkbox, Elements covers your photo with this mask. Here the blue shows the original area from the Final photo, and the lighter yellow shows the section (without the passerby) brought over from the Source photo. The brighter yellow is the actual stroke. (You can turn off Show Strokes if this bothers you.) If you look closely at the bottom-right corner of the image, you can see that the hand hasn't been deleted yet, but another drag with the pencil will do it. The mask is helpful if you have a hard time getting exactly the amount of source material you want, because the overlay gives you a better idea of where to erase or add material.

Merging Styles

Style Match is the latest addition to Adobe's ever-growing list of ways to merge images. Think about all the great photographers; each one has a distinctive style, and a lot of that comes from the way their images were treated in the darkroom or processed digitally. Style Match lets you create and duplicate your own style, or imitate one of your favorite photographers' styles. It gives you a way to say to Elements, "See this photo? I really like the way it looks. Do what you can to make my other photo look just like that."

You can produce a number of fun effects this way. And if you happen to be the executor of Ansel Adams's estate, don't worry: Not even a computer running Elements can take a casual snapshot and turn it into a serious work of art. In fact, what you actually get from using Style Match may be wildly different from what you expected, but that's part of the fun. You aren't just limited to using photos as sources, either; you can try blending effects from any kind of image. So if you did a digital painting and you'd like to copy that, you can use it as your source, although you're not going to get all the brushstrokes and textures.

Style Match is super easy to use. And if you don't have any carefully styled photos to use as sources, Adobe gives you some sample styles to use. Here's what you do:

1. **Open the photo you want to apply the style to, and then go to Enhance→ Photomerge→Photomerge Style Match.**

   Your photo appears in the "After" slot in the Style Match window.

2. **Choose a style to copy.**

   The Style Match window includes a new bin—the Style Bin—that appears in place of the Photo Bin. (To get back to the Photo Bin, click its button.) In this new bin are some sample images to get you started, but you can use any image as your source. To use one of your own images, click the green + button at the bin's upper left, and then choose between using a photo from the Organizer or one from your hard disk. If you choose your hard disk, in the window that opens, navigate to the image(s) you want and then click Open. In either case, the image(s) you choose get added to the Style Bin. To *remove* an image from the bin, click it and then click the trash can to get it out of your way.

TIP   If you want a better view of your image, you can collapse the Style Bin by clicking the down-pointing arrow on its upper right. To bring it back, just click the Style Bin button at the bottom of your screen.

3. Apply the style.

Drag the image you want to copy from the Style Bin to the Style Image slot on the left, and Elements automatically applies that image's style to your After photo. The result probably looks pretty bad (see Figure 11-8), but that's OK, because you're going to tweak things in the next step.

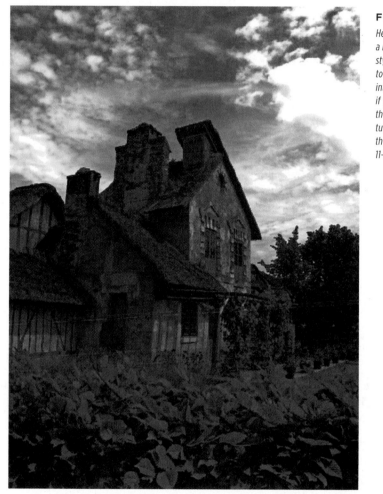

FIGURE 11-8.

Here's an example of what happens to a regular RGB photo when you copy the style from an old black-and-white photo to it. The RGB image's colors have an interesting, dramatic effect to them, but if you want to duplicate the coloring of the Sunset image in addition to its style, turn on the Transfer Tones checkbox in the Photomerge Style Match pane. Figure 11-9 shows the result.

4. **Try other styles, if you want.**

   Just drag a new image to the Style Image slot and Elements uses its style instead. Each time you add a new style, it *replaces* the previous one; the effect isn't cumulative. To go back to your original image, click the Reset button (the arching blue arrow and line) at the top of the Photomerge Style Match pane.

5. **Make any adjustments to the style.**

   The Photomerge Style Match pane includes a number of sliders you can use to tweak the effect on your image (they're explained in a moment). You can also use the Style Eraser to remove the style from part of your photo (if you want to apply it only to the background, for example), and the Style Painter to put back areas if you decide you took away too much. They work just like the regular Eraser and Brush tools, respectively, but they only apply (or remove) styles. You can adjust the size of these tools, and also their opacity (reducing the opacity can give you some interesting effects).

6. **When you like what you see, click Done.**

   It may take a few seconds for Elements to apply the style. When it's finished, it creates a layered file, so you can remove the style later by discarding its layer.

As mentioned above, the first version of your photo that appears after Elements applys a style may be pretty gnarly, but you have a whole panel full of ways to adjust things. You can use any of these settings to tweak the style, in addition to the Style Eraser and Style Painter tools (explained in step 5 above):

- **Style Intensity.** This slider always starts off at 100 percent, so the style is as strong as Elements can make it. Move the slider left if you want to reduce the effect.

- **Style Clarity.** This is a little like a contrast slider. Move it right for more intense contrast or left for a more blended look.

- **Enhance Details.** If you want a more posterized look (page 341), move this slider right. Moving it all the way to the left reduces the applied style to a kind of haze over your image.

- **Soften Stroke Edges.** The farther you move this slider to the right, the less sharp-edged your Style Painter or Style Eraser strokes will be.

- **Transfer Tones.** As mentioned earlier, this is probably the setting you'll want to go for first. Turn on this checkbox to also apply the *coloration* of the Style Image to your photo, not just its style. For example, if you use a sepia-toned Style Image on a color photo, your image will still be in color, just oddly darkened in spots. To convert your photo to a sepia image, turn on this checkbox. Figure 11-9 shows what it can do.

NOTE If your Style Image is colored, turning on Transfer Tones might create some pretty strange effects.

Style Match is fun, but it's not meant for doing serious retouching like getting the same adjustments onto a stack of photos. It works best on subjects like landscapes, although you can get some pretty funny results by first using Faces (page 369) and then running Style Match on the resulting image.

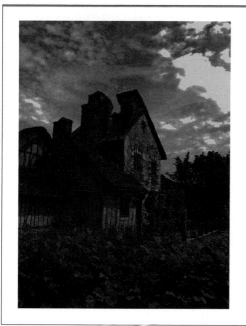

FIGURE 11-9.

Here's the cottage photo from Figure 11-8 again, only this time using the Sunset image with Transfer Tones turned on.

Correcting Lens Distortion

If you ever photograph buildings, you know that it can be tough getting good shots with a fixed-lens digital camera. When you get too close to the building, the lens causes distortion, as shown in Figure 11-10. You can buy special perspective-correcting lenses, but they're expensive (and if you have a pocket camera, they aren't even an option). Fortunately, you can use Elements' Correct Camera Distortion filter to fix photos after you take them. This is another popular Photoshop tool that Adobe transferred over to Elements, minus a couple of advanced options.

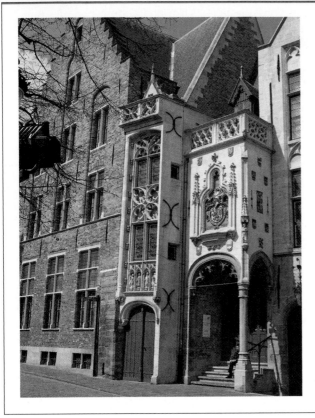

FIGURE 11-10.

Here's a classic candidate for Elements' Correct Camera Distortion filter. See how the buildings appear to lean back and to the right? This type of distortion is common when you're using a point-and-shoot camera in a narrow space that doesn't let you get far enough away from your subject. You can fix such problems in a jiffy with this filter.

Correct Camera Distortion is a terrifically helpful filter, and not just for buildings. You can also use it to correct the slight balloon effect you sometimes see in close-ups of people's faces (especially in shots taken with a wide-angle setting). You can even deploy the filter for creative purposes, like producing the effect of a fish-eye lens by pushing the filter's settings to their extremes.

Here are some telltale signs that it's time to summon Correct Camera Distortion:

- You've used the Straighten tool on your image but things still don't look right.

- The image's horizon is straight, but the photo has no true right angles. In other words, the objects in your photo lean in misleading ways. For instance, buildings lean in from the edges of the frame, or lean away from you.

- Every time you straighten to a new reference line, something else gets out of whack. For example, say you keep choosing different lines in the photo that ought to be level, but no matter which one you choose, something else in the photo goes out of plumb.

- Your image has a dark, shadowy effect in its corners (called *vignetting*). You can also use this filter to *create* vignetting for special effects.

Adobe has made this filter extremely easy to use. Just follow these steps:

1. **Open a photo, and then go to Filter→Correct Camera Distortion.**

    The dialog box shown in Figure 11-11 appears. Elements automatically places a grid over the image to help you align things.

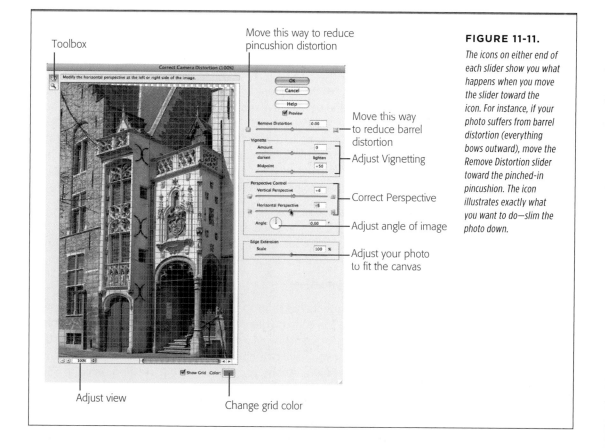

FIGURE 11-11.

The icons on either end of each slider show you what happens when you move the slider toward the icon. For instance, if your photo suffers from barrel distortion (everything bows outward), move the Remove Distortion slider toward the pinched-in pincushion. The icon illustrates exactly what you want to do—slim the photo down.

NOTE Even though Correct Camera Distortion is in the Filter menu, you can't reapply it using the Ctrl+F/⌘-F keyboard shortcut the way you can with most other filters—you always have to select it from the Filter menu.

2. **If necessary, use the Hand tool to adjust your photo in the window.**

You want a clear view of a *reference line*—something you know you want to correct, like the edge of a building. If the distortion is really bad, finding a really true reference line may be impossible, but try to find at least one line that's pretty closely aligned to the grid, so you can use it as a reference for changing the photo.

If your photo is too big or too small for a good view, you can also use the usual view controls (including zoom in and out buttons) in the dialog box's lower-left corner. The Hand tool adjusts both your photo and the grid, so you can't use it to position your photo *relative* to the grid. However, the Hand tool doesn't do anything unless you can't see your whole image in the window at once.

The Show Grid checkbox below the image window lets you turn the grid on and off, but since you're going to be aligning the image, you'll almost always want to keep it on. To change the grid's color, click the Color box next to the Show Grid checkbox.

3. **Make your adjustments.**

This filter lets you fix three different kinds of problems: barrel/pincushion distortion, vignetting, and perspective problems. These errors are the ones you're most likely to run into, and correcting them is as easy as dragging sliders around. The small icons on each side of the Remove Distortion and Perspective Control sliders show you how the photo will change if you drag the slider in that direction. You may need to make only one adjustment, or you may need many (the bulleted list that follows helps you decide which controls to use).

As you tweak these settings, watch the grid carefully to see how things are lining up. When everything is straightened to your satisfaction, you're done. To start over, Alt-click/Option-click the Cancel button to change it to a Reset button and return your photo to the state it was in when you summoned this filter.

4. **Scale the photo, if you wish.**

As you make adjustments, you'll probably notice some empty space appearing on either side of the canvas (the background area of your file). This often happens when Elements pinches and stretches a photo to correct distortion. To make things right, you have two options: Click OK and then crop the photo yourself using any of the methods you learned about starting on page 85, or use the Correct Camera Distortion dialog box's Edge Extension slider to enlarge the photo so it fills the image window. If you use the second method, Elements crops some of the photo, and you have little control over what it chops off. After all the effort you've put into using this filter, you may as well do your own cropping to get the best possible results.

5. **Click OK to apply the changes.**

   If you don't like the way things are turning out, then reset your photo by Alt-clicking/Option-clicking the Cancel button. If you just want a quick look at where you started (without undoing your work), toggle the Preview checkbox on and off.

The Correct Camera Distortion filter gives you a few different ways to adjust an image. Your choices are divided into sections according to the kinds of distortion they fix:

- **Remove Distortion.** Use this slider to fix *barrel distortion* (objects in your photo balloon out, like the sides of a barrel, as shown in Figure 11-12) and its opposite, *pincushion distortion* (your photo has a pinched look, with the edges of objects pushing in toward the center). Move the slider right to fix barrel distortion, or left to fix pincushion distortion.

TIP Barrel distortion is usually worst when you use wide-angle lens settings, while pincushion distortion generally happens when you use a telephoto lens that's fully extended. Barreling is more common than pincushioning, especially when you use a small point-and-shoot camera. You can often reduce barrel distortion in a small camera by simply avoiding your lens's widest setting. For instance, if you change the aperture setting from f2.8 to f5.6 (consult your owner's manual to learn how) or just zoom in a tad, you may see significantly less distortion.

- **Vignette.** If the photo has dark corners (usually caused by shadows from the camera's lens or a lens hood), you need to spend time with these sliders. Vignetting typically afflicts owners of digital single-lens reflex cameras, or people who use add-on lenses with fixed-lens cameras. Move the Amount slider right to lighten the corners or left to darken them. The Midpoint slider controls how much of the photo is affected by the Amount slider. Move it left to increase the area (to bring it toward the center of the photo), or right to keep the vignette correction near the corners. Consider turning off the Show Grid checkbox while you're working with these sliders so you have an unobstructed view of how you're changing the lightness values in the photo. (Turn it back on again if you have other adjustments to make afterward.)

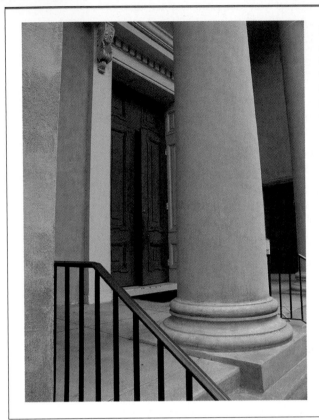

FIGURE 11-12.

A classic case of barrel distortion. This photo was already straightened with the Straighten tool, but things are still out of plumb; notice how the columns and walls lean in toward the top of the photo. You can even see a bit of a curve in the pillar on the far right. Barrel distortion is the most common kind of lens distortion, and you can easily fix it with the Correct Camera Distortion filter.

TIP Each of the adjustment sliders is accompanied by a box where you can type a number instead of moving the slider. If you want to make the same adjustments to several photos, take note of the numbers you used to fix the first photo, and then plug those numbers into the boxes for the other photos.

- **Perspective Control.** Use these sliders to correct objects like buildings that appear to be tilting or leaning forward or backward. It's easiest to understand these sliders by looking at the icons at their ends, which show the effect you'll get by moving the slider in that direction. The Vertical Perspective slider spreads the top of your photo wider as you move the slider left and makes the bottom wider as you move it right. (If buildings seem like they're leaning backward, move this slider left.) The Horizontal Perspective slider is for when your subject doesn't seem to be straight on in relation to the lens (for example, if it appears rotated a few degrees right or left). Move the slider left to bring the left side of the photo toward you, or right to bring the right side closer.

You can rotate the entire photo by moving the line in the Angle circle to the position you want, or by typing a number into the box. A small change here has a huge effect. Here's how it works: There are 360 degrees in a circle. Your photo's starting point is 0.00 degrees. To rotate the photo counterclockwise, start from 0.01, and then go up in small increments to increase the rotation. To go clockwise, start with 359.99, and then reduce the number.

- **Edge Extension.** As explained in step 4 above, when you're done fixing your photo, you're likely to end up with some blank areas along the edge of the canvas. Move the Scale slider right to enlarge your photo and get rid of those blank areas. (Moving the slider left shrinks your photo and enlarges the blank areas, but you'll rarely want to do that.)

  One important thing to keep in mind: Unlike the Zoom tool, the Scale slider changes the *actual* photo, not just your view of it. So when you click the Correct Camera Distortion dialog box's OK button after using this slider, Elements resizes and crops your photo. So if you want the objects in your photo to stay the same size, don't use this slider. Instead, just click OK, and then crop using any of the methods discussed starting on page 85.

The most important thing to remember when using Correct Camera Distortion is that a little goes a long way. For most photos, the best method is to start small and work in tiny increments. These distortions can be subtle, and you often need to make only subtle adjustments to correct them.

TIP   The Correct Camera Distortion filter isn't just for corrections. For example, you can use it to make your sour-tempered boss look truly prune-y by pincushioning him. (Just make sure you do it at home, not on your work computer!) Or you can add vignettes to photos for special effects, and use the filter on shapes (simplify them first; see page 422), artwork, or anything else that strikes your fancy.

Transforming Images

You'll probably end up using the Correct Camera Distortion filter for most of your straightening and warp-correcting. But Elements also includes a set of Transform commands, demonstrated in Figure 11-13, that come in handy when you want to make a change to just *one* side of a photo, or make final tweaks to a correction you made with Correct Camera Distortion. You can also apply these commands just for fun to create wacky photos or text effects. The following pages explain all your options.

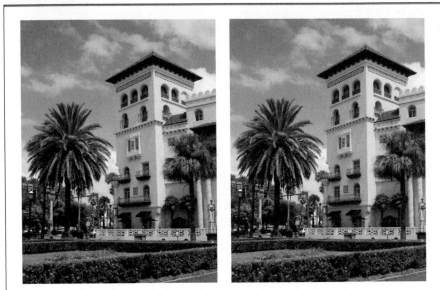

FIGURE 11-13.

Left: While you could use Correct Camera Distortion to straighten a slanting building like this one, sometimes it's easier to make straightforward corrections like this by switching to the Transform commands and just giving the object a yank to pull it where you want it.

Right: Here, it took only a dose of Skew and a bit of Distort to pull the building straight and make it tall again.

Skew, Distort, and Perspective

Elements gives you four Transform commands, including three specialized ones—Skew, Distort, and Perspective—to help straighten out objects in photos. They all move photos in different directions, but the way you use them is the same. When you choose a Transform command, the same box-like handles appear around your photo that appear when the Move tool is active. Just drag a handle in the direction you want the photo to move. Figure 11-14 shows how to use these commands.

To see the list of Transform commands, go to Image→Transform. Here's what they do:

- **Free Transform** is the most powerful Transform command because it includes all the others—you'll learn about it in the next section. Although Free Transform is the most capable command, it can also be the trickiest to use. You may find it easier to use one of the other Transform commands so you don't have to worry about inadvertently moving a photo in an unwanted direction.

- **Skew** slants an image. If a building in your photo looks like it's leaning to one side, for example, you can use this command to straighten it back up.

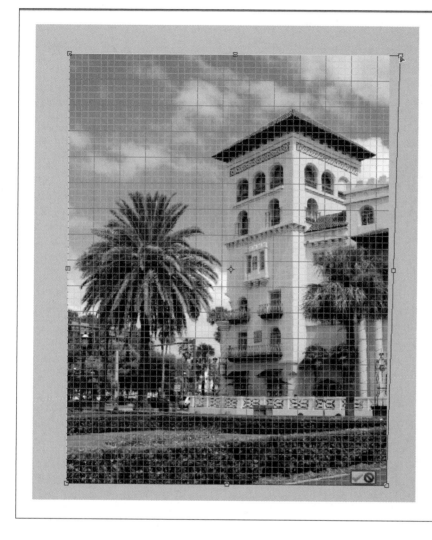

FIGURE 11-14.

Here's an example of how you'd use the Skew command to pull a building upright.

To apply the Transform commands, make sure you can reach the handles on the image's corners. If you're using tabbed windows (page 93), you're all set because you already have plenty of space around the image. But if you're working with floating windows (page 93), just drag the window's lower-right corner to enlarge it beyond the size of the actual image to give yourself room to pull.

> **NOTE** Transform commands work only on layers or active selections. So if you have only a Background layer, Elements automatically turns it into a regular layer when you use Transform commands.

- **Distort** stretches a photo in the direction you pull it. Use it to make buildings (or people) taller and skinnier, or shorter and squatter.

- **Perspective** stretches a photo to make it look like parts are nearer or farther away. For example, if a building in a photo looks like it's leaning away from you, you can use this command to pull the top back toward you.

All the Transform commands—including Free Transform—have the same Tool Options settings, shown in Figure 11-15.

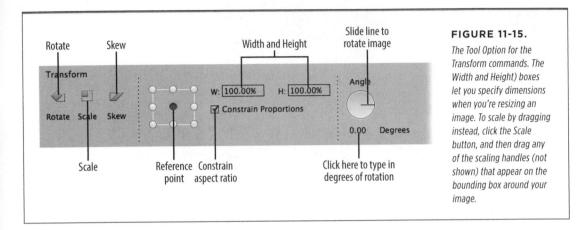

FIGURE 11-15.

The Tool Option for the Transform commands. The Width and Height) boxes let you specify dimensions when you're resizing an image. To scale by dragging instead, click the Scale button, and then drag any of the scaling handles (not shown) that appear on the bounding box around your image.

From left to right, here's what the Tool Options settings control:

- **Rotate.** Grab a corner of the image to make a free rotation (see page 83), or use the Angle setting (explained below) instead.

TIP If you Shift-drag while rotating an image, it turns in 15-degree increments.

- **Scale.** Click here to resize the image by dragging it.

- **Skew.** Click this icon, and then pull a corner of the image to the left or right, the way you do with the Skew command.

- **Reference point location.** This strange little doodad (shown in Figure 11-16) lets you tell Elements where the fixed point should be when you transform something; it's a miniature cousin of the Canvas Size dialog box's placement grid (page 109). The reference point starts out in the image's center, but you can tell Elements to move everything using the upper-left corner or the bottom-right corner as the reference point instead. To do that, click the button you want it to use as the reference.

FIGURE 11-16.

This nine-button icon in the Tool Options area is where you set the reference point for transformations, which tells Elements the central point to rotate around. (The dark button is the current reference point.) For example, if you want the photo to spin around its upper-left corner instead of its center, click the upper-left button, as shown here.

- **Width and Height.** You can resize the image by dragging, or by entering a percentage in the Width or Height box.

- **Constrain Proportions.** Turn on the Constrain Proportions checkbox to preserve the image's original proportions.

- **Angle.** To rotate the image by degrees, just click the number here and then type what you want. You can also grab the line in the circle and drag that around to rotate the photo.

In most cases, you can transform an object without paying much attention to these settings—just grab a handle and drag. Here's what you do:

1. **Position the image to give yourself room to work.**

   Position a photo so that you'll have room to drag the Transform handles far beyond its edges (Figure 11-14 explains how). If you're using tabbed windows, you probably have plenty of room.

2. **Choose how you want to transform the image.**

   Go to Image→Transform, and then select a command. It's not always easy to tell which one will work best for a given photo, so you may want to try all three in turn. You can always change your mind and undo your changes by pressing Esc before you accept a change, or by pressing Ctrl+Z/⌘-Z after you've accepted it.

   You can use Transform commands only on regular layers, so if your image just has a Background layer, the first thing Elements does is convert it to a regular layer. (You can apply Transform commands to a *selection* on a Background layer without converting it to a regular layer, though.) Once the Transform command is active, handles appear around your image.

3. **Transform the image.**

   Grab a handle and pull in the direction you want the image to move. You can switch to another handle to pull in a different direction. If you make a mistake, press Esc to return to the original photo.

4. **When you're happy with how the photo looks, accept the change.**

   Click the Commit button (the green checkmark) below your photo or press Return. If you decide not to apply the transformation after all, click the Cancel button (the red No symbol) or press Esc instead.

> **TIP**   Before clicking the Commit button, you can switch to another Transform command and add that transformation to the image, too.

Free Transform

Free Transform combines all the other Transform commands into one and lets you warp images in many different ways. If you aren't sure what you need to do, Free Transform is a good choice.

You use Free Transform exactly the way you use the other Transform commands, following the steps in the previous section. The difference is that with Free Transform, you can pull in *any* direction, using keystroke-drag combinations to tell Elements which kind of transformation you want to apply. Each of the following transformations does exactly the same thing it would if you selected it from the Image→Transform menu:

- **Distort.** To make the photo taller or shorter, Ctrl-drag/⌘-drag any handle. Your cursor turns into a gray arrowhead when you move it over a handle.

- **Skew.** To make the photo lean to the left or right, Shift+Ctrl-drag/Shift-⌘-drag a handle in the middle of a side. Your cursor turns into a gray arrowhead with a tiny double-headed arrow next to it.

- **Perspective.** To correct an object that appears to lean away from or toward you, press Alt+Ctrl+Shift/Option-⌘-Shift and drag a corner handle. You see the same gray arrowhead cursor as when you're distorting.

Free Transform is the most powerful of all the Transform commands, but when you're pulling in several different directions, it's easy to distort the photo. That's why some people prefer to use the simpler Transform commands and apply multiple transformations instead.

> **TIP** To transform only the *shape* of a selection (not its contents), try the Transform Selection command (page 168), which lets you make any of these changes to a selection's outline without calling up Free Transform. To change the *contents* of a selection, use the tools covered in this chapter instead.

Artistic Elements

Drawing with Brushes, Shapes, and Other Tools

I f you're not artistically inclined, you may feel tempted to skip this chapter. After all, you probably just want to fix and enhance your photos—why should you care about brush techniques? Surprisingly enough, you should care quite a lot.

In Elements, brushes aren't just for painting a moustache and horns on a picture of someone you don't like, or for blackening your sister's teeth in that old school photo. Lots of Elements' tools use brushes to apply their effects. So far, you've already run into the Selection Brush, the Clone Stamp, and the Color Replacement Brush, to name just a few. And even with the basic Brush tool, you can paint with lots of things besides color—like light or shadows, for example. In Elements, when you want to apply an effect in a precise manner, you often use some sort of brush to do it.

If you're used to working with real brushes, their digital cousins can take some getting used to, but there are many serious artists now who paint primarily in Photoshop. With Elements, you get most of the same tools as in the full Photoshop, if not quite all the settings for each tool. Figure 12-1 shows an example of the detailed work you can do with Elements and some artistic ability.

This chapter explains how to use the Brush tool, some of the other brush-like tools (such as the Erasers), and how to draw shapes even if you can't hold a pencil steady. You'll also learn some practical applications for your new skills (like dodging and burning photos to enhance them), and a super easy method of cropping photos in sophisticated, artistic ways—a technique scrapbookers love.

TIP If you have an iPad and like to fingerpaint, you can create drawings on your iPad in Adobe's Eazel app and send them directly to Elements to use in your projects. To learn more, head to *www.photoshop.com/products/ mobile/eazel*, or look for Eazel in the iTunes Store.

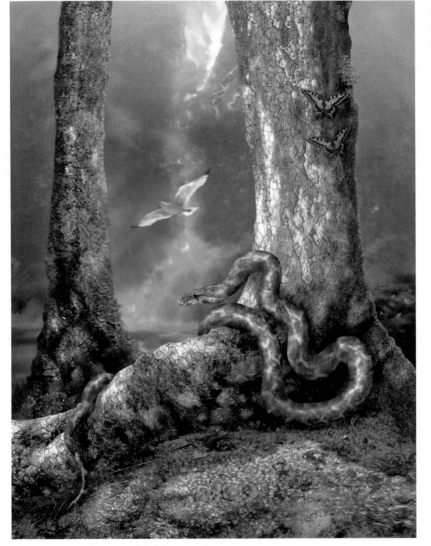

FIGURE 12-1.

If you learn to wield all of Elements' drawing power, you can create amazingly detailed artwork. This complex drawing by artist Jodi Frye was done entirely in Elements. You can see more of Jodi's work at her website, http://jodifryesgraphic images.weebly.com.

Picking and Using a Basic Brush

If you look at the Tools panel, you'll see the Brush tool at the upper left of the Draw section. (Don't confuse it with the Smart Brush, which looks like a house painter's brush and is in the Enhance section, or the Selection Brush, which is under the marquee tools up in the Select section.) To activate the tool, click its icon or press B.

The Brush shares its Tools panel slot with the Impressionist Brush and the Color Replacement tool. You can switch among them by clicking their icons in the Tool Options area, or by tapping the B key to cycle through them. You can read about the Impressionist Brush later in this chapter and about the Color Replacement tool on page 338. This section is about the regular ol' Brush tool.

The Tool Options (Figure 12-2) give you lots of ways to customize the Brush tool. Here's a quick rundown of these settings (from left to right):

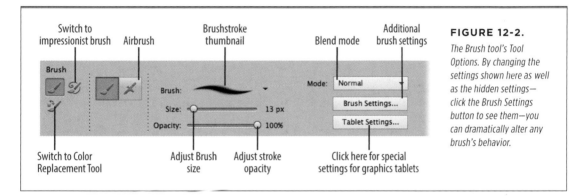

FIGURE 12-2.

The Brush tool's Tool Options. By changing the settings shown here as well as the hidden settings— click the Brush Settings button to see them—you can dramatically alter any brush's behavior.

- **Airbrush.** This pair of icons just to the right of the different brush tool icons lets you toggle the Brush tool as an airbrush. Click the pen-like airbrush icon on the right to use the Brush as an airbrush, and then click the normal brush icon on the left to switch back to a regular brush mode. Figure 12-3 shows how this works.

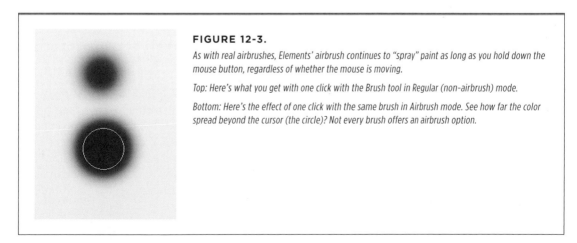

FIGURE 12-3.

As with real airbrushes, Elements' airbrush continues to "spray" paint as long as you hold down the mouse button, regardless of whether the mouse is moving.

Top: Here's what you get with one click with the Brush tool in Regular (non-airbrush) mode.

Bottom: Here's the effect of one click with the same brush in Airbrush mode. See how far the color spread beyond the cursor (the circle)? Not every brush offers an airbrush option.

- **Brushstroke thumbnail.** This squiggle shows the stroke you'd get with the current settings. Click it to display the Brush palette, where you can view and select Elements' brush *libraries,* which are basic brush collections. You can also download many more libraries from various websites (see page 598).

If you click the palette's drop-down menu, you'll see that you get more than just hard and soft brushes of various sizes (see Figure 12-4). You also get special brushes for drop shadows, brushes that are sensitive to pen pressure if you're using a graphics tablet—which you can also use with a mouse, but you won't have as many options—and brushes that paint shapes and designs.

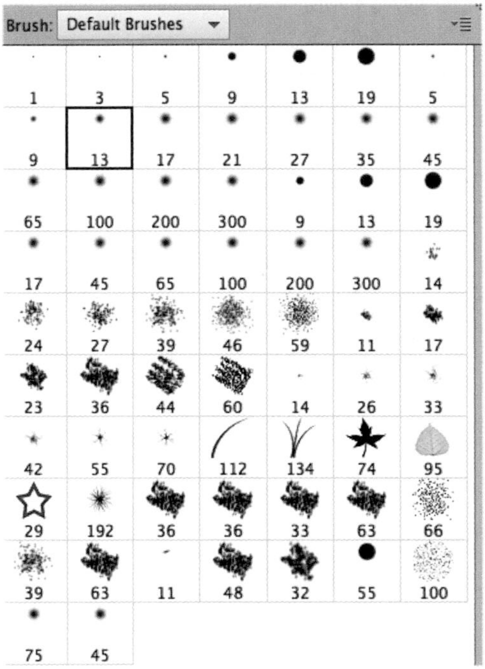

Brush:	Default Brushes ▾					
1	3	5	9	13	19	5
9	13	17	21	27	35	45
65	100	200	300	9	13	19
17	45	65	100	200	300	14
24	27	39	46	59	11	17
23	36	44	60	14	26	33
42	55	70	112	134	74	95
29	192	36	36	33	63	66
39	63	11	48	32	55	100
75	45					

FIGURE 12-4.

Elements gives you a pretty good list of brushes to choose from, and you can add your own. (Page 403 explains how to create brushes.) Here you see just one of the many brush libraries included with Elements, the Default Brushes. To see this view of your brushes, go to the upper right of the Brush palette, click the four-line square, and then choose Small Thumbnail from the pop-out menu. You can also drag the upper-right corner of the palette to resize it so you can see more brushes at once.

NOTE One very cool feature of Elements' brushes is that any changes you make to a brush are reflected in the little brushstroke thumbnail that appears in the Brush palette.

- **Size.** This slider lets you adjust the size of the brush cursor—anywhere from 1 pixel up to sizes that may be too big to fit on your monitor (the maximum is 2500 pixels in diameter or in the longest dimension). You can also click the pixel value and then type a new size. Figure 12-5 shows yet another way to adjust settings like brush size using your mouse. Or, as you're working, you can press the close bracket key (]) to quickly increase brush size, or the open bracket key ([) to decrease it.

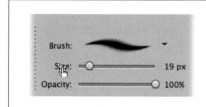

FIGURE 12-5.

You don't even need to grab a slider to adjust its setting. Just move your cursor over the word "Size," and the cursor changes into a pointing hand with a double-headed arrow. Now you can scrub (click and drag) back and forth right on the setting to make changes—left for smaller or less, right for larger or more. This trick works anywhere you see a slider.

- **Opacity.** This lets you control how thoroughly the brushstrokes cover what's beneath them. You can use the slider or type in any percentage you like, from 1 to 100. The maximum—100 percent—gets you total coverage (at least in Normal mode). Or you can scrub, as shown in Figure 12-5.

- **Mode.** Here's where you choose the brush's blend mode (you'll learn more about all the various modes later in this chapter). The mode you choose determines how the brush's color interacts with what's in your image.

- **Brush Settings.** Clicking this button brings up the Brush Settings palette, which offers oodles of ways to customize your brush, all of which are covered in the next section. If you're using the Brush tool for artistic purposes, it pays to familiarize yourself with these settings, since this is where you can set a chiseled stroke or a fade, for example.

- **Tablet Settings.** If you use a graphics tablet, click this button to see settings that let you tell Elements which brush characteristics should respond to the pressure of your stroke. (Page 595 has more about graphics tablets.)

> **TIP** If you ever want to return a brush to its original settings, click the four-lined square in the upper-right corner of the Tool Options area, and then choose Reset Tool from the drop-down menu.

To actually *use* the Brush tool, enter your settings, make sure the color you want to paint is the foreground color (page 247), and then simply drag across the image wherever you want to paint.

> **TIP** If you're used to painting with long, sweeping strokes, that technique can be frustrating in Elements. That's because when you undo a mistake (by pressing Ctrl+Z/⌘-Z), Elements undoes *everything* you've done while you've been holding down the mouse button. In tricky spots, you can save yourself some aggravation by using shorter strokes so you don't have to lose that whole long curve you painstakingly worked on just because you wobbled a bit at the end. (The Eraser tool [page 415] is handy for tidying up in these situations, too.)

One of the biggest differences between drawing with a mouse and drawing with a real brush is that, on a computer, it doesn't matter how hard you press the mouse. But if you've got a *graphics tablet,* an electronic pad that causes your pen movements to appear onscreen instantly, you can replicate real-world brushing, including pressure effects. Page 595 tells you all about using a tablet.

> **TIP** To draw or paint a straight line, simply click where you want the line to start, press and hold Shift, and then click at the end point; Elements draws a 1 straight line between those two points. Remember to click first and *then* press Shift, or you may draw lines where you don't want them.

TROUBLESHOOTING MOMENT

What Happened to My Cursor?

One thing that drives newcomers to Elements nuts is having the Brush cursor change from a circle to little crosshairs, seemingly spontaneously. This is one of those "It's not a bug, it's a feature" situations. Many tools in Elements offer you the option of what's called a *precise cursor*, shown in Figure 12-6. There are situations where you may prefer to see those little crosshairs so that you can tell *exactly* where you're working.

You toggle the precise cursor on and off by pressing the Caps Lock key. So if you press that key by accident, you may find yourself in precise-cursor mode with no idea how you got there. Just press Caps Lock again to turn it off.

There's one other way you may wind up with the precise cursor, and this time you have no choice in the matter. It happens when your image is so small in proportion to the cursor that

Elements *has to* display the crosshairs to show the brush in the right scale for your image. Zooming in usually gets your regular cursor back, unless you're working with a 1-pixel brush, which always uses crosshairs.

If you want, you can also elect to always see the crosshairs within the regular cursor circle. In the Preferences dialog box (Edit→Preferences→Display & Cursors/Adobe Photoshop Elements Editor→Preferences→Display & Cursors), in the Painting Cursors section, turn on "Show Crosshair in Brush Tip" and you'll always have a mark at the exact center of your brush. If you'd like to see a brush icon instead of a circle, choose Standard, and if you'd like the circle to always be as big as the entire brush stroke (as opposed to say, in the airbrush where the stroke normally extends beyond the actual circle), choose Full Size Brush Tip.

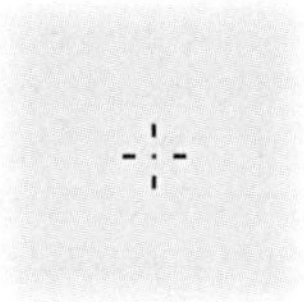

FIGURE 12-6.

Adobe calls these crosshairs the precise cursor. Elements sometimes makes your cursor look like this when you're zoomed way out on an image. To get the normal cursor back, try zooming in some, and read the box above for further advice.

Modifying Your Brush

When you click the Brush Settings button in the Tool Options area, Elements displays a palette that lets you customize your brush in a number of sophisticated and fun ways. (You'll run into a version of this palette for some of the other brush-like tools, too, like the Healing Brush.) Mastering these settings goes a long way toward getting artistic results in Elements:

- **Fade** controls how fast the brushstroke fades out—just the way a real brush does when it runs out of paint. A lower number means it fades out quickly (very few marks—see the Spacing bullet below), while a higher one means the fade happens slowly (more marks). Counterintuitively, leaving this setting at 0 means no fading at all—the stroke is the same at the end as it is at the beginning.

You can pick any number up to 9,999, so with a little fiddling, you should be able to get just the effect you want. If the brush isn't fading fast enough, decrease the number; if it fades too fast, increase it. A smaller brush usually needs a higher number than a larger brush does. And you may find that you need to set the brush spacing (explained in a sec) in the 20s or higher to make fading show any visible effect.

> **TIP** As you tweak the Brush Settings, the Tool Options area's brush thumbnail changes to reflect the new settings.

- **Hue Jitter.** Some brushes, especially the ones you can use to paint objects like leaves, automatically vary the color of their brushstrokes for a more interesting or realistic effect. This setting controls how fast the brush switches between the background and foreground colors. The higher the number (percentage) here, the faster the color varies; a lower number makes the brush take longer to get from one color to the other. Brushes that use hue jitter don't put down only the two colors, but a range of hues in between. Not all brushes respond to this setting, but for the ones that do, it's a pretty cool feature. Figure 12-7 shows how it works.

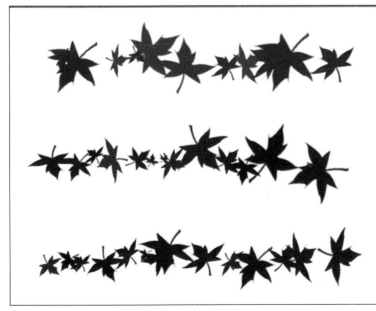

FIGURE 12-7.

Top: A brushstroke with no hue jitter.

Middle: The same brushstroke with a medium hue jitter value.

Bottom: The same brushstroke with a high hue jitter value. The colors used here are red and blue. It takes a fairly high number to get all the way to blue in a stroke this short. Some brushes, like this one, automatically do a little color shading, even without jitter turned on, as you can see in the top image here.

- **Scatter** means just what it sounds like: how far the marks get distributed in your brushstroke. When you paint with a brush in Elements, you're actually putting down many repetitions of the brush shape rather than a simple line. So if you set scatter to a low percentage, you get a dense, line-like stroke, whereas a higher value creates an effect more like random spots.

- **Spacing** controls how far apart the brush marks get laid down when you paint. A lower number makes them close together, a higher number farther apart, as shown in Figure 12-8. Scatter controls randomness, including how far the marks appear above and below the stroke itself, while Spacing just determines how frequently the brush makes a mark along the path of the stroke.

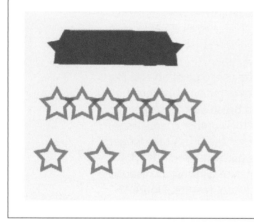

FIGURE 12-8.

The same brushstroke with the spacing set at 5 percent, 75 percent, and 150 percent (from top to bottom).

You may have wondered why some of the brushstroke thumbnails look like long caterpillars, when the brush should paint an object, like a star or a leaf. The reason? Cramped spacing. The thumbnail shows the spacing as Elements originally sets it. Widen the spacing to see separate objects instead of a clump.

- **Hardness** controls whether the brush's edge is sharp or fuzzy. This setting isn't available for all brushes, but when it is, you can choose any value between zero (the fuzziest) and 100 percent (the most defined edge).

- **Roundness** and **Angle.** Painters don't use only round brushes, and you don't have to in Elements, either. If you've ever painted with a real brush, you'll understand these settings right away. They let you create a more chiseled brush edge and then rotate it so that the edge isn't always facing the same direction.

Some of the brushes in Elements' libraries, like the calligraphic and faux-finish brushes, aren't round. But you can adjust the roundness of any brush to make it more suitable for chiseled strokes, as shown in Figure 12-9.

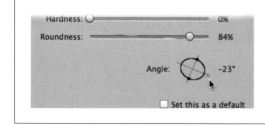

FIGURE 12-9.

Here's the bottom of the Brush Settings palette. To adjust a brush's angle and roundness, drag the black dots to make the brush rounder or narrower, and then grab the arrow and spin it to the angle you want. You can also type a number directly into either the Angle or Roundness box (or both).

The Brush Settings palette also includes a checkbox labeled "Set this as a default." Turn it on if you want to make all your brushes behave exactly the same way. Not all of the palette's settings are available for all brushes, though; some won't change and some will be grayed out for certain brushes.

TIP　If you're a by-the-numbers kind of person, you can click any of the numbers at the right ends of the sliders to turn them into text boxes where you can type in a number instead of using the slider.

Saving Modified Brush Settings

If you modify a brush and like your creation, you can save it as a custom brush. Elements lets you alter any existing brush and save the result—a great feature if you're working on a project that's going to last awhile and you don't want to keep modifying the settings. (Don't worry: When you modify an existing brush, Elements preserves a copy of the original.) To create a custom brush:

1. **Choose a brush to modify.**

   Select any brush in the Brush palette (Figure 12-4).

2. **Make the changes you want.**

   Change the brush's settings until you get what you're after. The brush thumbnail in the Tool Options area reflects your new settings.

3. **Tell Elements you want to keep the new brush.**

   Click the brush thumbnail to open the Brush palette, and then click the four-line square in the palette's upper-right corner and choose Save Brush. Elements asks you to name it; you don't *have* to, but named brushes are easier to keep track of. The name will appear as pop-up text when you hover your cursor over the brush's thumbnail in the Brush palette.

4. **Click OK.**

   The brush shows up in the palette at the bottom of the current list of brushes. If you make lots of custom brushes, you may want to create a special set for them.

Deleting a brush is pretty straightforward: Select it in the Brush palette, and then click the four-line square on the palette's right side and choose Delete Brush. Or you can Alt-click/Option-click the brush's thumbnail in the palette. (The cursor changes into a pair of scissors when you hold down the Alt/Option key; simply clicking with the scissors deletes the brush.)

You can also select something in an image and save it as a brush (the next section explains how). Just remember that brushes by definition aren't any specific color, so you save only the *shape* of the selection, not the color of it. The color you get when you use the brush is whichever color you choose to apply. If you want to save a *colored* sample, try saving your selection as a pattern (page 320) instead, or using the Clone Stamp (page 314) repeatedly.

Special Brushes

So far you've learned about brushes that behave pretty much as brushes do in the real world—they paint a stripe of something, whether that's color, light, or even transparency. But in the digital world, a brush doesn't have to be just a brush. With some of Elements' brushes, you can paint stars, flowers, disembodied eyeballs, gravel, or even rubber ducks with just one stroke, as shown in Figure 12-10.

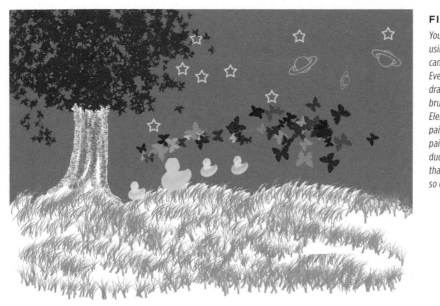

FIGURE 12-10.

You can digitally doodle using brushes, even if you can't draw a straight line. Everything in this lovely drawing was done with brushes that come with Elements. The leaves were painted with a brush that paints leaves, the yellow ducks come from a brush that paints ducks, and so on.

If you click a brush's thumbnail in the Tool Options area, you'll see the list of brushes in the current category and a drop-down menu that lets you investigate Elements' other brush sets. The brushes used in Figure 12-10, for example, came from several different categories. Many of them are in the Special Effects brush library, but there are others scattered around in the other libraries, too.

These special brushes respond readily to changes in the Brush Settings palette (covered earlier in this chapter). Your choices there can make a huge difference in the effect you get, like whether the brush paints swaths of smooth grass like a lawn, or scattered sprigs of dune grass, for instance. And if you're using a graphics tablet, many brushes are sensitive to pen pressure.

> **TIP** If you've tried some of the Special Effects brushes and found the results rather anemic, you can always go back once you've painted with them and punch up their color using a Multiply layer, just as you would with an overexposed photo (see page 221).

Making a Custom Brush

You can turn any picture, or selection within a picture, into a brush that paints the shape you've selected. Figure 12-11 shows what a cluster of flowers looks—and behaves—like when it's been turned into a brush. It's surprisingly easy to create a custom brush from any object you have a picture of:

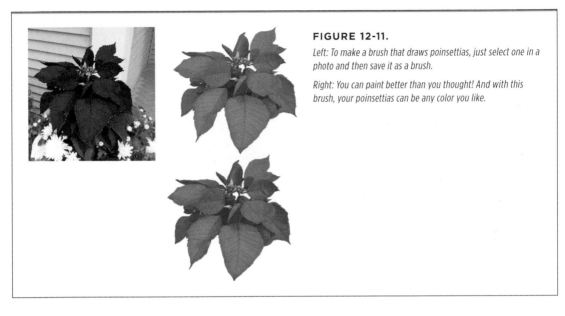

FIGURE 12-11.

Left: To make a brush that draws poinsettias, just select one in a photo and then save it as a brush.

Right: You can paint better than you thought! And with this brush, your poinsettias can be any color you like.

1. **Open the photo or drawing that includes what you want to use as a brush.**

   You can choose an area as large as 2500 pixels square. (You can resize your selection once it's a brush, just the way you can resize any other brush, so don't worry if it's a big area. That said, if you use a super-detailed brush at a tiny size setting, it may lose some definition.)

2. **Select the object or region you want.**

   Use any of the selection tools to do this. It's a good idea to inspect your selection with the Selection Brush in Mask mode, because any stray areas you include by mistake will get painted with each stroke—just as if you wanted them there.

3. **Create your brush.**

   Go to Edit→"Define Brush from Selection." A dialog box appears showing the selection's shape and asking you to name the new brush. Check the thumbnail to be sure it's exactly what you had in mind. If it is, click OK; if not, click Cancel and try again.

The new brush shows up at the bottom of your currently active list of brushes. If you want to get rid of it, simply Alt-click/Option-click the brush's thumbnail, or highlight the thumbnail, click the four-lined square in the upper-right corner of the Brush palette, and then choose Delete Brush.

◼ The Impressionist Brush

When you paint with the Impressionist Brush, Elements blurs and blends the edges of the objects in your photo, just like in an Impressionist painting. At least that's what's *supposed* to happen. This brush is very tricky to control, but you can get some really interesting effects with it, especially if you paint on a duplicate layer and play with that layer's Opacity setting. Usually, you'll want a really low opacity with this brush, or some of the curlier Style settings (explained in a sec) will make your image look like it's made from poodle hair. Changing the brush's Mode setting (page 409) can also help control the effect.

To activate the Impressionist Brush, press B or click the Brush tool's Tools panel icon, and then click this tool's icon in the Tools Options area (it's the one with the curlicue). This brush has most of the same Tool Options settings as the regular Brush, but if you click the Advanced button, you'll see three new settings:

- **Style** determines what kind of brushstroke effect the brush will create.

- **Area** tells Elements the diameter of the painting area, meaning how much area the actual stroke should cover. This is usually much larger than the size of the cursor itself.

- **Tolerance** controls how similar in color the pixels the brush passes over have to be before they're affected by the brush.

If you really want to create a hand-painted look, you may prefer the brushstroke filters (Filter→Brush Strokes); page 435 explains how to use them. The Impressionist Brush isn't really the best tool for creating true Impressionist effects, although its blurring qualities can sometimes be useful because it covers large areas faster than the Blur tool. The Smudge tool (page 411) is another excellent—though time-consuming—way to create a painted effect.

◼ The Pencil Tool

Basically just another brush, the Pencil tool lives at the lower-right corner of the Tools panel's Draw section. Click its icon (a pencil, of course) or press N to activate it.

The Pencil has many of the same settings as the Brush—like size, mode, and opacity—but it offers only hard-edged brushes. In other words, you can't draw fuzzy lines with the Pencil tool, not even the kind of lines you'd sketch with a soft pencil; the Pencil's lines are *always* well defined. This tool is handy when you want to work on a pixel-by-pixel basis.

You use the Pencil tool the same way you use any other brush. The big difference is the Auto Erase checkbox in the Tool Options area. Turning it on makes the Pencil paint with the background color over areas that contain the foreground color. But if you start dragging in an area that doesn't include the foreground color, it paints with the foreground color instead. This is really confusing until you try it. Take a look at Figure 12-12 for some help understanding this setting, or better yet, create a blank file and try it yourself.

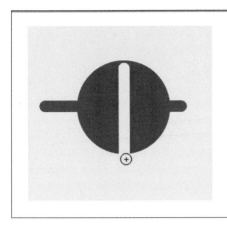

FIGURE 12-12.
The slightly confusing Auto Erase option was used to create two lines here: a horizontal one of the foreground color (purple) and a vertical one of the background color (light green). The horizontal line was drawn by starting with the cursor outside the purple circle (so the Pencil erased the green, leaving a purple line across the circle). The vertical line was drawn by starting inside the purple circle, causing the background color to be exposed.

The Paint Bucket

When you want to fill a large area with color in a hurry, the Paint Bucket is the tool for you. It's right below the Brush tool in the Tools panel's Draw section. If you click its icon or press its keyboard shortcut (K) and then click in your image, all the available area (either the whole image or the current selection) gets flooded with the current foreground color. It works something like the Magic Wand: Just as the Magic Wand *selects* only the color you click, the Paint Bucket *fills* only the color you click.

NOTE Make any Tool Options setting adjustments, discussed next, *before* clicking in your photo with the Paint Bucket tool.

Most of the Paint Bucket's Tool Options settings are probably familiar:

- **Pattern.** Normally, the Paint Bucket fills the affected area with the current foreground color, but click the square with diagonal lines on it to make this tool use a pattern instead. Choose an existing pattern from the Pattern palette (click the pattern thumbnail that appears to open it) in the Tool Options, or create your own, just as you would with the Pattern Stamp (page 320).

- **Opacity.** One hundred percent opacity gives you total coverage: Nothing shows through the paint you put down. Lower this percentage for a more transparent effect.

- **Tolerance.** This setting works the same way it does for the Magic Wand (page 155): The higher the number, the more shades the paint fills.

- **Mode.** You can use the Paint Bucket in any blend mode, as explained later in this chapter (page 409).

- **All Layers.** Turn on this checkbox and the paint fills any pixels that meet your criteria (determined by the tool's other Tool Options settings), no matter what layer they're on. (The Paint Bucket actually *paints* on the active layer, but with this setting turned on, it looks for pixels to change based on all the layers in your image.) To exclude a layer, click that layer's eye icon in the Layers panel to hide it. Don't forget that you can lock the transparent and translucent parts of layers in the Layers panel (see page 189).

- **Contiguous.** This is another option that should be familiar from the Magic Wand (page 155). If you leave this checkbox on, you change only areas of the chosen color that touch one another. Turn it off, and *all* areas of the color you click get changed, whether they're contiguous or not.

- **Anti-aliasing.** This setting smooths the edges of the paint. Leave it turned on unless you have a specific reason not to.

You can undo a Paint Bucket fill with the usual Ctrl+Z/⌘-Z.

> **TIP** You can sometimes improve blown-out skies by using the Eyedropper to select an appropriate shade of blue from another photo and then filling the blown-out areas of the sky in the photo you're trying to fix by using the Paint Bucket at a very low opacity.

◼ Dodging and Burning

Like Unsharp Mask, dodging and burning are old darkroom techniques used to enhance photos and emphasize particular areas. Dodging *lightens* the image and brings out hidden details in the range you specify (midtones, shadows, or highlights), and burning *darkens* the photo and brings out details in a given range. Both tools live with the Sponge tool in the Tools panel.

You may think that, given the Shadows/Highlights command, you don't need these tools. But they still serve a useful purpose because they let you make *selective* changes, rather than affecting the whole image or requiring tedious selections the way Shadows/Highlights does. To dodge or burn, you just paint your changes. Figure 12-13 shows an example of when you might need to work on a particular area. Of course, you can also make a selection and then use Shadows/Highlights on just that, which you may want to try in addition to dodging and burning.

Skillful use of dodging and burning can greatly improve your photos, although it helps to have an artistic eye to spot what to emphasize and what to play down. Use these tools along with the black-and-white conversion feature (page 343) to emphasize certain areas of your photos. Masters of black-and-white photography, like Ansel Adams, relied heavily on dodging and burning (in the darkroom, in those days) to create their greatest images.

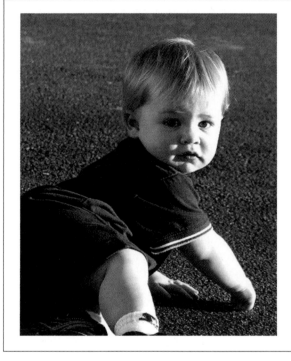

FIGURE 12-13.

Although the overall shadow/highlight balance of this photo is about right, the strong sideways lighting creates quite an imbalance over this little guy's face. Careful dodging and burning can really help fix these problems, as you can see in Figure 12-14.

Both the Dodge and Burn tools are really just variants of the Brush tool, except they don't apply color—they just *affect* the colors and tones that are already present in your photo. Adobe refers to them as the "toning tools."

One word of warning about these tools: Unless you use them on a duplicate layer, you can't undo their effects once you close the file, so be careful how you use them. Many people prefer to dodge and burn using the method described in the box on page 411 rather than with the actual Dodge and Burn tools, unless they're working on black-and-white photos.

TIP You may also want to try some of the Smart Brush's lighting settings (page 225) for making selective adjustments to just part of a photo. A little experimenting will give you a sense for which tools you prefer in different situations. Also, if you're aiming to copy a specific look from an already-corrected photo, try the Style Merge feature (page 376). It may not work, but it's worth a shot.

Dodging

You can use the Dodge tool to lighten parts of an image and to bring out details hidden in shadows. It's a good idea to create a separate layer when using this tool (Layer→Duplicate Layer or Ctrl+J/⌘-J) to preserve the original image in case you go overboard. (Be sure you apply the Dodge tool to a layer that has something on it, or nothing will happen.) Here's how to use it:

1. **Activate the Dodge tool.**

   Click the Sponge tool's icon at the lower right of the Tools panel's Enhance section or press O, and then click the Dodge tool's icon (the lollipop-like paddle) in the Tool Options. You'll see some of the usual brush settings, but with two differences: a Range setting that determines whether the tool works on highlights, midtones, or shadows; and an Exposure setting that determines the strength of the tool's effect.

2. **Adjust the tool's settings and then drag over the area you want to change.**

   Choose a low Exposure setting and then drag repeatedly over the area you want to change for a more realistic result (that's true for the Burn tool, as well), as shown in Figure 12-14. After you're done, if you think the tool's effect is too strong, you can always reduce the layer's opacity (as long as you're working on a duplicate layer).

Burning

The Burn tool works just like the Dodge tool but does exactly the opposite: It darkens. Use the Burn tool to uncover details in images' highlights. Of course, there have to be some details there for the tool to work with; if a photo's highlights are blown out, you won't get any results, no matter how much you apply the tool. The Burn tool is grouped with the Sponge and Dodge tools in the Tools panel; its icon is a curled hand.

Most of the time, you'll probably want to use the Dodge and Burn tools in combination. They can help draw attention to specific parts of a photo, but they work best for subtle changes. Applying them too vigorously—especially on color photos—creates an obviously faked look. Black-and-white photos (or color images converted to black and white) can generally stand much stronger contrasts.

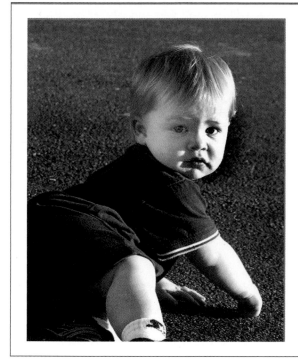

FIGURE 12-14.
Here's the boy from Figure 12-13 after a dose of the Dodge and Burn tools. The shadowed side of his face is easier to see, but the contrast is pretty flat there, while it's much too dramatic on the sunny side of his face. (The effects are deliberately too strong here to show you the perils of getting overzealous with either tool.)

See page 411 to learn a different method for selectively adjusting highlights and shadows. Both methods have advantages and disadvantages.

Blending and Smudging

You can control how Elements blends colors you add to an image with the colors that are already there. This section takes a look at two different blending methods: using *blend modes* to determine how the colors you paint change what's already in the image, and using the Smudge tool to mix parts of an image together.

Blend Modes

Blend modes are almost limitless in the ways they can manipulate images. They control how the color you add when painting reacts with the existing pixels in an image—whether you just add color (Normal mode), make the existing color darker (Multiply mode), or change the color saturation (Saturation mode).

Image-editing experts have found plenty of clever ways to use blend modes for some really sophisticated techniques. Thorough coverage of these techniques would turn this into a book the size of the Yellow Pages, but Figure 12-15 shows a few examples of how simply changing a brush's blend mode can radically alter your results.

Elements groups the blend modes according to the effects they have. You won't always see every group or all the choices, but generally speaking, in Elements menus (such as the Brush tool's Mode menu in the Tool Options area) the top group includes what you might call "painting modes," followed by modes for darkening, lightening, adjusting light, applying special effects, and adjusting color.

Keep in mind that the modes sometimes work quite differently with layers than with tools. In other words, painting with a brush in Dissolve mode may produce an effect quite different than creating a layer in Dissolve mode and painting on it.

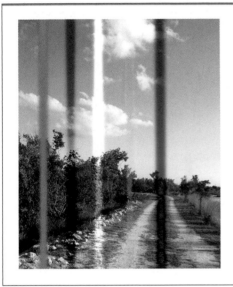

FIGURE 12-15.

This photo shows the effect of some of the different blend modes when used with the Brush tool. The same color was used to paint each of the vertical stripes, but each one used a different blend mode—you can see how different the results are. From left to right, the modes are Normal, Color Burn, Color Dodge, Vivid Light, Difference, and Saturation.

There are so many ways to combine blend modes that even Elements pros can't always predict the results, so experimenting is the best way to learn about them. They're really cool and useful once you get used to them, but if you're just starting out in Elements, there's no need to worry about them right away.

TIP If you'd like to learn more about each mode, you can find a lot of useful tutorials on the Web. A good place to start is *www.photoshopgurus.com/tutorials/t010.html*. (Ignore the section "Additional blend mode information"—that's only for Photoshop folks.)

Blend Modes Instead of Dodge and Burn

You can do a lot in Elements without ever touching blend modes. But if you take time to familiarize yourself with them, you might find they become a regular part of your image-editing toolkit. For instance, you may prefer the effect you get using a layer in Overlay mode to that of the Dodge and Burn tools.

To adjust a photo using a layer in Overlay blend mode, first make basic adjustments like Levels or Shadows/Highlights. Then, when you're ready to fine-tune the photo by enhancing details, here's what you do:

1. **Create a new layer.** Go to Layer→New→Layer or press Shift+Ctrl+N/Shift-⌘-N.

2. **Before dismissing the New Layer dialog box, choose the Overlay blend mode.** Select Overlay from the Mode menu, turn on the "Fill with Overlay-neutral color (50% gray)" checkbox, and then click OK. You won't see anything happen to your photo just yet.

3. **Set the foreground and background colors to black and white, respectively.** Press D to set the foreground and background squares to black and white.

4. **Activate the Brush tool.** Choose a brush (set to Normal mode) and set its opacity very low, maybe 17 percent or less. (You'll need to experiment a bit to see how low a setting is low enough.)

5. **Paint on the areas you want to adjust.** Paint with white to bring up the detail in dark areas and with black to darken overly light areas. (Remember that you can switch from one to the other by pressing X.) The detail in your photo becomes clearer just like magic.

Figure 12-16 shows the results of using Overlay mode on the image from Figure 12-13 so you can compare the results. This method has the added advantage of being adjustable—simply change the opacity of the Overlay layer to tweak the results. You can carry this technique to extremes for really interesting effects when you want an artistic (rather than realistic) result.

The Smudge Tool

The Smudge tool does just what you'd think: You can use it to smear the colors in an image as if you were rubbing them with your finger. You can even "finger paint" with it, if you feel the call of your inner preschooler. Adobe describes the effect of the Smudge tool as being "like a finger dragged through wet paint." It's sort of like a cousin to the Liquify filter (page 492), but with fewer options.

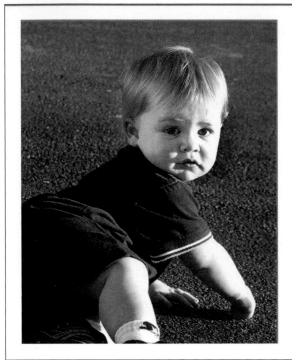

FIGURE 12-16.

Here's the little boy from Figure 12-13 again, this time after a dose of Overlay blending, as described in the box above. Unlike the results of using the Dodge and Burn tools (Figure 12-14), the color isn't grayish, but the contrast where shadowed areas meet bright ones still needs some work.

TIP Another great way to create drawn or painted effects in your photos is to try out the new Comic, Graphic Novel, and "Pen and Ink" filters, especially on a duplicate layer at a reduced opacity or in different blend modes.

If you want to turn photos into paintings (as in Figure 12-17), the humble Smudge tool is your most valuable resource. For really artistic smudging, you need a graphics tablet so you can vary the stroke pressure. (You can use this tool without a tablet, but the effect won't be nearly as good.) To learn more about this kind of smudging, you can find some excellent tutorials in the Retouching forum at Digital Photography Review (*www.dpreview.com*; search for *smudging*). The forums at *www.retouchpro.com* are another favorite hangout of expert smudgers.

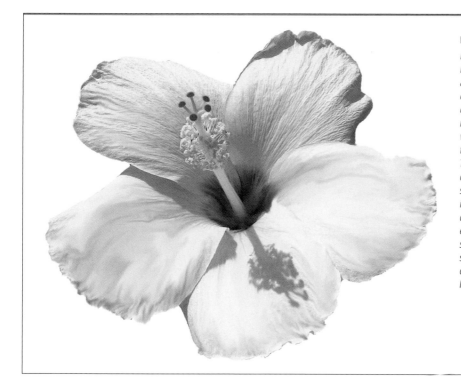

FIGURE 12-17.

In effect, the Smudge tool lets you turn a photo into a painting. With the help of a graphics tablet, you can join the ranks of the many skilled smudgers who create amazing effects using only this tool. The bottom three petals of this hibiscus blossom show preliminary smudging. The brushes you use determine whether the effect is smooth, as you see here, or more heavily stroked. To blend in other colors, use the tool's Finger Painting option.

TIP Scott Deardorff is one of the most talented smudgers out there. If you're serious about smudging, check out his DVDs and online training at *http://deardorfftraining.com*. Visit his website at *www.scottdeardorffportraits.com* to see some outstanding examples of what skilled hands can accomplish with the humble Smudge tool.

A warning: If you have a slow computer, there will be quite a lag between when you apply the Smudge tool and when you see its effect onscreen. This delay makes the tool tricky to control, because you have to resist the temptation to keep going over an area until you see results.

You'll find the Smudge tool hidden under the Blur tool in the Tools panel. Click the Blur tool's icon (the water drop) or press R and, in the Tool Options area, choose the Smudge tool (its icon, not surprisingly, is a finger that looks like it's painting).

The Smudge tool has mostly the same Tool Options settings as a regular brush, but it also includes the Sample All Layers checkbox, just like the Healing Brush and the Clone Stamp, as well as two additional settings:

- **Strength.** This setting does just what it says—it controls how much the tool smudges colors together. A higher number results in more blending.

- **Finger Painting.** Turning on this checkbox makes the Smudge tool smear in the current foreground color at the start of each stroke. When this box is turned off, the tool uses the color that's under the cursor at the start of each stroke. (Figure 12-18 shows the difference.) This option is useful for creating artistic smudges, like adding a contrasting color to help your strokes stand out more.

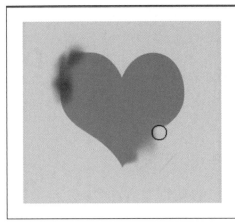

FIGURE 12-18.

The strokes on the left were done with the Smudge tool's Finger Painting checkbox turned on, which introduced a bit of the foreground color (orange, in this case) into the beginning of each stroke. This technique is really useful for shading and when you need to mix in just a touch of another color.

The smudging on the right was done with Finger Painting turned off, so it uses only the colors that are already in the image.

> **TIP** Use the Eyedropper (page 251) to sample parts of your image to add Finger Painting colors that harmonize well with the area you're smudging.

Once you've chosen your settings, smudge away.

> **NOTE** When using the Smudge tool, you only see results where two colors come together because it blends together the pixel colors where edges meet. So if you use Smudge in the middle of an area of solid color, nothing happens unless you've turned on Finger Painting.

■ The Eraser Tools

Everyone makes mistakes. That's why Adobe has thoughtfully included three different mistake-fixers in Elements. The Eraser, the Magic Eraser, and the Background Eraser share a slot at the upper right of the Tools panel's Draw section. You'll probably use all three tools at one time or another. This section explains what each one does.

Using the Basic Eraser

The standard Eraser tool is basically just another kind of brush tool, only it removes color instead of adding it. How it works varies depending on where you use it. If you use it on a regular layer, it replaces the color with transparency. If you use it on a Background layer or one in which transparency is locked, it replaces whatever color is there with the background color (see Chapter 6 for more about how layers work).

The Eraser's Tool Options settings are pretty much the same as for any other brush—including brush style, size, and opacity—with a couple of different twists:

- **Type.** This setting tells Elements what shape eraser you want to work with: Brush, Pencil, or Block. You can see the difference in how the Eraser is going to work by watching the brush-style preview in the Tool Options as you change modes. Picking Brush or Pencil mode lets you choose any brush cursor you like. The Brush option lets you make soft-edged erasures, while Pencil mode makes only hard-edged erasures. Choosing Block mode changes the cursor to a square, so that you can use it as you would an artist's erasing block—sort of.

- **Opacity** determines how much color gets removed; at 100 percent, it's all gone (or all replaced with the background color).

Here's how to use this tool:

1. **Activate the Eraser.**

   Press E or click the Eraser tool's icon in the Tools panel. The icon is a pink eraser, so it's easy to spot.

2. **Choose your settings.**

   In the Tool Options area, select a size, type, and opacity. (As noted earlier, the opacity setting works differently here than it does for regular brushes.)

3. **Drag anywhere in the image to remove what you don't want.**

   You may need to change the size of the Eraser a few times. It's usually easiest to use a small cursor (or the Background Eraser tool—page 417) to accurately clear around the edges of an object you want to keep, as shown in Figure 12-19. Then you can use a larger brush size to get rid of the remaining chunks once you don't have to worry about accidentally going into the area you want to keep.

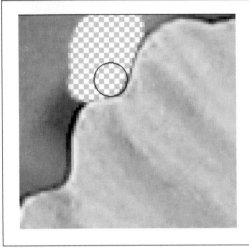

FIGURE 12-19.

Accurately erasing around an object usually means zooming way, way in so you can see which pixels the Eraser is changing.

TIP   You can use a selection (see Chapter 5) to limit where the Eraser operates.

Because it's tedious to erase around a long outline or to remove entire backgrounds, Elements has two other kinds of Erasers for those situations.

The Magic Eraser

Once you try the Magic Eraser, you're likely to wonder why the heck Adobe gave this pedestrian tool such an intriguing name. What's so magic about it? Not much, really. It's called "magic" because it works a lot like the Magic Wand tool in that you can use it to select pixels in a particular color or range (which you control with the Tolerance setting). Its icon even has the same little starburst as the Magic Wand's icon to remind you of the relationship.

The problem, as Figure 12-20 shows, is that the Magic Eraser doesn't do as clean a job as the other erasers. Still, it can be a big help in eliminating large chunks of solid color. Moreover, if you're lucky, you may be able to clean the edges right up with the Refine Edge dialog box (page 145) or the Defringe Layer command (page 167). (To use Refine Edge, you'll need to select the layer's contents, or click in the empty background area with the Magic Wand, and then choose Select→Inverse.)

It's typically best to use the Magic Eraser in combination with at least one of the other erasers if you're looking to achieve really clean results. One sometimes-useful side effect of the Magic Eraser is that, when you click a photo with it, Elements automatically turns the image's Background layer into a regular layer, just the way the Background Eraser (explained next) does. So if you want to do something to the remaining object that requires a regular layer—like applying a layer style (page 461)—this tool saves you a step.

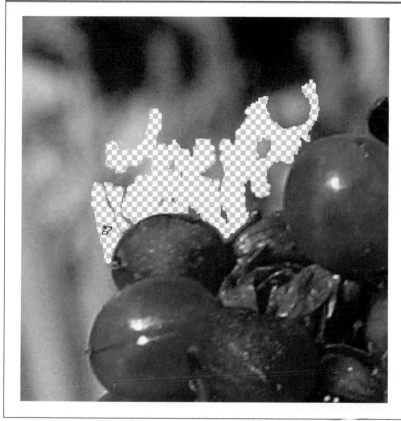

FIGURE 12-20.

Here's a close-up look at the Magic Eraser at work on the background behind a cluster of berries. A couple of clicks with this tool got rid of a chunk of the background, and setting the tolerance higher would've gotten even more. But if you look closely, you can see the disadvantage of this tool: The edges of the berries are fringed with dark, ragged areas it didn't eliminate. You may be able to clean up the edges with the Defringe Layer command (page 167) or Refine Edge dialog box (page 145), but those methods aren't always 100 percent successful.

The Background Eraser

Lots of people think *this* eraser deserves the name "Magic" much more than the Magic Eraser tool. This tool is a tremendous help when you want to remove all the background around an object.

The Background Eraser deletes all the pixels under your cursor (but outside the edges of the object) and renders the area it's used on transparent, even if it's a Background layer. (If you click with it on a Background layer, your computer may hesitate for a sec because it's busy transforming the Background into a regular layer.) Here's how to use it:

1. **Activate the Background Eraser.**

   Press E or, in the Tools panel, click the Eraser icon, and then choose the Background Eraser in the Tool Options area. (Its icon is an eraser with a pair of scissors next to it.)

2. **Choose a brush size.**

When you activated the Background Eraser, your cursor turned into a circle with crosshairs in its center. These crosshairs are important: They're the Background Eraser's "hot spot." Elements turns any color that you drag them over into transparency. The size of the cursor (the circle) changes depending on how large a brush you choose, but the crosshairs stay the same size. As you can see in Figure 12-21, with a large brush, there may be a lot of space around the crosshairs. That makes it easy to remove big chunks of the background at once, since everything in the circle gets eliminated.

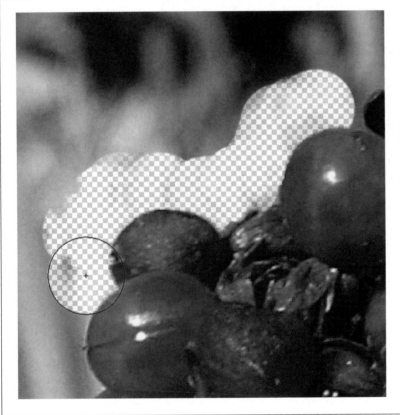

FIGURE 12-21.

The Background Eraser does a very careful job of separating these berries from their background. Just be sure to keep the little crosshairs away from the color you want to keep. Here, because the crosshairs are outside the red, only the background is getting removed. But if you moved the crosshairs over a berry, the Background Eraser would bite chunks out of it.

NOTE If *all* your brush tools start using crosshairs as their cursors (not just the Background Eraser), the box on page 398 tells you how to get back to the regular cursor.

---

3. **Drag in your photo.**

Move around the edge of the object you want to keep, being careful not to let the crosshairs touch the object itself, or else you'll start erasing that, too. If you make a mistake, just press Ctrl+Z/⌘-Z.

The Background Eraser has three Tool Options settings to help refine how it works (you may not need to change any of these settings to get the results you want):

- **Brush Settings.** If you want to use a different brush style, click this button and choose the settings you like. They're explained on page 395.

- **Tolerance.** This setting tells the Background Eraser how similar colors have to be for it to remove them. It's just like the Magic Wand's Tolerance setting (page 155).

- **Limits.** Do you want the Background Eraser to remove only contiguous color or *all* the patches of a certain color? This works exactly like the Magic Wand's Contiguous setting (page 155).

If you want to remove the background around an object, you may find it most effective to start by using the Background Eraser around the object's edges, and then switching to the other Erasers to clean up. The advantage of this method is that you don't have to clean up junk left over from the Magic Eraser. Plus it's easier to maneuver the Background Eraser than the regular Eraser, especially if you don't have a graphics tablet.

Drawing with Shapes

So many brush options and Adobe still isn't done—there's yet *another* way to draw things in Elements. The program includes the shape tools, a group of tools that share one slot in the Tools panel, which let you draw geometrically perfect shapes, regardless of your artistic ability. And not just simple shapes like circles and rectangles: You can draw animals, plants, starbursts, picture frames—all sorts of things, as shown in Figure 12-22. This tool should appeal to anyone whose grade-school "masterpieces" always got put up on the wall...behind the piano.

> **NOTE** When you draw a shape with one of the shape tools, Elements automatically fills it with color. If you're looking to add a simple, empty rectangle, square, circle, or ellipse rather than one filled with color, see the box on page 428 to learn how.

FIGURE 12-22.

Here are just a few of the shapes you can draw with Elements' shape tools, even if you flunked elementary school art class. These objects look even more impressive once you gussy them up with layer styles (page 461).

NOTE If you want to create text that follows the outline of a shape—to put words around the outside of a trombone, say—don't use the shape tools to create the path for the text. Use the "Text on Shape" tool (page 503) instead.

Turning yourself into an artist by using Elements' shape tools is easy. Just follow these steps:

1. **Open an image or create a new one.**

   You can add shapes to any file you can open in Elements.

2. **Activate the Shape tool.**

   Click the shape tools in the Tools panel (they're right above the Pencil tool in the Draw section) or press U. The shape tools are sometimes a little confusing to Elements newcomers because their Tools panel icon reflects the shape that's currently active—so it may be a rectangle, a polygon, or a line, for instance. (You'll see an irregular blue blob if you haven't used these tools before.)

3. **Select the shape you want to draw.**

   Use the icons on the left side of the Tool Options area to choose a custom shape, a rectangle, a rounded rectangle, an ellipse, a polygon, a star, or a line. (If you select the custom shape, you have *lots* of shapes to choose from; click the black-and-white shape currently displayed in the Tool Options to pick one from the pop-out menu.) All the shapes, and their accompanying options, are described in the following sections.

TIP   You can also add custom shapes by choosing them in the Graphics panel (page 524). There, just double-click the shape you want, or click the shape's thumbnail and then click Apply.

---

4. **Adjust your Tool Options settings.**

   Choose a color by clicking the color rectangle in the Tool Options or just use the foreground color, which automatically appears in the Tool Options area when you switch to the shape tools. Clicking the Tool Options' color rectangle brings up the Color Swatches palette. If you click the colored circle on the lower-right corner of the Swatches palette, you get the Color Picker instead (page 249).

   If you have special requirements, like a rectangle that's exactly 1″ x 2″, click Unconstrained and choose Fixed Size from the menu. Then enter a size for your shape in the boxes below the button.

   There's also a Tool Options setting that lets you apply a layer style (see page 461) as you draw the shape. Just to the right of the shape thumbnail, there's a white rectangle with a red slash through it. Click it and then choose the style you want from the Styles palette. To go back to drawing without applying a style, choose the square with the diagonal red line through it. (Sometimes you may need to reset the Shape tool to stop using a chosen style. To do that, click the four-lined square at the right of the Tool Options area and choose Reset Tool.)

5. **Drag in your image to draw the shape.**

   Notice that *how* you drag affects the final appearance of the shape. For example, the direction you drag determines its proportions. If you're drawing a fish, you can drag so that it's long and skinny or short and fat. Even with practice, it can take a couple of tries to get exactly the proportions you want.

TIP   If you're trying to create exact copies of a particular shape you've already drawn, use the Shape Selection tool (page 426) to create the duplicates.

The shape tools automatically put each shape on its own layer. If you don't want it to do that, or need to control how shapes interact, use the squares in the middle of the Tool Options area. They're the same as the ones for managing selections (page 142). Use them to add more than one shape to a layer, subtract one shape from another, keep only the area where shapes intersect, or exclude the areas where they intersect.

TIP The shape tools' Tool Options include a series of little squares just like the ones for the selection tools (page 142), only here they control drawing shapes instead of drawing selections. If you want to draw multiple shapes on one layer, for example, click the "Add to shape area (+)" button, which looks just like the "Add to Selection" button (see Figure 5-3 on page 142). That way, all the shapes you add end up on the same layer. (Shapes don't have to touch or overlap to use this option.)

Clicking the Simplify button in the Tool Options area turns any shape from a vector image (which is infinitely resizable) into a raster image (one that's drawn pixel by pixel). The box below tells you everything you need to know about the difference between these types of images, including why and when you'd want to make this change.

The following sections describe all the main shape categories and their special settings.

UP TO SPEED

Rasterizing Vector Shapes

Back in Chapter 3, you read about how the majority of images (definitely your photos) are just a bunch of pixels to Elements. These types of images are known as *raster* images. The shapes you draw with the shape tools work a little differently; they're what's called *vector* images.

A vector image is made up of a set of directions specifying what kind of geometric shapes your computer should draw. The advantage of vector images is that you can enlarge or shrink them without producing the kind of pixelation (blockiness) you get when you resize a raster image too much.

Shapes keep their vector characteristics until you *simplify* the layers they're on. Simplifying (which is also called *rasterizing*) just means that Elements turns the shape into regular pixels (in other words, into a raster image). Once you simplify vector images, they have the same resizing limitations as regular photos. For example, you can make the former vector image smaller without running into trouble, but you can't make it larger than 100 percent without losing quality, just as with a photo.

Sooner or later, you may want to transform a vector image to a regular raster image so you can do certain things to it, like apply filters or effects. If you try to do something to a vector image that requires simplifying (rasterizing) a layer, Elements generally asks you to do so via a dialog box. To rasterize the shape, just click OK, or click the Simplify button in the Tool Options. Remember that once you've rasterized a shape, if you try to resize, you won't get the clean, unpixelated results that you got back when it was a vector image. If you need to resize a simplified shape, it's easiest to start over with a new shape—if that's feasible. (This kind of situation is yet another good argument for using layers!)

Also, before you simplified the layer, you could change the shape's color by clicking the Tool Options area's color box, and the active shape would automatically change to the new color. After you simplify the layer, the shape totally ignores what you do in the Tool Options. Simplifying affects the *whole* layer—everything on it gets simplified. So once you simplify a shape, you have to select it and change its color the way you would with any detail in a photo.

The Graphics panel brings yet another wrinkle to the raster/vector situation—Smart Objects (page 518). The items in the Graphics panel (frames, backgrounds, and other doodads) act as vector objects, except that they may also seek out a particular place in the layer stack. Choose a background from this panel, for instance, and it knows to zip down and replace your former Background layer.

The Custom Shape Tool

This tool lets you draw a huge variety of different objects, as you can see in Figure 12-23. Its icon is the little irregular blue blob. Click it in the Tool Options area or keep pressing U until it appears in the Tools panel.

Once the Custom Shape tool is active, the Tool Options displays a black-and-white thumbnail labeled with the name of the current shape; click this thumbnail to display the Shape Picker. Various shapes automatically appear, but if you use the drop-down menu at the top of the Shape Picker, you get a lot more choices. To scroll through them all, choose All Elements Shapes.

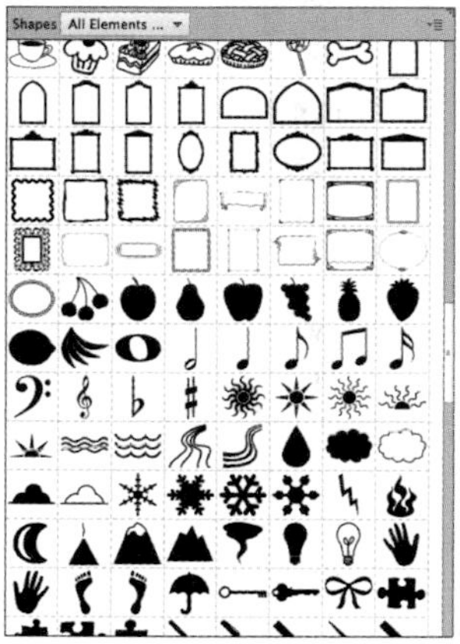

FIGURE 12-23.

Here are just a few of the shapes available when you use the Custom Shape tool. To expand the palette so you can see more shapes at once, drag its upper-right corner.

TIP The Shape Picker includes a copyright symbol you can use if you want something official-looking that's easy to enlarge and use as a watermark on your photos.

Clicking Unconstrained in the Tool Options area presents you with a menu that includes the following options:

- **Unconstrained.** This setting lets you control the proportions of the shape by dragging.

- **Defined Proportions.** Makes the shape keep its original proportions.

- **Defined Size.** The shape is always the size it was originally created to be—dragging won't make it bigger or smaller. Elements just plunks it down at a fixed size you can't control (except by resizing it after the fact).

- **Fixed Size.** Select this option and then enter the dimensions you want the shape to be in the W and H boxes. You can use inches, pixels, or centimeters as the unit.

In addition, the From Center checkbox lets you draw the object from its center rather than an edge.

Rectangle and Rounded Rectangle

The Rectangle and Rounded Rectangle tools work pretty much the same way, and they're both really popular for creating web-page buttons. To activate either tool, click the current shape tool in the Tools panel and then click the one you want in the Tool Options, or press U repeatedly until one of their icons appears in the Tools panel.

On the left side of the Tool Options area, you see the same colored rectangle and layer styles buttons that appear for the other shape tools. In addition, you can click the word Unconstrained for a drop-down menu that includes the following settings:

- **Unconstrained.** Elements selects this option automatically unless you change it. It lets you draw a rectangle with whatever dimensions you want; how you drag determines the proportions.

- **Square.** To draw a square instead of a rectangle, select this option before you start, or just hold down the Shift key as you drag.

- **Fixed Size.** This setting makes Elements draw a shape that's exactly the size you specify. Just enter the dimensions you want in the boxes below this menu in inches, pixels, or centimeters.

- **Proportional.** Use this setting if you know the proportions you want the rectangle to have, but not the exact size. For example, if you enter a width of 2 and a height of 1, then no matter where you drag, the shape will always be twice as long as it is high.

In addition, you have two checkboxes to help you further refine the rectangle.

- **From Center.** This setting lets you draw the shape from its center instead of from a corner. It's useful when you know where you want the shape but aren't sure how big it needs to be.

- **Snap.** This checkbox tells Elements to make sure that the edges of the rectangle fall exactly on the edge of a pixel to help create crisper-looking edges. It's available only for the Rectangle and Rounded Rectangle tools.

Most of the shape tools have similar options, though the Rounded Rectangle has one Tool Options setting of its own: *radius*, which is the amount (in pixels) that the corners are rounded off; a higher number means more rounding.

Ellipse

The Ellipse tool has the same Tool Options settings as the Rectangle tool. The only difference is that you can opt for a circle instead of a square. You can also draw a circle by pressing the Shift key while you drag.

Polygon and Star Tools

You can draw many kinds of regular polygons with these tools. Figure 12-24 explains the difference between them. Use the Tool Options area's Sides setting to control how many sides the shape has. Both these tools share a special setting:

- **Smooth Corners.** If you don't want sharp edges at the shape's corners, turn on this checkbox.

And the Star tool has a couple options of its own:

- **Indent.** Enter a percentage here to set how much the sides should be indented.

- **Smooth Indents.** Turn this checkbox on if you don't want sharp interior angles on your star.

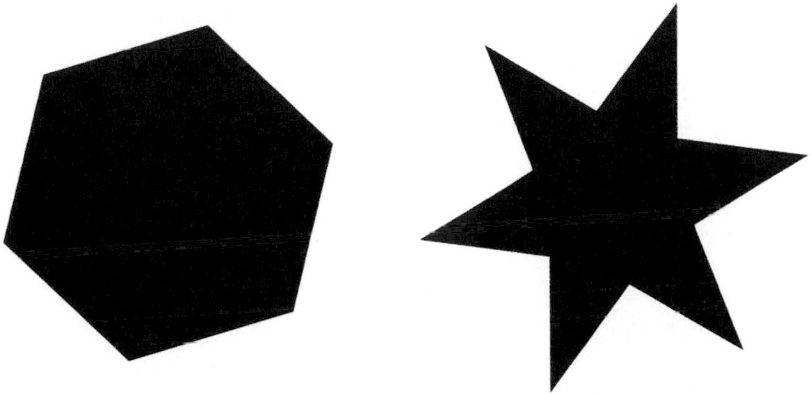

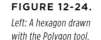

FIGURE 12-24.

Left: A hexagon drawn with the Polygon tool.

Right: Used with the same settings, the Star tool inverts the polygon's angles, so instead of a hexagon, you get a star.

Line Tool

Not surprisingly, you use this tool to draw straight lines and arrows. Specify the width of the line in pixels in the Tool Options. The Arrowhead menu lets you choose whether to have an arrowhead on the line at its beginning, end, or both. If you choose to add an arrowhead, these additional settings appear to help you control what it looks like:

- **W (Width) and L (Length).** These settings determine how wide and long the arrowhead is. The unit of measurement here is the percentage of the line's width, so if you enter a number lower than 100, the arrowhead will be narrower than the line it's attached to. You can pick values between 10 and 5,000 percent. If your length setting is too low, you'll get a shape that looks more like a T than an arrow.

- **C (Concavity).** Use this setting if you want Elements to indent the side of the arrowhead where it meets the line. This number determines the amount of curvature on the widest part of the arrowhead (see Figure 12-25). You can pick pick a number between –50 percent and +50 percent.

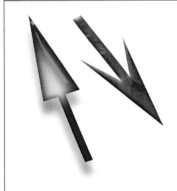

FIGURE 12-25.

Two arrows drawn with the Line tool. (Both arrows have layer styles applied to them so they don't look flat. You'll learn more about applying layer styles in the next chapter.)

Left: An arrow with no concavity.

Right: An arrow with concavity set to +50 percent.

TIP If you prefer fancier arrows, you'll find some in the Custom Shape tool's settings (see page 423).

The Shape Selection Tool

The gray arrow icon you see in the Tool Options area when you have any of the shape tools active is the Shape Selection tool. This is a special kind of Move tool that works only on shapes that haven't been simplified yet (page 422), as explained in Figure 12-26.

NOTE You can always use the Move tool, even on shapes that haven't been simplified, where you could use the Shape Selection tool instead.

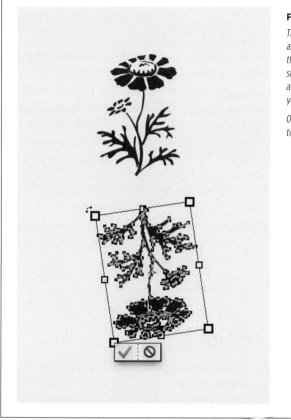

FIGURE 12-26.

The Shape Selection tool gives you the same kind of bounding box as the Move tool, and it works the same way, but only on shapes that haven't been simplified. You can also apply transformations like skewing and rotating (page 386) when the Shape Selection tool is active. (The Transform settings appear in the Tool Options area when you start rotating or pulling at the shape to change it.)

Once you simplify a shape's layer, you have to use the regular Move tool to move it around.

The Shape Selection tool is easy to use: Just activate it and then move your shape. (The shape doesn't even have to be on the active layer.) This may seem like an unnecessary tool, but it's very handy for some tasks, like making exact duplicates of shapes (simply Alt-drag/Option-drag a shape with this tool to copy it). You can also use the Shape Selection tool to combine multiple shapes into one by clicking the Tool Options area's Combine button. The Tool Options also include the same choices you have when using any of the shape tools: add, subtract, intersect, and exclude.

The Shape Selection tool works just like the Move tool: Drag a shape to move it, hold down Alt/Option while you drag to copy (instead of move) the original shape, drag the handles that appear around the shape to resize it, and so on. Unfortunately, you can't align and distribute shapes with this tool the way you can with the Move tool. So if you need to line things up, use the regular Move tool instead.

Drawing Outlines and Borders

If you've played around with the shape tools, you may have noticed that you can't draw shapes that are just outlines (that is, ones that aren't filled with color). No matter what you do, the shape is always solid. Even if you haven't ever touched a shape tool, you may be wondering how the heck to get a simple, plain-colored border around a photo.

The easiest way to create an outline is to make a selection using the Rectangular Marquee tool or another selection tool and then select Edit→Stroke (Outline) Selection. The Stroke dialog box pops up so you can enter a width for the line in pixels and choose a color. You'll also see choices for Location, which tells Elements where you want the line: around the inside edge of the selection, centered on the edge of the selection, or around the outside. (If you're bordering an entire photo, don't choose

Outside; if you do, the border won't show up because it'll be off the edge of the image.)

You can also choose a blend mode (page 409) for the outline and set its opacity. Using a mode can create a more subtle edge than a normal stroke does. The Preserve Transparency checkbox ensures that any transparent areas in the active layer *stay* transparent. When you're finished adjusting the dialog box's settings, click OK and then deselect (press Ctrl+D/⌘-D or just click someplace else in the image) to get rid of the marching ants, and you've got yourself an outlined shape.

Be sure to also check out some of the simple frame designs in the Graphics panel (page 524), which let you easily apply a border with just a few clicks.

The Cookie Cutter Tool

At first glance, you may think the Cookie Cutter is a pretty silly tool. But actually, it's so handy that you may use it all the time once you understand it. The Cookie Cutter creates the same shapes as the Custom Shape tool, but you use it to crop a photo to the shape you chose. Want a heart-shaped portrait of your sweetie? The Cookie Cutter is the tool for you. If you're a scrapbooker, just a couple of clicks can get you results that would take ages and a bunch of special scissors to create with paper.

If you're not into that sort of thing, don't go away, because hidden in the shapes library are some of the most sophisticated, artistic crop shapes around. You can use them to get the kinds of effects that people pay commercial artists big bucks to create—like abstract crops that give a jagged or worn edge to a photo (great for contemporary effects). You can also combine the result with a stroked edge, as explained in the box above, and maybe a layer style (page 461), too. Even without any additional frills, your photo's shape will be more interesting, as shown in Figure 12-27.

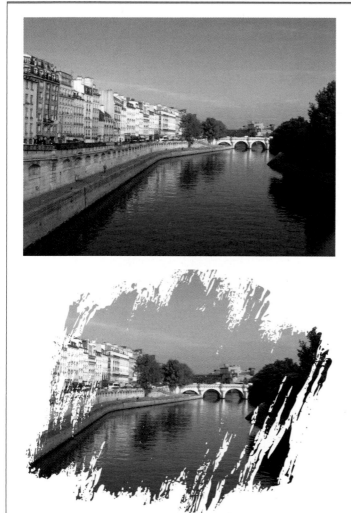

FIGURE 12-27

*A quick drag with the Cookie Cutter tool is all it took
to create the bottom graphic from the top photo.
If you want to create custom album or scrapbook
pages, you can rotate or skew the crops before you
commit them. (Page 385 explains how to rotate and
skew images.)*

TIP Elements also gives you a couple of other ways to create cutouts and fancy edge effects. In Windows, if you plan to print a cropped photo for use in a scrapbooking project, for example, check out the Picture Package feature (page 546). The frames there include some shape crops, and you can do everything right in the Organizer's Print dialog box, if those shapes work for you. (Despite the name, you can make a Picture Package with only one photo.) And the Graphics panel's Frames section (page 524) includes a bunch of crops, ranging from simple shapes like stars to elaborate edges that make a photo look like a half-completed jigsaw puzzle. And for an ultra-fancy effect, check out the Out of Bounds action in Guided Edit (page 460), which makes your subject look like it's stepping or flying out of the edges of the photo, and the Picture Stack Guided Edit, which makes a photo look like it's made from many photos piled together.

You use the Cookie Cutter just like the Custom Shape tool, but it cuts a shape from a photo, instead of drawing a shape:

1. **Activate the Cookie Cutter tool.**

   Click the Cookie Cutter in the Tools panel (it's at the bottom left of the Modify section, just below the Crop tool) or press Q.

2. **Select the shape you want your photo to be.**

   Choose a shape from the Shape Picker by clicking the black-and-white shape thumbnail displayed in the Tool Options area. You have access to all of Elements custom shapes, but pay special attention to the Crop Shapes category. Use the drop-down menu at the top of the Shape Picker to select a specific category of shapes, or choose All Elements Shapes.

3. **Adjust your Tool Options settings, if necessary.**

   You have the same shape-drawing options described earlier for the Custom Shape tool (page 423), so you can set a fixed size or constrain proportions, if you want. Click the Unconstrained button to see your choices.

   You can feather the edge of the shape, too. Just drag the Feather slider, or click the number to the right of the slider and then enter an amount (in pixels). (See page 156 for more about feathering.) Turn on the Crop checkbox to crop the edges of your photo so they're just large enough to contain the shape.

4. **Drag in your photo.**

   Elements puts a mask over the photo, and you see only the area that will still be there once you crop, surrounded by transparency.

5. **If necessary, adjust the crop.**

   You can reposition the shape mask or drag its corners to resize it. Although the cropped areas disappear, they'll reappear as you reposition the mask if you move it so that they're included again.

   Once you've created the shape, you'll see the Transform options (page 385) in the Tool Options area (which means that you can skew or distort the shape, if you want) until you *commit* the shape, as explained in the next step. You can drag the mask around to reposition it, or Shift-drag a corner to resize it without altering its proportions. It may take a little maneuvering to get exactly the parts of the photo that you want inside the shape.

6. **When you've got everything lined up just right, click the Commit button (the green checkmark) just below the image window or press Enter/Return.**

   If you don't like the results, click the Cancel button (the red circle) or press Esc instead. Once you've made your crop, you can use Ctrl+Z/⌘-Z to undo it and try something else.

TIP The Cookie Cutter replaces the areas it removes with transparency. If the transparency checkerboard makes it too hard for you to get a clear look at what you've done, temporarily create a new white or colored Fill layer beneath the cropped layer. Then simply delete the Fill layer once you're happy with your crop.

Filters, Actions, Layer Styles, and Gradients

There's a common saying among artistic types who use software in their studios: *Tools don't equal talent.* And it's true: No mere computer program is going to turn a klutz into a Klimt. But Elements has some special tools—*filters, actions,* and *layer styles*—that can sure help you fool a lot of people. It's amazing what a difference these features can make in the appearance of an image with only a couple of clicks.

Filters are a jaw-droppingly easy way to change how photos look. You can use certain filters for enhancing and correcting images, but Elements also gives you a bunch of other filters that are great for unleashing all your artistic impulses, as shown in Figure 13-1. (You can find the original photos—*rooftops.jpg* and *bauhinia.jpg*—on this book's Missing CD page at *www.missingmanuals.com/cds* if you want to play around with them yourself.)

Most filters have settings you can adjust to control how they change your photo. Elements comes with more than 100 different filters, so there isn't room in this chapter to cover each filter individually, but you'll learn the basics of applying filters and get in-depth coverage of some of the ones you're most likely to use. And Elements 11 includes a couple of great new filters that make it easy to make photos look like hand-drawn illustrations.

Actions, on the other hand, are like little macros or scripts designed to make elaborate changes to your image, such as creating a three-dimensional frame around it or making it look like a pencil sketch or an oil pastel. One of the best new features in Elements 11 is the Actions panel, which makes it easy to add and use actions. (You can also find a few actions in the Effects panel. They're also easy to apply—you just double-click a button—but you can't tweak their settings as easily as you can with filters, since effects are programmed to make specific changes.)

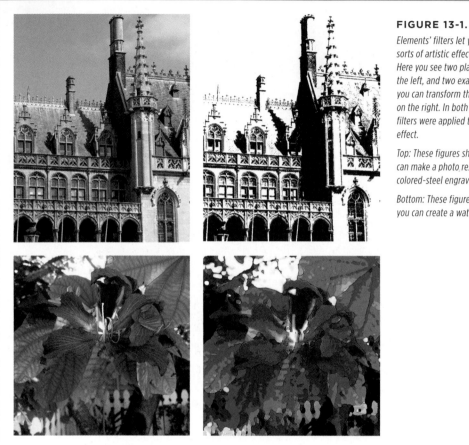

FIGURE 13-1.

Elements' filters let you add all sorts of artistic effects to photos. Here you see two plain photos on the left, and two examples of how you can transform them with filters on the right. In both cases, several filters were applied to build up the effect.

Top: These figures show how you can make a photo resemble a colored-steel engraving.

Bottom: These figures show how you can create a watercolor look.

NOTE Full-featured Photoshop lets you record and save your own actions and install actions created by others. You can use certain Photoshop actions in Elements, but you can't *create* actions in Elements.

Elements also gives you some spiffy new special effects in Guided Edit. If you've been using Elements for a while, you may think Guided Edit is just for beginners, but now there's plenty there even if you're an old pro. You can use it to create elaborate effects like the popular high-key and low-key looks for portraits, make an image look like it's made from a pile of separate photos, make a photo of a full-sized object or landscape look like a photo of a miniature version, or make a pop-art image à la Warhol. Page 458 has the lowdown.

Layer styles change the appearance of only one layer of an image (see Chapter 6 for more about layers). They're great for creating impressive-looking text, but you also can apply them to objects and shapes. Most layer styles include settings you can easily modify.

If you want to get really creative, you can combine filters, actions, and layer styles on the same image. You may end up spending hours trying different groupings, because it's addicting to watch the often unpredictable results you get when mixing them up.

The last section of this chapter focuses on *gradients*. A gradient is a rainbow-like range of color that you can use to color in an object or background. You can also use gradients and *gradient maps*—gradients that are distributed according to the brightness values in your photo—for precise retouching.

■ Using Filters

Filters let you change the look of photos in complex ways, but applying them is as easy as double-clicking. Elements gives you a ton of filters, grouped into categories to help you choose one that does what you want. This section offers a quick tour through the categories and some info about using a few of the most popular filters, like Noise and Blur.

To make it easy to work with filters, Elements lets you apply them from two different places: the Filter menu and the Effects panel. (The menu is the only place where you can see *every* filter; some filters, like the Adjustment filters, don't appear in the panel.) Elements also includes the Filter Gallery, a great feature that helps you get an idea of how your photo will look when you apply the artistic filters. Keep reading to learn about all three methods.

Applying Filters

In the Filter menu, you choose a filter from the list by category and then by name. In the Effects panel, thumbnail images give you a preview of what the filters do by showing how they affect a picture of a tree.

The cool thing about the Filter Gallery is that it shows you a preview of what a filter looks like when applied to *your* image. Some filters automatically open the Filter Gallery when you choose them from the Filter menu or Effects panel, though you can also call up the Gallery without first choosing a filter by going to Filter→Filter Gallery. You can't apply every filter from the Gallery, however—only some of the ones with adjustable settings.

> **TIP** You can easily apply the same filter repeatedly: Press Ctrl+F (⌘-F) and Elements applies the last filter you used, with whatever settings you last used. The top item in the Filter menu also lists the name of this filter (selecting it has the same effect as the keyboard shortcut: Elements applies that filter with the same settings you last used).

The filters do the same thing no matter which way you choose them. The next few sections explain your options in more detail.

THE FILTER MENU

The Filter menu groups your filters into 12 categories (Correct Camera Distortion [page 379] is all by itself at the top of the list, not in a category). There's a divider below the bottom category (Other). When you first install Elements, the Digimarc filter is the only filter below this line, but other filters you download or purchase will appear here, too.

When you choose a filter from this menu, one of three things happens:

- **Elements applies the filter.** This happens if the filter's name doesn't have an ellipsis (...) after it. Just look at the result in your photo, and if you don't like its effect, press Ctrl+Z/⌘-Z to undo it. If you do like it, you're done.

- **Elements opens a dialog box.** Filters that have adjustable settings have an ellipsis (...) after their names in the Filter menu. These filters (mostly corrective ones like Dust & Scratches) open a dialog box where you can tweak their settings. Adjust the settings while watching the small preview in the dialog box, and then click OK.

- **Elements opens the Filter Gallery.** Some of the more artistic, adjustable filters call up the Filter Gallery so you can see a large preview of what you're doing and rearrange the order of multiple filters before applying them. Page 437 explains how to use the Gallery.

Regardless of how you apply a filter, if you're not happy with its effect, you can undo it by pressing Ctrl+Z/⌘-Z. If you like it, just save your image.

> **TIP** Since you can't undo filters after you've closed your image, many people apply them to duplicate layers. Press Ctrl+J/⌘-J to create a duplicate layer.

EFFECTS PANEL

If you're more comfortable with visual clues when choosing a filter, you can find most filters in the Effects panel (Figure 13-2), which is, logically enough, also where you apply effects (page 456).

To call up the Effects panel, go to Window→Effects or click the Effects button at the bottom of your screen, and then click the Filters tab To find a filter, select a category from the panel's drop-down menu or choose Show All. The categories are the same as the ones in the Filter menu, except that Adjustments is available only through the Filter menu, and Sharpen appears in the panel but *not* the Filter menu. To apply a filter from the panel, double-click its thumbnail or drag the thumbnail onto your image.

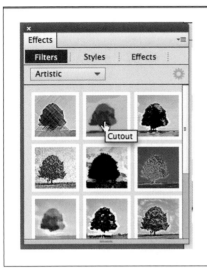

FIGURE 13-2.

The Effects panel shows you what the filters looks like when applied to the same picture of a tree. Click the panel's Filters tab, and then, from the drop-down menu (the one that says "Artistic" here), choose a category. Put your cursor over a filter's thumbnail (without clicking) to see a tooltip with the filter's name. If you know what you want a filter to do but don't know what it's called, scrolling through these thumbnail images can help you find the one you want. To apply a filter from this panel, double-click the appropriate thumbnail or drag the filter's thumbnail from the panel onto your image.

One drawback to applying filters from this panel is that you don't get a chance to adjust their settings. If the filter is one that has a dialog box or settings in the Filter Gallery, you don't see those here—Elements just applies the filter to your photo using the filter's current settings.

TIP If you prefer using the Effects panel but you also want to see the Filter Gallery, click the four-lined square on the panel's upper-right corner (or above it, if the panel is docked in the Panel Bin) and choose Automatically Show Filter Gallery.

■ THE FILTER GALLERY

The Filter Gallery (Filter→Filter Gallery), shown in Figure 13-3, is a popular feature. It gives you a large preview window, a look at sailboat thumbnails so you can tell what each filter does, and (most importantly) it lets you apply filters like layers: You can stack them up and change the order in which Elements applies them to the image. Changing the order can make a big impact on how filters affect images. For example, you get very different results if you apply Ink Outlines *after* the Sprayed Strokes filter rather than the other way around. The Gallery makes it easy to play around and see which order gives you the look you want. The layer-like behavior of the filters in the Gallery is only for previewing, though—you don't end up with any new layers after you apply the filter(s).

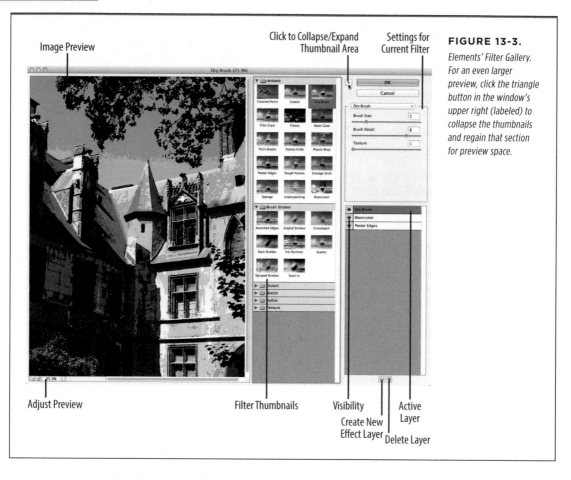

Image Preview

Click to Collapse/Expand
Thumbnail Area

Settings for
Current Filter

FIGURE 13-3.

*Elements' Filter Gallery.
For an even larger
preview, click the triangle
button in the window's
upper right (labeled) to
collapse the thumbnails
and regain that section
for preview space.*

Adjust Preview

Filter Thumbnails

Visibility

Active
Layer

Create New
Effect Layer

Delete Layer

The Gallery is more for artistic filters than for corrective ones. You can't apply the Adjustment or Noise filters from here, for instance. All the Gallery filters are in the artistic, brushstroke, distort, sketch, stylize, and texture categories. (The next section includes an overview of all the filter categories.)

TIP The Gallery usually opens full screen the first time you use it. If you want to shrink it down, drag its lower-right corner to resize the window.

The Filter Gallery window is divided into three panes. On the left is a preview of what your image will look like when you apply the filter(s). The center pane holds thumbnails of the different filters, and the right side contains the settings for the current filter. Your *filter layers* are at the bottom of the settings pane, where you can see what filters you've applied, add or subtract filters, and change their order.

> **NOTE** As noted above, you don't create any new, permanent layers when you use the Filter Gallery. Filter layers work something like regular layers (see Chapter 6), but they're just what you might call "working layers": They're only to help you figure out which order to apply filters in; they don't actually become new layers in your image. In other words, you have separate filter layers only until you click OK in the Filter Gallery; then all your chosen filters get applied to the image in the order you specified. You can't apply the filters, close your photo, come back later, and still see the filters as individual, changeable layers. And most important, the filters become part of the layer to which you apply them.
>
> Also, if you've used a recent version of the full-featured Photoshop, be aware that Elements doesn't create editable smart filters the way Photoshop does—it handles filters the way earlier versions of Photoshop (CS2 and below) did. Keep this in mind if you're trying to do something based on instructions written for Photoshop (directions you've found online, say).

In addition to letting you adjust the settings for a given filter, the Filter Gallery lets you perform a few other tricks:

- **Adjust your view of the image.** In the Gallery's lower-left corner, click the percentage or the up/down triangles (you see only one triangle in Windows) next to it to bring up a list of preset views to choose from. You can also click the + and – buttons to zoom in or out. Easier still, use Ctrl+=/⌘-= and Ctrl+minus/⌘-minus shortcuts to zoom in and out, respectively.

- **Choose a new filter.** Click a filter's thumbnail once, and Elements displays the settings for that filter and updates the image preview—usually. (See the box on page 443 for details.)

- **Add a new filter layer.** Each time you click the New Filter Layer icon (see Figure 13-4), Elements adds another filter layer.

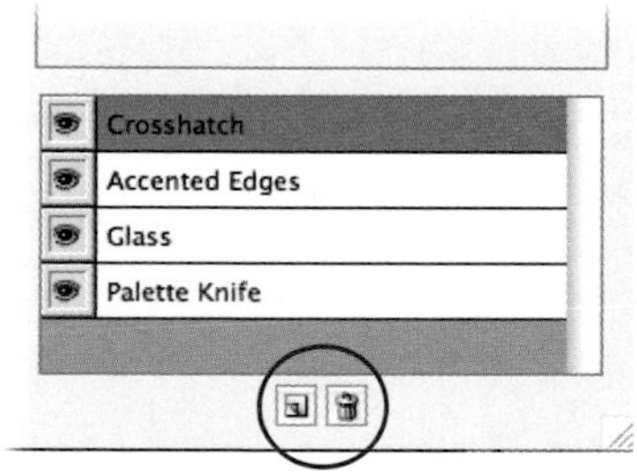

FIGURE 13-4

If you've used layers before (see Chapter 6), these circled icons should look familiar. In the Filter Gallery, the one on the left adds a new filter *layer to your image instead of a regular layer. Click the trash-can icon to delete a filter layer.*

The eye icons next to each filter layer turn visibility on and off just as they do in the Layers panel. Remember, filter layers don't show up as real layers in the Layers panel—only in the Filter Gallery.

- **Change the position of filter layers.** Drag them up and down in the stack to change the order in which Elements will apply them to your image.

- **Hide filter layers**. Click the eye icon next to a filter layer in the filter-layer panel to turn off its visibility, as in the regular Layers panel.

- **Delete filter layers.** Select any filter layer by clicking it, and then click the trash-can icon to delete it.

- **Change a filter layer's content.** You can change what kind of filter is in a particular layer. For instance, if you applied several filters and wish you could change the Smudge Stick filter to the Glass filter, you don't have to delete the Smudge Stick layer; just select it and then click the Glass filter's thumbnail in the middle pane to change that layer's contents.

Filter Categories

Elements divides filters into categories to help you track down the one you want. Some categories, like Distort, contain filters that vary hugely in what they do to photos. Other categories, like Brush Strokes, contain filters that are obviously related to one another. Here's a breakdown of the categories:

- **Correct Camera Distortion.** This isn't actually a category, but rather a single filter that lets you correct perspective distortion (think tall buildings) as well as vignetting (shadows) caused by your camera's lens. It's explained in detail on page 379.

- **Adjustments.** These filters apply photographic, stylistic, and artistic changes to photos. Most of them are explained on page 340; the Photo Filters are covered on page 294.

- **Artistic.** This huge group of filters can do everything from giving a photo a cut-from-paper look (Cutout) to making it resemble a quick sketch (Rough Pastels). You generally get the best results with these filters by using several of them or applying the same one several times.

- **Blur.** These filters let you soften focus and add artistic effects. They're explained on page 446.

- **Brush Strokes.** The filters in this category apply brushstroke effects and create a hand-painted look.

- **Distort.** These filters warp images in a variety of ways. The Liquify filter is the most powerful; page 492 explains how to use it.

- **Noise.** Use these filters to add or remove grain. They're explained on page 443.

- **Pixelate.** These filters break up an image in different ways, making it show the dot pattern of a magazine or newspaper's printed image (Halftone), or the fragmented look you see on television when a show conceals someone's identity (Mosaic).

NOTE The Color Halftone filter makes images look like they're made of many dots of color, like a magazine photo or other printed illustration, or comic-style pop art. But it's not the same as true halftone screening, which Elements can't do. So if the print shop you're working with needs a halftone, you need to either use the full-featured Photoshop or ask the printer to create the halftone for you.

- **Render.** This group includes a diverse bunch of filters that let you do things like create a lens flare effect and make an image look like fibers or clouds. The Lighting Effects filter, a powerful but confusing filter that's like a whole program in itself, helps you change the way lighting appears in your image. For a full rundown on what this filter does and how to use it, check out this book's Missing CD page at *www.missingmanuals.com.cds*.

- **Sharpen.** This category, which contains only the Unsharp Mask filter (page 254), appears in the Effects panel but not the Filter menu. (The sharpening commands are in the Enhance menu instead.)

- **Sketch.** These filters can make a photo look like it was drawn with charcoal, chalk, crayon, or some other material, or like it was embossed in wet plaster, photocopied, or created with a rubber stamp.

TIP Elements 11 brings two wonderful new Sketch filters for making photos look like illustrations: Comic and Graphic Novel. You can create some really interesting graphics by using these filters on a duplicate layer and then playing around with the blend mode, as shown in Figure 13-5. These filters aren't included in the Filter Gallery, just the Filters menu, and they're very processor-intensive. Even a new computer with plenty of RAM and a fast processor may take quite a while with these, but the end result is worth it.

- **Stylize.** These filters create special effects by increasing the contrast in a photo and displacing pixels. They can make a photo look radioactive, like the objects in it are moving quickly, or reduce it to outlines.

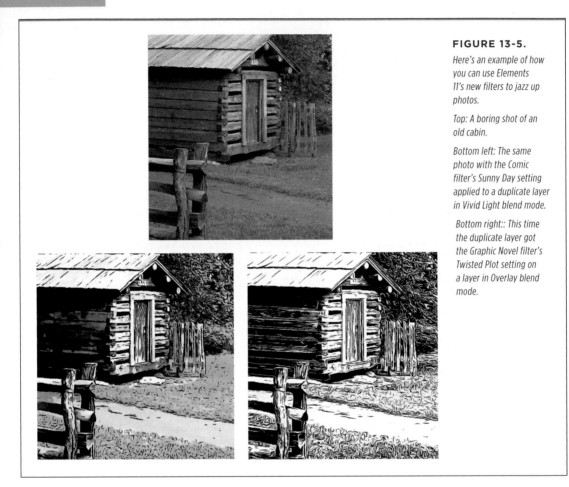

FIGURE 13-5.

Here's an example of how you can use Elements 11's new filters to jazz up photos.

Top: A boring shot of an old cabin.

Bottom left: The same photo with the Comic filter's Sunny Day setting applied to a duplicate layer in Vivid Light blend mode.

Bottom right:: This time the duplicate layer got the Graphic Novel filter's Twisted Plot setting on a layer in Overlay blend mode.

- **Texture.** These filters change the surface of a photo to look like it was made from another material. Use them to create a cracked finish, a stained-glass look, or a mosaic effect.

- **Other.** This is a group of technical, customizable filters. The High Pass filter is explained on page 259. You can use Offset to shift an image or a layer a bit, or to position tiled image layers.

- **Digimarc.** Digimarc is a company that lets subscribers enter their contact info into a database so that anyone who gets one of their photos can find out who holds the copyright. You can use this filter to check for Digimarc watermarks in photos.

You can find a number of filter plug-ins online, ranging from free to very expensive; page 598 suggests some places to start looking. When you install new filters, they appear at the bottom of the Filter menu.

> **NOTE** Filters are platform specific, which means you can't use plug-ins written for the Windows version of Elements if you're on a Mac and vice versa. And for Elements 11, Mac plug-ins have to be written specifically for *Intel* Macs; plug-ins written for older PowerPC Macs won't work (see page 38).

UNDER THE HOOD

Filter Performance Hints

If Elements could speak and you asked it about filters and effects, it would say, "Easy for *you*." Although you don't have to do much to apply them, the program has a huge amount of work to do. Elements is pretty fast, but if your computer is slow or memory-challenged, it can take a long time to apply filters or to update the preview.

You can speed things up by applying filters to a selection for previewing. (Filters that have their own dialog boxes—as opposed to the Filter Gallery—display a flashing line under the size percentage [below the preview area] to show their progress.) Here are a few other filter-related tips worth remembering:

- Filters don't do anything if they don't have pixels to work on, so be sure you're targeting a layer with something in it, not an Adjustment layer.

- If you apply a filter to a selection, you'll usually want to feather (page 156) or refine (page 145) the filtered edges to help them blend into the rest of the image.

- Option-click the Cancel button in the Filter Gallery or in any filter dialog box to turn it into a Reset button. Clicking Cancel closes the window, while Reset lets you start over without having to call up the filter again.

- If filters are grayed out in the Filter menu, check to be sure you're not in 16-bit mode (page 282) or in grayscale, bitmapped, or index color mode (all explained on page 42).

Practical Uses for Filters

Filters aren't only for creating fancy artistic effects. They're also great for fixing common problems in your images. This section covers how to use some of Elements' most popular and useful filters to correct photos and create a few special effects. For instance, you'll learn how to modify graininess to create an aged effect or to smooth out a repair job. And you'll find out how to blur photos to create a soft-focus effect or make objects look like they're moving.

■ REMOVING NOISE: GETTING RID OF GRAININESS

Noise, undesired graininess in an image, is a big problem with many digital cameras, especially ones that have small sensors and high megapixel counts, like most recent point-and-shoot models. It's rare to find a fixed-lens camera with more than 5 megapixels that doesn't have some trouble with noise, especially in underexposed areas.

If you shoot using the Raw format, you can correct a fair amount of noise right in the Raw Converter (page 264). But the Converter may give unpredictable results if you use it on JPEGs. And even Raw files may need further noise reduction once you've edited them after converting them.

Elements' Reduce Noise filter is (not surprisingly) designed to help get rid of noise. To run this filter, go to Filter→Noise→Reduce Noise. You get a dialog box with a preview area on the left and settings on the right. To apply the filter, first use the controls below the preview to set the zoom level to 100 percent or higher. (You need to see the individual pixels in the photo so you can tell how the filter is changing them as you tweak the settings.) Then adjust the filter's three sliders:

- **Strength.** This controls the overall impact of the filter, which reduces the same kind of noise as the Luminance Smoothing setting in the Raw Converter (page 281). The higher this setting, the greater the risk of softening your photo.

- **Preserve Details.** Using noise reduction can soften a photo and make it look blurry. This setting tells Elements how much care to take to preserve details.

- **Reduce Color Noise.** This control adjusts uneven color distribution in the image. You can set the slider pretty high without harming the photo.

The Remove JPEG Artifact checkbox tells Elements to minimize *JPEG artifacts*—the uneven areas of color caused by JPEG compression (see page 70). A mottled pattern in what should be a clear blue sky is a classic example of JPEG artifacting. Turn on this checkbox to help smooth things out.

For each setting, move the slider right if you want it to have more of an impact or left if you want less. Watch the effect in the preview area to see the changes. (You may notice a little lag time before the preview updates.) When you like what you see, click OK to apply the filter.

The Reduce Noise filter does an OK job on areas with a small amount of noise, like the sky in many JPEG photos, but it's not one of Elements' best tools. If your camera has major noise problems, you may need special noise-reduction software to tackle it. Some of the most popular programs are Noise Ninja (*www.picturecode.com*), Neat Image (*www.neatimage.com*), Topaz (*www.topazlabs.com*), and Noiseware (*www.imagenomic.com*), which all have demo versions you can download to try them out. If you do a Google search for "noise reduction software," you'll get a variety of other options as well, including several free programs.

■ ADDING NOISE: SMOOTHING OUT REPAIR JOBS

Elements also gives you a filter for *creating* noise. Why do that when most of the time you try to get rid of noise? One reason is when you're trying to age a photo: To make it look like it came from an old newspaper, for instance, you'd add some noise.

Another common use for noise is to help make repaired spots blend in with the rest of an image. If you've altered part of a photo in Elements, especially by painting on it, odds are good that the repaired area looks perfectly smooth. That's great if the rest of the photo is noise free, but if the photo is a little grainy, that smooth patch will stand out like a sore thumb. Adding a bit of noise makes it blend in better, as shown in Figure 13-6. Also, if you see color banding when you print, adding a little noise to the photo may help fix that.

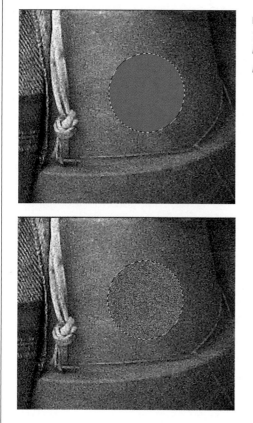

FIGURE 13-6.

Top: If you use the Average Blur filter in a repair on this noisy photo, the blended area stands out, making the repair obvious.

Bottom: Introducing some noise makes the change much less noticeable.

To add noise to a photo, start by selecting the area you want to make noisier. (Using a duplicate layer [Ctrl+J/⌘-J] for the noise is a good idea, since you can always undo changes if they're on their own layer.) Then, here's what you do:

1. **Call up the Add Noise filter.**

   Go to Filter→Noise→Add Noise to bring up the filter's dialog box.

2. **Adjust the filter's settings.**

   The settings are explained in the following list. Use the dialog box's preview area to check how the changes are affecting your photo.

3. **When you're satisfied, click OK.**

The Add Noise dialog box has three settings:

- **Amount**. This controls how heavy the noise will be. Drag the slider right for more noise or left for less. You can also type in a number; a higher percentage means more noise.

- **Distribution**. These buttons control how Elements distributes the noise in the image. Uniform is just what it says—the same all over. Gaussian produces a more speckled effect. (If you're adding noise to duplicate existing noise in a grainy photo, you probably want Gaussian distribution.) For an old-newspaper-photo look, try Uniform.

- **Monochromatic**. This setting limits you to grayscale noise. Take a look at the bottom-left image in Figure 13-7, and notice how many more colors you can see in the noise, compared with the solid green of the original. The bottom-left acorn's noise was applied with the Monochromatic setting turned off.

Noise can also help when you want to apply special effects to blocks of solid color, as shown in Figure 13-7, bottom right. If you try to apply the Angled Strokes filter to a solid color, you don't see the strokes. Adding noise first gives the filter something to work on. To make an abstract background for a project, you can create a blank file, add noise, and then run various filters on it.

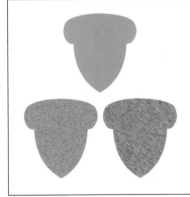

FIGURE 13-7.

Filters can really spruce up solid objects.

Top: Here's an unfiltered, solid green acorn drawn with the Custom Shape tool (page 423).

Bottom left: The same acorn after adding some uniform noise.

Bottom right: With the Monochromatic checkbox turned off, Elements mixes random colors into the noise. (Adding the Angled Strokes filter gave the acorn a lot more texture. If you don't add noise before applying this filter to a solid color, then nothing happens when you apply it.)

■ **GAUSSIAN BLUR: DRAWING ATTENTION TO AN OBJECT**

Probably the most frequently used of the Blur filters, Gaussian Blur (Filter→ Blur→Gaussian Blur) lets you control how much an image is, blurred. Besides using it on large areas, like the background in Figure 13-8, bottom, you can apply this filter at a very low setting to soften lines—useful when you're going for a sketched effect. To try out the different blurs, download *yellowbeak.jpg* from this book's Missing CD page at *www.missingmanuals.com/cds*.

When using the Gaussian Blur, you have to set the *radius,* which controls how much the filter blurs things; a higher radius produces more blurring. Use the filter's preview window to see what you're doing.

Gaussian blur is the classic way to isolate a subject from its background, but Elements 11 gives you an even better way to artistically blur a background, the new Lens Blur filter, described next.

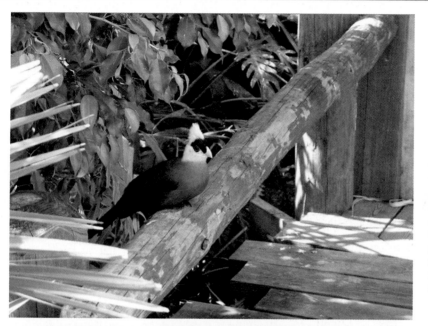

FIGURE 13-8.

Top: This little guy felt hidden enough to let the camera get pretty close, and he was almost right: It's hard to focus on him with all the stuff in the background. Blurring the background will center the focus on the bird rather than the distracting details.

Bottom: Applying the Gaussian Blur filter to the background makes the bird the clear focal point. To do this, select the bird, and then choose Select→Inverse before applying the blur.

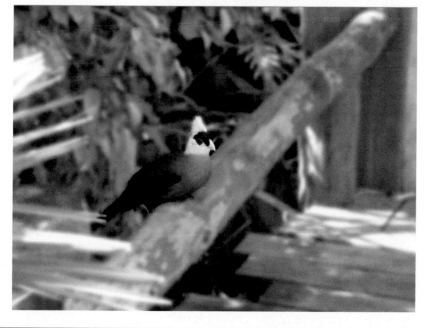

■ LENS BLUR: CREATING DEPTH OF FIELD

If you have a point-and-shoot camera, you know how hard it is to get your subject sharp and the background artistically blurred the way you can with larger DSLR (digital single-lens reflex) cameras. To create that effect after the fact, you could use a Gaussian blur as explained in the previous section, but the Gaussian Blur filter applies the exact same blur over the whole area you apply it to. If you look at a photo taken with a DSLR and a good lens, you'll notice that the amount of blurring (called the *bokeh* by those in the know) varies a bit. For example, the far distance is completely blurred, while you may still be able to distinguish objects immediately in front of and behind the focus area.

Full Photoshop has had a special filter, the Lens Blur filter, that helps to simulate a real bokeh a little better than a simple Gaussian Blur can, and now it's available in Elements, too. Using the Lens Blur filter is tricky, but with a little fiddling you can often get results that are closer to what you could do in a DSLR camera than you can get with a Gaussian Blur. In order to get the best results, though, you need to be comfortable with layer masking (page 202) and gradients (page 465). If you're just starting out with Elements, try the Depth Of Field effect in Guided Edit→Photo Effects; it's not in the same class as this filter, but the Lens Blur isn't for the faint of heart.

If you just go straight to the Lens Blur filter without doing anything to prepare your image for it, Elements blurs your entire image, so first you need to figure out the area you want to keep in focus. (If your goal is to create a soft-focus effect, then use a tiny amount of Lens Blur on the whole photo.) The very simplest way is to select what you want to keep in focus, go to Select→Inverse to select everything *but* that area, and then apply the Lens Blur filter. But if you do that, you'll just have a uniform blur all over, without the graduated effect you'd get in a fancy camera. To achieve that effect, here's what you need to do:

1. **Duplicate the layer you want to apply the blur to.**

   Go to Layer→Duplicate or press Ctrl+J/⌘-J.

2. **On the new layer, select the area you want to keep in focus, and then delete it.**

   Use any selection tool(s) of your choice, and then press Backspace/Delete to remove the selected area. By doing this, the original, sharp version of your subject will show through the blurred layer in the final image.

   At this point, you could go straight to the Lens Blur window (step 5), but if you want a really polished effect, you've still got a little more work to do.

3. **Create a layer mask for the new layer.**

   Make sure the new layer is active, and then click the Add Layer Mask icon in the Layers panel (the circle within a square).

4. **Fill the mask with a gradient.**

   Check to be sure the layer mask is active by clicking its icon in the Layers panel, and then press G to activate the Gradient tool (page 466) and choose a black-and-white gradient. Next, drag in the image so that the area you want in focus is in the black part of the gradient. (If you mess up, as long as the area you want is in a completely white area, you may be able to fix it with the Invert button as explained in the list of settings below.) You can turn off Background layer to see if you've got the right area masked out. Once you've got the gradient set up to your liking, disable the layer mask by right-clicking/Control-clicking its thumbnail in the Layers panel and choosing Disable Layer Mask. Then click the left thumbnail for the layer you applied the mask to (the duplicate layer you created in step 1) to make sure it's active.

5. **Call up the Lens Blur filter's window.**

   Go to Filter→Blur→Lens Blur. Your image opens all blurry despite your masking, but you'll fix that shortly.

6. **Adjust the filter's settings.**

   There are a lot of them, and they're explained after this list. For now, the most important one is the Source setting in the window's Depth Map section. Use the drop-down menu to choose Layer Mask, and your subject is back in focus. Now you can adjust the other settings.

7. **When you're happy with what you see, click OK.**

   You can turn the Background layer back on now, if you like, especially if you want to lower the opacity of the blur layer to reduce the effect. Figure 13-9 gives you a sense of what this filter can do.

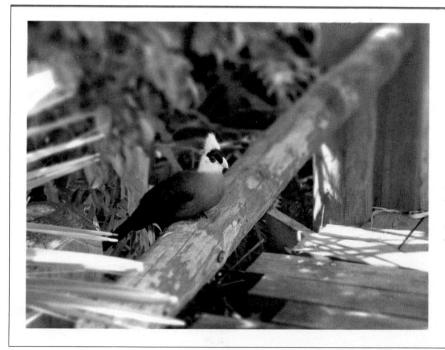

FIGURE 13-9.

Here's the bird from Figure 13-8 with the Lens Blur filter applied instead of a Gaussian Blur. In this instance, a radial blur was applied to help blur out the foreground as well as the background area. You can see that it would be a good idea to go back and edit the layer mask so that more of the deck would be affected by the blur, but this gives you a rough idea of how it works.

This filter's many settings can be a bit intimidating, but you really don't need to understand what many of their names mean. Just move the sliders till you like what you see. Here's what each section of the Lens Blur window does:

- **Preview.** Use the checkbox to toggle the preview off and on for a better look at how you're changing the photo. This filter uses plenty of processing power, so normally you'll want to leave the radio buttons set to Faster while you're working, and then switch to More Accurate for a last check when you think you're done moving the window's sliders.

- **Depth Map.** This is where you tell Elements what to use as the source point for the blur. You can choose None (everything's blurred), Transparency, or Layer Mask. The Blur Focal Distance slider is probably the most important slider in this window, because it tells the filter where to center the in-focus part of the photo. Remember, your layer mask is in shades of black and white. You can use the Blur Focal Distance slider to tell Elements which part of the masked area should be in focus. Black is 0 and white is 255, so if you chose 100, you'd be selecting an area covered by the medium-gray part of the mask. It's often easier just to click in the preview area to tell Elements where you want the most focused part to be; the focus shifts to the spot you click. The Invert checkbox swaps the effect, so what was in focus becomes blurred, and what was blurred becomes focused.

- **Iris.** This section may seem a bit confusing at first if you've never paid much attention to how a camera's lens operates. And really, the most important setting here is the Radius slider, which sets the maximum amount of blur in the image. So unless you know what you're doing, just focus on the Radius slider and just ignore Blade Curvature and Rotation (leave them at their original settings).

  But if you're interested, here's what they do: Think of a camera lens as working something like your eye. The iris area of your eye controls the size and (in some animals) the shape of the pupil. In the same way, the aperture of your camera is controlled by a mechanism also called an iris (*iris diaphragm*, actually). The overlapping blades that open and close so that light can reach the camera's sensor may be in many different patterns. This setting gives you some choice in just what kind of iris you want Elements to simulate. The Shape menu lets you choose what shape the iris should be. The Radius slider sets the maximum amount of blur in the image, Blade Curvature determines how round the iris is, and Rotation is how much the iris is rotated, since an iris is rarely a perfect circle, because of the blade configuration. Think of the iris in a cat's eye in bright light where the pupil is more like a slit than a circle—Rotation would tell Elements how much to rotate that from the perpendicular.

- **Specular Highlights.** These settings sound awfully complicated, but they're actually pretty simple. If you look at photos with a good bokeh, there tends to be a certain amount of light bloom—a kind of overbrightness in the very bright highlights. (If you look back at Figure 13-9, you can see examples on the deck and a couple of the leaves.) To mimic that, use the Brightness slider to determine how bright your out-of-focus highlights are, and the Threshold slider to determine how bright pixels must be in order for them to be affected by the Brightness slider.

- **Noise.** The Lens Blur filter creates a perfectly smooth effect where it applies. In order to make the blurred area match the rest of your image, you'll probably want to add a little bit of noise back in to make the filtered area blend in better. The controls in this section are the same as those for the Add Noise filter you read about on page 444.

While it's possible to get a nice blur with this filter, it's still not going to make a shot from your cellphone fool people into thinking you were using a DSLR with a top-quality lens. So don't feel bad if you decide you prefer the simplicity of using the Gaussian Blur filter after all.

> **NOTE** In addition to all the blurs discussed here, Elements gives you two other ways to blur photos, both found in Guided Edit→Photo Effects. One is the Orton Effect, named after the photographer who popularized this otherworldly, dreamy effect; if you've looked at any wedding photos recently, you'll recognize it. The other is the Tilt-Shift effect, which uses blurs to make your photos of full-sized objects look like pictures of miniatures instead.

■ RADIAL BLUR: PRODUCING A SENSE OF MOTION

As you can see in Figure 13-10, the Radial Blur filter creates a sense of motion. It has two styles: Zoom, which is designed to create the effect of a camera zooming in, and Spin, which produces a circular effect around a center point you designate.

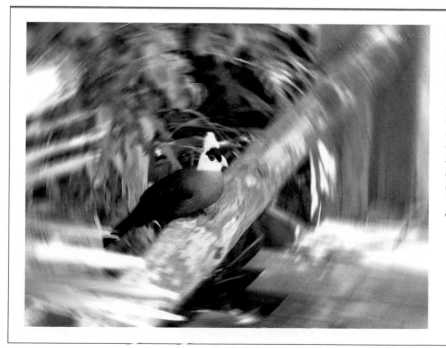

FIGURE 13-10.

A Radial Blur applied in Spin mode. As you can see, this filter can produce an almost vertiginous sense of motion. If you don't want to give people motion sickness, go easy on the Amount setting. A setting of 5 was used here, but unless you're looking for a psychedelic '60s effect, 1 or 2 is usually plenty.

The Radial Blur dialog box looks complicated, but it's really not. (Call it up by going to Filter→Blur→Radial Blur.) Unfortunately, Elements doesn't give you a preview with this filter, because applying it requires so much processing power. But the dialog box gives you a choice between Draft, Good, and Best quality. You can use Draft for a quick look at roughly what you'll get. Then undo it and choose Good for the final version. (Good and Best aren't very different except on large images, so don't feel you have to choose Best for the final version. However, with an up-to-date computer, you probably don't need to bother with Draft because your machine can whip up a final version a lot faster than computers could when this filter was first created.)

After choosing your blur method (Zoom or Spin), adjust the Amount slider, which controls how intense the blur will be. Next, click in the Blur Center box to tell Elements where you want the blur centered, as shown in Figure 13-11. Click OK when you're finished.

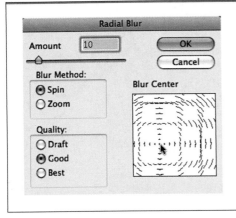

FIGURE 13-11.

The Blur Center box lets you pick a center point for the Radial Blur filter's effect. Drag the ripple drawing inside the box in any direction; here, the center point was moved just to the left and down from its original position in the center of the box.

■ COLOR CORRECTING WITH THE AVERAGE BLUR FILTER

If you've already given the Average Blur filter a whirl, you may be wondering what on earth Adobe was thinking when it created it. If you use it on a whole photo, the image disappears under a monochromatic soup, something like what you'd get by pureeing all the colors in the photo together.

Oddly enough, this effect makes this filter a great tool for getting rid of color casts (page 244). You can use the Average Blur filter to create a sort of custom Photo Filter (page 294) toned specially for the image you use it on. The secret is using blend modes (page 190). Here's how:

1. **Open a image and make a duplicate layer.**

   Press Ctrl+J/⌘-J or go to Layer→Duplicate Layer.

2. **Apply the Average Blur filter.**

   Make sure the duplicate layer is the active layer (click it in the Layers panel if it isn't), and then go to Filter→Blur→Average. Your photo disappears under a layer of (probably) unpleasing solid color, but you'll fix that in the next step.

3. **Change the blur layer's blend mode.**

   Set the unlabeled drop-down menu at the top of the Layers panel to Color. Already things are starting to look better.

4. **Invert the blur layer.**

   Press Ctrl+I/⌘-I to invert the layer's colors.

5. **Reduce the blur layer's opacity and do any other necessary tweaking.**

   Lower the Layers panel's Opacity setting to 50 percent or so. By now, the color should look right—no more color cast. Tweak if necessary, and then save your work.

> **TIP** You may want to add a Hue/Saturation layer if you find that, no matter how you adjust the blur layer's Opacity setting, the photo still looks a little flat.

The Average Blur filter is a particularly good way to color-correct underwater photos, where it's hard to get a realistic white balance using your camera's built-in settings.

■ IMPROVING SKIN TEXTURE WITH THE SURFACE BLUR FILTER

The Surface Blur filter is yet another way to blur images. At this point you may be thinking that you already have enough ways to eliminate details in your photos, but Surface Blur is actually really handy, especially on pictures of people. This filter is smart enough to avoid blurring details and areas of high contrast, which makes it great for fixing skin. If you want to eliminate pores, for instance, or reduce the visibility of freckles, this is your tool. And it's simple to use, too:

1. **Open an image and make a duplicate layer.**

   Press Ctrl+J/⌘-J or go to Layer→Duplicate Layer.

> **TIP** For best results, start by selecting the area you want to blur (see Chapter 5 for help with selections). Then make your duplicate layer from the selection so you can keep the details in the areas you *aren't* trying to fix. For example, select only the skin of your subject's face, leaving out the mouth and eyes so they won't be affected by the blur. Or, better yet, adjust the whole duplicate layer and then use a layer mask (page 202) to mask out the areas where you want to keep the details, or just erase those areas.

2. **Apply the Surface Blur filter.**

   Make sure your duplicate layer is the active layer (click it in the Layers panel if it isn't), and then go to Filter→Blur→Surface Blur. If necessary, move the dialog box out of the way so you can watch what you're doing in the main image window and in the dialog box's preview area.

3. **Tweak the filter's settings till you like the effect.**

   The dialog box's sliders are explained below. Be cautious—it doesn't take much to make your photo look like a painting. Click OK when the flaws are concealed as much as possible without losing important details like eyelashes.

4. **If you want, change the duplicate layer's blend mode and/or opacity.**

Use the controls near the top of the Layers panel for this step. If you want to eliminate blemishes, for example, try the Lighten blend mode.

The Surface Blur filter isn't hard to understand, but you usually have to do a fair amount of fiddling with its sliders to get the best balance between softening and preserving detail for a natural-looking effect. Here's what the sliders do:

• **Radius.** As with other filters, this setting controls the size of the area Elements samples for the blur. Move this slider left for a smaller blur or right for a wider blur.

• **Threshold.** This slider controls how different in tone the pixels have to be for Elements to blur them. A low setting means less blurring (fewer tones will be blurred); a higher setting means more blurring.

If you want to do a lot of experimenting, instead of dragging the sliders, try highlighting the number in each setting's box and then using the up and down arrow keys to adjust the effect.

NOTE Elements includes a whole tutorial especially for fixing portrait photos (although it uses the Smart Blur rather than Surface Blur). To try it out, go to Guided→Touchups→Perfect Portrait.

Applying Actions and Effects

If you hang around people who use Photoshop, you'll hear them talk about *actions* and how useful they are. An action is a little script—similar to a macro in a program like Word—that automates the steps for doing something, which can save tons of time. For example, imagine an action that applies your favorite filter and crops a photo to a certain size, or one that creates a complicated artistic effect, like a colorful watercolor look that would take many steps to do manually. Wouldn't it be great if you could use actions in Elements?

Well, in a way, Elements has always been able to use actions. The program has always included what were called *effects* and, under the hood, effects are really actions. For a long time the emphasis in Elements was on using effects rather than actions, but that's starting to change, with Adobe putting more emphasis on actions instead. You've always been able to add some Photoshop actions to Elements, although the process used to be complicated. But not anymore: One of the star features of Elements 11 is the new Actions panel, which (finally!) makes it just as simple to run actions in Elements as it is in Photoshop.

Using Actions

Adobe includes a few useful actions in Elements to get you started, and you can add your own, as explained later in this section. Here's how to run an action:

1. **Open a photo and then go to the Actions panel (Window→Actions).**

2. **Choose the action you want.**

   In the Actions panel, each little yellow folder is an *action set,* a group of related actions. Elements comes with sets that let you add captions (and canvas to display the captions), trim weight from your subjects, resize and crop photos, and apply special effects to them. Choose the specific action you want from a set by clicking its name. Figure 13-12 explains how it all works.

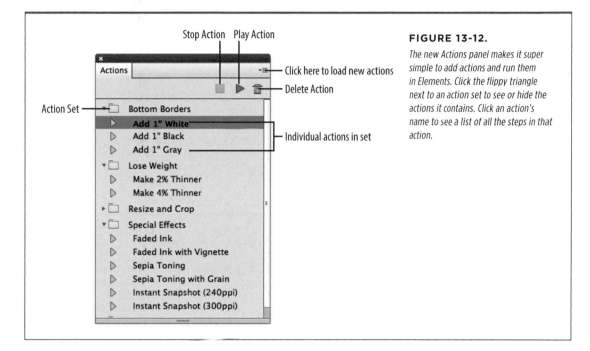

FIGURE 13-12.

The new Actions panel makes it super simple to add actions and run them in Elements. Click the flippy triangle next to an action set to see or hide the actions it contains. Click an action's name to see a list of all the steps in that action.

3. **Run the action.**

   Click the Play button in the panel's upper right, and Elements does its thing. The built-in actions happen pretty much instantly, but if you add actions from other sources, you may see pop-up dialog boxes that let you adjust settings for some steps. Just make any changes, click OK, and the action resumes and finishes up. If you want to stop an action while it's running, click the panel's Stop button. (You might do that if you prefer the look you get by using only part of an action, for example.)

   If you don't like the results, use the History panel to back up to before you started, or keep clicking the Undo button or pressing Ctrl+Z/⌘-Z to step backward through the action, and then try another one instead. (You can't step backward in the Actions panel.)

   That's all there is to it, except to save your file.

One of the best things about the Action Player is that you can easily add more actions to it. You can't create actions in Elements—you need Photoshop for that—but there are thousands of free actions on the Internet that you can download and add to Elements.

If you'd like to try installing actions, Red Steel is the action used to create the building image in Figure 13-1. You can download it from this book's Missing CD page at *www.missingmanuals.com/cds*. It works best on photos with lots of detail. On images with large blocks of color, the effect is more like pop art than a colored-steel engraving.

To add actions, just click the four-lined square at the upper right of the panel and choose Load Actions. In the dialog box that appears, find the action where it's saved on your computer, and then click Load. If you're tired of an action or a set, click its name in the panel, and then click the Delete button (the little trash can).

It's important to understand a few differences between actions in Photoshop and in Elements. Photoshop can run an action on a whole folder of images at once. In Elements, you're restricted to one photo at a time. Also, Elements can't fully perform actions that invoke Photoshop-only commands. For example, if you run an action that includes creating a history snapshot, you see the dialog box shown in Figure 13-13. If you like to play it safe, find actions written specifically for Elements. Page 598 tells you where to look for them.

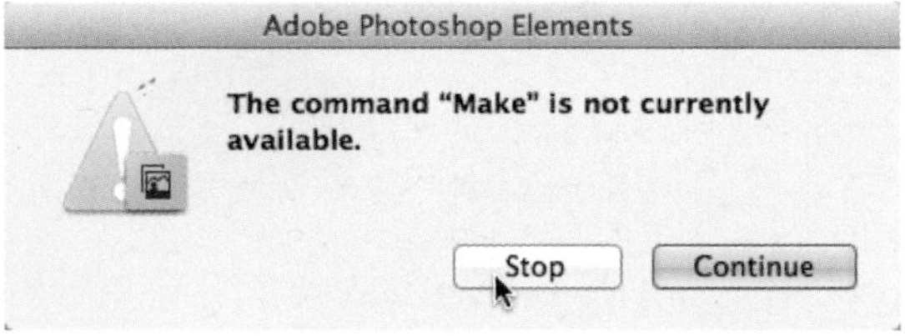

FIGURE 13-13.

When you run an action in Elements, you may see dialog boxes asking for your input as the action works through its steps. If you see this dialog box, you're trying to run an action that includes a step that Elements can't perform. You don't have to stop the action, but be aware that you won't get the same results as you would in Photoshop.

Effects

Like filters, Elements effects give you loads of ways to modify a photo's appearance—from adding lizard-skin textures to creating a pencil-sketch effect. Although you apply effects with a simple double-click, these clicks trigger a series of changes. Some effects involve many complex steps, but Elements works so quickly you might not notice all the changes it makes.

NOTE You usually can't customize or change an effect's settings—they're all or nothing.

You'll find effects in a few different spots in Elements:

- **The Effects panel** is home to some photo effects—like tinting (Figure 13-14)—and some vintage-photo looks. The panel is explained after this list.

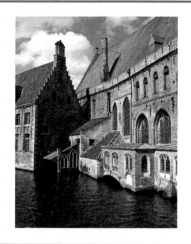

FIGURE 13-14.

The Effects panel lets you age a photo by applying an antique look to it, as shown here. This was a color photo that had the Vintage Photo effect applied to it.

- **The Graphics panel** houses some effects, but they work only on text. It's also where all the frames have gone, if you're looking for one you used to apply from the Effects panel. Page 524 has the scoop.

- **Guided Edit.** The past few versions of Elements have included a couple of fairly rudimentary special effects in this let-us-show-you-how section. In Elements 11, there are a lot more. If you're looking for an effect you've used in past versions of Elements, check Guided Edit; you may find it there. Page 458 tells you more about using Guided Edit.

To apply an effect from the Effects panel, choose Window→Effects, and then click the Effects tab at the top of the panel. Just as with filters, use the panel's drop-down menu to see all your choices or pick from only one category. The thumbnail images give you a preview of how each effect will change your image.

To apply an effect, double-click its thumbnail in the Effects panel or drag the thumbnail onto your photo. That's all there is to it. If you don't like the result, press Ctrl+Z/⌘-Z to undo it, since you can't do much to tweak it.

Here are a couple of effects-related tips to help you get the most out of these nifty-but-quirky features:

- A few effects flatten or simplify your image, so it's usually best to make a copy of your image, or wait until you're done making all your other edits, before applying an effect.

- Many effects create new layers; check the Layers panel once you're done applying them. If Elements added a layer for the effect, you may want to flatten your image to reduce the file size before printing or storing it. (See Chapter 6 if you need a refresher on layers.)

It's easy to add effects you've downloaded to the panel (see Chapter 19 for tips on where to find effects online). Simply click the four-lined square at the upper right and choose Load Effects, find the file on your computer, and then click Load. The effect appears in a category called My Effects. To get rid of it, right-click/Control-click its thumbnail in the panel and choose Delete Content. You can only add and delete effects one at a time using these techniques, though, not a set of effects. In Elements 11, you'd probably want to install them in the Actions panel instead, anyway.

> **TIP** If you want to apply an effect to only part of an image, check out some of the Smart Brush tool's options (page 225). Some of these are quite different under the hood from the effects described in this section, but the end result may be just what you're after.

Special Effects in Guided Edit

In addition to the special effects in the Actions panel, Elements includes two categories in Guided Edit that contain lots of interesting special effects. Elements carefully walks you through some fairly complex photo work in these edits, which can create some pretty impressive results, as you can see in Figure 13-15.

To get started, go to Guided→Photo Effects. Here are your choices:

- **Depth Of Field.** If you have a point-and-shoot or cellphone camera that takes photos where the entire image tends to be in focus, you can use this guided edit to simulate the kind of selective focus that's possible with a large-sensor camera like a DSLR (where your subject is in sharp focus and extraneous details aren't). You can also use the Lens Blur filter (page 448) to achieve this effect, but this Guided Edit is simpler.

- **High Key.** This edit helps you to create the look, especially popular for portraits, where the exposure is very bright, with low contrast and very few shadows. High key images are generally perceived as happy and upbeat.

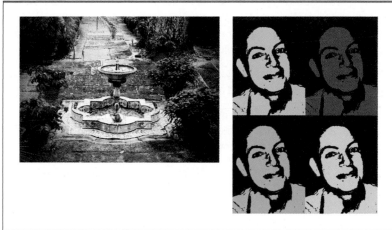

FIGURE 13-15.

Both of these images began with a simple color photo. Two clicks created this distinctive Lomo-style image (left), and creating the pop art portrait (right) was only a tad more complicated.

- **Line Drawing.** If you've tried the Pencil Sketch filter and weren't happy with the results, this guided edit gives you some help with additional tweaks to get a (somewhat) more realistic looking drawn effect.

- **Lomo Camera Effect.** The name of this effect may not mean anything to you, but if you click it in the Guided Edit panel, the example image's style should be familiar. Lomo was a brand of camera that produced photos that, technically speaking, weren't the greatest: They were oversaturated, had shadowy vignetted corners, and the registration (alignment) of the color channels was sometimes off, to name a few flaws. But people loved the strong personality of these images, and in recent years, making a photo look like it was taken with a Lomo has become popular. Figure 13-15 (left) shows an example of what Elements creates with this effect.

- **Low Key.** The opposite of a high-key photo, a low-key image is very dark and shadowy with lots of contrast. The emotions they convey are also darker and more thoughtful.

- **Old Fashioned Photo.** Use this to create a sepia-toned photo with an aged texture.

- **Orton Effect.** As explained on page 451, this edit uses a very soft focus to create a dreamlike mood.

- **Saturated Slide Film Effect**. You may be old enough to remember the ultra-saturated colors you could get by shooting certain types of slide film. This guided edit walks you through creating a similar look digitally.

- **Tilt-Shift.** A very fun effect that you see quite often, where the photo's focus zones are manipulated to make the subject look like a miniature (a car looks like a toy car, a house looks like a doll's house, and so on).

- **Vignette Effect.** Lets you create soft, shadowy corners in your photos. You can create either a dark or light vignette around your subject.

In addition, there are several fun effects in the Guided Edit panel's Photo Play section. Some of these are a bit complex, but once you've been through the process once or twice, it becomes very easy to create any of them:

- **Out Of Bounds.** This effect makes part of your subject look like it's moving out of the framed image, giving the photo a sort of 3-D look.

> **TIP** Good candidates for the Out Of Bounds effect are photos where there's a fairly strong color contrast between your subject and the background. For example, your daughter will be easier to select if she's playing soccer on a grass field than if she's running on a track amidst her classmates.

- **Picture Stack.** This makes a photo look like you took several shots of different bits of the subject and then arranged the pictures on a table so you could see the whole thing at once. You can choose whether there should be four, eight, or 12 pictures in the stack; adjust the size of the photos' borders; and change the background color, although you really don't see very much of it.

- **Pop Art.** This guided edit helps you create that '60s Andy Warhol look (like the one in Figure 13-15, right) with just a couple of clicks. It works best on photos of people or of objects with fairly simple lines rather than super-detailed subjects.

- **Reflection.** If you've seen any advertising in the past couple of years, you know this look, originally popularized by Apple. Start with a photo of an object with a simple background (or even none at all), and then follow the steps here to create a reflection beneath it, like it's standing on a shiny surface. This is especially great for gussying up photos for places like eBay.

> **TIP** While working on any of these Guided Edits, if you click the buttons that change the look of the image (by increasing the saturation, say) more than once, you can build up a much stronger effect than you get with just one click.

Adding Layer Styles

Like filters and effects, layer styles let you transform objects by giving them new characteristics such as drop shadows. Layer styles are especially useful for modifying individual objects, like text and buttons, because you can edit the text and change the button's shape even *after* you've applied the style.

Layer styles, as their name suggests, work on the contents of one layer rather than on a whole image. That's important: A layer style affects *everything* on a layer. So if you want to apply a layer style to just one object in your picture, select the object, and then put it on its own layer by pressing Ctrl+J/⌘-J (or going to Layer→New→"Layer via Copy") or Shift+Ctrl+J/Shift-⌘-J (or going to New→"Layer via Cut"). You can also mask out part of a layer (page 202) so that, when you apply a Layer Style to it, it affects only the visible part of the layer. Figure 13-16 shows what you can do with layer styles.

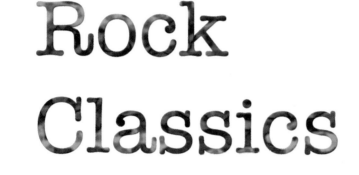

FIGURE 13-16.

It took only a double-click to create this funky retro-styled text. (The Batik style was applied here.)

You apply layer styles from the Effects panel (Window→Effects). Click the Styles tab at the top of the panel and then—from the drop-down menu—choose a category or select Show All, and find a style you like. Next, select the layer you want to modify by clicking its thumbnail in the Layers panel. Finally, back in the Effects panel, double-click the style's thumbnail or drag the style's thumbnail to your image. (The box on page 462 shows you how to modify a style's settings once you've applied it.)

> **TIP** Some tools, like the type tools, have Tool Options settings that let you choose a layer style.

Editing Layer Styles

Elements lets you customize layer styles, which can be a lot of fun. Start by applying a layer style to your image, and then you can edit it as much as you like. Just click the Style Settings icon in the Effects panel (the gear), double-click the Layer Style's icon in the Layers panel (the little italic *fx* to the right of the layer's thumbnail), or select Layer→Layer Style→Style Settings. In the Style Settings dialog box that appears, you can edit the following settings (see Figure 13-17):

- **Lighting Angle.** Not surprisingly, this setting controls the direction the light comes from, which determines things like where shadows fall. Think about how your shadow moves around depending on the sun's location at different times of day; changing the angle here has the same effect on your layer styles. (If you drag a shadow, as explained in the next item in this list, the angle degree number here and the line indicating the angle change automatically, but you can type a number or just drag the line in the circle if you'd rather do it that way.)

- **Drop Shadow.** You can change the shadow's direction, distance, opacity, or even its color. When the Style Settings dialog box is open, you can drag the shadow around in your image window until it's positioned where you want it.

- **Glow.** You can set the color, size, and opacity for both inner and outer glows, and turn each one on or off.

- **Bevel.** This lets you change the size or direction of the bevel.

- **Stroke.** A *stroke* is a border around the edge of the style (most folks simply call these "outlines"). You can change the color, size, and opacity of the stroke.

Elements lets you customize styles in so many ways that you can practically make your own style from an existing one. There's only one hitch: You can't change the standard settings for each style or save your custom style, so any changes you make affect the style only as you're currently applying it.

NOTE You can apply layer styles only to regular layers. If you try to apply one to a Background layer, Elements asks you to convert it to a regular layer first.

Here's a rundown of the choices available in each layer style category:

- **Bevels** give objects a 3-D look by making them appear raised from the page or embossed into it. Figure 13-18 shows how combining a bevel and a drop shadow can add dimension to a simple shape.

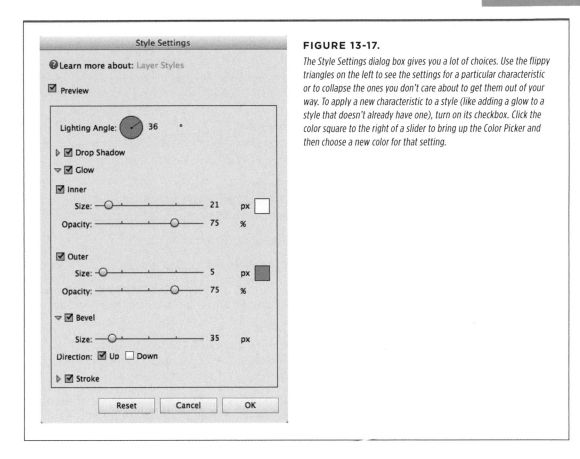

FIGURE 13-17.

The Style Settings dialog box gives you a lot of choices. Use the flippy triangles on the left to see the settings for a particular characteristic or to collapse the ones you don't care about to get them out of your way. To apply a new characteristic to a style (like adding a glow to a style that doesn't already have one), turn on its checkbox. Click the color square to the right of a slider to bring up the Color Picker and then choose a new color for that setting.

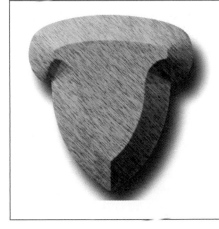

FIGURE 13-18.

Here's the acorn image from earlier in this chapter. Adding a bevel and a drop shadow gives it much more dimension and depth.

- **Complex** includes a variety of elaborate styles that make objects look like they're made from metal, cactus, or several other materials. These styles are particularly useful for applying to text.

- **Drop Shadows** add shadow effects that make an object look like it's floating above the page.

> **NOTE** To add a drop shadow to an *entire* photo, you have to also add canvas (see page 108) to give the shadow someplace to fall.

- **Glass Buttons** are supposed to make objects look like, well, glass buttons, but many people think they look more like plastic. They're useful for creating web page buttons.

- **Image Effects** give you tons of ways to transform photos, including fading them and making them look like the pieces of a puzzle or a tile mosaic.

- **Inner Glows** add light around the inside edge of an object.

- **Inner Shadows** give an object a hollow or recessed look by casting a shadow within it, rather than outside it the way drop shadows do.

- **Outer Glows** create the same kind of light effects that Inner Glows do, only around the outer edge of the object.

- **Patterns** apply an overall pattern to an object. Want to make something look like it's made from metal or dried mud, or to fill in a dull background with a vivid pattern? You'll find lots of choices here.

- **Photographic Effects** include traditional photographic techniques. You can add a variety of monochrome effects, like good, old-fashioned sepia.

- **Strokes** let you put a black or colored border around the edge of a layer, or an object on its own layer. They're great for making outlined text, too.

- **Visibility** changes the opacity and visibility of a layer. Use these styles to create a ghosted effect, or when you're applying multiple layer styles and want to use an object's outline without having the object itself visible.

- **Wow Chrome, Neon, and Plastic** styles make objects look like they're made from shiny chrome, outlined in neon, or made from plastic.

If someone sends you a file made using layer styles that you don't have, you can snag them for your own use by highlighting the layer with the styles applied to it, and then going to Layer→Layer Style→Copy Layer Style. To use these styles in your own image, click the layer you want to modify, and then choose Layer→Layer Style→Paste Layer Style. This command applies all the styles used in the original image to the layer you targeted. If you want to duplicate the styles from one layer to another within a single image, it's simpler. In the Layers panel, just Alt-click/Option-click the little *fx* icon on the layer whose styles you want, and drag it onto the layer you want to apply that style to. (If you simply drag the *fx* without pressing Alt or Option first, you'll move the layer style from one layer to the other rather than duplicating it.)

To remove a layer style, in the Layers panel, right-click/Control-click the layer it's applied to, and then choose Clear Layer Style or go to Layer→Layer Style→Clear Layer Style. These commands are all or nothing: If your layer has multiple styles, they all go away. To remove one style at a time, use the History panel (page 25) instead.

TIP To see what your image looks like without the styles you've applied to it, go to Layer→Layer Style→Hide All Effects.

You can download hundreds of additional layer styles from the Web (see page 598 for tips on where to look and how to install them). To add them, just click the little four-lined square at the Effects panel's upper-right corner and choose Load Styles; find the downloaded file on your hard drive and then click Load. You also delete styles using this same menu, but you have to delete the whole set—you can't just delete individual styles within it.

It's easy to get addicted to collecting layer styles because they're so much fun to use. You've been warned!

TIP In Elements 11, styles, effects, and actions you add by using the appropriate panel's four-line-square menu are automatically copied into Elements. That means you can move the originals wherever you like, so it's a good idea to keep a special folder with the originals for all your extra content. That way you'll always know where they are so you can back them up and also find them easily again if you need to reinstall them. (If you reinstall Elements, you'll need to reinstall all this stuff, too.)

▮ Applying Gradients

You may have noticed that a few of Elements' layer styles and effects apply a color tint that fades away at the edges of your layer or image. You can fade and blend colors in almost any way imaginable by using *gradients,* which let you create anything from a multicolored rainbow extravaganza to a single color that fades away into transparency. Figure 13-19 shows a few examples of what you can do with gradients. The only limit is your imagination.

You can apply gradients directly to your image using the Gradient tool, or create *Gradient Fill layers,* which are whole layers filled with—you guessed it—gradients. You can even edit gradients and create new ones using the Gradient Editor. Finally, there's a special kind of gradient called a *gradient map* that lets you replace the colors in your image with the colors from a gradient. This section covers the basics of all these tools and methods.

The Gradient Tool

If you want to apply a gradient to an object in your image, the Gradient tool (Figure 13-19) is the fastest way to go. This tool seems complicated at first, but it's actually easy to use. Start by activating it in the Tools panel (its icon is a black-and-white rectangle) or by pressing G. Figure 13-20 shows your Tool Options choices for this tool.

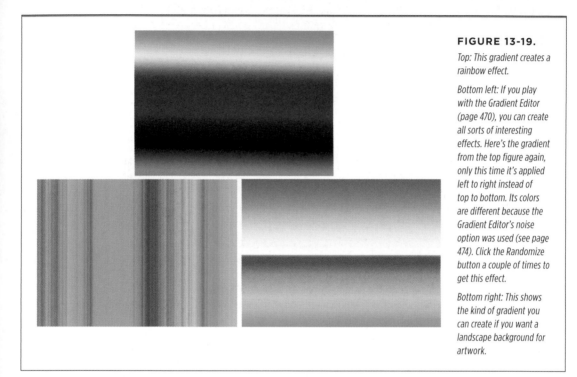

FIGURE 13-19.

Top: This gradient creates a rainbow effect.

Bottom left: If you play with the Gradient Editor (page 470), you can create all sorts of interesting effects. Here's the gradient from the top figure again, only this time it's applied left to right instead of top to bottom. Its colors are different because the Gradient Editor's noise option was used (see page 474). Click the Randomize button a couple of times to get this effect.

Bottom right: This shows the kind of gradient you can create if you want a landscape background for artwork.

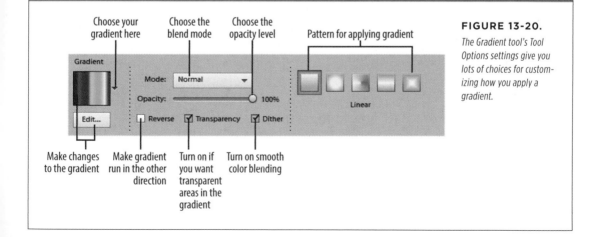

FIGURE 13-20.

The Gradient tool's Tool Options settings give you lots of choices for customizing how you apply a gradient.

Using the Gradient tool is as easy as dragging: Click where you want the gradient to begin, and then drag to the point where you want it to stop (you'll see a line connecting the beginning and ending points). When you release the mouse button, the gradient covers the available space.

For example, say you're using a yellow-to-white gradient. If you click to end the gradient one-third of the way into your photo, the yellow stops transitioning at that point, since you told Elements to stop the gradient there, and the remaining two-thirds of your photo get covered with white. In other words, something put down by the tool covers the entire space—your whole photo, in this case. Clicking stops the color *transition*—no more yellow beyond that point—but the gradient's end color fills in everyplace else. (Don't worry: This is much easier to understand once you try it.) Drag the gradient within a selection to confine it to that area so the entire photo or layer isn't affected by the gradient's colors.

> **TIP** The Gradient tool puts the gradient on the same layer as the image you apply it to, which means that it's hard to change anything about a gradient after you apply it. If you think you might want to alter a gradient, use a Gradient Fill layer instead.

Some of Elements' gradients use the current foreground and background colors, but Elements also offers a number of preset gradients with different color schemes. Click the arrow to the right of the gradient thumbnail in the Tool Options area to see a palette of different gradients, some of which use your foreground and background colors, and others that have their own color schemes. The gradients are grouped into categories; use the palette's drop-down menu to choose one to see what it contains. (You can work with the gradients in only one category at a time.)

You can download gradients from the Web and add them to your library using the Preset Manager (page 600); page 598 has suggestions of where to look online. You can also create your own gradients from scratch. Creating and editing gradients is explained later in this chapter, in the section about the Gradient Editor.

To apply a gradient with the Gradient tool, first make a selection if you don't want Elements to apply the gradient to your whole image. Then follow these steps:

1. **Choose the colors you want to use for your gradient.**

   Click the foreground and background color squares to choose colors. (Remember, some gradients ignore these colors and use their own preset colors instead.)

2. **Activate the Gradient tool.**

   Click its icon in the Tools panel or press G.

3. **Select a gradient.**

   Go to the Tool Options area, click the tiny arrow to the right of the gradient thumbnail, and then choose the one you want. (If you see the Gradient Editor window, you clicked the thumbnail itself; close the Gradient Editor and try again.) Then make any other necessary changes to the Tool Options settings (your options are explained in a moment), like reversing the gradient.

4. **Apply the gradient.**

   Drag in your image to mark where the gradient should run. If you're using a linear gradient, you can make it run vertically by dragging up or down, or make it go horizontally by dragging sideways. For Radial, Reflection, and Diamond gradients, try dragging from the center of your image to an edge. If you don't like the result, press Ctrl+Z/⌘-Z to undo it and try again. Once you like the way the gradient looks, you don't need to do anything special to accept it; just save your image before you close it.

You can customize gradients in several ways without even using the Gradient Editor. When the Gradient tool is active, the Tool Options area offers the following settings:

- **Gradient.** Click the arrow to the right of the gradient thumbnail to choose a different gradient.

- **Edit.** Click this button or the gradient's thumbnail to bring up the Gradient Editor (page 470).

- **Mode.** You can apply a gradient in any blend mode (see page 190).

- **Opacity.** If you want your image to be visible through the gradient, reduce this setting.

- **Reverse.** This setting changes the direction in which Elements applies the colors so that, for example, instead of yellow to blue (from left to right, say), you get blue to yellow instead.

- **Transparency.** If you want to fade to transparency anywhere in your gradient, turn on this checkbox. Otherwise, the gradient can't include transparent regions.

- **Dither.** Turn on this checkbox and Elements uses fewer colors but simulates the full color range using a noise pattern. This can help to prevent the gradient's colors from banding (having hard-edged transitions), making smoother transitions between them.

- **Gradient types.** These five buttons determine the way the colors flow in the gradient. From left to right, your choices are Linear (in a straight line), Radial (a sunburst effect), Angle (a counterclockwise sweep around the starting point), Reflected (from the center out to each edge in a mirror image), and Diamond. Figure 13-21 shows what each one looks like.

Gradient Fill Layers

You can also apply a gradient using a special kind of Fill layer (page 209). Most of the time, this method is better than using the Gradient tool, especially if you want to be able to make changes to the gradient after you apply it.

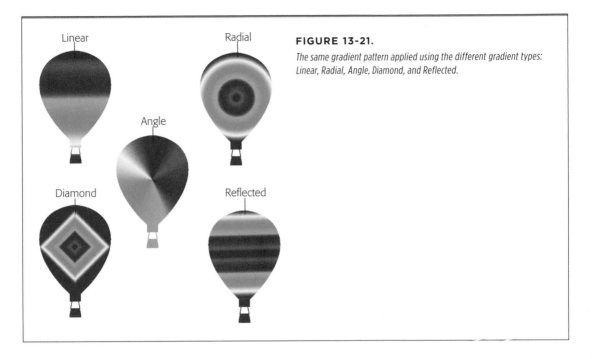

Linear

Radial

Angle

Diamond

Reflected

FIGURE 13-21.

The same gradient pattern applied using the different gradient types: Linear, Radial, Angle, Diamond, and Reflected.

To create a Gradient Fill layer, go to Layer→New Fill Layer→Gradient. The New Layer dialog box appears so you can set the layer's blend mode (page 190) and opacity. Once you click OK, Elements fills the new layer with the currently selected gradient, and the dialog box shown in Figure 13-22 pops up. You can change many of the gradient's settings here, or choose a different gradient altogether. Here's what each setting does:

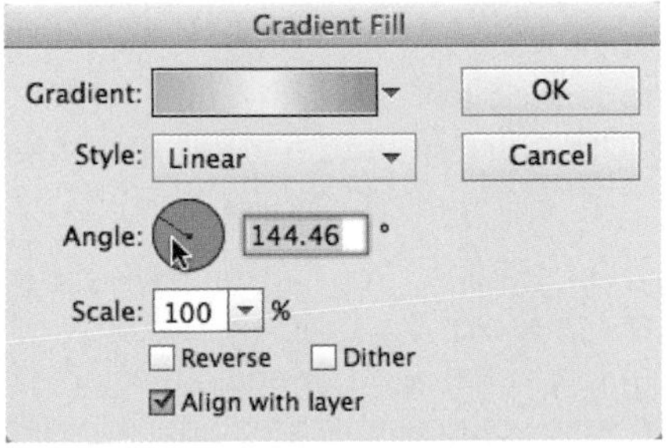

FIGURE 13-22.

The Gradient Fill dialog box gives you access to most of the same settings you find in the Tool Options area for the Gradient tool. The major difference is that with a Fill layer, you set the direction of the gradient by typing in a number for the angle or by changing the direction of the line in the circle as shown here (the cursor is pointing to the line you drag to change the angle). You don't get a chance to set the direction by dragging directly in your image as you do with the Gradient tool, but while this dialog box is onscreen, you can drag the gradient in your image to change where it transitions.

- **Gradient.** To choose a different gradient, click the arrow next to this thumbnail to see the Gradient palette. Use the palette's drop-down menu to choose a different gradient category.

- **Style.** You have the same choices here as for the Gradient tool (Linear, Diamond, and so on). Choose a different style and Elements previews it in the layer.

- **Angle.** This setting controls the direction the colors will run. To change the direction of the flow, enter a number in degrees or drag the line in the circle.

- **Scale.** This setting determines how large the gradient is relative to the layer. At 100 percent, they're the same size; at 150 percent, the gradient is bigger than the layer, so you see only a portion of the gradient in the layer. (For example, if you had a black-to-white gradient, you might see only shades of gray in your image.) If you turn off the "Align with layer" checkbox (explained in a sec), you can adjust the location of the gradient relative to your image by dragging the gradient.

- **Reverse.** Turn on this checkbox to make colors flow in the opposite direction.

- **Dither.** Use this setting to avoid banding and create smooth color transitions.

- **Align with layer.** This setting keeps the gradient in line with the layer. Turn it off and you can pull the gradient around in your image to place it exactly where you want it. At least, that's how it's *supposed* to work; you can usually drag while the dialog box is visible but not after you click OK.

When the gradient looks good, click OK to create the layer. You can edit it later by heading to the Layers panel and double-clicking the layer's leftmost icon (the gradient thumbnail). That brings up the Gradient Fill dialog box again, so you can change its settings or choose a different gradient.

Editing Gradients

Elements' Gradient Editor lets you create gradients that include any colors you like. You can even make ones in which the color fades to transparency, or modify existing gradient presets. Alas, the Gradient Editor isn't the easiest tool in the world to use. This section tells you the basics you need to get started. Then, as is the case with so many of Elements' features, playing around with the Gradient Editor is the best way to understand how it works.

You have to activate the Gradient tool to launch the Gradient Editor. After you activate the tool, in the Tool Options area, click the Edit button to see the Gradient Editor (see Figure 13-23).

The Gradient Editor opens showing the current gradient. You can choose a different gradient by picking from the thumbnails at the top of the Gradient Editor window, or by clicking the Preset menu at the upper left of the window and choosing a new category from the list. (You'll learn how to save your custom gradients later in this chapter.)

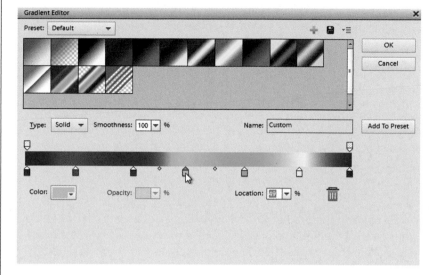

FIGURE 13-23.

The powerful and complex Gradient Editor. Here, the aqua stop (where the cursor is) was clicked to make it active. (The dark triangle above the stop is Elements' way of telling you it's the active stop.) The two tiny diamonds on either side of the active stop mark the midpoints of the transitions between the selected color and its neighbors. You can move these diamonds to change the midpoints.

To get started using the Gradient Editor, first choose your gradient's type and smoothness settings:

- **Type.** Your choices are Solid or Noise. Solid gradients are the most common; they let you create transitions between solid blocks of color. Noise gradients, which are covered later in this section, produce bands of color, as you might see in a spectrometer.

- **Smoothness.** This setting controls how even the transitions between colors are.

You do most of your work in the Gradient Editor's *Gradient bar,* the long colored bar where Elements displays the current gradient. The little boxes (called *stops*) and diamonds surrounding the Gradient bar let you control the gradient's color and transparency.

> **NOTE** The directions in this section are for editing solid gradients. Noise gradients work a little differently, as explained on page 474.

For now, you care about only the stops *below* the Gradient bar (the ones above it are explained in the next section). Each one is a *color stop;* it represents where a particular color falls in the gradient. (You need at least two color stops in a gradient.) If you click a stop, the pointed end turns gray to let you know that it's the active stop. Anything you do at this point will affect the area governed by that stop.

The color stops let you customize the gradient in lots of different ways:

- **Change where the color transitions.** Click a color stop and you see a tiny diamond appear under the bar. (If the stop isn't at an end of the gradient, you get two diamonds, one on either side of the stop.) The diamond is the midpoint of the color change. Diamonds always appear between two color stops. You can drag the diamond in either direction to skew the color range between two color stops so that it more heavily represents one color over another. Wherever you place the diamond tells Elements that that's where the color change should be half completed.

- **Change one of the colors in the gradient.** Click any color stop, and then click the Color rectangle at the bottom of the Gradient Editor to bring up the Color Picker. Clicking the down arrow on the corner of the Color rectangle brings up the Color Swatches palette. Choose a new color, and the gradient automatically reflects your change. You can also pick a new color by moving your cursor over the Gradient bar; the cursor turns into an eyedropper that lets you sample a color.

- **Add a color to the gradient.** Click anywhere just beneath the bar to indicate where you want the new color to appear. Elements adds a new color stop where you clicked. Then you can click the Color rectangle to choose a different color for the new stop. Repeat as many times as you want, adding a new color each time. To precisely position the new stop, enter a number (indicating percentage) in the Location box below the Gradient bar. For example, 50 percent positions a stop at the bar's midpoint. To duplicate an existing color from your gradient, click its stop, and then click below the bar where you want to use that color again.

- **Remove a color from a gradient.** If a gradient is *almost* what you want but you don't like one of its colors, you don't have to live with it. You can remove a color by clicking its stop to make it active. Then click the Delete button (the trash can) at the bottom right of the Gradient Editor, or just drag the stop downward off the bar. (The Delete button is grayed out if no color stop is active.)

■ TRANSPARENCY IN GRADIENTS

You can also use the Gradient Editor to adjust the transparency in a gradient. Elements gives you nearly unlimited control over transparency in gradients, and over the opacity of any color at any point in a gradient. Adjusting opacity in the Gradient Editor is much like using the color stops to edit the colors, but instead of color stops you use *opacity stops*.

NOTE Transparency is particularly nice in images for Web use, but remember that you need to save in a format that preserves transparency, like GIF, or you lose the transparency. (If you save the file as a JPEG, for example, the transparent areas become opaque white.) See page 533 for more about file formats for the Web.

The opacity stops are the little boxes *above* the Gradient bar. You can move an opacity stop to wherever you want and then adjust the transparency using the Gradient Editor's settings. Click above the Gradient bar wherever you want to add an opacity stop. The more opacity stops in the Gradient bar, the more points where you can adjust your gradient's opacity.

Here's how to add an opacity stop and adjust its opacity setting:

1. **Click one of the existing opacity stops (optional).**

   The new stop you're about to create will have the same opacity as the stop you click in this step, but you can adjust the new stop once you create it. (You can actually skip this step, but it lets you predetermine the opacity of your new stop.)

2. **Add a stop.**

   Click just above the Gradient bar where you want to add a stop. Then, if you want the new stop to be precisely positioned, enter numbers (indicating percentage) in the Location box below the Gradient bar. For example, 50 percent positions a stop at the bar's midpoint.

3. **Adjust the new stop's opacity.**

   Go to the Opacity box below the Gradient bar and either enter a percentage or click the arrow to the right of the number and then move the slider. To get rid of a stop, click it and then click Delete (the trash can) or drag the stop upward, away from the bar.

By adding stops, you can make a gradient fade in and out, as shown in the background of Figure 13-24, which has a simple, linear gradient that's been edited so that it fades in and out a few times.

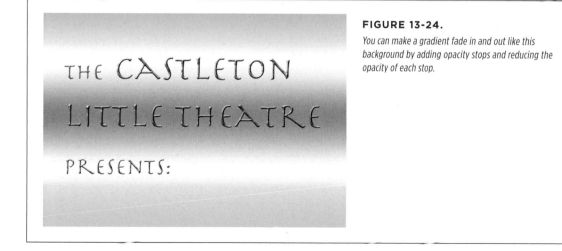

FIGURE 13-24.

You can make a gradient fade in and out like this background by adding opacity stops and reducing the opacity of each stop.

■ CREATING NOISE GRADIENTS

Elements also lets you create what Adobe calls *noise gradients*, which aren't speck-led as you might expect if you're thinking of camera noise. Instead, noise gradients randomly distribute their colors within the range you specify, giving them a banded or spectrometer-like look. The effect is interesting, but noise gradients can be un-predictable. The noisier a gradient is, the more stripes of color it contains, and the greater the number of random colors.

With the Gradient tool active, you can create a noise gradient by tweaking one of the sample ones that comes with Elements. First, go to the Tool Options area and click the down arrow to the right of the gradient's thumbnail; this opens the Gradient palette. Next, click the drop-down menu at the top of the palette and select Noise Samples. Look through the thumbnails that appear and click to select one you like. You can then edit it by clicking the Edit button in the Tool Options area to bring up the Gradient Editor.

> **TIP** If you want to create a noise gradient that's not based on one of Elements' Noise Sample presets, click the Option bar's Edit button to bring up the Gradient Editor, and then choose Noise from the Type menu.

Noise gradients have some special Gradient Editor settings of their own:

- **Roughness** controls how gradually the gradient transitions from color to color (see Figure 13-25 for details). A higher number not only means less-smooth transitions, but also more shades of color in the gradient.

FIGURE 13-25.

The amount of roughness in a noise gradient can make quite a difference in the effect you get.

Top: A solid gradient.

Middle: A noise gradient with the same colors and 50 percent roughness.

Bottom: A noise gradient with the same colors and 90 percent roughness.

- **Color Model** determines which color mode you work in—RGB or HSB. RGB gives you red, green, and blue color sliders, while HSB lets you set hue, saturation, and brightness (see page 250 for more about these settings).

- **Restrict Colors** keeps the gradient's colors from getting too saturated.

- **Add Transparency** puts random amounts of transparency into the gradient.

- **Randomize** adds random colors (and transparency, too, if you turned on that checkbox). Keep clicking the Randomize button until you see an effect you like.

Saving Gradients

After all that work, you probably want to save your gradient so you can use it again. You have two ways to save a gradient from the Gradient Editor:

- **Add it as a preset.** If you've made any changes to one of the preset gradients, the Name box has already changed to show the name "Custom." You can change it to a more descriptive name by highlighting the text and typing over it. Then click the Add To Preset button. Elements adds your gradient to the current category, and adds a thumbnail of it to the Gradient palette.

> **TIP** If you forget and click the Add To Preset button before naming your gradient (or if you just want to change its name), in the Gradient Editor, right-click/Control-click the gradient's thumbnail, and then choose Rename Gradient.

- **Save the gradient.** The Save button is the little floppy-disk icon at the upper right of the Gradient editor. When you click it, the Save dialog box appears and Elements asks you to name the set of gradients you're creating (called a *library*). This method resaves the entire library that's visible when you create your gradient, so you'll want to rename it so you don't save over the originals. You'll save it in a special Gradients folder, which Elements automatically takes you to in the Save dialog box. When you want to use the gradient again, click the Gradient Editor's Load button (the green + sign), and then select it from the list of gradients that appears. The new library appears at the bottom of the list of gradient libraries you see when you click the Preset menu.

> **TIP** You can also save and load gradients by calling up the Gradient palette (in the Tool Options area, click the arrow to the right of the gradient thumbnail) and then clicking the four-lined square in the palette's upper right.

Gradient Maps

Gradient maps let you use gradients in nonlinear ways. So instead of a rainbow that shades from one direction to another, with a gradient map, Elements substitutes the gradient's colors for the image's existing colors. You can use gradient maps for funky special effects as well as serious photo corrections.

When you create a gradient map, Elements plots out the brightness values in your image and applies those values to a gradient (light to dark). Then Elements replaces the existing colors with the gradient you choose, using the lightness values as a guide to determine which color goes where. That sounds complicated, and it is; but if you try it, you'll quickly see what's going on. Take a look at Figure 13-26, where applying a gradient map dramatically livens up a dull photo. But that's not all gradient maps are good for. They're also valuable tools for straight retouching. See the box on page 478 to learn how to use gradients to fix the color in photos.

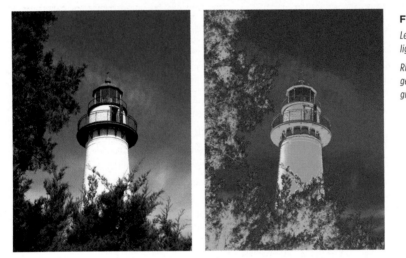

FIGURE 13-26.

Left: An ordinary shot of a lighthouse.

Right: The image becomes altogether different when you apply a gradient map adjustment.

You can apply a gradient map directly to an image by going to Filter→Adjustments→ Gradient Map or using the Smart Brush [page 225] (in the Tool Options area's Smart Paint setting [page 226], choose Special Effects→Rainbow Map). But most times, you'll want to use a Gradient Map Adjustment layer, because it's easier to edit after you've created the layer. Here's how:

1. **Create a Gradient Map Adjustment layer.**

   Go to Layer→New Adjustment Layer→Gradient Map. The New Layer dialog box appears so you can choose the blend mode and opacity for the new layer and name it if you want. Click OK, and Elements adds a gradient map to your photo, but don't worry if it's not what you had in mind. You can modify it by going to the Adjustments panel, shown in Figure 13-27.

2. **Select a gradient.**

In the Adjustments panel, you see a gradient whose colors are based on your current foreground and background colors. That gradient is the map that Elements made of the lightness/darkness values in your image. If you want your image to show color, choose a color gradient rather than a black- or gray-to-white one: At the right of the gradient thumbnail, click the arrow, and then choose a color gradient. Elements automatically replaces the colors in your image with the equivalent values from the gradient you chose, so you can click around in the gradient libraries and watch your image change.

The Dither checkbox adds a little random noise to make the gradient's transitions smoother. The Reverse checkbox switches the direction in which Elements applies the gradient to the map. For example, if you chose a red-to-green gradient, reversing it would put green where it would have previously been red, and vice versa. It's worth giving this setting a try—you can get some interesting effects.

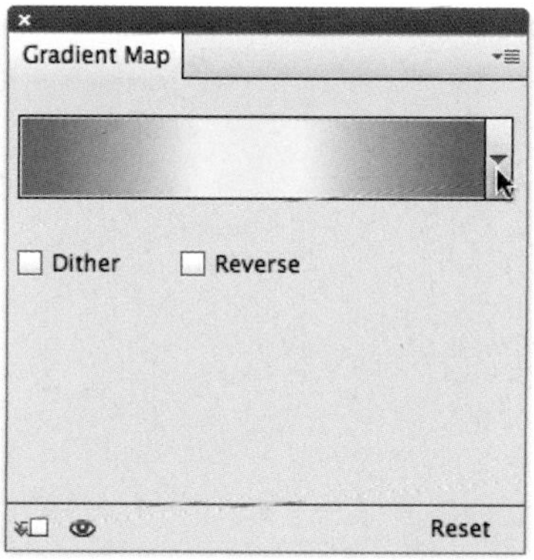

FIGURE 13-27.

The Gradient Map Adjustments panel. Click the tiny arrow to the right of the thumbnail (where the cursor is here) to see a drop-down menu of the available gradient patterns. Click in the thumbnail itself to bring up the Gradient Editor (page 470) if you want to make changes to the gradient you chose.

3. **Keep editing until you're satisfied with the result.**

When you like what you see, save the image. You can always go back and edit the gradient map layer (as explained in Figure 13-27) by clicking it in the Layers panel.

Remember that you can use gradient maps in any layer blend mode. You can spend hours playing around with gradient maps. Try adding other filters and adjustments to produce all sorts of strange results.

TIP Try equalizing your image (Filter→Adjustments→Equalize) after applying a gradient map adjustment—the colors can shift dramatically. Equalizing is a good thing to try if your gradient map makes your image look dull or dingy. You may need to merge the image's layers to get this command to work, since you can't equalize an Adjustment layer. (See page 341 for more about the Equalize command.)

Using Gradients for Color Correction

If you just want to use Elements to enhance and correct photos, you may think all this gradient business is a big waste of time. But gradients and gradient maps aren't just for introducing lurid colors into photos—they're also powerful tools for correcting images.

For instance, say you have a photo where one side is darker than the other and you want to apply an Adjustment layer so it affects only the dark side of the image. You can pull this off by bringing up the Adjustment layer's layer mask (see page 211), and then applying a gradient directly to the mask.

You can also use Gradient Map Adjustment layers in different blend modes to help balance out the colors in photos, although you may need to use the Gradient Editor to play with the distribution of light and dark values to get the best effect.

Gradient maps are also useful for colorizing skin in black-and-white photos. Set up a gradient based on three or more skin tones, and you can get a more realistic distribution of color tones than you can by painting.

Text in Elements

E lements makes it easy to add text to images. You can quickly create all kinds of fancy text to use in greeting cards, as newsletter headlines, or as graphics for web pages.

Elements gives you lots of ways to jazz up text: You can apply layer styles, effects, and gradients to it, or warp it into psychedelic shapes. And the Type Mask tools let you fill individual letters with the contents of a photo. Best of all, most type tools let you change text with just a few clicks (see Figure 14-1).

And that's not all. You also get three special tools for making artistic text: "Text on Selection," "Text on Shape," and "Text on Custom Path." With these tools, you can create text that swoops and turns, or make text run around the edge of an object. You can create very dramatic text effects with these tools, which are covered beginning on page 500. By the time you finish this chapter, you'll know all the ways Elements can add pizzazz to text.

Adding Text to an Image

It's a cinch to add text to an image in Elements. Just activate a Type tool, choose a font in the Tool Options area, and then type away. The type tools' icon in the Tools panel is easy to recognize: It's a capital T. (It lives at the bottom left of the Draw section, just to the left of the Pencil tool.) You can also activate it by pressing T.

Elements actually gives you *seven* different type tools, all of which you can see in the type tools' Tool Options: the Horizontal Type tool, the Vertical Type tool, the Horizontal Type Mask tool, the Vertical Type Mask tool, the "Text on Selection" tool, the "Text on

Shape" tool, and the "Text on Custom Path" tool. You'll learn about the Type Mask and "Text on..." tools later in this chapter (see page 500); this section focuses on the regular Horizontal and Vertical Type tools. As their names imply, the Horizontal Type tool lets you enter text that runs left to right, while the Vertical Type tool is for creating text that runs down the page.

When you use the type tools, Elements automatically puts the text you create on its own layer, which makes it easy to throw out what you've typed and start over. When a type tool is active, Elements creates a new Text layer each time you click in your image.

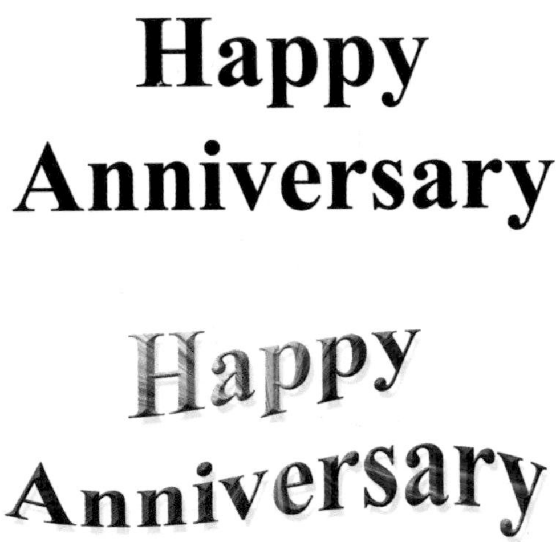

FIGURE 14-1.

With Elements, you can take basic text and turn it into the kind of snazzy headlines you see on greeting cards and magazine covers. It took only a couple of clicks—a couple of layer styles (Angled Spectrum and a bevel) and some warping—to turn these plain black letters (top) into an extravaganza (bottom).

TROUBLESHOOTING MOMENT

Why Does the Type Tool Turn My Photo Red?

If your image gets covered with an ugly reddish film every time you click it with a type tool, that means you've activated one of the Type *Mask* tools rather than one of the regular type tools. (Type masks, covered later in this chapter, are useful when you want to create text that's cut from an image.) To switch to the regular type tools, just click either of the first two icons at the left end of the Tool Options area.

The red mask may also appear if you try to add type to an image that's in Indexed Color mode, like a GIF. If you want to add text to a GIF, first go to Image→Mode→RGB and then type away. If you still need a GIF when you're done, then use "Save for Web" (page 554) to save your finished file.

Text Options

Activate either the Horizontal or Vertical Type tool, and then take a look at the many Tool Options settings (Figure 14-2). These choices let you control pretty much every aspect of your text, including its font, color, and alignment. Here are your options:

- **Font Family.** Choose a font from this unlabeled menu. Elements lists all the fonts installed on your computer. You can either click the arrow at the right end of this field to display a pop-out menu or, if you know the font you want, just start typing its name and Elements will automatically complete the name for you.

> **TIP** The font family pop-out menu mentioned above displays the word "Sample" in the actual fonts to make it easier for you to find one you like. You can adjust the size of these previews by going to Edit→Preferences→Type/ Adobe Photoshop Elements Editor→Preferences→Type.

- **Font Style.** Here's where you select from the styles available for your font, like bold or italic.

- **Size.** This is where you choose how big the text should be. Text is traditionally measured in *points*—that's what the "pt" here stands for. (The box on page 484 explains the relationship between points and actual size in Elements.) You can click the arrow and choose a preset size from this drop-down menu, or just type in the size you want into this field. And you aren't limited to the sizes shown in the menu—you can enter any number you want.

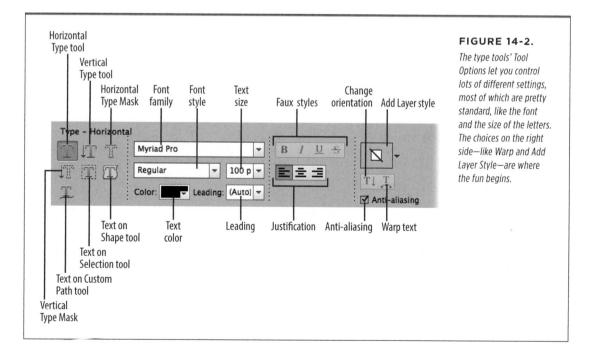

FIGURE 14-2.

The type tools' Tool Options let you control lots of different settings, most of which are pretty standard, like the font and the size of the letters. The choices on the right side—like Warp and Add Layer Style—are where the fun begins.

TIP If points make you nervous, you can change the type tools' units of measurement to millimeters or pixels by going to Edit→Preferences→Units & Rulers/Adobe Photoshop Elements Editor→Preferences→Units & Rulers.

- **Color.** Click this rectangle to bring up the color swatches. You can click a swatch to set the color of your text or click the rainbow-colored circle at the bottom right of the Swatches palette to open the full Color Picker. When you make a selection, the foreground color square changes to reflect your choice.

TIP When a type tool's cursor is active in your image (so you see a blinking line showing where letters will appear if you type), you can't use the standard keyboard commands to reset your foreground and background colors to black and white (X) or to switch them (D). (If you try to use the shortcuts, you'll simply type those letters in your image.) Instead, you have to click the relevant buttons in the Tools panel (page 247).

- **Leading.** This setting (whose name rhymes with "bedding") controls the spacing between the lines of text as measured in points. For horizontal text, leading is the difference between the *baselines* (the bottom of the letters) of each line. For vertical text, leading is the distance from the center of one column to the center of the column next to it. Figure 14-3 shows what a difference leading can make. Elements automatically sets the leading to Auto, which is the program's guess about what looks best. You can change the leading by choosing a number from the list or by entering the amount you want (in points, unless you changed the measurement unit in Elements' preferences).

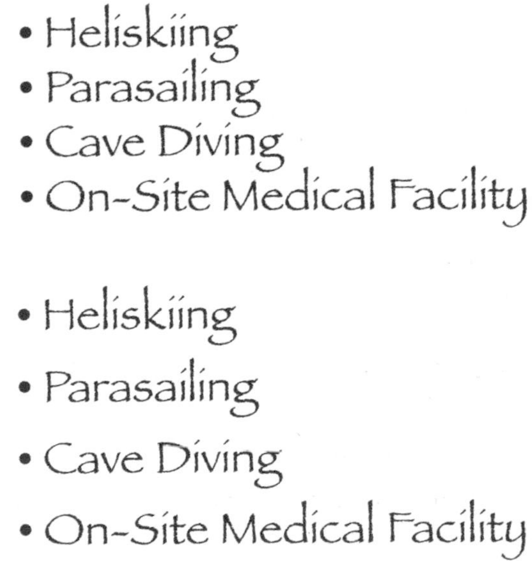

- Heliskiing
- Parasailing
- Cave Diving
- On-Site Medical Facility

- Heliskiing
- Parasailing
- Cave Diving
- On-Site Medical Facility

FIGURE 14-3.

Leading is the space between lines of text.

Top: A list of four items with Auto leading.

Bottom: The same list with the leading set to a higher number to make more space between the rows.

If you adjust the leading of vertical text, you change the space between the columns, rather than between letters within each column.

The box on page 487 explains how to tighten up the space between letters that are stacked vertically.

- **Faux Styles.** Yup, faux as in "fake." If your chosen font doesn't have a bold, italic, underline, or strikethrough version, you can tell Elements to simulate that style by clicking the appropriate icon here. (These options aren't available for some fonts.)

- **Justification.** These buttons tell Elements how to align the text, just like in a word-processing program. If you enter multiple lines of text, this is where you tell Elements whether you want it lined up left, right, or centered (for horizontal text). If you select the Vertical Type tool, you can align it along the top, bottom, or middle instead.

TIP If you're using the Vertical Type tool, each time you start a new column, Elements puts it to the left of the previous one, so your columns run from right to left. If you want vertical text columns that run left to right instead, you need to put each column on its own layer and position them manually. You can then use the Move tool's Distribute option to space them evenly (page 195).

- **Style.** You can add funky visual effects to text with layer styles (page 461) using this unlabeled button, which appears as a white square with a red slash through it. First, add some text to your image, and then click the Commit button (the green checkmark) below the text. Next, click the Style box and choose a layer style from the Styles palette. It's important that the text layer is active, but the letters shouldn't be highlighted. (If you see the Cancel and Commit buttons, Elements won't apply the style.) If you want to remove a style that you've just applied, click the four-lined square in the upper-right corner of the palette and choose Remove Style from the pop-out menu, or go to Layer→Layer Style→Clear Layer Style.

- **Orientation.** This button, which has a T with a down-pointing arrow next to it, changes text from horizontal to vertical, or vice versa. (You can't change the orientation of text that doesn't exist yet, so this setting is grayed out until you add some.) You can also change text's orientation by going to Layer→Type→Horizontal or Vertical.

- **Warp.** The little T-above-a-curved-line icon hides a bunch of options for distorting text in lots of interesting ways. There's more about this option on page 488. (The Warp Text command is also available from Layer→Type→Warp Text.) This button is grayed out until you actually type something.

- **Anti-aliasing.** This setting smooths the edges of the text, and you'll usually want it turned on. See page 487 for an explanation of antialiasing.

These two choices don't show up in your image until you've typed something:

- **Commit.** Click this green checkmark after you type on an image to tell Elements that, yes, you want the text to stay the way it is.

- **Cancel.** When you add text to an image, Elements automatically places the text on its own layer. Click this button (the red circle with a slash) to delete this newly created Text layer. This button works only if you click it *before* you click the Commit button. To delete text after you've committed it, head to the Layers panel and drag the Text layer onto the trash-can icon.

If you see either of these buttons in your image, that means you haven't committed your text, and many menu selections and other tools won't be available until you do. When you see these buttons, you're in what Elements calls *Edit mode,* where you can make changes to the text, but most of the rest of Elements' features aren't available to you. Just click Commit or Cancel to get the rest of the program's options back.

TROUBLESHOOTING MOMENT

How Resolution Affects Font Size

It's easy enough to pick a font size in the Text tool's Tool Options area. But you may find that what you thought would be big, bold, headline-size text is so tiny in your image that you can hardly see it. What gives?

In Elements, the actual size of text in an image is tied to the image's resolution. If you thought that choosing 72-point text would give you a headline that's an inch high, it will—but only if the *resolution* of your file is 72 pixels per inch (ppi). The higher the resolution, the smaller that same text is going to be. So if the resolution is 144 ppi instead, your 72-point text will print half an inch high. In a 216 ppi image, it'll be a third of an inch high, and so on.

If you're working with high-resolution images, you have to increase the size of your text to allow for the extra pixel packing that comes with increased resolution. It's not uncommon

to have to choose sizes that are *much* higher than anything listed in the Tool Options area's size menu. Don't be afraid of using really big sizes if you need them—just keep entering larger numbers in the size box until the text looks right in proportion to your image.

Another confusing thing about text in Elements is that the program creates text based on the *actual* size of an image, not your view size. So if you're zoomed way in on an image and you add some text that looks like it's a reasonable size, it may be much smaller when you print the image or see it at actual size. People often try to put very small text on a very big image and wonder why it's so hard to read. If you aren't sure about the actual size of your document, try going to View→Print Size before typing. This view offers only an approximation, but it helps you get a better idea of what the text will look like in the final version of the image.

Creating Text

Now that you're familiar with the choices in the Tool Options area, you're ready to start putting text in an image. You can add text to an existing image or start with a new, blank file (if you want to create text to use as a graphic by itself, say). To use either the Horizontal or Vertical Type tools, just follow these steps:

1. **Activate a type tool.**

   Click the type icon in the Tools panel or press T, and then select the Horizontal Type tool or the Vertical Type tool in the Tool Options area.

2. **Modify any settings you want to change in the Tool Options.**

   See the previous section for a rundown of your choices. You can make changes after you enter the text, too, so your choices aren't set in stone yet. Elements lets you edit text until you simplify the Text layer. (Page 422 explains what simplifying is.)

3. **Enter some text.**

Click in the image where you'd like the text to go and then start typing. Elements automatically creates a new Text layer for the text. If you're using the Horizontal Type tool, the horizontal line you see is the baseline the letters sit on. If you're typing vertically, the vertical part of the cursor is the centerline of the characters.

Type the way you would in a word processor, pressing Enter/Return to create new lines. Or, if you want Elements to *wrap* the text (adjust it to fit a given space), *drag* in the image with a type tool to create a text box before you start typing. Otherwise, you need to insert returns manually. If you create a text box, you can resize it to adjust the text's flow by dragging the box's handles after you finish typing. (You won't be able to do this anymore after you simplify the layer.)

As noted earlier, if you use the Vertical Type tool, you can't make the columns of text run left to right. So if you need several vertical columns of English text, enter one column and then click the Commit button. Then start over again for the next column, so that each column is on its own layer.

TIP Be careful about clicking when a type tool is active—each click creates a new Text layer. That's great if you're creating lots of separate text boxes to position individually, but it's easy to create a layer without meaning to. If you accidentally make a new layer, just delete it in the Layers panel, or merge it with an existing Text layer.

4. **If necessary, move the text.**

Sometimes the text doesn't end up exactly where you want it. Don't worry about that—as soon as you commit the text (as explained in the next step), the Move tool becomes active and you can drag the text where you want it. If you want to get back to the type tool, just click its Tools panel icon again.

TIP If it drives you nuts to have the Move tool popping up all the time, go to Edit→Preferences→General/ Adobe Photoshop Elements Editor →Preferences→General, and turn off "Select Move Tool after committing text."

5. **When you like what you see, click the green checkmark below the text (or click anywhere else in your image) to commit what you typed.**

When you commit text, you tell Elements that you accept what you've created. The type tool's cursor is no longer active in your photo once you commit.

If you *don't* like what you typed, click the Cancel button (the red circle and slash) below the text instead, and the whole Text layer goes away.

Once you've entered text, you can modify it using most of Elements' editing tools. You can add layer styles to it (page 461), move it with the Move tool, rotate it, change its color, and so on.

Editing Text

In Elements, you can edit text after you enter it, just like in a word processor. Elements lets you change not only the letters, but the font and size, too, even if you've applied lots of layer styles. You modify text by highlighting it and making the correction or by changing your settings in the Tool Options area. Figure 14-4 shows the easy way to highlight text for editing.

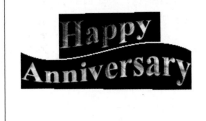

FIGURE 14-4.

If you change your mind about what you typed, no problem. Here, the text is highlighted so that the words can be edited. The best part is that you can change the text to say anything, and all the formatting stays exactly the same. (You can't do this after you simplify a Text layer, though.) If you find it hard to highlight text by dragging, go to the Layers panel and double-click the layer's text icon (the rectangle with the T in it). When you do, Elements highlights all the text on that layer so you can make changes.

TIP As mentioned earlier, you can see the word "Sample" in the font family menu (page 481) displayed in the actual fonts themselves. Even better, Elements gives you a quick way to preview what your particular text will look like in various fonts. First, highlight the text, and then click the name of the current font in the Tool Options area. Then use the up and down arrow keys to move around in the font list. Elements changes the highlighted words in your image so they appear in each font you choose as you go through the list.

You can make all these changes as long as you don't *simplify* the text. Simplifying is the process of changing text from a vector shape that's easy to edit to a rasterized graphic (see the box on page 422 for details). In this respect, text works just like the shapes you learned about in Chapter 12: Once you simplify text, Elements doesn't see it as text anymore, just as a bunch of regular pixels.

You can either simplify text yourself (by selecting Layer→Simplify Layer), or wait for Elements to prompt you to simplify, which it'll do when you try to do things to the text like apply a filter or add an effect. It's usually best not to simplify until you must.

TIP While the text effects that come with Elements don't simplify text, if you download effects, they may *automatically* simplify text without asking first. So make sure you've made all your edits to the text before using any effects you've downloaded.

■ SMOOTHING TEXT: ANTI-ALIASING

You read about anti-aliasing graphics in Chapter 5 (page 156). Anti-aliasing has a similar effect on text: It gets rid of any jaggedness by blending the edge pixels on letters to make the outline look smooth, as shown in Figure 14-5.

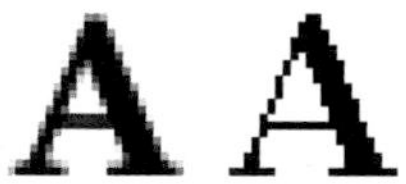

FIGURE 14-5.

An extremely close look at two versions of the same A. The left one has anti-aliasing turned on, making its edges smooth (well, smoother). The edges on the right one are much more jagged and rough looking.

Elements always starts you off with text anti-aliasing turned on, and 99 percent of the time you'll want to keep it on. The main reason to turn it off is to avoid *fringing*—a line of unwanted pixels that make text look like it was cut out of an image with a colored background.

TIP If your text looks really jagged even with anti-aliasing turned on, check your image's resolution: Text often looks poor at low resolution settings, just as photos do. See page 101 for more about resolution.

You turn anti-aliasing on and off with the Tool Options area's Anti-aliasing checkbox. You can also apply this setting by going to Layer→Type→Anti-Alias Off or Layer→Type→Anti-Alias On.

NOTE Once you simplify text, you can't change its anti-aliasing setting.

WORKAROUND WORKSHOP

Using Asian Text Options to Control Spacing

Spacing letters correctly when you're using the Vertical Type tool can be tough. Elements lets you adjust the leading (page 482), but with vertical text, that setting affects the spacing between *columns* of letters, not between the letters within a column. Also, sometimes you may want to adjust the spacing between letters written in horizontal text. Elements lets you make either of these fixes, but you need to enlist the help of the program's Asian Text Options—even if you're writing in English.

To get started, go to Edit→Preferences→Type/Adobe Photoshop Elements Editor→Preferences→Type, turn on the Show Asian Text Options checkbox, and then click OK. Now, the next time you click in an image with a type tool, you'll see the Asian Text options menu in the Tool Options area just below the alignment buttons (page 483). Click the Asian character or the down-pointing arrow to see a pop-out palette with three

options: *Tate-Chuu-Yoko, Mojikumi*, and a drop-down menu with percentages on it. You want the drop-down menu, which is for *Tsume*, a setting that reduces the amount of space around the characters you apply it to.

To apply Tsume, just highlight the characters you want to change in your image, and then select a percentage from the drop-down menu. (The higher the percentage, the tighter the spacing.) You can select a single letter or a whole word when using Tsume. Since it reduces the space all the way around each letter you apply it to, you can use it for either vertical or horizontal text, although for horizontal text, you'll probably use it to tidy up the spacing of just one or two letters. For vertical text, Tsume is a great way to tighten up the spacing of all the characters.

Warping Text

Elements lets you warp text in all sorts of fun ways. You can make it wave like a flag, bulge out, twist like a fish, or arc up or down, among other things. These complex effects are really easy to apply, and best of all, you can still edit the text once you've applied them. Figure 14-6 shows just a few examples of what you can do. If you add a layer style (explained on page 461), too, warping is even more effective.

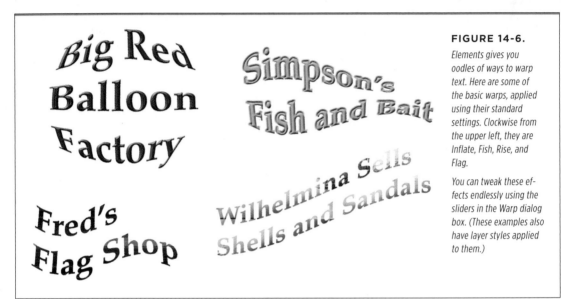

FIGURE 14-6.

Elements gives you oodles of ways to warp text. Here are some of the basic warps, applied using their standard settings. Clockwise from the upper left, they are Inflate, Fish, Rise, and Flag.

You can tweak these effects endlessly using the sliders in the Warp dialog box. (These examples also have layer styles applied to them.)

> **NOTE** Warping text is easy to do, but it's also a bit limited. You can control the amount of warp for the style you choose, but you can't just create a freeform style of your own. The section "Artistic Text" on page 500 has information about the special Elements text tools that give you much more flexibility than warping does.

To warp text, follow these steps:

1. **Enter some text.**

   Use the Move tool to reposition it, if necessary.

2. **Highlight the text you want to warp.**

   Make sure the Text layer is the active layer, or you won't be able to select what you typed. Click the Text layer in the Layers panel if it's not the active layer. To select all the text on the layer, double-click its icon in the Layers panel (the rectangle with the T in it).

3. **In the Tool Options area, click the Create Warped Text button.**

Make sure a type tool is active or you won't see this button (the T with a curved line under it). When you click it, the Warp Text dialog box, shown in Figure 14-7, appears.

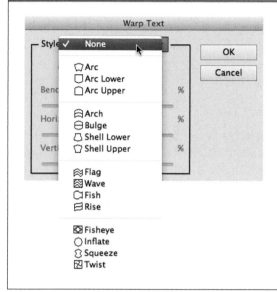

FIGURE 14-7.

As you can see, Elements gives you lots of ways to warp text. The sliders in this dialog box are grayed out until you select an option from the Style menu. After that, you can use the sliders to customize the effect.

4. **In the Warp Text dialog box, tell Elements how to warp the text.**

Select a warp from the Style drop-down list, and then make any changes you want to the sliders or the horizontal/vertical orientation of the warp (your options are described in more detail in a moment). Tweaking these settings can radically alter the warp's effect. Drag the sliders around to experiment, and watch your image to see the results. (You may have to drag the dialog box out of the way to get a good view.)

5. **When you come up with something you like, click OK.**

NOTE You can't warp text that has the Faux Bold style applied to it (you can warp all the other styles to your heart's content). If you forget and try to do so, Elements politely reminds you. The program even offers to remove the style and continue with your warp.

Elements gives you lots of different warp styles to choose from, and you can customize each one using the settings in the Warp Text dialog box. The settings are pretty straightforward:

- **Style.** This is where you choose a warping patterns, like Arc, Flag, or whatever. To help you select, Elements includes thumbnails in the list that show the general shape of each warp.

- **Horizontal/Vertical.** These radio buttons control the warp's orientation. Most of the time, you'll want to leave this setting the same as the text's orientation, but you can get interesting effects by warping the opposite way. A vertical warp on horizontal text gives more of a perspective effect, like the text is moving toward you or away from you. And you can get some really funky effects by putting a horizontal warp on vertical text.

- **Bend.** This is where you tell Elements how much of an arc you want, if you'd like to change it from Element's standard setting. Just type a percentage (click the existing number to type over it) or drag the slider.

- **Horizontal/Vertical Distortion.** These settings control how much the text warps in the horizontal and vertical planes. They give you precise control over just how and where the text warps. They work pretty much the same way as the Bend setting: Type in a negative or positive percentage or drag the sliders.

The best way to find the look you want is to experiment. It's lots of fun, especially if you apply a layer style first to give the text a 3-D look before warping it.

TIP Many of the warps look best on two lines of text, so that the lines bend in opposite directions. However, you can also get really interesting effects by putting two lines of text on separate layers and applying different warps to each one.

To edit a warp after you apply it, double-click the Text layer's Warp icon in the Layers panel (it's a T with a curved line under it). Doing that automatically makes the Text layer active and highlights the text on it. Then, in the Tool Options area, click the Create Warped Text button to open the Warp Text dialog box showing your current settings. Make any changes you want or set the style to None to unwarp the text.

■ Adding Special Effects

Besides warping text, you can apply all kinds of layer styles, filters, and special *text effects* to it to make your words look more elaborate. You can change the text's color, make the letters look 3-D, add brushstrokes for a painted effect, and so on. (There's more about layer styles, filters, and effects in Chapter 13.)

Elements gives you lots of different ways to add special effects to text. The following sections explain three of the most interesting: applying text effects, using a gradient to create rainbow-colored text, and using the Liquify filter to warp text in truly odd ways.

Text Effects

The Graphics panel (page 524) has a whole category dedicated to effects for text (Figure 14-8). You apply these effects just the way you apply any other effect: Select the Text layer in the Layers panel and then double-click the effect you want in the Graphics panel.

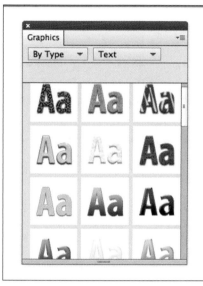

FIGURE 14-8.

The Graphics panel includes a whole section of text effects. Most—like Animal Fur Zebra and Denim—are unique to this section. Others, like Bevel, are just shortcuts for effects you could also achieve using layer styles, gradients, or other Elements tools.

If you've already applied layer styles to your text, it's hard to predict how much these effects will respect the existing layer styles. Some effects build on the changes you've previously made with layer styles, but most undo anything you've done before. Experimenting is the best way to find out what happens when you combine layer styles and effects.

Text Gradients

As you learned in Chapter 13, gradients fill text with a spectrum of color. The simplest way to get these rainbow effects is to apply one of the layer styles or text effects that include a gradient. But those methods don't give you any control over the gradient's colors or direction, so if you have a specific look in mind, you may have to start from scratch and do it yourself. The easiest way is to start with a type mask, as explained on page 495. But if you've already added some text to your image, as long as you haven't simplified the text, you can easily fill it with a gradient.

> **TIP** Heavier, chunkier fonts show off gradients better than thin, spidery ones. Fonts with names that end in Extended, Black, or Extra Bold are good choices, like Arial Black or Rockwell Extra Bold.

First, make sure you've got some text in your image, and then follow these steps:

1. **Create a new layer for the gradient directly above the Text layer.**

   You're going to clip these two layers together (page 198), which is why they need to be next to each other. To create the new layer, press Shift+Ctrl+N/Shift-⌘-N or go to Layer→New→Layer. In the New Layer dialog box, turn on the "Use Previous Layer to Create Clipping Mask" checkbox to clip this new layer to the Text layer below it, and then click OK.

   Look at the Layers panel to be sure the new layer is the active layer and that it's right above the Text layer. If it isn't active, give it a click in the Layers panel to highlight it.

2. **Activate the Gradient tool.**

   Click the Gradient tool in the Tools panel (or press G), and then choose a gradient in the Tool Options area. (See page 465 for more about how to select, modify, and apply gradients.)

3. **Drag across your image in the direction you want the gradient to run.**

   Because this layer is clipped to the Text layer, the gradient appears only in the text. If you don't like the result, press Ctrl+Z/⌘-Z and drag again until you like what you see.

That's all you have to do, except of course save your work if you want to keep it. If you like, you can also activate the Move tool and drag the gradient layer around till your text shows the color range you want. You won't see the gradient layer itself as you move it, but the colors of the text will change.

> **NOTE** You may have noticed that the Smart Brush tool (page 225) includes Rainbow Map as one of the adjustments you can brush onto an image. Sounds like it might be just the ticket for avoiding all this layer-creation business, doesn't it? Unfortunately, it applies a gradient *map* (see page 476) to an image, not a regular gradient. Because text is all the same tonal level, if you brush the Smart Brush's Rainbow Map onto some text, you'll just get a solid, one-color result, not a rainbow or a gradient at all.
>
> However, there are a couple of monochromatic gradients in the Graphics panel's text effects category, so you might want to check those out before trying the steps above. If you just want a single color that fades away, you'll save yourself some effort.

Applying the Liquify Filter to Text

The Tool Options area's Create Warped Text button (explained on page 488) gives you lots of ways to reshape text. But there's an even more powerful way to warp text: the Liquify filter (see Figure 14-9).

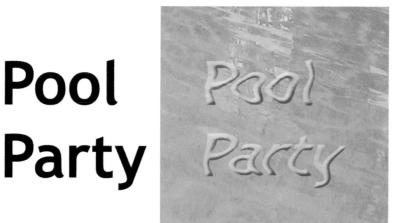

FIGURE 14-9.

The Liquify filter can reshape text in many different ways, including making it undulate like it's underwater (as shown here), making letters twirl around on themselves, or adding a flame-like effect.

Left: Plain black text.

Right: After adding a Wow Plastic layer style, you can use the Liquify filter's Turbulence tool to make the letters look like they're swimming.

> **TIP** You can use the Liquify filter to warp *anything* in an image—not just text. Use it to alter objects in photographs and drawings, for example: Fix someone's nose, make your brother look like E.T., give a scene a watery reflection, and so on.

To use the Liquify filter on text, you first need to simplify the Text layer by going to Layer→Simplify Layer (or, you can wait and click OK when the Liquify filter asks if you want to simplify); just remember that you can't edit text once you simplify it. Then, call up the Liquify dialog box by going to Filter→Distort→Liquify or double-clicking the Liquify filter's thumbnail in the Effects panel's Filter→Distort section. Either way, up pops yet another large Elements dialog box. Like most of them, it's fairly straightforward once you learn your way around it. In the upper-left corner is a little toolbox with some very special tools in it (see Figure 14-10). Each tool has its own keyboard shortcut (listed here in parentheses after the tool's name) that works only in this dialog box. From top to bottom, here they are:

- **Warp tool (W).** This lets you push the image's pixels in any direction, although it may take a fair amount of coaxing to create much of an effect.

- **Turbulence tool (T).** You can use this tool to create clouds and waves. Its effect depends on the Turbulent Jitter setting on the right side of the dialog box (explained in a moment); a higher number creates a smoother effect.

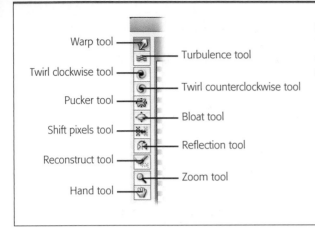

Warp tool

Twirl clockwise tool

Pucker tool

Shift pixels tool

Reconstruct tool

Hand tool

Turbulence tool

Twirl counterclockwise tool

Bloat tool

Reflection tool

Zoom tool

FIGURE 14-10.

The Liquify dialog box's toolbox. Along with the standard Hand and Zoom tools to help you adjust the view as you work, you get highly specialized tools found nowhere else in Elements.

- **Twirl Clockwise tool (C).** If you activate this tool and then click your image and hold down the mouse button, the pixels under your cursor spin clockwise. The longer you apply this tool, the more extreme the effect.

- **Twirl Counterclockwise tool (L).** The opposite of the Twirl Clockwise tool, this one makes the pixels under your cursor spin counterclockwise.

- **Pucker tool (P).** This tool makes the pixels under the cursor move toward the center of the cursor.

- **Bloat tool (B).** The opposite of the Pucker tool, this one makes pixels move *away* from the center of the cursor.

- **Shift Pixels tool (S).** The pixels you drag this tool over move perpendicularly in relation to the direction of your stroke. For example, if you drag from the top of an image straight down, the pixels you pass over move to the right. Alt-drag/ Option-drag to make them shift the opposite way.

- **Reflection tool (M).** Drag to create a reflection of the area the tool passes over. Overlapping strokes create a watery effect.

- **Reconstruct tool (E).** Pass this wonderful tool over areas where you've done too much liquifying, and they return to their original condition without undoing the rest of your changes.

- **Zoom (Z)** and **Hand (H) tools.** These are the same Zoom and Hand tools you find elsewhere in Elements.

Your image appears in the preview window in the center of the dialog box. You can adjust the view with the Zoom tool or by using the magnification menu in the lower-left corner of the dialog box.

> **TIP** It often helps to zoom in really close when using the Liquify filter. If you've added text to a large image, select the text with the Rectangular Marquee tool before activating the Liquify filter. That way you'll see only the selected area in the filter's dialog box, which makes it easier to get a high zoom level.

On the right side of the dialog box are the filter's Tool Options settings:

- **Brush Size.** You can enter a number as low as 1 pixel or as large as 600 here to change the size of your cursor.

- **Brush Pressure.** This controls how much the brush cursor affects the pixels you drag over. The range is from 1 to 100. The higher the pressure, the stronger the effect. If you're using a graphics tablet, turn on the Stylus Pressure checkbox so that the harder you press, the more effect you get.

- **Turbulent Jitter.** This controls how smooth your changes look. The higher the number, the smoother the effect.

- **Stylus Pressure.** Turn this on if you're using a graphics tablet and want the tool to be sensitive to how hard you press.

To use the Liquify filter, just pick a tool from the dialog box's toolbox, adjust the Tool Options (if you want), and then drag across your image. This is a processor-intense filter, so there may be a fair amount of lag time before you see results, especially if your computer is slow. Give Elements time to work.

If you like what you see in the dialog box's preview, click OK and wait a few seconds while Elements applies your transformations; then you're done. If you don't like what you see, you can always have another go at it. Click the Liquify dialog box's Revert button, which returns your image to the condition it was in before you started using the filter. Another option is Alt-clicking/Option-clicking the Cancel button to turn it to a Reset button that resets the dialog box's tool options *and* your image.

Type Masks: Setting an Image in Text

So far in this chapter, you've learned how to create regular text and glam it up by applying layer styles and effects. But in Elements, you can also create text by filling letters with the contents of a photo, as shown in Figure 14-11. (You'll find *sunset.jpg*, the photo used as the basis for Figure 14-11 and Figure 14-12, on this book's Missing CD page at *www.missingmanuals.com/cds*.)

The Type Mask tools work by making a selection in the shape of your letters. Essentially, they create a kind of stencil that you can then place on top of an image.

Once you've used these tools to create text-shaped selections, you can perform all sorts of neat tricks: emboss the text into an image (so that it looks like it's been stamped there); apply a stroke to the text's outline (useful if the font doesn't have a built-in outline option); or copy and move the text to another document entirely.

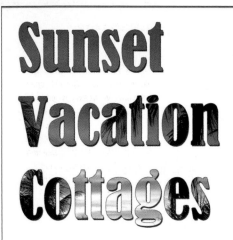

FIGURE 14-11.
Using the Type Mask tools, you can create text that's made from an image. These tools also let you emboss text into a photo (see Figure 14-13).

Using the Type Mask Tools

Here's how to create a type mask and lay it over an image so that the letters are filled with whatever is in the image:

1. **Open the image you want to appear inside the text.**

2. **Activate one of the Type Mask tools.**

   Click the type tool in the Tools panel or press T. Then select the Type Mask tool you want—horizontal or vertical—in the Tool Options area. The Type Mask tools behave just like the regular type tools: A horizontal mask goes across the page, a vertical mask goes up and down. The Type Mask tools also have the same Tool Options settings as the regular type tools, except for Color and Style. It's important to choose a really blocky font for the type mask, since you can't see much of the image if you use thin text.

3. **Click your image and start typing.**

   When you click, a red film covers the image. The red indicates the area that *won't* appear in the letters. By typing, you cut a selection through the red area (see Chapter 5 if you need a refresher on selections). In other words, instead of creating regular text, you're creating a text-shaped selection. You can see the shape of the selection as you type.

   It's hard to reposition the words once you've committed them, so take a good look at what you've got. While the mask is active, you can move it by dragging it, as explained in Figure 14-12.

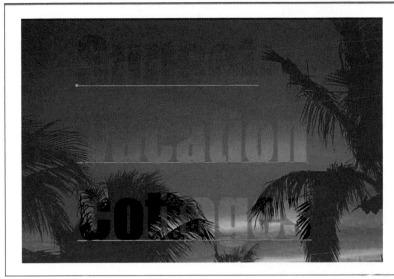

FIGURE 14-12.

Once you've activated the Type Mask tool and clicked in the image, you'll see this red mask appear over the picture. As you type, the text appears, as shown here. As long as you haven't committed the text yet, you can easily move it around by dragging it. You can also rotate or resize the letters by pressing Ctrl/⌘ and then grabbing a corner of the bounding box that appears. When you click the Commit button (the green checkmark), Elements turns the text into a text-shaped selection.

4. **Adjust the Tools Options settings until you like how the text looks.**

   Once you click the Commit button (the green checkmark below the text) in the next step, you can't alter the text as easily as you can with the regular type tools. That's because the regular tools create their own layers, while the Type Mask tools just create selections. Once you commit it, the text is just like any other selection—Elements doesn't see it as text anymore, so you can no longer change its size by highlighting it and picking a different size in the Tool Options, for example.

5. **When you're happy with the selection, click the Commit button.**

   When you click this button, Elements turns the outline of the text into an active selection. You can move the selection's outline by nudging it with the arrow keys, and use the Transform Selection command (page 168) to scoot it around in your image or to resize, transform, or rotate it. (This can make the letters look a little strange, though, so watch the effects carefully.)

6. **Remove the non-text portion of the image.**

   Go to Select→Inverse and then press Backspace/Delete to remove the rest of the image and create letters filled with the image. (If you don't perform this step, you'll just have a text-shaped selection to admire.) Or you can copy and paste the selection into another document.

   If you want a transparent background, double-click the Background layer in the Layers panel to turn it into a regular layer *before* you perform this step. Otherwise, the area outside the letters will be filled with the current Background color.

Figure 14-13 shows the effect of pressing Ctrl+J/⌘-J to place a type mask selection onto a duplicate layer of its own, and then adding layer styles to the new layer.

Creating Outlined Text

If the font you're using doesn't come with a built-in outline style (if it had one, it would appear in the Font Style menu, but very few font families have such a style), Elements gives you three ways to create outlined text. The Graphics panel's text effects (page 491) include an outline effect that you can apply with just a double-click. If you don't like what you get with that, you can also use the Stroke layer styles or the Type Mask tools to outline text. Both of these methods (which are explained in this section) are easy, but they're a bit more time-consuming than using the Graphics panel. On the plus side, they give you more control over the result. Use the layer styles method if you want the text's outline to be filled in; the type mask method gives you an empty outline.

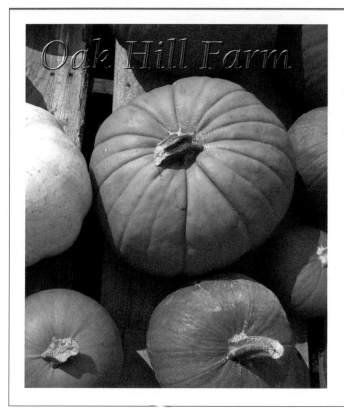

FIGURE 14-13.

By copying text to another layer, you can bevel or emboss it into your photo. This image shows something you need to watch out for—text that's kind of hard to see because it blends into the image. You may need to place your text a few times before it's positioned so that it's legible, or you can add a colored outline to make it stand out more, as described in the next section.

To add an outline to text with the Stroke layer style:

1. **Open an image or create a new one, and then activate a type tool.**

   Click the type tool's icon in the Tools panel or press T until you get either the Horizontal or Vertical Type tool (not the Type *Mask* tool).

2. **Adjust the Tool Options settings.**

   Select a font, size, style, and so on.

3. **Enter some text and commit it.**

   After you type the text, click the green checkmark below it.

4. **Apply a Stroke layer style.**

   Open the Effects panel (choose Window→Effects), click the word "Styles" at the top of the panel, choose Strokes from the panel's drop-down menu, and then double-click the style you want. Even if you don't like any of the Stroke styles, go ahead and pick one; you can edit the results in the next step.

5. **Edit the outline if you wish.**

   In the Layers panel, double-click the Text layer's layer style icon (the little *fx* to the right of the layer's name) to bring up the Style Settings dialog box, where you can change the width and color of the outline (see page 462).

Your other option is to use the Type Mask tool to create a text outline like the one shown in Figure 14-14. Here's how:

1. **Open an image or create a new one (if you just want the text by itself), and then activate the Type Mask tool of your choice.**

   Click the type tool's icon in the Tools panel or press T, and then select either of the Type *Mask* tools.

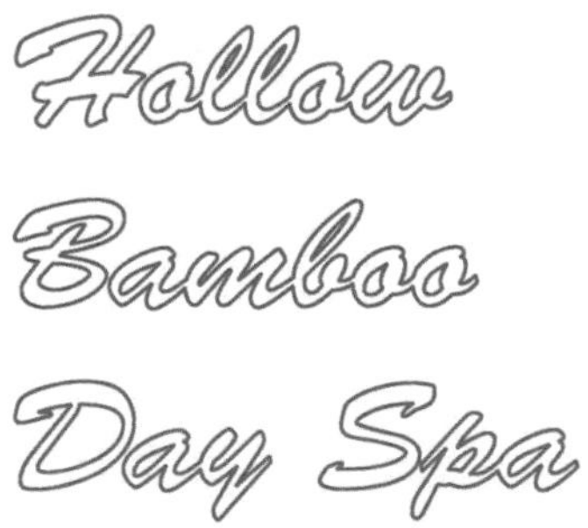

FIGURE 14-14.
The Type Mask tools let you create outlined text almost as quickly as ordinary text.

2. **Choose a font and size.**

   Use the Tool Options settings to pick a font you like, adjust its size, and so on. Outlined text works better with a fairly heavy font rather than a slender one, and bold fonts work better than regular ones.

3. **Enter some text.**

   Click in the image where you want the text to go, and then type away. If you want to warp the text (page 488), do that now, before you commit it.

4. **Click the Commit button (the green checkmark).**

   Be sure you like what you've got before you do this, because once you commit the text, it changes into a selection that's hard to edit. If you'd rather start over, click the Cancel button (the red circle with a slash) instead.

5. **Add an outline to the text.**

   Be sure the text selection is active, and then go to Edit→Stroke (Outline) Selection. In the Stroke dialog box, choose a line width in pixels and the color you want, and then click OK. (Page 428 has details about your other choices in this dialog box.) Your selection turns into an outline of the text you typed.

> **TIP** You can also create a hollow outline using the Stroke layer styles: Type some text, and then simplify the Text layer (Layer→Simplify). Next, go to the Effects panel and choose a stroke layer style in a contrasting color. Then select the color of the text itself (as opposed to the outline) with the Magic Wand (page 154; be sure to turn off the tool's Contiguous setting), and delete that color. The downside to this approach is that you can't edit the text once you simplify it.

■ Artistic Text

Since the early days of Elements, one of the biggest complaints about it has been that, for all the amazing things you can do with other parts of the program, its text-related features were pretty prosaic. You could glam up text with special effects, but it mostly ran left to right or straight up and down.

Elements now offers three tools for adding really fancy text to images: "Text on Selection," "Text on Shape," and "Text on a Custom Path." With these tools, you can make text curve, swoop, and turn, or even run around a circle. They really bump things up when it comes to adding text to images.

All three tools use a concept that used to exist only in full Photoshop: *paths*. A path is just what it sounds like. In the same way that your feet follow a path in the park, a path in Elements is a guideline for where text should go. The path is visible when you're creating it, adding text to it, or editing the Text layer, but it won't appear in the finished image. All folks will see is the cool way you've made the text snake around.

Adding Text to a Selection

The "Text on Selection" tool is pretty simple to use: Just select the object where you want the text and then type away. Here's how to get started:

1. **Open a photo in the Editor.**

    This tool doesn't work well on blank or solid-colored files. If you want to use one of those, use the "Text on Custom Path" tool (explained on page 505) instead, or create a selection before activating this tool (see page 502).

    You don't need to create a separate layer for this maneuver; the tool will automatically put the text on its own layer.

2. **Activate the "Text on Selection" tool.**

    Press T and then click its icon in the Tool Options area, which is a T with a dotted-line square around it.

3. **Select the object where you want the text.**

    When you first click the photo, you see a cursor that looks like the Quick Selection tool's—a circle with a crosshair inside it—and it works the same way. Drag over the area you want to select, and Elements finds the object's edges for you. Keep dragging to add to the area, or Alt-drag/Option-drag to remove part of the selection.

4. **Adjust the size of the selection and accept it.**

    You can use the Tool Options area's Offset slider to make the selection larger or smaller: Drag it left to reduce the size or right to increase it. (However, this slider makes a visible difference only if your image is fairly small; on larger, high-resolution images it has no effect.) When you like the selection, click the green-checkmark Commit button in your image or press Enter/Return to accept the selection. If you want to start over, click the red Cancel button instead or press Esc.

5. **Choose your Tool Options settings.**

    Pick a font, style (regular, bold, or whatever), size, and color, just as you would with the regular type tools.

6. **Enter some text.**

    When you committed your selection in step 3, the outline changed from marching ants to a solid line. That's the path for your text, and it's visible only when this tool is active; click over to another tool and the line disappears. It's just a working guideline, and it won't print, either.

    When you move your cursor close to the line, it changes to the text-insertion I-beam shown in Figure 14-15 to let you know that you can start typing. You can start anywhere on the path and type as much or as little as you want. Just be careful not to overrun the starting point if you type all the way around the selection, or you may lose some of the text.

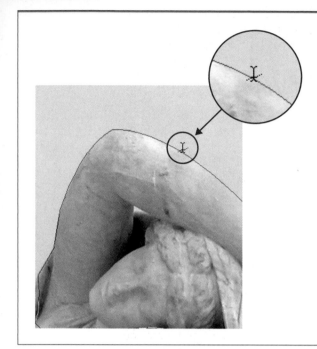

FIGURE 14-15.

When your cursor changes to this shape, you're ready to start typing. If you don't like where the text is going (say it's inside the selection and you want it outside, or vice versa), press and hold Ctrl/⌘ so that a little black arrow appears next to the cursor. Then drag so that it's inside or outside the path and your text will follow it. It's pretty tricky to see what you're doing sometimes because you also see the Move tool bounding box for the selection itself, but you want to be sure you see the I-beam cursor with the tiny arrow next to it before you start dragging.

7. **When you're through typing, click the green Commit button.**

   As with the regular type tools, you can't use Enter/Return to commit the text; you have to click the checkmark. If you don't like the way the text looks, click Cancel instead.

TIP Watch out that you don't overrun the beginning of your text when you're typing your way around the selection. If you do that, parts of the text will disappear. You may be able to backspace your way out of it, but if that doesn't work, you'll have to start over.

That's the basic way to use "Text on Selection", but there are a few tricks that make this tool much more useful than it first appears:

- **Use any kind of selection.** Although this tool gives you only the Quick Selection tool, you can actually create a selection with any tool, which is handy if your image doesn't give this tool much to work with. Just make a selection *before* you use this tool; that way, when you activate the "Text on Selection" tool, you should see the Commit and Cancel buttons in the image. (Click once inside the selection if you don't see them.) Click Commit and you've got yourself a path.

- **Move the text inside or outside the path.** Figure 14-15 explains how to change where the text appears.

- **Move the text's starting point.** If you start typing and then wish you'd started someplace else on the path, go ahead and commit the text anyway. Then make sure the Text layer is active (click it in the Layers panel if it isn't), and you should see an X at the beginning of the text's baseline. Grab that and drag it to move the text where you want it. (If you have trouble doing this, you can also click over to the Shape Selection tool [page 426] and grab the text with that instead.)

> **TIP** The X marks the start of the text, and there's a tiny, almost invisible circle that marks the end of it. If you type so much that the text circles back past your starting point, or if you drag the beginning of the text so it's past the circle, some of the letters you typed will disappear or the text will bunch up in weird places on the path. Find the circle and drag it farther away from the starting point and things should return to normal.

- **Resize the text.** If you wish you'd made the text larger or smaller or that you'd used a different font, that's easy to fix. With any of the text tools active, head over to the Layers panel and double-click the Text layer's icon to select all the text. Then, in the Tool Options area, change the text's font or size till you like what you see. (You can also use the Move and Transform tools on the text, but if you want to change only the letters and not the overall size of the selection, this is the best way to do it.)

- **Resize your selection.** Anytime after you create the selection but before you commit the text, you can hold down Ctrl/⌘ and you'll see the Move tool's handles appear in your image. Drag one, and the text will follow the new shape. Or, after you commit the text, you can use the Move tool to drag a handle. Both methods resize the selection as well as the letters. Just don't try to make the text a *lot* bigger this way, or it may start to look pixelated.

The one thing you can't do is adjust the spacing of individual letters, unfortunately. Despite this limitation, the "Text on Selection" tool is great for adding text to your images in ways that are much more interesting than boring straight lines.

Making Text Outline a Shape

You can also make text outline the shape of a heart or butterfly, for example. This is very popular for scrapbooking and projects like greeting cards. It works pretty much the same way as the "Text on Selection" tool, except you can start with a blank file, if you want. Figure 14-16 shows an example of what you can create.

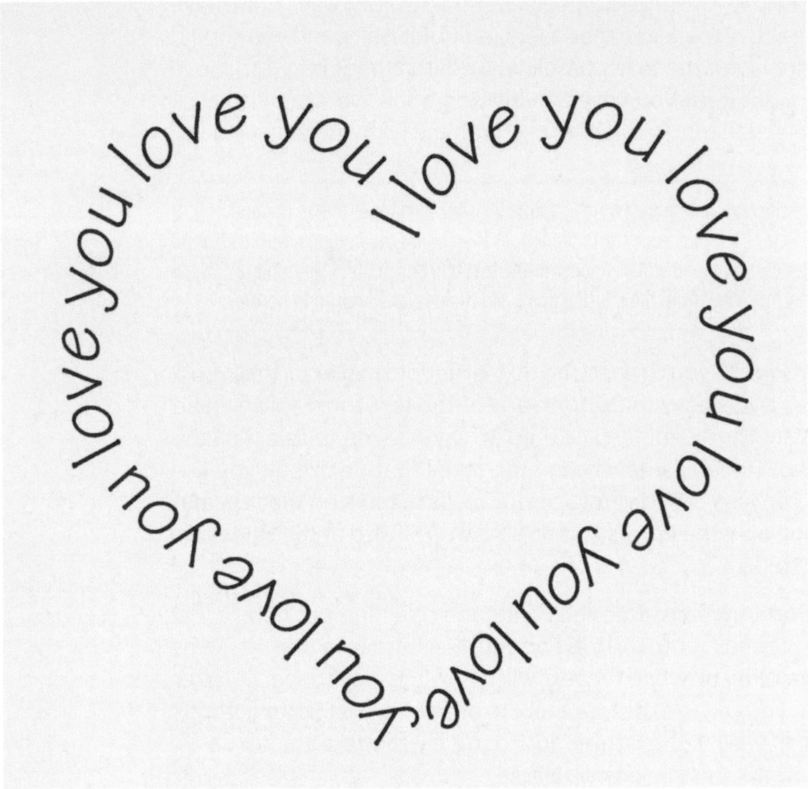

FIGURE 14-16.

Here's a basic example of what you can do with the "Text on Shape" tool. With a pointy shape like this, when you reach the tricky spots, adding a few extra spaces can help keep the letters from piling up in the narrow areas of the shape.

To get started, activate the "Text on Shape" tool by pressing T until you see its icon in the Tools panel, which is a capital T with a squiggly square around it. Then:

1. **In the Tool Options area, choose the shape you want.**

   You don't get to choose from *all* of Elements' shapes: Your only options are rectangle, rounded rectangle, ellipse, polygon, heart, speech bubble, and butterfly. However, the tip at the end of this section explains how to put text around other shapes.

2. **Drag In your image to draw the shape.**

   Once you let go of your mouse, the shape turns into a path, meaning it won't be visible as a shape in the finished image. It's only a guideline for entering text.

3. **Make your font choices in the Tool Options area, click the path where you want the text to start, and then type away.**

The Tool Options settings let you adjust the font, style, size, and color of the text.

4. **When you're done, click the green Commit checkmark.**

If you decide to forget the whole thing, click Cancel instead.

Some of the shapes put the text inside their paths and some put it outside, but you can use the technique explained back in Figure 14-15 to override this and put the text wherever you want it.

TIP You can put text around any shape you want, not just the ones available in the Tool Options area when the "Text on Shape" tool is active. Simply use the Custom Shape tool (page 423) to draw a shape. Next, create a new layer, get out the Magic Wand, and turn on the Sample All Layers checkbox. Then use the Wand to select the shape. Once you have a selection, switch to the "Text on Selection" tool and use it as explained in the previous section. You can delete the Shape layer when you're done if you don't want it to appear in your completed image.

Creating Your Own Path

There's yet another way to make text loop and curve, and it's the most flexible of all: creating a custom path for the text to follow. You can draw a path that's any shape you like, and it works just as well on a blank file as on an image file. In Elements 10 this was the hardest of the three "Text on…" tools to use. In Elements 11, it's probably the easiest. Here's how you use it:

1. **Activate the "Text on Custom Path" tool.**

Press T and then click this tool's icon, which is at the bottom left of the Tool Options area and looks like a T with a squiggle below it.

2. **Draw a path.**

When you activate this tool, your cursor changes to an old-fashioned fountain pen nib. (If it doesn't, head to the Tool Options area and click the pencil icon.) Simply drag to draw a path for the text. You can follow the outline of an object in a photo, or just draw freehand. Like the paths you can create with the Text on Selection and "Text on Shape" tools, what you draw here is a non-printing guideline for entering text.

If you like the path you draw, click the green Commit checkmark and skip to step 4. If you think your path is imperfect but salvageable, continue with step 3. And if you want to start your path over from scratch, click the red Cancel button and try again.

3. Refine the path.

If you aren't thrilled with how your path looks, that's OK, because it's easy to fix. In the Tool Options area, click the Modify button (the gray arrow). Figure 14-17 explains how it works. Once you've got the anchor points adjusted to your liking, click the green Commit checkmark. If you decide it would be easier to start over, then click the red Cancel button instead.

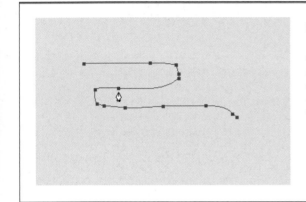

FIGURE 14-17.
When you click the Modify button, you see these little square anchor points, which are something like the ones for the Magnetic Lasso tool (page 158). Drag a point to move it; Alt-click/Option-click a point to remove it; or Shift-click to add a new one. By manipulating the points, you can smooth out a rather bumpy line like this one.

4. Add some text.

After you commit the path, the anchor points disappear and it seems like there's nothing else you can do, but if you move the cursor near the path, you see the I-shaped text-entry cursor appear. But before you start typing, go to the Tool Options and choose a font, style, size, and color. Then click where you want the text to start and type away.

5. Commit the text.

When you're through typing, click the green Commit button. (Click the red Cancel button instead to make the text go away.)

One of the really great things about the "Text on Custom Path" tool is that you can go back anytime and edit any aspect of your work, as long as you don't simplify it (page 422). Just make sure the Text layer is active and then click this tool's Modify button in the Tool Options area, and then you can drag the path all over the place. To edit the text, double-click the Text layer's T icon in the Layers panel to select it. You can also use all the techniques for moving and resizing listed in the "Text on Selection" section (page 502). This is a great tool for adding dramatic text effects to images.

Sharing Images

Creating Projects

If you're into making scrapbooks, greeting cards, or other photo concoctions, Elements is perfect for you. You can dress up pictures in all sorts of creative ways without any other software. Elements is crammed with add-on graphics, frames, and other special effects; it even lets you create multipage documents.

This chapter kicks off with an in-depth look at how to create photo collages. Once you've got those steps under your belt, all the other projects (summarized starting on page 519) use the same basic method. You'll also learn how to create photo books and calendars using Shutterfly, Adobe's online photo-printing partner. (If you aren't in the U.S. or Canada, you may see CeWe as your option for ordering photo books and calendars.) To learn how to create online albums [photo-filled web pages] and slideshows with Elements, flip to Chapter 18.

> **NOTE**   In Elements 11, most of the templates you use for these projects are actually stored online, so you'll need an Internet connection the first time you choose a new template. After that, the template is stored on your hard drive so you don't have to be online to use it, just like the artwork in the Graphics panel (page 524).

Photo Collages

The Create button (at the upper right of your screen in both the Editor and the Organizer) helps you make fancy pages featuring your photos, which you can then share as either printouts or digital files. Although Elements gives you lots of preset layouts to start from, you can customize every aspect of them to create projects that are totally your own.

One type of page you can create is a *photo collage*, which displays one or more photos, with or without a themed background. (Take a look at Figure 15-1 to get a glimpse of what you can do.) Elements starts you off with one basic template crammed with suggested photo placeholders, but you can add or remove photos, as well as change the background, frame styles, and other details.

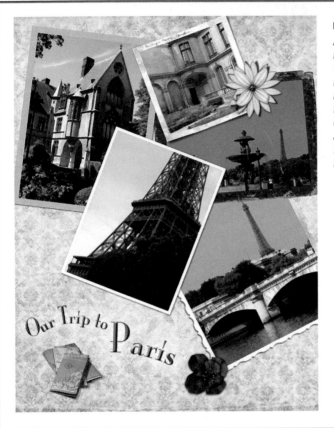

FIGURE 15-1.

All the artwork in this composition except for the photos came from the Graphics part of the Create panel. The photos were added first, their layers merged together, and then several filters were applied to give it a painted effect (see Chapter 13 for more about filters). The curvy text was created using the "Text on Custom Path" tool (page 505), and layer styles were applied to it. Finally, the remaining graphics (the flowers and the maps) were added to make them look like they're lying on a painted page.

To create a photo collage:

1. **Open some photos in the Editor or select them in the Organizer.**

   This step is optional, but if you preselect photos, Elements can automatically place them into the collage for you.

2. **Go to Create→Photo Collage.**

   If you start from the Organizer, Elements bounces you over to the Editor to create the collage. Don't be dismayed by the relatively small size of the window that appears when you start the project. Once you make choices here and then click OK, you'll be back to working in the main Editor window.

NOTE If you've edited any photos and haven't saved the changes, Elements won't place those images into your project. Instead, you see a warning that you need to save the file to use it. So, for example, if you have three photos open, two of which have unsaved changes, Elements will only automatically place the one saved image in your project. For that reason, it's best to make sure your images are all saved before you start a Create project.

3. **Choose a page size from the list on the left side of the Photo Collage window.**

   If you're confused about why it says "Print locally" above the size choices, it's to indicate that this is a project designed for you to print at home. (Some of the other projects, like photo books [page 519], offer online printing, and for those projects you'll see "Shutterfly" above the list of items you can order from them.)

TIP You can't easily rotate the collage sizes to change them from portrait orientation to landscape or vice versa, so if you start a collage and don't like the orientation for the size you choose (8½ x 11 inches is always portrait, for example), you may find it simpler just to create your collage by starting with a blank file in Expert Mode. You can do everything there that you can here—you just don't start out with a pre-designed project, so you have to add all the items you want to include instead of modifying things that are already there.

4. **In the middle of the Photo Collage window, select a theme.**

   Themes add coordinated backgrounds and frames for your photos, and in some cases, coordinated text styles as well. Click a theme's thumbnail to select it, and the right side of the window gives you a closer look at your choice.

   If you don't like any of the existing themes, it doesn't really matter, since you can change every detail once you get to the main Create window. So just pick the theme you dislike the least.

NOTE You may not see any choices other than the cluttered Basic one when you start your first collage, but that doesn't matter. You can quickly get rid of any extra frames in step 7 below.

5. **Tell Elements whether to automatically place your images in the collage.**

   If you leave the "Autofill with Selected Images" checkbox at the bottom of the window turned on, the pictures you chose in the Organizer or Photo Bin in step 1 automatically appear in the collage when Elements creates it. (If you didn't preselect any photos, the currently active photo in the Editor gets added, if you have any photos open there.) If *you* want to determine which photos go into which slots, turn off this checkbox.

NOTE Unlike some earlier versions of Elements, the Create projects in Elements 11 start with a fixed number of pages. If you've selected more photos than will fit in your current layout choice, Elements just doesn't place them, rather than automatically increasing the page count to accommodate the extra photos the way, say, Elements 8 did. A collage can only be one page long. So if you want more pages, create a separate file for each one.

6. **When you've made your choices, click OK.**

Elements sends you back to the main Create window and gets to work creating the collage. When it's done thinking, it displays the collage in the editing area.

If you preselected photos and left the Autofill checkbox turned on, Elements puts the photos into frames for you. (It puts each image in the collage on its own layer.) If you didn't select any photos (or if you didn't select enough to fill all the slots), you see "Click here to add photo or Drag photo here" inside each empty frame. That's fine, because you can add photos in step 8.

At this point, you're working in what Adobe calls Basic mode, explained in Figure 15-2.

7. **Choose a layout.**

After Elements creates the collage, the Create panel displays new options. At the bottom left of the panel is an icon labeled Pages. A collage has only one page, so when you click this icon, your page's thumbnail is displayed in its lonely glory. (For projects like photo books that have multiple pages, this is where you'd navigate among thumbnails of the project's different pages.)

If you like the preview that Elements shows you, there's no need to change anything. But if you click the Layouts icon below the Create panel, you see a bunch of alternative designs, grouped by the number of photos per page. To audition a different layout, either double-click its thumbnail or drag it onto the collage in the preview area. If you don't like it, undo it (Ctrl+Z/⌘-Z) and try another one.

TIP   If you plan to use only a couple of photos, one fast way to get rid of the extra photo slots in the Basic layout is to scroll down the Create panel till you see a layout with only one or two photos. Double-click the layout you want and the extra frames go away.

---

8. **Adjust the photos.**

If you haven't already picked photos for this project, drag a photo from the Photo Bin into a frame, or click an empty frame in the collage and then choose a photo from the dialog box that appears. (If you don't see the Photo Bin, click the Photo Bin button below the preview area to display it.)

Regardless of how you get photos into the collage, you can make a number of adjustments to them once they're there. The next section (page 514) explains everything you can do with photos and frames in a Create project, but for now, here are a couple of quick adjustments you can make:

- Once you click a frame, you should see the Move tool's bounding box around it. (If you want to see the Move Tool's Tool Options, just click the Tool Options button below the preview area.) Use the Move tool to stack your photos in the right order, and align or distribute them if you want.

- You can change a frame's style by clicking the Graphics button below the Create panel. Then, to change to a new frame, double-click the new style, or drag it onto the photo.

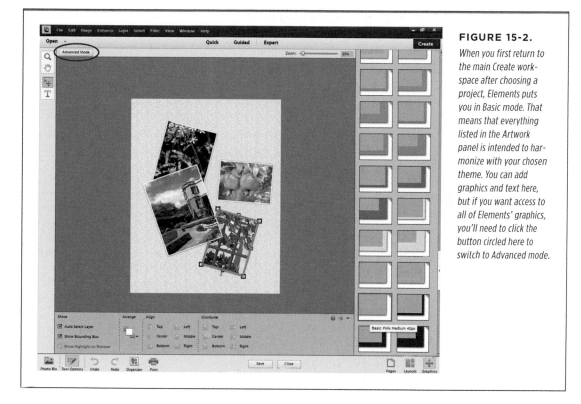

FIGURE 15-2.

When you first return to the main Create workspace after choosing a project, Elements puts you in Basic mode. That means that everything listed in the Artwork panel is intended to harmonize with your chosen theme. You can add graphics and text here, but if you want access to all of Elements' graphics, you'll need to click the button circled here to switch to Advanced mode.

9. **Customize the collage.**

   - This is the fun part. Click a photo in your collage and drag it into a different position. Or click the Graphics button below the Create panel and then drag art from the panel onto your collage (these graphics are vector images [page 422], so they'll look great no matter how big or small you make them). You can also add text to the collage.

   If you switch to Advanced mode (page 517), you can even flatten your image and use filters on the entire page. Figure 15-1 shows an example of what you can create with a photo collage.

10. **Finish up your collage.**

    When you're done, you have a couple of choices of what to do next:

    - Click Save at the bottom of the Create workspace to bring up the Save As window so you can name the project and save it. You can save it in any standard file format if it's a one-page collage, but for projects with more than one page (like calendars), you have to save it as a PSE file—a special format just for multi-page Elements documents (see the box on page 520 for details)—or a PDF file. (If you decide you don't like your collage, click Close at the bottom of the Create workspace instead and then tell Elements not to save your file when it asks.)

> **TIP** While you can wait till you're done to save your collage, you might want to use the Save button regularly as you work so you don't risk losing anything in case of a crash. You don't actually have to use the Save button at all—you can just click the Close button to leave Create and Elements will ask you about saving—but this route is a little risky, especially if you've put a lot of time into your project.

- You can also print your collage right from Create, the way you would any other file (see Chapter 16). Just click the Print button at the very bottom of the Elements window, or press Ctrl+P/⌘-P.

> **NOTE** Once you save a Create project, what happens the next time you open the file varies depending on what type of project it is. If you save and close a collage, for instance, the next time you open it, it will open in the regular Editor rather than Create. That's OK, because you can do anything you want to the collage in the Editor. This is also true for the other projects, like CD and DVD labels, that you can only print at home. On the other hand, projects you can order online, like photo books and greeting cards, always open back up in Create.

Customizing Your Project

There's almost no limit to what you can do in a photo collage. Anything you've read in the other chapters of this book works here, too. Plus you can do a few special things with photos in a collage. This section explains your options.

■ ADJUSTING PHOTOS AND FRAMES

Elements gives you a ton of ways to tweak the photos in a collage:

- **Rotate a photo in its frame.** Right-click/Control-click a photo and choose Rotate 90 Right or Rotate 90 Left to turn the photo 90 degrees clockwise or counterclockwise.

- **Adjust the way a photo appears in its frame.** Right-click/Control-click a photo and choose "Position Photo in Frame" (or just double-click it) to bring up the controls explained in Figure 15-3.

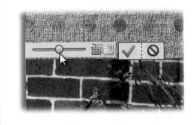

FIGURE 15-3.

When you double-click a photo in a Create project, you get these controls for adjusting it. (If you have trouble bringing them up, try clicking the Move tool in the Create workspace's toolbox before you double-click the photo.) You can resize the picture with the slider, rotate the photo by clicking the blue rectangles next to the slider, or search for a new photo by clicking the yellow folder icon. You can also drag a handle of the photo's bounding box to resize the photo or rotate it, just the way you'd use the Move tool. When it looks good, click the green checkmark to accept your changes.

- **Remove a photo from the collage.** Right-click/Control-click the photo and then choose Clear Photo. To remove the photo's placeholder and frame as well, just click the photo to select it and then press Backspace/Delete.

- **Remove a frame from a photo.** Right-click/Control-click and then choose Clear Frame.

- **Resize a frame.** You can resize a frame either before or after you put a photo into it. Click the frame once to bring up resizing handles, and then drag a corner handle to make the frame larger or smaller. You can also rotate a framed photo using these handles.

- **Resize a frame to fit a photo.** If you want to make a frame fit a photo, instead of the other way around, right-click/Control-click the photo and then choose "Fit Frame to Photo."

- **Edit a photo.** Right-click/Control-click the photo and choose Edit Quick; and Elements whisks your photo off to Quick Fix so you can make any last-minute fixes. When you're finished, click the "Back to Creations" button above the top left of the image preview area. (For some reason, the Edit Quick option is grayed out in certain types of projects. So it works for photo books, but usually not for collages.)

- **Add another photo.** Just drag a frame from the Create panel's Graphics section (you may need to click Graphics below the panel to see it) to a blank area of the collage, and then click within the frame to add a photo. (If you get too close to an existing frame, the new frame may replace the existing one. If that happens, just press Ctrl+Z/⌘-Z to undo it and then drag again, more carefully, to the blank spot.) You can also drag a photo into the collage from the Photo Bin.

- **Edit a frame's layer style.** Most of the Create panel's frames have layer styles applied to them. Right-click/Control-click a frame in the collage and choose Edit Layer Style to change things like the size of the frame's drop shadow. You can also edit the styles from the Layers panel in Advanced mode (page 517) the same way you'd edit any layer style (see page 462).

- **Add a filter to a photo.** If you click over to Advanced mode (see page 517), you get access to all of Elements' filters (page 435) so you can quickly create a brushed look or a rubber-stamp effect, for example. However, you have to simplify the photo's layer before you can use filters on it (page 422 explains simplifying).

■ ADDING GRAPHICS AND TEXT

It's really easy to add all sorts of embellishments to a collage. Click the Graphics button below the Create panel to see a long list of stuff designed to harmonize with your current theme. The list is divided into three categories:

- **Backgrounds.** If you don't like the look of the page's background, just drag in a new one. Drop it anywhere in the preview area (or just double-click the one you want), and Elements replaces the existing background with it. (Backgrounds are Smart Objects, which are explained in the box on page 518.)

- **Frames.** Elements includes some very fancy frames. Some of them tint your photo; you can tell which ones will do this by looking at the part of a frame's thumbnail where the picture will go—if it's colored red or blue, for example, then the photo will get tinted that color. Others cut your photo into various shapes. This section includes all kinds of interesting ways to frame your photos, so try a few to see which ones you like. Just double-click one or drop it onto a photo to use it.

- **Graphics.** You can add all sorts of clip art to your Create projects. The great thing about these graphics is that they're vector objects (page 422), so you can resize them as much as you want without having them go all pixely, as long as you don't simplify them (page 422). The thumbnails in the Graphics section may look a little funny and so may the graphics after you drag their handles to make them bigger, but once you press Enter/Return, they should settle down into perfect detail.

TIP If you don't like scrolling through all the Create panel's artwork, click the arrow to the right of a category's name to collapse that section and bring the next one up into view.

In Basic mode, there's a little toolbox on the left side of the Create workspace. In addition to the same Hand, Zoom, and Move tools you're already familiar with, you get the regular Elements type tools (page 479) so that you can add text to your collage as described in Figure 15-4. You can also zoom the view by using the slider above the right side of the preview area.

■ CREATE MODES: BASIC AND ADVANCED

When you first start working on a Create project in the main Elements window, you're automatically in Basic mode. That means the Create panel shows you only options (like frames and graphics) that Adobe thinks would work well in your particular project. And the only tools available to you on the left side of the screen are the Move, Zoom, Hand, and Type tools. (Figure 15-2 shows what Basic mode looks like.)

You can put together a pretty impressive project working in Basic mode, but Adobe knows that you may want to do a lot more with your project, so it created Advanced mode. To use this mode, click the Advanced Mode button above the left side of the preview area (circled in Figure 15-2). When you do, you get a whole different set of options. The regular Elements toolbox appears on the left side of the screen, along with the Layers panel on the right side. And when you click the Graphics button below the Create panel, you see *all* of Elements' graphics options, not just its suggested choices.

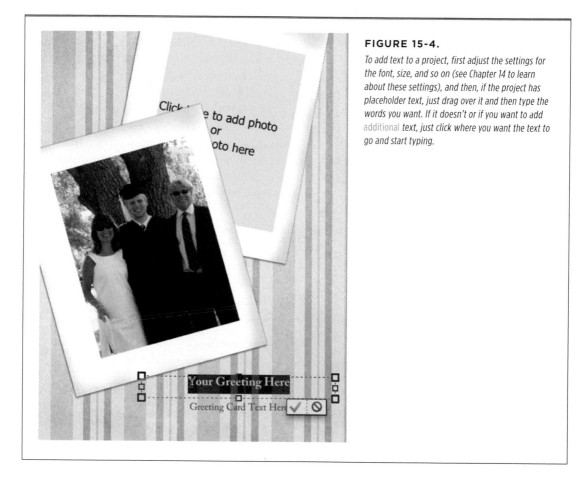

FIGURE 15-4.

To add text to a project, first adjust the settings for the font, size, and so on (see Chapter 14 to learn about these settings), and then, if the project has placeholder text, just drag over it and then type the words you want. If it doesn't or if you want to add additional text, just click where you want the text to go and start typing.

You can toggle back and forth between the two modes as much as you like. Simply click the button above the main preview area to change modes. As a general rule, there's not much point in sticking with Basic mode for collages, since your choices are limited and a bit random, but for projects like photo books, Basic mode offers handy groupings of coordinated content to add to your project.

Smart Objects

Smart Objects are one of the ways Adobe makes Elements' Create projects so fun and easy. Like their big-shot cousins in the full version of Photoshop, these objects seem to know where they are and what you're trying to do—and behave accordingly. Here are some examples of Smart Objects and what makes them so smart:

- When you apply a new background from the Graphics panel or the Graphics section of the Create panel, it automatically zooms down to the bottom of the layer stack to replace the existing background.

- The frames from the Graphics and Create panels automatically target your photos. Want to frame an image? Just go to the Graphics panel and double-click a frame. It automatically appears in your project, though you may need to adjust its size or the area that it frames once it's there.

- You can resize, transform, and distort objects from the Graphics panel's Graphics section as much as you want without affecting their quality. This behavior is something like how vector art works, but what's going on under the hood is quite different. (The preview may appear pixelated, but the actual object should be OK once you click the green checkmark Commit button.)

Anything you put into an Elements file in Expert Mode by choosing File→Place becomes a Smart Object, so you can do things like resize the object to any size. Also, anything you drag into one of the Create projects (photos, graphics, whatever) becomes a Smart Object. However, there are a few things you can do to Smart Objects only if you simplify them (page 422). For example, if you try to paint on a Smart Object, you just get the dialog box shown in Figure 15-5.

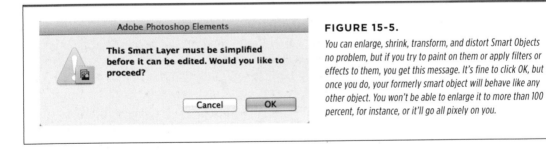

FIGURE 15-5.

You can enlarge, shrink, transform, and distort Smart Objects no problem, but if you try to paint on them or apply filters or effects to them, you get this message. It's fine to click OK, but once you do, your formerly smart object will behave like any other object. You won't be able to enlarge it to more than 100 percent, for instance, or it'll go all pixely on you.

NOTE In Elements 11, photo books and calendars are the only kind of Create projects that let you create a file with more than one page. You can't add pages to any kind of project except a photo book, and there's no way to add extra pages to a file in the Editor anymore.

■ Photo Books

Elements lets you create several sizes of pages to use in bound books of photos, which are a popular gift item. To get started, go to Create→Photo Book, and you'll see several different sizes to choose from. When you click a size on the left side of the Photo Book window, the right side changes to show details about it, as you can see in Figure 15-6. Most photo books are meant to be ordered online, but there's an 8½" x 11" size (well, technically 11" x 8½") that you can print at home. In fact, you can actually print *any* Create project on your home printer, if you like.

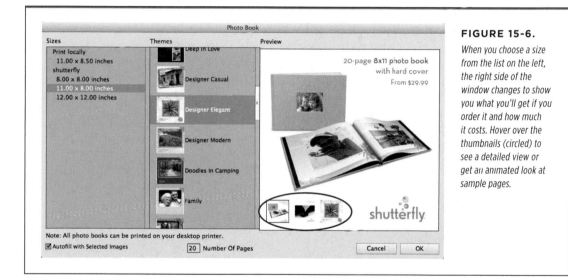

FIGURE 15-6.

When you choose a size from the list on the left, the right side of the window changes to show you what you'll get if you order it and how much it costs. Hover over the thumbnails (circled) to see a detailed view or get an animated look at sample pages.

About PSE Files

Anytime you create a multipage document in Elements, you get only one editable file format choice when it's time to save: PSE. (If you save your project as a PDF instead, you won't be able to go back and edit it later.) This special format has both advantages and disadvantages.

When you create a PSE file, you actually create a *folder* containing a separate .psd file for each page (or for each double-page spread if you're creating a photo book), and a PSE *project file* that contains all the info Elements needs to reassemble the document the next time you open it. That's handy when you're working in Elements, but the drawback is that hardly any other program can read these files. However, PSE files work just fine if you print at home or use Shutterfly for online printing; you can send them to Shutterfly as easily as you send JPEGs.

The rub comes when you want to use a different printing service. If you make, say, a book that you want to print at Lulu. com or MyPublisher.com, they don't accept PSE files—at least not as of this writing. Most printing services require PDF files instead. Fortunately, Elements can save your multipage PSE file as a multipage PDF that you can upload to your printing service of choice. (Be aware, though, that Elements creates *huge* PDF files.) Usually, you'll want to wait till you're through editing your project to create a PDF. So keep the file in PSE format as long as you still have work to do, and then save it as a PDF when you're ready to send it out to a printer other than Shutterfly. There's also an Export command under the File menu; select it and Elements saves all the pages of your photo book as separate JPGs or TIFs, or as a single PDF file.

At the bottom center of the Photo Book window is a box where you can enter the number of pages you want, if you know how long you want the book to be. However, the photo books from Shutterfly automatically start out with 20 pages, since that's the minimum number you need to order from it (Shutterfly's maximum is 100 pages plus the title page), so you can't delete pages to bring the total below 20. If you want to make a four- or 10-page book, then choose the 11" x 8½" "print locally" option.

NOTE The minimum number of pages required for books printed by Shutterfly is subject to change, so don't be surprised if one day you see a different number in that window. It just means it changed its minimum.

Creating a photo book is almost exactly like creating a collage (page 509). The only difference is that you have lots of pages to navigate through in the Create panel's Pages pane (click the Pages button below the panel to see it). Just click a different two-page spread to work on those pages. (Elements shows you the double-page spreads you'll see when the book is open.) You can also use the controls above the preview area to step through pages.

NOTE Photo books usually have a cutout front cover, so the first page is the title page.

To add pages to a photo book, in the Pages pane, click the thumbnail of the double-page spread you want to duplicate and then click the Add Page icon at the top of the Pages panel, as explained in Figure 15-7. To remove a double-page spread (you can't remove just one page), click its thumbnail and then click the trash-can icon. (Keep in mind that Elements won't let you go below the minimum number of pages for the Shutterfly books.) To change the order of pages in a photo book, drag their thumbnails around in the Pages tab.

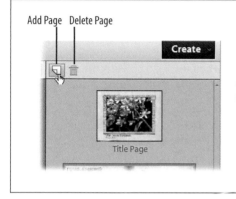

Add Page Delete Page

FIGURE 15-7.

To add another double-page spread to a photo book, click the thumbnail of a page with the layout you want (or the one most like it), and then click the Add Page icon. You can then drag the new page thumbnail to where you want it. (In Elements 11, photo books are the only type of file where you can add pages this way.) To delete pages, click their thumbnails, and then click the little trash can.

When you finish creating the book, you can click Save or Print as with a collage and, if you chose one of the Shutterfly options in the Photo Book window, there's also an Order button below the preview area that zips you over to Shutterfly so you can order the book from it. If you want to order the book from another company, just save the file in PDF format, which is accepted almost everywhere.

To save a photo book file, click the Save button. You need to choose the Photo Project Format if you want to edit the book again later. If you're already done editing, you can also save it as a PDF file. Or you can use the Export command as explained in the box on page 520. Photo book files have a special icon in the Photo Bin and Organizer that looks like a little stack of pages, but you can't expand it in the bin to see individual pages the way you could in some earlier versions of Elements.

TIP You can create a book of photos without using Elements' Photo Book feature at all. Just open a web browser and head to the Shutterfly website, upload your photos (as explained on page 528), and then have the company print them in its own style of photo book.

▊ Greeting Cards

For greeting cards, Elements lets you choose from several different layouts: some single-page options and several folded styles. And although they're all templates for cards from Shutterfly, you can also print them at home. The process for creating a card is the same as for a collage (page 509) or photo book.

▊ Photo Calendars

You can make very nice wall calendars in Elements. To get started, go to Create→Photo Calendar. In the Photo Calendar window, pick a month and year for the calendar's starting point and choose a theme for it. As with the other Create projects, you get a nice animated view of the style you choose.

After you click OK, you can customize each month in all the usual ways (add or remove photos, change the background, add artwork, and so on) explained earlier in this chapter. There's also a special way to customize specific dates, as Figure 15-8 explains.

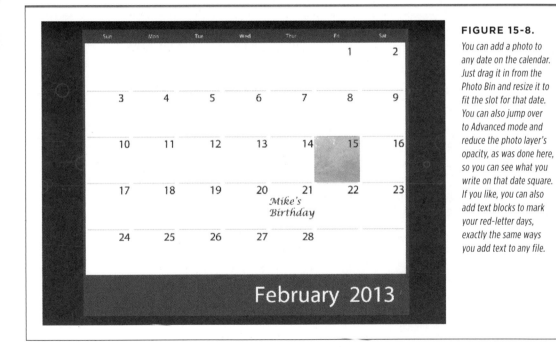

FIGURE 15-8.

You can add a photo to any date on the calendar. Just drag it in from the Photo Bin and resize it to fit the slot for that date. You can also jump over to Advanced mode and reduce the photo layer's opacity, as was done here, so you can see what you write on that date square. If you like, you can also add text blocks to mark your red-letter days, exactly the same ways you add text to any file.

Elements' calendars are designed to use a different photo or group of photos for each month, but if you want to see the same photo of your honey every month, you can do that, too. Just keep dragging it into the layout for each month where you want it to appear.

CD/DVD Jackets

Elements lets you create CD jewel case inserts and DVD inserts, which appear on the front and back of the case. To make a CD insert in either the Editor or the Organizer, just go to Create→CD Jacket.

The steps for creating a CD jacket are the same as for a photo collage (page 509) except that the layout choices are, of course, different. There's only one template, but you see several layouts when you click the Layouts button at the bottom of the window. Pay special attention to photo placement when choosing a layout; remember that the right side of the layout is the front cover. Turn the "Autofill with Selected Images" checkbox off or on to suit you.

Unfortunately, only the "2 Centered" layout even approximately marks out the general spine area, where most CDs display their titles. (Put your cursor over the various layouts—without clicking—to see what they're called.) If you decide to enter text that you want to appear on the spine, add a text block, and then either rotate the completed text into position with the Move tool, or switch to Advanced mode (page 517) and use the Rotate commands (page 78).

The DVD Jacket wizard (Create→DVD Jacket) is identical except for the layout choices.

CD/DVD Labels

You can create stick-on labels for CDs and DVDs with Elements and print them on blank label sheets from any office supply store. To get started, go to Create→CD/DVD Label. As with the CD/DVD jackets, Elements gives you one template with various choices in the Layouts pane. They all create a single label. When you're done, place your work into the template that goes with your specific brand of labels. (Most CD or DVD labels print two to a page.) The major brands, like Avery (*www.avery.com*) and Neato (*www.neato.com*), have free templates you can download from their websites to help you position the labels properly on the page.

While labels make your discs look great, it's risky to put a stick-on label on any disc you'll use in a computer because, if the label gets stuck in the disk drive, you may have to replace the drive. Consider using a marker to label discs instead, or buying printable discs if your printer can print on them.

■ Working with the Graphics and Favorites Panels

If you like all the graphics, frames, and other artistic goodies you can use in Create, you'll be happy to know you have access to all that stuff for *any* image, not just ones in Create projects. It all lives in the Graphics panel, which you can call up anytime in Expert Mode. You also get the Favorites panel, where you can keep the Graphics- and Effects-panel items you use most often. This section gives you a guided tour of both these panels.

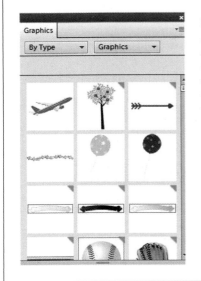

FIGURE 15-9.

Using the Graphics panel is very easy. Just use the left menu to choose how you want to search, and then use the right menu to refine your choice. Here you see the results of choosing By Type and Graphics. Notice that most of the thumbnails pictured here show a tiny blue banner at their upper-right corner. The first time you use a graphic marked with that banner, Elements has to download it, so you'll need an Internet connection. After it's been downloaded once, it's on your computer so it's always available, whether you're online or not.

The Graphics Panel

This panel got a makeover in Elements 11, so it's much easier to navigate through all the goodies it contains (see Figure 15-9). Here's how to use it to glam up your images:

1. **In Expert Mode, make sure the panel is visible.**

    If it's not already visible, go to Window→Graphics, or if you're in the Editor's Basic mode (as opposed to Create's Basic mode), click the Graphics button below the Panel Bin.

2. **Choose how you want to search for fun additions to your image.**

    At the top of the panel are two drop-down menus. In the left-hand menu, choose what you want to search by (like activity, word, or mood), or choose Show All to see everything in the panel.

3. **Refine your search.**

In the panel's right-hand drop-down menu, choose what you specifically want. What's in this menu changes depending on what you selected in the left-hand menu. So if you choose By Type on the left, you see Backgrounds, Frames, Graphics, and so on in this menu. If you choose By Mood on the left instead, the right-hand menu offers you choices like Active, Adventurous, Fun, Romantic, and Thoughtful.

> **NOTE** You can also search by name if you know what you're looking for. Choose By Word in the left menu and Elements presents you with a text box where you can type in the name or keyword for what you want. (To see the keywords associated with a particular item in the panel, right-click/Control-click it and choose Details from the pop-out menu.)

4. **Add the goody to your image.**

To use anything in the Graphics panel, double-click its thumbnail or drag it onto your image. Every item you add comes in on its own layer.

To remove what you've added, press Ctrl+Z/⌘-Z if you just added it, or click the object with the Move tool and then press Backspace/Delete. If you use the Backspace/Delete key, Elements asks if you want to "Delete the Layer"—you do, so click OK. (Chapter 6 is all about layers.) If you just hate a particular item in the panel and want it gone forever, right-click/Control-click it and choose Delete Graphics from the pop-out menu. (This is grayed out for online items that you haven't yet downloaded, logically enough.)

If that seems like a lot of navigation, check out the Favorites panel (described next) for a faster way to reach Graphics panel items you use a lot.

> **NOTE** The full Graphics panel isn't available in Create's Basic mode. Just switch over to Advanced mode (page 517) and you can use everything it contains.

The Favorites Panel

If you use the same effects, graphics, and styles over and over, you may find it tedious to keep navigating to them in the Graphics or Effects panels. Simplify things by saving your Graphics and Effects standbys in the Favorites panel. That way, you can get to them with just a click or two. To see the Favorites panel, go to Window→Favorites.

> **NOTE** Adobe has chosen to select a few favorites for you, so you'll probably want to delete their choices before you start adding your own.

To add an item to this panel, right-click/Control-click its thumbnail in the Graphics or Effects panel, and then choose "Add to Favorites," or just drag its thumbnail to the Favorites panel. To delete a favorite, right-click/Control-click its thumbnail in the Favorites panel and then choose "Remove from Favorites," or click it once to highlight it, and then click the trash-can icon at the top of the panel. (Unlike with the Graphics panel, trashing something here just removes it from the Favorites panel, not from Elements altogether.) If you forget what one of your favorites is for, right-click its thumbnail and choose Details to see a description of it.

Printing Photos

N ow that you've gone to so much trouble to make your photos look terrific, you no doubt want to share your masterpieces with other people. This chapter and the next two look at the many different options Elements gives you for sharing photos with the world at large.

This chapter covers the traditional method: printing photos. You can print them at home on an inkjet printer, take them to a kiosk at a local store, or order prints online. Elements makes it especially simple to use Shutterfly, Adobe's online printing partner. You also get an easy connection to several other popular online photo services (page 591). The best thing about ordering prints online is that you're not limited to just ordinary prints: You can create hardcover books, calendars, embarrassing t-shirts—you name it.

It's worth noting that while the basics of printing are the same whether you're using a Windows computer or a Mac, some things are a bit different between the two platforms. As you go through this chapter, you'll see the differences noted as they come up.

▊ Getting Ready to Print

Whether you're printing at home or sending photos to a printing service, you need to make sure your image files are set up to create good-looking prints.

The first thing to check is the photo's resolution, which controls the number of pixels per inch (ppi) in the image. If the photo doesn't have enough pixels, then the print will look grainy and pixelated. Most photo aficionados consider 300 ppi ideal; a quality print needs a resolution of at least 150 ppi to avoid the grainy look you see in low-resolution photos. See page 105 to learn how to check and—if necessary—tweak a photo's resolution.

> **TIP** Be sure to set the resolution to a whole number—using decimals may make some printers print black lines on your photos. For example, 247 ppi is fine, but 247.35 ppi may cause problems. (Older printers are most likely to have trouble with decimals.)

If you're printing on photo paper or sending photos out for printing, make sure the images are cropped to fit a standard photo paper size. (Cropping is covered starting on page 85.) And if you're printing at home, the paper and ink you use make a big difference in the color and quality of the prints. It may seem like just a marketing scam, but you really *will* get the best results by using the paper and ink your printer manufacturer recommends.

Ordering Prints

You don't need to own a printer to print photos, because there's no shortage of companies hoping you'll give them the privilege of doing it for you. You can order prints online or use a print kiosk at a local store. Elements makes it really easy to prepare photos for printing either way. Just save the photos in a compatible file format (see page 67 for more about picking a format). JPEG format is usually your best bet, but always check with the service you plan to use to see if it has any special requirements.

If you're going to physically take your photos somewhere for printing (as opposed to ordering them online), you can burn the photos to a CD to take in. Use the Organizer to export the photos to the desktop using the dialog box shown in Figure 16-1.

First, in the Organizer, select the photos. Then choose File→Export As New File(s) to call up the dialog box shown in Figure 16-1. Pick a new file format in the File Type section, if necessary (say you have TIFFs and the store wants JPEGs, for example). In the "Size and Quality" section, choose maximum quality (the Quality slider becomes active when you choose JPEG as the file type), and leave Photo Size set to Original. In the Location section, click the Browse button and choose your desktop. If you want to rename the files, type something in the Common Base Name field and Elements gives each exported file that new name followed by -1, -2, -3, and so on. When everything looks good, click Export, and Elements sends the files to your desktop so you can burn them to a CD. (The Windows version of Elements has always been able to do this, but this is the first time this Export command has been available in the Mac Organizer.) Then use your computer's CD-creation program to burn the exported photos to a disc, or just copy them to a memory card or a portable USB drive.

Adobe has partnered with the popular online photo-printing service Shutterfly to make it simple to upload photos directly from Elements. You can order prints, books, or any of the other photo-bearing items that they would love to sell you. Of course, you're free to use any *other* online printing service (see page 591 for some suggestions), but ordering from them isn't integrated right into Elements the way it is with Shutterfly. (Outside North America, you may see CeWe as your option for ordering prints online.)

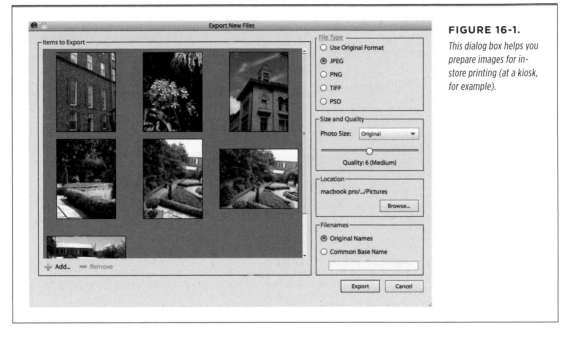

FIGURE 16-1.

This dialog box helps you prepare images for in-store printing (at a kiosk, for example).

Once you've edited some photos and are ready to place an order, just follow these steps (they're the same for both Macs and PCs):

1. **Select the photos you want to have printed.**

   Open them in the Editor, or select them in the Organizer. (Your photos don't have to be in the Organizer if you start from the Editor, and they aren't added to the Organizer automatically when you order prints.)

2. **Connect to Shutterfly and sign in.**

   You can order prints from Shutterfly from either the Editor or the Organizer:

   - **File menu.** Go to File→Order Prints→Order Shutterfly Prints.

   - **Create tab.** Go to Create→Photo Prints, and then choose Shutterfly from the list of options that appears.

   Regardless of where you start, Elements sends you to the Organizer (if you're not already there), prepares your photos, connects to Shutterfly, and opens the Shutterfly window. You need to log in before you can order, or to create an account if it's the first time you're using Shutterfly. An easy-to-follow series of guided question screens appears to help you set up an account and complete your order (see Figure 16-2).

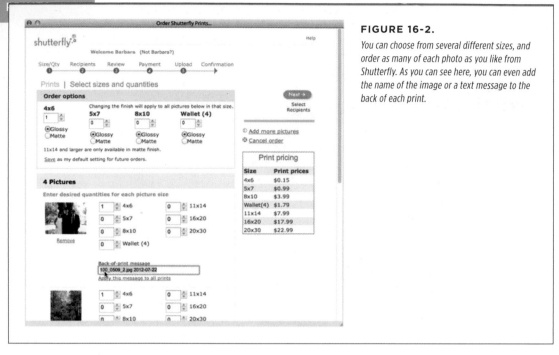

FIGURE 16-2.

You can choose from several different sizes, and order as many of each photo as you like from Shutterfly. As you can see here, you can even add the name of the image or a text message to the back of each print.

3. **Order your prints.**

Shutterfly lets you add or subtract photos, choose how many of each and which size, the finish you want, and so on. Then you enter info about the recipients (their names and addresses). It remembers whom you've sent photos to with previous orders, so you don't have to reenter Aunt Suzie's address each time. When your order is all set, enter your payment information, and in a few days you—or your lucky recipients—will receive an envelope of prints in the mail.

> **TIP** Elements automatically checks for updates to the online services and automatically notifies you about special promotions. You can stop it from doing either by heading to the Organizer and choosing Edit→Preferences→Adobe Partner Services/Adobe Elements 11 Organizer→Preferences→Adobe Partner Services and turning off the appropriate checkboxes in the "Check for Services" section.

Even though Elements makes ordering prints from Shutterfly really convenient, you can use Shutterfly without going through Elements, or use other online print services like Snapfish (*www.snapfish.com*). The real advantage of ordering from Elements is the convenience of being able to work right in the Organizer.

> **TIP** You can start an order right from Full Screen view (page 51). The Fix panel there has a "Mark for Printing" button that looks like a printer. Click it when you see photos you want to print. Then, when you return to the Media Browser from Full Screen view, a pop-up window offers you the choice of printing the photos at home or ordering prints. Click Order Prints and Elements prepares your photos and opens the Shutterfly window for you.

■ Printing at Home

If you prefer to print photos at home, Elements has you covered. It's quite easy to print from Elements, but this is one of the areas where your operating system makes a little bit of a difference. In Windows, you can print from either the Editor or the Organizer, and the process is pretty much the same from either, although you can only print groups of photos on a single page from the Organizer. On a Mac, all printing takes place from the Editor, no matter where you start.

Before you print, it's really important to be sure the resolution (ppi) of your photo(s) is what you want (see page 105 for more about resolution). It's also a good idea to do any cropping (page 85) before you call up the Print window. You can start from either the Editor or the Organizer, and (in Windows) once you're in the Print window, you can choose to create individual prints, a contact sheet of small thumbnails of all your photos, or a picture package of several sizes of prints. (On a Mac, if you want to create a contact sheet or picture package, you do so from the Editor's File menu; see page 547.) The following sections explain all your options.

Making Individual Prints

The basic process of printing from Elements is the same no matter where you start or what you're printing. You'll see a few differences between PCs and Macs if you're printing contact sheets or picture packages, which are covered later in this chapter, and there are a couple of minor ones, noted here, between how Windows and OS X handle all printing projects.

This section is about printing one photo per page from the Editor, since that method offers the most options. (To learn about the minor differences between printing from the Editor and from the *Windows* Organizer, see the box on page 537.) Once you understand how to make single prints from the Editor, you won't have any trouble with other kinds of printing. Both Windows and OS X require pretty much the same steps, but the order is slightly different.

■ PRINTING IN WINDOWS

1. **In the Editor, choose the photo(s) you want to print.**

   In the Photo Bin, select the photo(s) you want to print. If you don't select any, then Elements prints all your open photos. (You can add or remove photos once you're in the Print window, too—*if* the photos are already in the Organizer, as explained in Figure 16-3.)

2. **Go to File→Print or press Ctrl+P.**

   The Print window appears. It's divided into three main sections: On the left is a filmstrip-like view where you can add or remove photos you want to print (Figure 16-3). In the middle is a preview area where you see the image(s) you're going to print and some controls for rotating and adjusting the image(s); there's a blue outline around the area that's going to print. And on the right is a group of numbered settings, listed in the order you need to adjust them.

3. **Choose the printer you want to use.**

   Select it from the drop-down menu on the right side of the window (Step 1 listed there).

4. **Choose your printer settings.**

   On the right side of the Print window under Step 2 (Printer Settings), check to see what Elements proposes for the type of paper and the print quality. If you don't like its choices, click Change Settings. In the Change Settings window, adjust the settings to your liking. The window includes a setting to change the paper size, but you don't need to use it—you'll choose a size in the main Print window in the next step. Depending on your printer, you may have additional options here, like which paper tray you want the printer to use. If your printer can make borderless prints, you see a checkbox for that, too. Turn it on, and you'll see only borderless choices in the next step. When everything looks good, click OK.

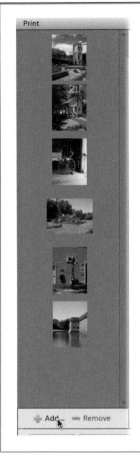

FIGURE 16-3.

On the left side of the Print window (shown here), you can add more photos to print, but only if they're already in the Organizer. Click the green + button, and a window opens that lets you browse through all your Organizer photos to choose ones to add. If you want to print photos that aren't in the Organizer, open them in Elements and then select them in the Photo Bin before you start the print process. If you decide not to print one of the photos in the Print window, click its thumbnail, and then click the red – button (which is grayed out here, because no photos are selected).

5. **Select a paper size.**

   Click the Select Paper Size menu (Step 3 in Elements' Print window) for a list of the sizes available for your printer. What's listed is determined by the printer you chose in Step 1, and by whether you turned on the Borderless checkbox in the Change Settings window. To change the page's orientation, click the button showing the orientation you want.

6. **Choose what kind of prints you want to make.**

   In the Print window's Step 4, choose whether to make individual prints, a contact sheet, or a picture package. In this example, you're making individual prints (one photo per page), so choose that. (If you want to make a contact sheet or a picture package, flip to page 544.)

7. **Select a print size.**

Use the aptly named Select Print Size drop-down menu (Step 5). If you don't want any of the preset sizes, choose Actual Size or Custom. If you choose the latter, the More Options dialog box appears showing the Custom Print Size settings, which are explained on page 539. Enter your choices and then click OK.

With the Print window's "Crop to Fit" checkbox turned on, Elements prints your whole image as large as it can be within the print size you chose, even if that means leaving empty space on some of the edges. So if you want to make your image fill the available space, leave "Crop to Fit" turned on and Elements trims the image to fit the print size you chose. Figure 16-4 shows the difference this setting makes.

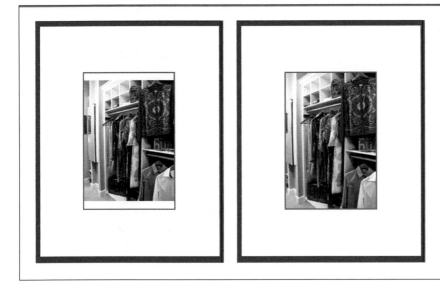

FIGURE 16-4.

Left: Here's how this photo will print with "Crop to Fit" turned off. Notice the white space at the top and bottom of the blue bounding box.

Right: Leave "Crop to Fit" turned on, and Elements enlarges the photo enough to fill all the space before cropping off the excess (here, it cropped the right and left edges).

Choose how many copies of each page you want to print.

If you want to make more than one copy of each print, enter a number in the Print box below the "Crop to Fit" checkbox. (Keep in mind that Elements prints this many copies of *every* print in this batch—you can't make three copies of one photo and two of another, for example.)

8. **Print your photo(s).**

Click Print and Elements prints the photo(s). If you change your mind, click Cancel or close the Print dialog box.

■ PRINTING IN OS X

1. **In the Editor, choose the photo(s) you want to print.**

   In the Photo Bin, select the photos you want to print. (If you don't select any, Elements prints all your open photos.) Just as in Windows, you can add photos in the Print window, as explained in Figure 16-3, but they have to be in the Organizer.

2. **Go to File→Print or press ⌘-P.**

   The Print window appears. It's divided into three main sections: On the left is a filmstrip-like view where you can add or remove photos you want to print (Figure 16-3). In the middle is a preview area where you see the image(s) you're going to print and some controls for rotating and adjusting the image(s); there's a blue outline around the area that's going to print. And on the right is a group of numbered settings, listed in the order you need to adjust them.

3. **Choose the printer you want to use.**

   Select it from the pull-down menu on the right side of the window (this step is labeled "1").

4. **Select a paper size.**

   In Step 2 in Elements' Print window, click the Select Paper Size menu for a list of the sizes available for your printer. What's listed is determined by the printer you chose in the previous step. If you want to change the page's orientation, click the button showing the orientation you want.

5. **Select a print size.**

   Use the aptly named Select Print Size drop-down menu (Step 3). If you don't want any of the preset print sizes, choose Actual Size or Custom. If you choose the latter, the More Options dialog box appears showing the Custom Print Size options, which are explained on page 539. Enter your choices and then click OK.

   The Print window's "Crop to Fit" checkbox makes Elements print your whole image as large as it can be within the print size you chose, even if that means leaving empty space at some of the edges. So if you want to make your image fill the available space, leave "Crop to Fit" turned on and Elements trims the image to fit the print size you chose. Turn back to Figure 16-4 to see the difference this setting makes.

6. **Choose how many copies of each page you want to print.**

   If you want to make more than one copy of each print, enter a number in the Print box below the "Crop to Fit" checkbox. (Keep in mind that Elements prints this many copies of *every* image in this batch—you can't make three copies of one photo and two of another, for example.)

7. **Print your photos.**

   After you adjust Elements' Print window's settings and click the Print button, you see *OS X's* Print dialog box, where you make your final print setting choices—like paper profile (more on that in a minute) and color management. Figure 16-5 explains how it works.

First, choose the printer you want to use from the top pull-down menu. Next, click Show Details (if you're using Lion or Mountain Lion) or the blue down-arrow button to the right of the printer's name (if you're using Snow Leopard or earlier) to expand the dialog box (see Figure 16-5), and then choose paper and color options from the pull-down menu that starts out set to Layout.

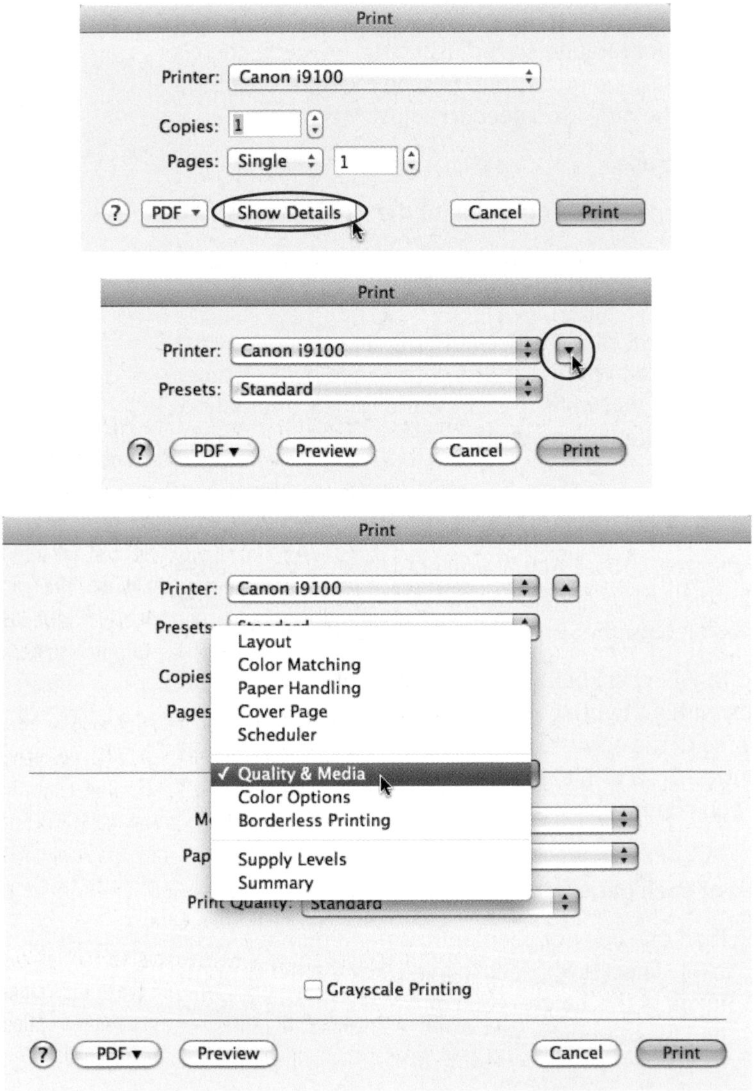

FIGURE 16-5.

Use the OS X Print dialog box to choose paper and print-quality settings.

Top: In OS X 10.7 (Lion) or 10.8 (Mountain Lion), click the Show Details button circled here to expand the window so you can see all your options.

Middle: In older versions of OS X, click the arrow (circled) to do the same thing.

Bottom: In any version of OS X, you then use these various pull-down menus in the expanded dialog box to make your choices.

Your paper and color options vary depending on the kind of printer you have. Selecting a paper profile may sound complicated, but it's usually as simple as selecting the kind of paper you plan to use (Photo Paper Plus Glossy, say) from a list of choices. Setting color options can be as easy as choosing "high-quality photo" from a list of quality settings, and usually you'll have someplace to specify Printer Color Management, although probably not in the same menu item.

When everything is set, click Print and Elements prints your photo(s).

That's the basic process for printing from Elements. If you're in a hurry or not fussy, you can use it to get a handful of prints in short order. But odds are that you're using Elements precisely because you *are* fussy about your photos, and you may want to tweak several other settings. The next sections cover all the ways you can customize things like how the photo sits on the page, its color management, and so forth.

NOTE Elements' Print window isn't *color managed* (page 230), which means that what you see in the window isn't necessarily the same as the colors you'll get when you print. The window's preview is just meant to show you where on the page the photo is going to print (which is the subject of the next section).

THE SIMPLE LIFE

Printing from the Windows Organizer

In Windows, if you want to make individual prints in the Organizer, start by selecting the photo(s) in the Organizer's Media Browser rather than in the Editor's Photo Bin. Other than that, the process for printing individual images is exactly the same whether you start in the Editor or the Organizer except for three details, which all involve clicking the More Options button at the bottom of the Prints window;

- **Image positioning.** The Editor always prints one photo per page, regardless of the relative sizes of the photos and your paper, while the Organizer may place more than one photo on a page if there's room. If you want to restrict the Organizer to placing only one image on a sheet, then click the More Options button, make sure Printing Choices is selected on the left side of the window, and then turn on the One Photo Per Page checkbox. Also, if you print from the Editor, you can turn off the Print window's Center Image checkbox to reposition your photo. (This checkbox isn't available if you start from the Organizer—Elements is totally in charge of positioning your photos.)

- **Max Print Resolution.** If you start the printing process from the Organizer, when you're in the Print window and go to More Options→Custom Print Size, you'll see a box labeled Max Print Resolution. (The Editor's Print window just lists your image's print resolution in pixels per inch.) If you don't make a change here, anything you print from the Organizer will print at 350 ppi or less (see page 105 for more about resolution and why this may matter). Normally, that's just fine.

- **Color Management.** If you open the Print window from the Editor and go to More Options→Color Management, you'll see many options (see page 541). If you start in the Organizer, however, the More Options dialog box just presents you with the current *color space* (see page 234) for your image and a drop-down menu set to "Same as Source." Leave that setting as is.

Another handy Organizer feature is that you can mark photos for printing in Full Screen view (page 51). When you return to the Media Room, a pop-up window gives you the option of printing your photos or ordering prints online (page 528).

Positioning Your Image

In both the Windows and Mac versions of Elements, there are two main ways to adjust the relationship between an image and the paper you print it on. Elements' Print window has some controls for rotating and sizing the image, which are normally all you'll need. You can even scoot the photo around within the preview area to determine which *part* of it will print if you don't want to print the whole image. And if you like, you can also call up the Page Setup dialog box, which is the same for all programs on your computer. The following sections explain your options. (Quick reminder: In Windows, Elements lets you position your image only if you start from the Editor; if you print from the Organizer, Elements decides where to put the image.)

■ PRINT WINDOW SETTINGS

When you open Elements' Print window, you see your photo in a white preview area surrounded by a blue outline (called a *bounding box*). The white area represents the paper, and the blue box shows the printing boundaries of the photo. The blue outline doesn't get printed. (Incidentally, Adobe's official name for the area inside the blue outline is the Print Well, in case you run into it in any tutorials.) Your first impulse may be to grab the photo and try to adjust its placement on the page. But if you do this, rather than moving the blue box, you just move your image *within* the box. You need to pay attention to your cursor to see just what you're going to move, as Figure 16-6 explains.

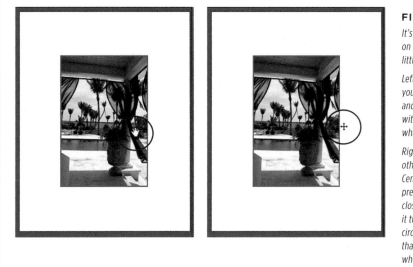

FIGURE 16-6.

It's easy to move a photo around on the paper, but you have to be a little careful.

Left: If you grab the photo itself, you get the hand cursor (circled) and you'll simply move the image within the print outline and change what part of the image will print.

Right: To move the photo to another spot on the page, turn off the Center Image checkbox below the preview, and then move the cursor close to the edge of the photo till it turns into the crossed arrows circled here. These arrows indicate that you can drag the photo to wherever you want it.

To reposition a photo on the page (to print a small photo on the upper-left corner of a large piece of paper, for example), just turn off the Center Image checkbox and then drag the bounding box wherever you want it, or enter the amount of distance from the top and left edges of the page in inches, centimeters, millimeters, points, or picas.

In addition to moving the bounding box itself, there are several ways to change how your image appears within it. Here's what you can do:

- **Rotate the photo.** Below the preview area are the same rotation icons you see elsewhere in Elements. Click one to rotate the photo within the bounding box. (If you want to rotate the box on the page, leave the Image Only checkbox turned off. If you turn it on, then the bounding box stays put and the image rotates within it.)

- **Resize the photo.** If you don't want to print the whole image, zoom in on part of it by using the slider below the preview to control which part of it appears in the box. Be careful with this feature: You can easily enlarge the image beyond a reasonable pixel density. (When you click Print, Elements will warn you if the image is going to print at less than 220 ppi, but as a general rule it's best to take care of any resizing *before* you open the Print window.)

- **Reposition the photo in the box.** As mentioned above, you can drag the image around in the preview area to determine which part of it will print. (You can also accidentally drag the image almost out of view. If that happens, just choose a different print size in the right part of the window, and then switch back to the original size. Elements recenters your image in the bounding box each time you change this setting.)

> **TIP** If you turn on the "Crop to Fit" checkbox on the right side of the Print window, Elements crops based on the *original* position of the image; it doesn't take into account any dragging that you do. In other words, you can't control the part of your photo that gets printed if you use "Crop to Fit."

- **Make the image and print size the same.** If you decide to make a 4 × 6-inch print of an image that's the right aspect ratio (shape) for a 5 × 7-inch print, you'll end up with some empty space on the edges because the print size and the aspect ratio aren't equivalent. There are two ways around this. You can turn on "Crop to Fit," and Elements will chop off the edges of the photo. Or, if you've already cropped the image to a photo-paper size, head to the Select Print Size drop-down menu and choose Actual Size. You can also use a custom size, as explained next.

- **Pick a custom print size.** Either choose Custom from the Print window's Select Print Size menu, or click the More Options button and then click Custom Print Size; either way, you see the More Options dialog box's Custom Print Size options. There, you can type the exact height and width you want to print in inches, centimeters, millimeters, points, or picas.

- **Make the image fill the paper.** If you click the Print Window's More Options button and then click Custom Print Size, you can turn on the "Scale to Fit Media" checkbox, and Elements makes your image larger or smaller so that all of it fits into your desired page size. (You may need to use your operating system's Page Setup dialog box—described next—to change the page's orientation after choosing this option.)

■ **THE PAGE SETUP DIALOG BOX**

In the lower-left corner of Elements' Print window, there's a Page Setup button. Click it to bring up your operating system's Page Setup dialog box. Normally, you don't need to use this dialog box at all in Elements—choosing your printer in the Print window's Step 1 area takes care of things. But once you've got everything set up in Elements' Print window, you can use Page Setup to override Elements' settings. You can also select a printer here, but normally choosing a printer in Elements' Print window changes the Page Setup dialog box to match.

Additional Print Options

Elements includes a number of other useful ways to tweak a photo, like putting a border around it, printing crop marks as guides for trimming the printed version, or even flipping it for printing as an iron-on transfer. You'll find the following settings by clicking the Print window's More Options button and then, on the left side of the dialog box that appears, clicking Printing Choices:

- **Photo Details.** You can print the image's shot or creation date, filename, and/ or caption on the page with the photo by turning on the relevant checkbox(es) here. (When you click Apply, the Print Window's image preview changes to show where the text will get printed, so if the More Options dialog box is in the way, move it over so you can see what happens as you check these boxes.) Caption text is what you entered in the Organizer, or you can go to File→Info in the Editor to add a caption in the Description field.

- **Border.** If you want to add a border to the photo, turn on the Thickness checkbox and then enter a size for the border (in inches, millimeters, or points). Elements shrinks the photo to accommodate the border, even if there's plenty of empty space around the picture, so you may need to enlarge the photo a bit before printing to get the size you originally chose. Click the white square that appears to bring up the Color Picker so you can choose a border color. If the page has empty space you want to fill with a background color, then turn on the Background checkbox and click its color square to bring up the Color Picker.

- **Iron-on Transfer.** Turn on the Flip Image checkbox to reverse your image horizontally. You'd use this when printing transfers for projects like t-shirts.

- **Trim Guidelines.** The Print Crop Marks checkbox lets you print guidelines in the margins of the photo to make it easier to trim. These marks are useful mainly for trimming bordered photos so that the borders are perfectly even.

Color Management

When you print from the Editor, Elements gives you several advanced color-related settings if you click the Print window's More Options button and then click Color Management on the left side of the dialog box that appears. If you're content with the way your prints look without adjusting these settings, just be happy and ignore them. But if you don't like the color you're getting from Elements, then use these advanced controls to make adjustments.

TIP Color management is a dauntingly complicated subject. The advice in the following pages should be enough to get you started, but if you're determined to learn more, a good place to start is *Real World Color Management* by Bruce Fraser, Chris Murphy, and Fred Bunting (Peachpit Press). It's geared toward Photoshop, but it's the standard reference on the subject, and much of it applies to Elements as well.

WORKAROUND WORKSHOP

Economical Print Experiments

If you've just gone out and bought top-quality photo paper, you may be suffering from a bit of sticker shock and perhaps are even thinking, "Oh yeah, great. Now I'm supposed to use this stuff up experimenting? At that price?"

The good news is that, while you have to bite the bullet and sacrifice a sheet or two, you don't need to waste a whole box. Try this: Make a small selection somewhere in a photo you want to print, press Ctrl+C/⌘-C, and then go to File→New→"Image from Clipboard." You get a new file with only a small piece of the photo in it; this is your test print. Next, go to File→Print, turn off the Center Image checkbox, and then drag the partial

photo to the page's upper-left corner. Then try printing the page using Elements' standard settings.

If the print looks good, then you're ready to print the whole photo. If, on the other hand, you don't like the result, then press Ctrl+P/⌘-P to bring up the Print window again. This time, drag the test print over to the right a little bit. Adjust your settings (keeping track of the changes you make), and then print again on the *same* piece of paper. Your new test prints out beside the first one. Keep moving the test area around on the page, and you can try out quite a few different combinations of settings, all on one sheet of paper.

You may remember from Chapter 7 that Elements is a *color-managed* program, which means it tries to coordinate the color settings used by various devices and programs: your image file (which may retain color settings applied by your camera), your monitor, Elements, and your printer. Sometimes you need to step in and help Elements decide which settings are best, since different devices and programs can have different interpretations of what certain colors look like.

Color management may sound intimidating, but you already did some when you chose a paper type and print quality. Now your most important decision is whether you want Elements or your printer to manage the photo's color settings. (You can let Elements *and* your printer have a say in color management, but that almost always mucks things up.) The good news is that Elements does its best to keep you from double-managing color, and it tries to make managing the color in your prints as painless as possible.

You have four main color-management choices to make in the More Options dialog box:

- **Color Handling.** Here's where you decide who's going to be in charge: your printer (Printer Manages Colors) or Elements (Photoshop Elements Manages Colors). The choice you make here determines your options in the rest of these settings. Elements also gives you some hints about your printer settings, as you can see in Figure 16-7.

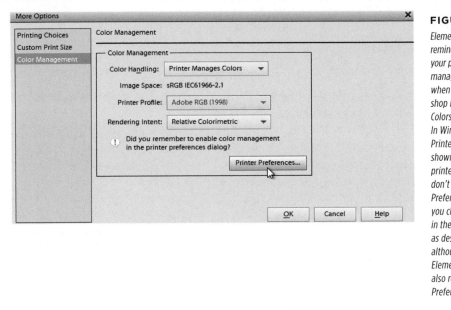

FIGURE 16-7.

Elements thoughtfully reminds you to turn off your printer's color-management feature when you choose Photoshop Elements Manages Colors in this window. In Windows, click the Printer Preferences button shown here to adjust your printer's settings. (Macs don't have the Printer Preferences button, since you change these settings in the OS X Print window, as described on page 536, although the text in the Elements Print window also refers to "Printer Preferences" for Macs.)

- **Image Space.** This setting shows you which, if any, color space your file is tagged with (for example, sRGB or Adobe RGB). You don't actually choose anything here—this line is purely informative. (See page 233 for more about color spaces.)

- **Printer Profile.** This setting is grayed out unless you chose Photoshop Elements Manages Color in the Color Handling menu. If Elements is managing the color, then you can choose the profile you want from this list, which shows all the profiles Elements can find on your computer.

- **Rendering Intent.** Use this setting to tell Elements what to do if your photo contains colors that fall outside the range of the color space you're using; your choices are explained in the box on page 544.

The easiest way to set up color management, and a good way to start, is to choose Printer Manages Color. This means that Elements hands the photo over to your printer and lets the printer take care of the color-management duties. Then all you need to do is select the proper paper profile and settings for your printer. Selecting a paper profile may sound kind of technical, but actually, you've probably already done it.

In Windows, you picked a paper profile back in Printer Settings→Change Settings (step 4 on page 532). It's usually as simple as choosing, say, Photo Paper Plus Glossy from the list of options there. If you already chose a paper type and print quality in

Elements' Print window, your printer preferences should have changed to reflect them. However, your printer may offer some additional choices that are worth exploring. In the More Options dialog box's Color Management section, just click the Printer Preferences button to view these settings, or, in Elements' Change Settings dialog box (page 532), click the Advanced Settings button. The exact wording in the dialog box that appears differs depending on what kind of printer you have, but Figure 16-8 shows a typical printer's settings.

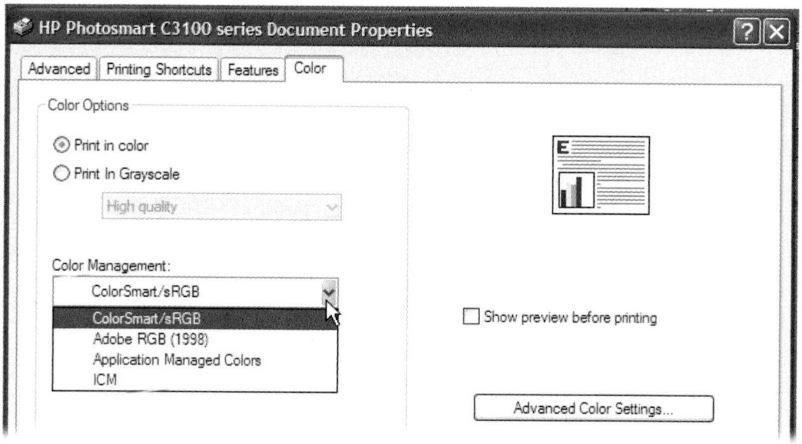

FIGURE 16-8.

Setting up color management in your printer's settings is easy. Here, just leaving this particular HP printer's menu set to ColorSmart/sRGB is all it takes. If you plan to let Elements manage color, you'd choose Application Managed Colors instead. Different brands of printers have different names for their color-management systems, so you'll have to hunt around in the window a bit, but it's usually pretty simple to figure out which option you want.

On a Mac, you make your paper profile choices in the OS X Print window, as explained back on page 536. Your options are similar to the ones in Windows; you just get to them in a different place.

> **TIP** If your camera takes photos in sRGB and you've been editing them using Elements' No Color Management or "Always Optimize Colors for Computer Screens" setting (Edit→Color Settings), then don't choose Adobe RGB for the printer profile, as the colors may shift drastically. If for some reason you want to change the color space for the printer, first go to Image→Convert Color Profile, and then apply the Adobe RGB profile to the photo. If you aren't absolutely sure that your printer understands Adobe RGB (many inkjets don't) and you don't have a compelling reason for changing the color setting, then it's best to leave things alone.

You can configure Elements' color settings in a zillion different ways, and you may need to experiment a bit to find what works best. (See the box on page 541 for advice on how to cheaply test out a bunch of different print settings.) If you go looking around for more info, you'll find that this subject is very controversial—everyone has a different approach that's the "right" one. But in fact, many different options can lead to good results.

What's Your Intent?

For most people, the Rendering Intent setting in Elements' More Options dialog box is the most confusing of the color-management options. Here are the basics you need to know to choose a setting.

Sometimes a photo may contain colors that fall outside the color boundaries of the print space you're using; in other words, the print space can't properly display those colors. The Rendering Intent setting tells Elements what to do if it runs into colors like that. You have four choices:

- **Perceptual** tells Elements to preserve the relationship between the colors in the image—even if that means it has to visibly shift some colors to make them all fit.

- **Saturation** makes colors very vivid—but not necessarily very accurate. This setting is more for special effects than for regular photo printing.

- **Relative Colorimetric** tries to preserve the colors in both the source and the output color spaces by shifting things to the closest matching color in the printer profile's space. This is Elements' standard setting, and it's usually what you want because it keeps colors as close as possible to what you see onscreen.

- **Absolute Colorimetric** lets you simulate another printer and paper. This setting is for specialized proofing situations.

Printing Multiple Images (Windows)

Elements also lets you print from the Windows Organizer, which gives you many more output options than the Editor, including the ability to print several photos on one page. You can create contact sheets of thumbnails and picture packages (like you'd order from a professional photographer), and easily add all kinds of fancy borders to the photos (by choosing a frame in the Print window's settings) in the Organizer. (You can *begin* creating a contact sheet or a picture package in the Editor, but Elements bounces you over to the Organizer for the actual printing.)

> **NOTE** To learn how to print a bunch of images on a Mac, skip to page 547.

Contact Sheets

Contact sheets show thumbnail views of multiple images on a single page. They're great for creating a visual reference guide to the photos you've archived on a CD, for instance. Or you may want to print a contact sheet of all the photos on a memory card as soon as you download the photos to your computer, even before you edit them (see Figure 16-9).

To print a contact sheet, select the photos you want to print and then choose File→Print. In Elements' Print window, go to the "Select Type of Print" menu and choose Contact Sheet. (If you start from the Editor, Elements asks if you want to go to the Organizer, which is where you print Contact Sheets.) The window changes to include a "Select a Layout" section, and you can use the following settings to customize your contact sheet:

- **Columns.** Here's where you decide how many columns of photos to have on a page (up to nine). The more columns, the smaller the thumbnails. Even if you have only one image currently selected, increasing the number of columns shrinks the thumbnail.

- **Show Print Options.** Turn on this checkbox and you can decide whether to have Elements print the image's date, caption (any text in the image's Description field), and/or filename below each thumbnail. You can also add page numbers if you're printing multiple pages. (If all your photos fit on one page, then the Page Numbers checkbox is grayed out.)

You can add and remove images as explained earlier (page 531), and you can click a photo in the layout and use the slider to zoom, just as with individual prints. When you like the layout, click Print.

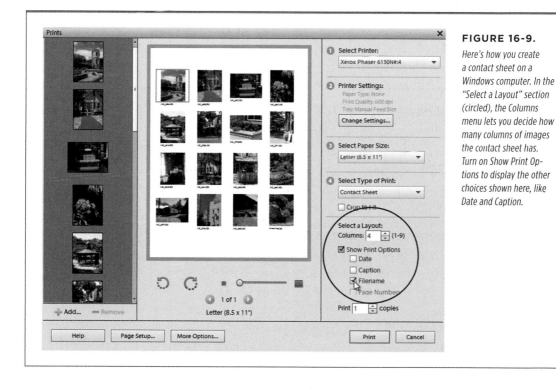

FIGURE 16-9.

Here's how you create a contact sheet on a Windows computer. In the "Select a Layout" section (circled), the Columns menu lets you decide how many columns of images the contact sheet has. Turn on Show Print Options to display the other choices shown here, like Date and Caption.

> **TIP** You can also start in either the Editor or the Organizer by going to Create→Photo Prints→Contact Sheet. The only advantage to doing it this way is that the Print window opens with Contact Sheet already selected as the type of print.

Picture Packages

Elements' Picture Package tool lets you print several images on one sheet. You can print a package that's one photo printed repeatedly, or one that includes multiple photos.

To get started, in the Organizer, select the images you want to print and then press Ctrl+P to call up the Prints window. Then go to the "Select Type of Print" section and choose Picture Package. Next, under "Select a Layout," pick which composition style you want (choices include four 3″ × 5″ photos, two 5″ × 7″ photos, and so on). Then choose a frame, if you want one, from the "Select a Frame" menu. Add photos to your package by clicking the Add button in the lower-left corner of the window.

> **TIP** You can also start a picture package in either the Editor or the Organizer by going to Create→Photo Prints→Print Picture Package. The only real advantage to going that route is that the Print window opens with "Picture Package" preselected in the section labeled "4."

Figure 16-10 shows you how to change the layout of the photos once they're on the page. If you turn on the Fill Page With First Photo checkbox, then you get a whole page dedicated to each photo showing multiple sizes of the image, instead of various photos on each page.

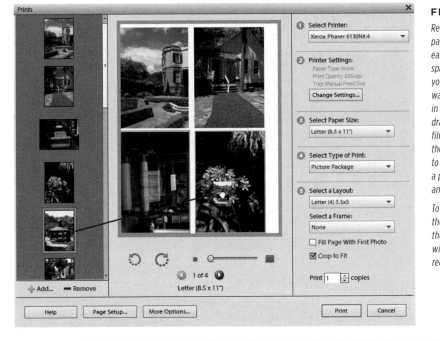

FIGURE 16-10.

Reorganizing a picture package is drag-and-drop easy. If there's empty space in the layout and you want to fill it, or you want to change the photo in a particular slot, just drag a thumbnail from the filmstrip on the left into the slot where you want to use the photo, or drag a photo from one slot to another.

To remove a photo from the package, click it on the left side of the main window and then click the red Remove button.

You can select a photo in the layout and then use the rotation buttons and the zoom slider to tweak it. If you turn on the "Crop to Fit" checkbox, Elements crops your photos to fit their slots, but you're probably better off doing any cropping yourself in the Editor instead. When you've got the photos arranged the way you want, click Print.

> **TIP** The box on page 552 has info on creating your own custom picture package.

Printing Multiple Images (Mac)

The Mac version of Elements gives you even better options for printing multiple images, because you can save your completed projects for future use. This section explains how to create contact sheets and picture packages.

Contact Sheets

Contact sheets show a bunch of thumbnails of different photos. You can use them to keep track of the photos on a CD or as a record of all the photos you took in one shooting session, for example. The plug-in that comes with Elements makes it a snap to create a contact sheet that's laid out the way you want. To create a contact sheet:

1. **Collect your photos.**

   You can make a contact sheet of all your open photos or all the photos in a folder. So decide which photos you want to use and open them in the Editor, or put them together in a folder.

2. **Call up the Contact Sheet dialog box (Figure 16-11).**

   Press Option-⌘-P, or go to File→Contact Sheet II. (Confusingly, there's no Contact Sheet I option—it was replaced by this one many versions of Elements ago.) You can also go to Create→Photo Prints→Print Contact Sheet in either the Editor or the Organizer, although you'll get bounced over to the Editor to actually create the contact sheet. If you preselect photos in the Organizer, they open in the Editor and you can choose to include them all in step 3.

3. **Choose your settings.**

   You have lots of options:

   - **Source Images.** This is where you pick which photos to include. You can select the files currently open in the Editor or files in a certain folder.

   - **Document.** Here's where you select the overall page settings. Set the page size in inches, centimeters, or pixels. Then enter a resolution and choose between RGB and grayscale color mode (see page 42). The Flatten All Layers checkbox doesn't affect your originals—it just creates a contact sheet where text and images are on the same layer—so you can leave it turned on to keep the file smaller.

- **Thumbnails.** These settings control how the thumbnails are laid out. Choose whether you want the pictures to go across the page or down (as they're being laid out), how many columns and rows you'd like, and whether you want Elements to figure out the spacing between images or to set the spacing yourself. Turn on the Rotate For Best Fit checkbox to make Elements rotate the thumbnails so they fit on the paper most efficiently. (If you don't like having photos improperly oriented, leave this setting off.)

- **Use Filename As Caption.** Turn on this setting if you want the name of each photo to appear as a caption. Your font choices are Myriad Pro, Minion Pro, or Lucida Grande. Getting a font size you like may take some experimenting.

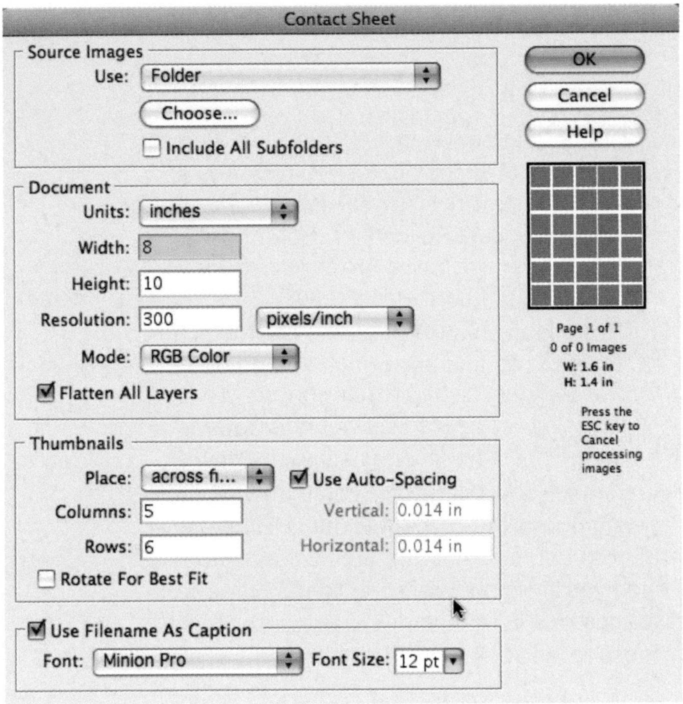

FIGURE 16-11.

You can customize a contact sheet by adjusting things like the amount of space between the thumbnails. As you tweak these settings, the layout preview on the right side of the dialog box changes to reflect your choices, and Elements keeps a running tally of the number of pages needed to fit your photos in the current layout.

4. **Click OK to create the contact sheet.**

   Elements goes to work and you see your images flash back and forth. The contact sheet thumbnail in the Photo Bin updates to show each photo as Elements places it.

TIP If you change your mind about making a contact sheet while Elements is working, press the Esc key.

5. **Save or print your contact sheet.**

Your finished contact sheet is just like any other file: You can save it in the format of your choice, print it out, burn it to disc along with the photos it contains—whatever. If you included so many photos that they don't all fit on one page, then Elements creates a separate file for each page.

Picture Packages

You can also print a group of pictures, called a picture package, on one page. You can make packages that feature one photo printed in several different sizes, or packages that include more than one photo. Here's how:

1. **In the Editor, go to File→Picture Package.**

   You can also start from either the Editor or the Organizer by going to Create→Photo Prints→Print Picture Package, though you end up in the same Picture Package window in the Editor.

   You don't need to select any photos first, but you may want to open photos in the Editor before starting, since the Picture Package, like the Contact Sheet, ignores the Organizer. So it's often simplest to open the photos or collect them into a folder to make them easy to find before you start this process.

2. **Choose your photo(s).**

   The Picture Package dialog box's Use drop-down menu is where you select the pictures you want in the package. If you choose lots of files, Elements adds as many pages as necessary to fit them all in. You can use a single file, a folder of photos, the frontmost open photo, or all open photos. Elements starts by filling the entire layout with copies of one photo, but you can change that in step 4 if you want more than one image per page.

3. **Choose your page size and layout settings.**

   Elements gives you lots of options:

   • **Document.** This is where you pick the overall settings for the package. You can set the page size (12" × 18", 8" × 10", 10" × 16", or 7.5" × 10.9"), layout (how many photos appear on one page and their sizes), resolution, and whether to use RGB or grayscale color mode (see page 42). The Flatten All Layers setting works the same way as it does for contact sheets (see step 3 on page 547). The page size options are all photo paper sizes, but you can print the 8" × 10" layout on standard 8½" × 11" paper.

- **Label.** This is where you tell Elements whether to put text on the photos. If you don't want any text, leave the Content menu set to None. If you want text, you can use the filename, copyright, description, credit, or title from the file's metadata (see page 48), or enter custom text. The other options are for the text itself: font, size, color, opacity, and position. If you don't want black text, click the color square to bring up the Color Picker. The Rotate menu lets you tell Elements to rotate the text so that, if your photos print sideways, say, the text still prints right-side up on the photo. And you can use the Opacity and Position settings to create a watermark.

If all these options aren't enough for you, check out the next section, which explains how to customize a picture package even further.

4. **Adjust the placement of the photos.**

Figure 16-12 explains how to change the contents of a particular placeholder (Adobe calls them *zones*). Keep clicking zones to put as many different shots on a page as you have zones to hold them.

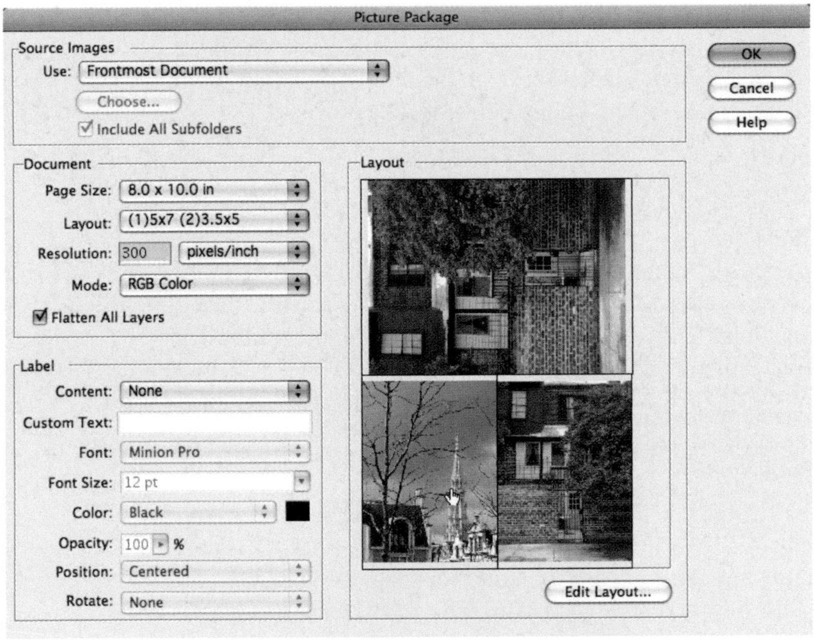

FIGURE 16-12.

To add a new photo or replace an existing one, click any box in the Layout section of this dialog box and then choose the new photo in the "Select an Image File" dialog box that appears. (You can't rearrange photos by dragging them from one zone to another.) An even easier way to slot in a new photo is to drag it in from the Finder and then drop it in the right zone; Elements opens the image and replaces the existing photo with it.

5. **When everything is arranged to your liking, click OK to create the package.**

If your settings required more than one page to fit the photos, then Elements creates a separate file for each page. You can print them or save them in any format that suits you, just like a single photo.

■ CUSTOMIZING A PICTURE PACKAGE

You're not limited to the picture-package layouts Elements offers. You can customize a layout in all sorts of ways and then save it to use again. Start by choosing the built-in layout that's closest to what you want. Then click the Edit Layout button in the Picture Package window's bottom right to call up the dialog box shown in Figure 16-13.

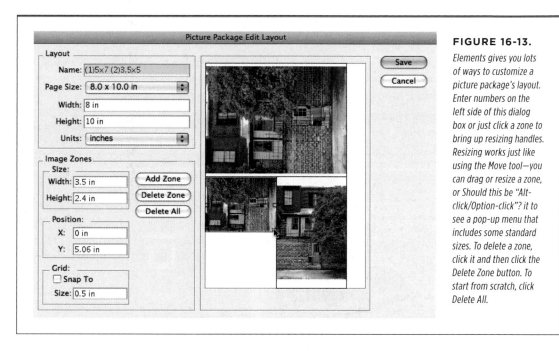

FIGURE 16-13.

Elements gives you lots of ways to customize a picture package's layout. Enter numbers on the left side of this dialog box or just click a zone to bring up resizing handles. Resizing works just like using the Move tool—you can drag or resize a zone, or Should this be "Alt-click/Option-click"? it to see a pop-up menu that includes some standard sizes. To delete a zone, click it and then click the Delete Zone button. To start from scratch, click Delete All.

You can choose a preset page size or type in a custom size in inches, centimeters, millimeters, or pixels. And as Figure 16-13 explains, you can also change the size and location of the images in the package. (The boxes for typing in custom sizes are grayed out until you select a zone.)

If you click a zone and then click Add Zone, Elements creates an additional zone instead of replacing the one you clicked. If there's no space that's big enough for the new zone, Elements just dumps the new zone on top of the existing layout and leaves you to sort things out. Simply delete an existing zone to make room for the new one. The Snap To checkbox in the dialog box's Grid section helps you line up the zones.

When you're happy with your custom layout, name it by typing something in the Name box, and then click Save. (Be sure to give your layout a new name so you don't overwrite the built-in layout you started with.) Make sure you save it in Applications→Adobe Photoshop Elements 11→Support Files→Presets→Layouts. That way, your new layout will show up in the list of preset layouts.

If this method of customizing a picture package doesn't meet your needs, the box below explains another way to create a custom package.

Creating Your Own Package

You may find that you want a layout for your picture package that's different from any of the choices Elements offers. Fortunately, you can easily make your own picture package from scratch on either a Mac or a PC:

1. **Save all the photos you want to use at the same resolution.** See page 105 for more about setting a file's resolution.

2. **In the Editor, create a new document (Ctrl+N/⌘-N or File→New).** Make sure it's the size you want the finished package to be and that it has the same resolution as your photos. You can save time by choosing the Letter preset size from the New dialog box's Size menu; that size is already set to 300 ppi.

3. **Bring each photo into your new file.** Drag the photos from the Photo Bin and then position them as you wish, or just copy (Ctrl+C/⌘-C) and paste (Ctrl+V/⌘-V) them. Each photo comes in on its own layer, so it's easy to reposition them individually. Once the photos are in the new document, you can use the Move tool or Scale command (page 388) to resize them.

When you have all the photos positioned and sized, save the combined file, and then print it. You can make the file smaller by flattening it first (Layer→Flatten Image), but flatten it only if you don't think you'll want to tweak the layout later.

In Windows, you can also create new layouts in the Organizer. Go to *C:\Program Files [Program Files(x 86) for 64-bit operating systems]\Adobe\Elements 11 Organizer\Assets\locale\en_US \ layouts* (the "en_US" part will be different if you aren't in the United States) and choose the layout that's closest to what you want. (You might want to audition the different layouts in Elements first and make note of the one that's most like what you want, so you'll know which file to open.) Open the file in a text editor (like Notepad), save it with a new name, and then make your changes. When you're done, save the changes, and then put the new file into the same folder as the original. If you're not sure about what to change, the layouts folder has a helpful ReadMe file that explains what to do.

Email and the Web

Printing photos is great, but it costs money, takes time, and doesn't do much to instantly impress your faraway friends. And to many people, printing is just so 20th century. Fortunately, Elements comes packed with tools that make it easy to prep your photos for onscreen viewing and to email them in a variety of crowd-pleasing ways.

■ Image Formats and the Web

Back in the Web's early days, making graphic files small was important because most Internet connections were as slow as snails. Nowadays, file size isn't as crucial; your main obligation when creating graphics for the Web is ensuring they're compatible with the web browsers people use to view them. That means you'll probably want to use either of the two most popular image formats, JPEG or GIF, though PNG is also an option:

- **JPEG** (Joint Photographic Experts' Group) is the most popular choice for images with lots of details, and where you need smooth color transitions. Photos are almost always posted on the Web as JPEGs.

> **TIP** JPEGs can't have transparent areas, although there's a workaround for that: Fill the background around the image with the same color as the web page you want to post it on. That way, the background blends into the web page, giving the impression that the object is surrounded by transparency. See Figure 17-4 (page 559) for details on this trick.

- **GIF** (Graphics Interchange Format) files are great for images with limited numbers of colors, like corporate logos and headlines. Text looks much sharper in GIF format than it does as a JPEG. GIFs can also include transparency.

- **PNG** (Portable Network Graphic) is a web graphics format that was created to overcome some of the disadvantages of JPEGs and GIFs. There's a lot to like about PNG files: They can include transparent areas, and this format reduces the file size of photographs without losing data, as happens with JPEG files (see page 70 for more about that). PNG files' big drawback is that only newer web browsers handle them well. Old versions of Internet Explorer are notorious for not supporting the PNG format, so if you've potentially got viewers with ancient computers, then you probably don't want to use PNGs.

Elements makes it a breeze to save images in any of these formats using the Save For Web dialog box, explained next.

Saving Images for the Web or Email

If you plan to email your photos or put them up on your website, Save For Web is a terrific feature that takes any open image and saves it in a web-friendly format. It also gives you lots of options to help maintain maximum image quality while keeping file size to a minimum. Save For Web aims to create as small a file as possible without compromising the image's onscreen quality.

Save For Web creates smaller JPEG files than you can get by using the Save As command because it strips out the image's EXIF data, the information about your camera's settings (see page 48). To get started with Save For Web, in the Editor, go to File→"Save for Web" or press Shift+Alt+Ctrl+S/Shift-Option-⌘-S. The dialog box shown in Figure 17-1 appears.

The most important point to remember when saving images for the Web is that the resolution (measured in pixels per inch, or ppi) is completely irrelevant. You only care about the image's pixel dimensions, such as 400 × 600. If you're working with a photo that you've optimized for print, you almost certainly want to downsize it; Save For Web makes that a snap.

Elements gives you lots of useful tools in the Save For Web dialog box, like the Hand and Zoom tools for adjusting the view. But the main attraction is the before-and-after image preview in the two main preview panes. On the left is your original, and to its right you see what the image will look like after you save it. The file size is listed below each image preview.

NOTE In the Save For Web dialog box, the preview panes may sometimes be stacked one above the other rather than side by side, depending on the size of your image and its orientation.

Toolbox

File format and quality settings

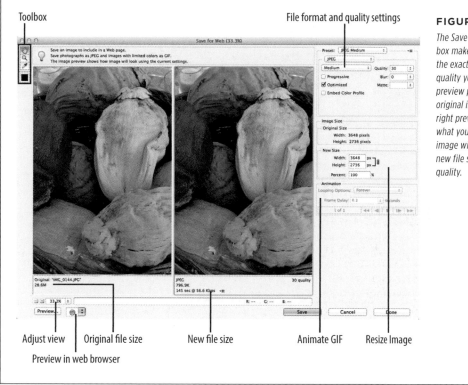

FIGURE 17-1.

The Save For Web dialog box makes it easy to get the exact image size and quality you want. The left preview pane shows the original image, and the right preview pane shows what your web-friendly image will look like at its new file size, format, and quality.

Adjust view   Original file size   New file size   Animate GIF   Resize Image

Preview in web browser

Below the left corner of the right-hand preview is an estimate of how long it will take to download the image at that size. You can adjust the download time by modifying your assumptions about your recipient's Internet connection speed, as shown in Figure 17-2. You can also change the zoom percentage (using the Zoom menu in the dialog box's bottom left), but you should usually stick with 100 percent because that's the size your image will be on the Web.

The upper-right part of the dialog box has your file format and quality choices (what you see varies a bit depending on which format you've chosen). Below that are your options for resizing the image. If you want to create animated GIFs (those tiny moving images you see on web pages), then tweak the settings in the Animation section, which are explained in detail on page 561.

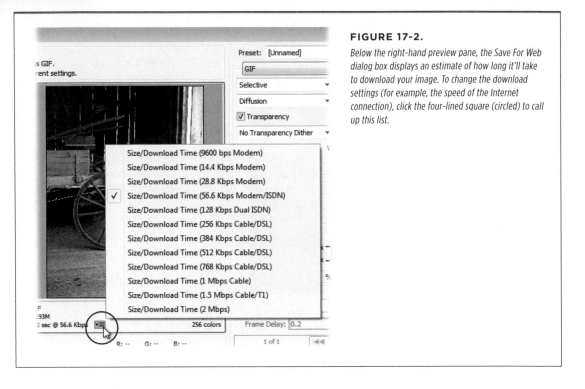

FIGURE 17-2.

Below the right-hand preview pane, the Save For Web dialog box displays an estimate of how long it'll take to download your image. To change the download settings (for example, the speed of the Internet connection), click the four-lined square (circled) to call up this list.

Using Save For Web

When you're ready to use Save For Web, follow these steps:

1. **In the Editor, open the image you want to modify.**

2. **Launch the Save For Web dialog box.**

   Go to File→"Save for Web" or press Shift+Alt+Ctrl+S/Shift-Option-⌘-S. If you're working with a large file, you may see a dialog box stating, "The image exceeds the size Save for Web was designed for," along with dire-sounding warnings about slow performance and out-of-memory errors. Just click Yes to tell Elements that you want to continue anyway. Unless you're using a seriously underpowered, antique computer, you won't have any problems.

3. **Choose format and quality settings for your web image.**

   Use the Preset drop-down menu to choose a format. Your choices are explained in the following section.

4. If necessary, resize the image.

To make sure that anyone can see the whole image, no matter how small her monitor, in the New Size section, enter 650 pixels or less for the longest side of the photo. (650 pixels is about the largest size that fits on small monitors without scrolling. If your friends all have big, new monitors, you can go much larger.) As long as the Constrain Proportions checkbox is turned on, you don't have to enter the dimension for the other side of the photo—Elements fills it in automatically.

You can also resize the image by entering a percentage in the New Size section (for example, typing *90* shrinks your image to 90 percent of the original size). When you finish entering the new dimensions, click Apply.

NOTE   Remember, if any of your friends don't have broadband, large photos can take a long time to download on dial-up connections. Elements helps you out by telling you the download times for various connections, as explained in Figure 17-2.

5. Check the results.

Look at the file size again to see if the new file is small enough, and use the Hand tool to scoot the image around in the preview area to take a close look at it. Use Elements' file-size optimization feature (explained in Figure 17-3), if necessary. You can also preview the image in your actual web browser (see page 561). There's no Undo option in the Save For Web dialog box, but you can Alt-click/Option-click the Cancel button to change it to a Reset button.

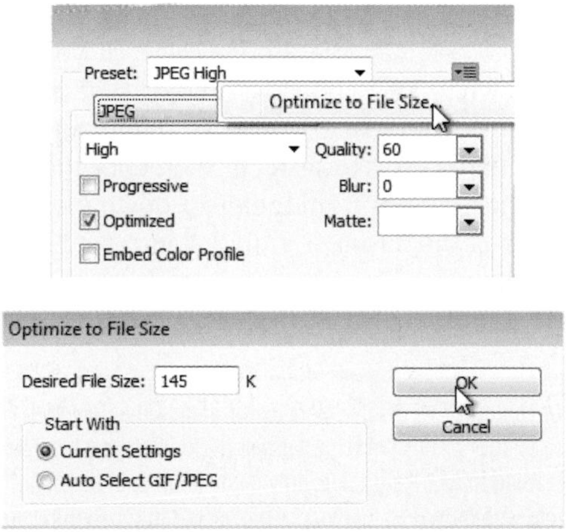

FIGURE 17-3.

Save For Web's file-size optimization feature is helpful when you need to send a file someplace that puts limits on your total file size.

Top: Click the four-line square in the upper right of the Save For Web dialog box and then choose "Optimize to File Size." Elements displays the dialog box shown in the bottom half of this figure, where you can enter your desired file size.

Bottom: The "Optimize to File Size" dialog box uses kilobytes as its unit of measurement. Simply enter the size you want (in kilobytes) in the Desired File Size box. Below that, picking Current Settings tells Elements to start with whatever settings you've entered in the main Save For Web window, like the format and quality. Auto Select GIF/JPEG means you want Elements to decide between GIF and JPEG for you. Once you finish making your selections, click OK, and Elements shrinks the image to the size you requested.

6. **When everything looks good, click Save.**

Name the new file, and then save it wherever you like.

> **TIP** If you want to process several photos in Save For Web with the same settings, Press the Alt/Option key to change the Help button to a Remember button, and then click it. That way, the next time you open Save For Web, it'll have your current settings preselected. (At least that's what it's supposed to do, although it doesn't always work properly.) If you want Save For Web to remember your settings but you don't actually want to save the current photo, just click Done and Save For Web should open with the same settings next time you call it up.

■ SAVE FOR WEB FILE FORMAT OPTIONS

You can reduce an image's file size by changing the length and width of the image, as explained in step 4 above. But you can also make a file smaller by adjusting its quality settings. The quality options you see in the Save For Web dialog box vary depending on which format you choose to save the file as:

- **JPEG.** Elements offers you a variety of basic JPEG quality settings: Low, Medium, High, Very High, and Maximum. You can then fine-tune the quality by entering a number in the Quality box (not surprisingly, a higher number means higher quality). Medium is usually good enough if you're saving for Web use. If you're using Save For Web to make JPEG files for printing, then use Maximum instead.

  If you turn on the Progressive checkbox, then your JPEG loads from the top down. This option was popular for large files when everyone had slow dial-up connections, but it makes for a slightly larger file, so it's not as popular today. You can also embed a color profile in the image by turning on the checkbox to do so. (See page 235 for more about color profiles.)

  Since JPEGs can't include transparency, the Matte menu lets you set the color of any area that's transparent in the original (see Figure 17-4). (If you don't pick a matte color, Elements uses white.) By choosing a color that matches the background of your web page, you can make it *look* like the image is surrounded by transparency. You have three ways to select a color: Click the arrow to the right of the Matte box and then choose from the drop-down menu; use the Eyedropper tool on the left side of the Save For Web dialog box to sample a color from your image, and then choose Eyedropper Color from the Matte drop-down menu; or click the Matte box to call up the Color Picker.

> **TIP** Elements' Color Picker lets you limit your choices to web-safe colors by turning on the Only Web Colors checkbox in its lower-left corner. But do you *have* to stick to this limited color palette for web graphics? Not really. You need to be seriously concerned about keeping to web-safe colors only if you know that the majority of people looking at your image will be using *very* old web browsers. All modern browsers can cope with a normal color range. (Getting colors to display consistently in all browsers is another kettle of fish entirely, as the next section explains.)

- **GIF.** The fewer colors a GIF contains, the smaller its file size. You can use the Colors box to set the number of colors, either by clicking the down arrow on the right edge of the box to scroll to the number you want, or just typing it in the box.

  If you turn on the Interlaced checkbox, then your image downloads in multiple passes (sort of like an image that's slowly coming into focus). With today's computers, interlacing isn't as useful as it used to be on slower machines. If you want to keep transparent areas transparent, then leave the Transparency checkbox turned on. If you don't want transparency, then choose a matte color the way you do for a JPEG (see the previous bullet point). If you're creating a GIF that you plan to animate, turn on the Animate checkbox. (You need a layered file to make an animated GIF; page 561 has the details.)

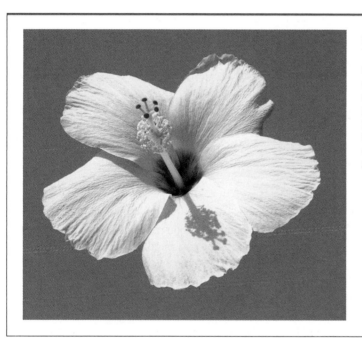

FIGURE 17-4.

When you save an image in JPEG format, the transparent areas aren't preserved. But Elements helps you simulate transparency by letting you choose a matte color, which replaces the transparency. By choosing a color that's identical to your web page's background, you can simulate transparency. For example, the purple matte around this hibiscus blossom will blend into the purple background of the page it's bound for.

Dither is an important setting because the GIF format works by compressing and flattening large areas of colors. When you use dithering, Elements blends existing colors to make the image look like it has more colors than it actually does. For instance, Elements may mix red and blue pixels in an area to create purple. You can choose how much dither you want by entering a percentage. Depending on your image, you may not want any dithering; in that case, set the Dither field to 0 percent. (Dithering makes for a larger file, but in these days of large files and fast connections, the difference in size is minuscule, so you'll usually want to use it.)

New in Elements 11, you can choose the kind of dithering used for both the image itself and for any transparent areas by selecting from the menus directly above and below the Transparency checkbox, respectively, although 99 percent of the time you won't need to bother with these settings. But if you're interested, Diffusion, the basic setting, applies dithering in a random pattern that is the least noticeable of the choices. Pattern applies dithering in a square pattern, something like the pattern of a halftone, and Noise is something like Diffusion, except that Diffusion disperses the effect over partial adjacent pixels, while Noise restricts it to staying within pixels. The Transparency dither options affect only partially transparent pixels.

Web Snap is a setting that lets you tell Elements you want only the antique web-safe colors in your image (see the note on page 558), as is Lossy. Leave the Lossy setting off—there's no sense in causing a GIF to lose data.

> **NOTE** If you've used Elements before, you may notice that in Elements 11 GIF and PNG-8 have longer names in the Preset menu with "128 Dithered" added to them. They're still the same old GIF and PNG-8 you knew from previous versions.

- **PNG-8.** This option, the more basic of your PNG choices in Elements, gives you pretty much the same options you get with GIF.

  With both PNG-8 and GIF, you get advanced options for how to display colors (specifically, to have Elements generate the color lookup table, which probably doesn't mean anything to you unless you're a web-design maven). The menu below the file-format menu lists your options. You can safely ignore this menu (Elements chooses Selective unless you change it), but if you're curious, here are your choices: Selective favors broad areas of color and keeps to web-safe colors; Perceptual favors colors to which the human eye is more sensitive; Adaptive samples colors from the spectrum appearing most commonly in the image; and Restrictive keeps everything within the old 216-color web palette.

- **PNG-24.** This is the more advanced level of PNG. Technically, both PNG formats let you use transparency, but more web browsers understand transparent areas in PNG-24 files than in PNG-8 files. Your other save options with this format are the same as some of those for JPEGs.

> **NOTE** The Preset menu includes an Original option, but unfortunately it's not very useful. All it does is to make both preview areas show the original format—it doesn't let you see a complete view of your photo without the second preview.

Previewing Images

Elements gives you a few different ways to preview how an image will look in a web browser. You can start by looking at the image in any browser you have on your computer (see Figure 17-5).

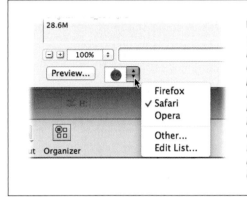

FIGURE 17-5.

To preview an image in a web browser, click the icon to the right of the Preview button in the bottom left of the Save For Web dialog box to launch your computer's standard web browser. (Once you've used it, the button displays your preferred browser's icon, or the one for the last browser you used for previewing in Elements.) Or you can click the arrow next to this icon and then choose a browser from the list. The first time you click this arrow, you may need to pick Edit List and then click Find All to use the browser you want. Elements sniffs out every browser on your computer and adds what it finds to this menu. (Sometimes the Windows version of Elements finds only Internet Explorer, so you have to add other browsers, like Firefox, manually via the Add button in the Browsers window. On Macs, Elements is pretty good about finding them all.)

To add a new browser, in the Save For Web dialog box, click the arrows shown in Figure 17-5, and then choose Edit List. In the Browsers dialog box that appears, click the Add button and navigate to the one you want. If you want to have *all* your browsers listed, then click Find All. From now on, you can pick any browser in the list to make Elements launch the browser with your image in it.

NOTE   If you've used previous versions of Elements, you may notice that Adobe has dropped the ability to preview using different color options like Standard Windows or Macintosh Color. That's probably because it was never a very good approximation of what your image would look like in real life. (You need only take a stroll down the monitor aisle at your local electronics store to see what a wacky bunch of color variations are possible.) You really can't control how other people will see your image without going to their homes and adjusting their monitors for them.

■ Creating Animated GIFs

With Elements, it's easy to create *animated GIFs,* those little illustrations that make web pages look annoyingly jumbled or delightfully active, depending on your taste. If you've ever seen a strip of movie film or the cels for a cartoon, Elements creates a similar series of frames with these specialized GIFs.

Animated GIFs are made up of layers, with a separate layer for each frame. Save For Web creates the actual animation, which you can preview in a web browser.

NOTE It's a shame that you can't easily animate a JPEG the way you can a GIF. Most elaborate web animations involving photographs are done with Flash, which is another program altogether. (You can learn a little
more about Flash on page 571; if you want the full story, pick up a copy of *Flash CS6: The Missing Manual*.)

The best way to learn about animated GIFs is to create one. Here's how to make
twinkling stars:

1. **In the Editor, set the foreground color to some shade of yellow and the
   background color to black.**

   See page 247 if you need help setting these colors.

2. **Create a new document.**

   Press Ctrl+N/⌘-N. In the New dialog box, set the size to 200 pixels × 200 pixels,
   choose RGB for the color mode, and then choose Background Color for the
   background contents. Finally, set the resolution to 72 ppi and then click OK.

3. **Activate the Custom Shape tool (page 423) and choose a star shape.**

   In the Tool Options area, click the down arrow to the right of the Shape field
   to open the Shapes palette. Then click the drop-down menu at the top of the
   palette and select Nature. Double-click the Sun 2 shape, which is in the top row,
   second from the left.

4. **Draw some stars.**

   Drag to draw one yellow star, and then, in the Tool Options area, click the "Add
   to shape area" button (page 421) before drawing four or five more stars. (This
   puts all the stars on the same layer, which is important, since that way you won't
   have a bunch of layers to merge.)

5. **Merge the star layer and the Background layer.**

   Choose Layer→Merge Down. You now have one layer containing yellow stars
   on a black background, like the bottom layer in Figure 17-6.

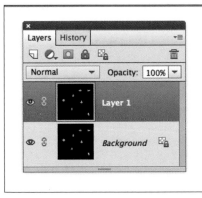

FIGURE 17-6.

*This animated GIF has only two frames, which makes for a pretty crude animation. The more
frames you have, the smoother the animation, but the bigger the file, too. On a tiny image
like this one, size doesn't matter, but with a larger image, your file can get huge pretty fast.*

6. **Duplicate the layer.**

Choose Layer→Duplicate Layer and then click OK. You now have two identical layers.

7. **Rotate the top layer 90 degrees.**

Go to Image→Rotate→Rotate Layer 90° Left (not the regular "90° Left" command). You should now have two layers with stars in different places on each one.

8. **Animate your GIF.**

Go to File→Save For Web, and in the dialog box that appears, turn on the Animate checkbox. (If you don't see the Animate checkbox, make sure GIF is selected in the box below the word "Preset"; if it isn't, select it from the drop-down menu.) In the Animation section, adjust the time between frames, if you want. Leave the Looping Options menu set to Forever so the animation repeats over and over (otherwise your animation plays just once and then stops).

9. **Preview the animation.**

You can use the arrows in the Animation section to step through your animation one frame at a time, but for a more realistic preview, view the image in a web browser as explained in the previous section. The stars should twinkle. (Well, OK, they flash off and on—think of twinkle lights.)

10. **Save the animation, if you like, by clicking Save in the Save For Web dialog box.**

You can reopen and edit GIF files in Expert Mode and see all the layers they include. Save them as PSD files to preserve their layers. If you make any changes, be sure to use Save For Web to reanimate it.

ON THE WEB

Creating Web Buttons

Elements makes it a snap to create buttons to use on web pages. Here's how:

1. **Create a new blank file (File→New→Blank File).** In the New dialog box's Preset menu, choose Web and then pick a size you like. In the Background Contents menu, choose Transparent. Then click OK.

2. **Set the foreground color square to the color you want to use for the button, and use a shape tool to draw the shape you want.** It helps to choose Actual Pixels for your view size when doing web work, because that shows you the same size you'll see in a web browser.

3. **Apply one or more layer styles (page 461) to make your button look more 3-D.** Bevels, some of the Complex layer styles, and the Wow layer styles are all popular choices.

4. **Add any necessary text using a type tool (page 479).** You may want to apply a layer style to the text, too.

5. **Save the file as a GIF.**

Emailing Photos

Elements makes emailing photos you have stored in the Organizer a piece of cake. With just a few clicks, the program preps the image(s), fires up your email program, and attaches the image(s) to an outgoing message. (Of course, you can also email images without Elements' help, and you may prefer that method since you get more freedom to specify settings like file size.)

> **NOTE** Elements can prep your image and automatically launch your email program only if you're using Windows Live Mail (in Windows 7), Vista's Windows Mail, Outlook Express or Outlook (in Windows XP), or Adobe's own mail server in any version of Windows. (It's a bit annoying that you can't use Windows Live Mail anywhere but in Windows 7, but that's how Adobe set things up.) On a Mac, your choices are OS X's Mail, Entourage, or Outlook 2011. The first time you use one of Elements' email features, you get a pop-up window asking you to choose one of these programs. If you want to change the program later, in the Organizer, go to Edit→Preferences→Sharing.
>
> Elements' email features don't work with other email programs like Yahoo Mail or Thunderbird, so if you want to use a program like that, just use that program's Attach button instead. (You can export an image from the Organizer to your desktop to make it easier to find.)

If you use Windows, you have quite an array of formatting choices for emailing photos: You can send simple attachments or prearranged groups of photos, frame the photos, change their background color, and so on. On a Mac, not so much, unfortunately.

All emailing in Elements 11 starts from the Organizer's Share menu. Here are your main choices there:

- **Email Attachments (Mac and Windows).** This is the most traditional option, where you send each photo as a standard attachment.

- **Photo Mail (Windows only).** Elements lets you send emails formatted in *HTML*, the programming language used to create web pages. This option gives you all kinds of fancy design options, and your photo gets embedded in the body of the email—it's basically like emailing someone a custom-built web page featuring your image.

    The catch is that the recipient has to be using a mail program that understands HTML. Most newer email programs fit the bill, but if you're emailing someone who uses ancient software like AOL 4, then your email formatting won't appear correctly. An even larger problem, though, is that if your recipient has her email program's HTML option turned off, then your email doesn't appear with all its formatting intact. Page 567 has more info about Elements' Photo Mail options.

- **PDF Slide Show (Mac and Windows).** This option creates a basic PDF-format slideshow of your images. All you have to do is name the slideshow (see page 569).

You need to choose the kind of email you want to send before you start. To pick, click the one you want in the Organizer's Share menu. The basic process is pretty similar for all the different types and is explained in detail below. There's one really annoying aspect of sending images from Elements, though: The messages you send include an ad for Elements.

Individual Attachments (Mac and Windows)

To send photos as regular email attachments, just follow these steps:

> **NOTE**   In Elements 11, all sharing starts in the Organizer. If you don't use the Organizer or you want to email photos that aren't in the Organizer, just use the Attachments button in your regular mail program.

1. **In the Organizer, select some photos (optional), and then go to Share→Email Attachments.**

   You can preselect photos before you start or add or change them once the Email Attachments panel appears; Figure 17-7 explains how.

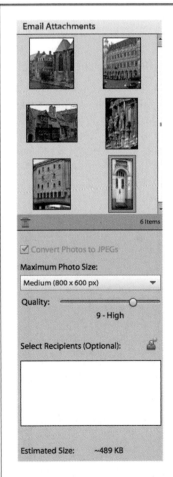

FIGURE 17-7.

The Organizer's Email Attachments panel is pretty easy to use. You can start with one photo or a group, as shown here. To send more photos, just drag the images' thumbnails from the Media Browser into the Email Attachments panel. Remove photos you don't want by highlighting them in the panel and then clicking the little trash can below the thumbnail area. Drag your photos in the panel to change their order.

In the Email Attachments panel, below the image thumbnails, is some info that can help you decide how many photos to send and how large to make them:

- **Number of Items.** Indicates how many photos you've selected to send.

- **Convert Photos to JPEGs.** JPEG is the best format for emailing photos, so you can turn on this checkbox to have Elements make JPEG versions of the images you've selected. (If the photos are already JPEGs, then the option is grayed out.) If you want to convert only some of your photos to JPEGs, select their thumbnails before you turn on this checkbox.

- **Maximum Photo Size.** This tells Elements how large you want the emailed photos to be. Remember that it can take a really long time to download a large image with a dial-up Internet connection, and many email providers have a 10 MB limit per mailbox. If you need to change the size, then use this drop-down menu to choose a new one.

- **Quality.** If you're just emailing photos for viewing onscreen, then you can get away with a lower Quality setting than you can for photos that the recipient is going to print.

Below these settings, at the very bottom of the panel, is Elements' calculation of how large the attachment will be.

NOTE Elements doesn't do anything to warn you if you're sending a humongously large attachment, so it's up to you to pay attention to how large a file you're making with all the photos you're including. Unless your friends have dial-up connections, a 1 MB attachment is no big deal these days, but some Internet service providers still limit attachment sizes to 5 MB or less.

2. **Address the email (optional).**

   Decide whether you want to enter the recipient's email address now. You can:

   - **Do nothing.** Wait until Elements is through, and then type the address in the completed email before you send it.

   - **Select Recipients.** Elements keeps a Contact Book—a list of people you regularly email—so you can simply select names from the list. (The box on page 567 has more about this feature.) If you haven't used Elements' email feature before, then start by clicking the Edit Contacts button (the little silhouette just above the Select Recipients section) and entering your recipient's contact info.

   - **Edit Contacts.** To enter a new recipient or change the information for someone in your list, then click the Edit Contacts button (the silhouette), and enter the new info in the Contact Book.

3. **To finish, click Next.**

Elements launches your email program, creates a new message, and attaches the files for you. You can then add your own text to the message or make any changes to the recipient(s) in your email program.

Elements' Contact Book

The Organizer makes it easy to call up the addresses of people you regularly email by keeping a Contact Book. Anytime you send email to a new recipient, you first have to add the address to the Contact Book by clicking the Edit Contacts button (the silhouette) in the Email Attachments panel. (You can also get to the Contact Book by choosing Edit→Contact Book in the main Organizer window.)

Once you've got the Contact Book window open, click the New Contact button to add an address. Then you can type in a name, email address, phone number, and other contact info. To edit or delete a contact, just highlight it in the list and then click the relevant button.

You can also create groups of names in the Contact Book, for times when you want to send the same photo to several people at once. To do this, click New Group, enter a name for the group, select entries in the Contact Book, and then click Add. The people's names go into the Members list. To remove a name from the group, highlight it in the Members list and then click Remove.

In Windows, Elements makes it easy to coordinate the Contact Book with your existing address book. You can choose to import addresses from Vista's Windows Mail, Microsoft Outlook, or Outlook Express, as well as any that you've saved as vCards (a digital business card format) in other programs. Just click Import and choose your source. You can also export your Contact Book addresses as vCards to use them in other programs. This is another feature that isn't in the Mac version yet, although OS X's Address Book can import and export vCards for you.

Photo Mail (Windows only)

Elements also gives you a ton of options for gussying up your photos if you choose Share→Photo Mail. As mentioned earlier, Photo Mail is actually HTML mail. When you send HTML mail, your message gets formatted using a *template*, a stationery design in which your photo appears.

NOTE Mac folks, there's no need to fret because you don't have Photo Mail. If you use OS X's Mail, you've got some pretty fine templates right there. Just start a new message and then click Show Stationery at the upper right of the New Message window to see a bunch of Apple-designed formatting choices.

The process for sending Photo Mail is pretty much the same as for email attachments (page 565), but in the first panel you can choose whether to display captions along with the photos, and you don't get the option of converting the photos to JPEGs; Elements controls that.

After you've chosen your photos and (optionally) your recipients, click Next and the Stationery & Layouts wizard (a series of guided question screens) presents a long list of stationery theme categories with several choices in each. The preview window updates to show each one as you click it. You can add a caption to any photo in this window by highlighting the text above the photo and typing what you want. When you find a style you like, click Next.

In the next window, you have a choice of several different page layouts. Below the layouts, you can choose a typeface from a list of five common fonts. Click the box to the right of the font's name to choose a color for the text. You can also customize the frame or border around the photos, as shown in Figure 17-8. Each time you make a change in the left pane of the window, Elements updates the preview so you can see just what you're getting.

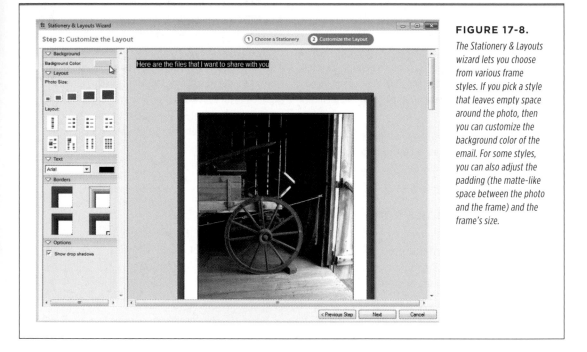

FIGURE 17-8.

The Stationery & Layouts wizard lets you choose from various frame styles. If you pick a style that leaves empty space around the photo, then you can customize the background color of the email. For some styles, you can also adjust the padding (the matte-like space between the photo and the frame) and the frame's size.

When you've adjusted everything to your liking, click Next. (Click Cancel if you don't want to send the email after all, or Previous Step if you want to go back and choose a different theme.) Elements creates your ready-to-send email. You can make any changes to the message and address just as you would to any other email—and send it off like any other email, too.

PDF Slideshows (Mac and Windows)

You can also email a group of photos as a slideshow. Elements uses the popular PDF format, which lets your recipients page through each slide using the free, ubiquitous Adobe Reader program available from *http://get.adobe.com/reader* (or, on a Mac, in OS X Preview, if they prefer). They just open the PDF and view the photos one by one.

To create a slideshow from the Organizer, select the photos you want to include, and then go to Share→PDF Slide Show. In the PDF Slideshow panel that appears, Elements offers you a choice of sizes and quality, just as you have for sending photos as email attachments. Name the slideshow, enter a message or recipients if you like, and then click Next. Elements generates a standard email message with the slideshow attached. At this point you can add your own message text (and delete the advertising for Elements, if you like). As with regular attachments, pay attention to the size of the PDF that Elements has created to make sure you won't choke your recipient's inbox.

> **NOTE** On Windows computers, you have another way to create slideshows: the Slide Show Editor, which is covered in more detail on page 580. On Macs, the Share menu is your only slideshow option in Elements, but don't forget that you can also make slideshows in iMovie, iPhoto, and iDVD if you want something more deluxe.

Online Albums
and Slideshows

I n the last chapter, you learned how to email photos. But what if you've got le-
gions of friends—do you have to email your pictures to everyone individually? Not
with Elements, which makes it incredibly simple to post images online, either at
Adobe's Photoshop Showcase site or a number of popular social-networking and
photo-sharing sites.

You can create fancy online albums complete with professional-looking effects,
courtesy of *Flash*, the ubiquitous Adobe program that's responsible for zillions of
nifty online animations. If you use Windows, Elements can also help you put together
elaborate slideshows, complete with slick between-photo transitions like wipes and
dissolves, clip art, and even audio. In this chapter, you'll learn the ins and outs of all
these ways of sharing photos.

> **NOTE** Alas, the fancy slideshows didn't make it into the Mac Organizer, but Apple fans can still make online
> albums and PDF slideshows.

■ Online Albums

Adobe calls these "albums," but the online albums you create from Elements aren't
just boring, grid-like rows of photos like you see on most photo websites. Instead
they're elaborate, Flash-based displays in which your photos do things like appear
in an animation of an old-fashioned school notebook or spiral down the screen.

Sharing a New Album

If you've signed up to use Photoshop Showcase (page 9), Adobe makes it super easy to share albums there, right as you create them:

1. **In the Organizer, go to Share→Online Album.**

   In the Share panel on the right side of the Organizer, choose Create New Album.

2. **Choose how you want to share the album.**

   You can opt to send your completed album to Photoshop Showcase or export it to your hard drive so you can use another method to put it on your own website (more about that below). If you use Windows, you can also burn the album to a CD or a DVD. (Mac users can do this by choosing "Export to Hard Disk" and then burning the disc in the Finder.) These options are explained in more detail after this list.

   Click Next to move to the next pane.

3. **Name your new album and add photos to it.**

   Type a name for the new album, and, if you wish, choose a category for it. (Album categories are optional, so unless you make so many albums you'd have trouble keeping track without more organization, you can skip choosing a category.) If you selected photos before you started this process, they'll appear in the Content tab on the right side of the Organizer. If you didn't, simply drag the photos you want to include in the album from the thumbnails area onto the Content tab. You can then drag the photos around to rearrange them in the album. To delete a photo you don't want included, click the photo to highlight it, and then click the trash-can icon near the bottom of the Share panel. Shift-click or Ctrl-click/⌘-click to select multiple photos.

   When you've got all the photos in the order you want, click OK to move to the next step. You'll see a dialog box that says "Please enter the details for Sharing this album." Just click OK. Elements thinks for a bit, and then displays a preview of your album in the main Media area. Don't be alarmed if music starts playing—some templates include music. You can turn it off by clicking the musical note icon in the preview's lower left.

4. **If you wish, change the album's template.**

   Elements starts you off by displaying a preview of your album in the main part of the Organizer window. If you don't like the template Elements picked, go to the "Select a Template" menu above the preview area and choose a template category, and then double-click the various template thumbnails that appear below the menu. Use the slider below the thumbnails to move back and forth through the category's available slideshows. The main part of the Organizer window displays a large preview of what your photos will look like in the selected template.

Most templates play automatically, and others are interactive, as explained in Figure 18-1. (When you create the album, Elements applies the last template style you clicked.)

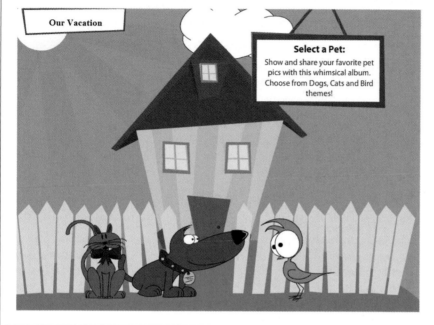

FIGURE 18-1.

Some of the album styles automatically start playing their slideshows, while others, like the Pet Gallery template shown here, are interactive. Your friends choose the pet (dog, cat, or bird) they want to scamper into the house to accompany your photos as they look through them.

5. **Change any settings for the album.**

   Some albums have "ghosted" settings panels that come into focus when you move your cursor over them. Others have tabs you can click within the preview to make changes. The settings you can change depend on the template: You may be able to tweak only the title that appears, or to do things like change the kind and color of the paper Elements uses for the virtual notebook pages.

6. **Choose the sharing options you want in the Sharing pane.**

   Even though you already chose a sharing option when you started the album, this is where you make your final choice (you can pick a different sharing option here than you chose when you started the album, if you change your mind). This is where you will have the opportunity to provide the information that Elements needs to finish the job, like the folder where you want to save the finished album, for example. Your options are explained in detail after this list.

7. **Click OK.**

   Elements either sends your album off to Photoshop Showcase or exports it (or not) in the way you chose in step 6.

Before you finalize your album, you have to choose a sharing method from the Sharing tab. Here are your choices:

- **Photoshop Showcase.** If you have an account at Photoshopshowcase. com (see page 9), Elements sends your album there so you can share it online. You can choose to make it public or to send a private link to your friends and family so that only they can see it.

- **Export to CD/DVD (Windows Only).** Elements asks you to choose the drive to use to burn the disc, and enter a name (a.k.a. label) for the CD or DVD. When you click OK, Elements asks you to insert a disc. Put one in, and then click OK. Elements burns the disc and then asks if you want to verify it; you do. Finally, it reminds you to label the completed disc before it ejects it.

  Discs made this way play on computers, not on DVD players. If your friends use Windows, the disc should play automatically when they put it into their computers. If that doesn't work (sometimes the loading animation loops endlessly and the slideshow never runs), or if they're using Macs, tell them to open the disc, navigate to the Root folder, and then double-click the *index.html* file inside that. The slideshow will then play in their web browser.

> **TIP** If you have a Mac, you can still burn an album to a disc. Just export it to your hard disk and then burn it to a disc using the Finder.

- **Export to Hard Disk.** This option makes Elements save your album to a folder on your hard drive. In the Sharing tab, click the Browse button to choose a location for the album and then click OK. This creates an album that plays right on your computer, even when you aren't connected to the Internet. To play it, open the folder where Elements saved it and then double-click the file named *index.html*. Your web browser opens and the slideshow runs there. If you want to upload the album to your website, use an FTP program to do so, the same way you would send any other file to your site.

- **Do Not Share.** Elements creates your album, but it exists only in the list of albums in the Organizer rather than being exported so you can share it with others.

Sharing Existing Albums

It's also easy to share existing albums from the Organizer's Share menu or the Albums/Folders panel:

- **Share menu.** In the Organizer, click the Share menu and select Online Album. Elements presents you with the Online Album pane described above, where you can create a new album or choose an existing album from the list and then select how you want to share it. The rest of the process is the same as the one for sharing a new album (page 572).

- **Albums panel.** To display the Albums/Folders panel (page 49), click the Show button at the bottom left of the main Organizer window. In the panel, right-click/Control-click an album's name, and then choose whether to have Elements export it to Photoshop Showcase, your hard disk or, in Windows, to a CD or a DVD.

The process for any of these options is similar to the one described in the previous section. You can change templates, rearrange the photos, add or remove photos, and so on, exactly the way you can when creating a new album.

◼ Slideshows

Online albums are about the easiest way to make fancy slideshows to share with people in other places, but maybe you want more control than they give you, or perhaps you want to add features like your own music or panning and zooming over the photos à la Ken Burns. Elements makes it easy to create very slick little slideshows—even some with music and transitions between the images—that you can play on your computer or send to friends. Elements' Slide Show Editor lets you create really elaborate slideshows, but unfortunately it's still available in only the Windows version of the program.

If you have a Mac or if you prefer the simple life, you can quickly create a plain-vanilla PDF slideshow in about as much time as it takes to email a photo. PDF slideshows are really straightforward to create, but you can't add audio to them or control how the photos transition. On the plus side, you can send PDF slideshows to anyone, regardless of what operating system they use. As long as your recipients have Adobe Reader (which is free) or another PDF-viewing program, they can watch your show.

The Windows-only Slide Show Editor, on the other hand, lets you indulge your creativity big time. You can add all sorts of snazzy transitions, mix in sound (background music or narration), add clip art, pan around your photos, and so on. It's a bit more complex to work with the Slide Show Editor than to make a PDF slideshow, but the real drawback to the Slide Show Editor comes in your choices for the final output: The slideshow file you create isn't as universally compatible as available in only, as explained later in this chapter.

The easiest slideshow of all, though, is the kind you can make in the Organizer's Full Screen view, where it's a snap to create a full-featured slideshow with just a couple of quick settings adjustments. But you can show this kind of slideshow only to people who can see your computer monitor—you can't save it and email it or post it on the Web.

> **TIP** If you plan to create a simple PDF slideshow, then you need to do all your photo editing beforehand. The Full Screen view and Slide Show Editor methods, on the other hand, let you edit as much as you like before finalizing the slideshow.

Choosing a Slideshow

A couple of versions ago, people sometimes slammed Elements for not offering much in the way of slideshows. Now the program gives you so many slideshow options that you might get overwhelmed trying to decide on one. Here are some suggestions to help you out:

- **Slideshows on your computer.** The fastest way to create a slideshow to display on your computer screen is to use the Organizer's Full Screen view, as explained below.

- **Slideshows for the Web.** If you want to share the slideshow on the Internet, create an online album (page 571).

- **Slideshows with audio.** If you use a Windows computer and you want the slideshow to have a narrated soundtrack, use the Slide Show Editor to create the show (page 580), and then burn it to a disc to share with friends, who can watch the show on their computers using Windows Media Player. (On a Mac, you can use iMovie to do this.)

- **Slideshows for people who aren't comfortable with technology.** You've got two options here, neither of which

is guaranteed to prevent Uncle Joe from complaining that he can't see pictures of his new grandniece. You can create an online album (page 571) and then send him a disc or email him a link, but he'll need a web browser with Flash installed. The simple PDF slideshow (page 569) is also pretty straightforward, but your recipients need to have Adobe Reader or another PDF viewer to watch it. For the severely techno-challenged, consider a printed photo book, described on page 519.

Finally, if you still don't think Elements offers enough choices, ProShow Gold from Photodex (*www.photodex.com*) is probably the most popular slideshow program for Windows. On a Mac, if iMovie, iPhoto, and iDVD don't work for you, FotoMagico (*www. boinx.com*) is the next step up. And if you don't like Elements' photo albums, jAlbum (*www.jalbum.net*) is a popular free alternative for both Mac and Windows, although these days many people just create online slideshows using one of the photo-sharing services mentioned on page 591.

Full Screen View

Elements gives you a really easy way to create impressive little slideshows to play on your computer, which could come in handy if you want to play a retrospective of Mom and Dad's life together during their 50th wedding anniversary party, for example. Whether you're using a Mac or a Windows machine, you do this via the Organizer's Full Screen view, and you have all kinds of options for music and fancy transitions between the images. To get started:

1. **In the Organizer, select the photos and videos you want to use in the slideshow, and then go to Full Screen view.**

   If you want the photos displayed in a particular order, put them into an album (page 55) and rearrange them there. Then press F11/⌘-F11 or click the Slide Show button below the image thumbnail area. (If you have a Mac with a short keyboard without the 10-key pad on the right—one like a laptop or the current Bluetooth keyboard—you need to add the fn key to all keystroke combos that use the F-keys on the top row of the keyboard.)

If you'd rather display more than one image at a time, press F12/⌘-F12 instead to start your slideshow in Side-by-Side view, which shows two images at a time.

2. **In Full Screen view, adjust the slideshow's settings.**

Use the control strip across the bottom of the screen (shown in Figure 18-2) to control how Elements presents your slideshow. (You won't see the control strip until you move your mouse over the photo being displayed.) Your options are explained after this list.

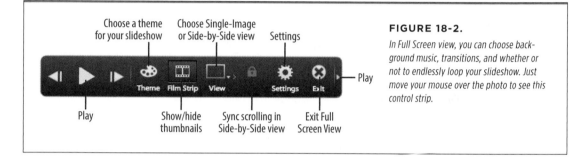

FIGURE 18-2.

In Full Screen view, you can choose background music, transitions, and whether or not to endlessly loop your slideshow. Just move your mouse over the photo to see this control strip.

3. **Run the slideshow.**

Click the Play button or tap your space bar to start the slideshow. To pause it, click the Pause button or press your space bar again. To exit Full Screen view and get back to the Organizer, click the X at the right end of the control strip or press Esc.

Here's what the buttons in the control strip (Figure 18-2) let you do:

- **Theme.** Click this button to choose from among four kinds of transitions between slides: Classic (one photo simply gives way to the next), Fade In/Out, Pan & Zoom (Elements pans across each photo), or 3D Pixelate, which puts an elaborate glittery dissolve between each image. Move your cursor over each transition's thumbnail to see a demo of it, and then click the radio button under the one you want.

You can't change the background color in Full Screen slideshows—it's always black (unless you choose the 3D Pixelate transition, in which case it's white).

- **Film Strip.** Use this button to toggle a thumbnail view of all the images in your slideshow across the bottom of your screen.

- **View.** Click the appropriate icon to choose between a single-image view or seeing two photos side by side or one above the other.

TIP You can use the F11 / ⌘-F11 and F12 / ⌘-F12 shortcuts while your slideshow is running to switch between Single-Image and Side-by-Side view.

- **Sync.** When you're in a double-image view, this button (which looks like a padlock) lets you tell Elements to pan and zoom over the two images in exactly the same way. (This button is grayed out when you're in Single-Image view.)

- **Settings.** Click this gear icon to change the music for your slideshow (or choose None if you don't want any). Elements comes with a few built-in songs, but you can use any compatible audio file (MP3, WAV, AC3, AAC, or WMA format) that's on your computer. If the audio file you want to use isn't in the Background Music menu, click the Browse button to find it. You can opt to play any audio captions included in your files (see page 587), display text captions, or allow Elements to resize the slideshow's photos and videos so they fit onscreen (yes, videos play here, too, if you include them in the show).

  You can also choose to display a strip of thumbnails of all your photos along the bottom of the screen (the control strip's Film Strip button does the same thing). Use the Page Duration box to determine how long each photo stays on the screen.

- **Exit.** Press Esc or click this button to end the show.

Those are the controls you normally see, but if you click the arrow at the right end of the control strip, it expands to include these additional choices:

- **Fix.** Click this for a pop-out panel where you can apply all the quick fixes you can make in the main Organizer window (page 116).

- **Organize.** You can tag photos or sort them into albums right in Full Screen view. Just click this button for a pop-out panel with a list of albums and your most commonly used tags (page 53).

- **Info.** This button brings up the same information about the current photo that you would see in the Information pane in the main Organizer window. (If you're using a two-image view, Elements puts a blue outline around the image it's displaying information about.)

It hardly takes any time to set up a slideshow this way, and all you have to do once you get it going is stand back and accept compliments for your impressive display. The disadvantage to this kind of slideshow, obviously, is that you can't share it with anyone who doesn't have access to your computer. But Elements gives you a bunch of ways to make slideshows to send to other folks, as explained in the rest of this chapter.

TIP If you want a fancier slideshow than you can create in Full Screen view, create an online album (see page 571) and export it to your hard disk. To play it there, open the folder where you saved it and double-click the file named *index.html*.

PDF Slideshows

Elements gives you two ways to create PDF slideshows. The first, the simple PDF slideshow, is very basic—just a quick run-through of the photos you choose. But if you have a Windows computer, you can make a PDF that's slightly more elaborate using the Slide Show Editor.

■ SIMPLE PDF SLIDESHOW

To start a simple PDF slideshow, in the Organizer, go to Share→PDF Slide Show. Creating the slideshow is as easy as sending an email. You can read more about it on page 569. This slideshow has no transitions, no clip art, and no custom text, but it's the most compatible kind of slideshow you can make in Elements, which means that almost anyone you send it to will be able to view it. And you can easily create a reasonable-sized file so anybody can watch it, no matter how underpowered their computer.

■ MAKING A PDF IN THE SLIDE SHOW EDITOR (WINDOWS ONLY)

The other way to create a PDF slideshow isn't as intuitive as the method just described. The next section has all the details of how to create a show in the Slide Show Editor. When you're done, you can choose between saving it as a Windows Media Video (WMV) file or a PDF. If you want to preserve the show's multimedia bells and whistles, then you need to choose WMV. But then there's that tantalizing PDF option.

You may think this PDF slideshow sounds like the best of both worlds—a very compatible format and all the fancy effects you added with the Slide Show Editor. Unfortunately, that's not quite how it works. When you create a PDF this way, you lose the pan-and-zoom feature (page 587), the audio, and the transitions you selected, though Elements preserves any custom slides, text, and clip art you added. On the whole, it's best to use this feature when you've created a full-scale slideshow but one or two of the people you want to send it to can't open Windows Media Video files. The people who get the PDF version can't see everything the WMV recipients do, but it's faster than trying to recreate a separate version for the WMV-challenged.

To create a PDF using the Slide Show Editor, just follow the instructions in the following section. When you're ready to create the PDF, click Output, and on the left side of the Slide Show Output dialog box that opens, choose "Save As a File." On the right side of the dialog box, click the PDF File button. This displays a series of settings just for your PDF:

- **Slide Size.** This setting starts out at Small. If you're going to burn a CD, then you can choose a larger size. If you want to email the final file, go with Small or Very Small. You also have a Custom choice for when you want to create a size that's different from the presets.

- **Loop.** Turn this on, and the slideshow repeats over and over until your viewer stops it by pressing Esc.

- **Manual Advance.** If you want recipients to be able to click their way through the slideshow instead of having each slide automatically advance to the next one, turn this on.

- **View Slide Show after Saving.** Turn on this setting, and as soon as Elements is through creating your slideshow, it launches Adobe Reader so you can watch the results of your work.

TIP To make a PDF from an existing slideshow project file, in the Media Browser, right-click the slideshow's thumbnail, and then choose Edit. Once the Slide Show Editor opens, click Output→"Save As a File."

When you've got everything set the way you want it, click OK to bring up the Save As dialog box. Simply name your file and then save it.

The Slide Show Editor (Windows only)

The Slide Show Editor lets you add audio, clip art, and nifty slide-to-slide transitions to your slideshows. You also get several different ways to share the completed slideshow, including making a video CD (VCD) or—if you also have Premiere Elements—a DVD that your friends can watch using a regular DVD player.

To get started, in the Organizer, select the images you want to include. You may want to set up an album (page 55), which lets you control the order of the images. (You can change the order once they're in the Slide Show Editor, but for large shows, it saves time if you have things arranged in pretty much the correct order when you start.) You can also start with a single photo and, once you're in the Slide Show Editor, click the Add Media button to add more images. In any case, once you've got the photo(s) selected, go to Create→Slide Show.

■ SLIDE SHOW PREFERENCES

Once you choose to create a slideshow, Elements presents you with the Slide Show Preferences dialog box (Figure 18-3) before displaying the actual Slide Show Editor. You can click right past this dialog box if you like, but it has some useful options for telling Elements how you want it to handle certain aspects of all your shows, like the duration of each slide and the background color. (You can change these settings for a particular show in the Slide Show Editor itself.)

In the Slide Show Preferences dialog box, you can adjust the following:

- **Static Duration.** This determines how long Elements displays each slide before it moves on to the next one.

- **Transition.** This setting tells Elements how to move from one slide to the next. You get many different styles to choose from, like a pinwheel effect or having the next slide move into view from the side. When you choose a transition from the pop-out menu, the dialog box shows you what that transition looks like, as explained in Figure 18-3.

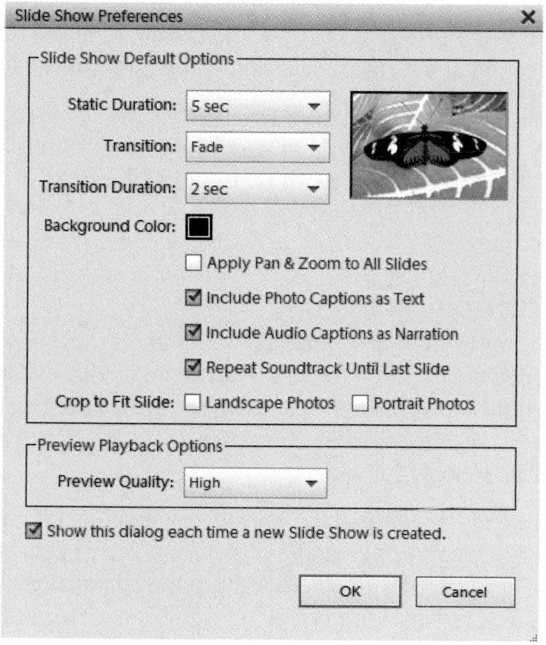

FIGURE 18-3.

This dialog box lets you set the slide duration and background color for all your slideshows. It's also a great place to audition different transitions. To see what a particular transition does, select it from the Transition drop-down menu and Elements plays it in the little preview area on the right. If you choose a transition here, then Elements automatically applies it to every slide. But you can override this setting for individual slides in the Slide Show Editor's storyboard by clicking the transition you want to change and choosing a different one.

- **Transition Duration.** Use this to set how fast the transitions happen.

- **Background Color.** If you want a different background color, click this square to bring up the Color Picker.

- **Apply Pan & Zoom to All Slides.** If you set up the Pan & Zoom feature (explained later in this chapter) for one slide, turn this on and the camera swoops around *every* slide.

- **Include Photo Captions as Text.** To display a photo's Caption field, turn on this checkbox. (This works in reverse, too—you can hide the captions by turning off this checkbox.)

- **Include Audio Captions as Narration.** If you've recorded audio captions for your slides (page 587), leave this checkbox turned on if you want your audience to hear them.

- **Repeat Soundtrack Until Last Slide.** Leave this checkbox turned on, and if the slideshow is longer than the soundtrack, Elements repeats your song(s) as many times as necessary.

- **Crop to Fit Slide.** Turn on either of these checkboxes (for landscape- and portrait-oriented photos) and, if an image is too large for its slide, then Elements chops off the excess. However, it's best to do any cropping (page 85) yourself before creating a slideshow.

- **Preview Quality.** This setting controls the quality of the preview you see while working on the show; it doesn't affect the quality of the final slideshow.

Once you're through setting these preferences, click OK. If you don't want to see these settings every time you start a new show, then just turn off the "Show this dialog each time a new Slide Show is created" checkbox. You can call up the dialog box again anytime you're in the Slide Show Editor by going to Edit→Slide Show Preferences.

■ USING THE SLIDE SHOW EDITOR

After you click OK in the Slide Show Preferences dialog box, Elements launches the Slide Show Editor. It's crammed with options, but everything is laid out logically—in fact, it's pretty similar to the Editor window. There's a menu bar across the top, but most of the commands here are available elsewhere via a button or a keystroke (like pressing Ctrl+Z to undo your last action).

The preview area on the left side of the window displays the slide you're currently working on. There's a Panel Bin on the right side of the screen, and you can collapse it by going to the View menu and turning it off there. (You turn it on again in the same place.)

At the bottom of the window is a strip called the *storyboard,* where Elements displays your slides and the transitions between them. (If you didn't preselect any photos, the storyboard just says "Click Here to Add Photos to Your Slide Show.") Click a slide or transition here and its properties (duration, background color, pan-and-zoom settings) appear in the Panel Bin. To hide the storyboard, go to the Slide Show Editor's View menu and turn off the checkmark next to its name. You can unhide it again there, too.

TIP To add photos to your slideshow, click the Add Media button at the top of the Slide Show Editor window. The advantage to bringing photos in this way (as opposed to selecting them before creating the slideshow) is that you can pick photos, videos, and audio clips that *aren't* in the Organizer by clicking this button and then choosing either the "Photos and Videos from Folder" or "Audio from Folder" option, and then navigating to the files you want. You can even edit photos right in the Slide Show Editor. The disadvantage of using the Add Media button is that you have to choose each photo separately or you have no control over the order in which Elements brings them into the show.

The Slide Show Editor lets you finesse your show in lots of different ways. For instance, you can do the following:

- **Edit slides.** Just click an image in the preview window, and then, using the choices that appear in the Properties panel (Figure 18-4), you can rotate the slide, resize it, crop it, and apply Auto Smart Fix (page 123) and Auto Red Eye Fix (page 121) to it. If you want to do more substantial editing, then just click the More Editing button, and Elements whisks the slide over to Expert Mode.

> **NOTE** The Properties panel changes depending on what you select in the storyboard or the main preview area. The panel always includes settings that are relevant to the item you've selected.

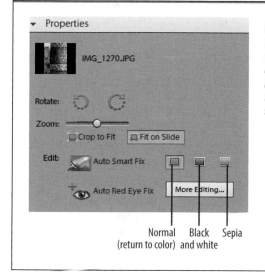

FIGURE 18-4.

The three little rectangles in the Slide Show Editor's Properties panel let you change a photo to black-and-white, sepia, or back to color again (if you change your mind). To make a slide to black-and-white or sepia, just click the button for the effect you want. To undo a color change you make here, click the Normal button. The changes you make with these buttons affect only the slide, not the original image.

- **Change durations.** In the properties Elements displays is a number indicating how long a slide appears onscreen before it transitions to the next one. Click the number to see a pop-up menu that lists various durations (if you want to enter your own number rather than selecting from the menu, just click the current duration number to turn it into an active text box where you can type what you want). You can assign different durations to each slide, if you want. If you want to choose a duration that isn't between 3 and 7 seconds, choose Custom from the pop-up menu and type the number of seconds you want. You can also use the drop-down menu that appears next to the slide's thumbnail in the Properties panel.

TIP If you've lost the duration and Pan & Zoom properties because you clicked over to the slide's Edit or Text properties (described in the following sections), you can get back to them by clicking once in the preview area outside the slide itself.

- **Pick transitions.** Elements gives you lots of different ways to get from one slide to the next. These transitions appear in the storyboard and are represented by small thumbnail icons between the slides they connect. (The icon changes to reflect the current transition style when you choose a new one.)

    On the right side of each transition icon is a tiny black triangle. (If you mouse over it, it lights up to make it easier to see.) Click it to see a pop-out menu listing all of Elements' transitions, and then choose the one you want.

    Transitions have their own Properties panels, which appear when you click a transition in the storyboard. You can choose how long a transition takes and, for some transitions, the direction it moves.

If you like to make long slideshows, you'll appreciate Elements' Quick Reorder feature, explained in Figure 18-5. When you switch over to the Quick Reorder window, you see all your slides in a view that looks like a contact sheet, making it easy to reposition slides that would be annoyingly far apart if you had to move them in the storyboard. In Quick Reorder, you just drag them to another spot in the lineup without the hassle of scrolling.

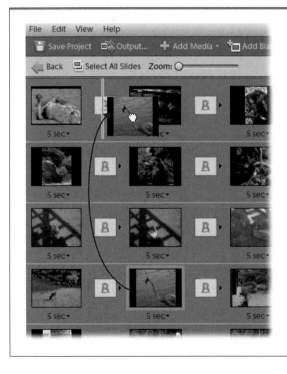

FIGURE 18-5.

You can reorder slides by dragging them in the storyboard, but if you have more than a few slides, all that scrolling can be a pain. The Quick Reorder window, shown here, makes the process easier. Just click the Quick Reorder button in the lower left of the Slide Show Editor (just above the storyboard) to bring up what looks like a contact sheet of your slides. Then drag any picture to its new location. You see a vertical blue line (like the one next to the flamingo image being moved here) indicating the photo's new position. When you're done, in the window's upper-left corner, click Back to return to the main editing window.

You can also change the order of all your slides by using the Slide Order drop-down menu below the Properties panel, although your choices there are limited. If you start a slideshow by first selecting photos in the Organizer, then the Slide Order menu reads From Elements Organizer, but you can choose Date (Oldest First), Date (Newest First), Random, Folder Location, Custom (this is what you see if you manually drag slides to new locations), and Reset (which puts your photos back in the order they were in when you first brought them into the Slide Show Editor).

■ ADDING SPECIAL EFFECTS

Elements gives you all kinds of ways to gussy up your slideshow, including adding clip art, text, and sound. If you want a slide that lists credits, for instance, start by creating a blank slide. (To do that, click the existing slide right before the spot where you want the new blank slide to go, and then, above the preview area, click the Add Blank Slide button.) Elements adds a blank slide to the right of the slide you selected, and you can then add whatever you want to it—like credits, for instance. Here's a rundown of what you can add to a blank slide (or to any slide, for that matter, as shown in Figure 18-6). Just click the relevant tab (Graphics, Text, or Audio) in the Extras panel at the top right of the Slide Show Editor to see these options:

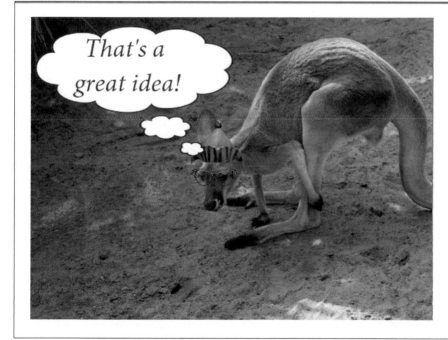

FIGURE 18-6.

You can add all sorts of clip art to slides, as well as create slides that include only *clip art or text. If you'd like to angle clip art (like the hat and glasses here) to make it fit your subjects better, the tip on page 586 explains how.*

- **Graphics.** Elements includes a whole library of clip art you can add to slides. The art is divided into categories: animals, backgrounds, costumes, and so on. To see what's in the different categories, use the tiny scroll bar on the right side of the Extras panel to scroll through them, or click the flippy triangle to the left of a category's name to expand or collapse that category. Use the backgrounds on blank slides, because they cover the whole slide; you can add the rest of the clip art to slides that already have something on them. To add a piece of clip art to a slide, just drag it into the preview area and it appears on the slide surrounded by a bounding box. You can grab the corners of the box and drag them to resize the clip art, or use the Size slider in the Properties panel. You can also reposition the art by dragging it. To remove it, right-click it on the slide preview, and then choose Delete.

> **TIP** If you play around with Elements' clip art costumes (hats, outfits, and glasses that you can paste onto your pictures), you may notice that you can't rotate the clip art on the slide. If you want to adjust the angle of any of the costumes, here's a workaround: All the art lives in *C:\ProgramData\Adobe\Elements Organizer\11.0\Slideshow Graphics* if you have Windows 7 or Vista, or *C:\Documents and Settings\All Users\Application Data\Adobe\Elements Organizer\11.0\Slideshow Graphics* in Windows XP. (Program Data and Application Data are hidden folders, so you need to turn on hidden folder viewing to see them—the tip on page 600 explains how.) Open the slide in Expert Mode, and then add the clip art to it there by importing it from the Slideshow Graphics folder described above. Then use the Move tool to place the clip art just so, and use the Transform commands (page 385) to adjust its shape as needed. When you're done, you can re-import the image into the Organizer as a version and then use that version in your slideshow. Better yet, open the clip art images themselves in Expert Mode, change them, and then save them as PNG files under new names in the same folder as the originals; that way, they appear right in the Slide Show Editor's clip art section along with the originals.

- **Text.** You can add text to slides and apply a number of fancy styles to it. Click the Text tab at the top of the Extras panel, and then double-click the text style you like; the Edit Text window pops up. (If Elements launches the slideshow preview instead, just press Esc to get back to the Slide Show Editor and try again). Type in what you want to add to the slide and then click OK. The text appears in the slide, surrounded by a blue bounding box, which you can use to place the text. Alternatively, you can drag a text style onto a slide and then, in the Properties panel, click the Edit Text button to enter your words.

> **TIP** When the Edit Text window is active, you can't click OK by pressing Enter—doing that just creates a line break in the text. You need to actually click the OK button with your mouse.

When you add text, the Properties panel displays settings for changing the text's font, size, color, and style. You can even choose a different drop-shadow color if you're using shadowed text. If you want to edit text later on, just click the letters on the slide to bring back the bounding box and display the text settings in the Properties panel.

- **Audio.** You can record narration for your slideshow by clicking the slide you want to add your voice to, and then, in the Extras panel, clicking the Audio tab. Elements then displays the recording window shown in Figure 18-7. Of course, you need a computer with a built-in mic or some kind of microphone hooked up to your PC to record your voiceover.

If those aren't enough options for you, you can add a couple of other snazzy extras to your slideshow:

- **Music.** If you want, you can add a full-scale soundtrack to a slideshow. To do that, click the link at the bottom of the Slide Show Editor window that says "Click Here to Add Audio to Your Slide Show." In the window that opens, navigate to the audio file you want and then click Open. You can choose any MP3, WAV, AC3, AAC, or WMA file on your computer.

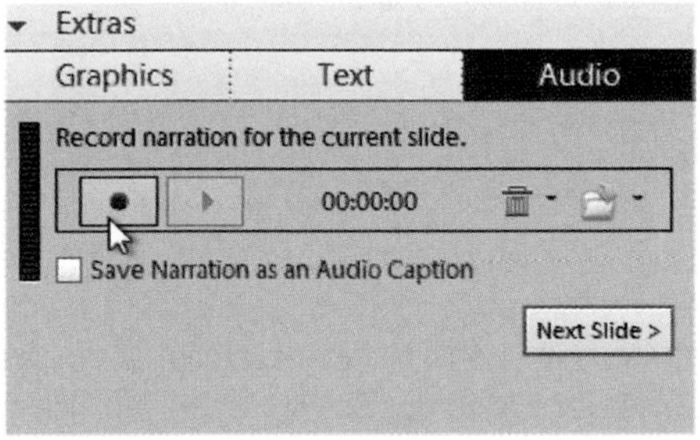

FIGURE 18-7.

Adding narration to slides is pretty simple. Just click the red Record button and start talking, and then click it again when you're done. Click the Play button to review what you did. If you don't like how things turned out, click the trash-can icon, and then choose Delete This Narration. To permanently save your narration as an audio caption for the original photo, turn on the "Save Narration as an Audio Caption" checkbox. You can also click the folder icon to the right of the recording controls to import an existing audio caption to use with this slide.

You can even make the slideshow fit the duration of the music, if you like. At the top of the storyboard, click Fit Slides To Audio and Elements adjusts the duration of your slideshow to last the length of the song. Or, if you'd rather repeat a short audio clip over and over, go to Edit→Slide Show Preferences, and then turn on Repeat Soundtrack Until Last Slide. If you don't turn on either of these settings, then Elements doesn't make any attempt to synchronize the soundtrack and the slideshow.

> **TIP** If you have problems getting the Organizer to play one of your audio files, then you may have better luck if you use an audio program to re-encode the file as a variable bit-rate MP3. (Check the audio program's options or help files for instructions on how to do this.) If that doesn't do it, make sure there isn't any kind of DRM (digital rights management) restriction on the file, like a limit on the number of devices on which you can play it. If there is, Elements won't like the file.

- **Pan & Zoom.** Filmmaker Ken Burns popularized this technique, where the camera moves around a still photo, giving the impression of motion. To create this effect in Elements, in the storyboard, just click the slide you want to pan over and then, in the Properties panel, turn on the Enable Pan & Zoom checkbox.

The Properties panel displays two little thumbnails labeled Start and End. Click the Start thumbnail to choose where to begin panning over the photo. A green box appears in your photo to show where Elements will begin panning over it. To change the starting point, drag the box to another spot or drag a corner to resize it.

Then click the End thumbnail in the Properties panel and repeat the process with the red box that appears to set the end point for panning and zooming. To edit the effect, just click either thumbnail again to bring back the box. You can also click the buttons between the thumbnails to change the start and end positions. From top to bottom, these buttons copy the starting point to the ending point, copy the ending point to the starting point, and swap the starting and ending points.

You can control the zoom level by resizing the start and end boxes. A small box makes the camera zoom in to fill the slide. For example, an end box that's larger than the start box makes the camera zoom out.

> **TIP** Panning and zooming may look pretty jerky when you preview your slideshow, but don't worry about that—it should be smooth in the final version.

You can also pan more than once on a slide. To do that, click "Add Another Pan & Zoom to this slide." If you want all your slides (or selected slides) to use the same pan and zoom you just set up, then go to the Edit menu and choose "Apply Pan & Zoom to Selected Slide(s)" or "Apply Pan & Zoom to All Slides."

> **TIP** While Elements doesn't give you a way to create scrolling credits, you can fake them by creating a slide with a list of people on it, and then applying the pan-and-zoom effect to the slide multiple times. So, for example, the first pan would zoom from the full frame to the first line or two of credits; then you'd apply another pan (without changing the zoom level) to move down to the next couple of lines, and so on, as many times as necessary to give all the people in the list their moment of glory.

■ SAVING AND SHARING YOUR SLIDESHOW

After all the work you've done creating a slideshow, needless to say, you want to save it. (If you forget, Elements reminds you to do so when you exit the Slide Show Editor.)

> **TIP** To watch a full-screen preview of your slideshow, click the aptly named Full Screen Preview button above the preview area or press F11. Press Esc to get back to the Slide Show Editor window.

Before saving, you need to decide what you want to do with the slideshow: burn it to a CD, email it as a file, and so on. It's important to remember that no matter what you choose (except for saving as a PDF), you're going to end up with a Windows Media Video (WMV) file. That doesn't matter as long as everyone you want to share it with has a computer or a DVD player that uses a recent version of Windows Media Player. (It's part of the Windows operating system [if you've disabled Windows Update, you can download the latest version from Microsoft.com]; for Macs, you can find a free plug-in at *http://tinyurl.com/crm9xx2*.)

If you want to send a slideshow to someone who *doesn't* have a way to view WMV files, your options are to create a PDF file as explained on page 579; to upload your slideshow to YouTube (*www.youtube.com*) or Vimeo (*http://vimeo.com*) and send the link to your friends; or to use other software to change the format to something your recipients can use, like QuickTime. (You can upload to YouTube or Vimeo right from the Organizer: Just go to the Share menu.) You can also upload video to Adobe's Photoshop Showcase from this menu.

To see your Output options, click the Output button at the top of the Slide Show Editor window. Elements opens the dialog box shown in Figure 18-8, where you can choose from several ways to save and share your slideshow:

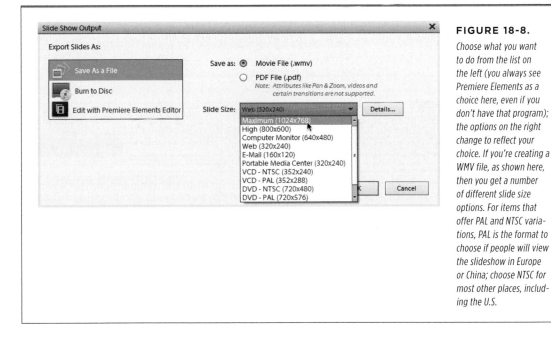

FIGURE 18-8.

Choose what you want to do from the list on the left (you always see Premiere Elements as a choice here, even if you don't have that program); the options on the right change to reflect your choice. If you're creating a WMV file, as shown here, then you get a number of different slide size options. For items that offer PAL and NTSC variations, PAL is the format to choose if people will view the slideshow in Europe or China; choose NTSC for most other places, including the U.S.

- **Save As a File.** Choose this option to save your slideshow to your hard drive as a PDF or WMV file. If you select WMV, you get several size and quality options. Select the one that best suits how you plan to share the slideshow. (If you're curious about the various options, pick the one you want to know more about and then click the Details button; Elements displays a pop-up window with info about that size and its suggested uses.) The PDF options are explained on page 579.

- **Burn to Disc.** You can use Elements to create a video CD (VCD), a disc that plays in a DVD player just like a regular DVD, but you don't need a DVD recorder to create it (because you're just using a plain old CD). The downside is that VCD is a tricky format—the quality is just plain awful, and you can expect to have problems getting the discs to play in many DVD players. If you want to send VCDs, you may want to make a short test slideshow for your friends to be sure they can watch one before you invest a lot of time in creating a large project.

> **TIP** If you'd like to check which players can handle VCDs, or if you just want to know more about the format, head to *www.videohelp.com/vcd*, where you'll find information and links to lists of compatible players.

You can include more than one slideshow on the same disc if you turn on the "Include additional slide shows I've made on this disc" checkbox. Then click OK to bring up the "Create a VCD with Menu" window and select the slideshows you want to include. In that window, you have to pick between the NTSC or PAL formats for your disc. Choose PAL if you're sending the disc to Europe or China; choose NTSC for most other places, including the United States. Then click Burn and Elements gets to work.

> **NOTE** If you also have Adobe's Premiere Elements program (and a drive that can create DVDs), then you can send your slideshow to Premiere Elements to make a *true* DVD. If you have a DVD burner but not Premiere Elements, you can output the slideshow as a WMV file, and then use any other DVD-authoring software you've got loaded on your PC. If you have a DVD burner, you almost certainly got some kind of authoring software with it.

- **Edit with Premiere Elements.** You can send a slideshow over to Premiere Elements for more editing. (You see this option even if you don't have Premiere Elements installed, but clicking it just displays a dialog box suggesting you install Premiere Elements.)

> **NOTE** If you'd like Elements to keep an editable version of your slideshow that you can work on later, save it as a project file by clicking Save Project in the Slide Show Editor. To edit an existing slideshow, in the Organizer, right-click the slideshow's thumbnail and choose Edit from the pop-up menu. Elements opens it in the Slide Show Editor so you can make changes. If you don't save the project file, you won't have an editable slideshow anymore. (You can't edit PDFs or WMVs in the Slide Show Editor.)

A Few More Ways to Share

The Organizer's Share menu makes it simple to post your photos to several other sites besides Adobe's Photoshop Showcase so your friends can view your photos online. You can quickly send photos to sites like Facebook and SmugMug right from within Elements. (The items in the Share menu change depending on Adobe's current partnerships, so you might see slightly different options from the ones listed below.) Once you post photos, you and your friends can order not only prints, but also t-shirts, mugs, bags, and other items with your photos on them. (Exactly what you can order depends on which service you use.) Here's a quick rundown of what you can do with each site, and what it'll cost you:

- **Facebook.** To upload photos to your Facebook page, just select photos in the Organizer and go to Share→Facebook. The first time you do this, you're given the option of importing the email addresses of your Facebook friends to your Contact book (page 567).

- **YouTube.** You can send videos from the Organizer right to your YouTube account. (You don't need a YouTube account to watch videos on the site, but you do need a free account to *upload* videos there.) This option appears even if you don't have Premiere Elements installed.

- **Video to Photoshop Showcase.** This option lets you easily upload videos to Photoshop Showcase (page 9); you don't need to have Premiere Elements installed.

- **Vimeo.** If you have an account with this popular video-sharing site, you can upload your videos right from the Organizer, even if you don't use Premiere Elements.

- **SmugMug Gallery.** SmugMug offers a lot of different gift items that you and your friends can order. You can try it free for 7 days, and your friends can order prints and merchandise without a paid account. If you want to maintain a gallery here, it's $40 a year for a basic account after the trial period expires.

- **Flickr.** This is a really popular photo-sharing site where you can create galleries and slideshows and order different kinds of merchandise featuring your photos. Basic accounts are free.

- **Adobe Revel.** If you have a Revel account (see page 9), you can access it by selecting this item in the Organizer's Share menu.

To upload a photo to any of these sites, just select the image or video in the Organizer, click the Share button, and then choose the one you want. (You can also select and upload more than one photo at a time.) You'll be asked to sign in if you already have an account, or to create one if you don't. Each site has a simple-to-use wizard that walks you through the process of creating an account (and another one for uploading photos once you have an account), and they also have tours so you can look around before you decide to join. If you aren't sure which one(s) to try, ask your friends which one they like. Each site has pros and cons, so you may want to try them all before you decide.

> **TIP** If you use Windows and you have an iPhone, an iPod Touch, or an iPad, Elements makes it easy to share your photos that way, too. If you used your iPhone to take pictures and you want to get them into Elements or if you're using your iPod, iPhone, or iPad to move photos from another device to your computer, just connect your i-gadget to the computer and then use the Photo Downloader (page 29) to send them straight to the Organizer, or download them via Windows Explorer and then go to the Organizer and choose File→Get Photos to bring them into Elements. Even better, if you've signed up for Apple's free iCloud service (*www.apple.com/icloud/setup/ pc.htm*), your Pictures/My Pictures folder should contain a folder called Photostream. Your i-gadget photos appear there automatically, and you can set that as a watched folder (page 35) for the Organizer, too, so your photos go directly into Elements.
>
> To send photos or albums to your iPod, iPhone, or iPad, either to show them off to your friends or to transport them to another device or computer, if you use iCloud, just put them in your Photostream folder. If not, connect the i-gadget to your computer, and then go to iTunes→Photos→"Sync photos from"→Photoshop Elements.
>
> (For Macs, the way is still via iPhoto/iTunes.)

Additional Elements

Beyond the Basics

So far, everything in this book has been about what you can do with Elements right out of the box. But as with many things digital, there's a thriving cottage industry devoted to souping up Elements. You can add new brushes, shapes, layer styles, actions, and fancy filters. Best of all, a lot of what's out there is free. And many of the tools are designed to make Elements behave more like Photoshop.

This chapter looks at some of these extras, how to manage the stuff you collect, and how to know when you really need the full version of Photoshop instead. You'll also learn about the many resources available for expanding your knowledge of Elements beyond this book.

▉ Graphics Tablets

Probably the most popular Elements accessory is a *graphics tablet*, which lets you draw and paint with a pen-like stylus instead of a mouse. A tablet is like a souped-up substitute for a mouse: You control the onscreen cursor by drawing directly on the tablet's surface—an action that many artists find offers them greater control. If trying to use the Lasso tool with a mouse makes you feel like you're trying to write on a mirror with a bar of soap, then a graphics tablet is for you.

Most tablets work like the one shown in Figure 19-1, where you use the stylus on the tablet just as you would a mouse on a mousepad. Any changes you make appear right on your monitor.

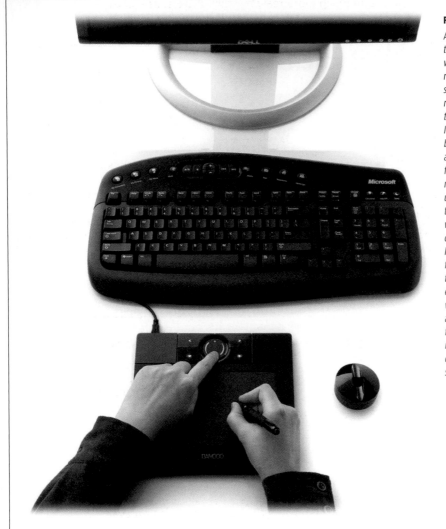

FIGURE 19-1.

A Wacom Bamboo tablet in action. The working area is inside the rectangle on the tablet's surface. The buttons and ring at the top of the tablet let you do things like zoom and scroll. For basic photo retouching, a small tablet is usually fine. If you want to do more drawing and like using sweeping strokes to draw, then you may want a larger model. You can also buy tablets that let you use your fingers for input, like a laptop trackpad. But for photo editing, you'll be happier with one that comes with a pen-like stylus, since the stylus lets you be more precise when doing things like making selections.

NOTE Some deluxe-model graphics tablets act as monitors and let you work *directly* on your image—but you need to budget close to $1,000 for that kind of convenience.

For most people, it's much easier to control fine motions with a tablet's stylus than with a mouse. And when you use a tablet, many of Elements' brushes and tools become *pressure sensitive*—the harder you press, the darker and wider the line becomes. So a stylus lets you create much more realistic paint strokes, as shown in Figure 19-2.

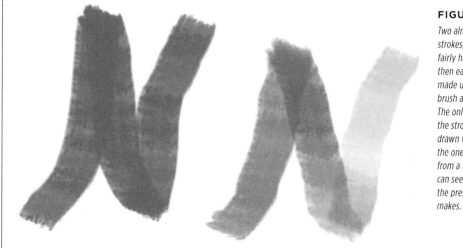

FIGURE 19-2.

Two almost identical paint strokes, starting with fairly hard pressure and then easing up. Both were made using the same brush and color settings. The only difference is that the stroke on the left was drawn with a mouse, and the one on the right came from a tablet stylus. You can see what a difference the pressure sensitivity makes.

When using the Brush tool, you'll see a Tablet Settings button in the Tool Options area that lets you access the tool's tablet options. Many brushes and tools are automatically pressure sensitive when you hook up a tablet. The tablet settings let you choose whether to let the pressure control the size, opacity, roundness, hue jitter, and scatter for the brushes. (See page 395 for more about brush settings.)

With a tablet, you can also create hand-drawn line art—even if you don't have an artistic bone in your body—by placing a picture of what you want to draw on the surface of the tablet and tracing over it. And, if you find constant mousing troublesome, you may have fewer hand problems when using a tablet's stylus. Most tablets also come with a wireless mouse, which works only on the surface of the tablet. Or you can use your regular mouse on a mousepad or on your desk the way you always do, and just switch back and forth between the stylus and the mouse.

Tablets now start at less than $100, a big drop from what they used to cost. There are lots of different models, and their features vary widely. Sophisticated tablets offer more levels of sensitivity and can even respond when you change the *angle* at which you're holding the stylus.

Wacom, one of the big tablet manufacturers, has some pretty nifty tablet demos on its website (*www.wacom.com*). You can't actually simulate what it's like to *use* a tablet, but the animations give you a good idea of what your life would be like if you were to go the tablet route.

■ Stuff from the Internet

You have to spend some money if you want a graphics tablet, but there's a ton of free (and not free) stuff—tutorials, brushes, textures, and layer styles, for example—available online that you can add to Elements. (Most of these add-ons say they work with Photoshop, but since Elements is based on Photoshop, you can use most of them in Elements, too.) Here are some popular places to go treasure hunting:

- **Adobe Exchange** (*www.adobe.com/cfusion/exchange/index.cfm*). On Adobe's own website, you can find hundreds of downloads, including more layer styles than you could ever use, as well as brushes, textures, and custom shapes to use with the shape tools. Many are free once you register. This site is one of the best resources anywhere for extra stuff, although these days it's horribly confusing to navigate. About 99 percent of the items listed are made specifically for Photoshop, but Photoshop's brushes, swatches, textures, shapes, and layer styles work in Elements, too. (See this book's Missing CD page at *www.missingmanuals.com/cds* for help installing your finds.)

- **Simple Photoshop** (*www.simplephotoshop.com*). Home of the popular (but not free) Elements+ add-on tools and some tutorials.

- **MyJanee** (*www.myjanee.com/tutorialselements.htm*). You'll find lots of tutorials and free downloads on this site.

- **Sue Chastain's site** (*www.graphicssoft.about.com*). Another site with lots of downloads and many tutorials.

- **PanosFX** (*www.panosfx.com*). Panos Efstathiadis produces some wonderful actions (see the next section for more about actions) for Photoshop, and he has adapted many of them for Elements as well. Some are free; some cost a few bucks.

- **optikVerve Labs** (*www.optikvervelabs.com*). This is the home of virtualPhotographer, one of the most amazing *plug-ins* (add-ons) for Elements. Best of all, it's free. Alas, this plug-in works only in Windows, not on Macs.

- **Grant's Tools** (*www.elementsvillage.com*). This has long been the most popular set of free add-on tools for Elements. These days, it's easiest to find the most up-to-date version via the forums at Elements Village. Just look for the Grant's Tools thread at the top of the General Elements Discussion forum.

- **ShutterFreaks** (*www.shutterfreaks.com*). This website has a number of Elements add-ons. Some are free, but most cost a few dollars. You'll find tutorials here, too.

- **CoffeeShop** (*www.thecoffeeshopblog.com*). Offers free brushes, frames, patterns, and tutorials for Photoshop and Photoshop Elements.

- **The Pioneer Woman** (*www.thepioneerwoman.com/photography/category/ photoshop-elements*). Here you can find very popular free Elements actions for special image effects.

- **Texas Chicks** (*www.texaschicksblogsandpics.com*). Another site with lots of great actions and tutorials for Elements.

- **Alibony** (*www.alibony.com*). Lots of Elements tutorials, actions, brushes, and effects, many of which are geared for scrapbooking projects.

- **ActionCentral** (*http://atncentral.com*). Many free actions here. Most are for Photoshop, but there are a number that work in Elements as well.

If you're willing to pay a little bit, you've got even more choices. You can find everything from more elaborate ways to sharpen photos to really cool collections of special edges and visual effects. Prices range from "donationware" (pay if you like it) to some sophisticated plug-ins that cost hundreds of dollars. You can also buy books like the ones in Peachpit Press's *Wow!* series, which have loads of illustrations showing the styles available on the included CD.

> **NOTE** Elements 11 is based on Photoshop CS5, so CS5 downloads are compatible with it. Plug-ins and other goodies designed for older versions of Photoshop or Elements usually work with newer versions, but not the other way around. For example, a brush made for Photoshop CS5 works in Elements 11 but not in Elements 3. Also, remember that Mac plug-ins don't work in Windows, and vice versa, but many plug-ins offer two versions, one for each operating system.

> When downloading a plug-in, check with the developer to make sure it will work with Elements 11, especially if it costs money. If you're using Windows Vista or Windows 7, check the plug-in's compatibility with them, as well. Mac folks who still use OS X 10.6 (Snow Leopard) should remember that Elements doesn't run in Rosetta (see page 38), so any plug-ins you buy need to be Intel-native, meaning they're not written for older PowerPC Macs. (This shift away from Rosetta doesn't have any effect on actions, layer styles, shapes, brushes, and gradients—only plug-ins.) So most plug-ins that are more than a few years old won't work with Elements 11.

With so many goodies available, it's easy to get overwhelmed trying to keep track of everything you've added to Elements. Your best bet is to make backup copies of anything you download so you'll have it if you ever need to reinstall Elements. Elements also includes a Preset Manager (Figure 19-3) that can help you keep track of certain kinds of downloads. To launch it, in the Editor, go to Edit→Preset Manager.

> **NOTE** If you download actions, check to be sure that they're compatible with Elements 11. It's safest to use actions written specifically for Elements, but actions for Photoshop will work as long as they don't include steps Elements doesn't understand. (Incidentally, many of the add-on tools you can download are based on actions.)

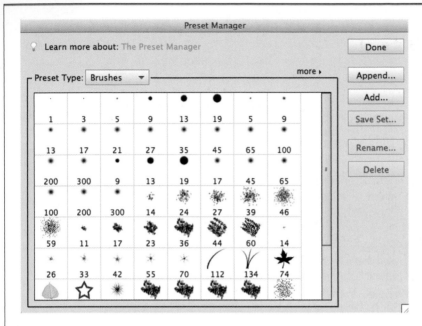

FIGURE 19-3.

Elements' Preset Manager is a nifty feature that lets you see all your brushes, swatches, gradients, layer styles, patterns, and effects in one place. You can use it to change which groups are loaded, add or remove items, and so on—the same way you would when using the Brush tool.

TIP In Windows, you have to turn on hidden files to see some of Elements' folders. In Windows 7, go to Control Panel→Appearance and Personalization→Show Hidden Files and Folders. In Vista or Windows XP, it's Classic View→Folder Options→View→Show Hidden Files and Folders.

When You Really Need Photoshop

You can do a ton with Elements, but some people need the full version of Photoshop instead. For example, if you want to write your own *actions* (little scripts, like macros, that automate certain things in Photoshop) or if you have to work extensively in CMYK mode, then you need Photoshop.

When you send a file to a print shop, the printer usually tells you it needs to be a *CMYK* file. CMYK is the color mode used for commercial printing—it stands for Cyan, Magenta, Yellow, and blacK, which are the colors professional printers use. You can't convert files to CMYK in Elements, so if you need CMYK files on a regular basis, it's worth the extra price of Photoshop to avoid the aggravation. If you only occasionally need CMYK, you might just ask the print shop about converting the file for you for an additional fee.

Photoshop gives you more of everything: more choices, more tools, more settings, more types of adjustment layers, and so on. But for most people, Elements is probably plenty.

Beyond This Book

You can do thousands of interesting things with Elements that are beyond the scope of this book. The Help menu gives you access to dozens of interesting tutorials right within Elements. Also, bookstores have loads of titles on Elements and Photoshop, and a lot of tasks are the same in both programs. And you can find all kinds of specialized books on everything from color management to making selections to scrapbooking.

In addition, you'll find hundreds of tutorial websites. Besides those mentioned earlier in this chapter, here are some other popular sites:

- **Adobe** (*www.adobe.com*). You'll find plenty of free online training for Elements here, and you can get to a lot of it from the Help menus in the program itself. You'll also find many video tutorials on Adobe TV (*http://tv.adobe.com*).

- **Photoshop Roadmap** (*www.photoshoproadmap.com*). This site has tutorials and plug-ins for Photoshop, but there's a big section of Elements tutorials, too.

- **Photoshop Support** (*www.photoshopsupport.com/elements/tutorials.html*). Despite the name, this site isn't run by Adobe. It has a whole section of Elements tutorials.

- **YouTube** (*www.youtube.com*). Yep, that's right: You can find videos about almost *anything* on YouTube, including lots of Elements tutorials, including some from the Adobe folks themselves.

- **Photoshop Elements User** (*www.photoshopelementsuser.com*). This is the website for a subscriber-only print newsletter, but it includes some free video tutorials, a forum, and a good collection of links. This is the only publication specifically for Elements. Its forums, the most active ones out there for questions about creative projects in Elements, are hosted at *www.elementsvillage.com*.

- **PhotoLesa** (*www.photolesa.com*). The website of Photoshop maven Lesa Snider includes many well-written Elements tutorials.

- **LVS Online** (*www.lvsonline.com*). This site offers popular, inexpensive online courses in Elements.

If you search around online, you're sure to find a tutorial for any project you have in mind. Although many of them are written for Photoshop, in most cases, you can adapt them for Elements. If you get stuck or need help with any other aspect of Elements, there's an active online community that will have an answer for you. Besides the sites already mentioned, try these:

- **Adobe Support forum** (*http://forums.adobe.com/community/photoshop_elements*). This is the official Adobe Photoshop Elements User-to-User forum. It's your best bet for getting answers without calling Adobe support.

- **Digital Photography Review** (*www.dpreview.com*). This site has a bunch of camera-specific forums. You can also get a lot of Elements answers in the Retouching forum if you specify in your question that you've got Elements rather than Photoshop, although, sadly, the quality of the posts there has fallen off in the past year or two.

- **RetouchPRO** (*www.retouchpro.com*). The forums here cover all kinds of retouching and artistic uses of Elements and Photoshop. They also host frequent webcasts about digital imaging.

- **Photoshop Creative** (*www.photoshopcreative.net*). Another forum for Elements enthusiasts.

Many sites are devoted to scrapbooking using Elements. A good place to start is Scrapper's Guide (*www.scrappersguide.com*), a commercial site run by Linda Sattgast.

No matter what you're looking for—add-ons, tutorials, communities—try a Google search, and you'll no doubt find a site that has what you want.

There's no question about it: Once you get familiar with Elements, it's addictive. Lots of other folks have found out how much fun this program is, so you shouldn't have any trouble finding the answer to any question you have.

The only limit to what you can do with Elements is your imagination. Enjoy!

> **NOTE** If you'd like to learn how to add layer styles, shapes, and actions to Elements, head to this book's Missing CD page at *www.missingmanuals.com/cds* for the lowdown.

Appendixes

Installation and Troubleshooting

> **NOTE** Head to this book's Missing CD page on *www.missingmanuals.com/cds* to download two more appendixes: "The Organizer, Menu by Menu" and "The Editor, Menu by Menu."

Installation and Troubleshooting

Elements is easy to install and is pretty trouble-free once it's up and running. This appendix describes some things you can do to ensure a smooth installation, and provides cures for most of the little glitches that can crop up once you're using the program.

Like printing, installing Elements works quite a bit differently depending on whether you have a Windows computer or a Mac. This is partly due to the differing ways the two platforms install programs. But another big difference is that, on a Mac, you get asked to create an Adobe ID (see page 609) during the installation process; the installer then registers your copy of Elements. In Windows, on the other hand, you create an Adobe ID from the Welcome screen or from within Elements itself when you run the program for the first time (see page 608).

Regardless of what kind of computer you have, you need to install Elements when you're logged into an administrator account on your machine. (If you've never done anything to change your account and there's only one account on your computer, it's almost certainly an administratior account.)

> **NOTE** If you have a previous version of Elements on your computer, you don't need to remove it before installing Elements 11. All versions of Elements run completely separately, so you can keep older versions if you want.

Make sure you have your Elements serial number handy before you start the installation process. You can install Elements without a serial number, but only as a 30-day trial; when your 30 days are up, the program stops working. If you have a retail version of Elements, the serial number is on the label on the install disc's case, or there may be a redemption code on your receipt instead, which you use to obtain a serial number (the directions for how to do this should be listed along with the code). If you got the program bundled with something else (maybe with a scanner you bought, for example), you'll usually find the serial number on the paper sleeve the disc is in. (It's not a bad idea to write the serial number right on the disc so you'll always have it around if you need to reinstall.) Regardless of where you bought the program, the box contains both the Mac and Windows versions of Elements 11. Just insert the disc for the version you want to install. If you downloaded Elements from Adobe, you can install it on two computers but they must both use the same platform; in other words, two Windows computers or two Macs, not one of each. And if you bought the Mac App Store version, you can install it on as many Macs as you own, but no Windows computers.

> **TIP** Once you install and register Elements, Adobe hangs onto a record of your serial number, so if you ever misplace it, you can get it from Adobe. Also, when Adobe releases new versions of Elements, it usually offers a rebate for registered owners of previous versions. And if you agree to let Adobe send you email, it often offers discounts on other programs, like on the full version of Photoshop, in case you want to move on to that later.

If you use Organizer, Elements stores your catalog of images separately from its program files. That means you can install and uninstall Elements as many times as you like without damaging or losing your existing catalog (if you have one from a previous version of Elements). However, it's a good idea to back up any existing catalogs from older versions before installing Elements 11.

When you first install Elements 11, if the Organizer doesn't automatically find your existing catalog, go to File→Manage Catalogs→Open. Then navigate to your catalog (usually called something like "My Catalog") and open it. Elements automatically makes a backup copy of the catalog and adds "-1" to its name (My Catalog-1, for example). The Organizer then uses your existing catalog (the one *without* the -1 in its name). Just remember that any changes you make in Elements 11 won't appear in the backup version of your catalog (the one *with* "-1" in its name).

■ Installing Elements in Windows

Before you install Elements, it helps to make sure your PC is ready to receive its newest addition. First of all, if your computer is on a network, take it off the network temporarily. (You can go back on as soon as you've installed Elements.) Also, it's important to disable any antivirus software, as well as *any* products from Symantec, whose programs tend to quarrel with Adobe software during installations. You can turn all these programs back on as soon as you've finished installing Elements.

If you have other versions of Elements on your computer, it's a good idea to make a complete backup of the Organizer catalogs for those versions before you start, just in case (see page 72 for info on backing up). After you do that, here's how to run the installer:

1. **Put the install disc in your computer's drive, or, if you downloaded Elements, expand the file by right-clicking it and choosing Extract.**

   If you insert the disc, the installer window should open automatically. If it doesn't, then double-click the disc's icon or right-click it and then choose Open.

   If you have the downloaded version, double-click the extracted Elements 11 folder. Then double-click Setup.exe to start the installer. (In Windows 7, you won't see the .exe extension, but the file type says Application.)

2. **Choose a language and then click OK.**

   This determines the language that Elements will use. After you click OK, the installation wizard (a series of guided question-and-response screens) opens.

3. **In the License Agreement window, read and accept the license agreement.**

   There's a language choice menu here, too, but it affects only the language in which the agreement is displayed, not the language for Elements itself.

4. **Enter your location and the serial number you got with Elements.**

   Choose your country from the drop-down list. If you have a retail version of Elements, the serial number is either on the label on the install disc's case, or you got a redemption code on your receipt instead, which you use to obtain the serial number (the directions for how to do this should be listed along with the code). If you got the program bundled with something else (a graphics tablet, for example), you'll usually find the serial number on the paper sleeve the disc is in. (It's not a bad idea to write the serial number on the disc itself so that you'll always have it around if you need to reinstall.) If you downloaded the program, Adobe emailed you the serial number. (You can install Elements without a serial number, but it will only run as a trial for 30 days, and then stop working.) Once you've entered your info, click Next.

5. **Choose where you want the installer to put Elements.**

   Unless you have a specific reason not to (if you install all your programs on a separate drive, for example), just go with the location the installer suggests by clicking Next.

6. **Click Install to begin the installation.**

   The installer gets to work. When it's done, click Finish to exit the installer, and then restart your computer.

7. **Activate Elements.**

   You do this by launching the program for the first time, as explained next.

The installer creates a desktop shortcut to Elements. To launch the program, double-click the shortcut or right-click it and then choose Open.

The first time you start Elements, you see a screen asking you to create or log into your Adobe ID. Enter your info to register Elements. You'll also be asked to choose your country. Elements also needs to activate itself (see page 610), but you don't have to do anything about this except let the program connect to the Internet at least once.

If you don't register, and you change your mind later, go to Editor→Help→Registration to call up that window again so you can register.

■ Installing Elements on a Mac

There's not much you need to do prior to installing Elements on a Mac, but if you have any antivirus software or any Symantec/Norton products running, you should disable those before you start. (Remember to turn them on again when you're through installing Elements.)

If you want to remove very old versions of Elements (Elements 4 or earlier) from your computer, just drag their folders from Applications to the Trash. For more recent versions, you have to remove them by running their uninstallers. For Elements 6, the uninstaller is the same as the installer. In the first installer screen, simply choose Remove Adobe Photoshop Elements Components, click Next, and then click Install. (If you don't have the disc or download file to get to the installer, there's an emergency uninstaller in Applications→Utilities, but it's much better to use the Elements disc's installer if you can.) For Elements 8, 9, and 10, you'll find the uninstaller in Applications→Adobe Photoshop Elements [8, 9, or 10]→Uninstall Adobe Photoshop Elements [8, 9, or 10].

To install Elements 11:

1. **Put the install DVD in your Mac's DVD or combo drive, or double-click the .dmg file you downloaded to expand it.**

   Double-click the DVD icon or the .dmg file to see the disc's contents.

   NOTE If you bought the Mac App Store version of Elements, it installs automatically when you download it. And you don't have to activate your copy of Elements (page 610), either; you can download and install it on every Mac where you use the same App Store account.

2. **Double-click the Adobe Photoshop Elements 11 folder.**

3. **Double-click the Install icon.**

4. **Choose the language you want to read the software agreement in.**

   Give the agreement a quick read and then click Accept.

5. **Enter your serial number and select the language you want Elements to use, and then click Next.**

If you have a retail version of Elements, the serial number is either on the label on the install disc's case, or you got a redemption code on your receipt instead, which you use to obtain the serial number (the directions for how to do this should be listed along with the code). If you got the program bundled with something else (a graphics tablet, for example), you'll usually find the serial number on the paper sleeve the disc is in. (It's not a bad idea to write the serial number on the disc itself so that you'll always have it around if you need to reinstall.) If you downloaded the program, Adobe emailed you the serial number. (You can install Elements without a serial number, but it will only run as a trial for 30 days and then stop working.)

Elements has a multilanguage installer. Choose the language you want Elements to use.

6. **Create an Adobe ID if you don't have one, or enter your Adobe ID if you do.**

After you're done, click Next. If you aren't ready to do this, you can click Skip This Step instead, or just click Next without typing anything. (If you don't create an ID now, you see a reminder screen when you start Elements.) Creating an Adobe ID (or logging into an existing one) registers Elements for you, so it's a good thing to do, as explained in the next section.

7. **Adjust your installation settings, if you like.**

The Install Options screen lets you change where the installer puts the program on your computer, but unless you have a specific reason to do so (if you install all your programs on a separate drive, for instance), just agree to the location the installer suggests, which is your Mac's main Applications folder. The Elements updater always expects to find the program there, so you'll have fewer problems with updates if you don't change anything on this Options screen.

8. **Click Install.**

Enter your OS X account password when the installer asks for it. The Elements installer does its thing, which takes a few minutes (you can watch its progress in the window).

9. **Click Done to close the installer or click the Adobe Photoshop Elements 11 button to start using the program.**

Clicking the Photoshop Elements button takes you to the Welcome screen, explained on page 5. The first time you launch the Editor, you'll be asked to select your country.

TIP It's a really good idea to repair your Mac's permissions after installing Elements. (Repairing permissions is a simple housekeeping task that helps make sure everything runs smoothly.) Go to Applications→Utilities→Disk Utility; in the list that appears on the left, click your hard drive's name and then click Repair Permissions. This can take quite a while, so don't fret, and don't freak out over all the messages you may see scrolling through the window while it's running—they're normal.

To launch Elements, go to Applications→Adobe Photoshop Elements 11, and then double-click the Elements program icon (the turquoise square with the outline of two overlapping photos on it), or if you're using 10.7 (Lion) or 10.8 (Mountain Lion) and prefer a different route, go to the Dock→Launchpad and single-click the Elements icon. This opens the Welcome screen. If you want to launch the Editor, it's hidden away in Applications→Adobe Photoshop Elements 11→Support Files.

To keep Elements in the Dock, simply click and hold the program's Dock icon while Elements is running and choose Options→"Keep in Dock" from the pop-out menu, or drag the program's icon—*not* the whole Elements folder—into the Dock when Elements *isn't* running. If you add Elements to the Dock and then change your mind about having it there, just drag the program's icon out of the Dock and watch it vanish in a puff of smoke.

■ Activation

In addition to installing Elements, you also need to activate it. That's a process where Elements collects information about the computer you install it on and sends that info to Adobe. Why? Because your installations are physically tied to the computers Adobe knows about. Adobe lets you install your copy of Elements on two different computers. If you want to install it on a third computer, you have to *deactivate* it on one of the other two first. This is a change from early versions of Elements, where your license to use the program had the same restrictions but Adobe didn't actually *do* anything to keep you from installing Elements on 20 computers.

You don't have to register Elements (though the benefits of registering include a record of your serial number [see page 605]), but you do need to activate it. The good news is that you don't have to do anything special to activate Elements except let the program go online at least once. (If you don't normally allow your computer online or you have a firewall that blocks outgoing connections, make sure that Elements can connect or the program will stop working after 30 days.) To check whether your copy of the program has been activated, open the Editor's Help menu; if it contains a Deactivate item, you're all set.

You can run Elements for a while without activating it, but it just runs as a 30-day trial, and when your month is up, that's it unless you activate it. If you uninstall Elements, remember to deactivate it first. You can do that by going to Help→Deactivate in the Editor before you uninstall Elements, or by turning on the Deactivate checkbox in the uninstaller window. After that, you won't be able to use Elements on that machine again until you reactivate it by reentering your serial number and letting Elements contact Adobe again.

You *can* uninstall and reinstall Elements on the same machine without deactivating it first, but it's safest to deactivate each time you uninstall. That way, if something happens before you reinstall, like a major system crash that requires you to get a whole new hard drive, you won't have any problems. It's especially important to deactivate Elements if you're selling your computer or replacing your hard drive so you don't go over the two-computer installation limit.

If you run into any problems activating your copy of Elements, the only solution is to contact Adobe.

■ Scratch Disks

The calculations Elements makes behind the scenes are really complex, and the program needs a place to write stuff down while it's figuring out how to change your images. If the task at hand is too heavy-duty for your system's main memory to cope with alone, Elements uses what's called a *scratch disk*—unused space on your hard drive—when it's busy making your photos gorgeous.

You probably have just one hard drive in your computer, and in that case Elements automatically uses that drive as its scratch disk. That's fine, and Elements can run very happily like that.

TIP If you use Windows, you can make Elements *really* happy by keeping your hard drive defragmented and making sure there's plenty of free space available for the program to use. To defragment in Windows 7 or Vista, go to Control Panel→"System and Security"→Administrative Tools→"Defragment your hard drive." In Windows XP, it's Control Panel→"Performance and Maintenance"→"Rearrange items on your hard disk to make programs run faster."

If you're fortunate enough to have a computer with more than one internal drive, you can designate a separate disk as your scratch disk to improve Elements' performance. Just keep in mind that the scratch disk needs to be as fast as the drive Elements is installed on, or there's no point in setting up a special scratch disk. If you have a USB external drive, for instance, forget it—USB isn't fast enough (even USB 3.0), so just leave your main drive as the scratch disk.

To assign a scratch disk, in the Editor, go to Edit→Preferences→Performance/Adobe Photoshop Elements Editor→Preferences→Performance and choose your preferred disk(s). You can select up to four disks to use as scratch disks.

■ Troubleshooting

If Elements behaves badly from the moment you install it, then something probably went funky during installation. That's easy to fix: Uninstall Elements and reinstall it.

To uninstall Elements, first deactivate it (in the Editor, select Help→Deactivate, or just turn on the Deactivate checkbox on the Uninstaller's first screen). Then, in Windows 7 or Vista go to Control Panel→"Uninstall a Program" (in Windows XP, Control Panel→"Add or Remove Programs") and remove Elements. On a Mac, go to Applications→Adobe Photoshop Elements 11→Uninstall Adobe Photoshop Elements 11. Then reinstall the program.

Fortunately, Adobe makes good software that looks after itself pretty well. There is, however, one simple procedure you can perform if Elements starts acting funny: Delete your *preferences file*, which is where Elements keeps track of your preferred settings for the program. Deleting this file fixes the overwhelming majority of problems that may develop. You'll most likely need to delete the preferences file when dealing with Editor-related problems.

> **NOTE** There's one downside to throwing out your preferences file: Once Elements supplies you with a replacement file (which it generates automatically), you'll have to redo any changes you made to things like window behavior and other preferences. Your panels also go back to their original locations, so you'll need to rearrange them again if you pulled any of them out of the Panel Bin. But deleting the preferences file doesn't affect your image files at all.

Deleting preferences is much easier in Elements 11 than in previous versions. In the Editor, just go to Edit→Preferences→General/Adobe Photoshop Elements Editor→Preferences→General, and click the "Reset Preferences on next launch" button. You'll see a rather scary warning that "This cannot be undone." Just click OK. As explained above, it's not a big deal to delete preferences. Then quit the Editor and start it again.

It's much less common to need to reset the Organizer's preferences, but if you want to do that, it's easy, too: When you're in the Organizer, go to Edit→Preferences→General/Adobe Elements 11 Organizer→Preferences→General, and then click the Restore Default Settings button at the bottom of the window.

Index